DECIPHERING THE NEW
ANTISEMITISM

STUDIES IN ANTISEMITISM
Alvin H. Rosenfeld

DECIPHERING THE NEW
ANTISEMITISM

—⁂—

EDITED BY

ALVIN H. ROSENFELD

INDIANA UNIVERSITY PRESS

Bloomington & Indianapolis

This book is a publication of

Indiana University Press
Office of Scholarly Publishing
Herman B Wells Library 350
1320 East 10th Street
Bloomington, Indiana 47405 USA

iupress.indiana.edu

The paper used in this publication meets the minimum requirements of the
American National Standard for Information Sciences—Permanence of
Paper for Printed Library Materials, ANSI Z39.48-1992.

Manufactured in the United States of America

Library in Congress Cataloging-in-Publication Data

Deciphering the new antisemitism / edited by Alvin H. Rosenfeld.
    pages cm. — (Studies in antisemitism)
    Includes index.
    ISBN 978-0-253-01865-6 (cloth : alk. paper) — ISBN 978-0-253-01869-4 (ebook)
1. Antisemitism—History—21st century—Congresses. 2. Antisemitism—
Congresses. I. Rosenfeld, Alvin H. (Alvin Hirsch), [date]- editor.
    DS145.D435 2016
    305.892'4—dc23

                                                              2015020756

1 2 3 4 5 20 19 18 17 16 15

For Diane Druck
With Gratitude and in Friendship

Contents

PART IV. *Regional Manifestations*

Acknowledgments

UNDER THE AUSPICES OF Indiana University's Institute for the Study of Contemporary Antisemitism (ISCA), forty-five scholars from ten countries came together in Bloomington in April 2014 for four days of intensive analysis and discussion of the recent upsurge of anti-Jewish hostility. The chapters of this book are revised versions of many of the papers presented at this gathering, the second international scholars' conference on antisemitism that ISCA has convened.

I thank all of the conference participants for their important critical insights into the challenging subject matter before us and for the exceptional display of collegiality that marked our deliberations. I am grateful to Ira Forman, the U.S. State Department's special envoy to combat and monitor antisemitism, who spoke to conference participants and especially invited guests about his work on the evening before our sessions formally began.

I am particularly grateful to M. Alison Hunt, who was invaluable in more ways than one in helping me organize the conference and prepare many of the conference papers for subsequent publication. I can hardly thank Alison enough for being such a congenial and efficient coworker—a pleasure to have by my side from start to finish.

Special thanks likewise go to Janet Rabinowitch for carefully reading and editing all of the book's chapters. Janet's professional expertise as an editor is of the highest order and is matched by her personal graciousness and generosity. I am hugely appreciative of all her efforts on this volume's behalf.

I also thank Melissa Deckard, Janice Hurtuk, Tracy Richardson, and Melissa Hunt for their steadfast assistance in helping with a range of conference-related details.

My deepest gratitude goes to the following benefactors, whose generosity, in addition to being of direct practical help, is the best vote of confidence in our work that I could possibly hope for: the Justin M. Druck Family (sponsoring benefactor), Hart and Simona Hasten, David Semmel and Jocelyn Bowie, Monique Stolnitz, Tom Kramer, Marija Krupoves-Berg and Dr. Daniel Berg, Irwin Broh, Gale Nichols, Roger and Claudette Temam, and Carole Silverstein and Dr. Bruce Silverstein.

—ᴔ—

Few undertakings are more dispiriting for scholars than the study of antisemitism. For lifting the hearts and strengthening the resolve of conference participants, it is a pleasure to acknowledge the special contributions of Marija Krupoves-Berg, Daniel Stein, Svetla Vladeva, Dena El Saffar, and Tim Moore, whose inspired performances of Jewish music helped us through some difficult days.

Finally, I am most grateful to President Michael McRobbie, Provost Lauren Robel, and dean of the College of Arts and Sciences Larry Singell for their support of the work of the Institute for the Study of Contemporary Antisemitism. Indiana University is one of only two institutes of higher learning in the United States that houses a research institute of this kind. It is both a privilege and a pleasure to work at a university whose administrative leadership is as understanding, cooperative, and supportive of such new initiatives as these distinguished colleagues are.

Alvin H. Rosenfeld

DECIPHERING THE NEW
ANTISEMITISM

Introduction

ALVIN H. ROSENFELD

THIS BOOK ADDRESSES a disturbing phenomenon that was largely unforeseen in the recent past but has since grown to be one of the most highly charged developments of our time: the upsurge of antisemitism on a global scale. Such hostility has increased significantly since the end of the previous century, and while it takes a variety of forms and poses different challenges in different parts of the world, it is always a threat and needs to be taken seriously—and not only by Jews. This latter point was made clear in a brief but telling statement issued in July 2014 by the foreign ministers of France, Germany, and Italy. They condemned the "anti-Semitic rhetoric and hostility towards Jews [and] attacks on people of the Jewish faith and synagogues" that were taking place almost daily in their countries and elsewhere in Europe. Recognizing the ominous nature of these occurrences, they pledged to do "everything we can to ensure that our citizens can continue to live in peace and security, free from anti-Semitic hostility."[1] By themselves, obviously, these words would not put an end to the escalation of antisemitism in European societies. But presented as a premonitory warning to all of their citizens, and intended not only to calm the rattled nerves of French, German, and Italian Jews, the foreign ministers' statement was neces-

1

sary and timely. It was also politically wise, for it is well-known that the pathologies that animate antisemitism do not focus their destructive energies only on Jews but, if left unchecked, inevitably end up targeting others, as well, and can create high levels of social chaos and disruption.

Jonathan Sacks, the former chief rabbi of Great Britain, expanded on this latter point in these terms: "Antisemitism has been the early warning signal of a society in danger.... The politics of hate that begins with Jews never ends with Jews.... Ultimately, this campaign amounts to an attack on Western democratic freedoms as a whole. If not halted now, it will be Europe itself that will be pushed back to the Dark Ages."[2]

Without minimizing the grounds for Rabbi Sacks's apprehension—much of what he says is warranted—most informed observers of contemporary antisemitism do not anticipate a return to the Dark Ages. They do, however, debate whether analogies can be properly drawn between what is happening in Europe today and what took place on the continent in the 1930s. Despite the growing popularity in some countries of far-right-wing parties that are overtly antisemitic, there is no evidence to date of an established politics of discrimination against Jews on the governmental level. On the social and cultural levels, however, antisemitic comments are now commonplace and are no longer heard only on the margins of society. Anti-Zionist vilification and anti-Jewish censure circulate freely in the media, in politics, in certain churches and trade unions, and on university campuses. Such hostile rhetoric has also become a familiar feature of anti-Israel street demonstrations and frequently accompanies and no doubt helps to fuel the many attacks on Jews and Jewish institutions that have been occurring on a regular basis. Violence of this sort becomes especially prominent when talk of Israel and the Holocaust comes to the fore.

In an effort to clarify these developments, the French philosopher Bernard-Henri Lévy identifies three contemporary sources of today's antisemitism: anti-Zionism, Holocaust denial, and competitive victimhood. He sees these as the main tenets of a "moral atomic bomb" in the making and predicts that when these three will be assembled, "the conflagration will be fearsome."[3]

It is impossible to know if the frightening scenario that Lévy projects will become a reality anytime soon. The forms of anti-semitism that he singles out, however, are all in evidence today, as are numerous other manifestations of anti-Jewish hostility. The taboos that formerly held such animus in check have weak-ened and, in some circles, fallen altogether, and charges about Jewish "control" of the media, international finance, and politi-cal power, which not long ago were considered unacceptable in mainstream society, are now openly expressed. Passions can be-come especially intense when the focus shifts to Israel, a country now firmly demonized in some quarters and regularly and un-fairly condemned for an array of human rights violations of the worst sort, including racism, apartheid, ethnic cleansing, crimes against humanity, and even genocide. Charges of this extreme kind follow a script drafted at the United Nations Conference against Racism held in Durban, South Africa, in the summer of 2001 and have been repeated almost nonstop since then. The cu-mulative impact of these damning accusations has been, in effect, to criminalize the State of Israel and, more broadly, to offer what Lévy calls "a new system of justification" for today's antisemitism.

Once it finds a place in the public sphere, antisemitism is always a potentially destructive force, and it should never be granted sanction or justification. Its ideas have been discredited time and again, and those who promote them are usually linked to political and religious currents of thought that most people find noxious. Nevertheless, under one guise or another, antisemitism is a dy-namic and growing force today. It needs to be carefully studied and, wherever possible, effectively contested and combatted.

Motivated by the conviction that scholars can help to meet these challenges, forty-five scholars from ten countries came together at Indiana University in April 2014 for a series of intense discussions organized by the university's Institute for the Study of Contemporary Antisemitism. Meeting over four days, conference participants aimed to critically examine the various manifestations of today's antisemitism, to decipher what defines and motivates it, and to assess its directions and consequences. The chapters of this book grew out of the papers delivered at that conference. They focus on a range of topics, including the role of intellectuals in fostering antisemitic ideas and ideologies; the cultural, intellectual, political, and religious contexts in which these ideas develop and prosper; the links between anti-Zionism and antisemitism; the political manipulation and exploitation of Holocaust memory and the propagation of Holocaust denial; the responses of international organizations and institutions to contemporary antisemitism; and regional manifestations of antisemitism. Because the problem is broad and multifaceted, the scholars addressing it here represent a wide range of academic disciplines and bring a deep and diverse body of learning to bear on the issues at hand.

We live at a time when a politics of hatred is spreading around the globe, and antisemitism is a prominent feature of the ideological foundations of such hatred. The contributors to this book and I hope that these essays might help readers better understand the nature of this hostility and the urgency of mitigating some of its most serious threats.

NOTES

1. "Statement by the Foreign Ministers of Italy, France and Germany on Anti-Semitism," Federal Foreign Office, press release July 22, 2014, http://www.auswaertiges-amt.de/EN/Infoservice/Presse/Meldungen/2014/140722-Antisemitismus.html?nn=479796.

2. Jonathan Sacks, "Europe's Scary New Anti-Semitism," Wall Street Journal, October 4, 2014.

3. Bernard-Henri Lévy, "Today's Anti-Semitism Is a Ticking Time Bomb," New Republic, October 8, 2014.

PART I

Defining and Assessing Antisemitism

ONE

Antisemitism and Islamophobia

The Inversion of the Debt

PASCAL BRUCKNER

Something new was happening here: the
growth of a new intolerance.
It was spreading across the surface of the
earth, but nobody wanted to know.
A new word had been created to help the
blind remain blind: *Islamophobia.*
To criticize the militant stridency of this religion in its
contemporary incarnation was to be a bigot.
A *phobic* person was extreme and irrational in his views,
and so the fault lay with such persons
and not with the belief system that boasted
over one billion followers worldwide.

—Salman Rushdie, *Joseph Anton: A Memoir*

IN 1910, a French drafter for the Ministry of the Colonies, Alain
Quellien, published *Muslim Politics in Western Africa* (*La Politique
musulmane dans l'Afrique occidentale*].[1] Aimed at a specialist audience, it offered temperate praise of Koranic religion, regarded as
"practical and permissive" and best suited to the natives, whereas
Christianity was considered "too complicated, too abstract, too
austere for the primitive and materialistic mentality of the Negro." Observing that Islam, through its civilizing influence, con-

tributed to European penetration, that it "dragg[ed] populations out of fetishism and degrading practices," the author urged his readers to abandon the prejudices that equated that faith with barbarism and fanaticism. He denounced the "islamophobia" rampant among colonial personnel: as he put it, "to sing the praises of Islam is as unfair as unjustly denigrating it." On the contrary, the religion should be treated impartially. In that instance, Quellien spoke as an administrator concerned with public order: he blamed the desire of Europeans to demonize a religion that maintained peace in the Empire, whatever were the various kinds of abuse—slavery, polygamy—it gave rise to. Since Islam was the best ally of colonialism, its followers had to be protected from the nefarious influence of modern ideas and their ways of life respected. Another colonial official, serving in Dakar, Maurice Delafosse, wrote around the same time that "no matter what those who endorse Islamophobia as a principle of colonial administration may claim, France has nothing more to fear from Muslims in Western Africa than from non-Muslims [...]. There is no justification for Islamophobia in Western Africa, whereas Islamophilia, understood as a preference granted to Muslims, might create a sense of mistrust in non-Muslim populations, which happen to be the most numerous."[2] However, the terms *Islamophobia* and *Islamophilia* remained scarcely used, except by scholars, until the beginning of the 1980s. At that point, the term Islamophobia began to gain use as a political tool in the aftermath of the 1979 Islamic Revolution in Teheran. A floating signifier in search of meaning, the term Islamophobia can indeed refer to two different things: either the criticism of Islam or discrimination exerted against the followers of the Koran. A word is not the property of the person who first used it but of those who have reinvented it so as to popularize its use. A newcomer in the semantic field of antiracism, that term is governed by three principles I dwell on here: the inviolability principle, the equivalence principle, and the substitution principle.

THE INVIOLABILITY PRINCIPLE

In October 2013, in Istanbul, the Organisation of Islamic Cooperation (OIC), which is funded by several dozen Muslim countries that shamelessly persecute Jews and Christians at home, addressed a call to Western countries in the persons of Hillary Rodham Clinton and Catherine Ashton, demanding that freedom of expression, that fundamental right, be restrained when dealing with Islam, since it resulted in far too negative a representation of that religion as oppressive to women and bent on an aggressive proselytism.[3] The petitioners were willing to turn the criticism of Islam into an international crime, recognized as such by the highest authorities. Such a call, already formulated in Durban as early as 2001, has been repeated almost every year since. Doudou Diène, the UN special rapporteur on racism, in his September 14, 2007, address to the Human Rights Council in Geneva, branded Islamophobia as "constitut[ing] the most serious form of religious defamation."[4] Six months earlier, the very same Human Rights Council had likened that kind of defamation to outright racism and demanded a ban on any kind of gibe directed at prophets and religious symbols, while condemning Zionism as a form of racial discrimination and apartheid. The goal of the council's March 2007 statement was twofold: First, to silence Western countries, which were held guilty of three capital sins, namely colonialism, secularism, and sexual equality. Second, to forge a domestic policing instrument that can be leveled at those enlightened Muslims who dare to criticize their faith, denounce fundamentalism, or call for certain reforms: reform of family law, instituting gender equality, the right to apostasy and/or conversion, the right not to believe in God, the right not to observe Ramadan, and the right not to follow religious rules. This action by the council made it necessary to stigmatize young women who want to free themselves from the veil and go about in public without shame, their heads uncovered; to blast the

French, the Germans, and the British with family backgrounds in Turkey, the Maghreb, or Africa who claim the right not to care about religion and who do not automatically feel themselves to be Muslims because they are of Pakistani, Moroccan, Algerian, or Malian descent. To block any hope of a change in the land of Islam, these renegades, these alleged traitors, have to be exposed to public condemnation of their coreligionists, silenced, and admonished for being imbued with colonial ideology. And all this with the approval of the useful idiots of both left and right, who are always on the lookout for a new racism and who are deeply convinced that Islam is the last oppressed subject in history. We are witnessing the fabrication on a global scale of a new crime of opinion analogous to the crime that used to be perpetrated by "enemies of the people" in the Soviet Union. It is a crime that silences contradictors and shifts the question from the intellectual or theological level to the penal level, every objection, mockery, or reservation being subject to prosecution.

But a mystery remains: that of the transubstantiation of religion into race. That is the trickiest part of the operation, although it seems to be on the verge of success: as everyone knows, a great, universal religion like Islam or Christianity gathers a wide array of populations and thus cannot be reduced to a specific race. To talk of Islamophobia, then, amounts to generating serious confusion between a distinctive set of beliefs and those who adhere to it. Criticizing or attacking Islam or Christianity would therefore result in smearing Muslims and Christians. Now, the denunciation of a creed, or the rejection of dogmas one judges absurd or false, is the very foundation of intellectual life: does it make any sense to talk of anticapitalist racism, antiliberal racism, or anti-Marxist racism? In a democracy, one has a right to reject all religious denominations, to regard them as fallacious, backward, or stultifying. Here is a clear counterexample: whereas Christian minorities living in some of the lands of Islam are persecuted, killed, or forced into exile, the word *Christianophobia*, which was coined by UN drafters, has not been widely adopted. Such a terminological dearth seems strange: we have a hard time picturing Christianity as other than a conquering and intolerant religion, although in the Near East and as far as Pakistan it is today a martyred religion. In France, a country with an anticlerical tradition, one can make fun of Judeo-Christianity, mock the pope or the Dalai Lama, and represent Jesus and the prophets in all sorts of postures, including the most obscene, but one must never laugh at Islam, on pain of being accused of discrimination. Why does one and only one religion escape the climate of raillery and irony that is normal for the others?

At this juncture, there appears the strangest element of this story: the enlistment of a part of the U.S. left in the defense of Islam. That is what one might call the neo-Bolshevik bigotry of Marxism's lost zealots. The left, which has forsaken everything it once believed in—the working class, the third world—clings to this last illusion: Islam, considered the ultimate religion of the poor, represents, for a certain number of disenchanted activists, the last utopia, after the fall of communism and the fiasco of Third Worldism. In the gallery populated by the exemplary characters of history, the Muslim has replaced the Prole, the Wretched of the Earth, the Guerillero. He is now the one figure embodying hope for justice on this planet, transcending borders and parochialism, the only champion, according to his supporters, of social justice. What Marx considered the "opium of the people" has become the indispensable viaticum. Feminism, equality between men and women, the intellectually vivifying effect of doubt, the spirit of inquiry, all that has been traditionally associated with a progressive position, is trampled upon. Such a political stance leads to an uncompromising worship of any Muslim ritual or practice, most notably the Islamic veil, which has been literally glorified and exalted to such an extent that, for some commentators, an unveiled Muslim woman who claims her right not be veiled can only be a traitor, a Harki, or a knave bought by colonial authorities. Here, it would be appropriate to dwell further on what has been called Islamo Leftism, the hope, entertained by a revolutionary fringe, of seeing Islam become the spearhead of a new insurrection, engaged in a "Holy War" against global capitalism, something reminiscent of what happened in Baku in 1920, when Bolshevik leaders, including Zinoviev, called, alongside Pan-Islamists, for a Jihad against Western imperialism. As an illustration of such a trend, one may refer to the following reflection of the philosopher Pierre Tevanian, who seriously maintained that "it has been statistically established that racist, xenophobic, Islamophobic opinions are more common among Whites than among non-Whites. [. . .] One must also acknowledge that the panels of Muslim respondents are clearly more progressive than the rest of the population with respect to questions relating to social welfare, redistribution of wealth, racism and xenophobia" and, finally, that 93 percent of Muslims in France voted for the socialist candidate in May 2012.[5] That is a very strange claim, inasmuch as it racializes the whole issue to the extent that it links political opinions to skin color or religious denomination.

THE EQUIVALENCE PRINCIPLE

Edward Said, in *Orientalism,* recalls that in the cartoons that appeared after the 1973 war, the Arabs, depicted with hook noses, standing near a gas pump, "were clearly Semitic": "The transference of a popular anti-Semitic animus from a Jewish to an Arab target was made smoothly, since the figure was essentially the same."[6] In short, according to Said, in the Western Christian world, hostility toward Islam went hand in hand with antisemitism, and it thrived coming from the same source. Philosopher Enzo Traverso explains that "Islamophobia, for the new racism, plays the role that once was that of Anti-Semitism": the rejection of the immigrant, perceived, since the colonial era, as the other, the invader, the foreign body that cannot be assimilated by the national community, "the specter of Judeo-Bolshevism being replaced by that of Terrorism." In such a perspective, Traverso claims, Islamophobia is part and parcel of what could be called "the Anti-Jewish archive […], a catalogue of stereotypes, images, places, representations, stigmatizations conveying a perception and an interpretation of reality that condense and organize themselves into a stable and continuous discourse. As a discursive practice that can shift the object on which it bears, Anti-Semitism indeed transmigrated towards Islamophobia."[7] Here are some other symbols of such a transformation: back in 1994, in Grenoble, young Muslims protested against the ban of the Islamic scarf from schools by wearing armbands with the crescent of Islam in yellow, on a black background, together with this inscription "When is our turn?," an allusion to the yellow star that the Jews were compelled to wear under the Nazi occupation of Europe. And when militant Islamists, suspected of sympathizing with the Algerian jihadist groups during the Algerian civil war of the 1990s, were placed in detention in the summer of 1994, confined to barracks in northern France, they immediately hoisted a banner labeling the place a "Concentration Camp." Tariq Ramadan, the Swiss fundamentalist preacher who once served as Tony Blair's adviser, explains that the present situation of Muslims in Europe is similar to that of the Jews in the 1930s. That is indeed an astounding temporal shortcut: 2014 is already 1933. To criticize Islam, to deny the respect of its integrity, amounts to nothing less than preparing a new Holocaust, clothing oneself in the garb of Hitler's executioners. Referring to the prohibition of the Islamic veil in French schools, former London mayor Ken Livingstone declared that he was "determined London's Muslims should never face similar restrictions. It marks a move towards religious intolerance which we, in Europe, swore never to repeat, having witnessed the devastating effects of the Holocaust (…). Have the French forgotten what happened in 1940 when they started to stigmatize the Jews?"[8] There are also contemporary

scholars who want to address jointly the construction of the
"Jewish Problem" and that of the "Muslim Problem." Christian
Europe, Gil Anidjar argues, conceived its enemy as "structured
by the Arab and the Jew, that is to say, by the relation of Europe
to *both* Arab *and* Jew."[9] According to Edward Said, it was Ernest
Renan who, while building the science of Orientalism, gave support to the Semitic hypothesis invented by the historian August
Ludwig von Schlozer. Renan's work on Semitic languages, Said
maintains, is akin to "a virtual encyclopedia of race prejudice
directed against Semites (i.e. Moslems and Jews)."[10] Accordingly,
there would exist a link between European integration and the
rise of Islamophobia comparable, according to Shlomo Sand, to
"the role played by political Judaeophobia in nation-building in
Europe" during the nineteenth century.[11]

Why put antisemitism and Islamophobia on a par? Or, to frame
things differently, why does everyone, especially the antisemites, want to be a "Jew" today? It is to attain the status of the oppressed, because Europeans have a Christian vision of the Jews
as the crucified people par excellence. It is also to elevate the
tiniest conflict to the level of the fight against Nazism and to
associate the smallest critic of the Muslims with the far right.
Fundamentalists thereby seek to obtain for their faith a sort of
perpetual immunity, so as to position themselves beyond criticism. Entire groups barricade themselves into communitarian
fortresses to justify their nonintegration into the countries in
which they live. Just as antisemitism has outlived its object by
Judaizing the goyim in places where all traces of Jewish presence
have disappeared or been reduced to a handful of people, the
desire to be Jewish, for many populations and groups, becomes
acutely competitive as one struggles to attain the prestige of being the elect. Generally, one can distinguish between two major
types of antisemitism: the religious type, of Christian inspiration, blaming the Mosaic people for having killed Jesus and per-

sisting in the error of denial after the evangelical revelation; and the nationalist type, denouncing stateless minorities as a source of impurity that is prejudicial to the health of the nation. A third, more surprising, kind has been added to these two traditional objections in the post–World War II era: the envy of the Jew as a victim, the paragon of misfortune. In this way, the Jew becomes the model and the obstacle; he usurps a position that should, by all rights, redound to the Blacks, the Palestinians, the Muslims, the Russians, the Poles, and so on. The suffering of the Jews has become the universal measure of suffering, its characteristic features—pogroms, diaspora, genocide—are claimed by everyone, and the Shoah has become the founding event that provides access to the understanding of mass crimes. But it has also given rise to a calamitous misinterpretation: it fascinates people not as an abomination but as a treasury from which they think they can draw advantages, the occasion of being singled out by misfortune, a distinction, the potential for winning an inalienable immunity. Hence the striking success of the word *Holocaust* and its misuse over the past two or three decades: being able to say that you are the object of a new Holocaust means shining the brightest floodlights on your own case; it also means purloining the maximum misfortune and declaring oneself its only legitimate owner, expelling all others. Accordingly, one deals here with a symbolic contest for the control of a highly coveted market: that of antiracism. To put things differently, antisemitism constantly feeds on its own refutation. It is regularly revived not despite Jewish suffering but because of it, and it is eager to appropriate that suffering one way or another. It is as if other populations, denying the Jews the privilege of annihilation, are claiming that "Auschwitz happened to us." The result is the ambivalence of the negationism that wrests the Shoah from the Jews only to give it back to more deserving groups or races: Africans, Palestinians, Muslims. The dead are interchanged, but the event remains the same.

THE SUBSTITUTION PRINCIPLE

In other words, the Shoah has become a monstrous object of covetous lust. We have not so much sensitized public opinion to a major abjection as we have fed a perverse metaphysics of the victim. From this comes the frenzied effort to gain admission to this very closed club and the desire to dislodge those who are already part of it. Consider this circa-2005 statement by Sir Iqbal Sacranie, secretary general of the Muslim Council of Britain until 2006, who proposed replacing Holocaust Memorial Day with Genocide Day: "The message of the Holocaust was 'never again' and for that message to have practical effect on the world community, it has to be inclusive. We can never have double standards in terms of human life. Muslims feel hurt and excluded that their lives are not equally valuable to those lives lost in the Holocaust time."[12] In short, and to put it bluntly, it is now time to change victims. In the contest for the world title of best outcast, the Muslim must replace the Jew, all the more so because the latter not only failed to live up to his status but because he has himself become, with the creation of the state of Israel, an oppressor. In short, the idealization of the Jew has paved the way for his later vilification, or, to put it differently, the Judaization of the Muslims necessarily leads to the Nazification of the Israelis. You have the good Jew of old, scattered through the Diaspora, eternally persecuted, and the bad Israeli, settled in the Near East, domineering and racist. As Traverso candidly admits, in times past Jews and Blacks fought shoulder to shoulder in antiracist and anticolonialist movements; then the Jews crossed the "color line" and became "White," that is, the oppressor.[13] The true Jew now speaks Arabic and wears a checkered keffiyeh, while the other Jew is an impostor who claims title to land and has lost what Charles Péguy called the moral magistracy of martyrdom. Just one quotation, among tens of thousands, I cite this statement made by the activist and former diplomat Stéphane Hessel in a January 2011 interview with the

German newspaper *Frankfurter Allegemeine Zeitung*. Comparing the German occupation of France during World War II with the Israeli occupation of Palestinian territories, he declared that "the German occupation was, when compared with the present occupation of Palestine by the Israelis, a relatively harmless occupation, apart from exceptions like the arrests, detentions and executions, as well as the theft of art treasures." In other words, when Jews constitute themselves as a state, not only do they act like Nazis, but they are worse than the Nazis! Here, one is faced with a clear case of symbolic expropriation: it is our turn, say the fundamentalists; the Jews must be evicted from antisemitism and the Muslims put in their stead. Once the equivalence principle is established, the elimination principle sets in, an insidious but effective process. By so doing, Islam can present itself as the creditor of the whole of mankind: we owe it everything because of all the abuse it has endured since the Crusades. It is a matter of transferring the West's moral debt from Jews to Muslims because of the colonial trauma, because of the occupation of Palestine by Zionists, and, finally, because of the despicable image plaguing the religion of the Prophet Muhammad.

How is one to react to what could be called a genuine case of semantic racketeering? First, by claiming that one should be clear about the debts one is talking about, namely those that are not to be repaid but acknowledged as such and handed down. Those are the genuine debts that are to be honored, and Europe is indeed indebted to Judaism, which has always been part of its history. Islam belongs to the French and European landscapes; accordingly, it is entitled to freedom of religion, to protection by public authorities, to adequate places of worship, and to respect, provided it itself respects republican and secular rules, does not claim extraterritorial status, specific rights, special arrangements for Muslim women in swimming pools and gyms, segregated education, or any other sort of favor or privilege. Those who believe must be protected, but protected also are those who do not

believe, the apostates, the skeptics; hence my suggestion, formulated in 2002, to create a vast system of assistance dedicated
to those who dissent from Islam, an initiative that presupposes
the right to question the doctrine freely, just as is the case with
Christianity, Judaism, or Buddhism. The very notion of Islamophobia, which is primarily directed against those who dissent
from the Koran, is invoked as a legitimate foundation for an academic discipline so as to secure for Islam a status that any other
religion in the modern world is denied: an exemption status. Obligations would be imposed on all great religious denominations
except Islam, which would be allowed to persevere in its being,
unchanged, immutable. Beyond that, the most intolerant religion
demands the privilege of never being challenged, on pain of being
charged with racism! Of course, one must denounce as unacceptable the religious persecutions endured by Muslims and call for
their punishment. But the same should be true for Christians,
Jews, Hindus, and Buddhists living in Muslim countries. To normalize the presence of Islam at home amounts to granting it the
very same status as any other religion; neither foolish demonization nor blind glorification is called for. It is not the first time that
fanaticism speaks the language of human rights and clothes itself
in the victim's garb so as to prevail. As Shakespeare famously put
it, "The Devil can cite Scripture for his purpose."[14]

In this last respect, all the great religions lost their place of
honor a century ago. Today they are several among many in a
multiplicity of religions. That is apparent in any U.S. city, where
one encounters unending stretches of Baptist, Catholic, Lu-
theran, and other denominational churches, sitting alongside a
synagogue or a Hindu temple. Is this a sign of bigotry? It is first
and foremost evidence of civil peace, of a pacified coexistence of
the various expressions of the divine. As Voltaire put it, "when
there is only one religion, tyranny rules; when there are two religions, war reigns; when there are many, liberty comes." The best
one can hope for Islam, in the interest of all, is neither "phobia"

nor "philia" but benevolent neutrality in a community open to all faiths. But that is exactly what Islamic fundamentalists refuse, for it would mean that Islam becomes only one religion among many others. Islam does not consider itself the heir of earlier faiths but rather their successor that invalidates them forever. It cannot be the equal of all other religions since it deems itself superior to all of them. That is indeed the problem!

NOTES

The epigraph to this chapter is from Salman Rushdie, *Joseph Anton: A Memoir* (Toronto: Vintage Canada, 2013), 344.

1. Alain Quellien, *La Politique musulmane dans l'Afrique occidentale* (Paris: E. Larose, 1910).

2. Maurice Delafosse, *Revue du monde musulman* 11, no. 5 (1910): 57, quoted in Abdellali Hajjat and Marwan Mohammed, *Islamophobie* (Paris: La Découverte, 2013), 73.

3. Soeren Kern, "OIC Blames Free Speech for 'Islamophobia' in West," Gatestone Institute, 11 Dec. 2013, http://www.gatestoneinstitute.org/4088/islamophobia-oic-free-speech.

4. Habib Siddiqui, "Reflection on the Report of Bigotry in Europe." *Asian Tribune*, 24 Sept. 2007.

5. Pierre Tevanian, *La Haine de la religion* (Paris: La Découverte, 2013).

6. Edward Said, *Orientalism* (London: Penguin Classics, 2003), 286.

7. Enzo Traverso, *La Fin de la modernité juive. Histoire d'un tournant conservateur* (Paris: La Découverte, 2013).

8. Ken Livingstone, address, Assembly for the Protection of Hijab (Pro-Hijab), London's City Hall, July 12, 2004, quoted in Pnina Werbner, "Veiled Interventions in Pure Space: Honour, Shame, and Embodied Struggles among Muslims in Britain and France," *Theory Culture Society* 24 (2007): 161–186.

9. Gil Anidjar, *The Jew, the Arab: A History of the Enemy* (Stanford, Calif.: Stanford University Press, 2003), xi, quoted in Hajjat and Mohammed, *Islamophobie*, 185.

10. Edward Saïd quoted in Hajjat and Mohammed, *Islamophobie*, 188; the authors themselves do not endorse his hypothesis.

11. Shlomo Sand, "From Judeophobia to Islamophobia," *Jewish Quarterly* 57, no. 1 (2010), 60–61, quoted in Hajjat and Mohammed, *Islamophobie*, 194.

12. Among the victims of the "Arab Muslim" genocide, Sacranie includes the Palestinians and the Iraqis but not the Kurds gassed by Saddam Hussein. After the Fatwa against Salman Rushdie had been issued, he also declared that death would be too sweet for him and that he should instead be tormented until the end of his life.

13. Enzo Traverso, "Les Juifs et la ligne de couleur," in *De quelle couleur sont les Blancs? Des "petits Blancs" des colonies au "racisme anti-Blancs,"* ed. Sylvie Laurent and Thierry Leclère (Paris: La Découverte, 2013), 253–261.

14. William Shakespeare, *The Merchant of Venice*, 1.3.

TWO

The Ideology of the New Antisemitism

KENNETH L. MARCUS

DEPENDING ON ONE'S PURPOSES, antisemitism may be defined as an attitude, a set of practices, or an ideology. Attitudinal
definitions are helpful for survey research. Definitions that are
based on actions or practices are useful for practical purposes,
such as monitoring and evaluation. But whatever else it is, antisemitism is also an ideology, a "conception of the world," in
Sartre's phrase.[1] Ideological definitions are best for understanding why antisemitism persists, how it reaches such virulence,
and how we might ultimately defeat it. To define antisemitism
as an ideology is to facilitate a deeper understanding of how
distorted perceptions of "the Jews" arise and the work these
perceptions do to shape broader worldviews. This is as true for
contemporary manifestations of antisemitism, which focus on
Israel as the "collective Jew," as it is for older variants. Ideological definitions tend to emphasize the process by which Jewry,
individually and collectively, is worked up into a distorted construct. What is interesting here is not so much the nature of the
construct, or the difference between reality and illusion, but
rather the process itself.

OBJECTIONS TO THE
IDEOLOGICAL APPROACH

Some antisemitism scholars object that this approach elevates "vicious and degraded sentiments" to "the status of an ideology." To scholars of ideology, however, "vicious and degraded sentiments" are precisely the business of ideologies. Critics of this approach also argue that antisemitism lacks the coherence or sophistication of a genuine political philosophy. "Antisemitism," Anthony Julius argued, "cannot claim the equivalent of a St. Paul, a Locke, *or a Marx*" (emphasis added). For this reason, Julius insists that antisemitism "is not an ideology; it is instead a protean, unstable combination of received ideas, compounded by malice."[2]

Despite Julius's claim, we cannot help but note the fact that antisemitism can indeed claim a "Marx." In fact, it may claim Karl Marx, whose essay "On the Jewish Question" is a milestone in the history of antisemitism. (Indeed, when this chapter was first read in conference, Paul Berman insisted that antisemitism may claim St. Paul, as well.) Much could be and has been written on the infection of Western philosophy with antisemitism. Even if this were not the case, however, to define antisemitism in ideological terms does not imply that it has the coherence of a philosophical treatise. Rather, the notion is that antisemitism is a way in which people make sense of the world, even if their conceptions are often distorted or nonsensical. To paraphrase Zygmunt Bauman, ideological antisemitism treats "the Jew" as a window rather than as a picture on the wall. This applies with equal force to the new antisemitism, highlighting the constellation of false ideas and images surrounding what may be called the "collective Jew." What is interesting here is not just the distorted view of Israel but the way in which Israel becomes central to a distorted worldview.

IDEOLOGICAL DEFINITIONS AND
THE NEW ANTISEMITISM

The new antisemitism projects traditional conceptions of "the Jew" onto Israel as the collective Jew. For this reason, traditional definitions of the ideology of antisemitism apply fully to its new manifestation. Following the work of Theodor Adorno and Helen Fein, we may define antisemitism as a set of negative attitudes, ideologies, and practices directed at Jews as Jews, individually or collectively, based upon and sustained by a repetitive and potentially self-fulfilling latent structure of hostile erroneous beliefs and assumptions that flow from the application of double standards toward Jews as a collectivity, manifested culturally in myth, ideology, folklore, and imagery, and urging various forms of restriction, exclusion, and suppression.[3]

This definition builds on Adorno's formulation: "This ideology [of antisemitism] consists . . . of stereotyped negative opinions describing the Jews as threatening, immoral, and categorically different from non-Jews, and of hostile attitudes urging various forms of restriction, exclusion, and suppression as a means of solving 'the Jewish problem'" (emphasis omitted).[4] Adorno's definition, although less influential than it once was, shows surprising contemporary relevance as a characterization of the relationship between antisemitism and anti-Zionism, especially if the word *Israel* is substituted for *Jewish* and *the Jews*. Thus, the ideology of the new antisemitism would include *stereotyped negative opinions describing the Jewish state and its members, supporters, and coreligionists as threatening, immoral, and categorically different from other peoples, and of hostile attitudes urging various forms of restriction, exclusion, and suppression as a means of solving the "Israel problem."* The relevancy, cogency, and resonance of this substituted language arises not only because some of the same "stereotyped negative opinions" classically directed against Jews are now directed against Israel, but also because these stereo-types are applied for the same purposes of "restriction, exclusion, and suppression" as a means of resolving a supposed "Jewish problem," which turns out in fact to be a gentile problem.

Helen Fein's work further develops this ideological conception, defining antisemitism "as a persisting latent structure of hostile beliefs towards Jews as a collectivity manifested in individuals as attitudes, and in *culture* as myth, ideology, folklore, and imagery, and in *actions*—social or legal discrimination, political mobilization against Jews, and collective or state violence—which results in and/or is designed to distance, displace, or destroy Jews as Jews" (some emphases omitted).[5] Fein's definition enables us to consider the use of anti-Israel "myth, ideology, folklore, and imagery," which mediates between anti-Jewish attitudes and anti-Israel social, legal, political, and military action. In sum, anti-Israelists do not harbor animus against the actual state of Israel, nor do they address the actual historical ideology of Zionism. Rather, they direct their antagonism at complex social constructs that stand in for the state of Israel and for the idea of Zionism, just as classical antisemites direct their hostility at false constructs of the Jewish people.

IDEOLOGY, IGNORANCE, AND CYNICISM

When we view antisemitism as an ideology, we are able to analyze one of its most distinctive features, namely, the irrational willingness of highly educated and intelligent non-Jews to strongly defend so many false, groundless, and completely implausible beliefs about Jews, such as the persistent belief that Jews kill gentile babies in order to use their blood to bake Passover matzo or that Jews entirely fabricated the extermination of six million Jewish victims during the Holocaust.[6] Similarly, it is otherwise difficult to imagine the extraordinarily widespread belief in the authenticity of The Protocols of the Elders of Zion despite scholarly consensus that they are a thinly plagiarized version of Maurice Joly's Dialogue in Hell between Machiavelli and Montesquieu.

These are not idle historical curiosities. The blood libel and Holocaust denial have both appeared in some form or other on U.S. college campuses in the twenty-first century. The Protocols meanwhile are once again a publishing phenomenon throughout the world. As recently as 2004, the retailing giant Walmart defended its decision to stock that famously fraudulent work, observing that "the Protocols were taken seriously by the Russians and by people in America like the famed industrialist Henry Ford," which "seems to give it validity."[7] At other times and places, as in Nazi Germany, extraordinary numbers of ordinary people maintain such blatant absurdities at the center of their worldview. Worse, these false beliefs motivate the vilest of actions, turning these people, in extreme conditions, into mass executioners.[8]

A rich intellectual tradition explores the manner in which ideology can function as a mechanism for supporting inequitable social relationships. "What persuades men and women to mistake each other from time to time for gods or vermin," Terry Eagleton explained, "is ideology."[9] Eagleton's evocative definition highlights an important aspect of the concept of ideology, that is, its tendency (in some formulations) to create dangerous illusions. This tendency is reflected in the theory of false consciousness, which describes the divergence between social reality and our distorted representations of it. That is to say, theorists have produced an extensive literature to explain how people are deluded to see the world in ways that sustain inequitable social arrangements. This literature can illuminate the ways in which people form distorted representations of Jewish identity.

One important lesson in this literature, indebted more to the work of Freud, is that the ideology of hatred is a symptom of repressed desire.[10] Generally speaking, the cause can be found in some wish that one perceives as shameful and comes to disown.

In Freudian theory, such desires always return in some form, often disguised or distorted. Typically, one projects the desire in distorted form onto another person or group, whom one comes to despise for representing the very desire that one has rejected. This projection is the origin of hatred and its ideologies.

Another critical element is that, to be kept in the thrall of a distorted ideology, individuals must be unaware of its effects on society. The new antisemitism exhibits nothing so much as an ability to disguise its true nature, even from those who are most engaged in its dissemination.[11] This fact opens up the possibility that an ideological critique, by dissolving this naïveté, may weaken the hold that an ideology (like antisemitism) has on those who espouse it. In other words, it creates the possibility that ideologically based hatreds may be resolved through a procedure that can "lead the naïve ideological consciousness to a point at which it can recognize its own effective conditions, the social reality that it is distorting, and through this very act dissolve itself." Traditionally, ideological critique has operated by identifying the blank spots in texts, explicating what must be repressed if a system is to sustain its consistency.[12]

This notion has been challenged by those who argue that ideologies have evolved in postmodern society in ways that no longer rely on naïveté. In his influential Critique of Cynical Reason, Peter Sloterdijk has argued that ideology's primary mode is now cynical.[13] Sloterdijk maintains that those who profit from the dominant ideology now understand full well how the world works and choose to overlook the inequities from which they benefit as well as the myths and illusions on which those inequities are based. In other words, the haves know that their spectacles distort social reality, but they do not remove them, because they have more to lose by doing so. Is antisemitism now sustained, in some parts of the world, by this enlightened false consciousness? It is not hard to imagine that some in the Middle East are aware of the fictional character of works such as the Protocols but nevertheless appreciate their role in sustaining negative attitudes toward Israel. If so, then traditional procedures of ideological critique will not be effective for them. To address this problem, a more sophisticated version of ideological critique moves beyond the fantasy that enlightened false consciousness preserves, focusing instead on the unseen sources of ideological fantasy.[14]

The source of ideological fantasy is not the undistorted reality that is misrecognized by ideological lenses. It is not the face behind the mask but rather the need that people have to mask one another. It is not, in other words, merely the image of "the Jew" that violent antisemites hold when they look on the anguished faces of their victims. It is also the desire to turn living, breathing people into monsters that can be tortured and destroyed. The ideological distortion has been described as a double illusion: it consists first in working people up into fantastic versions of themselves and second in overlooking the way this illusion structures our relationship to the real world.[15] The "ideological fantasy" of antisemitism is this double illusion in which first the Jew disappears behind "the Jew," and then the underlying trauma that caused this distortion is forgotten.

IDEOLOGY AND MISINFORMATION

A frequent response to the new antisemitism is to call for more rather than less speech, and specifically for speech that corrects the factual errors that antisemitic speech is thought to contain. In one representative example, in November 2011, a Jewish undergraduate student complained to University of California at Santa Cruz administrators that a film shown at his campus vilifies Jews and Jewish values. In response, administrators denied that the university is, on balance, biased against Jews and assured the student: "You too can develop a program on the Middle East for presentation on the campus." The message was that the best response to anti-Jewish hostility is a pro-Israel informational campaign. Indeed, a further implication is that those who oppose antisemitism should engage in debate, a free exchange of ideas, with those who promote antisemitic canards. Similarly, a decade ago, when a student newspaper at the University of California at Irvine expressed the view that Jews are genetically inferior to non-Jews, the university urged Jewish students to present their views of the issue, as if it were a proper subject for debate.[16] Exponents of this position go so far as to insist that those who oppose Holocaust denial should engage in public debates with Holocaust deniers themselves, providing a public platform for the deniers to disseminate their odious ideology.[17]

This approach harkens to a viewpoint that was commonly accepted not only within the Jewish community but also among those scholars and activists who were more generally concerned with problems of prejudice and discrimination during the 1930s and early 1940s. For example, Gunnar Myrdal argued in his pathbreaking 1944 volume, An American Dilemma, that widespread education could vanquish prejudice: "White prejudice can change, for example, as a result of an increased general knowledge about biology, eradicating some of the false beliefs among whites concerning Negro racial inferiority. If this is accomplished . . . education will then be able to fight racial beliefs with more success."[18] Several years later, this position was articulated by Hilda Taba, then the director of the American Council on Education's Intergroup Education Project. Taba wrote that educators "know . . . that a person's attitude toward Jews and Negroes is determined to a considerable extent by the degree to which he is adequately informed about these groups."[19]

At the time, this position was largely dominant within the Jewish communal world. The leaders of Jewish communal organizations generally believed, as one group put it at the time, that "the lack of information was basically responsible for group hostilities."[20] Their assumption was that prejudiced people accepted anti-Jewish stereotypes because they lacked accurate information about or firsthand experience with Jews. Jewish leaders believed at that point that they could eliminate prejudice by teaching white U.S. gentiles about the various ethnic, racial, and religious groups within the United States. Historian Naomi W. Cohen argues that this approach meshed well with secular Jewish ideas about education: "Their Enlightenment heritage had led them to believe that secular education shaping young impressionable minds was the surest way to capture the humanistic truths of which the philosophers spoke. As the clouds of ignorance lifted, irrational prejudice, like that directed against the Jew, would also vanish."[21]

During this period, both the Anti-Defamation League and the American Jewish Committee devoted considerable resources to an education campaign that pursued this strategy, despite the fact that their professional staff members had already begun to doubt its wisdom. For example, during the 1930s, the American Jewish Committee funded Franz Boas and other anthropologists whose worked debunked Nazi racial science. This approach was largely abandoned, for many reasons, during the late 1940s to 1950s.[22] Psychologists such as Bruno Bettelheim argued that, since antisemitism is the product of psychological factors, it is unlikely to be altered by superficial educational or propaganda techniques. John Slawson, an executive vice president of the American Jewish Committee at that time, admonished a conference of Jewish communal professionals that "recent psychological studies . . . reinforce the contention advanced by many of us that there is indeed a vast difference between selling goods and ridding the American population of prejudice against the Jew."[23] More pointedly, Bettelheim and Janowitz insisted that educational efforts "concentrated on disseminating correct information and . . . disproving the accusations of the intolerant" fail to address the psychological roots of prejudice.[24] Similarly, Adorno argued that antisemitism could not be resolved through "apologetic refutation of errors and lies." Dismissing the view that antisemitism was "based primarily on distortion of facts which some individuals have mistakenly accepted as true," they criticized informational programs as being "distinguished for their lack of success."[25]

In more recent years, Slavoj Žižek has demolished the case for informational programs with an even more trenchant critique. "Let us examine antisemitism," he begins. "It is not enough to say that we must liberate ourselves from so-called 'anti-Semitic prejudices' and learn to see Jews as they really are—in this way we will certainly remain victims of these so-called prejudices." Žižek's reason for this is essentially the same as Bettelheim's and Morris's. In this way, Žižek too argues that informational campaigns fail to address the psychological roots of antisemitism. His argument is somewhat more nuanced, however, as it acknowledges that even truthful claims can be used to advance a pernicious ideology. "Let us suppose, for example, that an objective look would confirm—why not?—that Jews really do financially exploit the rest of the population, that they do sometimes seduce our young daughters. . . ." Here again, Žižek is nothing if not outrageous. "Is it not clear that this has nothing to do with the real roots of our antisemitism?" Žižek here reminds us of Lacan's proposition concerning the pathologically jealous cuckold: "even if all the facts he quotes in support of his jealousy are true, even if his wife really is sleeping around with other men, this does not change one bit the fact that his jealousy is a pathological, paranoid construction."[26]

These insights are confirmed by both historical studies and empirical research. For example, when historians conclusively demonstrated that *The Protocols* are a fraudulent document, their publisher nevertheless persisted in espousing the work's deeper "truth." Sergei Silus, the Russian religious writer responsible for *The Protocols'* first unabridged publication, brushed away questions of veracity: "Let us admit that the Protocols are a forgery. Cannot God make use of a forgery in order to illuminate the iniquity of what is about to occur? Cannot God, in response to our faith, transform the bones of a dog into the relics of a miracle? He can thus place into the mouth of a liar the annunciation of a truth."[27] Similarly, Günther Jikeli's studies of young male European Muslims confirm Žižek's thought experiment in the context of contemporary Germany, France, and England. Those European Muslim participants who are explicitly hostile to Jews as Jews sometimes call for the extermination of the Jewish people, regardless of the apparent virtues of individual Jewish people. Jikeli illustrates this with the transcript of an interview with Bashir, a representative fifteen-year-old Muslim in Berlin:

> BASHIR: [I] would ... say ... that the damned Jews should be burnt ... Maybe there are Jews who are kind or so, I don't know.
> INTERVIEWER: And those who are kind, should they be burnt, too?
> BASHIR: Yes.
> INTERVIEWER: Why?
> BASHIR: Because they are Jews nevertheless. Jews are, a Jew is a Jew anyway.[28]

This response sheds light on why factual information is insufficient to break the grip of ideological fantasy. In Žižek's terms, it "is why we are ... unable to shake so-called ideological prejudices by taking into account the pre-ideological level of everyday experience." The basis of that argument is that "the ideological construction always finds its limits in the field of everyday experience—that it is unable to reduce, to contain, to absorb and annihilate this level."[29] But that is surely not the case.

In Leon Wieseltier's more concise formulation, "Prejudice is not a mistake; it is a fiction. Mistakes can be corrected, but prejudice can only be fought. Anti-Semitic beliefs about the Jews are not merely false; they are also, for those who believe them, unfalsifiable."[30] When told that The Protocols of the Elders of Zion are "vicious nonsense," Martin Heidegger reportedly responded, "But the dangerous international alliance of the Jews still exists."[31] If one is in the grip of an antisemitic (or Islamophobic) ideology, one will find confirmation all around. Žižek explains this with a thought experiment about a typical German man in the late 1930s who had a kindly Jewish neighbor named Stern: "He is bombarded by anti-Semitic propaganda depicting a Jew as a monstrous incarnation of Evil, the great wire-puller, and so on. But when he returns home he encounters Mr. Stern, his neighbor, a good man to chat with in the evenings, whose children play with his. Does not this everyday experience offer an irreducible resistance to the ideological construction? . . . The answer is, of course, no."[32] Why is the answer "no"? Because antisemitism, whatever else it is, is also an ideology.

When we are in the grip of an ideological illusion, as opposed to a mere mistake of fact, we will tend to view "facts" in a way that fits our preformed ideas. "How then," Žižek asks, "would our poor German, if he were a good anti-Semite, react to this gap between the ideological figure of the Jew . . . and the common everyday experience of his good neighbor, Mr. Stern?" He would answer the question in a way that reconciles the evidence of his sense to the preconceptions of his ideology: "His answer would be to turn this gap, this discrepancy itself, into an argument for antisemitism: 'You see how dangerous they really are? It is difficult to recognize their true nature. They hide it behind the mask of everyday experience—and it is exactly this hiding of their real nature, this duplicity, that is a basic feature of the Jewish nature.'"[33] Indeed, this has been the reaction of antisemites since ancient times, as in the case of Saint John Chrysostom, who insisted that Jews mix truth with falsehood in a virulent cocktail "in the same way that those who mix lethal drugs smear the lip of the cup with honey to make the harmful potion to drink." This imagined quality underlies the deepest Jew hatred. "This," said Saint John, "is why I hate the Jews."[34]

ANTISEMITISM AND SOCIAL TRAUMA

The challenge, then, is to identify the fundamental trauma that yields the antisemitic ideology. The theories of projection and displacement can help with this task. According to projection theory, aversions arise as a means for people to resolve or at least ameliorate their internal conflicts.[35] The theory is that people often repress or disown desires that then return as projections onto other people or groups. For example, a person who is internally conflicted about greedy or sexual impulses might project those impulses on members of another group, whom he or she will then see as possessing those attributes. Those who have aggressive desires that are suppressed by the demands of their own superegos may project those desires onto Jewish people. "Antisemitism," wrote Max Horkheimer and Theodor Adorno, "is based on false projection."[36] The "displacement" theory is also sometimes known as the "ventilation" theory or the "aggression-resentment" theory. According to this theory, prejudice results from the externalization or displacement of aggression.[37] Simply put, people who are frustrated by personal disappointment take their frustration out on other persons or groups, who are often seen as scapegoats for their misfortunes. The greater the frustration, the greater the aggression that is vented on others. Empirical studies have shown, for example, that non-Jewish Americans who are distrustful of politicians and perceive themselves to be victims of economic forces are more likely to exhibit antisemitic attitudes than others.[38]

Socioeconomic trauma may also trigger a repetition of extreme prejudice. For example, some theorists have associated racial prejudice with the prejudiced person's fear of economic failure. Among them are Bettelheim and Janowitz, who argued that there is a strong correlation between racial and religious intolerance and anxiety about unemployment and other forms of downward economic mobility.[39] Similarly, Ackerman and Jahoda argued that "a strongly competitive society gives permanent cause for social anxiety to everyone, even to those who have achieved material success." Ackerman and Jahoda shrewdly theorized that the key role of these tensions could be discerned in the acquisitive traits that prejudiced persons projected onto Jews, for example, stinginess, greed, social ambitions.[40] More grandly, Žižek argues that antisemitism arises when the class struggle is mystified or displaced and its cause is projected onto "the Jews."[41] We should not expect the same traumas to play out in the same way in each instance. The underlying element is that every society contains deep social conflicts which under certain circumstances may give rise to distorted or prejudiced views of that society's "other." In Western societies, when such conflicts develop, there is always an available stock of anti-Jewish delusions that can serve this function.

THE NEW ANTISEMITISM AS NODAL POINT

While many forms of prejudice can be found in Western society, antisemitism has played a distinctive function. It is neither a discrete phenomenon—something unrelated to other biases and conceptions—nor a mere generic manifestation of some broader problem, such as racism or xenophobia. On the one hand, antisemitism is too closely related to other notions to be studied in isolation. On the other, antisemitism is too distinctive in its virulence, repetitiveness, and ideological character to be reduced to a mere manifestation. In fact, antisemitism plays a central role, in both old and new manifestations, in a broader constellation of ideological elements. This does not render antisemitism unique, since other ideologies have played similar roles, but it does give Jew-hatred a defining quality absent in most other forms of animus.

The best way to understand the central role that antisemitism plays in many worldviews is to recognize its role as a "nodal point" that quilts together a multitude of proto-ideological elements, or floating signifiers, and fixes their meaning.[42] Slavoj Žižek, Ernesto Laclau, and Chantal Mouffe have developed this idea of ideological nodal points, drawing on the psychoanalytic work of Jacques Lacan and the linguistics of Ferdinand Saussure, to explain how meaning is established within the free flow of signification by certain privileged signifiers which fix meaning within a signifying chain.[43] Žižek, while demonstrating little understanding of the new antisemitism, nevertheless cogently explains that ideology consists of a multitude of elements that may be defined in various ways. The "nodal points" in an ideological field fix their meaning and tie them together in a manner that appears coherent:

> Ideological space is made of non-bound, non-tied elements, "floating signifiers," whose very identity is "open," overdetermined by their articulation in a chain with other elements—that is, their "literal" signification depends on their metaphorical surplus-signification. Ecologism, for example: its connection with other ideological elements is not determined in advance; one can be a state-oriented ecologist (if one believes that only the intervention of a strong state can save us from catastrophe), a socialist ecologist (if one locates the source of merciless exploitation of nature in the capitalist system), a conservative ecologist (if one preaches that man must again become deeply rooted in his native soil), and so on; feminism can be socialist, apolitical; even racism could be elitist or populist ... The "quilting performs the totalization by means of which this free floating of ideological elements is halted, fixed—that is to say, by means of which they become parts of the structured network of meaning."[44]

To say that antisemitism is a nodal point is to observe that it gives specificity to related ideological elements while giving unity to an assemblage of otherwise unrelated political stances.

This observation helps us to understand how antisemitism has functioned, at various times and places, as a cultural code for resistance to a broader range of social developments. For example, it has been observed that nineteenth-century European antisemitism functioned as a code for the political identity of those who opposed modernity, while twenty-first-century right-wing Hungarian antisemitism serves as a code for opposition to parliamentary democracy.[45] In the same way, contemporary left-wing anti-Israelism serves as a code for opposition to globalism, Americanism, or Western liberalism.[46] In each case, antisemitism has sutured a broad range of hostilities.

According to this approach, there are many nodal points that may unify contemporary Western ideological fields. This theory helps to explain why seemingly disparate political ideas seem to cohere together so closely in the ideologies of many people. Social and political ideas are bundled and tied together by unifying themes or ideas. The ideology that emerges as a "nodal point" gives meaning to the remainder of the field, as Žižek explains: "If we 'quilt' the floating signifiers through 'Communism,' for example, 'class struggle' confers a precise and fixed signification to all other elements: to democracy (so-called 'real democracy' as opposed to 'bourgeois formal democracy' as a legal form of exploitation); to feminism (the exploitation of women as resulting from the class-conditioned division of labour); to ecologism (the destruction of natural resources as a logical consequence of profit-orientated capitalist production); to the peace movement (the principal danger to peace is adventuristic imperialism), and so on." In this sense, the struggle of ideology is a contest to determine which nodal point will unify the remainder of the free-floating political elements.[47] For earlier generations, grand ideologies like Marxism or radical feminism presented an overarching theory into which other ideas were accommodated. In our "post-ideological age," after the fall of communism, there has been no explicit ideology that commands the respect of large numbers of Western intellectuals. Traditionally, antisemitism played precisely that role for the masses, which is why it was fittingly described as the "socialism of fools." In recent years, the new antisemitism has played a similar role for some Western intellectuals as well.

This is the manner in which anti-Israelism has totalized free-floating elements of the contemporary global left. Anti-Zionism has been closely related to elements within what Alvin Rosenfeld has called "a diverse range of intellectual and ideological currents—Islamism, Third-Worldism, Marxism, postmodernism, multiculturalism, post-colonialism, anti-Americanism, [and] certain strains of feminism." These intellectual trends are important, because several of them have helped to form "the political identities and thinking of two or more generations of American academics, especially those situated in humanities and social science departments."[48] Ernest Sternberg explains the phenomenon in his classic article, "Purifying the World." Echoing the old joke about Jews and bicyclists, Sternberg asks, "Why Israel?" The clue, Sternberg suggests, is in the astonishing variety of groups held together in the new anti-Western coalition: post-Christian humanitarians, third-worldists, Islamists, Arab Nationalists, and anti-globalizers of various sorts. "This," Sternberg explains, "is the movement's ticklish problem: how to keep so much diversity in check. If Empire is too abstract as a nemesis, and the United States seems too formidable, Israel represents a scapegoat manageable enough in size, and devilish enough in the popular imagination."[49]

Antisemitism serves as a nodal point in the sense that it provides a central inexplicable figure by means of which everything else can be explained. "All comes from the Jew," as Édouard Drumont wrote in a bestselling nineteenth-century tract, and "all returns to the Jew."[50] Similarly, the ideology of contemporary Muslim antisemitism sees the Jews as the source of all catastrophes; "There is no disaster in the world that was not caused by the Jews," wrote journalist Safaa Saleh in 2011 in the Egyptian government newspaper Al-Gumhouriyya.[51]

> What does Hitler do in Mein Kampf to explain to the Germans the misfortunes [p. 18] of the epoch, economic crisis, social disintegration, moral "decadence," and so on? He constructs a new terrifying subject, a unique cause of Evil who "pulls the strings" behind the

scene and is the sole precipitator of the series of evils: the Jew. The
simple evocation of the "Jewish plot" explains everything: all of
a sudden "things become clear," perplexity is replaced by a firm
sense of orientation, all the diversity of earthly miseries is conceived as the manifestation of the "Jewish plot."[52]

Similarly, contemporary Islamic antisemitism, like its Nazi pre-
cursor, sees Jewry as the root of evil responsible for such diverse
phenomena as Marxism, psychoanalysis, materialism, pornography, sociology, sexual permissiveness, and the degradation of
morals.[53]

It must be acknowledged that this approach can be taken to
unsupportable extremes. For example, Žižek argues that antisemitism goes so far as to attain the "zero-level (or the pure form)
of ideology, establishing its elementary coordinates: the social
antagonism ('class struggle') is mystified or displaced so that
its cause can be projected onto the external intruder."[54] Žižek,
characteristically, is engaged here in a bit of hyperbole, since he
is really arguing that antisemitism is a particular manifestation
that fully embodies the concept of ideology—or more precisely
his own Marxist conception of that concept—rather than that
it is coequal with the universal concept itself (as would be implied by the notion of zero-level). Nevertheless, the basic insight
is accurate. Although antisemitism may not be the "pure form"
of ideology, it has been the paradigmatic case of ideological hatred throughout Western history. Indeed, it has been the form
of prejudice that has most frequently played a defining role in
forging a worldview for Western societies.

David Nirenberg confides that he was motivated to write his
magisterial history of *Anti-Judaism* by his conviction that we
"live in an age in which millions of people are exposed daily to
some variant of the argument that the challenges of the world
they live in are best explained in terms of 'Israel.'"[55] Many people
today make sense of the world in terms of the alleged dangers
and evils of Israel and Zionism. This is not merely an attitude,

although it often manifests itself in emotional responses. Nor is it best understood in terms of the conduct to which it gives rise, although the world's treatment of Israel cannot be understood in any other way. Instead, the way in which Israel is treated today forms a broader ideology that parallels the historic treatment of the Jew. For this reason, the new antisemitism must be addressed at its psychological and ideological core. Here it is not merely about "the Jew," individually or collectively, but about a way of bringing sense out of the world's chaos and of responding to the traumas of social division.

NOTES

Some portions of this chapter are drawn from Kenneth L. Marcus, *The Definition of Antisemitism* (New York: Oxford University Press, forthcoming 2015).

1. Jean-Paul Sartre, *Anti-Semite and Jew,* trans. George C. Becker (New York: Schocken Books 1995), 17.

2. Anthony Julius, *Trials of the Diaspora: A History of Antisemitism in England* (Oxford: Oxford University Press, 2010), xlii, xliv, xlii.

3. Kenneth L. Marcus, "The Definition of Antisemitism," in *Global Antisemitism: A Crisis of Modernity,* ed. Charles Asher Small (Leiden, the Netherlands: Martinus Nijhoff Publishers, 2013), 109.

4. T. W. Adorno et al., *The Authoritarian Personality* (New York: Harper, 1950), 71.

5. Helen Fein, "Dimensions of Antisemitism: Attitudes, Collective Accusations, and Actions," in *The Persisting Question: Sociological Perspectives and Social Contexts of Modern Antisemitism,* ed. Helen Fein (Berlin: De Gruyter, 1987), 67.

6. Marvin Perry and Frederick M. Schweitzer, *Antisemitism: Myth and Hate from Antiquity to the Present* (New York: Palgrave Macmillan, 2002), 74.

7. Deborah Lipstadt, "*The Protocols of the Elders of Zion* on the Contemporary American Scene: Historical Artifact or Current Threat?," in *The Paranoid Apocalypse: A Hundred-Year Retrospective on "The Protocols of the Elders of Zion,"* ed. Richard Landes and Steven T. Katz (New York: New York University Press, 2012), 172–185. Walmart subsequently reversed this decision after initially resisting public pressure, insisting that it had "not

seen [a] clear and convincing version" of evidence that *The Protocols* were a forgery (ibid., 172).

8. Daniel J. Goldhagen, *Hitler's Willing Executioners: Ordinary Germans and the Holocaust* (New York: Knopf, 1996), 455.

9. Terry Eagleton, *Ideology: An Introduction* (London: Verso, 2007, rev. ed.), 2.

10. Niza Yanay, *The Ideology of Hatred: The Psychic Power of Discourse* (New York: Fordham University Press, 2013), 20.

11. American Psychological Association, *Resolution on Anti-Semitic and Anti-Jewish Prejudice* (adopted by the APA Council of Representatives August 2005, amended August 2007), http://www.apa.org/about/policy/antisemitic.pdf.

12. Slavoj Žižek, *The Sublime Object of Ideology* (London: Verso, 1989), 24, 26.

13. Peter Sloterdijk, *Critique of Cynical Reason,* trans. Michael Eldred (Minneapolis: University of Minnesota Press, 1987).

14. Žižek, *Sublime Object of Ideology,* 26.

15. Ibid., 30.

16. U.S. Commission on Civil Rights, *Briefing Report on Campus Anti-semitism* (Washington, D.C.: U.S. Commission on Civil Rights, 2006), 66.

17. Deborah Lipstadt, *Denying the Holocaust: The Growing Assault on Truth and Memory* (New York: Free Press, 1993), 1–2.

18. Gunnar Myrdal, *An American Dilemma: The Negro Problem and American Democracy* (New York: Harper, 1944), 1:76.

19. Hilda Taba, "What Is Evaluation Up to and Up against in Intergroup Education?," *Journal of Educational Sociology* 21 (September 1947): 19–24, 21, quoted in Stuart Svonkin, *Jews against Prejudice: American Jews and the Fight for Civil Liberties* (New York: Columbia University Press, 1997), 63–64.

20. "Community Relations Agency Involvement in Intergroup Education" (March 1953): 1–2, quoted in Svonkin, *Jews against Prejudice,* 41, 63.

21. Naomi W. Cohen, *Encounter with Emancipation: The German Jews in the United States, 1830–1914* (Philadelphia: Jewish Publication Society of America, 1984), 91, quoted in Svonkin, *Jews against Prejudice,* 75–76.

22. Svonkin, *Jews against Prejudice,* 41–42, 63, 53–61.

23. John Slawson, "Programming Community Relations in the Present Period," paper delivered at NCRAC Fifth Plenary Session, Atlantic City, New Jersey (March 15–17, 1947), 7, quoted in ibid., 54.

24. Bruno Bettelheim and Morris Janowitz, *Dynamics of Prejudice: A Psychological and Sociological Study of Veterans* (New York: Harper, 1950), 4–6.

25. Adorno et al., *Authoritarian Personality,* ix, 93, 973.

26. Žižek, *Sublime Object of Ideology,* p. 48, 48–49, 49.

27. Sergei Silus quoted in Richard Landes and Steven T. Katz, "Introduction: The *Protocols* at the Dawn of the 21st Century," in Landes and Katz, *Paranoid Apocalypse,* 8.

28. Günther Jikeli, "Antisemitism among Young European Males," in *Resurgent Antisemitism: Global Perspectives,* ed. Alvin H. Rosenfeld (Bloomington: Indiana University Press, 2013), 284.

29. Žižek, *Sublime Object of Ideology,* 49.

30. Leon Wieseltier, "Old Demons, New Debates," in *Old Demons, New Debates: Antisemitism in the West,* ed. David I. Kertzer, 1–8 (Teaneck, N.J.: Holmes & Meier, 2005), 3.

31. Elżbieta Ettinger, *Hannah Arendt/Martin Heidegger* (New Haven, Conn.: Yale University Press, 1995), quoted in Anthony Julius, *Trials of the Diaspora: A History of Antisemitism in England* (Oxford: Oxford University Press, 2010), 58.

32. Žižek, *Sublime Object of Ideology,* 49–50.

33. Ibid.

34. John Chrysostom, *Discourses against Judaizing Christians,* trans. Paul W. Hawkins (Washington, D.C.: Catholic University Press, 1979), 6.6.10–11, quoted in David Nirenberg, *Anti-Judaism: The Western Tradition* (New York: W. W. Norton, 2013), 113.

35. Elisabeth Young-Bruehl, *The Anatomy of Prejudices* (Cambridge, Mass.: Harvard University Press, 1996), 53.

36. Max Horkheimer and Theodor W. Adorno, *Dialectic of Enlightenment: Philosophical Fragments,* ed. Gunzelin Schmid Noerr and trans. Edmund Jephcott (Stanford, Calif.: Stanford University Press, 2002), 154.

37. Ibid., 52.

38. Ibid., 53.

39. Bettelheim and Janowitz, *Dynamics of Prejudice,* 58–61, 76–85.

40. Nathan Ackerman and Marie Jahoda, *Antisemitism and Emotional Disorder* (New York: Harper, 1950), 8–9, quoted in Svonkin, *Jews against Prejudice,* 38–39.

41. Slavoj Žižek, *The Year of Dreaming Dangerously* (London: Verso, 2012), 23.

42. Žižek, *Sublime Object of Ideology,* 95.

43. Ernesto Laclau and Chantal Mouffe, *Hegemony and Socialist Strategy: Towards a Radical Democratic Politics,* 2nd. ed. (London: Verso, 2001), 112.

44. Žižek, *Sublime Object of Ideology,* 95–96.

45. András Kovács, "Antisemitic Prejudice and Political Antisemitism in Present-Day Hungary," *Journal for the Study of Antisemitism* 4, no. 2 (2013): 443, 464.

46. Ernest Sternberg, "Purifying the World: What the New Radical Ideology Stands For," *Orbis,* winter 2010, 61.

47. Žižek, *Sublime Object of Ideology,* 96.

48. Alvin H. Rosenfeld, "Responding to Campus-Based Anti-Zionism: Two Models," in *Antisemitism on the Campus: Past and Present,* ed. Eunice G. Pollack (Boston: Academic Studies Press, 2011), 414, 416, 417.

49. Sternberg, "Purifying the World," 81.

50. Édouard Drumont quoted in Robert Wistrich, *A Lethal Obsession: Antisemitism from Antiquity to the Global Jihad* (New York: Random House, 2010), 6.

51. Safaa Saleh quoted in Matthias Küntzel, "The Roots of Antisemitism in the Middle East: New Debates," in Rosenfeld, *Resurgent Antisemitism,* 283.

52. Slavoj Žižek, *For They Know Not What They Do: Enjoyment as a Political Factor* (London: Verso, 2008), 17–18.

53. Wistrich, *Lethal Obsession,* 6.

54. Žižek, *Year of Dreaming Dangerously,* 23.

55. Nirenberg, *Anti-Judaism,* 471.

A Framework for Assessing Antisemitism

Three Case Studies
(Dieudonné, Erdoğan, and Hamas)

GÜNTHER JIKELI

SCHOLARS OF ANTISEMITISM often describe antisemitic incidents and developments in detail, sometimes including an analysis of possible sources. Much work has also been done to make the case that some statements, incidents, or individuals are indeed antisemitic. In this chapter, I argue that, in times of rising antisemitism, more research is needed to go one step further and assess, within their context, the potential impact and threat of antisemitic attitudes, incidents, individuals, or organizations under investigation.

I propose a framework to assess the potential consequences that arise from contemporary manifestations of antisemitism and apply it to three case studies: French comedian Dieudonné M'bala M'bala, Turkish President Recep Tayyip Erdoğan, and the Palestinian terrorist organization Hamas. The first two are antisemitic individuals in very different power positions. The third is an antisemitic organization that governs territory in Gaza. The evaluation shows not only that these manifestations pose a serious threat to Jews and non-Jews but also explains the nature of these threats and the factors that contribute to their different negative impacts now and potentially in the future.[1] I also identify which factors might help to contain the threats.

EVALUATION FRAMEWORK

Social psychology has shown that attitudes can predict *intentions* for possible behaviors that, depending on circumstances, might then be translated into *actual* behavior.[2] However, there is a major difference between someone who believes that all Jews are rich and someone who wants to build an organization to kill Jews, although both are antisemites. We should therefore analyze attitudes carefully, including their strength and quality.[3] What are the specific qualities of antisemitic attitudes and stereotypes? Helen Fein notes that the attribution of alleged Jewish violations to an intrinsic or racial quality and the accusation of a Jewish world conspiracy have motivated attempts at categorical elimination of the Jews. She further distinguishes between conventional stereotypes without (direct) hostile effect and intrinsically hostile accusations that demonize and dehumanize Jews and justify violence or discrimination against Jews.[4] Some antisemitic beliefs are used to justify not only discrimination against Jews but the annihilation of Jews. Gavin I. Langmuir identifies these notions as chimeric and distinguishes them from xenophobic assertions.[5] Antisemitic chimeric assertions that have no empirical basis whatsoever portray Jews as "inhuman or subhuman monsters who fall outside the norm of humanity of the ingroup. […] Jewish existence has been or is much more seriously endangered because real Jews have been converted in the minds of many into a symbol that denies empirical reality and justifies their total elimination from earth."[6]

Daniel Goldhagen developed a framework for a qualitative assessment of antisemitic beliefs with regard to antisemitic action.[7] He suggests three parameters. The first captures beliefs about the essence of Jewishness, the perceived source of the Jews' malicious qualities such as race, religion, culture, or social environment. These beliefs have implications for how the antisemite analyzes the "Jewish question" and what he or she prescribes as appropriate courses of action. Goldhagen's second parameter is how preoccupied or obsessed an antisemite is with Jews. This parameter represents the centrality of antisemitic views in a person's consciousness between latent and manifest, or the strength of antisemitic attitudes.[8] The third parameter represents the putative perniciousness of the Jews. To what extent are Jews perceived as a threat? The wish for annihilation increases alongside the antisemite's sense of the Jewish threat.

Additionally, antisemitic movements, from Nazism, to communism, to Islamism, have shown that antisemitic attitudes lead to particularly threatening behavior if they are part of a revolutionary wish to change society.

Taken together, these reflections on the *quality* of attitudes leading to the intention of antisemitic behavior can be captured with seven questions:

1. What antisemitic actions are explicitly or implicitly advocated or tolerated?
2. What are the fears and putative perniciousness of Jews?
3. Are the antisemitic beliefs part of a revolutionary wish to change society?
4. How strong and obsessive are antisemitic attitudes?
5. How chimeric and delusional are the attitudes?[9]
6. What is the perception of Jewishness (socialization or culture, faith, and race) and how strong is the conception of the Jews as one entity?
7. To what extent are Jews dehumanized and demonized?

Assessing How and Where Antisemitism Is Manifested

In addition to the quality of antisemitic attitudes, we should assess how and where antisemitism is manifested. Antisemitism becomes more dynamic and threatening if it advances from individual action to a level of social exchange, or if antisemitism is organized collectively. Where is antisemitism voiced or manifested? What is the level of social organization of antisemitism? Fein's definition of antisemitism differentiates between attitudes, culture, and actions by individuals, a collective, or the state.[10] Some scholars distinguish between manifest antisemitism such as assaults, damage to properties, and hate speech, and latent antisemitism in everyday discourses where antisemitism is often voiced indirectly and through insinuations.[11] Due precisely to the fact that they are not recognized and not actively discredited as antisemitism, they are able to enhance the dissemination of antisemitic beliefs.[12] Latent forms of antisemitism can contribute to a shift in discourses, resulting in a shift of social norms of tolerance of antisemitic actions and verbal expressions.[13]

However, antisemitism in organized form, particularly from state actors or governments, has the highest destructive potential due to governmental power. Additionally, the type of government and its willingness to maintain the rule of law (and to ensure equal rights for Jews) are important background factors. We can distinguish four categories of antisemitic manifestations with different implications for an assessment of its threats:

1. Individual actions
2. Communication, discourses, and culture
3. Organized actions performed collectively, including political mobilization
4. Institutionalized actions and state violence

Assessing the Cultural and Historical Contexts

If overt antisemitic action and verbal expression depend on "the situation of the moment," as Theodor W. Adorno and others put it, it is worth defining the situation more precisely.[14] Structural opportunities are important for antisemitic behavior in politics, culture, and discourse.[15] The cultural context in which antisemitism occurs is an important background factor for a prognosis of further antisemitic behavior. What is more, prior history of genocides and instability has proven to be highly relevant for an assessment of the threat of genocides. An analysis of more than a hundred incidents of genocides and mass violence has shown that an "exclusionary ideology," prior violence and discrimination against the target group, as well as the regime type and its willingness to maintain the rule of law, are some of the key indicators for genocide.[16] Nico Voigtländer and Hans-Joachim Voth found a surprisingly long historic consistency of antisemitic violence on a local level, explaining this as persistence of antisemitism in cultural traits. In the first half of the twentieth century, antisemitism was particularly widespread in German cities and towns where pogroms had occurred during the Black Death in the fourteenth century.[17] Assessing the contexts of antisemitism, we should therefore also ask: What beliefs about social norms and restrictions (of antisemitic actions) might encourage or hinder antisemitic behavior? What are the local, regional, and national histories of antisemitism? What has been the impact of the antisemitic individual, organization incident, or manifestation of attitudes so far? This last question obviously necessitates listening to those who are the immediate targets of antisemitism.

Assessing the Influence of Actors Who Endorse, Tolerate, or Oppose Antisemitism

To evaluate the potential influence of both antisemites and those who oppose antisemitism, it is essential to know who the potential perpetrators and opponents are and their relative numbers. Surveys of antisemitism usually collect data on the percentage of a certain population who agree or disagree with antisemitic statements. Disagreement with antisemitic statements in a survey does not necessarily mean opposition to it. An individual who does not agree with an antisemitic statement might tolerate it as an opinion that he or she simply does not share. Interestingly, some studies of antisemitic attitudes during the period when National Socialism was virulent in Germany show not a significant rise in antisemitic attitudes but rather a rise of indifference toward antisemitism.[18] Therefore, Fein asks: "Can we assume that the execution of antisemitic programs depends on the growth in the number of antisemites or the decline in resistance to antisemitism (anti-antisemitism)? How we estimate the weight of the indifferent, neutral, and/or those with 'weak' or mixed attitudes depends on which assumptions we choose."[19] Those with indifferent attitudes might join in antisemitic actions for opportunistic reasons, whereas those who oppose antisemitic attitudes might oppose and avert antisemitic actions depending on their number and influence. Leo Löwenthal points out that the lack of resistance to the National Socialists in the Weimar Republic, which became obvious during his studies in the 1930s, was a decisive and foreseeable factor for catastrophe—rather than rising antisemitism in the German population.[20] Helen Fein suggests that both the dominant tendency and the size and stability of "anti-antisemitic" factions should be studied. She further highlights the importance of other variables for predicting behavior such as power, interests, resources, and sanctions.[21] Others highlight that antisemitism is particularly dangerous if combined with political goals or if voiced as political goals.[22] In summary, to predict antisemitic action, the following characteristics of those who endorse, tolerate, or oppose antisemitism are relevant: numbers, stability, influence in society (including support by governmental and nongovernmental organizations), interests, political articulations, and possible sanctions they might face.[23]

It is the combination of the different factors and dimensions that makes antisemitism an eminent threat for Jews, civilized society, and humanity in general. A comprehensive assessment of the quality, forms and spheres, and actors helps us to evaluate the threats realistically without downplaying them or panicking. The suggested framework serves as a first step to move from implicit judgments about the dangers of antisemitic manifestations toward an explicit evaluation through a qualitative assessment of antisemitism, summarized in table 3.1.

ASSESSING ANTISEMITISM IN THREE CASE STUDIES

This evaluative framework is now applied to three case studies: French comedian Dieudonné M'bala M'bala, Turkish president Recep Tayyip Erdoğan, and the Palestinian terrorist organization Hamas. The threat is very different in these three cases. Previous studies have discussed only some aspects of their antisemitism, failing to see the full picture.

Most publications about Dieudonné's antisemitism document his antisemitic behaviors but fail to analyze both the quality of his antisemitic views and his impact. The most comprehensive work, *La Galaxie Dieudonné,* by Michel Briganti, André Déchot, and Jean-Paul Gautier, does provide a wider context and an analysis of Dieudonné's multiple connections to extremists, and unmasks his goal of an extreme right revolution against the "Empire" behind his talk in the name of the underdog. However, the study addresses the quality of Dieudonné's antisemitism only partly, failing to see its centrality in his worldviews.

Erdoğan's antisemitic utterances have been criticized, but no one has assessed how deep his antisemitic convictions are and what we might expect of future actions of this head of state of 77 million people.

There are also a number of deficiencies in the analysis of Hamas's antisemitism that might be made good with more comprehensive questions. Assessing the depth and strength of Hamas's antisemitism might provide insights into the limitations of agreements with this organization.

Only a thorough evaluation, including questions in all dimensions of antisemitism, can determine what kind of actions we can expect in each case and what factors contribute to the potential negative impact.

TABLE 3.1. EVALUATIVE FRAMEWORK: DIMENSIONS OF ANTISEMITISM

1st Dimension
Quality of Antisemitic Beliefs

· What kind of actions are directly or indirectly incited by the antisemitic beliefs? Is the intent genocidal?
· What antisemitic actions are advocated or tolerated?
· What are the fears and putative perniciousness of Jews?
· Are the antisemitic beliefs part of a revolutionary wish to change society?
· How strong and obsessive are antisemitic attitudes?
· How chimeric and illusionary are the attitudes?
· What is the perception of Jewishness (socialization or culture, faith, and race) and how strong is the conception of the Jews as one entity?
· To what extent are Jews dehumanized and demonized?

2nd Dimension
Forms and Spheres of Antisemitic Manifestations

How is antisemitism manifested?
· In individual actions?
· In communication, discourses, and culture?
· In organized actions; including political mobilization?
· In institutionalized actions and state violence?

3rd Dimension
Context

· What are the cultural, social, and historical contexts?
· What beliefs about social norms and restrictions (of antisemitic actions) might encourage or hinder antisemitic behavior?
· What are the local, regional, and national histories of antisemitism?
· What has been the impact of the antisemitic individual, organization, incident, or manifestation of attitudes so far?
· What are reactions of the Jewish communities?

4th Dimension
Factions of Individuals and Organizations

· Who endorses, tolerates, or opposes antisemitism?
· What is the estimated number of antisemites and what kind of impact and power do they have?
· What is the estimated number of those who are indifferent to antisemitism? What factors might influence them in supporting or opposing antisemites?
· What is the estimated number of anti-antisemites and what kind of impact and power do they have?

The Case of Dieudonné M'bala M'bala

Dieudonné M'bala M'bala, a French comedian and political activist, is a convicted antisemite and Holocaust denier. He was born in France in 1966 to a Cameroonian father and a French mother. He made his career as a stand-up comedian in France in the 1990s, together with his childhood friend, Jewish comedian and actor Élie Semoun. After their eventual split, Dieudonné, as he was known by then, continued with successful one-man shows and appeared in some movies. Since 1999 he has run the Théâtre de la Main d'Or in Paris, which regularly hosts his stand-up comedy and political events and meetings. However, his shows and other public appearances have become increasingly controversial and antisemitic.

His shift from an artist working closely with a Jewish comedian and an antiracist activist in the late 1990s to one of the most outspoken antisemites among public figures in France can be traced in his professional work as a comedian and his political activism. Today, his activism, his conspiracist worldview, his work as a comedian, and a unique and successful marketing strategy, including regular video messages, are inextricably interwoven. His antisemitic tirades, his alliances to the Far Right, black supremacists, and Islamists including Mahmoud Ahmadinejad are well-documented elsewhere and have been discussed in media such as the *New Yorker,* the *New Statesman,* and the *New York Times.*[24] It will suffice here to recall some of his most controversial statements and acts in recent years before assessing his potential impact on antisemitism.

In 2002, in an interview with a monthly regional magazine from Lyon, he described "the Jews" as the worst of all sects and a "fraud." In 2003, he appeared live on France's second- largest public television channel, France 3, with a sketch culminating in a Hitler salute, disguised as a "Jewish Orthodox settler." Some weeks later he gave an interview to the cultural magazine the

Source in which he talked about the "Jewish lobby" that might ban him from television, accusing a Jewish television presenter of "funding the Israeli army who doesn't hesitate killing children." In 2005, he described, in a press conference in Algeria, Holocaust remembrance as "memorial pornography" and the Central Council of French Jews as a "mafia" that had "total control over the exercise of French policy." He further accused "Zionists" of controlling French cinema and preventing him from making a film about the slave trade. In 2008, he invited Holocaust denier Robert Faurisson to one of his shows. His 2010 show *Mahmoud* (standing for Mahmoud Ahmadinejad) has an openly antisemitic tone, caricaturing Judaism as "the religion of profit" and Jews as slave traders (a now constant theme in his appearances), ridiculing "official" versions of the Holocaust and praising Mahmoud Ahmadinejad and Hamas leader Khaled Meshaal, both of whom he had previously met in person. In 2012, Dieudonné made his directorial debut in a film called *L'Antisémite* (*The Antisemite*), starring himself and featuring Faurisson. The film is an antisemite's daydream, using numerous antisemitic tropes and culminating in the wish for extermination of the Jews. An important part of the movie is the mocking and "killing" of remembrance of the Holocaust.[25] The movie was produced by the Iranian company Yahod Setiz. It was not screened in French cinemas, but it is commercialized on the internet. Dieudonné's antisemitism became internationally known when professional soccer player Nicolas Anelka performed the offensive quenelle, a modified Nazi salute pointing downward, to celebrate scoring a goal for the English Premier League club West Brom in December 2013.[26] Dieudonné invented and popularized the quenelle, widely regarded as being antisemitic. He claims that it is "a kind of up yours gesture to the establishment." However, he believes that "the establishment" is run by Jews. He also said that he wants "to put a quenelle into Zionism's butt"—equating "Zionism" with Judaism. Many of his followers recognize his antisemitic messages, and it has become commonplace to perform the quenelle in public areas, including Holocaust memorials and outside of Jewish institutions. Tens of thousands of followers take a picture of their quenelle performance and post it on social media, encouraged by the ceremonies and awards that Dieudonné arranges.

French authorities took decisive action against M'bala M'bala following a preview of his 2014 live performance, *Le Mur [The Wall]*, in which he expressed his wish that the Jewish radio journalist Patrick Cohen had been gassed. The show was canceled in many cities after French Interior Minister Manuel Valls sent a memo in early 2014 to all police prefects in France pointing out the antisemitic content of the show.[27] Dieudonné responded to the accusation of antisemitism in a widely watched video message with a remarkable statement: "Antisemite? I'm not of that opinion . . . I'm not saying I'd never be one . . . I leave myself open to that possibility, but for the moment, no . . . I don't have to choose between the Jews and the Nazis. I'm neutral in this affair. . . . Who provoked whom? Who robbed whom?"[28] However, he changed his show slightly and continues his regular performances three times per week in his theater in Paris in addition to shows in other parts of France and abroad.

Dieudonné also participated in a number of national and European elections. He started his political career during the national elections in 1997 when he campaigned against a National Front candidate. In 1998 he headed the Liste des Utopistes (the Utopians) in regional elections. He attempted to run in the 2002 and 2007 presidential elections. At the European Parliament elections in 2004, he was a candidate for the extreme left-wing party Euro-Palestine, which he left shortly afterward due to disagreements with party leaders over his alliances to the extreme right. In 2009 he was head of the Liste antisioniste (the Anti-Zionist Party), close to the Zahra Center, a Shi'ite Islamist organization with links to Iran and Hezbollah. Another candidate and close friend was Alain Soral, a well-known ideologue of the extreme right. Dieudonné stood again for elections with the same party in the 2012 national elections. He has never won a seat and his parties have been fringe groups without any political leverage, but his election campaigns have gained him some publicity. In November 2014, he and Soral founded the party Réconciliation nationale (National Reconciliation). Jean-Yves Camus, an expert on the extreme right, described the main goals of the party as "the radical opposition to Judaism, the Jewish community, and Israel."[29]

Assessing Dieudonné M'bala M'bala's Antisemitism

What kind of action is incited by Dieudonné's beliefs? M'bala M'bala does not publicly call for violence against Jews, but he has repeatedly downplayed and denied antisemitic violence in France and antisemitism by Hamas and Hezbollah and, more recently, showed solidarity with the murderer of Jews in the kosher supermarket in Paris in January 2015.[30] However, his apparent wish for the annihilation of the Jews and of particular Jews often surfaces.[31] He contends that "Zionists," meaning Jews, are in control of the current "establishment" and "empire," bringing wars, exploitation, and censorship.[32] He evidently sees himself as being the center of a revolutionary fight against "the establishment"—controlled by the Jews, or "Zionism" as he often puts it.[33] He claims to be personally persecuted by the "Jewish lobby," which he alleges is trying to kill him socially. Additionally, M'bala M'bala frequently uses antisemitic stereotypes such as allegations that Jews are greedy and clannish and often blames Jews for the black slave trade. His antisemitic expressions and presumably his antisemitic attitudes have grown stronger and more outspoken during the last decade. His obsession with Jews, Judaism, and Zionism can now be observed in almost all of his shows and public statements. His descriptions of Jews are highly chimeric and have no basis whatsoever in reality. He implicitly uses his "humor" as an excuse for his statements based on associations and obsessions rather than logic. His representation of Jewishness tends to be racist, and he poses Jews as one entity throughout history and space. M'bala M'bala increasingly demonizes all Jews and uses "Zionists" and "Jews" almost interchangeably.[34] He has compared Jews to rats and dogs.[35] His declarations that he wants to free France and the world from "Zionism" are a thinly veiled expression of the wish for the annihilation of Jews. We can therefore conclude that M'bala M'bala's antisemitic attitudes are genocidal in intent, well beyond the aim of excluding or discriminating against Jews. Nevertheless, he seems to hold back from even blunter statements and other antisemitic behavior, at least for the time being.[36]

Where and how does he voice his antisemitism? M'bala M'bala acts as an individual in his shows, public appearances in mainstream media, and video messages. His shows are attended by thousands of people in France and abroad, and hundreds of thousands watch his video messages, some of which exceed a million views. His appearances on television have dwindled due to his openly antisemitic statements. However, his views are often covered by the press, albeit scandalized in recent years. By January 2014, the vast majority in France (87 percent) had heard of Dieudonné M'bala M'bala; 16 percent of the overall population and 22 percent of those under the age of thirty-five had a positive view of him.[37] In September 2014, 64 percent thought that the government was right to ban Dieudonné's show earlier that year. However, 46 percent agreed with Dieudonné that there is not enough discussion about black slavery, and 23 percent agreed with him that "Jews control the media" and that there is too much discussion about the Shoah.[38] M'bala M'bala presents himself as a rebel against "the system" and uses his role as a comedian and "humor" as a tool to disseminate hate messages that would otherwise be rejected. He thereby allows antisemitic sentiments to be voiced publicly, which is part of his appeal. Additionally, he has been active in politics, particularly in the Anti-Zionist Party. He cooperates with influential antisemites from the extreme right and with Islamists, and he uses his theater for political events and meetings. Although he has secured some funding from Iran, his political alliances are with fringe groups in France, with the exception of the National Front. However, the new party leader since 2011, Marine LePen, daughter of her predecessor Jean-Marie LePen, sees him as a pariah. M'bala M'bala has been exceptionally successful in disseminating his antisemitic messages with his song "Shoananas," which mocks the Holocaust, and even more so with the popularization of the quenelle. Thousands of people perform the gesture in public and post it on social media or send it to M'bala M'bala, who organizes ceremonies and prizes for participants. This can be seen as a modern and unconventional form of organized antisemitic action.

What are the cultural, social, and historical contexts? M'bala M'bala's antisemitic messages fall on fertile ground within parts of the French population (and in other francophone countries). They link to widespread antisemitic stereotypes; 51 percent of the French population agreed in 2013 that "Jews have too much power in the business world," and 44 percent thought that "Jews still talk too much about what happened to them in the Holocaust."[39] Additionally, Dieudonné portrays himself as a victim of racism and as an underdog, attempting to appeal to people of Arab and African heritage. He often refers to competing victimhoods (viz., opposing victims of slavery and colonialism against victims of the Holocaust) in his rants against Holocaust remembrance. Moreover, he often wraps his antisemitic messages in anti-Zionist, antireligious, and "anti-communitarist" views, all of which have been traditionally strong in France.[40] Historically, antisemitic actions have occurred in French society for many centuries. Moreover, M'bala M'bala uses grievances of blacks and people of North African background to incite hatred against remembrance of the Holocaust, which he sees as being imposed by "Zionists."

The impact of M'bala M'bala's antisemitism on France's half-million-strong Jewish communities has added to hostility among significant parts of the French population. M'bala M'bala's dissemination of hatred against the Jews, deeply offensive remarks about the Holocaust, and personal attacks against some Jews have led to an outcry and strong reactions by Jewish leaders and organizations.

Lastly, we must look at his supporters and adversaries in order to assess his impact. M'bala M'bala is supported by radical intellectuals and politicians of the extreme right, such as Alain Sorel and Jean-Marie LePen, but also by the Iranian regime and other Islamists and Arab nationalist leaders. (He awarded a golden quenelle to Bashar Al-Assad in 2013 for his anti-Zionism and anti-imperialism.) However, he is financially independent.[41] M'bala M'bala has a large following, many of them antisemites, as evidenced by their performances of the quenelle outside venues related to Judaism or the memory of the Holocaust and by their comments on Dieudonné M'bala M'bala's blog, messages, and videos. Other fans just tolerate his antisemitism, appreciate the supposed ambiguity, or still believe that his attitudes are funny. A major source of financial and moral support, his fan community also contributes to his social acceptability. His shows are frequently sold out. His fan community connects through social media and is active in French-speaking countries, including Canada and a number of African countries. Some of his followers are prominent. While a large majority in France (71 percent in early 2014) has a negative opinion of Dieudonné M'bala M'bala, some tolerate his antisemitism and interpret his comments as ambiguous, antiestablishment, anti-Zionist, or satirical. At least since 2014, M'bala M'bala has faced strong opposition from the government that, as noted earlier, led to the cancellation of one of his shows in a number of cities. Mainstream media frequently condemn M'bala M'bala's antisemitism and denounce his affiliation to the extreme right, while often overlooking his affiliation to Islamists. Action has also been taken in the judicial system. M'bala M'bala has been convicted on numerous accounts for his antisemitic comments since 2007. This has led to his further marginalization, and a number of public figures have distanced themselves from him.

To conclude, M'bala M'bala's impact and ability to organize antisemitic action, which became obvious with his successful campaign of the quenelle, has long been underestimated. Although he faces strong opposition for his antisemitism, he has found efficient ways to disseminate his genocidal antisemitic views, particularly under the disguise of humor, anti-Zionism, and attacks on Holocaust remembrance, all of which he will most likely continue. In a preview of his 2015 show, he announced his goal, embedded in a revolutionary posture: to "free France from Zionism."[42] While it is unlikely that he will gain any political leverage in the near future, he should not be underestimated in his role as a rabble-rouser, inciting hatred and softening publicly accepted limits of antisemitism in France and francophone countries.

The application of the presented framework reveals that his antisemitism is genocidal in intent and is not limited to individual actions but rather to exploring new forms of organized action. It also exposes that some of his themes such as "Jewish power," the mocking of the Holocaust, and anti-Zionism can be related to commonly held views in France and therefore have the potential to resonate in society. The framework also shows that he faces opposition and that limiting his possibilities are necessary to reduce or contain his negative impact.

The Case of Recep Tayyip Erdoğan

Another prominent figure who has long espoused antisemitic views is Recep Tayyip Erdoğan. Elected president of Turkey in August 2014, he served as the Turkish prime minister from 2003–14 and was the longtime leader of the ruling Justice and

Development Party (AKP). Erdoğan has often been described as a "moderate Islamist" due to his commitment to democratic procedures. However, he and his party have been working slowly but effectively to change the secular nature of the Turkish state and his commitment to democracy has increasingly been questioned in recent years. Erdoğan's antisemitism has become public on a number of occasions, often disguised as anti-Zionism. A closer look reveals that his antisemitism is deeply rooted in his political and general worldviews and that he acts upon his antisemitic views.

Back in 1974 he wrote, directed, and played the lead role in the play *Mas-Kom-Ya,* which presented Freemasonry, Communism, and Judaism as evil. To this day, Erdoğan's muse is Necip Fazıl Kısakürek, an antisemite and fierce enemy of secular Turkey. Kısakürek translated and published *The Protocols of the Elders of Zion* and praised Henry Ford's antisemitic pamphlet *The International Jew.* He also wrote a political platform that included the following: "With this commandment every measure is to be taken in order to bring the Turkish homeland to a state in which its only inhabitants are Muslims and Turks and to cleanse it from head to toe of traitors and darker forces. Chief among these treacherous and insidious elements to be cleansed are the Dönmes and the Jews. After the Dönmes and Jews, next in line are the Greeks, Armenians and various small minority groups."[43] The Dönmes are Crypto-Jews whose ancestors were followers of the so-called messiah Sabbatai Zevi in the seventeenth century. The accusation of being a Dönme has become an antisemitic insult in Turkey.[44] Erdoğan has praised Kısakürek as a guide for himself and future generations at a party gathering.[45]

Erdoğan became politically active in the 1970s in the Islamist National Salvation Party (MSP), led by Necmettin Erbakan. Erbakan, a fierce antisemite and outspoken Islamist, became his political mentor until the late 1990s, when Erdoğan turned away from Erbakan's anti-Western rhetoric.[46] Erdoğan's antisemitism

is less outspoken compared to the late Erbakan; however, his public rants against Israel and Jews since at least 2009 are telling.
Erdoğan accused Israel of "barbarism that surpasses Hitler" during its ground invasion of Gaza in summer 2014. In 2013, following
mass protests in cities around the country, Turkey's financial mar-
kets were turbulent, and Erdoğan laid the blame on the "interest
rate lobby." His deputy, Beşir Atalay, specified: "There are some
circles that are jealous of Turkey's growth. They are all uniting,
and on one side is the Jewish Diaspora. You saw the foreign media's attitude during the Gezi Park incidents; they bought it and
started broadcasting immediately."[47] These verbal attacks were
followed by unprecedented demands by the authorities against
Istanbul traders to hand over all email traffic with foreigners.
During the protests against the government's handling of Soma's
coal mine disaster in 2014 that led to more than three hundred
deaths, Erdoğan downplayed the tragedy and insulted protesters, victims, and their families. One of his insults ("Why are you
running away, spawn of Israel?") against a fellow countryman
shows how his obsession with Jews and Israel has translated into
his brutal language. A few days later, the pro-Erdoğan Islamist
newspaper *Yeni Akit* directly accused the Jewish-controlled media and Israel of responsibility for the tragedy.[48]

Obsession with Jews also influences Erdoğan's foreign policy.
Partners and enemies are chosen for ideological reasons rather
than based on what advances national interests. His close ties to
Gaddafi were founded partly on their common hatred of Israel.
Erdoğan received Gaddafi's International Human Rights Awards
of 2010 after deliberately provoking a crisis in Turkish-Israeli relations. The crisis amplified when the vessel *Mavi Marmara* of
the Turkish organization IHH (İnsani Yardım Vakfı) with ties to
Hamas and to the Turkish government, tried to break the Israeli
sea blockade on Gaza. The vessel departed with Erdoğan's approval, and nine Turkish citizens subsequently died in the violent clash with the Israeli army. Most media worldwide blamed

Israel. However, Erdoğan was not satisfied with the reports and invoked the classic antisemitic stereotype of Jews running the media: "When the word 'media' is pronounced, Israel and Israel's administration comes to mind. They have the ability to manipulate it as they wish."[49]

When Egyptian president Mohamed Morsi (Muslim Brotherhood) was ousted in July 2013, Erdoğan told party members: "Israel is behind the coup in Egypt, we have evidence." He then referred to a 2011 meeting in France between an Israeli justice minister and a "French Jewish intellectual" (later identified as Bernard-Henri Levy), opining that even if the Brotherhood won at the ballot box, he would not personally regard this as democratic and he would "urge the prevention of them coming to power . . . by all sorts of means."[50] In the mind of an antisemite, the case is clear: In Erdoğan's words: "Who is behind this? Israel." In 2009, he had insulted Israeli president Shimon Peres at Davos with a modernized blood libel, accusing Israelis of deliberately killing Palestinian children. Despite lip service to international audiences, Erdoğan clearly not only tolerates but actively endorses antisemitism.

Assessing Recep Tayyip Erdoğan's Antisemitism

What kind of action is incited by Erdoğan's beliefs? Erdoğan's antisemitic attitudes are harder to assess than M'bala M'bala's because, as a statesman of the Turkish Republic, he has been relatively careful in his comments about Jews. Even at the time he made the antisemitic comparison between Hitler and Israel, he tried to assure the Turkish Jewish community: "Jews in Turkey are our citizens. We are responsible for their security of life and property."[51] However, he also publicly urged community leaders to issue statements against the Israeli government, thereby feeding the antisemitic stereotype that Jews are not loyal citizens.[52] In combination with a demonization of Israel, this can be a dangerous accusation. Jewish communities in many countries have been attacked with this argument. The Jews of Turkey are undoubtedly, and understandably, uneasy and feeling insecure about their safety.

Erdoğan tries to distinguish the Jewish community in Turkey (which he tends to see as a monolith), but he seems to suspect Turkish Jews in general of alliances to Israel. Erdoğan's anti-Zionist expressed attitudes are highly delusional and chimeric, as the above examples have demonstrated, and he has used anti-semitic tropes, such as Jews as child killers. Although he has not publicly challenged Israel's right to exist, he has demonized Israel on numerous accounts, calling it a "terror state," comparing it to Hitler, and accusing it of genocide and, in the words of Bernard Harrison, of "utterly exceptional crimes."[53] What is more, he has supported Hamas, a terrorist group devoted to the annihilation of Israel and the killing of Jews. He sees Turkish interests threatened by alleged Israeli conspiracies and believes that the world press is run by Israel.[54] The frequency and passion with which he utters antisemitic remarks reveals a strong obsession with Jews and the Jewish State. Domestically, his antisemitic beliefs do not seem to be part of his visions to change society, although he frequently cites intellectuals who have wanted to rid Turkey of Jews. His anti-Israel foreign policy, however, is partly influenced by the idea of fundamental change in the region and the goal to build on Turkey's Ottoman imperial past.[55] Erdoğan's antisemitic views call for action in at least two areas: putting pressure on Jewish communities in Turkey, and attacking Israel. This is precisely what he and his government have been doing since about 2005, including, albeit half-hearted, direct military threats against Israel on at least two occasions.[56]

The way in which Erdoğan's antisemitism is manifested relates to his position as Turkey's most popular leader since 2003. Unsurprisingly, his public comments invoking antisemitic stereotypes, conspiracy theories, and hatred against Israel have an important impact. Additionally, he has not only failed to condemn blunt antisemitic comments and Holocaust denial in the press, he has also publicly supported the authors of such articles.[57] Antisemitic themes are also disseminated in state-sponsored media. Beyond his antisemitic statements, Erdoğan's antisemitic actions have been most apparent in his support of Hamas leaders, whom he has hosted in Turkey, and in his support of Hamas in its 2010 attempts to break the Israeli sea blockade.

What is the context of Erdoğan's antisemitism in Turkey, and who in Turkey are the antisemites, the anti-antisemites, and the indifferent? Although Turkish officials often claim that antisemitism has no place in Turkey, referring frequently to the accommodation of the Sephardic Jews of Spain at the end of the fifteenth century in the Ottoman Empire as well as the positive role of Turkish diplomats in the rescue of Jews during the Holocaust, this history does not reflect reality today. Antisemitism is part and parcel of Turkish Islamist ideology. Prominent antisemitic themes among Turkish Islamists are conspiracy theories about crypto-Jews, the abolishment of the caliphate and the creation of modern Turkey as a Jewish plot, and anti-Zionism and conspiracy theories about Israel, such as accusations that Israel has expansionist intentions—including Turkish soil. On the basis of a biblical verse it is claimed that Israel wants to expand from the Euphrates to the Nile and thus supports the Turkish-Kurdish separatist and terrorist organization Partiya Karkerên Kurdistan (PKK). Conspiracy theories about the "Israel lobby" instigating an alleged coup against the Islamist government and conspiring for the "Ergenokon plot" are also disseminated. However, Erdoğan's antisemitism falls on fertile ground beyond Islamists. Antisemitism has become widespread in Turkey, and opposition to it is low. According to a 2014 Anti-Defamation League survey, 69 percent of the population harbor antisemitic attitudes. This corresponds to a survey from 2008, when 68 percent had a "very unfavorable opinion of Jews," up from 59 percent in 2006. Antisemitic books such as the *Protocols of the Elders of Zion* (published

in Turkish 114 times between 1946 and 2012, mostly by Islamists)
and *Mein Kampf* (which in 2005 sold more than 100,000 copies
within two months) are popular and easily available. Antisemitic movies and television series such as the *Valley of the Wolves*
and *Ayrilik* are endorsed by state media.[58] Most dispiriting of
all, few individuals apart from a handful of intellectuals and
some human rights activists seem to be bothered by this state
of affairs. The small Jewish community, which is directly targeted, dares not speak up. However, even some Islamists such
as Mehmet Şevket Eygi and Abdurrahaman Dilipak have noted
that antisemitic ideas have corrupted thought in political Islam,
and member of parliament Aykan Erdemir from the opposition
Republican People's Party admitted in early 2014 that twelve
years of Erdoğan rule have significantly advanced antisemitism
in Turkey.

To conclude, Erdoğan's 2014 election as the president of Turkey is likely to have further negative consequences for Turkey's
Jews, Israel, Turkey's society, and even Turkey's interests. The
pressure on Turkey's Jews to distance themselves from Israel will
probably rise. So far, antisemitism has not been institutionalized in secular Turkey. However, there are fears that Erdoğan
will push for further Islamization of Turkey in his new role and
that religious minorities will be discriminated against or not sufficiently protected from hate crimes.[59] Turkish-Israeli relations
have deteriorated since Erdoğan took power, harming both Israeli and Turkish interests, such as discussion of a potential gas
pipeline from Israel to Turkey. This highly beneficial economic
project might be indefinitely stalled due to political tensions.[60]
What is more, Turkey's strong support for Hamas for ideological
reasons not only harms Israel but might also have negative diplomatic consequences for Turkey.[61] Lastly, the rise of antisemitic
attitudes and conspiracy theories in Turkey under Erdoğan adds
to a climate of religious and political intolerance that will be difficult to reverse.[62]

The application of the presented framework shows that Erdoğan's antisemitism is not genocidal but nevertheless dangerous for Turkish Jews and that his irrational and impulsive anti-Zionism poses an incalculable risk, particularly in his position as the leader of the Turkish Republic. The assessment also reveals that there is almost no opposition within Turkey and that antisemitism has been growing under Erdoğan. Opposition against Erdoğan's antisemitism thus needs to come from outside, and internal opposition needs to be supported.

The Case of Hamas

Hamas was founded in 1987 as an offshoot of the Muslim Brotherhood in Palestine to fight Israel and to establish an Islamic state in its place. It is considered a terrorist organization in many countries; countries that do not consider it a terrorist organization include Iran, Turkey, Qatar, Russia, and China. Hamas-led terrorist operations against Israel include suicide bombings, abductions, and rocket attacks. After the 2005 withdrawal of Israel from Gaza, Hamas won elections in the Palestinian Territories and took power in Gaza in fierce and violent battles against Fatah in 2007. It has since governed over Gaza's 1.82 million residents in authoritarian rule.

Assessing the impact of Hamas's antisemitism might demonstrate particularly well the usefulness of an evaluative framework. The framework suggested here reveals the dangers of its antisemitism on the highest levels and in multiple dimensions. The first dimension, the quality of antisemitic beliefs, can be answered unambiguously. In addition to frequent use of antisemitic stereotypes from "the rich and exploitative Jews," to child killers, to world conspiracy theories, Hamas has repeatedly called not only for the annihilation of Israel but for the killing of all Jews. It has done so in Hamas's official and unofficial oral and written statements. Hamas' antisemitic attitudes can therefore be described as genocidal in intent; however, some of its representatives may

offer coexistence if Jews were to accept living as a protected minority under the rule of a benevolent Muslim state.[63] The Hamas
charter provides ample evidence of vicious antisemitism. It directly aligns itself with the *Protocols of the Elders of Zion* with its
antisemitic world conspiracy theories, calling for the complete
destruction of Israel and for the killing of Jews: "Hamas has been
looking forward to implement Allah's promise whatever time it
might take. The prophet, prayer and peace be upon him, said:
The time [of redemption] will not come until Muslims will fight
the Jews (and kill them); until the Jews hide behind rocks and
trees, which will cry: O Muslim! there is a Jew hiding behind me,
come on and kill him!" (article 7).[64] More countless recent examples are the following: Hamas spokesman Osama Hamdan's
public claim in August 2014 that Jews use Christian blood to
make matzos; in May 2014, a Hamas television show for children
calling for the killing of Jews; a Hamas cleric's vow in July 2014
on Al-Aqsa TV to exterminate all Jews "until the last one"; and the
dissemination of a music video in November 2012 by Hamas's Al-
Qassam Brigades in which killing Jews is presented as a form of
worship.[65]

These examples show that Hamas's antisemitism is manifested
in all spheres: in individual actions, in communication and culture, in organized action, and in violence from the government.
The cultural and historical contexts are embedded in radical Islamism: antisemitism is an integral part of it.[66] What is more,
Hamas's hatred of Jews and incitement to murder are part of a
narrative of "resistance against the Zionist occupation" that has
become integral to Palestinian national ideology and that is often accepted in Western media. Additionally, Hamas sees itself
explicitly in the tradition of the pogroms in the 1930s, and hatred
and violence against Jews have been a regular occurrence in the
region since that time. The impact of Hamas's antisemitism has
been that no Jews can live in territory governed by Hamas, and
other minorities are also under serious threat. Hamas has killed

hundreds of Jews in Israel. Hamas propaganda efforts have contributed to an anti-Zionist view of the Palestinian-Israeli conflict in Western media. Incitement to murder of Jews has been legitimized in this context in other parts of the world, eroding standards of putting limits to antisemitism. Attacks against Diaspora communities in times of heightened conflicts between Israel and Hamas are an indirect result of Hamas propaganda (and its acceptance). Jewish communities worldwide frequently highlight the threat of Hamas.

In Gaza, Hamas does not tolerate opposition and frequently kills dissidents. Therefore (and also due to propaganda efforts), opposition to Hamas's antisemitism within Gaza is almost nonexistent. Other factions of Palestinian society are even more radical in their hatred, such as Islamic Jihad, or, like Fatah, share radical antisemitic attitudes. Other minorities, such as the small community of Christians in Gaza, are themselves under threat. The only reason that Hamas's genocidal antisemitic intentions are not fully put into practice is the military response by the Israeli army. Military confrontations with Israel have shown that Hamas's intention of killing Jews is stronger than its will to protect the population in Gaza or even the security of its own fighters, making a policy of deterrence by the superior Israeli military power difficult. The military support particularly by Iran, whose regime is seeking to arm Hamas with ever deadlier weapons, as well as the possibility of a Hamas takeover in the West Bank, add to a serious security risk for Israel. The political and financial support from Qatar and Turkey helps Hamas sustain its power and makes it difficult to isolate Hamas internationally. In the case of Turkey, Hamas poses a security threat to the diaspora community, and its open or concealed cooperation with the Turkish government can pose a security threat to the Jewish state as demonstrated by the *Mavi Marmara* incident.

The assessment shows that Hamas's genocidal threat against Jews in Israel and beyond is proportional to Hamas's military strength. It is driven by ideologically hardened attitudes, and the murder of Jews is one of the core aims of the organization. While Hamas is active in other countries, such as the United States and Europe, it has not yet been engaged in terrorist attacks beyond the Middle East. However, this might change.

CONCLUSIONS

The three case studies illustrate the usefulness of the presented evaluative framework in a comprehensive assessment of the threat posed by individuals and organizations. The framework helps us look into the different dimensions of antisemitism and to identify particular threats. The evaluation might even lead to practical conclusions for those who fight antisemitism. In the case of Dieudonné M'bala M'bala, we can deduce that the impact of his antisemitism can only be contained as long as he stays a marginal figure. Legal and other actions that restrict the dissemination of his antisemitic ideas are therefore likely to be effective. Recep Tayyip Erdoğan's threat, particularly as the president of Turkey, against the Jewish community in Turkey must be watched closely. His anti-Zionist antisemitism is deeply rooted in his convictions, and he will not hesitate to support further violent and nonviolent action against the Jewish State if he is not forced to do otherwise by his international partners. Lastly, the evaluation of Hamas's antisemitism shows that the organization's deeply irrational antisemitism is at the core of this organization. Its violent actions against Jews will stop only if it is physically prevented from carrying out its goals, which are ultimately genocidal.

NOTES

1. The delusional and obsessive character of antisemitism makes it a danger for the whole society, sometimes leading to aggressive destruction, self-destruction, and barbarism. Persecution of individuals based on anti-

semitic ideas can quickly become endemic. Additionally, antisemitism is a worldview full of conspiracy, hindering individuals from taking responsibility and from making constructive and rational decisions. The wish for a better world and a better society is transformed into the wish for the death of Jews, who are imagined to be the source of all evil. Antisemitism, if widespread, becomes a major factor for social, political, and economic stagnation at best, and death and destruction at worst.

2. Icek Ajzen and Martin Fishbein developed the theory of reasoned action/ planned behavior that uses attitudes towards a certain behavior and the subjective norm and beliefs about restrictions to predict behavior. Icek Ajzen and Martin Fishbein, "The Influence of Attitudes on Behavior," in *The Handbook of Attitudes,* ed. Dolores Albarracin, Blair T. Johnson, and Mark P. Zanna (Mahwah, N.J.: Lawrence Erlbaum Associates, 2005). Other models highlight the influence of the strength of attitudes. Russell H. Fazio, "Multiple Processes by Which Attitudes Guide Behavior: The MODE Model as an Integrative Framework," ed. Mark P. Zanna, *Advances in Experimental Social Psychology* 23 (1990): 75–109. Studies have shown that implicit and explicit manifestations of attitudes predict different forms of behaviors. Explicitly expressed attitudes predict behaviors that are deliberate or planned, while implicit attitudes are useful in predicting behaviors that plausibly occur spontaneously. Anthony G. Greenwald and Brian A. Nosek, "Attitudinal Dissociation. What Does It Mean?," in *Attitudes. Insights from the New Implicit Measures,* ed. Richard E. Petty, Russell H. Fazio, and Pablo Briñol (New York: Psychology Press, 2008), 78.

3. However, attitudes cannot be observed directly but only perceived through some kind of action, such as the response to questions in a survey or interview.

4. Helen Fein, "Dimensions of Antisemitism: Attitudes, Collective Accusations, and Actions," in *The Persisting Question: Sociological Perspectives and Social Contexts of Modern Antisemitism,* ed. Helen Fein, 73–74 (Berlin: De Gruyter, 1987).

5. Langmuir defines chimeric assertions only as antisemitic in distinction to xenophobic assertions. Whereas his distinction is convincing in identifying the specification of antisemitism in National Socialism, his views on the roots of both slavery and the Holocaust as results of chimeric assertions are doubtful.

6. Gavin I. Langmuir, "Towards a Definition of Antisemitism," in Fein, *Persisting Question,* 112, 127.

7. Daniel Goldhagen, *Hitler's Willing Executioners* (London: Abacus, 1997), 35–37.

8. Research on the general relation between attitudes and behavior confirms this assertion as it has shown stronger influences of attitudes on behaviors with rising strength of attitudes. Attitudes can be defined as learned associations in memory between an object and a positive or negative evaluation of that object. Hence attitude strength is equivalent to the strength of this association. Fazio, "Multiple Processes by Which Attitudes Guide Behavior." Strong attitudes are usually understood as the degree of accessibility. The stronger the attitude, the more likely it is that it will be automatically activated. Thus, manifest attitudes can be understood as strong attitudes. A number of empirical studies have shown a correlation between the strength of attitudes and their influence on respective behaviors. Moreover, strong attitudes are less likely to change over time. Jon A. Krosnick and Richard E. Petty, "Attitude Strength: An Overview," in *Attitude Strength: Antecedents and Consequences,* ed. Jon A. Krosnick and Richard E. Petty, 1–24 (Mahwah, N.J.: Lawrence Erlbaum Associates, 1995); Martin Fishbein and Icek Ajzen, *Predicting and Changing Behavior: The Reasoned Action Approach* (New York: Psychology Press, 2010); Stuart Oskamp and Wesley Schultz, *Attitudes and Opinions* (Mahwah, N.J.: Lawrence Erlbaum Associates, 2004).

9. "Chimeric assertions [. . .] attribute with certitude to outgroups characteristics which have never been empirically observed. Another characteristic of chimeric assertions, which sharply distinguishes them from xenophobic assertions, is that they apply to all real individuals who can somehow be identified as members of the outgroup." Langmuir, "Towards a Definition of Antisemitism," 112.

10. Fein, "Dimensions of Antisemitism," 67.

11. Wolfgang Benz, "Antisemitismus: Zum Verhältnis von Ideologie und Gewalt," in *Antisemitismus—Geschichte und Gegenwart,* ed. Samuel Salzborn (Giessen: Netzwerk für politische Bildung, Kultur und Kommunikation, 2004), 33–50, 35. Werner Bergmann and Rainer Erb, "Kommunikationslatenz, Moral und Öffentliche Meinung. Theoretische Überlegungen zum Antisemitismus in der Bundesrepublik Deutschland," *Kölner Zeitschrift für Soziologie und Sozialpsychologie* 38 (1986): 226; Werner Bergmann, "Politische Psychologie des Antisemitismus. Kritischer Literaturbericht," in *Politische Psychologie Heute,* ed. Helmut König (Opladen, 1988), 217–234; Lars Rensmann, *Demokratie und Judenbild. Antisemitismus in der politischen Kultur der Bundesrepublik Deutschland* (Wiesbaden: Westdeutscher Verlag, 2005), 78; Wolfgang Frindte, *Inszenierter Antisemitismus. Eine Streitschrift* (Wiesbaden: VS Verlag für Sozialwissenschaften, 2006), 126.

12. Salomon Korn, "Die Wut hinter der Maske. Vom latenten und manifesten Antisemitismus: Versuch über das 'deutsche Schweigen,'" *Die Zeit*, April 7, 2002, http://www.zeit.de/2002/28/200228_antisemitismus.xml.

13. Micha Brumlik, Hajo Funke, and Lars Rensmann, *Umkämpftes Vergessen: Walser-Debatte, Holocaust-Mahnmal und neuere deutsche Geschichtspolitik* (Berlin: Das Arabische Buch, 2000).

14. Theodor W. Adorno, *The Authoritarian Personality* (New York: Harper, 1950).

15. Rensmann, *Demokratie und Judenbild*, 38, 211.

16. Barbara Harff, "Countries at Risk of Genocide and Politicide 2012," in *Guiding Principles of the Emerging Architecture Aiming At the Prevention of Genocide, War Crimes, and Crimes Against Humanity*, Genocide Prevention Advisory Network Conference Report (Arlington, Va.: Genocide Prevention Program at George Mason University's School for Conflict Analysis and Resolution, 2012), 5–12. Curiously, the Holocaust has not been included in the comparative analysis of factors leading to genocides and mass violence. See Jay Ulfeder, *Assessing Risks of State-Sponsored Mass Killing*, Research report for the Political Instability Task Force (PITF) funded by the Central Intelligence Agency (Science Applications International Corporation (SAIC, 2008) or Barbara Harff, "No Lessons Learned from the Holocaust? Assessing Risks of Genocide and Political Mass Murder since 1955," *American Political Science Review* 97, no. 1 (February 2003): 57–73. It is therefore not surprising that the irrationality, a distinguishing aspect of antisemitism, is neglected in such assessments.

17. Nico Voigtländer and Hans-Joachim Voth, *Persecution Perpetuated the Medieval Origins of Anti-Semitic Violence in Nazi Germany*, Working Paper Series (Cambridge, Mass.: National Bureau of Economic Research, 2011), http://papers.nber.org/papers/w17113.

18. Ian Kershaw, "The Persecution of the Jews and German Popular Opinion in the Third Reich," in Fein, *Persisting Question*, 317–353.

19. Fein, "Dimensions of Antisemitism," 83.

20. Helmut Dubiel and Leo Löwenthal, *Mitmachen Wollte Ich Nie: Ein Autobiographisches Gespräch mit Helmut Dubiel*, 1st ed. (Frankfurt am Main: Suhrkamp, 1980).

21. Fein, "Dimensions of Antisemitism," 82–84.

22. Adorno, *Authoritarian Personality*.

23. The categories of antisemites, those indifferent to antisemitism, and anti-antisemites are usually not homogeneous and need to be further disaggregated to evaluate their specific influence on levels of antisemitic behavior.

24. Jean-Paul Gautier, Michel Briganti, and André Déchot, *La Galaxie dieudonné. Pour en finir avec les impostures* (Paris: Éditions Syllepse, 2011); Dominique Albertini, "Dieudonné, l'antisémitisme mot à mot," *Liberation,* July 2014; Jean-Yves Camus, *Quand l'humour ne fait plus rire . . .* (Paris: Akadem, 2013), http://www.akadem.org/sommaire/themes/politique/anti semitisme/mythes-judeophobes/quand-l-humour-ne-fait-plus-rire-17-12 -2013-56016_137.php. Alexander Stille, "The Case of Dieudonné: A French Comedian's Hate," *New Yorker,* January 10, 2014; Andrew Hussey, "Dieudonné's War on France: The Holocaust Comedian Who Isn't Funny," *New Statesman,* January 30, 2014; Maïa De La Baume, "A Jester Who Trades in Hate: Dieudonné, French Comic Behind 'The Anti-Semite,'" *New York Times,* June 22, 2012, sec. Movies.

25. In the film *The Antisemite,* Dieudonné M'bala M'bala and Robert Faurisson drive a truck and run over a figure symbolizing the Shoah.

26. After a public outrage, some years earlier French American NBA basketball player Tony Parker had apologized for making the gesture.

27. The memo, dated January 6, 2014, is available at circulaire.legifrance .gouv.fr/pdf/2014/01/cir_37810.pdf.

28. Dieudonné M'bala M'bala, https://www.youtube.com/watch?v=9n Oo8vgZ26c, December 31, 2013.

29. "Jean-Yves Camus: Quel poids pour le nouveau parti d'Alain Soral et Dieudonné?," interview by Alexandre Devecchio, *Le Figaro,* October 21, 2014.

30. Dieudonné M'bala M'bala has been convicted of apology of terrorism for his declaration "Je me sens Charlie Coulibaly" (I feel like Charlie Coulibaly). Amady Coulibaly is the name of the terrorist who shot four Jewish shoppers at a kosher supermarket in Paris, January 9, 2015. "Je suis Charlie" was a slogan shared by millions to express their solidarity with the victims at the journal *Charlie Hebdo,* January 7, 2015.

31. See his film *The Antisemite* and his show *Le Mur* [*The Wall*].

32. In early 2014 he declared in an interview with the blogger Mireille Tchiako, "France is run by a Zionist lobby." https://mireilletchiako.word press.com/2014/02/16/dieudonne-je-suis-venu-communier-avec-mes -ancetres/. In interviews with Iranian TV channels (Press TV in 2010 and Shahar in 2014), he details his accusations against the "Zionist lobby" in France, allegedly responsible for the French educational system and atheism. In 2010, he declared "Zionism divides humanity in order to rule. . . . They have instigated all the wars and all disorder on the planet. They were involved in the black slave trade," documented by the Middle East Media Research Institute (MEMRI), http://www.memritv.org/clip_transcript

/en/95074.htm, April 7, 2010. M'bala M'bala frequently replaces the word "Jews/Judaism" with "Zionists/Zionism." He has explained his political rational behind it: "I don't pronounce the word 'Jew.' After my different trials, I have understood that this word could be misconstrued, whereas with 'Zionist' no interpretations are possible," my translation, quoted by Pierre-André Taguieff, *La Judéophobie des Modernes: Des Lumières au Jihad mondial* (Paris: Odile Jacob, 2008), 427. However, in another interview, with the website Sirat Alizza, widely circulated in 2010, he used the word "Jew" directly, saying "the biggest fraudsters of the planet are all Jews."

33. Jacques Tarnéro, *Antisémitisme/antisionisme. Mots, masques, sens, stratégie, acteurs, histoire* (Paris: Études du Crif, nr. 30, July 2014).

34. This results in bizarre statements, such as "Zionism killed (Jesus) Christ" (my translation), Dieudonné M'bala M'bala on Iranian TV Sahar 1, February 10, 2011. On the same occasion, he explained that he is engaged in combating Zionism in France and described Zionism as the "most evil thing we have in us" and believes that it has replaced Christian values in Europe. "Zionism is the quest for manipulation and lies . . . it is the opposite of the values of Christianity and Islam" (my translation), http://www.dailymotion.com/video/x16855_interview-de-dieudonne-mbala-mbala-a-la-tv-iranienne-sahar-1-2_news?start=127.

35. The comparison to rats is at https://www.youtube.com/watch?v=BA-6uCOdrvo. Regarding rats, M'bala M'bala said in a 2010 interview: "The big frauds of the planet are all Jews. . . . You have to be Jewish to have the freedom of speech in France. This is a reality. And saying the opposite means being afraid. But we are not afraid anymore. They did everything to us. They draggled us, they put us into a state of slavery. They colonized us. . . . Death is more comfortable than submission under these dogs." My translation, http://www.7sur7.be/7s7/fr/1527/People/article/detail/1095062/2010/04/20/Dieudonne-Les-plus-grands-escrocs-sont-des-juifs-video.dhtml.

36. M'bala M'bala has called for nonviolence and repeatedly said that he is not an antisemite because he "doesn't have the time."

37. Ifop for metro, "La Cote d'opinion de Dieudonné," January 9, 2014, http://www.ifop.fr/media/poll/2459-1-study_file.pdf.

38. Dominique Reynié, "L'antisémitisme dans l'opinion publique française" (Paris: Fondapol, 2014), 15.

39. Anti-Defamation League (ADL), "The ADL GLOBAL 100: An Index of Anti-Semitism," 2014, http://global100.adl.org/http://global100.adl.org/. For more detailed figures from a 2014 survey, see Reynié, "L'antisémitisme dans l'opinion publique française."

40. Jews have been accused of "communitarism" since the French Revolution. "We must refuse everything to the Jews as a nation and accord everything to Jews as individuals," famously said Clermont-Tonnerre in speech on religious minorities in 1789.

41. His earnings from his shows and the sale of merchandise are substantial. The estimated turnover for 2012 was 1.8 million euros. However he has recently been accused of fraud and faked bankruptcy to avoid payment of fines and taxes. Les Echos, "Dieudonné, un homme d'affaires avisé?," LesEchos.fr, January 10, 2014.

42. Sylvain Mouillard, "Au nouveau Spectacle de Dieudonné, 'système, juifs et homos,'" *Liberation,* June 27, 2014, http://www.liberation.fr/societe/2014/06/27/au-nouveau-spectacle-de-dieudonne-systeme-juifs-et-homos_1051708.

43. For more details see Rıfat N. Bali's outstanding book on the issue. Rıfat N. Bali, *Antisemitism and Conspiracy Theories in Turkey* (Istanbul: Libra Kitap, 2013).

44. Rıfat N Bali, *A Scapegoat for All Seasons: The Dönmes or Crypto-Jews of Turkey* (Istanbul: Isis Press, 2008).

45. S. Singer, "Erdogan's Muse: The School of Necip Fazil Kisakurek," *World Affairs* 176, no. 4 (2013): 81–88.

46. On Erbakan as a fierce antisemite, see Rıfat N. Bali, "Antisemitism in Contemporary Turkey," in *Resurgent Antisemitism: Global Perspectives,* ed. Alvin H. Rosenfeld (Bloomington: Indiana University Press, 2013), 308–336.

47. "Turkish Deputy PM Says Jewish Diaspora behind Gezi Protests," *Today's Zaman,* July 2, 2013, http://www.todayszaman.com/_turkish-deputy-pm-says-jewish-diaspora-behind-gezi-protests_319776.html.

48. "Pro-Erdogan Paper Blames Mine Disaster on the Jews," Haaretz.com, May 21, 2014.

49. "Dünyada medyayi Israil yönetiyor," Milliyet, June 11, 2010, translated by Rıfat N. Bali, quoted in Bali, "Antisemitism in Contemporary Turkey," 319.

50. Suzan Fraser, "Erdogan: Israel Behind Egyptian President Mohammed Morsi's Ouster," *Huffington Post,* August 20, 2013, http://www.huffingtonpost.com/2013/08/20/erdogan-israel-egypt_n_3784716.html?utm_hp_ref=world.

51. "Turkey Replies to American Jewish Congress for Demanded Award," *Daily Sabah,* July 29, 2014, http://www.dailysabah.com/politics/2014/07/29/turkey-replies-to-american-jewish-congress-for-demanded-award.

52. Rıfat N. Bali, "The Decline of the Jewish Community in Turkey," *Jerusalem Center for Public Affairs: Changing Jewish Communities*, no. 63 (January 6, 2011).

53. Bernard Harrison, "Anti-Zionism, Antisemitism, and the Rhetorical Manipulation of Reality," in Rosenfeld, *Resurgent Antisemitism*, 8–41.

54. "When the word media is pronounced, Israel and Israel's administration comes to mind. They have the ability to manipulate it as they wish," Erdoğan said in 2010, quoted in Bali, "Antisemitism in Contemporary Turkey," 319.

55. See Ahmet Davutoğlu's (Erdoğan's close ally and former Turkish president and now Turkish prime minister) vision of Turkish foreign policy. Ahmet Davutoğlu and SAM (Center), *Principles of Turkish Foreign Policy and Regional Political Structuring*, 2012.

56. Simon Henderson, "Turkey's Threat to Israel's New Gas Riches," September 13, 2011, http://www.washingtoninstitute.org/policy-analysis /view/turkeys-threat-to-israels-new-gas-riches.

57. See Bali, "Antisemitism in Contemporary Turkey," 321.

58. Bali, *Antisemitism and Conspiracy Theories in Turkey*.

59. Christians have also been under attack in Turkey. See John Eibner, "Turkey's Christians under Siege," *Middle East Quarterly*, March 1, 2011, http://www.meforum.org/2907/turkey-christians.

60. Dov Friedman, "Turkey's Leaders Are in Danger of Scuttling a Major Natural Gas Project with Israel," *Business Insider*, August 7, 2014.

61. Jonathan Schanzer and Michael Argosh, "Lying Down with Dogs," *Foreign Policy*, August 20, 2014.

62. See for example Burak Gümüş and Ahmet Baran Dural, "Othering through Hate Speech: The Turkish-Islamist (v)AKIT Newspaper as a Case Study," *Turkish Studies* 13, no. 3 (2012): 489–507.

63. Meir Litvak, "Mashaal: Hamas Is Ready to Coexist with Jews, But Not the Occupation," interview by Ariel Ben Solomon, *Jerusalem Post*, July 28, 2014, http://www.jpost.com/Operation-Protective-Edge/Mashaal -Hamas-is-ready-to-coexist-with-Jews-but-not-the-occupation-369140.

64. Translated by Raphael Israeli, The Hebrew University, Jerusalem, http://fas.org/irp/world/para/docs/880818.htm. This translation of article 7 is not much different in substance than the English translation provided by the Islamic Association for Palestine, http://www.google.fr/url?sa=t&r ct=j&q=&esrc=s&source=web&cd=11&ved=0CCAQFjAAOAo&url=http %3A%2F%2Fwww.txnd.uscourts.gov%2Fjudges%2Fhlf2%2F09-29-08%2 FHamas%2520Charter%25203.pdf&ei=7fUPVfyyMIL_uNXVgYAB&usg

=AFQjCNFizSqqkEeohC98gYojY3Y-I9jhKg&sig2=cBKTw_XynEwHL
d4sIl_cvg&bvm=bv.88528373,d.d24&cad=rja.

65. Molly Wharton, "Hamas Spokesman Does Not Retract Claim that Jews Use Christian Blood to Make Matzos," *National Review Online,* August 4, 2014, http://www.nationalreview.com/corner/384567/hamas-spokesman-does-not-retract-claim-jews-use-christian-blood-make-matzos-molly; children's show at https://www.youtube.com/watch?v=57Q8K5 TmivM; extermination avowal at http://palwatch.org/main.aspx?fi=157 &doc_id=12218; music video at http://palwatch.org/main.aspx?fi=987&fld _id=987&doc_id=8086.

66. Robert S. Wistrich, *A Lethal Obsession: Anti-Semitism from Antiquity to the Global Jihad* (New York: Random House, 2010); Gilles Kepel, Jean-Pierre Milelli, and Pascale Ghazaleh, *Al Qaeda in Its Own Words* (Cambridge, Mass.: Belknap Press of Harvard University Press, 2008); Klaus-Michael Mallmann and Martin Cüppers, *Nazi Palestine: The Plans for the Extermination of the Jews in Palestine,* trans. Krista Smith (New York: Enigma Books, 2010); Michael Kiefer, *Antisemitismus in den islamischen Gesellschaften. Der Palästina-Konflikt und der Transfer eines Feindbildes* (Düsseldorf: Verein zur Förderung Gleichberechtigter Kommunikation, 2002); Jochen Müller, "Von Antizionismus und Antisemitismus. Stereotypenbildung in der arabischen Öffentlichkeit," in *Anitsemitismus in Europa und in der arabischen Welt. Ursachen und Wechselbeziehungen eines komplexen Phänomens,* ed. Wolfgang Ansorge (Paderborn: Bonifatius, 2006), 163–182.

FOUR

Virtuous Antisemitism

ELHANAN YAKIRA

SINCE ABOUT THE TURN of the millennium, the number of publications dealing with different aspects of antisemitism—its history, its manifestations, its "resurgence," its rapport with phenomena such as "post- or anti-Zionism," anti-Israelism, and so forth —has been steadily growing.[1] Undoubtedly, something was happening at the beginning of the new millennium to prompt this kind of attention. What was believed to have practically disappeared after the Second World War, and also was deeply discredited and delegitimized, has newly become an important factor of contemporary culture. Notably, most obviously in the Islamic and Arab worlds but also in the West, we have been witnessing what has been dubbed a "resurgence of antisemitism," the rise of a "new antisemitism," and the like. Naturally, abundant writing and talk about this phenomenon have ensued. Much of it is historiographical in nature, monitoring contemporary antisemitic events and discourses, looking for its roots in "traditional" Jew hatred or for analogies between the older and more recent forms of antisemitism, or discussing the links between antisemitism and anti-Zionism or anti-Israelism.[2] Attempts to go beyond mere description usually take the form of either a historical search for causes or, less frequently, psychological or sociological explanations. The results, often interesting and illuminating, do not resolve the conundrum of Jew hatred, which is, as Robert Wistrich has called it, the longest hatred. I do not pretend to be able to solve this conundrum. I wish, rather modestly, to turn the attention of the reader to one characteristic of antisemitism that seems quite extraordinary and which, although not unknown, merits more attention than it usually receives: the fact that it has always been, in the past as well in the present, a phenomenon of high culture.

Although certainly very old, anti-Judaism, just like contemporary anti-Israelism, is not necessarily, at least not always, "hate." We all know the hateful discourse, and of course actions, hate-crimes, or otherwise violent acts, which seem to be resurgent all around us and which target Jews, Israelis, Zionists, and sometimes their allies, too. Harassment, insults, and aggressions are quite common on the streets of Paris and its suburbs and on U.S. and Canadian campuses, and occasional acts of vicious violence are also part of the everyday reality of many contemporary Western countries. This is certainly the most conspicuous aspect of anti-Judaism, as well as the most disquieting, the aspect that needs most of all to be addressed not only theoretically, but also politically and through law enforcement. In a sense, however, it is not what makes antisemitism the specific phenomenon it is. Ugly, sometimes murderous violence has often marked the history of the relationships between Jews and their neighbors, especially since the beginning of the second millennium. Pogroms, riots, looting, raping, and killing; expulsions, discrimination, ghettoization; sedition and incitement of ignorant mobs to turn their frustrations against Jews; manipulation of popular feelings, of deep-rooted images and stereotypes by regimes of all kinds and by unscrupulous politicians and propagandists of all colors—all this, and more, is the stuff of which the history—or histories—of what we call antisemitism is made. It is only natural that such phenomena are the main concern of the man in the street, the media, the politician, the community leader, and also the scholar.

But there has always been more to it. Jews are far from being the only victims of xenophobia, racism, and intercommunal and inter-confessional hatreds and violence; as we have unfortunately come to know, Jews may also harbor such hostile feelings and perpetrate such acts. Still, there are good reasons to think that antisemitism is a specific phenomenon; and one way in which this specificity can be deciphered is to look beyond hatred. In fact, "hatred," "phobia," "envy," and other notions depicting different affects may not be sufficient to make antisemitism intelligible. They are certainly part of it, but arguably not what gives it its specific nature, what makes of it not only the oldest hatred, but also the strangest and most incomprehensible. Perhaps we can get a better grasp of what antisemitism is if we indeed look beyond affects and give more attention to its less dramatic aspects. Looking beyond the affectivity of antisemitism, beyond the violence, stupidity, and malice, may permit a better grasp of its deeper essence.

In what follows, I shall refer to this beyond-hatred antisemitism as "virtuous antisemitism."[3] Roughly speaking, it seems that one can distinguish between two subcategories of virtuous antisemitism. The first is virtuous in a negative way; the second is more positive. By the first I mean the benign kinds of anti-Judaism. For there are definitely many nonviolent, even antiviolent negative attitudes toward Jews, which may often reflect more or less fictional images of "the Jew." Such images can be semi-aesthetic and often appear in the form of a silent and unsaid discomfort in dealing with Jews; their direct impact is usually harmless.[4] Some Jews and many Israelis are often deaf to these attitudes. Acknowledging them takes experience but also greater perceptiveness, sharper sensitivity to nuances of language and behavioral codes than many of us are capable or perhaps willing to marshal. Some, Jews and non-Jews alike, unconsciously suppress their feelings toward this form of anti-Jewishness or deliberately choose to ignore it or to accommodate to it; quite a few—here we talk, of course, of Jews—would even internalize it and themselves become, for instance, uncomfortable with Judaism in general or some of its aspects.[5] Setting aside barbarism, namely violence, hatred, or other forms of blatant anti-Judaism discourses and of anti-Jewish practices, and even though not always easily heard, there is often beneath the civilized surface—in Europe and, probably to a lesser degree, at least more recently, in the United States as well—an unpleasant murmur that never goes away. Some Jews seem to have a special gift for a certain deafness toward this murmur. This probably is common more among those whom Bernard Lazare, and, after him, Hannah Arendt, had called the parvenu, and whom Jean-Paul Sartre, in his remarkable *Réflections sur la question juive,* described as the nonauthentic Jew.[6] But in normal or less troubled times, also "authentic Jews" would perhaps not always be very keen on listening to it.

In his *Réflections,* Sartre portrayed, beside the figures of the authentic and inauthentic Jew, a rather familiar brand of "antisemite": the one who manifests unharmful, benign, even gentle and humanistic opposition to Jews. This type of person is precisely the antisemite we often tend to disregard, to endure and tolerate as we endure and tolerate other nuisances, unpleasant but usually perceived as more or less innocuous inconveniences. I use here the term *opposition* rather than, for example, *hatred,* because this kind of antisemitism is indeed often not hatred. Sartre was certainly thinking of an "antisemitism" he knew well, the kind of attitude shared by many whom he knew from his social environment and that even was his to some extent.

Sartre's antisemite did not hate Jews. He never would have even so much as dreamed of hurting Jews, let alone of committing anything remotely resembling the horrific things that were happening in Europe, to some extent in France itself, when he was writing that essay, or shortly beforehand. By this famous capacity for self-deception, the *mauvaise foi* that has been such a central theoretical element of Sartre's existentialism, the benign antisemite tells himself—and others—that "the Jew" is such and such, or has such and such (unpleasant) qualities or habits, and so on, thereby justifying to himself the kind of unpleasant feelings, the vague repulsion perhaps he or she feels in the presence of a Jew or when the abstract, necessarily more or less fictional, idea of "the Jew" presents itself to him or her. Defended by the same *mauvaise foi,* the gentle antisemite convinces himself, or herself, that his/her attitude toward Jews has nothing to do with the horrific crimes—about which he may sincerely feel profound horror—that others commit against Jews. Implicitly, Sartre's essay, it seems, denounces such attitudes.

Réflections was written during or immediately after the war. It contains only one rather casual allusion to the mass murder of the Jews by the Nazis. Many readers of this essay were quite puzzled, or even taken aback, by what seemed a banalization of antisemitism, a strange refusal to talk about the real thing, namely the destruction of European Jewry. I believe Sartre was more subtle, more sophisticated than that, and in particular more attentive to the real consequences of antisemitism. Although it is not altogether clear what he knew about the murder of Jews, Sartre probably did hint to his reader that he knew what the real consequences of antisemitism were and perhaps implied that the underlying murmur was not as innocent as it appeared to be. Without saying it in so many words, he was arguably (or at least this is a lesson the reader can draw from the essay), pointing, on the one hand, to a pervasive element of European civilization, implying also, on the other hand, that the ultimate evil of the mass killing of the Jews was conditioned by this inoffensive, and in itself, benign "soft" and civilized antisemitism.

—⁕— —⁕— —⁕—

In addition to the "low," often banal forms of Jew hatred, beside the discrimination, persecution, and violence, but also beside the benign, common, more or less softer kinds of popular antisemitism, beside the repugnance and dislike, beside the aristocratic aesthetic uneasiness provoked by the figure of "the Jew"—there also exist higher forms of anti-Judaism (and nowadays of anti-Israelism), the "tainted greatness" I mentioned above. It is to these "high" anti-Jewish discourses, frames of mind, and cultural and intellectual structures, the second type of "virtuous antisemitism" according to the typology I propose here, that I wish to turn now. It is *positively virtuous:* not just benign, bourgeois, nonviolent resentment, but anti-Judaism coming from the heights of culture. In a way, this is where the paradoxes of antisemitism become most visible, and it is with this kind of anti-Judaism, more than in the violence of the mob or the *mauvaise foi* of the ordinary, normative person, that the full darkness of the conundrum of antisemitism becomes apparent.[7]

The notion, or metaphor, of "high" I use here can have two different meanings. It can refer to what is sometimes called high culture; it can also refer to high moral grounds. The positively virtuous antisemite would belong, for example, to an intellectual elite; he or she could be a respected, even distinguished member of a savant community; a good, even great artist; a spiritual leader; an important politician or an influential ideologue. But he might also be an antisemite from a stance that can be described—bizarrely, implausibly, weirdly—as authentic moral decency. Virtuous antisemitism may be authentically innocent.

Anti-Jewishness (and anti-Israelism) is indeed quite common among the class of clerks and among the cultural and intellectual elites of European societies. Insofar as antisemitism can be said to be a specific phenomenon, or a cluster of phenomena, it was in fact created by intellectuals. It is rooted in the first centuries of the Common Era, and there are good reasons to think—in fact many historians do think—that there is a continuity between the early and later antisemitisms of the elites. More than thematic, however, this continuity is *structural;* the very fact that since its appearance as a specific phenomenon, and through all the vicissitudes of its long history, anti-Judaism has always been a characteristic of high culture, a "structural" element.[8] Church historians disagree about whether Christian anti-Judaism was the result of an actual missionary competition among the first Christians and the established Jewish communities in the Hellenistic and then Roman antiquity, or whether the theologians of the early church forged an image of Jewish religion that had little to do with the real Jews, as a central means of stabilizing its own still-hesitant and insecure identity.[9] I am not qualified to take a stand on this question; in any case, it does not have much bearing on my central claim that from its very beginnings antisemitism as a generalized animosity toward Judaism has been endemic to elites, apparently imprinted upon Christianity by elites rather than engendered by a popular movement. Normally, we tend to attribute xenophobias to mobs (or to demagogues who draw their strength from mobs). Antisemitism, as an essential characteristic of Christian civilization, was conceived by Christianity's spiritual founders, many of them undoubtedly exceptional men. No outstanding force of imagination is needed to understand the ideological urgency to delegitimize the "Old Covenant" in the early Church's struggle to theologically consolidate and auto-legitimize itself as the "New Covenant" and the "True Israel." This project obviously needed considerable intellectual toil, and it is consequently no wonder that Christian antisemitism originated as a defining element of the Church's elite and spiritual leadership. Whatever this may mean for the ideological foundation of Christianity and whatever speculation this may suggest about how constitutive a role and place the opposition to Judaism has in Christian consciousness—and subconsciousness—is beyond the scope of this chapter; what is relevant for us here is that from its inception, antisemitism, as a specific historical phenomenon, has as its place of preference the ideology of spiritual leadership.

The permanence of this characteristic of antisemitism makes one suspect that behind what is described as a "legitimate" criticism of Israel's politics (and it is sometimes just that), there often lurks an anti-Zionism and anti-Israelism that are at bottom new versions of antisemitism.[10] The transformations that antisemitism as a trait of high culture has gone through, why and how it has been transmitted and remained stable, may pose serious questions to the historian. Many of these questions are probably not fully answerable. It is, however, undeniable that since the times of the Church fathers, of Marcion and Origen of Alexandria, for example, Pope Innocentius III (1160/1161–1216) passing by Luther and his contemporary rival, the great humanist Erasmus, Bossuet in the seventeenth century: the highest and most influential religious authorities of the Church—the Catholic Church and then the reformed churches and their many denominations—have more often than not been deeply anti-Jewish.[11] But Voltaire, with his famous *écrasez l'infame,* was not less anti-Jewish, and neither were Baron d'Holbach, Balzac, and Dostoyevsky. One can add T. S. Eliot, Ezra Pound; or Hegel and Kant among the philosophers, and, closer to us, Gotlob Frege, Wittgenstein, and many others.

The idea is simple and the facts are largely known. One could easily, just by going through any of the many histories of antisemitism, compose a long list that would include many of the Christian West's most illustrious intellectual, political, religious, literary, or artistic figures who were—it can be argued that this is still, mutatis mutandis, the case—anti-Jewish and sometimes simply antisemitic.

―ᴡ―   ―ᴡ―   ―ᴡ―

It would be too easy, but also wrong and counterproductive, to dismiss all these intellectual lights—and other lesser known or unknown figures—as charlatans, hypocrites, or crooks, as abject or stupid, or as cynical manipulators of popular prejudices and frustrations. Among antisemites, there are of course many such types. Like Samuel Johnson's famous patriotism, antisemitism has often been the scoundrel's refuge. This, however, is only part of the story, and not necessarily the more interesting one. For among the "virtuous antisemites" are many who are not simply prominent cultural, intellectual, or spiritual figures, even leaders, but also people of otherwise deep and authentic decency. These people are not only representative of "high culture," but they also occupy—in a real sense and said without irony—the "high moral ground."

I shall look here at two such figures, Blaise Pascal (1623–1662) and Ernest Renan (1823–1892). Chosen more or less at random but undoubtedly reflecting my own personal and professional biases, both happen to be French. They are, however, not unlike many other intellectual figures from different periods, countries, traditions, and national cultures. Both men's anti-Judaism is so complex, ambiguous, and equivocal that it can hardly be referred to as antisemitism. No wonder that both, although not absent altogether from the literature on antisemitism, draw relatively very little attention from its historians.[12]

The quasi-absence of Pascal and Renan in this literature is symptomatic. On the one hand, it is indeed very doubtful that the term *antisemitism,* with all its symbolic charge, but also with its more properly theoretical connotations, is applicable to them; it certainly does not apply to either one, if we understand by *antisemitism* a kind of hatred. On the other hand, and although marking the extreme limits of the phenomenon, both still belong to the cultural and ideological spaces we designate by this term, and first of all by their direct and indirect, certainly unintended, contribution to its perpetuation and to its becoming the murderous kind of phenomenon it has since become.[13] They may in fact be said to occupy, each of them in his own specific way, a peculiar, but also typical, place in the multifaceted and complex, indeed paradoxical, space of what we call antisemitism. They represent one of its most peculiar, perhaps unique, facets, the one that is perhaps the most difficult to understand, to cope with, to form coherent judgment or take a moral stance about, but that is perhaps also the expression of antisemitism's deepest essence. Both were exceptional men in many ways and outstanding scholars, and their influence on modern France in particular, and on European civilization in general, was considerable. Most importantly, both were men of uncontested intellectual honesty and of personal integrity.

Pascal was a great man of science and a mathematician and, later in his short life, an apologist for Catholic Christianity and a non-systematic philosopher-theologian; Renan was a great philologist, historian, and theorist of religions, a specialist in the Hebrew language, a historian of early Christianity and of the ancient People of Israel, but also a secular humanist and, after a period of monarchism, a skeptical democrat and moderately liberal (in the French sense of the word) republican.[14] There are of course significant differences between the two, not only in respect to their personal religious faith, but also, and more importantly, in regard to the two very different moments in the history of antisemitism to which each respectively belongs.[15] Pascal was most deeply affected by the looming demise of an old world on the threshold of a secularized modernity, one of the most intelligent, sophisticated, and articulate apologists for Christianity and, indeed, for faith in general. In his defense of Christianity, he also reproduced the themes of the Christian—more accurately, Augustinian—theology of Judaism and Jewish history. Renan was active during the period that gave birth to modern, racist but secular, antisemitism. Both men were deeply preoccupied with the Jewish faith and with its place in, or over and against, European Christian civilization. Both men's attitudes toward Judaism are extremely equivocal, almost contradictory.

In Pascal's *Pensées*, the Jewish people, its history, its prophets, and Biblical prophecy in general occupy a very important place. In perhaps as much as a quarter of the text there are either short allusions to Jewish matters or quite long elaborations. The approximately eight hundred fragments found among Pascal's papers after his death, which were grouped together under the title "Pensées," were mostly meant, as is well known, to serve as a comprehensive project of an apologetics for the Catholic religion. Much of the theology of this project is based on close and extensive reading of the Bible—both the Jewish Bible and the New Testament. Pascal was, however, also very interested in postbiblical Jewish history and literature. There are hundreds of citations, allusions, and often lengthy discussion of the Hebrew Bible, especially the prophets, of the *Mishnah*, the *Talmud*, and the *Midrashim* and of a few Jewish thinkers and *Parshanim* (exegets).[16]

Pascal's preoccupation with the Jewish people was purely theological. The Jewish presence in France in the first half of the seventeenth century was very limited, with Jewish communities almost exclusively in southern France and in Alsace and Lorraine. It is possible that Pascal had never met a Jew. Very generally, Pascal's theological interpretation of the Jewish fact is based on a few main tenets: the Hebrew Bible's testimony of revelation is trustworthy; the Jews misinterpreted it and hence refused to acknowledge Jesus as the Messiah announced by their own scripture; their understanding of the divine revelation given to them—and only to them—was formalistic and legalistic, carnal and not spiritual; their misery is a punishment for their stubborn refusal to accept the new covenant, but their prolonged existence in misery is a testimony to their sins and the truth of Christianity.

An important element of Pascal's highly complex, sophisticated, and subtle apologetics is his attempt to give a kind of historical justification for the "truth" (which is itself a complex philosophical-theological notion in his thought) of Christianity. It is based, in a way that puts it within the Augustinian tradition, on the one hand, and the sixteenth- and early seventeenth-century Christian erudite Hebraism, on the other, on a hermeneutics of the Hebrew Bible and of the history of the Jewish people. In Pascal's view, thus, the Bible—both the Hebrew and the Christian—and in line with traditional Christian readings, does not talk of anything except Christ. The words of the prophets in particular, but the history of ancient Israel, as well, have a hidden meaning, which becomes comprehensible only with the coming of Jesus. Despite the Jews' refusal to acknowledge this truth, not only the ancient scripture, but also the Jews' understanding and loyalty to it, as well as the ancient Jews themselves are admirable. Moreover, the *fact* of the survival of the Jewish people through its postbiblical long and terrible history and, in particular, its perseverance as, precisely, Jewish, is not only an immensely significant fact from a religious—Christian—point of view but also an incomparably admirable fact from a human and moral point of view. Jewish history deserves not only admiration but also compassion. Thus, to take just one example of the numerous pronouncements one can find in the *Pensées* and its annexes are these sections:

> 617 (390): Perpetuity. Think that since the beginning of the world, waiting for the Messiah or his adoration has subsisted without interruption; [...] that [Moses and the prophets] said that the Law that they had was there only as long as that of the Messiah was waited for; that until now it has been perpetual, but that the other one will last eternally [...]

> 618 (456): This is a fact. While all the philosophers are divided into different sects, there is in one corner of the world people who are the most ancient of the world, who declare that everybody is in an error, that God has revealed to them the truth that will subsist always on the earth. Indeed, all the sects have disappeared, this one lasts always, and since 4000 years. [...]

> 619 (454): [...] The encounter with this people astonishes me, and seems to me worthy of attention. I consider this Law that they boast having received from God, and I find it admirable. This is the first law of all the others, and even before the word law was used among the Greeks. [...] I find it strange that the first law in the world is also found to be the most perfect [...]

620 (451): Advantages of the Jewish people. In this encounter, the Jewish people draw my attention first by a quantity of admirable and singular things that are visible there.

640 (311): It is an astonishing thing, worthy of strange attention, to see the Jewish people subsisting since so many years, to watch it always in misery. It is necessary for the proof of Jesus Christ both that it subsists for proving him and that it be in misery, since they crucified him. [...][17]

The Hebrew translator of the *Pensées* added the following footnote at this point: "One may be puzzled by the fact that such a great philosopher as Pascal adopts such a dubious justification of the persecutions of the Jews. On the disastrous consequences of this position for the Jews, including the indifference of the Christian world during the last Shoah, see M. Hay, *The Prejudices of Pascal*, 1962."[18]

In fact, the full ambiguity and equivocation of Pascal's position can be easily grasped here: the admiration, respect, and compassion on the one side; the justification of the suffering, misery, and persecution on the other—justification, it has to be noted, that extends to the future and not only to the past. Yet, it has also to be noted, and emphasized, that in Pascal's writings there is no trace of malice, let alone hatred, toward the Jews but, on the contrary, not only admiration, but also compassion. This is undoubtedly a clear case of "virtuous antisemitism."

My second example is Ernest Renan.[19] One can hardly exaggerate the breadth and depth of his scholarship or his importance and influence. Although his intellectual and spiritual itineraries were the opposite of Pascal's, and notwithstanding the risk of anachronism and, in particular, the incommensurable difference between the two regarding knowledge of Jewish history, sources, and, of course, the Hebrew language and the Hebrew Bible, there are still remarkable parallelisms between Renan's scientific and rationalist vision of the civilizational role of the Jewish people and Pascal's apologetic theology of the Jewish history. The first

thing to emphasize is that, just as in Pascal's case, so for Renan
there is no animosity either toward the Jewish people as a historical fact or toward the Jewish religion. Unlike Pascal, Renan
knew Jews, there was a non-negligible presence of Jews around
him, and he refers sometimes explicitly to his encounters with
Jews; but there is no trace of anything that can be described as
antisemitism in his attitude toward the Jews as a concrete reality
of Republican France. Beyond all this, and most importantly,
Renan's theory about the historical role of the Jewish people—
and of the "Semites" in general—reproduces, in a secularized
form, some of the major themes of the Christian (in its Augustinian version) theology of the Jewish fact, which has also been
Pascal's.

Not unlike Pascal, Renan often expresses great wonder in the
face of the spectacle of an obscure, simpleminded desert tribe
that miraculously invented monotheism. There is no explanation of the appearance of belief in a single God in the midst of a
civilization—the Semitic civilization—that lacked any sophistication and subtlety and was in fact incapable of real intellectual
and spiritual creativity. The invention of monotheism by the ancient Hebrews can thus indeed be considered a natural miracle.
Again secularizing old themes, Renan admires the great tenacity
of the Jewish people and its loyalty to the one God and to His
revealed Law. There is, however, great (and typical) ambiguity
here. Although admirable in some sense, the Jews' unflinching
loyalty and tenacity were, thinks Renan, the results of the static,
unchanging nature of the Jewish people. Its existence was unhis-
toric. What changed everything was the appearance of Christ,
who, although coming from this people, opened a new historical
phase, in which the great monotheistic treasure, which the Jews
had conserved but did not know how to spread, began to evolve,
acquired a history, and has become a universal asset. This, however, has been done not by the Semites (or Jews) but by the Indo-
Europeans (or Aryans).

As Maurice Olander masterfully shows in all its subtlety and complexity, Renan develops this secularized conception of the Jewish people and of its history within a general cultural anthropology. On the basis of his immense knowledge of the Semitic languages and, in particular, of Hebrew, he constructs an elaborate and sophisticated theory of civilization divided into two main branches; other cultures do not fully merit to be considered "civilizations." Although participating together in the one civilizational human endeavor, the two nevertheless differ profoundly. The main expression and perhaps essence of these two civilizations is linguistic: the division of languages into two main families—Hindu-European and Semitic—draws the distinction between them. Study of the two types of language permits us to understand their differences, in particular with regard to their religions. Renan uses more or less indiscriminately linguistic notions and notions such as "race," which was then becoming quickly the anchor of the pseudoscience of ideological antisemitism. Thus, as he sees it, while the Aryan "races" have the talent for full spiritual and intellectual developments, the "Semitic" are devoid of such capacities, so that they could not have appreciated the value and significance of their own invention of monotheism. The "Semites" invented monotheistic religion but were incapable of going beyond this invention in order to develop real spiritualty, real linguistically conditioned philosophical, scientific, or literary culture.

In the spirit of the times, Renan often uses the ambiguous notion of "race"; but, especially when he confronts the emerging racial ideologies and abuses (nationalistic and, before long, antisemitic) of the (pseudo-)scientific imagination from which this notion grew, he often warns that "race" has to be understood as a fundamentally linguistic—and not ethnographic, let alone biological—notion.[20] However, there is an essential connection between language and the "spirit" of the human groups using the languages, and through this he can, he thinks, list the positive or negative qualities allegedly pertaining to such groups. And the Semites are incapable, because of the nature of their languages, of formulating abstract concepts, forming metaphysics, or performing any intellectual creative work. After they received the monotheistic donation, the Jewish people did not participate in the progress—scientific, spiritual, and so on—of humanity, and remained immobile as a kind of relic, the custodian of a fixated and petrified monotheism.

Antisemitism is often thought to be a form of hatred. If so, these two great Frenchmen, these two great *men,* Pascal and Renan, were not antisemites. They did not hate Jews, nor did they hate the Jewish religion. Their greatness was real, and their intellectual honesty beyond question. How then to explain, indeed how to describe, what name we should call their very questionable, bizarre, retrospectively dangerous, acceptance of what was, in the last analysis, not much more than rather stupid prejudices? How to name these two good, intelligent men's different, and yet similar discourses about the Jews? Not hate, and not really antisemitism. For lack of a better term, I refer to this quite unique kind of animus as an intellectual dislike of Judaism.

My aim is not to offer a systematic explanation of this animus. I do not pretend to *understand* virtuous antisemitism. But something important, even grave, concerning antisemitism in general seems to transpire through this pervasive dislike of Judaism. The best one can do is expose its gravity. In order to do so, we must first say what it is *not.* Both Pascal (somewhat anachronistically) and Renan can be said to be "public—or *engagés*—intellectuals." Blaming the figure of the "intellectual" for betraying his vocation or of not living up to the standards he preaches to others—in the manner of Julian Benda's *La Trahison des clercs,* Paul Johnson's *Intellectuals,* or Raymond Aron's "The Opium of the Intellectuals," for example—has been a common theme ever since "opinion" has become a central factor in shaping the public sphere and ever since the "intellectual" has made his appearance in it. There is often much truth in the critique of the intellectual, although, of course, this criticism is usually done by intellectuals as well. It is, however, of no use to us here. Our paradigmatic Pascal or Renan was morally and intellectually impeccable. There was no malice in their attitude toward the Jews, and, at least in Pascal's case, one can observe a kind of compassion and generosity. Neither man was an opportunist, cynic, coward, "useful idiot," or excessively naive. They did not belong to a "chattering class," and they cannot be blamed for simple moral or political blindness. Their "virtuous antisemitism" was something else.

Yet, and as virtuous as they may have been, they can still be said to have contributed, despite themselves perhaps, to the solidification and perpetuation of the real, not-at-all virtuous antisemitism, or to the Christian legacy of hatred of the Jews. Unlike other forms of hate, xenophobia, or racism, opposition to the Jews has always been ideological, and antisemitism has always pretended to be a matter of "discourse" or "doctrine." As "discourse" antisemitism has some recognizably characteristic traits. Thus, for example, experience shows that it has always been immune to rational arguments. It cannot be disproved or argued down; no apologetic, or any other kind of polemics, can convince the antisemite that he or she is wrong. Like Popper's pseudoscience, antisemitism cannot be refuted, and the antisemite, if he or she uses language, and not fists, clubs, or knives, would always have answers, or "explanations," for every argument brought against him or her. As many of us have had this experience, it is beyond discussion. No *convincing* of its wrongness is possible. There are then good reasons to suspect that antisemitism is not *really* about opinions, positions, facts, or anything that can be conceived in cognitive terms but is, as Sartre suggested in his *Réflexions,* indeed an *affect.* This, arguably, is the case when antisemitism assumes the form of "theory." The full non-triviality of this phenomenon can be grasped through virtuous antisemitism, especially when one takes into consideration the deeply absurd nature of anti-Jewish ideologies and of many antisemitic pronouncements, on the one hand, and, on the other, the fact that otherwise serious, even esteemed, writers accept them as truths beyond question. Immune to criticism, anti-Jewish discourse does not usually respect the elementary rules of rational discourse; a favorable reception is assured no matter what nonsense is said.[21]

As suggested above, antisemitism has always been the affair of elites. One of the elites' main functions is to produce discourse and doctrine. This, arguably, is one of the main sources of antisemitism's longevity, its elasticity, and its extraordinary capacity to change and adapt itself to the Zeitgeist of the moment. Apparently, there is a typical dialectic here. It is often maintained that human societies entertain what we call myths, or narratives, or differently dubbed anonymous formative forces, subrational by definition, that are thought to determine much of what people think and do. The antisemite's consciousness, then, would be "socially constructed." Our virtuous antisemite would thus be both a victim and a contributor to the antisemitic myth. Innocent anti-Judaism such as Pascal's or Renan's seems to transcend personal responsibility or individual perversity and to point to a trans-individual sphere that is often called civilization. Now dealing with civilizations and their constitutive myths, the historian or the sociologist of cultures, or the human scientist in general, ideally avoids judging—that is, bearing *moral* judgment on—the human collectivities he or she studies. This means that collective forms of thinking and behaving are thought to lie outside the sphere of moral considerations.

But can antisemitism, virtuous or not, even in its most benign forms, be considered from a point of view of moral neutrality? I believe not. To make my point, I turn once more to Jean-Paul Sartre's attempt to draw a phenomenological-moral portrait of the "antisemite." Based on his notion of *mauvaise foi* and on his existentialist philosophy of the inescapability of freedom and choice, Sartre's antisemite, although of the benign kind, is still fully responsible not only for the moral and intellectual faults of his, or her, antisemitism, but also for the consequences he or she did not envisage, such as, say, deportation and murder. But *mauvaise foi* and self-deception still do not confer full intelligibility on the unlikely fact that highly intelligent, sophisticated, civilized, and, in particular, decent and honest, people can adhere to abject absurdities of the kind the antisemitic discourses are made of. Surely no one is immune to the vice of self-deception. But we assume that neither Pascal nor Renan were anti-Jewish by hiding from themselves some truth they should have been aware of. Pascal in particular, but also Renan, was innocent of the affectivity-pretending-to-be-thought of the self-deceiving, or simply corrupt, intellectual.

There is, however, another lesson one can retain from Sartre. As he puts it, man is always *en situation*, historically, sociologically, politically, and so on. And antisemitism can certainly be considered to be such a situation. These are known facts: Since its appearance as a specific phenomenon during the first centuries of the Common Era, the opposition to Judaism has been a constitutive element of Christianity. The long and painful history of its relations with Judaism began as a complex play of appropriation and negation, as a struggle, indeed, of auto-legitimation and of creating and affirming an identity, maybe of overcoming deep ideological and moral insecurity, through a systematic affirmation of Christianity's moral, spiritual, and theological superiority over Judaism. This, in a nutshell, was a "situation" into which both Pascal and Renan were thrown. Despite being "situated," men are always, so thought Sartre, responsible for what they do, indeed for what they are. This applies also to the ways views about Jews are determined by culture or tradition. And in fact, although a constitutive element of Christian civilization, there have always been those who resisted better than others the antisemitic temptation. If there were Marcion and Manichean anti-Jewish theologians, there also was a St. Augustine;[22] if there have been Voltaire and de Holabach, there have also been Rousseau and Montesquieu. If antisemitism is indeed a constitutive element of European civilization, and if, within this civilization, even the virtuous often entertain antisemitic feelings and anti-Jewish (pseudo-)opinions, it is still the case that there have always been those who found the moral resources needed to resist the collective voice of resentment, or the cultural valuating of anti-Judaism. Man, in other words, is always free to be or not to be all antisemite; man is always responsible for his antisemitism.

This means that antisemitism is a *moral fact*. The notion of "moral fact" is complex. Some (e.g., Hume and Humean philosophers) would even regard it as an oxymoron. Taken as a legitimate concept, however, it would mean that there is a need, nay an imperative, to take a moral stance, or simply to *judge,* in our case, the "situated antisemite." By definition, there is no way to remain morally neutral toward a moral fact, even when one tries to be scientifically objective. Antisemitism, in other words, cannot be reduced only to its history or studied as a purely sociological fact. This also means, more importantly, that a moral fact is unintelligible, as a *fact,* outside the space of moral judgment: Those who do not *judge* it do not *understand* it. Those who, facing the antisemite, insist on retaining ideal scientific purity, untainted, as it were, by moral considerations, commit not only a moral, but also an intellectual, even theoretical, fault.

I have presented nothing particularly controversial so far. As a moral fact, antisemitism is judged to be evil. It also provokes such feelings as indignation, anger, disgust, and frustration. Indeed, indignation is the common presupposition of practically all writing on anti-Jewish phenomena. But the notion of "virtuous antisemitism" raises unexpected difficulties. We usually consider as moral facts only what can be attributed to human agency. Natural calamities may be horrible, but we would usually not consider them as *moral* facts. The case of the virtuous antisemite is more complex and ambiguous, and it can leave one perplexed. We presume that Pascal and Renan were good men, yet their respective discourses on the Jews were bad. Neither man provokes, however, indignation, anger, disgust, or any other feeling of that sort. Yet, and notwithstanding the historical contexts, large and narrow, in which they lived and worked, what they wrote on the Jews seems morally wrong. Consequently, what we feel is wonder, bewilderment, incomprehension, perhaps a kind of sorrow. We are at a loss when we face the need to form an opinion and take a stand. Put differently, we cannot comply with the moral and theoretical need to judge.

We feel we need to dissociate the act from its actor or agent. We do not condemn Pascal and Renan for any wrongdoing, but we do condemn—morally judge to be a kind of evil—what both wrote on the Jewish religion, on the Jewish people, and on Jews. We can be ironic about it, more or less indulgent, dismiss or even ignore it, but the question remains. And we have to acknowledge that we commit here a serious fallacy of moral reasoning: Pascal and Renan are one thing, their intellectual dislike of Jewishness, another. Was then their greatness, after all, untainted by their Jewish animus? But since evil cannot be detached from its agent, we face, at the end of this short incursion into virtuous antisemitism, a philosophical conundrum. Trying to avoid falling into the pitfall of moral relativism, it is not at all clear how one is to conceptualize this strange divorce between the agent and the act. Virtuous antisemitism, it can be argued, is where one encounters "pure" antisemitism: no hatred, no pernicious affectivity, purely intellectual. Virtuous antisemitism reveals the conceptual opacity of anti-Jewishness in general and shows it to be a philosophical anomaly. We lack the right categories under which to subsume it. Maybe this is the reason that philosophers have so little to say about anti-Judaism. Maybe anti-Judaism is also anti-philosophy, that is, anti-thought. Beyond this aporetic imposed silence, we can only add one sad positive conclusion: What becomes evident here is the cultural thickness of antisemitism: it is so deeply rooted in Western (and nowadays Muslim) civilization, that even such good men as Pascal and Renan grew up with this perversion built into their innermost constitution and somehow were unable to resist its encroachment into their thinking.

NOTES

1. In this chapter, I shall confine myself to the Western tradition of antisemitism, namely to anti-Judaism as it has evolved mainly in the Christian and post-Christian world in central and western Europe and North America. There are other traditions of antisemitism, for example in the eastern European churches and elsewhere, lately and most importantly, of course in the Arab and Muslim worlds. I shall not deal with these traditions here, although much of what will be said here probably applies to them, as well.

2. On a few other occasions I have argued that anti-Israelism has the same structure and the same moral import as antisemitism; both are basically a license to kill, and specifically to kill Jews. In what follows I'll assume that both belong to the same family of phenomena, and I do not distinguish between the two. My main purpose in this chapter is to point to one such "structural" element that is common to both ideologies and this is arguably and in many ways unique, adding thus force to the claim that anti-Israelism is a new form of antisemitism.

3. My thanks to Catherine Chatterley for bringing to my attention a collection of essays done with an apparently similar idea in its origin: see Nancy A. Harrowitz, ed., *Tainted Greatness: Antisemitism and Cultural Heroes* (Philadelphia: Temple University Press, 1994). Among the "cultural heroes" dealt with in that volume, I would mention here Luther, Mircea Eliade, Lombroso, Wagner, Heidegger, Ezra Pound, Maurice Blanchot, and a few more. Pascal and Renan—of whom more later on—are either not mentioned at all (Pascal) or once, in passing (Renan) in *Tainted Greatness*.

4. Anthony Julius, in his comprehensive study of British antisemitism, makes the following distinction between four kinds of antisemitism that have, he says, English provenance, but that actually apply to other cultural and historical contexts, as well: radical antisemitism of defamation, expropriation, murder, and expulsion; a literary antisemitism, or antisemitic discourse continuously present in British literature; a modern quotidian antisemitism of insult and partial exclusion; the new configuration of anti-

Zionism. There is a partial congruence between Julius's three last kinds of antisemitism and my virtuous antisemitism.

5. We often talk of this phenomenon in terms of "self-hate," although more often than not the term is arguably misleading. It was notably Theodor Lessing who made this term famous in his classic *Der Jüdische Selbsthass* (Berlin: Jüdischer Verlag, 1930); see also Sander L. Gilman, *Jewish Self-Hatred: Anti-Semitism and the Hidden Language of the Jews* (Baltimore, Md.: Johns Hopkins University Press, 1986).

6. Jean-Paul Sartre, *Réflexions sur la question juive* (Paris: Gallimard, 1954). Sartre's depiction of the antisemite deserves more serious attention than it usually receives. See Jonathan Judaken, *Jean-Paul Sartre and the Jewish Question: Anti-Semitism and the Politics of the French Intellectual* (Lincoln: University of Nebraska Press, 2006), notably chapter 4.

7. There is an intended irony in talking of "dark conundrum" here. Yirmiahu Yovel, a philosopher from Jerusalem and formerly my teacher and then colleague, published a comprehensive and illuminating study of Hegel's and Nietzsche's respective attitudes toward the Jews and Judaism: *Dark Riddle: Hegel, Nietzsche, and the Jews* (State College: Penn State University Press, 1998). Hegel, much more than Nietzsche, qualifies perfectly as a virtuous antisemite in the sense I am trying to articulate here. Karl Rosenkranz, Hegel's biographer, writes that Judaism—not antisemitism—was Hegel's "dark riddle."

8. We know that among the pre-Christian Hellenistic and Latin authors, resentment toward the Jews existed, as well. What such authors found odd was mainly the obstinacy to remain loyal to the Jewish one God and to retain Jewish customs and ways of life. See notably Menahem Stern, *Greek and Latin Authors on Jews and Judaism* (Jerusalem: Israel Academy of Sciences and Humanities, 1974–1984); see also David Nirenberg, *Anti-Judaism: The Western Tradition* (New York: Norton, 2013), chapter 1. Pre-Christian hostility toward the Jews was arguably different from Christian anti-Judaism, and, as most historians of antisemitism would undoubtedly agree, antisemitism as a specific phenomenon was born with Christianity.

9. The classical and still highly authoritative statement about the inner-Christian origin and nature of the early Christian *contra Judaeos* literature is Adolf von Harnack's; see Paula Fredriksen, *Augustine and the Jews: A Christian Defense of Jews and Judaism* (New Haven, Conn.: Yale University Press, 2010); Nirenberg, *Anti-Judaism*, chapters 2–3.

10. In a paper read at the first conference organized by the Indiana University Institute for the Study of Contemporary Antisemitism, I claimed that anti-Zionism is antisemitism by being made, as it were, of the same

moral stuff. Generally speaking, taxing anti-Israelis with the charge of antisemitism is often counterproductive and becomes immediately an arm in
the hands of the self-proclaimed critics of Israel, who are often, of course,
themselves Jews. Anti-Israelism as a historical phenomenon has its own irreducible specificity. However, what bring the two phenomena together as
two different manifestations of one more general and continuous history
are what can be described as structural invariables—one such invariable
is the moral scandal involved in the two (what I dubbed in the aforementioned article as an implicit, or implied *license to kill*); another one is the
fact that both are often "virtuous" in the sense I try to develop here. See
Elhanan Yakira, "Antisemitism and Anti-Zionism as a Moral Question,"
in *Resurgent Antisemitism: Global Perspectives,* ed. Alvin H. Rosenfeld
(Bloomington: Indiana University Press, 2013).

11. On Innocentius III, see for example Kenneth Stow, "Hatred of Israel
or Love of the Church: The Pope's Attitude to the Jews," in *Antisemitism
through the Ages,* ed. Shmuel Almog (Jerusalem: Zalman Shazar Center,
1980, in Hebrew).

12. A partial list of authors about antisemitism who either ignore the
two completely or mention briefly one of them includes Jules Isaac, Léon
Poliakov, David Nirenberg, Shmuel Ettinger, Shmuel Almog, Georges
Ben-Soussan, Robert S. Wistrich, Albert S. Lindemann and Richard S.
Levy (as editors), and Hannah Arendt.

13. In a public conference presented in 1883, when racist antisemitism
was already apparent, Renan is already apparently aware of the demons
unleashed by the use—his own use, too—of the notion of "race," and
he warns against it. See *Le Judaïsmz comme race et comme religion* (Paris:
Calman Lévy, 1883).

14. Renan's five-volume *Histoire d'Israël* 1887–1893 (the last two volumes
appeared after Renan's death) is considered one of his major works.

15. Pascal began his adult life as a man of the world and a scientist, but
after his famous conversion he devoted himself to religion; Renan had begun his intellectual and spiritual itinerary with a religious vocation but left
the orders as a young man to devote his life to science.

16. See for example David Wetsel, "Pascal and Holy Writ," in *The Cambridge Companion to Pascal,* ed. Nicholas Hammond, 162–181 (Cambridge:
Cambridge University Press, 2003). Wetsel complains of the neglect by
readers of Pascal of his scriptural exegesis (162). This neglect, however, is
not as absolute as may seem from Wetsel's remark; beside his own works,
one could learn much for example from a number of the essays in L. Bove,
G. Bras, and E. Mécholan, eds., *Pascal et Spinoza. Pensées du contraste: de la*

géométrie du hasard à la nécessité de la liberté (Paris: Éditions Amsterdam, 2007). On the other hand, Pascal's theology of the Jewish fact is practically absent from the secondary literature, despite the considerable attention he himself paid to it; most probably, because of the problematic, namely anti-Jewish, nature of this theology. Pascal used mainly the Vulgate Latin translation of the Bible (but also a Latin translation and a French translation). His close acquaintance with the Hebrew Bible was also the result of his participation in the working sessions of the Port-Royal group, in which was prepared what would become "the first complete Catholic translation of the Bible, commonly known as the Sacy Bible (1672–1723)" (Wetsel, "Pascal and Holy Writ," 168). His knowledge of postbiblical Jewish literature is secondhand and was derived mostly, probably exclusively, from a medieval anti-Jewish polemical work, *The Glaive of Faith* by Raymundus Martini (1285–1220; the full Latin title is *Pugio Fidei advesus Mauros et Judaeos*). In an earlier study (in Hebrew), the great Talmudic scholar Saul Liberman shows that despite its polemical nature, the *Pugio Fidei* is based on a serious study of traditional Jewish sources, some of them lost since, and can still be of use to contemporary research (see the introduction to the Hebrew translation of the *Pensée* by Joseph Ur, *Hagigim;* הגיגים (Jerusalem: Magnes, 1976).

17. My translation. The first numbers refer to the older, Brunschvicg edition (Paris: Hachette, 1897) and the second to the newer, Lafuma edition (Paris: Éditions du Seuil, 1963).

18. Joseph Ur, trans., *Hagigim,* 141. I have not consulted the Hay work that Ur mentions.

19. In what follows, I draw mainly from Maurice Olender's remarkable study, *Les Langues du paradis. Aryens et Sémites. Un couple providentiel* (Paris: Éditions du Seuil, 1969), also translated by Arthur Goldhammer as *The Languages of Paradise: Race, Religion, and Philology in the Nineteenth Century* (Cambridge, Mass.: Harvard University Press, 2009. See also Léon Poliakov, *Le Mythe aryen* (Paris: Calman-Lévy, 1971), 208–210.

20. See for example Poliakov, *Le Mythe aryen* and *Le Racism* (Paris: Seghers, 1976), 72–73.

21. This is one more "structural" feature by which anti-Israelism and anti-Zionism constitute a continuation of traditional antisemitism. In both cases, it seems sometimes that there is some pre-established immunity licensing the most questionable, indeed incredible, and often outright false allegations and claims directed against Jews and now also against Israel. While writing this chapter, I dipped into one of the latest deliveries in the growing anti-Zionist literature, Giani Vattimo and Michael Marder's collec-

tion of essays grouped under the title *Deconstructing Zionism: A Critique of Political Metaphysic* (London: Bloomsbury, 2013). This preposterous volume contains articles by such luminaries as Vattimo himself, of course, but also Slavoj Žižek, Judith Butler, Luce Irigaray, and a few others unknown to me. The chapters I have already read—it takes some stamina to go through this material—move between the outrageous to the confused and ridiculous. One feels almost ashamed to need to refute or answer this surrealist production, allegedly based on an alleged refutation (or "deconstruction") of the proposed two-state solution to the Israeli-Palestinian conflict (thus elevated to the range of "ontology") through a sometimes explicitly stated, sometimes elegantly silenced call for the demise of the "Jewish State." For a critical review of this book, see Gabriel Noah Brahm, "The Philosophy behind 'BDS': A Review of 'Deconstructing Zionism: A Critique of Political Metaphysics,'" in http://www.fathomjournal.org/reviews-culture/the-philosophy-behind-bds/. See also Renate Holub, "Italian Heidegger Affairs," in Harrowitz, *Tainted Greatness,* 173–189. In this fascinating and funny little essay, the author speaks of a number of Italian Heideggerians, among them Vattimo.

22. In *Augustine and the Jews,* Fredriksen tries to show, contrary to received opinions, that during the later stages of his writing, Augustine developed a pro-Jewish theology. It was, however, typically and essentially equivocal: deep respect for the ancient Hebrews and their religion, and an opposition to any persecution on the one hand, theological justification of this defense based on the accusation of not recognizing the Messiah and on the idea that the Jew's misery is a testimony of the superiority of Christianity, on the other. Pascal is definitely within the Augustinian tradition in general, and also with regard to the theological doctrines about Judaism.

PART II

Intellectual and Ideological Contexts

FIVE

Historicizing the Transhistorical

Apostasy and the Dialectic of Jew Hatred

DORON BEN-ATAR

TOM PAULIN'S 2001 POEM "Killed in Crossfire" established the gold standard for contemporary Jew hatred:

We're fed this inert
this lying phrase
like comfort food
as another little Palestinian boy
in trainers jeans and a white teeshirt
is gunned down by the Zionist SS
whose initials we should
—but we don't—dumb goys—
clock in that weasel word *crossfire*

In a few vicious verses, Paulin weaves old themes of blood libel, Jewish clannishness, and "Zionist SS." But before unleashing the hateful words, Paulin took cover in the words of a Jew. Above the poem, Paulin inserted the following quotation from Victor Klemperer's June 13, 1934, diary entry: "To me the Zionists, who want to go back to the Jewish state of 70 AD (destruction of Jerusalem by Titus), are just as offensive as the Nazis. With their nosing after blood, their ancient 'cultural roots,' their partly canting, partly obtuse winding back of the world, they are altogether a match for the National Socialists."[1] The use of Klemperer was of course strategic. His long diaries became a strange best seller in Germany in the 1990s. In a phenomenon that few could fathom and none could explain, the pedantic Klemperer became the Anne Frank of post-unification Germany—the perfect Jewish victim who was not even much of a Jew—Klemperer converted to Protestant-ism in 1912, and even the years of persecution and the murder of family members did not diminish his distaste for Jews. Here was a "good" Jew—a real "credit to the race." And now Paulin could publish his hate freely—after all, what he said was no different from what Victor Klemperer noted in 1934. Even the Jews admit it: the Zionists are Nazis.[2]

Klemperer, of course, could not be blamed for providing cover for Paulin. The entry was from 1934 and, however offensive, Klem-perer wrote it when Nazism seemed like just another pogrom—not the mad attempt to kill every Jewish woman, man, and child. But in taking cover under Klemperer, Paulin has picked up on an increasingly popular motif in contemporary anti-Zionist dis-course: Jews denouncing Israel.

The controversy over the "new antisemitism" centers on Is-rael, which is often a stand-in for the Jews as a whole in attract-ing animosity. "We live in an age," writes David Nirenberg, "in which millions of people are exposed daily to some variant of the argument that the challenges of the world they live in are best explained in terms of 'Israel.'"[3] Anti-Zionists angrily reject the charge. They complain that antisemitism is directed against Jews, not against the "colonial" state of Israel, whereas they are critics and/or enemies of a particular political entity. They have nothing against Jews per se. How can they be antisemitic with so many Jews in their ranks? They charge that the equation between Israel and Jews is fallacious and aimed at discrediting legitimate criticism of Israel and stifling free speech. Judith Butler, for ex-ample, began writing *Parting Ways* in order "to debunk the claim that any and all criticism of the state of Israel is effectively Anti-Semitic." And Avi Shlaim, in a passage evoking the worst charge of all against Jews—deicide—declared that Israel's apologists, "not content with the thirty pieces of silver . . . insist on retaining the crown of thorns."[4] That is, of course, a patently false charge. Opposition to Israeli policies is not antisemitic. No one in his or her right mind has ever argued that it is, and Butler, Shlaim, and their allies know that. Their project is not criticism but bringing about the end of Zionist Israel.

Is that goal antisemitic? Not if one maintains the racial definition of Jew hatred that led to the invention of the word in the late nineteenth century. Antisemitism modernized Jew hatred in classifying it as a secular opposition to an essentialist racial group. Racial antisemitism, however, was just one manifestation of anti-Judaism, and was exceptional in the sense that in its purest form it denied Jews the possibility of opting out. Nonracial Jew hatred, from antiquity to the present, makes distinctions between "bad" Jews who stubbornly refuse to see the light, from Christianity to multiculturalism, and "good" Jews who do. Employing racially modeled antisemitism to analyze the predominantly nonracial contemporary Jew hatred fails to account for the return of the old model that grants individuals the possibility of redemption by separating from the Jewish collective. The term *antisemitism,* however, remains in use, to denote irrational religious, political, cultural, and social hostilities to Judaism as a religion and also to the Jewish collective. The effort to make a radical distinction between hostility to Jews and to Israel is disingenuous. You cannot wish harm on more than half of world Jewry and claim it is not anti-Jewish. To many people, Israel, however flawed, represents Jewish identity and collectivity in the world.

The intense focus on the wrongdoings of one country, the Jewish state, cannot be understood as wholly separate from the two thousand years of anti-Judaism. Indeed, Jehuda Reinharz's and Monika Schwarz-Friesel's study of a decade of hate mail sent to the Central Council of Jews in Germany and to the Israeli embassy in Berlin concluded that it is "impossible to distinguish between anti-Semitism and anti-Israelism. Modern anti-Semites have turned 'the Jewish problem' into 'the Israeli problem.' They have redirected the 'final solution' from the Jews to the State of Israel, which they see as the embodiment of evil." The findings are not surprising. Opposing Israel's existence not only denies the right of Jews to self-determination; it legitimates attacks on Jewish people and institutions all over the world.[5]

The list of progressive anti-Zionist Jews is long and growing, featuring university professors, journalists, human rights activists, and political agitators. The position is fashionable; the seeming righteousness of their apostasy can turn obscure scholars into intellectual celebrities. Getting a Jew to support anti-Israeli measures protects against charges of antisemitism. As Emanuele Ottolenghi wrote, "in a world where identities matter, a Jewish or Israeli background of critics against Israel provides a powerful alibi to those who support, endorse, and articulate the denial of Israel's right to exist." Britain's National Committee (BNC) for Palestinian Boycott, Divestment, and Sanctions (BDS) denied that it is antisemitic, pointing out that "many Jewish organizations and prominent Jewish academics and cultural figures around the world are . . . our allies and partners." *Zionism Unsettled*, the Presbyterian study guide found unacceptably offensive even by the national Presbyterian organization that voted to divest from Israel, uses the writings of Jewish intellectuals to narrate much of its hateful content. And even the *New York Times*, which has been highly critical of Israel for years, has taken to employing the strategy. Reporting on the strong public reaction to the 2013 decision of the American Studies Association to boycott Israeli academic institutions, journalist Tamar Lewin, seeking to dispel the notion that the boycott had anything to do with antisemitism, pointed out that supporters of the boycott include "some prominent Jewish professors."[6] If some Jews vilify Israel, then it must be all right to do so.

Jewish kosherizers fill their invectives with quotations and references from Jewish texts to delegitimize Zionism and Israel.

Jewish Voice for Peace, for example, publishes a regular commentary blog titled the *Palestinian Talmud,* which incorporates biblical stories and Talmudic quotes into an all-out demonization of Israel. Critics generally discount such claims to a place in the Jewish tradition and conversation. Robert Wistrich, the preeminent historian of modern antisemitism, dismissed the Jewishness of the "heroic dissidents" who demonize Israel and Zionism. Their Judaism, he wrote, "is so skin-deep that it scarcely extends beyond their willingness to denigrate Israel."[7] I don't share this view. To be sure, some professions of concern for Israel's impact on Jewish culture and religion, such as by the notoriously secular historians Avi Shlaim and Ilan Pappe, are not credible.[8] But there are many in the emerging anti-Zionist community for whom Jewish ancestry, learning, and practice are central and cherished features of their identity. They are carving a new place in the geography of both Judaism and anti-Judaism. Defined by the tropes of personal narratives of disillusionment, and fetishized Judaism and "Jewish values," they kosherize a seismic shift in contemporary discourses about Judaism, Jews, and Israel.[9]

INTIMATE INSIDERS

There has always been a degree of intimacy between antisemites and their special Jews. Heinrich Himmler warned the SS officers that while each German may have "his decent Jew," no exception could be made for anyone's special Jew.[10] Favorite Jews were divided into two groups—those known personally who received special dispensation and those who "dared to tell the truth" about other Jews. Hitler, for example, had both. He was attached to his mother's doctor, Eduard Bloch, and kept in touch with him even after he became the infamous antisemitic Führer. At a 1937 Nazi conference in Berchtesgaden, Hitler inquired about Bloch in front of the entire gathering, declaring, "(Bloch) is an Edeljude (noble Jew). If all Jews were like him, there would be no Jewish question." Following the annexation of Austria (*Anschluss*) in 1938, Hitler arranged to have Gestapo guards posted outside Bloch's home for three months in order to protect him until the doctor secured a visa to emigrate to the United States.[11] Hitler also had a favorite Jewish philosopher, Otto Weininger, whom he described as "a profoundly unhappy man of great integrity who perished of his own philosophy."[12]

This intimacy contrasts with the view of anti-Judaism articulated by David Nirenberg in his masterful study of the western tradition of anti-Judaism. Nirenberg focuses on the ideology of anti-Judaism; on haters like Luther, Shakespeare, and Voltaire who had little to no contact with actual Jews and for whom anti-Judaism was a rhetorical abstraction, a weapon in their theological, cultural, and philosophical battles with rivals where the label *Jew* and *Judaizer* stood for all that was wrong and immoral. Nirenberg's work does not account for the violent passion of anti-Judaism precisely because he treats it as an abstraction devoid of connection to actual Jews or Judaism. He succumbs to the fallacy popularized by Hannah Arendt, who diagnosed Eichmann as a passionless gray bureaucrat rather than the fanatical antisemite that he was.[13]

Anti-Judaism is sufficiently large to include both abstracters and zealots. It takes both to sustain the longest hatred. These distinctions are not an exclusive binary of either/or. Antisemites like Voltaire articulated both passionate and dispassionate expressions of Jew hatred. But whereas abstracters, as Nirenberg documents, didn't really care about the Jews or what they said, passionate haters liked to footnote their animosity with Jewish sources. Hitler, for one, said, "I am an innocent lamb compared to revelations by Jews about Jews. But they are important, these disclosures of the Jew's most secret, always totally hidden qualities, instincts, and character traits. It isn't I who say this, it is the Jews themselves who say it about themselves, about their greed for money, their fraudulent ways, their immorality, and their sexual perversions."[14]

Anti-Judaism emerged as a powerful historical force in the context of the contest between Judaism and Christianity in late antiquity. Since then, however, the hatred has spread and mutated to cultures and times that have little to do with the theological disputations with Christianity or the sociological realities of Jewish existence. The manifestations of anti-Judaism differ, but its hold on human imagination seems to transcend specific historical circumstances.

Nothing human is of course transhistorical. And yet, an emphasis on the concrete in the study of anti-Judaism often obscures the true dimensions of its visceral force. Scholars document manifestations and explain the phenomena in relation to specific historical circumstances. And so we learn that the hostility of late antiquity is not related to the popularity of *Mein Kampf* in modern Japan; that the 1066 murderous riots in Granada, the 1903 Kishinev pogrom, and the 1941 *Farhud* of Baghdad, are three distinct, independent historical events; and that the rhetoric of Martin Luther's *The Jews and their Lies* has nothing to do with Mahmoud Ahmadinejad's Holocaust denial and calls to wipe Israel off the map. Conventional wisdom, on the other hand, insists on the unity of Jew hatred. It is common for academics to follow Hannah Arendt and sneer at popular notions of eternal antisemitism.[15] Yet, concretization alone is not only counterintuitive, it limits the depth of our analysis. Anti-Judaism is both concrete and general. Denial of the connection between different varieties and elements of Jew hatred is just as fallacious as insisting on a quasi-mystical, ahistorical antisemitic force. Thus, my examination of contemporary Jewish allies of the new antisemitism considers them in the context of present discourse and as descendants and followers of former Jewish kosherizers of anti-Judaism.

Anti-Judaism is dialectical; it emerges between and among Jews and non-Jews. It is tied to the Jewish condition of being simultaneously part of the world and apart from it. Apostasy plays an important role in this relationship. In each generation, some Jews opt out of their communities for full-fledged participation in surrounding cultures. These converts sometimes turn on their coreligionists with great passion.[16] The apostate becomes a crucial informer—the intimate insider who has seen the light and takes on the mission of exposing the alleged vileness of Jews to the unsuspecting world. Sometimes apostates officially sever their ties to Jews and Judaism, and at other times they take on the mantle of the "good" Jew or "right kind" of Jew—the "credit to the race." Their anti-Jewish campaigns and denunciations give credibility, authenticity, and legitimacy to anti-Judaism.

Consider, for example, the first known blood libel—the 1144 killing of William of Norwich. The boy's uncle initially circulated the rumor that local Jews killed the boy, but he failed to provoke a response. Nearly three decades later, a minister from across England traveled to Norwich and set out to turn the boy into a saint. That clergyman, Thomas of Monmouth, published *The Life and Miracles of Saint William of Norwich* in 1173, in which he charged that the local Jews crucified the boy in an act reminiscent of the biblical deicide. His narrative relied on the testimony of one Theobald, a converted Jew, who confirmed not only the details of William's murder, but also claimed that each year the local Jews get together to select the community in which they'll perform the ritual murder and crucifixion of a Christian boy. "The words of a converted Jew," Monmouth wrote, provide the indisputable proof; "we reckon to be all the truer, in that we received them as uttered by one who was a converted enemy and had also been privy to the secrets of our enemies."[17]

In the thirteenth century, King Louis IX held the infamous Talmud trial in Paris. Nicholas Donin, a former Yeshiva student who "exposed" the vile nature of the Talmud, set the proceedings in motion. Donin provided proof texts that the Talmud blasphemously attacks Jesus and the Virgin Mary. The court ruled that the book was blasphemous and ordered the burning and banning of the Talmud, leading to the actual destruction of numerous books in medieval Europe. A few decades later, the mantle of the former insider-turned-denouncer of Judaism passed to Pablo Christiani, who persuaded King James I of Aragon to force Jews to attend his proselytizing sermons, Pope Clement IV to destroy all surviving volumes of the Talmud in Europe, and King Louis IX of France to enforce the requirements for Jews to wear identifying badges in public.[18]

Apostate testimony thus kosherized the blood libel, forced conversions, and led to the destruction of Jewish sacred texts—the most prominent assaults on Jewish life in the medieval and early modern eras. There were many lesser-known, former Jews who likewise turned on former brethren, leading to expulsions, riots, forced conversions, and destruction of Jewish learning. And the content of apostates' denunciations of Jews and Judaism evolved in concert with the evolution of antisemitism. As Enlightenment thinkers assaulted Jewish backwardness and clannishness and defined the Jew as the anti-citizen, Jewish critics decried the very same qualities in their communities and urged fellow Jews to embrace full assimilation and confine Jewishness to the private sphere. Some Jews saw in the emancipation the opportunity for complete assimilation and criticized the "bad" Jews who hung on to their traditions. By nature, these latter Jews were seen as dishonest, uncivilized, and money-grubbing. Jews then had to free themselves from their backward traditions and abandon Judaism.[19] The following century, as western antisemitism centered on the evils of industrial capitalism, Karl Marx, descended from a long line of rabbis, decried, "What is the secular basis of Judaism? *Practical* need, *self-interest*. What is the worldly religion of the Jew? *Huckstering*. What is his worldly God? *Money*." Marx called for "the emancipation of mankind from *Judaism*" (original emphasis).[20]

Even the most racist antisemites of the turn of the twentieth century had their Jewish kosherizers. Jewish admirers doted on the viciously antisemitic composer Richard Wagner, tolerated his repeated threats and insults, and vouched for him against critics who did not appreciate his prejudice.[21] And Otto Weininger confirmed racial antisemites' worst ideas of Jews. The wunderkind of Viennese intellectual circles declared in his book *Sex and Character* that Jews were effeminate perverts, "saturated in femininity," of "slavish disposition," who believe in "nothing," and are cynically dedicated to material pursuits. Small wonder that "the bitterest Antisemites are to be found among the Jews themselves," because, according to Weininger, they are the only ones with the intimate knowledge of how corrupt and perverse they are.[22] Weininger converted to Protestantism but could not bear his inner Jewish self and committed suicide a year later in the same house in which his hero Beethoven died. His suicide was regarded by Third Reich ideologues as the only honorable way for a Jew to cleanse the world of his existence.

BETWEEN DISSENT AND APOSTASY

Contemporary dissidents come out of a powerful tradition of self-criticism that goes back to the founding experiences and texts of Judaism. The Hebrew Bible stands as the single most critical indictment of Jews as individuals and as a nation. Prophets denounced the moral and religious failings of Israel and prescribed expulsion and death. Jeremiah even commanded not to weep for the dead, for they received their just punishment. Rabbinic Judaism is all about dissent and disputation. Authors of the Talmud not only included minority opinions in their discussion of Jewish law, but even gave a place of honor to its most famous apostate—Elisha Ben-Abuyah. This mixture of orthodoxy and dissent has come to define Judaism. As Gershom Scholem writes, "It is precisely the wealth of contradictions, of differing views, which is encompassed and unqualifiedly affirmed by tradition. There are many possibilities of interpreting the Torah, and tradition claimed to comprise them all. It maintains the contradictory view with astounding seriousness and intrepidity, as if to say that one can never know whether a view at one time rejected may not one day become the cornerstone of an entirely new edifice."[23]

Controversial outcasts in one generation are sometimes recast as moral and just authorities later. The Jews of Paris burned the works of Maimonides, arguably the most respected Jewish philosopher and theologian of all time. Indeed, one could easily construct the last two millennia of rabbinic Judaism as a series of dialogues with apostasy, from Hillel to Mordechai Kaplan, from Rabbi Akiva to Adin Steinsaltz.

Engaging in intellectual disputations and moral criticism are very different from joining forces with antisemites. Yet, an analysis of Jewish kosherizers needs to be tempered by honoring the Jewish tradition of dissent and social criticism and by recognizing the inglorious history of the way in which some Jewish communities have dealt with dissenters. The Talmud struggles to make sense of the excommunication of two great sages—Rabbi Eliezer and Akavya ben Mahalalel—who refused to go along with the majority opinion. The Jewish community of Amsterdam excommunicated Baruch Spinoza in 1665 for expressing doubts about God and his exclusive relationship with Moses—opinions that most modern Jews, even observant ones, share. And while the battle with heresy and apostasy was primarily theological, and these theological disputations, including excommunications, persist, emancipation, secularization, and the rise of Jewish nationalism altered the nature of Jewish identity and Jewish heresy and unleashed a new kind of overreaction to self-criticism. Who could forget the absurd vilification of Philip Roth for his portrayal of some Jewish characters in his fiction?

The well-meaning women and men who kosherize modern anti-Zionism are not the medieval converts who turned on their family and friends. Some Israeli policies are controversial and merit critical scrutiny and even condemnation. Anti-Zionists kosherize antisemitism only when they endorse the destruction of Israel, when they employ old antisemitic tropes to describe Israel's relationship with the world, and when they conflate Zionism and Nazism.[24] Scholarly analysis of the phenomenon must be moderated by the recognition that offensive rhetorical excesses and efforts to silence critics have not been the exclusive domains of progressive anti-Zionists. Some nationalist demagogues resort to the N (for Nazi) word to describe critics of Israel. Some campus Hillels refused to show the award-winning film *Five Broken Cameras* because it narrates a partisan Palestinian perspective on the separation barrier. And, lest we forget, intolerant bigots have physically assaulted so-called Jewish traitors. The specter of Yitzhak Rabin's assassin, Yigal Amir, must always be in front of us as we examine this painful phenomenon.[25]

My argument is with the learned women and men who consider themselves proud descendants of Jewish dissenters who stood up to power and sided with the weakest—the foreigner, the orphan, and the widow.[26] They claim they do not want anything more than for Jew and Arab to live together in peace and harmony in a peaceful Palestine, which will come to pass as soon as the militarist apparatus of the allegedly settler colonial state of Israel is dissolved and its Zionist ideology defeated. In portraying Israel as the reactionary enemy of human progress, they echo two millennia of anti-Jewish tropes. Early Christian theologians created the supersession model—that is, that God's covenant with Christ and his followers replaced the earlier one he had with Israel. The secular ideologies that followed merely substituted the vocabulary of supersessionism: capitalists accuse Jews of communism, communists of being capitalists; nationalists of being anti-nation, internationalist of being hyper-nationalists, and antiglobalization activists for their supposed intimacy with international finance; racists for being a polluted hybrid, antiracists for their clannish exclusivity. Some contemporary radical critics acknowledge that their denunciations of Israel, as Butler put it, "can excite those who would condemn not only Israel, but Jews more generally in the spirit of anti-Semitism." Rabbi Brant Rosen, cochair of the Rabbinical Council of Jewish Voice for Peace, joined the Palestinian solidarity movement despite being "really worried that I was making my bed with antisemites," though in his opinion this is not the case.[27] The evils of Israel, they believe, justify their most unethical alliances with propagators of Jew hatred.[28]

They often trace their intellectual roots to Hannah Arendt, whom they see as the preeminent cosmopolitan Jewish thinker who "exposed" the evils of Zionism in *Eichmann in Jerusalem*. Avraham Burg dedicated *Defeating Hitler* to Arendt, "who knew and understood before anyone else," and Judith Butler calls her "a resource for post Zionism."[29] It does not matter that Arendt invented an Eichmann who did not exist, that she did not attend much of the trial, that she was cruelly intolerant of the sufferings of the survivors who testified in the trial, and that she defamed the Judenräte (Jewish Councils). *Eichmann in Jerusalem* embodies the primary ideological principles of modern kosherizing: the denial of Israel's right to try Eichmann in the name of Europe's dead Jews; the minimization of antisemitism as a factor in the Final Solution; the claim that the Holocaust was a human rather than a Jewish catastrophe; the suggestion that organized Jewry actually aided the Final Solution; and the characterization of the Israeli justice system as a crude arm of the Zionist political establishment. And they certainly love her decisive answer to Gershom Scholem's accusation that she lacked love of Israel: "I do not 'love' the Jews, nor do I 'believe' in them," is the motto of many present-day anti-Zionist progressives.[30]

THE NARRATIVE OF DISILLUSIONMENT

Contemporary kosherizers share a narrative of disillusionment. Once, they recall, they believed in Zionism and in the righteousness of Israel. But then they saw what was "really" taking place and had, usually after painful soul-searching, had second thoughts. Many invoke a youth spent in Jewish homes and Hebrew school, where they learned of the wonders of Zionists making the desert bloom only to find out later in life that the tiny beleaguered virtuous state of their youth is actually a powerful military force that "routinely engages in ethnic cleansing and state brutality." Historian Tony Judt, who spent a couple of years in Israel in the mid-1960s, couldn't bear its "parochialism, its self-obsession, its resort to violence as a first solution to everything," not to mention that he didn't particularly fancy being surrounded by "the presence of other Jews."[31] Alisa Solomon, who together with Tony Kushner edited the anthology *Wrestling with Zion: Progressive Jewish-America Responses to the Israeli-Palestinian Conflict,* grew up in a Hebraist family and came to recognize the "evils" of Israel during the siege of Beirut of 1982. In a video featuring other equally "sobered" Jews, English professor Bruce Robbins explains that he grew up thinking Israel was good, but going there and seeing the separation barrier made him think of the Holocaust.[32]

Few men embodied the hopes of the Israeli peace movement more than Avraham Burg. Son of the notoriously witty and warm leader of the hawkish National Religious Party and longtime government minister Yosef Burg, Avraham joined the Peace Now movement during the 1982 Lebanon War. In February 1983, as activists marched on Prime Minister Menachem Begin's office to demand the resignation of Defense Minister Ariel Sharon, a right-wing extremist tossed a hand grenade into the crowd of protesters, killing Emil Grunzweig and injuring, among others, the son of the interior minister.

The younger Burg's stand against a cabinet that included his father and his willingness to put his body on the line in the name of peace quickly turned him into the promise of the left. Here was a young graduate of the nationalist Hesder (הסדר) Yeshivas, a combat officer in the paratroopers, who turned against the settlement movement that numbered most of his friends and peers. And unlike other Yeshiva graduates who joined the peace movement, Burg did not take off his *kippah* (yarmulke). To the contrary, he continued to wear the knitted *kippah*, culturally associated with the most ideological segment of the settlement movement, Gush Emunim (Block of the Faithful). He joined the Labor Party and rose like a meteor in its ranks. In a country that was growing increasingly religious and nationalist, Burg emerged as a most unusual electoral asset. Here was a man who could unite religious and secular and lead the left to electoral victory and the nation to peace. A close ally of dovish Shimon Peres, he became a Labor member of the Knesset in 1988, director of the Jewish Agency in 1995, and chairman of the Knesset in 1999. Alas, the promise of the early years did not materialize, and his popularity declined as rapidly as it rose. In 2003 he tried and failed to become the leader of the Labor Party. The following year, with his political career at a dead end and his reputation sullied by embarrassing revelations of incompetence, greed, political intrigues, and questionable personal ethics, he retired from political life at the age of forty-nine.

Burg's dramatic and embarrassing decline coincided with the violence of the Second Intifada, which discredited the Oslo Accords and delivered a blow to the Israeli peace camp, from which it has yet to recover. Many lost faith in the peace process, others clung to the Oslo promise, and a few moved to the right. Burg, on the other hand, underwent a total conversion. The former great hope of dovish Zionism turned on the public that rejected him with the vengeance of an adolescent spurned lover.[33] Four years after his retirement, he published *Defeating Hitler* (the 2009 English translation is titled *The Holocaust Is Over; We Must Rise from Its Ashes*), which traded heavily in contemporary tropes of antisemitism.[34]

The Holocaust plays a prominent role in the discourse of many Jewish anti-Zionists. Modern effective kosherizers do not deny the Jewish dimension of the catastrophe, but they insist that it

originated in racism and nationalism—sentiments they now find
in the Jewish state. Their historical narrative of Zionism begins
with the Holocaust. Israel, declared Tony Judt shortly before his
death, would not have come into being without the Holocaust.[35]
And as some see it, Zionists drew the wrong lesson from the catastrophe. As Alan Sokal stated, "You can react to the Holocaust
by saying never again will it happen to us, or by saying never
again should it happen to anyone."[36] The solution to the tragedy of
European Jewry, they explain, echoing familiar Arab arguments,
should not have come at the expense of the Palestinians. They
deny the connection of Jews to Zion, the presence of the Jewish community in Eretz Yisrael through the ages, and the nearly
seven decades of pre-1948 Arab-Jewish conflict in Palestine. They
subscribe to a mystical, ahistorical view of the relationship between the Arabs and the land. The Palestinians, according to this
ahistorical logic, are innocent victims of Hitler's atrocities. The
Jews are their Nazis.

Burg follows this trope. *Defeating Hitler* does not necessarily
have to draw the comparison between Jews and Nazis, except that
Burg does. From the title page through its long and meandering
polemics, Burg echoes figures, such as Paulin, who are given to
equating Israelis and Nazis. Israel, Burg argues, is following in
Germany's footsteps from the rise of Bismarck to the collapse of
the Weimar Republic. Burg shows an initial reluctance to characterize Israel as the modern incarnation of Nazism. But a few
pages later he turns to a passionate listing of all the wrongs of occupation, without a single qualifier about circumstances, context,
or agency of the other side, dropping all caution, and equating
Israel with Nazism. The gas chambers are not in Israel yet, but
the structure, language, and ideology that created them are. He
doesn't see a national conflict with the Palestinians, only Israeli
oppression and injustice.[37] He predicts the coming passage of
racial Nuremberg laws in Israel. He refers to the Israeli policy in
the West Bank as an *Anschluss* to echo Hitler's 1938 annexation

of Austria, considers the desire for a Jewish state to be racist, and compares the settlement of Jewish immigrants in the West Bank to Hitler's policy of settling *Volksdeutsche* in territories conquered from Poland in 1939. He even equates the Israeli Commando Unit 101 (which operated in the 1950s in response to *fedayin* attacks, i.e., guerilla terrorist attacks) to a German unit by the same number that executed Jews and committed large-scale atrocities in wartime Poland. Unit 101 did indeed kill innocent civilians, most notably in Qibya in 1953, but any military organization sometimes commits atrocities, which is very different from acting in accord with Nazi policy and actions. The comparison to the Nazis, in short, is unfounded and obscene.[38]

According to Burg, the civilized nations of the world have internalized the lessons of the Holocaust and are committed to global human rights, whereas Israel has adopted a cynical realpolitik policy that uses the history of the persecution of Jews to justify its oppression of Palestinians and fend off any criticism as reincarnation of the old hatred. Israel is a nation that lives by its sword and worships death. "Ultimately we became like all of the world's other violent thugs." To Burg, Israelis have grown so accustomed to the sounds of war that we can "no longer hear that horrible sound . . . of distorted morality of the nation of victims that permits it to do everything—especially to sacrifice the lives of others." In his view, Israelis cannot see the suffering of others because they are so involved with their own history of suffering. Antisemitism, according to Burg, is a minor unimportant phenomenon that gets blown out of proportion by organizations whose entire raison d'être rests on perpetuation of a paranoid myth. The Anti-Defamation League (ADL), he glibly declares, sees every swastika or desecrated headstone as a cause for a celebration, or at least for a news conference. If there is antisemitism in the world, he declares, it stems from Israel's treatment of the Palestinians. Burg writes: "The world has changed its nature and character. The superpowers of the world, most of the Christian denominations, and a significant portion of the world's citizenry took an oath of 'never again' sixty years ago and they mean it."[39]

Burg is obviously no hater of Jews. He longs for his father's world—the German Jewish Rechavia neighborhood in Jerusalem—the gentle and peaceful Judaism that has been replaced in his view by paranoid militarism. National Jewish self-determination is not necessary. He oddly sees the Jewish sojourn in Europe in nearly millennial terms of fruitful coexistence interrupted only by the horrible twelve years of Nazism.[40] Even as he plays the Nazi card repeatedly against Israel, he charges the Israeli establishment with continued and cynical use of the Holocaust, championed most famously by that "Jewish Polish demagogue 'Mr. Holocaust,' Menachem Begin."[41]

Sometimes when Burg speaks of Israel he uses the pronoun "we," suggesting that he does not separate himself from the Israeli collective. At other times Burg condemns Zionism as racist, and at still others he declares that Zionism should advance to a post-Zionist liberal universalism. Burg continues to reside in Israel, although he sees himself first as a citizen of the world, second as a Jew, and only third as an Israeli. The former head of the Jewish agency also acquired in 2007, through his wife, a French passport and recommended that all Israelis follow suit—an odd choice given that nearly half of contemporary Jews in France admit to considering emigration because of the rising tide of antisemitism.[42] In a missionary tone, he sets himself above his countrymen whose "eyes are blind, their ears are deaf and their leaders are flaccid and weak."[43] He charges that Zionism and Israel are traitors to the Jewish traditions of "equality, freedom and brotherhood," and that Israeli policy in "the land of our ancestors is a blasphemy of the legacy of Abraham, Isaac and Jacob."[44]

Burg believes that the Holocaust subverted Judaism's course. It turned the universal and humanist tradition into a tribal nationalist one. He feels most connected to the antinational German Reform movement, which, as he understands it, eliminated all references to Zion and turned Judaism into a purely spiritual and humanitarian tradition, following that of the biblical prophets.[45] Burg sees racism and chauvinism of the worst kind creeping in on the Israeli right. Indeed, there are extremes in the Israeli political spectrum, including political initiatives, which, if enacted, can undermine equality. There are also radical vigilantes who engage in sometimes violent, retaliatory anti-Arab campaigns. A concern with these developments is warranted, but the conclusions that Burg draws from is not. What makes Burg's text unpersuasive and offensive is his intense and constant comparisons of Israel to Nazi Germany; his insistence that Israel is on the cusp of embodying the worst elements of Nazism; and his use of the occasional graffiti that celebrates the racist Rabbi Meir Kahana and marginal radical texts of some extreme rabbis as representatives of the Israeli mainstream.

Avraham Burg has become one of the most popular kosherizers of modern anti-Zionism. He cherishes the role, declaring, "If Israel-haters used me, that's fine as far as I am concerned."[46] Indeed, Burg readily accepts invitations to speak for groups that openly call for the destruction of Israel and has even expressed empathy and understanding of suicide bombers.[47] He has the perfect credentials for a contemporary kosherizer: the family pedigree, the knitted *kippah,* the combat service in an Israel Defense Forces (IDF) elite unit, and an intimate knowledge of the circle of Israel's decision makers. Who can better expose the purported evils of Zionism? He looks around the world and sees love, tolerance, and humanism and finds no danger lurking. The world is basically good, the Israeli Pangloss insists. People are good. The Jews do not have enemies. It is time to put away our fears and trust our fate to the goodwill of the international community. As Burg sizes matters up, Israel and the Jews are the racists and warmongers.[48]

Burg is a modern-day Shabtai Tzvi, the seventeenth-century Jewish messianic pretender who converted to Islam. Burg's transformation, like Tzvi's, aims to save the Jews from their maddeningly frustrating history, expressing a surprising faith in the world that has rejected him. Like Tzvi, Burg seems unaware of the sudden break he has made with Jews and their history. Tzvi and his followers, after all, created a separate community of believers that held on to the Shabbatean mission as distinctly Jewish for centuries afterward, regarding their leader's conversion as the first step in the millennial vision. Burg's sense of Jewishness is equally millennial. He believes that history will prove him right. He likens himself to Yochanan Ben-Zakai, the sage who resuscitated rabbinic Judaism from the ashes of the political folly of the rebellion against Rome. Ben-Zakai, however, never actively aided the enemies of his people. Burg has.

FETISHIZING THE JEWISH CANARY

Whereas radical critics of Israel are disingenuous when they claim that Zionists paint every criticism of Israel as antisemitic, their critics are equally disingenuous in denying any relationship between the Israel occupation and hostility to Israel. As long as events in Judea and Samaria continue to pit ugly exchanges between Israeli soldiers and settlers and Palestinian civilians, conscientious and committed Jews will struggle to disassociate themselves and their faith from the realities of occupation.

Unlike former apostates who turned their back on Judaism, an important segment of contemporary kosherizers claim an intimate connection to Jewish identity and history. "The Nicholas Donins and Pablo Christianis of our own time," writes Cynthia Ozick, "run to embrace their Jewish ties even as they besmirch them." Unlike the traditional anti-Zionist Ultra-Orthodox community, which has always rejected Zionism as false messianism, current kosherizers are modern women and men who harken back to the iconic prophet Amos, who prophesized Israel's destruction because the cup of its sins had overflown. "Speaking hard truths to power," writes Brant Rosen, "is a venerable Jewish tradition that dates back to the prophets."[49] He and others of a like mind see Judaism involved in a Manichaean struggle between good cosmopolitanism and evil nationalism, and they narcissistically cast themselves as the virtuous defenders of the true faith.[50]

"Inspired by Jewish tradition." With these words, the most controversial and important contemporary Jewish anti-Israeli organization begins its mission statement. Jewish Voice for Peace (JVP) appears on the ADL's top ten anti-Israel organizations, though it insists it is an organization defined by Jewish values of "peace, social justice, equality, human rights, respect for international law, and a U.S. foreign policy based on these ideals."[51] JVP opposes discrimination against Arabs or Jews. It condemns both the occupation and terrorism, although primarily it concerns itself with the sins of Israel. The struggle, according to its executive director Rebecca Vilkomerson, "is not about the end of Israel, but a vision for justice that all of us can be proud to say we've played a role in encouraging."[52] Yet this supposed evenhandedness is not borne out by an examination of the organization's statements and activities. JVP endorses all nonviolent campaigns against Israel, including those that seek to destroy Jewish national self-determination. It may envision a country named Israel existing, but that country would have very little in common with present-day Israel.

JVP fetishizes an imagined Judaism and "Jewish values." As Vilkomerson admits, "We talk about Jewish values, but we say that these are our Jewish values." Informed by cultural radicalism and postmodern sensibilities about power, colonialism, and nationalisms, JVP activists imagine a multiethnic, multicultural utopia replacing the "racist colonial settler state of Israel." They invent an aestheticized Judaism—a psychological and intellectual state of mind—that is divorced from the actual Jewish collective and from the experience of Jews as individuals and as a people.

To them, the "good" Jew is not the strong Israeli defending his home but the stateless, cosmopolitan, alienated Jew; humanity's canary in the coal mine; the one who has not been debased by the trappings of power and particularist solidarities; the ally of the weak and unfortunate whoever and wherever they are.[53]

A cast of the who's who of the Jewish radical intelligentsia serves on the JVP advisory council: philosophers Noam Chomsky and Judith Butler, filmmaker Udi Aloni, playwrights Tony Kushner and Eve Ensler, political critic Naomi Klein, historian Avi Shlaim, Talmudic scholar Daniel Boyarin, and others. Butler has replaced Chomsky at the head of the Jewish anti-Israel coalition, although she has not stooped to Chomsky's defense of Holocaust denial.[54] Among the most celebrated figures in the U.S. academy, she has cast herself as the American Foucault: transgressive, openly gay, obtuse, employing obfuscating rhetoric, and always swinging to the left of the cultural left. Butler ventured into the Jewish fray late in the 1990s and became prominent in the aftermath of September 11 and the onslaught of the Second Intifada. She is the most visible supporter of the boycott Israel campaign, going as far as objecting to having Kafka's papers housed in the National Library in Jerusalem because interested scholars would have to fill out an Israeli library form, thereby compromising the boycott of the state.[55]

Butler's involvement in the anti-Israel campaigns has endowed the movement with radical chic. A self-identified Jew, Butler describes herself as "a scholar who gained an introduction to philosophy through Jewish thought, and I understand myself as defending and continuing a Jewish ethical tradition that includes figures such as Martin Buber and Hannah Arendt. I received a Jewish education in Cleveland, Ohio at the Temple under the tutelage of Rabbi Daniel Silver where I developed strong ethical views on the basis of Jewish philosophical thought." It was this education that led to her "ethical and political resistance to Zionism." In 2012 she published *Parting Ways: Jewishness and the Critique of Zionism,* a philosophical treatise that centers on saving Judaism from Zionism. Her work draws on secular Jewish thinkers of the twentieth century: Sigmund Freud, Martin Buber, Hannah Arendt, Jacques Derrida, Walter Benjamin, Immanuel Levinas, and others. She admits that her "opposition to Zionism requires the departure from Jewishness as an exclusionary framework for thinking both ethics and politics."[56]

Most Jews have never heard of Butler, but her prominence in the academy makes her the most important Jewish kosherizer of contemporary anti-Zionism. She has become a lightning rod to both defenders and enemies of Israel. Her involvement in the 2013 BDS conference at Brooklyn College was front-page news. Butler epitomizes a certain version of the gentile's Jew—the "credit to the race." Persona non grata in many Jewish circles, she is honored by others as the humanist philosopher who represents what "good" Judaism could become in the twenty-first century; hence, her receiving the prestigious Theodore W. Adorno Award.[57]

JVP believes that an international boycott of Israeli products and institutions can force Israel to change its policies vis-à-vis the Palestinians. It supports BDS and organizes divestment campaigns all over the United States. Vilkomerson denies that the BDS campaign is antisemitic.[58] The BDS movement, however, does not merely protest the occupation. It demands to undo the state created in 1948.[59] Its leader, Omar Barghouti, openly declares that the "racist apartheid state of Israel" has no right to exist and has accused Israeli soldiers of hunting Palestinian children for sport—a clear echo of the blood libel. Political science professor As'ad AbuKhalil is even clearer: the "real aim of BDS is to bring down the state of Israel. . . . That should be stated as an unambiguous goal. There should not be any equivocation on the subject. Justice and freedom for the Palestinians are incompatible with the existence of the state of Israel."[60]

All too often, JVP activists find themselves in coalitions with Holocaust deniers, Islamists, crackpots who actually believe in the *Protocols of the Elders of Zion,* advocates of the elimination of Israel, and leaders of terrorist organizations. Butler has voiced support for Hamas and Hezbollah—openly antisemitic organizations that declare their desire to eliminate Israel and target Jews anywhere in the world—because, as she put it, "their fight against imperialism makes them members of the 'global left.'" She has contributed a chapter to a book that voiced understanding for Mahmoud Ahmadinejad's call to wipe Israel off the map. Vilkomerson joined a 2014 hate-fest at New York University that featured speakers known for outlandish conspiratorial views of Israel.[61] And the BDS coalition includes some openly antisemitic groups and individuals. Activists' profound identification with the Palestinian struggle against Israel frequently puts them in the company of unsavory characters and organizations. They are moved by the real plight of the Palestinians living under Israeli occupation, though they construct a Manichaean narrative of a struggle between evil colonists and virtuous native victims. They stand against the identification of Judaism and collective Jewish identity with Israel. Zionism, as Avi Shlaim declared, "is the real enemy of the Jews."[62]

JVP has grassroots appeal among some young and disaffected U.S. Jews. It is an exclusively Jewish organization, from staff to membership. And it is growing. It claimed to have amassed some 140,000 supporters by the beginning of 2014, over four thousand dues-paying members, and nearly forty chapters in universities all over the United States. During the summer Gaza war of 2014, 60,000 additional supporters added their names to JVP's online condemnations of Israel. There is talk of JVP developing Hebrew schools, JVP summer camps, and more.[63] Growing numbers of educated young people in the United States are attracted to its view of a multicultural Judaism that eschews Jewish particularism for universal human solidarity. Israel, in contrast, is seen to stand for the opposite: its pro-Jewish laws and practices, its official insistence that Orthodoxy is the only legitimate form of

Judaism, and its claim to speak for all Jews wherever they are.[64] As a consequence, some university Hillels are struggling to define their relationship to JVP. The national organization's instructions that local Hillel chapters not sponsor speakers and events who call for the destruction of Israel has brought the Swarthmore, Vassar, and Wesleyan chapters to break with the organization and declare themselves "open" Hillels. And while other chapters have not officially decamped, JVP student groups are making inroads into Hillel's leadership councils.[65]

In its culture and practices, JVP is in tune with the emerging anti-institutional mood that is shaking the foundations of the Conservative and Reform movements in the United States. As the 2013 Pew "Survey of Jewish Americans" starkly demonstrated, some Jews eschew affiliation with synagogues and other established Jewish institutions altogether, and others join independent minyanim (unaffiliated small groups) divorced from the broader Jewish community. The young women and men who join the JVP, according to Vilkomerson, embody this attitude. Although some may come from observant homes, these activists prefer a connection to Jewish practices and spirituality that is independent of the traditional congregational Sunday schools' emphasis on Israel and the Holocaust. Whereas older activists underwent the "disillusionment" process that shook the foundation of their connection to Judaism, younger Jewishly literate activists in the United States may be perfectly comfortable with a Judaism without Israel.[66]

JVP activists who join organized communities tend to find a home in Reconstructionist synagogues. The JVP rabbinical council, led by Rosen, who recently stepped down from the pulpit of the Jewish Reconstructionist Congregation in Evanston, Illinois, and Margaret Holub, of the Mendocino Coast Jewish Community in California, is composed mostly of Reconstructionist rabbis.[67] JVP is gaining strength within Reconstructionist Judaism. Half of the 2013–2014 entering class at the Reconstructionist

Rabbinical College in Boston, according to Vilkomerson, affiliates with JVP. Perhaps this is not surprising. Mordechai Kaplan, after all, set out to eradicate what he saw as chauvinist elements from modern Judaism, changing the blessing one says over the Torah, thanking God for giving Jews a way to become close to Him instead of the traditional expression of gratitude for choosing Jews over all other nations. Kaplan understood Judaism as primarily a civilization—one among many equal ones in the world. It is unlikely, however, that the rational Zionist Kaplan would recognize this new brand of Reconstructionist Judaism. The movement born of the desire to center modern Judaism on peoplehood and their civilization has developed a group within it defined by the rejection of Jewish national solidarity. The earlier anti-superstitious engagement has been replaced by a fetishized spiritual quest that seeks to dilute Jewish distinctiveness: the Judaism of the JVP, as Rabbi Rosen put it, is founded upon "a universal vision that ultimately sees Jewish identity rooted in universal values."[68]

JVP's growth coincides with the resurgence of the New Left. It identifies with the Occupy movement that held long-term sit-ins, most famously on New York's Wall Street in the fall of 2011. Vilkomerson described the Kol Nidrei prayer service held by hundreds of Jewish protesters as the most moving religious moment of her life. The movement nourishes a fantasy of progressive Jews who long to reconnect to the imagined past of their grandparents— the unionized workmen's circle Jew who fought the robber barons at home and Franco's Fascist troops in Spain. Zionism displaced these good causes with the bad nationalist one. Tony Kushner bemoaned the "calamity," that is, Zionism, that has "driven international Jewish culture from its progressive base."[69] According to Daniel Boyarin, Zionism has created a state so flawed that it has subverted two millennia of Jewish ethics. Redemption through territorial sovereignty, he wrote, "must either be infinitely deferred . . . or become a moral monster."[70]

In contrast to sovereignty and autonomy, kosherizers fetishize diaspora powerlessness. Exile long defined, and for some Jews continues to define, Jewish existence, and there is a significant body of work, dating from the twelfth-century Spanish philosopher Yehuda Halevi to the twentieth-century German-Jewish thinkers Franz Rosenzweig and Martin Buber, that demarcates the natural Jewish condition as exilic.[71] To some German-Jewish intellectuals around the turn of the twentieth century, diasporism might have made sense. Jewish self-determination seemed beyond reach, and they imagined a vibrant Jewish existence in a tolerant Europe. As history developed, however, it turned out otherwise.

Diasporism wishes away the destructive aspects of twentieth-century history. In the view of committed diasporists, this world is safe. Jews do not have powerful enemies. Pipik, the imposter in Philip Roth's satiric *Operation Shylock,* described the arrival of the trains carrying Israeli Jews back to Poland:

> You know what will happen in Warsaw, at the railway station, when the first trainload of Jews returns? There will be crowds to welcome them. People will be jubilant. People will be in tears. They will be shouting, "Our Jews are back! Our Jews are back!" The spectacle will be transmitted by television throughout the world. And what a historic day for Europe, for Jewry, for all mankind when the cattle cars that transported Jews to death camps are transformed by the Diasporist movement into decent comfortable railway carriages carrying Jews by the tens of thousands back to their native cities and towns.[72]

Roth, of course, parodied the idea that antisemitism would disappear if the Jews left the Middle East. The New Agey theology of the kosherizers, however, casts banishment from the ancestral land as a religious calling. These congregations tend not to read the traditional prayer for the state of Israel, nor do they include the statement "we were exiled because of our sins," which is part of the daily prayer service, though individual members who lead services sometimes revert to the traditional forms.[73] Inverting Psalms 137's recollection that during the Babylonian exile "we sat and wept when we remembered Zion," JVP's fetishized Judaism denies Israel's central place in both ritual and contemporary Jewish life.

JVP's Judaism considers the religious connection to Eretz Yisrael as symbolic, not real. The longing for return is understood as merely representational. Nineteenth- and twentieth-century racial antisemitism, according to the diasporist narrative, gave birth to a twisted racialist Jewish nationalist movement that broke with thousands of years of Jewish tradition. According to Corey Robin "it fucks Jews up" to have a state. Zionism, writes JVP's deputy director Cecilie Surasky, "is on the wrong side of history." The Zionist aim to normalize the Jewish condition, according to Boyarin, involved replacing the effeminate characteristics of diaspora Judaism with masculine militarism. Butler argues that,

> not only is there substantial evidence that dispersion is the mode in which Jews have in fact survived; but that the idea that "dispersion" is a threat to Jews that must be overcome often relies on the notion that "dispersion" is a form of exile from the homeland (a condition of *galut* that can only be reversed through "returning" to the homeland). If dispersion is thought not only as a geographical situation but also as an ethical modality, then dispersion is precisely the principle that must be "brought home" to Israel/ Palestine in order to ground a polity where no one religion or nationality may claim sovereignty over another.[74]

Whereas Rosenzweig and Buber dedicated their work to Jewish cultural particularism, contemporary diasporism is a political act of assimilating into an imagined tolerant multicultural mosaic. When Judith Butler declares, "my politics are profoundly diasporic," she is turning outward because she believes that "the relation with the non Jew is the core of Jewish ethics." Daniel and Jonathan Boyarin believe that the Jewish diasporic condition forced Jews to develop "tactics of survival" which "belonged by

nature to women." Zionism betrayed the Jewish tradition because it is essentially masculine. "In resisting through becoming
'Muscle Jews,' it could be argued, the early Zionists were simply
assimilating and capitulating to general European values . . . ,
while through maintaining themselves as weak and passive, the
Torah Jews of Eastern Europe were engaged in a more successful act of cultural resistance to the hegemony of Christian culture." They call for rejecting masculine Zionism for a diasporic
view "in which the absence of the phallus is a positive product
of cultural history and not a signifier of disease." Or Rosen, in
a more straightforward fashion, celebrates the "intrinsic beauty
and genius of the Jewish conception of peoplehood: in a time
of profound upheaval and crisis we spiritualized the concept of
homeland and redefined ourselves as a globally based, multiethnic, multi-cultural nation that viewed the entire world as its
'home.' The concept of exile became, in a sense, a spiritual prism
through which we viewed the world and our place in it."[75]

JVP activists and intellectuals wish to see the end of Israel
as the national home of the Jewish people. "Am Yisrael" (the
people of Israel), Rosen points out, "existed many years before
there was a Medinat Yisrael (the state of Israel)." And the effort
to create a safe place for Jews has failed. Zionists created "an
over-militarized garrison state with an *über* nationalist culture
in the Middle East," but Israel, Rosen argues, remains the most
dangerous place in the world for Jews.[76] Zionism, according to
Butler, pits Judaism "against the diversity that defines democracy, and . . . betrays . . . the obligation of co-habitation with those
different from ourselves." Coexistence "can only begin with the
dismantling of political Zionism," starting with the return of the
Arab refuges of 1948.[77] Nothing short of an all-out eradication of
Zionism would satisfy diasporic Jewish ethics. Jews must return
to their natural position as a dependent minority.

Israel, in this view, will be replaced by a multicultural paradise in Palestine, modeled after the supposedly benign Ottoman

Empire that preceded European colonialism. Udi Aloni believes that "we can offer no greater good to the world than to build a new society on a foundation of multiple ethnic and religious distinctions."[78] Boyarin calls for replacing Zionism with a "diasporic consciousness . . . of a Jewish collective as one sharing space with others, devoid of exclusivist and dominating power." He imagines "an Israel in which individual and collective cultural rights would become an essential part of its structure, no longer coded as a Jewish State but as a bi-national, secular, and multicultural one." The only remaining moral path is "the renunciation of near exclusive Jewish hegemony," by which Boyarin means eradicating the Zionist foundations of Israel. It will be a beautiful paradise that "allows a formulation of Jewish identity not as a proud resting place, indeed not as a 'boast,' but as a perpetual, creative, diasporic tension." And while JVP does not advocate the removal of the Jews living in Israel back to Europe, or as Roth famously put it, "Last year in Jerusalem! Next year in Warsaw!," it imagines them living as a minority in an amicable, tolerant Arab Middle East. And what happens if this utopian vision of peace and harmony doesn't come to pass? There isn't really a plan B.[79]

JVP turns Jewish texts and holidays against Israel. It declared Tisha B'Av 2013, a day on which Jews lament the destruction of the temples, a Day of Action against Israel. Reconstructionist rabbinical student Jessica Rosenberg announced the launching of a new ritual of reading Palestinians lamentations, including one commemorating the libelous charge of a 2003 IDF massacre in Jenin. And in North Carolina, activists followed prayer by lobbying the board of directors of TIAA-CREF, the largest retirement insurer of academics, to adopt the BDS investment criteria. The contradiction between mourning past losses of Jewish sovereignty while working to bring about the destruction of the contemporary one is lost on activists who elevate support for Israel's enemies into a religious calling. As Rosen declares, "Standing with Palestinians is the most Jewish thing I can do."[80]

A FRANKIST MOMENT?

Gershom Scholem drew clear distinctions between the two early modern Jewish heretical messianic movements: the Shabbateans and the Frankists. Both Shabtai Tzvi and Jacob Frank declared themselves messiahs who would bring redemption to their oppressed brethren. Both converted from the faith in what they believed was a necessary step on the road to salvation. The Shabbateans continued to envision themselves as part of the Jewish mission even after the conversion to Islam, holding on to their unique liminal standing for over a century afterwards The Frankists were an altogether different phenomenon. Jacob Frank did not convert because his life was in danger. In fact, he probably converted a few times, to Islam and Catholicism, whenever and wherever it suited his needs. Frank capitalized on the residue of mystical Shabbatean sentiments in some Jewish Polish communities, declared himself a messiah, and, playing upon antisemitic sentiments in the Polish Catholic church, received special dispensation to create a cult of followers of ethnically Jewish Trinitarian Christians. Notwithstanding the financial and sexual scandals that permeated the cult, what's most striking about the Frankists, who, unlike the Shabbateans, rapidly dissolved in the larger Polish Catholic surroundings, was the alliance they struck with the enemies of Poland's Jews. In an orchestrated public disputation with the rabbis of Lvov in 1759, the Frankists stated that the Talmud teaches that the Jews need Christian blood, and that whoever believes in the Talmud is bound to use it. In their desire to "wreak vengeance on their rabbinic persecutors," the Frankists kosherized the blood libel.[81]

Modern apostates fantasize about a utopian Jewish existence that is wholly divorced from two millennia of Jewish history. They argue that the destruction of Zionist Israel would be a first step toward the creation of this sociocultural paradise. They call for the untangling of Judaism from Zionism, and as Israel's international isolation grows, they undertake a Frankist transition into the mainstream, all in the name of superior claims to Jewish ethics. In the liminal space they occupy they play an important role in kosherizing anti-Zionism.

Kosherizers are mostly ignored, denounced, and shunned by the Jewish mainstream. Perhaps there is no room in the community for radical dissenters who, however well meaning, wish to return the Jewish people to a state of a dependent minority. In the emerging narrative, however, these "courageous progressives" are becoming "the right kind of Jews," whereas the mainstream of world Jewry is increasingly associated with an illegitimate, reactionary nationalist regime and ideology. In elite intellectual circles, warring against Zionism is becoming the only appropriate Jewish ethical path. The next pogrom has already been kosherized.

NOTES

Thanks to Rebecca Wilkomerson and Brant Rosen for agreeing to be interviewed despite their full cognizance that I do not share their points of view. Udi Aloni, likewise, knew I am critical of Jewish Voice for Peace (JVP) and still connected me to the group's leadership and answered my questions. I thank the following for reading earlier drafts and offering useful commentary: Nimrod Aloni, David Bell, Henry Cohen, Susan Neiman, Debbie Pollak, Alvin Rosenfeld, Rabbi Benjamin Scolnic, and Elhanan Yakira.

1. Tom Paulin, "Killed in Crossfire," *Observer,* February 17, 2001, accessed January 15, 2014, http://www.theguardian.com/books/2001/feb/18/poetry.features1.

2. For analysis of the pernicious uses of the Holocaust in anti-Israel rhetoric, see Alvin H. Rosenfeld, *The End of the Holocaust* (Bloomington: Indiana University Press, 2011), chapter 9, and Daniel Jonah Goldhagen, *The Devil that Never Dies: The Rise and Threat of Global Antisemitism* (New York: Little, Brown, 2013), chapter 12.

3. David Nirenberg, *Anti-Judaism: The Western Tradition* (New York: Norton, 2013), 471.

4. Judith Butler, *Parting Ways: Jewishness and the Critique of Zionism* (New York: Columbia University Press, 2012), 1; Avi Shlaim, "The War of

the Israeli Historians," accessed February 5, 2014, http://users.ox.ac.uk
/~ssfc0005/The%20War%20of%20the%20Israeli%20Historians.html.
Having used this antisemitic "thirty pieces of silver" trope when deliver-
ing the lecture at Georgetown University on December 1, 2003, Shlaim
later uploaded it onto the Oxford website. The offensive language does not
appear in the published essay in French, "La Guerre des historiens israé-
liens," *Annales. Histoire, Sciences Sociales* 59 (Jan.–Feb. 2004): 164; Emanuele Ottolenghi, "Present-Day Antisemitism and the Centrality of the Jewish Alibi," in *Resurgent Antisemitism: Global Perspectives,* ed. Alvin H.
Rosenfeld (Bloomington: Indiana University Press, 2013), 465n98.

    5. Ofer Aderet, "Study: In Germany, Anti-Semitic Hate Mail Doesn't
Come from the Far-Right," *Haaretz,* February 25, 2014, accessed February 26, 2014, http://www.haaretz.com/jewish-world/jewish-world-news
/.premium-1.576189. Many scholars of modern antisemitism consider
anti-Zionism to be antisemitism in all but name. David Hirsh points out
that close scrutiny reveals that "Anti-Zionism has a tendency to present
the crimes and failings of the Jewish state as the whole and necessary
truth of the Jewish state, which is analogous to the way that antisemitism
presented the crimes and failings of particular Jews . . . as the whole and
necessary truth of all Jews in general." David Hirsh, "Anti-Zionism and
Antisemitism: Cosmopolitan Reflections," *Yale Initiative for the Interdis-
ciplinary Study of Antisemitism Working Paper Series* (2007), 14. See also
Edward H. Kaplan and Charles A. Small, "Anti-Israel Sentiment Predicts
Anti-Semitism in Europe," *Journal of Conflict Resolution* 50 (August 2006):
548–561. I share Bernard Lewis's opposition to the automatic conflation
of antisemitism and anti-Zionism. "Even the frequently reiterated Arab
intention of dismantling the state of Israel and 'liquidating the Zionist society' is not, in itself, necessarily an expression of antisemitism. In the view
of most Arabs, the creation of the state of Israel was an act of injustice, and
its continued existence a standing aggression. To those who hold this view,
the correction of that injustice and the removal of that aggression may be
legitimate political objectives." "The New Anti-Semitism," *New York Review of Books,* April 10, 1986.

    6. Ottolenghi, "Present-Day Antisemitism and the Centrality of the
Jewish Alibi," 425; "BNC Responds to French Prime Minister: BDS Promotes Justice and Universal Rights," BDS Movement: Freedom Justice
Equality, February 25, 2010, accessed November 21, 2013, http://www.bds
movement.net/2010/bnc-responds-to-french-prime-minister-bds-promotes
-justice-and-universal-rights-645#sthash.PPKJslaG.dpuf; *Zionism Unsettled* cites Mark Ellis and Avraham Burg on the use of the Holocaust by

Zionism, Ian Lustig on how Zionism is yesterday's truth and thus an obstacle to Jewish welfare and security, Akiva Eldar on the Jewish pathology of victimhood that allows Israel to brutalize Palestinians, Brant Rosen on his new "liberation" theology; Ilan Pappe on the Nakba; David Myers on Netanyahu's philosophy and more. Donald Wagner and Walter T. Davis Jr., *Zionism Unsettled: A Congregational Study Guide,* booklet and DVD (Eugene, Ore.: Pickwick Publications, 2014). Tamar Lewin, "Prominent Scholars, Citing Importance of Academic Freedom, Denounce Israel Boycott," *New York Times,* December 26, 2013.

7. Robert Wistrich, *A Lethal Obsession: Antisemitism from Antiquity to Global Jihad* (New York: Random House, 2010), 527; Ottolenghi, "Present-Day Antisemitism and the Centrality of the Jewish Alibi," 434; Anti-Defamation League, "Profile: Jewish Voice for Peace" (New York: ADL, 2013), 2, accessed February 1, 2014, http://www.adl.org/assets/pdf/israel-international/Profile-Jewish-Voice-for-Peace.pdf. Elie Wiesel likewise condemned the Jewish intellectuals who "shamelessly use their Jewishness to justify their attacks against Israel." "A Mideast Peace—Is It Impossible?," *New York Times,* June 23, 1988.

8. Ilan Pappe, "Reclaiming Judaism from Zionism," *Electronic Intifada,* October 18, 2013, accessed October 18, 2013, http://electronicintifada.net/content/reclaiming-judaism-zionism/12859.

9. The third pillar of contemporary anti-Zionist discourse targets the supposed villainy of the American Jewish establishment in general, and the American Israel Public Relations Committee (AIPAC) in particular. Indeed, AIPAC has come to stand for the secret Jewish cabals of medieval times, and it has become almost an article of faith in liberal circles to denounce the influence of the Jewish lobby and accuse it of disloyalty. John J. Mearsheimer and Stephen M. Walt, who authored the charge that a Zionist cabal controls U.S. foreign policy—first as an article, "The Israel Lobby," *London Review of Books* 28 (March 23, 2006): 3–12, and then as the book, *The Israel Lobby and U.S. Foreign Policy* (New York: Farrar, Straus and Giroux, 2008)—are not Jewish, but shortly after their treatise was published Tony Judt rushed to defend it in the *New York Times,* "A Lobby, Not a Conspiracy," April 19, 2006; and *Tikkun* editor Rabbi Michael Lerner found in this modern rendition of the *Protocols of the Elders of Zion* an echo of the biblical prophets of ancient Israel. "The Israel Lobby," *Tikkun* (September–October 2007), accessed December 22, 2014, http://www.tikkun.org/article.php/Lerner-the-israel-lobby. When New York mayor Bill DeBlasio met with AIPAC representatives and uttered a political cliché about his

door being open to hear them, fifty-eight "courageous" Jews published a letter countering that "your job is not to do AIPAC's bidding when they call you to do so. AIPAC speaks for Israel's hard-line government and its right-wing supporters, and for them alone; it does not speak for us." Daniel Treiman, "Letter from Jewish Liberals Slams de Blasio over AIPAC Address," JTA, January 29, 2014, accessed January 30, 2014, http://www.jta.org/2014 /01/29/news-opinion/the-telegraph/letter-from-jewish-liberals-slams-de -blasio-over-aipac-address#ixzz2tWNqZ74W. Jewish journalist John Judis has recently faulted the Jewish lobby for manipulating Harry Truman into supporting partition. *Genesis: Truman, American Jews, and the Origins of the Arab/Israeli Conflict* (New York: Farrar, Straus and Giroux, 2014). The absurdity of this evaluation of Jewish power in the 1940s is obvious to anyone familiar with the most basic facts of U.S. history. According to this twisted logic, Jews couldn't get the administration to do anything about the Holocaust, but within two years they somehow came to dominate U.S. foreign policy. For an excellent journalistic analysis of the pro-Israel American sentiment and its relationship to AIPAC see Yair Rosenberg, "U.S. Policy Is Pro-Israel Because Americans Are Pro-Israel, Not Because of AIPAC," *Tablet,* February 27, 2014, accessed February 27, 2014, http:// www.tabletmag.com/jewish-news-and-politics/164223/why-american -policy-is-pro-israel/2.

10. "Heinrich Himmler Speech to SS Officers, Poznan, Poland, October 4, 1943," *Holocaust-History.org,* accessed November 25, 2013, http:// www.holocaust-history.org/himmler-poznan/speech-text.shtml.

11. Hitler quoted in Ron Rosenbaum, *Explaining Hitler: The Search for the Origins of Evil* (New York: Random House, 1999), 146–149. On the relationship between Hitler and Block, see Rudolph Binion, *Hitler among the Germans* (DeKalb: Northern Illinois University Press, 1984); Robert G. L. Waite, *The Psychopathic God: Adolf Hitler* (New York: Bantam Books, 1977), 188–189, and Gertrude Kurth, "The Jew and Adolph Hitler," *Psychoanalytic Quarterly* 16 (1947): 11–32.

12. As cited by Brigitte Hamann, *Hitler's Vienna: A Dictator's Apprenticeship* (New York: Oxford University Press, 1999), 227.

13. Nirenberg, *Anti-Judaism.* See also Michael Walzer, "Imaginary Jews," *New York Review of Books,* March 20, 2014.

14. Hans Frank's recollection of what Hitler said in 1937, as cited by Hamann, *Hitler's Vienna,* 230.

15. D. Hirsh, "Anti-Zionism and Antisemitism," 15; David Nirenberg, "Anti-Judaism as a Critical Theory," *Chronicle of Higher Education,* Janu-

ary 28, 2013, accessed March 15, 2014, https://chronicle.com/article/Anti
-Judaism-as-a-Critical/136793/.

16. Cynthia Ozick, "Apostasy, Then and Now," in *Israel's Jewish Defamers; The Media Dimension,* ed. Andrea Levin (Boston: Committee for Accuracy in Repo, 2008), 19–24; Todd M. Endelman, introduction, in *Jewish Apostasy in the Modern World,* ed. Todd M. Endelman (New York: Holmes & Meier, 1987), 14–15.

17. Thomas of Monmouth, *The Life and Miracles of St. William of Norwich,* ed. Augustus Jessopp and Montague Rhodes James (Cambridge: Cambridge University Press, 1896), 94.

18. *The Trial of the Talmud: Paris, 1240,* Hebrew texts translated by John Friedman, Latin texts translated by Jean Connell Hoff, historical essay by Robert Chazan (Toronto: Pontifical Institute of Mediaeval Studies, 2012), 102–121; William Chester Jordan, "The Crown and the Jews: Marian Devotion and the Talmud Trial of 1240," in *Ideology and Royal Power in Medieval France: Kingship, Crusade, and the Jews,* 61–76 (Aldershot, U.K.: Ashgate, 2001); Jeremy Cohen, "The Mentality of the Medieval Jewish Apostate: Peter Alfonsi, Hermann of Cologne, and Pablo Christiani," in Endelman, *Jewish Apostasy in the Modern World,* 36–37.

19. Michael Mack, *German Idealism and the Jew: The Inner Anti-Semitism of Philosophy and German Jewish responses* (Chicago: University of Chicago Press, 2003), 72–89.

20. Karl Marx, "On *The Jewish Question,* II: Bruno Bauer, 'The Capacity of Present-day Jews and Christians to Become Free,' *Einundzwanzig Bogen aus der Schweiz,* pp. 56–71," accessed March 10, 2014, http://www.marxists
.org/archive/marx/works/1844/jewish-question/.

21. *Wagner's Jews,* produced, written, and directed by Hilan Warshaw, DVD (New York: Overtone Films, 2013).

22. Otto Weininger, *Sex and Character by Otto Weininger,* authorized translations from the 6th German edition (New York: G. P. Putnam's Sons, 1907), 304, 311, 313, 321.

23. Gershom Scholem, "Revelation and Tradition as Religious Categories in Judaism," in *The Messianic Idea in Judaism and Other Essays on Jewish Spirituality* (1971, reprint New York: Schocken Books, 1995), 290.

24. Natan Sharansky has argued that criticisms of Israel qualify as antisemitic when they involve three Ds: 1. Demonization: "when comparisons are made between Israelis and Nazis and between Palestinian refugee camps and Auschwitz." 2. Double standard: when Israel is singled out for human rights violations that are committed by other countries. 3. Dele-

gitimization: when "Israel's fundamental right to exist is denied—alone among all peoples in the world." I accept the first and third criteria. I reject the double standard defense, for it suggests that criticism of Israeli policies is not legitimate if some rogue brutish regime is doing worse. "3D Test of Anti-Semitism: Demonization, Double Standards, Delegitimization," *Jewish Political Studies Review* 16 (fall 2004), accessed March 22, 2014, http://jcpa.org/phas/phas-sharansky-fo4.htm. The U.S. Department of State's official definition of antisemitism addresses the double standard question in a more precise manner. U.S Department of State, *Defining Antisemitism,* fact sheet, June 8, 2010, accessed March 22, 2014, http://www.state.gov/j/drl/rls/fs/2010/122352.htm.

25. Marianne Hirsch, "The Sound of Silencing in the Academe," *Chronicle of Higher Education,* February 3, 2014, accessed February 3, 2014, http://chronicle.com/article/The-Sound-of-Silencing-in/144339/.

26. The rants and antics of Gilaad Atzmon, Roger Waters, Max Blumenthal, Michael Neumann, Mark Ellis, and their ilk discredit rather than kosherize antisemitism. It is unfair to associate the thoughtful critics I engage in this article with such people.

27. Butler, *Parting Ways,* 203; Brant Rosen, Skype interview with the author, February 21, 2014. Rosen gives the Palestinian solidarity movement a clean bill of health, though he sets the bar for antisemitism rather low: at Gilad Atzmon and Holocaust denial.

28. Labeling someone an antisemite employs a psychological typology that reduces people into a defined personality model. We are all more complicated than that. This chapter focuses on concrete antisemitic acts and speech, not on antisemites, with the exception of known pathological cases such as Hitler, Himmler, Eichmann, and Ahmadinejad.

29. Avraham Burg, *Lenatzeach et Hitler,* in Hebrew (Tel Aviv: Yediot Sfarim Press, 2007), dedication. All citations from Burg's book are my translations; Butler, *Parting Ways,* 35. Butler dedicates two chapters of the book to engaging Arendt, though her discussion narrowly tries to fit Arendt into her political agenda. Susan Neiman has written a more nuanced analysis of Arendt's *Eichmann in Jerusalem,* one that does not gloss over the historical errors and yet is highly appreciative of Arendt's formulation of the problem of modern evil, *Evil in Modern Thought: An Alternative History of Philosophy* (Princeton, N.J.: Princeton University Press, 2002), 267–281, 299–310. For an excellent critical discussion of the place of Arendt scholarship in radical Israeli discourse, see Elhanan Yakira, *Post-Zionism, Post-Holocaust: Three Essays on Denial, Forgetting, and the Delegitimation of Israel,*

trans. Michael Swirsky (New York: Columbia University Press, 2010). On Arendt's complex relationship to Zionism and Jews, see Elhanan Yakira, "Hannah Arendt, the Holocaust, and Zionism: A Story of a Failure," *Israel Studies* 11 (fall 2006): 31–61; Bernard Wasserstein, "Blame the Victim— Hannah Arendt among the Nazis: The Historian and Her Sources," *Times Literary Supplement* 5558 (October 9, 2009), 13–14. On Arendt's misreading of Eichmann see Bettina Stangneth, *Eichmann before Jerusalem: The Unexamined Life of a Mass Murderer,* trans. Ruth Martin (New York: Alfred A. Knopf, 2014).

30. Judith Butler centers her discussion of Arendt on this reply. *Parting Ways,* chapter 5.

31. Merav Michaeli, "Tony Judt's Final Word on Israel," *Atlantic,* September 14, 2011, accessed March 17, 2014, http://www.theatlantic.com/inter national/archive/2011/09/tony-judts-final-word-on-israel/245051/?single _page=true. Judt's end-of-life tirade exposed, as Jeffery Goldberg put it, his "contempt for Jews, his blatant dishonesty, and his support for the radical Arab vision of a Judenrein–Middle East." "Tony Judt's Last Interview on Israel," *Atlantic,* September 14, 2011, accessed March 17, 2014, http://www .theatlantic.com/international/archive/2011/09/tony-judts-last-interview -on-israel/245062/. For an analysis of Judt's passionate anti-Zionism see Benjamin Balint, "Future Imperfect: Tony Judt Blushes for the Jewish State," in *The Jewish Divide over Israel: Accusers and Defenders,* ed. Edward Alexander and Paul Bogdanor (New Brunswick, N.J.: Transaction, 2006), 65–76.

32. Bruce Robbins, *Some of My Best Friends Are Zionists,* accessed February 3, 2014, http://www.bestfriendsfilm.com/. Robbins belittles antisemitism, titling his film *Some of My Best Friends Are Zionists* to echo the clichéd characteristic of Antisemites in denial who quip "some of my best friends are Jewish." Robbins explains, however: "the title is meant to be polyvalent. We recognize that statements of the form 'some of my best friends are X' are usually considered to be racist. In choosing to pass through or to allude to a racist site of enunciation, we are of course being ironic, but in a serious way and in part at our own expense. We are trying to distance the film from the self-righteousness that is so difficult to avoid when one feels one has discovered a political truth that inexplicably remains obscure to those around one." Bruce Robbins, "Some of My Best Friends Are Zionists," *Jadaliyya,* October 26, 2011, accessed February 3, 2014, http://www.jadaliyya.com /pages/index/2945/some-of-my-best-friends-are-zionists. The film is nothing if not self-righteous, which makes the title appropriate rather than ironic.

33. Burg seemed to have modeled himself after the famous Talmudic apostate Elisha ben Abuyah, who, as legend has it, rejected the Torah, embraced Hellenism, and worked for the Romans during the Bar Kochba rebellion. In an interview with Hagai Segal in Israel's Knesset channel on December 2, 2013, Burg declared that had he lived in the days of the second temple he would have been, like Elisha ben Abuyah, a proud Hellenizer and that Mattityahu, the leader of the Hasmonites, was a murderous racist zealot—a rabbi Kahana of sorts. Conversation between Avraham Burg and Hagai Segal, Arutz 7, broadcast January 21, 2013, accessed April 9, 2014, http://www.inn.co.il/News/News.aspx/266425.

34. David Remnick, an outspokenly harsh critic of Israel himself, characterized the book's argument as "a kind of undergraduate universalism, a table talk at once snobbish and half-baked." "The Apostate: A Zionist Politician Loses Faith in the Future," Letter from Jerusalem, New Yorker, July 30, 2007, accessed April 9, 2014, http://www.newyorker.com/reporting/2007/07/30/070730fa_fact_remnick?printable=true&currentPage=all.

35. Merav Michaeli, "Tony Judt's Final Word on Israel," Atlantic, September 14, 2011, accessed March 20, 2015, http://www.theatlantic.com/international/archive/2011/09/tony-judts-final-word-on-israel/245051/. The fallacy that Zionists triumphed because the world felt guilty over the Holocaust has been refuted many times by historians. It is, however, a fallacy that's quite popular among pro-Arab activist like Judt, who had little expertise in the history of Zionism.

36. Alan Sokal quoted in Robbins, "Some of My Best Friends Are Zionists."

37. Burg, Lenatzeach et Hitler, 60–75.

38. Burg's logic is reminiscent of Jacqueline Rose's argument that Hitler and Herzl were both inspired to write Mein Kampf and Der Judenstaat by the same Wagner performance they both attended in Paris. For an excellent analysis of Rose, see Alvin H. Rosenfeld, "Progressive" Jewish Thought and the New Anti-Semitism (New York: American Jewish Committee, 2006), 9–12.

39. Burg, Hitler, 31, 60, 176, 47, 11. This last statement by Burg is particularly offensive given the number of genocides that have taken place in the world since the end of World War II.

40. Burg, Hitler, 50. Burg follows writer Amos Elon, who late in life turned nostalgic for the golden age of German Jewry, writing The Pity of It All: A Portrait of the German-Jewish Epoch, 1743–1933 (New York: Metropolitan Books, 2002). But whereas Elon's work is shrouded in sadness and

longing for a world destroyed by the Holocaust, Burg's longing is rather upbeat, congruent with his view that the Holocaust was an aberration never to be seen again and that antisemitism is, for all intents and purposes, dead.

41. Burg, *Hitler,* 169. As Elhanan Yakira pointed out, "the instrumentalization of the Holocaust is much more common among the enemies of Israel, of Zionism, and of Jews in general, than by all the latter." "Anti-Israelism and Neo-Antisemitism," unpublished essay. I thank Professor Yakira for sharing his essay with me prior to its publication.

42. Ari Shavit, "Get Kritot," *Haaretz,* June 6, 2007, accessed April 9, 2014, http://www.haaretz.co.il/1.1416131.

43. Avraham Burg, "Even I—an Israeli—Think Settlement Goods Are Not Kosher: Preventing the Mislabelling of Products as 'Made in Israel' Would Be a Giant Leap for Middle East Peace," *Independent,* June 7, 2012, accessed April 9, 2014, http://www.independent.co.uk/voices/commentators /avraham-burg-even-i—an-israeli—think-settlement-goods-are-not-kosher -7821011.html.

44. Burg, *Hitler,* 170–171, 103.

45. Ibid., 44.

46. Burg quoted in Wistrich, *Lethal Obsession,* 540. It should be noted that while Burg supports boycotts and sanctions against Jewish settlements in the West Bank, he does not support the more general BDS call that does not distinguish between the Israel of the pre and post 1967 borders. Burg, "Even I—an Israeli—Think Settlement Goods Are Not Kosher." Burg does lend his voice to more radical groups such as the Elders, chaired by Desmond Tutu, on June 28, 2013, accessed January 18, 2014, http://www.the elders.org/article/putting-green-line-back-map.

47. Burg wrote:

> Israel, having ceased to care about the children of the Palestinians, should not be surprised when they come washed in hatred and blow themselves up in the centres of Israeli escapism. They consign themselves to Allah in our places of recreation, because their own lives are torture. They spill their own blood in our restaurants in order to ruin our appetites, because they have children and parents at home who are hungry and humiliated. We could kill a thousand ringleaders a day and nothing will be solved, because the leaders come up from below—from the wells of hatred and anger, from the "infrastructures" of injustice and moral corruption.

"The End of Zionism," *Guardian,* September 15, 2003, accessed January 30, 2014, http://www.guardian.co.uk/world/2003/sep/15/comment.

48. "Court Decides: Burg Will Not Get a Car and Personal Driver," *Ynet,* May 14, 2007, accessed April 9, 2014, http://www.ynet.co.il/articles /0,7340,L-3399880,00.html. Burg's convictions have not stopped him from living off the state of Israel and taking the Jewish Agency to court in a failed effort to have it provide him with a car and chauffer for the rest of his life. As writer Yossi Klein Halevi commented: "You don't take all the perks of the Zionist movement and refuse to relinquish them and then repudiate the most cherished notions of Zionism at the same time. There's something smarmy about it. He is so totally out of touch with Israeli reality that I'm appalled that he ever had any positions of Israeli authority." Halevi quoted in Remnick, "Apostate."

49. Ozick, "Apostasy, Then and Now," 20; Brant Rosen, "Does the ADL Have a Monopoly over Jewish Values?," *Palestinian Talmud,* August 20, 2013, accessed March 12, 2014, http://palestiniantalmud.com/page/2/.

50. I contrast modern kosherizers with the self-hate phenomena that were brilliantly analyzed by Sander Gillman in his seminal work, *Jewish Self-Hatred: Anti-Semitism and the Hidden Language of the Jews* (Baltimore, Md.: Johns Hopkins University Press, 1986). See also Paul Reitter, "Karl Kraus and the Jewish Self-Hatred Question," *Jewish Social Studies,* new series, 10 (autumn 2003): 78–116; Z. Diesendruck, "Antisemitism and Ourselves," *Jewish Social Studies* 1 (October 1939): 399–408; Sara Honig, "Another Tack: The Otto Weininger Syndrome," *Jerusalem Post,* April 6, 2010.

51. "Mission Statement," *Jewish Voice for Peace,* accessed February 10, 2014, http://jewishvoiceforpeace.org/content/jvp-mission-statement. The list of the top ten anti-Israel organizations in the United States, according to ADL president Abraham Foxman, "represents the worst of the worst anti-Israel groups." These groups "lob any and every accusation against Israel, including charges of Nazi-like crimes, 'apartheid' policies, ethnic cleansing, war crimes and genocide. Their accusations are rarely, if ever, balanced with an acknowledgement of Israel's repeated efforts to make peace with the Palestinians, or the legitimate terrorism concerns faced by Israeli citizens." "News: Ranking the Top 10 Anti-Israel Groups in 2013," press release, ADL, October 21, 2013, accessed March 12, 2014, http://www .adl.org/press-center/press-releases/israel-middle-east/adl-lists-top-ten -anti-israel-groups-in-america.html.

52. Rebecca Vilkomerson, "Ken Stern and the American Jewish Committee's Integrity Problem," *MuzzleWatch,* August 8, 2012, accessed February 12, 2014, http://muzzlewatch.com/2012/08/30/ken-stern-and-the -american-jewish-committee%E2%80%99s-integrity-problem-by-rebecca -vilkomerson/.

53. Rebecca Vilkomerson, interview with the author, January 27, 2014. I focus on Jewish Voice for Peace, but other strongly identified and observant Jews share its positions, although they are not on the organization's official council. The list is long and getting longer. See, for example, Mark Oppenheimer, "A Conflict of Faith: Devoted to Jewish Observance, but at Odds with Israel," *New York Times,* February 14, 2014.

54. Paul Bogdanor, "The Devil's State: Chomsky's War against Israel," and "Chomsky's Ayatollahs," in Alexander and Bogdanor, *Jewish Divide over Israel,* 77–114, 115–134.

55. Shmoop Editorial Team, "Judith Butler's Bio," *Shmoop University,* 11 November 2008, accessed January 21, 2014, http://www.shmoop.com /judith-butler/bio.html. Judith Butler, "Who Owns Kafka," *London Review of Books* 33, (March 3, 2011): 3–8.

56. Butler, *Parting Ways,* 20, 2; "Judith Butler Responds to Attack," http:// www.egs.edu/faculty/judith-butler/articles/i-affirm-a-judaism-that-is-not -associated-with-state-violence/; Shmoop Editorial Team, "Judith Butler's Bio." Unlike Burg, Rosen, and even Boyarin, Butler's narrative of disillusionment is rather untraumatic; someone in college challenged her homegrown inclination to be pro-Israel and she came to see the light. Her intellectual roots are in the radical cultural politics of the GLBTQ liberation struggle. Butler comes across a bit phony when she invokes Yiddishisms as if they have always been a feature of her vocabulary. For example, she opened her remarks to the overwhelmingly non-Jewish BDS conference at Brooklyn College with "What a Megillah!," which came across as inauthentic. "Judith Butler's Remarks to Brooklyn College on BDS," *Nation,* February 7, 2013, accessed March 20, 2014, http://www.thenation.com/article /172752/judith-butlers-remarks-brooklyn-college-bds#.

57. On September 11, 2012, the City of Frankfurt awarded Judith Butler the Adorno Prize, which is tantamount to awarding the prize named after one of the most famous refugees from Nazism to a Jew who advocates the elimination of the state of Israel. For an excellent critique of Butler's arguments, see Cary Nelson, "The Problem with Judith Butler: The Political Philosophy of BDS and the Movement to Delegitimize Israel," in *The Case against Academic Boycotts of Israel,* ed. Cary Nelson and Gabriel Noah Brahm (Chicago: MLA Members for Scholars Rights, 2014), 164–201.

58. Vilkomerson interview. For a critique of this view of the boycott see Emily Budick, "When a Boycott Is Not Moral Action but Social Conformity and the 'Affectation of Love,'" in Nelson and Brahm, *Case against Academic Boycotts of Israel,* 85–103.

59. BDS states its goals as follows: "1. Ending its occupation and colonization of all Arab lands occupied in June 1967 and dismantling the Wall; 2. Recognizing the fundamental rights of the Arab-Palestinian citizens of Israel to full equality; and 3. Respecting, protecting and promoting the rights of Palestinian refugees to return to their homes and properties as stipulated in UN Resolution 194." BDS, "Introducing the BDS Movement," accessed March 15, 2014, http://www.bdsmovement.net/bdsintro. The third goal obviously involves dismantling modern Israel.

60. See Omar Barghouti's interview with Silvia Catori, "Omar Barghouti: No State Has the Right to Exist as a Racist State," *Political Writings Silvia Catori,* December 6, 2007, accessed April 2, 2014, http://www.silvia cattori.net/article345.html. As'ad AbuKhalil, "A Critique of Norman Finkelstein on BDS," *English alakhbar,* February 17, 2012, accessed April 12, 2014, http://english.al-akhbar.com/blogs/angry-corner/critique-norman -finkelstein-bds. Brant Rosen, however, argues that BDS must be understood in terms of the power imbalance between Israelis and Palestinians. "Though a movement like BDS might feel on a visceral level like just one more example of the world piling on the Jews and Israel, we need to be open to the possibility that it might more accurately be described as the product of a weaker, dispossessed, disempowered people doing what it must to resist oppression." "Is BDS Antisemitism?," Shalom Rav: A Blog by Rabbi Brant Rosen, April 1, 2009, accessed April 2, 2014, http://rabbibrant .com/2009/04/01/is-bds-anti-semitism/.

61. Shmoop Editorial Team, "Judith Butler's Bio"; Gianni Vattimo and Michael Marder eds., *Deconstructing Zionism: A Critique of Political Metaphysics* (New York: Bloomsbury, 2013); program of New York University's American Studies Program Annual Conference, Feb. 28–March 1, 2014, accessed April 9, 2014, http://4.bp.blogspot.com/-zd7PycvmdyM/Uwo LN6jGbaI/AAAAAAAAcdo/VQxS8WtcGJ8/s1600/asa+nyu.jpg. Even though her statement of support for Hamas and Hezbollah is on the record, Butler has denied she meant anything normative in her description of these organizations. "Judith Butler Responds to Attack." Given Butler's politics, the denial strikes me as disingenuous spin. To my knowledge she has not explained why she chose to republish a chapter from *Parting Ways* in *Deconstructing Zionism.*

62. Avi Shlaim, "Why Zionism Today Is the Real Enemy of the Jews," *International Herald Tribune,* February 4, 2005.

63. Jason Horowitz, "Can Liberal Zionists Count on Hillary Clinton?," *New York Times,* December 21, 2014; Vilkomerson interview.

64. Peter Beinart has argued that Israeli policies are the cause of the growing rift between assimilating young Jews, Israel, and the U.S. Jewish establishment. Peter Beinart, "The Failure of the American Jewish Establishment," *New York Review of Books,* June 10, 2010; Peter Beinart, "The American Jewish Cocoon," *New York Review of Books,* September 26, 2013. I believe that criticism of the controversial Israeli policies provide the vocabulary of alienation. The roots lie in deeper sociocultural developments, in the broader U.S. society and within the Jewish community. For an insightful analysis of these trends see Daniel Gordis, "Conservative Judaism: A Requiem," *Jewish Review of Books,* winter 2014.

65. The national Hillel instructed local university chapters to "not partner with, house, or host organizations, groups, or speakers that as a matter of policy or practice: Deny the right of Israel to exist as a Jewish and democratic state with secure and recognized borders; Delegitimize, demonize, or apply a double standard to Israel; Support boycott of, divestment from, or sanctions against the State of Israel; Exhibit a pattern of disruptive behavior towards campus events or guest speakers or foster an atmosphere of incivility." Hillel International, Hillel Israel Guidelines, accessed April 4, 2014, http://www.hillel.org/jewish/hillel-israel/hillel-israel-guidelines. The leadership of Wesleyan's Jewish students community broke with the national Hillel organization because its guidelines "have resulted in the barring of speakers from organizations such as Breaking the Silence and the Israeli Knesset from speaking at Hillels without censorship, and has resulted in Jewish Voice for Peace and other Jewish organizations not being welcome under the Hillel umbrella or in the Jewish community that gathers in those spaces." "Wesleyan Jewish Community Student Leaders Stand with Open Hillel," press release, April 2, 2014, available at *Mondoweiss,* http://mondoweiss.net/2014/04/chaperones-wesleyan-declares.

66. Vilkomerson interview.

67. Other rabbis on the JVP rabbinical council affiliate with the Jewish Renewal Movement. Rabbis on the council generally do not hold a pastoral position in Jewish congregations but are activists in a variety of left-wing causes. I take their claims to rabbinical status, learning, and authority at face value.

68. Rosen interview.

69. Bruce McLeod, "An Interview with Tony Kushner," *Iowa Journal of Cultural Studies,* 1995, 143–153.

70. Daniel Boyarin, *A Radical Jew: Paul and the Politics of Identity* (Berkeley: University of California Press, 1997), chapter 10, in *Poetry Genius,* ac-

cessed November 29, 2013, http://poetry.rapgenius.com/Daniel-boyarin-a
-radical-jew-paul-and-the-politics-of-identity-chap-10-answering-the-mail
-toward-a-radical-jewishness-annotated. Boyarin, an observant Orthodox
Jew without a shul or community, believes that the purpose of his Orthodox
observance is to express his "own radical commitments to social, economic,
and ethnic solidarity and equality." Boyarin champions BDS campaigns and
Palestinian solidarity movements, and there are student allegations that he
has covered for a Berkeley Arab colleague who vouched for the truthfulness
of *The Protocols of the Elders of Zion*. Menachem Kellner, "Daniel Boyarin
and the Herd of Independent Minds," in Alexander and Bogdanor, *Jewish
Divide over Israel,* 167–176; Oppenheimer, "Conflict of Faith"; Alan Brill,
"Daniel Boyarin and Orthodoxy: An Interview," Book of Doctrines and
Opinions: Notes on Jewish Theology and Spirituality, December 27, 2011,
accessed November 29, 2013, http://kavvanah.wordpress.com/2011/12/27
/daniel-boyarin-and-orthodoxy-an-interview/.

71. Udi Aloni, *What Does a Jew Want? On Binationalism and Other Spec-
ters,* ed. Slavoj Žižek (New York: Columbia University Press, 2010), 22–23;
Butler, *Parting Ways,* 37. It should be noted that Rosenzweig understood
the Jewish condition as a mission that transcends the physical world—not
as a positive theological construct.

72. Philip Roth, *Operation Shylock: A Confession* (New York: Simon and
Schuster, 1993), 45.

73. Rosen interview; Brant Rosen to Doron Ben-Atar, email March 20,
2014.

74. Phoebe Maltz Bovy, "Is Corey Robin the Ultimate Facebook Lefty,
Twitter Radical, and Anti-Zionist Scourge?," *Tablet Magazine,* accessed
January 7, 2015, http://tabletmag.com/jewish-news-and-politics/188090
/straight-outta-chappaqua; Cecile Surasky, "Tracking Efforts to Stifle
Open Debate about U.S.-Israeli Foreign Policy," MuzzleWatch, accessed
December 31, 2014, http://muzzlewatch.com/; Daniel Boyarin, *Carnal
Israel: Reading Sex in Talmudic Culture* (Berkeley: University of California
Press, 1995); Daniel Boyarin, *Unheroic Conduct: The Rise of Heterosexual-
ity and the Invention of the Jewish Man* (Berkeley: University of California
Press, 1997); Yaron Peleg, "Heroic Conduct: Homoeroticism and the Cre-
ation of Modern, Jewish Masculinities," *Jewish Social Studies* 13 (fall 2006):
31–58; Butler, *Parting Ways,* 6.

75. Aloni, *What Does a Jew Want?,* 215; Butler, *Parting Ways,* 99, 115;
Daniel Boyarin and Jonathan Boyarin, *Powers of Diaspora: Two Essays on
the Relevance of Jewish Culture* (Minneapolis: University of Minnesota

Press, 2002), 37, 45, 46, 69; Brant Rosen, "More Heat than Light: My Response to Rev. Chris Leighton," Shalom Rav, February 26, 2014, accessed March 1, 2014, http://rabbibrant.com/.

76. Rosen interview.

77. "Judith Butler's Remarks to Brooklyn College on BDS"; Butler, *Parting Ways*, 4, 7.

78. Aloni, *What Does a Jew Want?*, 15.

79. Boyarin, *Radical Jew*, chapter 10; Rosen interview; Roth, *Operation Shylock*, 158.

80. Jessica Rosenberg, "What If We Really Wept: Days of Fasting, Days of Action," Palestinian Talmud, July 12, 2013, accessed March 1, 2014, http://palestiniantalmud.com/2013/07/12/what-if-we-really-wept-days-of-fasting-days-of-action/; Rosen interview; Vilkomerson interview. The ADL views JVP as a cynical organization. On the Tisha B'Av stunt, it wrote, "This exploitation of Jewish tradition to promote an anti-Israel agenda is classic JVP." "Jewish Group to Hold Anti-Israel Protests on Tisha B'Av," ADL, July 16, 2013, accessed April 9, 2014, http://blog.adl.org/international/jewish-group-to-hold-anti-israel-protests-on-tisha-bav.

81. Gershom Scholem, "Redemption through Sin," in *Messianic Idea in Judaism and Other Essays on Jewish Spirituality*, 83.

Literary Theory and the Delegitimization of Israel

JEAN AXELRAD CAHAN

IN 2009 AN ISRAELI HISTORIAN, Shlomo Sand, published *The Invention of the Jewish People*. It was perhaps the most striking title in a slew of books with similar titles published since the 1990s.[1] It is tempting to dismiss Sand's work on grounds of poor scholarship, but the book's international success warrants a more considered response. In France and in the United States the book sold well (according to Amazon.com rankings); in 2009, in France, it was awarded the Prix Aujourd'hui, a prestigious prize whose list of laureates includes Raymond Aron, Marek Halter, Alain Minc, Jean-Francois Revel, and many other distinguished writers on history and politics.[2] According to Michael Berkowitz, Sand's book "elicited a thunderous response that has yet to abate."[3] Simon Schama has predicted that "very soon, expect to hear on campuses, in news programs on the radio and occasionally in TV programs that the Jewish people are a myth. This stuff used to be said by the neo-Nazi loonies who inhabit this world, but now we have a Jewish son of Holocaust survivors, professor from an Israeli university, ideologue whose ideology so blinds him to the basic identity of the Jewish people that he has put this lie into the mainstream."[4] In an authoritative review of Sand's book, Anita Shapira explicitly set aside questions about conceptual underpinnings and instead demonstrated the weakness of the empirical evidence for Sand's theses.[5] But those concerned about the delegitimization of Israel ought to try to understand more fully the conceptual underpinnings of the work of Sand and other like-minded scholars. They involve a double conceptual assault on the bases of Jewish identity: negation of the Jewish religion and negation of Jewish nationhood. Both negations rely on ill-defined notions of myth and seek to undermine distinctions between reality and fiction on the ground that such distinctions are usually politically motivated. In this chapter I focus on the denial of the fact/fiction distinction in the development of Jewish nationhood.

—※— —※— —※—

A substantial literature has come into being on "nations and nationalism" in the modern era (post-eighteenth century). Two of the most prominent theorists in this field were (and remain) the historian Eric Hobsbawm (1917–2012) and the social anthropologist Ernst Gellner (1925–1995). They took the lead in arguing that modern nations rest on mythical foundations; that all tradition is "invented"; and that modern nation-states are only interested in a "usable past," that is, one that serves political purposes. Two main inferences about Jewish nationhood have been drawn from these claims: Jewish historical narratives as they have been transmitted for generations have been deeply distorted by the aim of achieving social cohesion, and it is extremely doubtful whether a Jewish people can be said ever to have existed at all before the artificial construction of modern Israel through the Zionist movement (this is Sand's argument).

Questioning of the historical bases of the Jewish nation received a major impetus from Spinoza's critique of religion and religious texts. Spinoza underscored the fabricated quality of much biblical history, the dispensability of historical narratives for religion, and the exclusionary character of the Jewish nation.

To some extent, his ideas were a beneficial influence in the development of critical modes of studying history. But what we see increasingly often now is not the view that *some* historical claims are exaggerated or false; rather, we see an attitude that there is *no* distinction to be made between real history, or facts, and fiction. This is a problem not only for the Jewish people and for Israel; it affects the writing of U.S. history and that of many other national collectivities. There is a critical difference, however: while the existence of Greece, for example, does not depend on the historical accuracy of the Homeric epic poems, and obliteration of the distinction between reality and fiction in an Oliver Stone movie does not trouble the United States unduly, for Israel there are immediate practical consequences. There are daily problems in establishing and transmitting facts about contemporary as well as historical events in the Israeli-Palestinian conflict: operations like Cast Lead, an armed conflict in the Gaza Strip between Israeli troops and Palestinian combatants, which took place in December 2008 and January 2009; the apparent death of a young boy, Muhammad Al-Dura, during the Second Intifada in September 2000 (television footage of the crossfire in which al-Dura was killed became the object of much controversy; the disputed footage ultimately resulted in several trials in France); attempted weapons shipments by Hamas and Hezbollah; Israel's role or lack thereof in the death of Yassir Arafat and other historical events. These events and reports about these historical events have been drenched in doubt as to the veracity of facts and images, and in retaliatory violence. But there is a longer-term consequence, too, for even well-educated citizens of Western nations can be led to doubt the historical case for Israel's legitimacy. The halls of academe are traveled by large numbers of *bien-pensants* who have virtually no knowledge of Jewish and Israeli history and are quite uninterested in the historical facts and justifications for many of Israel's positions and policies. They don't see the relevance of adequate historical knowledge or even acknowledge that it is possible; instead, they prefer to indulge in a very presentist moral indignation.

Another consequence of discounting or discarding the real, historical dimension of Jewish religion and nationhood is the (sometimes unstated) preference for the international or cosmopolitan, secular-liberal, Jew. To those who favor such a type, a Jew more attached to what he understands as his history-based, traditional religion and land is regarded as too "tribal," too particularistic, and willing to sacrifice such larger, more universal goals as world peace for allegedly parochial concerns. This attitude pervades the work not only of the authors discussed in this chapter, but the large scholarly literature on religious fundamentalism, the history of religions, and the history of European philosophy.[6]

A small group of mutually reinforcing authors—Benedict Anderson, Edward Said, and Hayden White—has sought to vitiate distinctions between fiction and reality. Their work has, either intentionally or unintentionally, influenced authors like Shlomo Sand. Their writings have been much discussed elsewhere since the 1980s, but the extent to which their conceptual work has helped undermine the historical "case for Israel" has not been fully appreciated to date. Also noteworthy is how the "standard model" of internationalist, socialist critique of nationalism has been modified: the new cosmopolitanism often incorporates an inverted relation between the socioeconomic base and the cultural-political superstructure.[7] Under the old Marxist scheme, the economic base generated religious and political fictions and was reflected in cultural products of the superstructure; under many contemporary schemas, a set of fictions and myths organizes the nation-state and its material energies and powers. In effect, the ideological superstructure now secures the material base. But the nature of the fictions produced has also changed: whereas Feuerbach and Marx thought of religious, political, and cultural fictions along the lines of *cognitive* error, which could be replaced by scientific understanding of human society and economics, the critics I consider here tend to regard religion and national history (including but not limited to the Jewish instance) as a fiction that is more a *political and moral* error, a set of ill-intentioned, that is to say, imperialist, lies. As against this, science or a long-term, intersubjective process of rational communication would be ineffective; it must be met with the most intense moral and political resistance. After surveying the work of the authors mentioned above, I return, in a concluding section, to what I take to be the implications for Israel's legitimacy.

THE INFLUENCE OF ERICH AUERBACH

The work of contemporary critics of Israel and its historical claims reveal the influence of a handful of literary theorists: Erich Auerbach, Benedict Anderson, Hayden White, and Edward Said. It is no coincidence that they are often cited together, because Anderson, Said, and White explicitly model themselves on Auerbach. The precise nature of Auerbach's influence, however, is not often discussed and is perhaps not what it first appears to be.

Born and raised in a well-to-do, assimilated Jewish family in Berlin, Auerbach took refuge from the National Socialist regime in Istanbul. There, in the early 1940s, he composed, largely on the basis of memory, his great work, *Mimesis: The Representation of Reality in Western Literature.* The most commonly admired features of Auerbach's work are his vast erudition; his "fragmentary" method of focusing on selected phrases and words to carry the analysis of a whole epoch, movement, or style (it comports well with postmodern approaches); his effort to examine the role of popular, that is, nonelite or nonaristocratic characters; his historicism; and his notion of *figura.* Two other features are striking: the effort to link what Marxists might call social formations with literary, ideational superstructures; and the fascination with the religion of Christianity. For Auerbach, as for many other "non-Jewish" Jews of his era—Hannah Arendt, Hans Jonas,

Karl Löwith, Theodor Adorno—discussion of religion almost always meant discussion of Christianity, and rarely Judaism. Nonetheless, *Mimesis* opens with a famous chapter contrasting the Hebrew Bible very subtly and sympathetically with Homer's *Odyssey*. Usually read as a study of Jewish-Hebraic versus Greek literary styles and methods, the chapter also includes a distinction between what Auerbach calls innocent lying and political lying. "Pagans" are entitled to be liars in some sense, but the authors of the Bible are not. It would be of no significance, says Auerbach, if Homer turned out to be a liar, that is to say, if his narratives turned out to be historically inaccurate or false. But this is not the case for the author or authors of the Hebrew Bible, where "the religious purpose necessitates an absolute claim to historical truth." The nature of authority is such that without complete and absolutely objective truth, the Elohist would have been perceived as a cynical political liar or propagandist; Homer, by contrast, would merely have appeared as an innocent liar. According to Auerbach, "the Bible's claim to truth is tyrannical; it excludes all other claims."[8] Thus we see that Auerbach, unlike some of his imitators in the study of literary history, is not prepared to relinquish all distinction between myth and religion or between history and literary fiction.[9] For him, the Jewish religion depends on the historical correctness of the biblical narratives in a way that ancient Greek religion did not depend on the historicity of the Homeric epics. Since the publication of *Mimesis,* the historical accuracy of the Homeric writings has indeed come into question, but this does not seem to have affected the contemporary state religion of Greece or Greece's national unity.

BENEDICT ANDERSON'S *IMAGINED COMMUNITIES*

The old base-superstructure model, originally put forward by Marx and apparent in much looser form in Auerbach, is emulated by Benedict Anderson in his *Imagined Communities* (1984).

This widely admired book, written by an international-relations expert, seeks to overturn standard accounts of the development of modern nationalism. Unlike others with a similar ambition, Anderson does not see Europe as the main locus of this development, but Caribbean, South American, and South Asian societies. Along the way he puts forward various claims that demand our attention.

At one time, according to Anderson, there were "large sacral spaces" and empires permeated by "sacred silent languages" such as Sanskrit, Greek, Latin, and Hebrew. (This immediately raises a question: could the ancient Hebrew–speaking society plausibly be considered an empire?) Together with the universal languages there existed vast empires and social hierarchies that were assumed to be natural. Gradually the spatially vast empires, the universal languages, and the sociopolitical hierarchies broke down into smaller units—nations—speaking newer, more provincial, languages. The breakdown occurred mainly because of the emergence of "print capitalism," a combination of a new economic mode of production and new technologies for distributing information and ideas. Crucially, what could be printed and promulgated now were ideas about the past, an "image" of antiquity that, in Anderson's view, usually had little resemblance to any past reality. The image of antiquity transmitted a sense of past unity that was usually fictional. For example, the English could now write about William the Conqueror as the founder of their nation, even though he had not been English and did not even speak English. Print capitalism thus allowed various groups and classes to *imagine* nationhood: "Out of the American welter came these imagined realities: nation-states, republican institutions, common citizenships, popular sovereignty, national flags and anthems, etc." By the mid-nineteenth century, the "Euro-Mediterranean empires" were "sidling" toward national identification; the Romanovs discovered they were Russian, the Hohenzollerns that they were German. This type of national identification on the part of the governing elites was later transformed into "official nationalism," defined by Anderson as "an anticipatory strategy adopted by dominant groups which are threatened with marginalization or exclusion from an emerging nationally-imagined community." Thus old elites, who in the nineteenth century, if not earlier, began to feel threatened by developing popular nationalism, fell back on "official nationalism" in order to maintain their grip on power. Official nationalism involves compulsory, state-controlled primary education, state-organized propaganda, official rewriting of history, and militarism. Anderson concludes that "the imagined community has . . . spread out to every conceivable contemporary society," including those claiming to be socialist or communist. Indeed, nationalism is especially likely to appear after a communist revolution, because it "emanat[es] from the state and serv[es] the interest of the state."[10]

For Anderson, as I have described his views so far, a fundamental distinction between fiction and reality seems to persist; his point about images of antiquity (e.g., William the Conqueror) being used for modern official nationalism depends on it. But it is by no means clear that Anderson holds to the distinction firmly. He begins by differentiating himself from Ernest Gellner, saying that he prefers the phrase "'imagined' community" to Gellner's "'invented' nations." He points out that Gellner "assimilates 'invention' to 'fabrication' and 'falsity,' rather than to 'imagining' and 'creation.'" Anderson insists that "communities are to be distinguished, not by their falsity/genuineness, but by the style in which they are imagined." But later in the book Anderson does slide into language that suggests that falsity and fabrication are at the heart of nation building. He wonders, "[why do people feel] *attachments* for the *inventions* of their imaginations?" (emphasis added) and quotes approvingly a statement that most nationalisms and empires were "the product of deliberate invention, resulting from a theory." Anderson's discussion of the French Revolutionary historian Michelet is also permeated by the suggestion that the French nation was a product not merely of Michelet's imagination, but of an effort to *fabricate* relations with the dead. He rejects Michelet's stated aim of providing for posterity an interpretation of the acts and words of those who had died in the revolution without realizing "the significance of the events." For Anderson, this effort, like historical accounts of the St. Bartholomew's Day Massacre of 1572, is ultimately only a "systematic historiographical campaign deployed by the state and the school system to remind of antique slaughters now part of 'family history.'" It would be preferable, in Anderson's view, to write like Fernand Braudel, who composed a voluminous history of the epoch of Philip II without once mentioning "la Saint-Barthélemy," even though the massacre took place in the middle of that epoch. It would be preferable because "the deaths that matter are those myriad anonymous events . . . which permit him [Braudel] to chart the slow-changing conditions of life for millions of anonymous human beings of whom the last question asked is their nationality."[11]

In this way, Anderson denies any place for individual, family, or even local memory and interpretive history. Obviously not only is this approach completely contrary to Jewish tradition and habit, it does not fit any nation, group, or individual who cannot or does not want to fall into forgetfulness or remain completely uncomprehending of certain events.

Moreover, Anderson utilizes the concept of imagination to explain, mainly to himself, how it is that individual human beings can form communities at all. Any community has to be imagined, he maintains, because "the members of even the smallest nation will never know most of their fellow-members, meet them, or even hear of them, yet in the minds [sic] of each lives the image of their communion."[12] This is the conceptual crux of the matter. But it is no more than the old philosophical problem of knowledge of the external world: How can I know that a world exists at all outside my mind? Perhaps, like Descartes observing a ball of wax apparently before him, I am deceived about this? How do I transcend the limits of my own mind to have knowledge of another mind outside it? This philosophical problem, as far as I know, has not been solved. Therefore, anyone may be mistaken not only in regard to the existence of an entire community, however small—he or she may also be sadly misinformed about the existence of apparently close family members and "the image of communion" shared with them. Seen in the light of the old philosophical problem, the question of how nations can be held to exist is no different from how anything else can be held to exist. The positing, creative power of imagination might be one solution, but it is not one that most philosophers would accept, since imagination is an unreliable faculty and is not usually regarded as a source of certain knowledge.

Moreover, by privileging the role of imagination, as opposed to other factors in the emergence of nations, we risk ending up exactly where a fair amount of the historiography of ancient Israel has ended up: doubting its historical existence, geographic location, and distinctive religion and culture. Although Anderson, unlike other authors whom we consider here and who have been influenced by him, is not interested in Israel or the Middle East, he does venture the opinion that "Zionism marks the reimagining of an ancient religious community as a nation."[13] In other words, Israel was, historically speaking, never a nation but only a religious community; therefore, its life and claims should be treated as products of *contemporary* imaginings.

EDWARD SAID ON NATIONALISM
AND JEWISH INTELLECTUALS

Said, like Anderson, revered Auerbach and emulated him in writing about broad correlations between social and political realities, on the one hand, and literary culture on the other. In the course of this work, Said also relied on the works of Anderson,

Hobsbawm, and Gellner. Like them, he came to insist on the imaginary, invented aspects of national histories. It has also been accurately suggested that Said adapted Auerbach's concept of *figura* to fit his own case.[14] Specifically, he took the classic Jewish notions of exodus and exile, among others, and applied them to the Palestinians and their experiences. But more important for my theme is his challenge to the facticity of histories that didn't suit his advocacy of the Palestinian cause.

Though brought up as a Protestant, Said at some point became explicitly secular: "We should begin with acknowledgement of a world map without divinely or dogmatically sanctioned spaces, essences, or privileges. It is necessary, therefore, to speak of our element as secular space and humanly constructed and interdependent histories that are fundamentally knowable, but not through grand theory or systematic totalisation.... [Human experience is] ... accessible enough *not* to need the assistance of extra-historical or extra-worldly agencies to illuminate or explain it" (original emphasis).[15] It is not clear about whom Said is speaking here, but in any case this is exactly what Jews traditionally have maintained: history is not explicable or interpretable without a certain concept of God; indeed, knowledge of God itself depends on certain historical narratives; and the Jewish religion is intimately related to a certain geographical area. As the distinguished scholar Gerhard von Rad put it: the Bible is a report of an ongoing effort on the part of the Jewish people to interpret their own history to themselves.[16] Said, however, insists that since human beings construct their own history, mainly for political ends, they are fully capable of explaining it out of their worldly resources, so to speak. Western-educated historians produce "fabricated identities" that can and should be challenged or dissolved through an historical method that has "contestatory force."[17]

Consequently, Said is irked by Jews' attachment to the Land of Israel and what he calls their talent for specificity. This talent may be contrasted with the broad capacity of the imperial West to create "imaginative geographies," to divide the world mentally as well as materially on the basis of certain linguistic and textual representations of "the other." These representations are both largely imaginary and directed by powerful material and political interests. The Jews and Zionism, while utilizing Western-style imagination, also display an "almost unbearable concreteness."[18] Zionism succeeded because it was "*a policy of detail,* not simply a general colonial vision" (original emphasis). "It was a specific territory with specific characteristics, that was surveyed down to the last millimeter, settled on, planned for, built on, and so forth, *in detail*" (original emphasis). Thus, Said sees Zionism as a product of imagination and fiction, as are all imperialisms, and at the same time as possessing a sinister level of concreteness and materialism. But further, "a main ideological necessity for such a program was acquiring legitimacy for it, giving it an archaeology and a teleology that ... completely outdated the native culture ... to enclose the territory with the oldest and furthest reaching of possible 'realities.'" In other words, the historical narratives of the Jews, based on their central sacred text as well as archaeology and other intellectual "devices," are merely a means of legitimating the Jews' return to Palestine and Zionism's territorial expansionism. Archaeological findings that might support or illuminate the historical and continuous Jewish presence in Palestine are to be regarded as politically expedient rather than factually correct. Said concludes that the Palestinian Arabs were unable to resist modern Jewish nationalism effectively because they "always opposed a general policy on general principles. . . . Even to this day the Palestinian political position . . . does not sufficiently try to meet the detail of the Zionist enterprise."[19] Auerbach, too, had noted the concreteness of the Hebrew language and Bible compared to other texts. But when it comes to love of specific places, it is unlikely that Christians are any less attached to Bethlehem or Muslims to Mecca. Said wrongly singles out the Jews in this matter of geographical and historical specificity.

According to Said, then, Zionism's success has been to sub-stitute its own constructed reality, its history and Westernized culture, for the Palestinian Arab narrative and reality: "Israel is the norm, Israeli ideas and institutions are the authentically native ones ... Palestinians are a quasi-mythical reality ... a pro-paganda reality."[20] Ultimately, one perceives that Said's oeuvre is permeated by doubt as to whether there can be a true repre-sentation of anything. Do all the imaginings and constructions of culture-producers amount to anything true? To be fair, Said acknowledges that his own reconstructions of Palestinian Arab history are of dubious verisimilitude: "I realized that the world I grew up in, the world of my parents, of Cairo and Beirut and pre-1948 Talbieh, was a made-up world. It wasn't a real world. It didn't have the kind of objective solidity that I wanted it to have."[21] But mostly this type of doubt is directed at Western scholars and writers and at Zionists who have co-opted their concepts and methods. The problem with Orientalism is not that it presents a *false* picture, and the true one could be known in principle. "[Rather] 'the Orient' is itself a constituted entity." Western con-ceptions of the Orient, including Palestine of course, amount simply to a system of ideological fictions and myths. Zionists have colluded in the promulgation of this useful fiction: "The common denominator between Weizmann and the European anti-Semite is Orientalism."[22]

As against the imperialism of the Zionists, and imperialism in general, Said would like to see a politics and an epistemol-ogy of nomadism. Certain great Europeans have been capable of the kind of internationalism or universalism that Said has in mind: his beloved Auerbach, Goethe, Adorno, Camus, Austen, and others. These were all writers who resisted or transcended nationalist tendencies; they participated in world literature in order to construct a different cultural reality within it, though on some level they may have remained entrenched in "European bourgeois humanism."[23] They knew that "the dense fabric of secular life is what can't be herded under the rubric of national identity or can't be made entirely to respond to this phony idea of a paranoid frontier separating 'us' from 'them'—which is a repetition of the old sort of orientalist model."[24] They also knew that all culture is hybrid, and increasingly so: "Exile, far from being the fate of nearly forgotten unfortunates who are dispossessed and expatriated, becomes a thing closer to the norm, an experience of crossing boundaries and charting new territories in defiance of the classic canonic enclosures, however much its loss and sadness should be acknowledged and registered. . . . To paraphrase a remark made by Erich Auerbach in one of his last essays, our philological home is the world, and not the nation or even the individual writer."[25] This outlook enables Said to assert the following:

1. That the Jewish return to Palestine is an ongoing injustice because the land was already inhabited by Arabs (he ignores the fact that Jews also lived there) and they could have been "accommodated" elsewhere.
2. "I don't find the idea of a Jewish state terribly interesting. The Jews I know—the more interesting Jews I know—are not defined by their Jewishness. I think that to confine Jews to their Jewishness is problematic. . . . Once the initial enthusiasm for statehood and aliyah subsides, people will find that to be Jews is not a lifelong project. It's not enough."[26]
3. "I'm the last Jewish intellectual. . . . All your other Jewish intellectuals are now suburban squires. From Amos Oz to all these people here in America. So I'm the last one. The only true follower of Adorno. Let me put it this way: I'm a Jewish-Palestinian."[27]

The ligature between the second and third of these extraordinary statements is the notion that the best, and indeed only respectable, kind of Jew is the non-Jewish Jew, the nonreligious, non-Zionist, cosmopolitan, left-wing intellectual.

A thoroughgoing critique of Said has been carried out by several distinguished scholars.[28] Pertinent to my discussion of the effects of eliminating the reality/fiction distinction, I would simply argue that Said is wrong about Talbieh. The pre-1948 neighborhood that he "constructed" in his mind or imagination was not *entirely* nonexistent, not *pure* fiction. It can be shown, through empirical evidence, to have existed in an objective, physical sense, but also probably in more emotional and "figurative" ways that were quite similar to how Said recalled it. There are or were likely other individuals who recalled it as he did, and intersubjective comparisons could be made. Similarly, Jews' recollections of prewar Vienna or Kraków, or of Shiloh and Hebron, are not pure fiction, either. The point here is that memory—individual, or collective at some level—while fallible and requiring correction, is not *necessarily only* a source of false and self-serving beliefs. Actually existing places and events may be described through oral and written histories containing significant admixtures of exaggeration, error, and illusion, but these histories may also contain veridical reports of material facts and authentic expressions of the "feel" of a place and time. The "end-product" of historical narration is not *necessarily* fiction or fantasy, and it does not preclude historians from remaining awake to new evidence and interpretations.

HAYDEN WHITE AND AUERBACH'S *FIGURA*

Similar issues are raised by the literary theorist Hayden White, who also takes Erich Auerbach's work as a starting point. In *Figural Realism: Studies in the Mimesis Effect* (1999) as well as in *The Content of the Form* (1987), White lays out a theory of both literary modernism and the nature of narrative history. His main thesis is that literary narrative and historical narrative are extremely similar, in that they both employ literal as well as tropological linguistic elements. Ultimately, both are engaged in a type of writing that White calls "figural realism." In making this argument, he seeks to explicate and theoretically extend Auerbach's concept of *figura*. White explains that what are ordinarily understood as objectively existing historical facts and events are "really" entities so deeply imbued with figurative language and theoretical assumptions that it cannot be claimed that they exist in any mind-and-language-independent sense. Distinctions between objective facts and valuational meanings must break down. Some examples of White's claims follow.

> In realistic, no less than in imaginary, discourse, language is both a form and a content. . . . This liberates historiographical criticism from fidelity to an impossible literalism and [shows] the extent to which [historical discourse] constructs its subject matter in the very process of speaking about it.

> Literary discourse may differ from historical discourse by virtue of its primary referents, conceived as imaginary rather than real events, but the two kinds of discourse are more similar than different since both operate language in such a way that any clear distinction between their discursive form and their interpretive content remains impossible.

> Stories are told or written, not found. And as for the notion of a true story, this is virtually a contradiction in terms. All stories are fictions.[29]

White sees Auerbach as the originator of figural realism. In *Mimesis* and the famous later essay "Figura," Auerbach showed how medieval Western Christian thought—the hegemonic culture—regarded Jewish history, personages, and texts as prefigurations of later historical developments of great significance to the West. Events were both complete in themselves and indicators of a meaning that would only be revealed later.[30] Literary modernism, a relatively recent exemplar of figural realism as White understands it, was a "reaction to earlier realisms." Literary modernism dismissed "the rigid opposition between history and fiction": "Modernism . . . [set aside] . . . the longstanding distinction between history and fiction . . . in order to image a historical reality purged of the myths of such 'grand narratives' of fate, providence, *Geist*, progress, the dialectic and even the myth of the final realization of realism itself."[31] However, White seems uncertain as to what we should conclude from Auerbach's work concerning the relation between socioeconomic change on the one hand and cultural change on the other. He concludes that literary change is both a passive reflection of and a more active response to changes in the social order, and he goes on to claim that cultural modernism "permitted" totalitarianism. This process may also be seen in certain aspects of Zionism: "The totalitarian, not to say fascist, aspects of Israeli treatment of the Palestinians on the West Bank may be attributable primarily to a Zionist ideology that is detestable to anti-Zionists, Jews and non-Jews alike."[32] Nonetheless, Zionism is "fully comprehensible" to White as a "morally responsible response to the meaninglessness of a certain history," just as the Palestinian aim to "mount a politically effective response to Israeli policies" is also an attempt to endow their history with meaning. This interplay of responses, White continues, raises the question of whether it is possible to construct a narrative—literary or historical—that is free of political aspirations and motivations: "[this] brings us back to the question of the political or ideological implications of narrativity itself as a modality of historical representation." He concludes that there is no escape from the value-ladenness of historical narrative, where "value-laden" means "politically motivated," and any aspiration to objectivity and realism in an ideologically neutral or impartial sense is a mere facade for the "disciplinization of historical studies," that is, orientation toward a certain point on the political spectrum.[33]

This vitiation of any distinction between fiction and reality goes further than Auerbach himself was willing to go. He states repeatedly that this is not his intention: "The figures of Isaac, Jacob etc. were removed from their earthly and political contexts and made into *figura futurorum* by patristic exegetes." And speaking about characters in the *Divine Comedy:* "We must always be careful not to deny their earthly historical existence altogether, not to confine ourselves to an abstract, allegorical interpretation." Auerbach insists that "quite apart from the misunderstanding of poetic reality that such a judgment [that fiction and reality are one and the same] shows, it is surprising to find so deep a chasm between reality and meaning. Is the *terrena* Jerusalem without historical reality because it is a *figura aeternae Jerusalem*?" Auerbach, regarded by his acolytes Anderson, Said, and White as the archetype of the cosmopolitan, displaced (where displacement is an intellectual gain though a geographic loss) Jew, is here firmly insisting on the reality of the particulars of Jewish history, the particular persons and places that are central to Jewish history, religion, and self-understanding. For Auerbach, figural writing arose out of religious developments in the West, whereas mythical and symbolic writing was more common in ancient, pagan, and secular societies.[34]

INVENTION OF THE JEWISH PEOPLE?

It is tempting to set aside Anderson, Said, and White and their notions of fiction as an Americanized version of impenetrable debates in French intellectual history on the nature of the literary imaginary and relations between literature and politics. But while the epistemological claims of the Americans have not led to the kind of "theoretical terrorism" of the French, the effect of their writings on academic scholarship about Israel and the perceived legitimacy of the State of Israel ought not to be underestimated.[35]

Academic work that utilizes some of the ideas of the authors discussed above, as well as that of Hobsbawm and Gellner, ranges from ancient to contemporary history and politics. Thus we find the well-known historian Shaye J. D. Cohen writing that "Jewishness . . . is imagined; it has no empirical, objective, verifiable reality to which we can point . . . Jewishness is in the mind. In the felicitous phrase of Benedict Anderson, we are speaking of an 'imagined community.'"[36] This general attitude reaches a sort of culmination in Shlomo Sand's book.[37]

Sand attempts a large-scale survey of the development of modern nationalism, in this case Jewish nationalism or Zionism. He notes his debt to Anderson, saying that "the moment I began to apply the methods of Ernest Gellner, Benedict Anderson and others . . . the materials I encountered in my research were illuminated." Like Anderson, he proposes an explanation of nationalism in which socioeconomic forces are mirrored in cultural superstructures. Historians, archaeologists, and anthropologists uncover material bases, and their work is then "cosmetically improved by essayists, journalists and novelists."[38]

From Sand's point of view, the work of most other Israeli historians has been deeply ideological and wrong. Their aim has been to "promote a homogeneous collective" in order to justify the disenfranchisement of non-Jewish Israelis; "to provide . . . a long narrative" connecting modern Jewish Israelis to their purported ancestors of thousands of years ago. But "such a close connection . . . has never actually existed in any society," and therefore the "agents of memory worked hard to invent it." Contrary to popular belief, the Jews have never been a nation; at most, Jews in different parts of the world have shared a "belief-culture." This is not the place to examine the confusion of terms and ideas utilized by Sand to press his case: the reduction of nationhood to blood ties and the rejection of ethnicity as a basis of nationality; the removal of religion as one of the components of ethnicity; the conflation of an undefined term 'myth' with all aspects of religion; one-sided reading of Ernst Renan, and others; what counts as mainstream social anthropology. My concern here is Sand's pervasive assertion that the concept of Jewish nationhood is nothing but a "huge universe of culturally constructed truth," a set of "national fantasies."[39]

According to Sand, the "imagined origin" of the Jewish nation
represented in the Hebrew Bible was and remains merely an instrument in conflicts with hostile neighbors. Ethnicity is "entirely
fictitious" and is not any kind of "natural" community; nations
are the result of conscious social and cultural "projects," such
that "a nationalist theology of the intellectuals" usually becomes
"a nationalist mythology for the masses." It was Anderson's and
Gellner's merit, according to Sand, to have articulated this claim
in an especially perceptive way. In the case of the Jewish nation,
this means that the work of the great historians, especially in the
nineteenth century (Graetz and Dubnow) and early twentieth
century (Baer and Baron), amounted only to "historiographical
explorations" of "the fascinating invention of 'the Jewish nation.'"
The study of history actually became a substitute for traditional
religion: for those Jews who could not accept either Jewish religious "mythologies" or the growing Western European nationalisms with their Christian past, "the only option was to invent and
adhere to a parallel national mythology—a conception of a putative kingdom in its own homeland." In that way, the Jews would
then cease to be "merely a religious community that lived in the
shadow of other, hegemonic religions." The kingdom of David;
the lives of the patriarchs and other personalities of the tanakh;
the exodus from Egypt; the exile in Babylonia; the exile after
the destruction of the Second Temple—they are all almost completely imaginary, fictitious, and serve only to legitimate the "rise
of the modern Jewish nation" and its discrimination against non-
Jewish inhabitants of the territory of present-day Israel and the
West Bank. The Zionists "needed to erase existing ethnographic
textures, forget specific [geographically differentiated] histories,
and take a flying leap backward to an ancient, mythological and
religious past." The contemporary state of Israel "does not serve
a civil-egalitarian demos but a biological-religious ethnos that is
wholly fictitious historically but dynamic, exclusive and discriminatory in its political manifestation."[40]

CONCLUDING ANALYSIS

That Sand's reading of other scholars is tendentious is not difficult to discern. But his work presents a deeper, conceptual problem. This is his uncritical use of the epistemological notion of "construction." Every narrative concerning the past, every purported collective memory, is regarded as a fiction derived purely from the self-serving motives of one or another group of Jews (the motives of Palestinian Arabs are not discussed). For Sand, both historical and religious narratives are reducible to political myths of a virtually Sorelian type; that is, they are deliberately constructed in order to be instruments of social cohesion to the point of fascism.

At best, this is an unnuanced application of the idea that reality is socially constructed. This idea, which has a complicated history itself, posits that races, genders, mental illnesses, and even subatomic particles in physics, have never existed outside the minds and intentions of certain social groups.[41] Sand and our other writers on nationalism place nations on the long list of nonnatural, socially constructed facts and entities. For Sand, the modern concept of a nation emerged no earlier than the eighteenth century and has been retro-jected onto the ancient world by "higher political and intellectual powers." Like "race" and "gender," the concept "nation" is thought to "pick out" certain social groups in order to legitimize certain power relations and contemporary policies of discrimination. But "pick out" from what? The background, one might suppose, is an otherwise undifferentiated humanity. But it seems that for Sand the background consists of a set of "fragmentary though persistent subidentities," including tribes, tiny kingdoms, religious communities, or "low strata that did not belong to the political and cultural elites."[42]

A first point to notice is that while Sand clearly objects to the socially constructed—and to his mind fictional—concept of a nation, he apparently does not object to the arguably equally socially constructed—and by his logic equally fictional—concept of class, or low and high social strata. But is there any reason to suppose that classes are somehow more "natural" than nations?

Second, Sand and Said have relied on a form of argument that confuses the origin of a concept or argument with its truth or validity. Sand and Said not only would not recognize this confusion as an error, but they insist on using it as a key methodological principle. For them, the fact that historical narratives may be *motivated* by certain social and political interests *entails* that they are completely false. For Anglo-American analytic philosophers, by contrast, this would not *necessarily* be the case. For the latter, evidentiary factors would have to be brought into the judgment as to whether or not a belief is justified, and not all methods of gathering evidence are equal.

Sand uses the "evidence" that the Jewish exile after the destruction of the Second Temple did not occur exactly as described in Jewish religious texts to claim that there was *no* exile; for him, the story of the exile was a fiction motivated by and grounded purely in political purposes. Following that reasoning, we would have to conclude that there was no Palestinian refugee problem, either, because that also did not happen exactly as initially described by Arab sources. Events that did not take place in exactly the manner in which their first historians reported cannot simply be erased from history by calling them literary or political fictions. But to say that some mistaken or even imagined elements may have entered a historical narrative is an order of magnitude different from saying that all national history is entirely fictional, and in particular that the historical bases of Jewish claims to Israel's territory are strictly imaginary. That is why I ventured to say that Said is wrong about Talbieh. While it turned out not to be exactly as he remembered it, his memory being heavily colored by emotion and imagination, nonetheless it does exist in a physical sense and may even exist in the minds of others in the way that he recalled it. This is verifiable to some degree, through interpersonal comparison and communication. Should or can we banish the Talbieh of Said's memory to the realm of pure fiction, as he himself did? Again, I think not. By the same token, neither should Jewish memories of Hebron and Shiloh be dismissed.

There is one final question to consider: is the legitimation crisis facing Israel different from that of Pakistan, the Federal Republic of Germany, or any other recently "constructed" country, when we consider the effects of the attitudes to historical narrative described above?

In one way, the case of Israel is different. The state of Pakistan, for example, does not depend on historical arguments to the same degree that the state of Israel does. Much of the Muslim population of Pakistan was largely transferred there around 1947 for practical reasons; it does not have a record of habitation there going back thousands of years, though the area itself may have been inhabited (by others) as long or longer than the area known as Canaan. The decisions to "view with favor" the establishment of a Jewish homeland and subsequently the state of Israel were supported by Britain and the "international community" in large part because of the historical claims of the Jews; to dismiss those claims today is to greatly weaken the case for Israel's legitimacy. If history and fiction/fabrication/falsehood are indistinguishable, Israel's historical legitimacy vanishes. But that is what some of the scholars I have cited intend.

However, in another way the case of Israel is not different from that of any other nation, whether it has been in existence for millennia or merely since the nineteenth century. All nations and nation-states incorporate collective memory and history into their respective identity. In contrast to those who think that "invented traditions" are only "functional for" a dangerous level of social integration, I don't think there is a *necessary* connection between collective memory and expansionist, aggressive nationalism.

Sand, Said, and others reject Zionism as a remnant of nineteenth-century nationalism, which was later transformed into European imperialism and fascism. In their minds, to cling to

nationhood is to run great political risks and to remain attached
to groups and ideas that are morally arbitrary. By contrast, to
pursue a cosmopolitan, egalitarian political reality that does not
interrupt itself at territorial borders—and especially not at the
Green Line—is a deliberate, constructive human action and is
morally principled.[43] Nonetheless the rigid connection, implied
by these authors, between a sense of national unity and imperialist aims, can be resisted. There are alternative conceptions of
national identity that are both intellectually open and compatible
with what I would maintain is a still-practicable political liberalism. To remain a liberal and democratic state, Israel does not
have to repudiate its historical narratives (or its religion). Like all
historical narratives, these are open to correction and revision.
But believers in the Jewish nation can transmit and utilize history
in a critical, open, intersubjective way. They do not have to, and
for the most part they do not, rely on fabrications and fictions.

Literary theories about the relationship of fiction and reality
might be viewed as esoteric, and the work of the authors discussed in this chapter is, at present, mainly of interest and import
for the academic world. But although there is often a long delay
between the composition of a theoretical work and the percepti-
bility of its wider influence in society and politics, such influence
can eventually be discerned. Thus it is not surprising to find the
following views expressed by a well-educated Palestinian in response to the Israeli journalist and writer Ari Shavit:

> There is no balance between my right and your right. At the outset,
> the Jews had no legal, *historical* or religious right to the land. The
> only right they had was the right born of persecution, but that right
> cannot justify taking 78 percent of land that is not theirs. It cannot
> justify the fact that the guests went on to become the masters. At
> the end of the day, the ones with the superior right to the land are
> the natives, not the immigrants. [emphasis added]
>
> And look at the road signs [between Gedera and Hadera]. Most
> of them are in Hebrew and English, not Arabic. Because what you

want is for tourists to travel around the country and believe that there really is a Jewish state here. . . . That's why you find us [Arabs] so difficult. To keep your nice little fiction of a European-Jewish state, you try to hide our existence.[44]

The view of the Israeli-Jewish state as a fictional state may not be the verifiably direct result of a reading of any of the authors discussed (though it is likely that Said had some influence), but it is at least plausible that the basic tendency of the work I have been describing has contributed to a wider view, in more educated and self-conscious sectors of Arab societies, that Israel is in some sense provisional. Whether this should be counted as a form of antisemitism is debatable. But I would say that the problem is deeper than that: it is a view of Israel and the Jews as unreal. Here, we are in the realm of metaphysics and epistemology, and of truth, which goes beyond a clash of cultures and nations. Such a view may result, however, as it has in the past, in attempts at an extremely material and brutal form of denial and suppression of Israel and the Jews.

NOTES

1. Other works with a "family resemblance" to Sand's book include Uri Ram, "Zionist Historiography and the Invention of Modern Jewish Nationhood: The Case of Ben-Zion Dinur," *History and Memory* 7, no. 1 (1995); Keith W. Whitelam, *The Invention of Ancient Israel: The Silencing of Palestinian History* (London: Routledge, 1996); Michael Prior, *The Bible and Colonialism: A Moral Critique* (Sheffield, U.K.: Sheffield Academic Press, 1997). Gabriel Piterberg, *The Returns of Zionism: Myths, Politics and Scholarship in Israel* (London: Verso, 2008) could also be mentioned. The family resemblance consists in emphasizing the role of imagination in the construction of historical fictions for political purposes, and the fraudulent nature of these national fictions. A somewhat different but related argument, also relying on Anderson's notion of an imagined community, is made by Leora Batnitzky in *How Judaism Became a Religion: An Introduction to Modern Jewish Thought* (Princeton, N.J.: Princeton University Press, 2011), in which the author maintains that "the modern concept of religion was created in tandem with the modern nation-state" (112).

2. Pierre Assouline, "Comment Shlomo Sand a reinvente le people juif," http://passouline.blog.lemonde.fr/2010/02/23/comment-le-peuple -juif-a-invente-shlomo-sand//.

3. Michael Berkowitz, review of *The Invention of the Jewish People,* http://www.history.ac.uk/reviews/review/973.

4. [Simon Schama], "Shlomo Sand Ridiculed by Historian Simon Schama," http://www.jewlicious.com/2009/11/shlomo-sand-ridiculed-by -historian-simon-schama/.

5. Anita Shapira, "Review Essay: The Jewish-People Deniers," *Journal of Israeli History* 28, no. 1 (March 2009): 63–72.

6. This is also a principal thesis of Jean-Francois Lyotard's *Heidegger and the Jews,* trans. Andreas Michel and Mark S. Roberts (Minneapolis: University of Minnesota Press, 1990). Lyotard uses a lowercase "J" deliberately to indicate the cosmopolitan type he has in mind.

7. Thus Eric Hobsbawm feels compelled to reiterate somewhat defensively that material forces are primary in the development of nationalism. See the concluding essay in Eric Hobsbawm and Terence Ranger, ed., *The Invention of Tradition* (1983; reprint Cambridge: Cambridge University Press, 2013).

8. Erich Auerbach, *Mimesis. Dargestellte Wirklichkeit in der Abendlandischen Literatur* (Bern: Francke, 1958), 19.

9. Auerbach is here independently addressing a problematic also raised by Yehezkhel Kaufmann in *The Religion of Israel: From Its Beginnings to the Babylonian Exile,* trans. and abridged by Moshe Greenberg (Chicago: University of Chicago Press, 1960); first published as *Toldot Haemunah Ha'israelit* (Tel Aviv: Bialik Institute-Dvir, 1937–1956). The question is whether and how religion may be differentiated from myth. Kaufman seems often to be regarded today as an apologist for Zionism rather than a distinguished Bible scholar.

10. Benedict Anderson, *Imagined Communities: Reflections on the Origin and Spread of Nationalism* (London: Verso, 1983), 81, 101, 159.

11. Ibid. 6, 6, 141, 155, 198, 205.

12. Ibid., 6.

13. Ibid., 149n16.

14. See also Aijaz Ahmad, *In Theory* (London: Verso, 1992), 163; Bill Ashcroft and Pal Ahluwalia, *Edward Said* (London: Routledge, 2001).

15. Edward Said, "Figures, Configurations, Transfigurations," *Race and Class* 32, no. 1 (1990): 11.

16. Gerhard von Rad, *God at Work in Israel,* trans. John H. Marks (Nashville, Tenn.: Abingdon, 1980).

17. Said, "Figures, Configurations, Transfigurations," 12.

18. Edward Said, *Culture and Imperialism,* cited in Ashcroft and Ahlu-walia, *Edward Said,* 92.

19. Edward Said, *The Question of Palestine* (1979; reprint New York: Vintage Books, 1992), 95, 95, 86, 95.

20. Ibid., 36.

21. Edward Said, "My Right of Return," Edward Said interviewed by Ari Shavit for *Haaretz.* Retrieved from http://www.MiddleEast.org, 8/26/2000, 9.

22. Edward Said, *Orientalism* (New York: Pantheon Books, 1978), 322, 306.

23. Edward Said, *Culture and Imperialism* (New York: Knopf, 1993), 316.

24. Said cited in Ashcroft and Ahluwalia, *Edward Said,* 104.

25. Said, *Culture and Imperialism,* 317.

26. Said, "My Right of Return," 6.

27. Ibid., 10.

28. Edward Alexander, "The Professor of Terror," *Commentary* (1989); Bernard Lewis, "The Question of Orientalism," *Islam and the West* (New York: Oxford University Press, 1993); Aijaz Ahmad, *In Theory: Classes, Nations, Literatures* (London: Verso, 1992).

29. Hayden White, *Figural Realism: Studies in the Mimesis Effect* (Baltimore, Md.: Johns Hopkins University Press, 1990), 4, 6, 9.

30. Ibid., 95.

31. Ibid., 100.

32. Hayden White, *The Content of the Form: Narrative Discourse and Historical Representation* (Baltimore, Md.: Johns Hopkins University Press, 1987), 80.

33. Ibid., 80, 80, 80, 81, 82.

34. Erich Auerbach, "Figura," in *Scenes from the Drama of European Literature: Six Essays* (Gloucester, Mass.: Peter Smith, 1973), 65, 73, 74, 63. In this connection I disagree somewhat with David Nirenberg, who has argued that "nowhere in these published works did Auerbach himself explicitly relate his questions about the Western 'representation of reality' to 'Jewish questions,' though we know from his letters that precisely such a relation weighed heavily on his mind." See David Nirenberg, *Anti-Judaism: The Western Tradition* (New York: W. W. Norton, 2013), 468.

35. Richard Wolin, *The Wind from the East: French Intellectuals, the Cultural Revolution, and the Legacy of the 1960s* (Princeton, N.J.: Princeton University Press, 2010), 246.

36. Shaye J. D. Cohen, *The Beginnings of Jewishness: Boundaries, Varieties, Uncertainties* (Berkeley: University of California Press, 1999), 5.

37. Benedict Anderson's influence has not been limited to academic writings. It can be seen, for example, in the efforts of Richard Falk, professor emeritus of international law and United Nations special rapporteur on human rights in the Palestinian territories. He is the author of innumerable official reports, as well as journalistic screeds, severely critical of Israel. He admiringly invokes Anderson's notion of an imagined community while revealing that, although of Jewish background, he has at various times been "inspired and enlightened by the practices and wisdom of Christian, Buddhist, Islamic, Hindu, Taoist, and indigenous peoples." The "Old Testament," outside of the prophetic writings, is nothing but an account of "the often bloody exploits of the ancient Israelites." Although he does not here seem to question the historicity of the text, it does not appear to be more than a political tool (see http://richardfalk.wordpress.com/tag/benedict-anderson).

38. Shlomo Sand, *The Invention of the Jewish People,* trans. Yael Lotan (London: Verso, 2009), xi, 15.

39. Ibid., 15, 14.

40. Ibid., 54, 71, 75, 255, 307.

41. The history of this philosophical stance no doubt includes Kant and Hegel, some existentialist influences, and Nietzsche: "What is called a 'nation' in Europe today, and is really rather a *res facta* than a *res nata* (and occasionally can hardly be told from a *res ficta et picta*) is in any case something evolving, young and easily changed." Friedrich Nietzsche, *Beyond Good and Evil,* in *Basic Writings of Nietzsche,* ed. Walter Kaufmann (New York: Modern Library, 2000), 378.

42. Sand, *Invention of the Jewish People,* 27.

43. For the distinction between morally principled as opposed to morally arbitrary attitudes toward nationhood I am indebted to the writings of Kwame Anthony Appiah, especially his "Cosmopolitan Patriots" in *For Love of Country: Debating the Limits of Patriotism,* Martha C. Nussbaum with respondents, ed. Joshua Cohen (Boston: Beacon Press, 1996).

44. Mohammed Dahla, quoted in Ari Shavit, *My Promised Land: The Triumph and Tragedy of Israel* (New York: Spiegel and Grau, 2013), 314–315, 314.

Good News from France

"There Is No New Antisemitism"

BRUNO CHAOUAT

A POSTCOLONIAL TURN?

ANY PROCLAMATION that antisemitism has faded away in France and elsewhere in the West is belied by episodes such as the Dieudonné affair and the pompously named Day of Wrath, a protest against the French president and the entire so-called system that gathered tens of thousands onto the streets of Paris.[1] A fringe group of demonstrators used the occasion to shout such slogans as "Jews, get out, France does not belong to you," a video of which quickly went viral on YouTube.[2] More tragic are the 2012 targeting and killing of a rabbi and three Jewish children in Toulouse. A repetition of the Toulouse murders occurred in May 2014 at the Jewish Museum in Brussels. We have seen episodes such as the "comedy" shows of Dieudonné M'bala M'bala, which drew a wide public until they were shut down by French authorities.

Yet the thesis that antisemitism has almost entirely vanished has been put forth by several French intellectuals, including the historian of the Holocaust and of German Jewry, Enzo Traverso, who, after a career in the French university system is now a professor in the United States. While in this chapter I focus on Traverso's rhetorical strategies as paradigmatic of new antisemitism minimization or denial, Traverso follows a certain trend represented by intellectuals and public figures, such as Eric Hazan, Alain Badiou, Guillaume Weill-Raynal, and Ivan Segré, who have written skeptically on the resurgence of antisemitism since about 2000.[3] I analyze the rhetorical strategies of this new denial of antisemitism by focusing on Traverso's 2013 *La Fin de la modernité juive. Histoire d'un tournant conservateur* (The end of Jewish modernity: History of a conservative turn).[4]

Traverso's thesis runs as follows: the revolutionary, universalistic, critical calling or mission that for two centuries had been the grandeur of European Jewry, was made obsolete by the birth of the state of Israel, which represented a historic break, a dialectical counterpart to the Holocaust. These two watershed events put an end to the persecution, the marginalization, the incongruity of the Jews—elements that had brought about the Jewish gift for critique. But now, according to Traverso, a page has turned: antisemitism has been eradicated. The Golden Age of Judaism, of Jewish genius, had taken place between 1750 and 1950—a period that Traverso calls "Jewish modernity" and whose end he sees in the founding of the state of Israel. Good, authentic Jewishness has yielded to a negative avatar. It is the time of the "Jewish Jew" or Zionist, who is, in Traverso's view, the reactionary Jew, the "Jew of order," the law-and-order Jew. Traverso's "Judaism of order" and "return to order" concepts are left vague and imply that Judaism, during its most authentic two centuries ending in 1950, embodied a principle of disorder, of subversion and anomy. This view amounts to an inversion of the antisemites' essentialization of the Jew, the simple placement of a plus sign before their negative essentialization—a gesture typical of philosemitic essentialism.

Traverso does not even save Hannah Arendt from such opprobrium, although she had the good sense to reject Zionism and criticize the Israeli establishment's exploitation of the Eichmann trial. For she appears in his eyes to have gone rotten as a result of her "Americanization."

Lest it may seem that this Jewish return to order means going back to the nationalism, say, of a Charles Maurras, we should think again. Traverso does not shy away from inconsistencies, since he sees the United States as a state without a national tradition, and reminds us that that is precisely what Arendt liked about the United States. Thus America represents the very opposite of a key element of Western civilization. Yet defending the West is the charge he levels against Jews who support the United States and Israel. The "Jewish world," Traverso further argues, has lost its universalistic, critical, and revolutionary compass. It has gone off course and veered to the right. Jews exploit the Jew hatred of the exploited, whose hatred is seen as understandable, if not excusable, given the socioeconomic exclusion and racial discrimination of which they are the victims. The Judeophobia of the exploited is thus transformed by Jewish hands into a weapon against Palestinians, a means of promoting the reactionary Americano-Zionist cause.

As already noted, according to Traverso, antisemitism is dead after the Shoah. (Here's a one-liner: "it's easy to get rid of antisemitism; just get rid of the Jews." But that lame witticism does not reflect reality, because a shortage of Jews in any given place does not seem to inoculate against Jew hatred.) Antisemitism has been replaced, as current dogma has it, by Islamophobia in France and in Europe generally. The Palestinians are the new Jews of the Middle East. Traverso's main point is that antisemitism and the struggle against it have fallen out of fashion and have been replaced respectively by racism and the "postcolonial" cause. Here is his conclusion: "The birth of postcolonialism coincided with the ending of the Jewish cycle of critical thought in Europe. This development took place at a few generations' remove from the Holocaust and decolonization, when the cumulative effects of these two breaking-points became manifest."[5] There is almost a new theology of supersession operating here—a secular theology, to be sure. The "Jewish cycle" has been replaced with a postcolonial one. The sole value of the Jewish cycle had resided in its revolutionary, universalistic, critical horizon, which once exhausted was to be supplanted by another revolutionary cycle, dubbed "postcolonialist" by Traverso. This new postcolonial cycle assumes the place of the Jewish one, just as in Christian doctrine the Jew according to the Spirit dethroned the Jew according to the flesh.

Traverso ends his book on a quip by the Egyptian American academic Edward Said, a bon mot he takes quite seriously. In an interview with the Israeli daily *Haaretz,* Said asserted he was the "last Jewish intellectual," immodestly concurring with Alain Badiou's *Portées du mot Juif,* whereby the premier implication of the word *Jew* is the universal calling designated thereby.[6] If a Jew is most of all a "non-Jewish Jew," and if, for Freud, Moses was an Egyptian, could not Said the Egyptian be a Jew?[7]

GOOD JEW, BAD JEW

In *La Fin de la modernité juive,* Traverso explains why Jews are hated, why they are attacked on the street, why Jewish children and their teacher were executed in a Toulouse schoolyard. For him, they were targeted not as Jews but as "conservatives," "colonizers," and "imperialists." This is an age-old, sleight-of-hand case of anti-Jewish logic. Jews are hated because of their hatred of others. In his important *Anti-Judaism: The Western Tradition,* historian David Nirenberg traces the origin of the myth of Jewish misanthropy back to nowhere other than ancient Egypt and to the importation of its lore to Greece by Hecataeus of Abdera circa 300 BCE.[8] There is nothing new under the Western sun.

Traverso's book merits close scrutiny as symptomatic of a new tendency conceptually to divide Jews, to "split the Jew." It is a formidable Machiavellian strategy of ideological intimidation aimed at dividing the Jew into a positive figure (anti-Zionist, diasporist, universalist) and a negative one (particularist, Zionist).

Traverso starts by positing two Jewish "archetypes" (a characterization that I dispute). Emblematic of the first is Trotsky, the Jewish revolutionary. The second is embodied by the American Kissinger, the powerful, "imperialistic" Jew. Regarding Trotsky, one may wonder whether he is good qua Jew or qua revolutionary, that is, a post-Jewish, non-Jewish Jew à la Deutscher. In turn, the "bad" Jew Kissinger (bad in Traverso's scheme of things) is a repulsive figure: an American, Zionist, rich, powerful. Traverso's book thus carries a warning to those Jews whose questionable taste leads them to identify with the latter figure.

Unfortunately, this friendly advice has come a little too late, it would appear, for Traverso sees Jews as already having chosen their camp—that of reaction and domination: "Today the axis of the Jewish world has moved from Europe to the United States and Israel."[9] Jews shouldn't complain; the "Jewish world" has sealed its own destiny; they should have stayed in the bosom of European modernity, critique, and revolution, even though modernity had rejected them. While the Holocaust ruined the dream of symbiosis between Europe and the Jews, the persecution of Jewish apparatchiks of the Soviet bloc as Zionists was a paradoxical reward for their support for the Bolshevik revolution.

From this allegedly incontrovertible allegation that the Jewish world has become staunchly Atlantist, conservative, Americano-Zionist, Traverso engages in a kind of free association leading to this inference: "Antisemitism has ceased pervading national cultures and has yielded its place to Islamophobia, the dominant form of racism at the beginning of the twenty-first century, but also to a new Judeophobia engendered by the Israeli-Palestinian conflict."[10] Traverso takes Pierre-André Taguieff's denunciatory term, "the new Judeophobia" (*la nouvelle judéophobie*), and deforms its meaning so as to deny the existence of antisemitism. For Traverso, the new Judeophobia is "engendered"—it has a rational, political cause in the Israel-Palestinian conflict, whereas Islamophobia has no such mooring. It is simply "racism," an irrational hatred with no justifiable cause or origin. In Traverso's reasoning, hatred of Muslims cannot be understood as related in the slightest to the rise of radical Islam, a movement that is no less political, after all, than Zionism, and could thus (in Traverso's interpretive schema) offer a logical explanation or even justification for Islamophobia. But for Traverso, hatred of Muslims can in no way be traced to Muslims themselves and their radicalization, whereas the cause for Judeophobia is to be found among Jews who identify with Zionism and the state of Israel.

Traverso speaks of the "Jewish world" cavalierly, since it is hard to know whether he means the Jewish communities of Europe, or of the United States, or of the entire planet; the expression seems to designate the entire diaspora and, of course, the state of Israel. Whatever the definition, this Jewish world has supposedly become anti-critical. That is to say, it has sold out: having once been a force for progress and subversion of power, it is now on the side of power and world domination. Traverso does not say with any precision when this shift from an ethical Judaism to an ethnic Judaism took place. But it clearly marks the end of what he repeatedly calls "Jewish modernity," which has run out of steam: "Jewish modernity has completed its trajectory. After having been the Western world's main source of critical thought, at the time when the West was the center, Jews now find themselves, through a kind of paradoxical reversal, at the heart of its mechanisms of domination."[11] Thereupon follow the names of four Jewish personalities who have heeded the "call to order," who have fallen prey to the siren song of political reaction, and been swept along by the shift to conservatism: Henry Kissinger (as we have seen), Leo Strauss, Raymond Aron, and Ariel Sharon. This Borgesian enumeration, heterogeneous to say the least in combining a diplomatic strategist, a military man, and two philosophers, drawn from three geographical, historical, and political realms (the United States, France, and Israel), would be quite funny if it did not serve to delegitimize, or even censor, nonrevolutionary Jewish thought.

While he was alive, Sharon had been Europe's bogeyman, both physically and politically. Novelist Nathalie Azoulai, in *Les Manifestations* (The demonstrations), grasps well what the French antisemitic unconscious could make of the resemblance between the name Sharon and the word *charogne* (lit. "carrion," but also a disgusting person). At the time of the invasion of Iraq by coalition forces in 2003, she wrote this: "Many nights I have dreamt that Sharon had a name different from Sharon, a name that recalled something other than the odor of rotting flesh, or vultures circling over bleeding children. I am sure that the association with *charogne* is heard in his name, and that were it something else, his reputation would not be so tarnished."[12] In recent times, no one more than Sharon has summoned up the image of the Jew according to the flesh, the abject Jew from whom, paradoxically, salvation was to come, a Christian doctrine lavishly re-elaborated by Léon Bloy. Writing after the publication of Édouard Drumont's antisemitic classic, *La France juive* (*Jewish France*), but before the Dreyfus affair, Bloy shows at once contempt and admiration for the Jewish people: "Their miserable flesh, which has resisted admixture for so great a number of centuries, all too clearly attests to their wondrous, exceptional position within humanity."[13]

The name Aron seems dragged in by the rhyme with that of Sharon; there is no other explanation for the juxtaposition. Strauss and Aron; Kissinger and Sharon; two philosophers and two adipose politicians—the mention of their names side by side could be drawn from traditional antisemitic literature, because these personalities have little in common except their Jewish births. This strategy of invidious association has the added advantage of delegitimizing not only any unrevolutionary system of thought, but more particularly anticommunism and antitotalitarianism. For Aron was a giant in this area of French intellectual life, having introduced Arendt's work in France in his 1965 *Démocratie et totalitarisme* (*Democracy and Totalitarianism*) and explaining the totalitarian system in terms of ideology.[14] Turning Aron and

Strauss into cynical warlords, ideologues of domination, colonialism, and investment capitalism because they opposed the two major twentieth-century totalitarianisms is a way of silencing any dissonant voice, presenting any critique of totalitarianism as imperialist, colonialist, fascist: a tried-and-true Stalinist method.

For Traverso, the great "turn toward conservatism" took place gradually and began with the Six-Day War of 1967 (even though the Jewish revolutionary cycle had supposedly ended in 1950). The morphing of Jews into conservatives or reactionaries (the two terms are interchangeable for Traverso, for whom not being a revolutionary means being a reactionary) culminated in the 1980s or 1990s, according to the nebulous chronology well-suited to his imprecise theory. What about the involvement of Jews in the U.S. civil rights movement, which took place well beyond 1950? We could also mention the fact that the American Jewish Committee—which Traverso would have to classify as conservative and on the right because of its support for Israel—called for desegregation in 1949, compared segregation to the Nuremberg laws, and, faithful to its ethical principles, has taken an official position in favor of immigration reform and the legalization of undocumented workers. But for Traverso, to think, philosophize, and theorize means necessarily to advance the cause of revolution, and (in the Jewish case) to promote an identity that could be called "post-Jewish" or, following Deutscher, Jewish non-Jewish.

THE RETURN OF THE ORIENTALIST
TROPE IN POSTCOLONIAL THEORY

Is antisemitism in decline? Has it disappeared? Indeed, it has, replies Traverso. He concedes that it may reappear from time to time, here and there. So let us examine how he interprets Mohammed Merah's 2012 murder of three Jewish children and their teacher in a Toulouse schoolyard. (Merah earlier shot four French soldiers of North African and Caribbean origin in Montauban—

his actions against Jews and against other minorities serving in
the French armed forces are obviously related, but my focus here
is antisemitism.) Traverso writes of such acts and their attendant
rhetoric: "These are abominable crimes and insane words that
we cannot place into the long list of violent actions linked to
exclusion and persecution, for those same violences strike those
who commit such criminal acts, which are precisely their reaction to them."[15] Let us deconstruct this logical concatenation
of such (perhaps deliberate) obscurity. Merah has committed
"abominable crimes" and uttered "insane words." The latter, just
quoted by Traverso, are the arguments Merah gave to the police
besieging him, whereby he justified his acts as retribution for the
killing of Palestinian Muslim children by "Jews."[16] But Traverso
maintains that "we cannot place" Merah's crimes "into the long
list of violent actions linked to exclusion and persecution," by
which we must understand that they cannot be inscribed within
the history of antisemitism. Killing Jewish children in a schoolyard because they are Jewish is thus not, for Traverso, an antisemitic act. It is something altogether different: simply a reaction
by a victim of exclusion.

It is untenable from a logical point of view to explain antisemitic murders as reactions to socioeconomic exclusion. One
could possibly imagine, though not condone, acts of such inten-
tionality perpetrated against the rich or people of "pure" French
blood, but that is beside the point. Rather, on a purely factual
plane, Merah cannot be considered marginalized. How often do
those left out of the system spend, as he did, vacations in the
French mountains, on the Swiss border, skiing with friends?[17]
And even if he were one of the excluded, could the same not be
said of one of his two brothers, Abdelghani, whose courage Traverso would have been better advised to hail? Abdelghani has
chosen an existential and ethical path diametrically opposed to
his brother's, by denouncing hatred of Jews and of the French
republic on television, face fully visible to the audience.[18]

Such apologetics for violence contain a grave error of philo-sophical reasoning, an error, alas, ever more frequent within con-temporary sociology: the marginalized who commit illegal acts cannot be criminals but are reacting to their marginalization. For argument's sake, let's say such people are indeed marginalized. If, in reaction to their marginalization they rob, beat, or murder someone, they nonetheless are committing criminal acts. An un-intentional, particularly redundant caricature of such arguments is put forth by sociologist Michel Wieviorka and endorsed by Traverso: "This hatred of Jews is a logical result of ghettoization, of a combination of socio-economic marginalization and racist discrimination, accentuated by a profound sense of having been pushed aside, closed off, relegated elsewhere."[19] Thus Merah hated Jews because he was hated. But even if "pure-blooded" French-men hated Merah, does this mean that Jews hated him? Accord-ing to this apologetic sociology, it follows that hatred was mu-tual, that Muslims hate Jews as a reaction to Jews' hating them. Why, therefore, should it surprise us when Jews and their places of worship are attacked, since these Jews identify with a criminal state? Anti-Jewish terrorism on French soil is but a continuation, on another battleground, of Palestinian resistance to the Zionist occupier: "Confusion is carefully maintained by spokespeople for Jewish communities who, claiming to represent Jewry as a whole, display unconditional support of Israeli policy. Their to-tal identification with the state of Israel ultimately promotes the negative equation that leads antisemites to desecrate a synagogue because they see in it a symbol of the 'Jewish state.'"[20] Yet again Traverso takes great care not to push such logic to its ultimate conclusion, which would excuse Islamophobia. If aggression against Jews in France or desecration of their synagogues can be explained away as so many attacks on symbols of an allegedly colonial, racist state in the Middle East, why cannot violence on Muslims be explained or excused as acts against those who on European soil represent the Taliban in Afghanistan or Hamas in

Gaza? Such arguments are, of course, part of the pathetic arsenal of right-wing extremists, but are they any more pathetic than the attempt to explain away antisemitism in France by blaming acts perpetrated by Israel? An obvious double standard is at work. Violence on Jews can be blamed on its victims, but Islamophobia can only be attributed to Jewish, Zionist, or neocolonial racism. However you grasp these arguments, they end up, terrifyingly enough, blaming Jewish victims, accusing Jews of instigating hatred against themselves, making Jews into accomplices to or even the main disseminators of Islamophobia and the socioeconomic marginalization of Muslims.

Indeed, Traverso offers us his explanation for the state of tension and resentment Muslims feel regarding Jews, emotions that lead them far astray, legally and morally, into deeds so terrible as the murder of children. These are "abominable crimes," says Traverso, but as we have seen, he does not put them in the same category as past violence and other exactions against Jews: "Immigrants of postcolonial origin and their descendents number several million in Europe, yet they have no public visibility except on some sports fields, or as artists and writers. Through a kind of back-and-forth, the marginalization from which they suffer was put into place in parallel with a new respectability gained by Jews. From this background of exclusion emerges a new Judeophobia. It targets a minority that, after having embodied for centuries a figure of otherness internal to the Western world, has now become a symbol for the latter."[21] Let us leave aside the question of whether the "visibility" of some Muslims as "artists or writers"—part of an intellectual élite—suggests they might not be so lacking in influence on society, as Traverso claims. The origin of the "new Judeophobia" is, he asserts, the attainment and new respectability of the Jews. By "respectability" Traverso can only mean Jewish money and power, respectability being for him pejorative, as are money and power. True respectability is reserved for those who disdain and resist the pseudo-respectability of the

bourgeois order of money and power. Jews were loved and love-
able as long as they embodied "otherness internal to the Western world," when they were figures of marginality and not yet
"respectable" (i.e., bourgeois). Thus Traverso beseeches them to
become, once again, the outsiders within the West—something
they never were except in the antisemitic unconscious or philosemitic romanticism. Alas, Jews are now on the side of power, and
Muslims occupy the position Jews had in the past. How could,
therefore, Muslims not hate Jews, the very "symbol," as Traverso
puts it, of the Western world?

Is Traverso's thought dictated by unconscious antisemitism?
I don't think so, even though he goes so far off the rails as to
draw up a list of "Jews of order," incoherent and unworthy of an
historian. A philosemite he doubtless is, but his philosemitism
is grounded in a romanticizing of diasporic Judaism—a romanticizing that always risks reproducing the essentializing of the
Jew that characterizes antisemitism. Several years ago, Traverso
published a book that strings together all the topoi of diasporic
romanticism, *La Pensée dispersée. Figures de l'exil judéo-allemand*
(Diasporic thought: Figures of Jewish German exile) a reflection on German Jewishness, exile, displacement, and world citizenship placed under the double legacy of Isaac Deutscher and
Edward Said.[22]

Rather than diagnosing his case as the result of unconscious
antisemitism, I'd rather attribute it to ideological blindness or political perversion. As Alain Finkielkraut and Pierre Vidal-Naquet
showed at the time of the sinister Faurisson affair, Holocaust
deniers cannot place the Shoah and its gas chambers into an ideological framework structured around class struggle; therefore, to
them the Shoah did not happen.[23] Likewise, for deniers of antisemitism, that form of hatred cannot emanate from the marginalized; it can originate only among those in power, and primarily as
a result of nationalism. Traverso is willing to accept the existence
of a Jew hatred linked to marginalization and socioeconomic

discrimination, but he calls it Judeophobia and not antisemitism, for him a phenomenon too deeply enmeshed within the structure of the nation-state.

The perverse result of such reasoning is as follows: if Jews have become conservatives, defenders of Western values, nationalists, or cultural supremacists, they too can be antisemites. Indeed, we often enough come across the allegation that Zionism is the ultimate form of antisemitism. It occurs in the writings Gil Anidjar and can be traced back at least to Edward Said, a fact I return to shortly.[24] So great a misappropriation of the term *antisemitism* can only serve to relativize, minimize, or deny antisemitism, as others have done and continue to do regarding the Shoah.

As soon as the term *Jew* has been emptied of its specificity, it becomes quite easy to find a "new Jew" embodied by Muslims or, as they are sometimes called, "migrants"—not even "immigrants," since those in question are often enough French-born. (Let us note that the term *migrant* is usually applied to Muslims, Africans, and Arabs, which is a way of denying the existence of other immigrant groups, such as Asians.) This superimposition of Jew and Muslim is made all the easier, perhaps on an unconscious plane, by the use of the word *Muselmann* in concentration camp argot and by the internalization of the Orientalistic category of "Semite." Thus Traverso writes: "In contemporary Europe, the migrant essentially presents Muslim traits. For the new racism, Islamophobia plays the role formerly assigned to antisemitism."[25] Whereupon he paints a portrait of today's Muslim as a mirror image of yesterday's pious Jew, replete with beard, kaftan, and a wife with veiled hair—since the two "outsiders," Jew and Muslim, are supposedly equivalent in the racist, colonial imaginary.

This strategy of equating Jews of yesteryear with Muslims of today, of making Islamophobia the latest avatar of antisemitism, is only possible if the word *antisemite* is understood literally as *anti-Semite*. But the existence of a Semitic race or peoples is a racist and Orientalistic conception. If it were not so, hatred of

Arabs and Muslims would indeed simply be antisemitism. And those who speak of a "new antisemitism," especially present in Europe today, would be trying to deflect attention from the most common, current form of racism: Islamophobia.

This sophistry has it that "Semites" are indistinguishably Jews and Arabs. However, since Jews are no longer colonized but allegedly colonizers, neither victims nor the embodiment of a diasporic principle of subversion, it is they who are the anti-Semites, with a hyphen. The entire argument dates at the very least from the extensive adoption of Edward Said's theses, and most of all, from the 1978 publication of his *Orientalism*.[26] That book has become a kind of Gospel in and of itself, heralding uncontestable truth regarding the perspective the racist West brought to bear on Muslim otherness. The dogma is widespread not only on U.S. campuses but also among a certain European intelligentsia. Here is what Said wrote:

> The transference of a popular anti-Semitic animus from a Jewish to an Arab target was made smoothly, since the figure was essentially the same. . . . The Arab is conceived of now as a shadow that dogs the Jew. In that shadow—because Arabs and Jews are Oriental Semites—can be placed whatever traditional, latent mistrust a Westerner feels towards the Oriental. For the Jew of pre-Nazi Europe has bifurcated: what we have now is a Jewish hero, constructed out of a reconstructed cult of the adventurer-pioneer-Orientalist . . . , and his creeping, mysteriously fearsome shadow, the Arab Oriental.[27]

Said superimposes Jews and Arabs in a play of shadows expressed in convoluted prose. But his purpose is not to condemn a European racist and colonialist mentality that gives credence to the idea of a Semitic race. Rather, Said himself endows that conception with a pretense of reality. For how else should we interpret the phrase "Arabs and Jews are Oriental Semites"? Said may be engaging in a kind of indirect quotation of racist discourse; nonetheless, this phrasing shows how racial rhetoric, the racialization

of politics and of society, is a return of what is repressed in postcolonial theory.

"The Jew of pre-Nazi Europe," the Jew Traverso celebrates as
the Jew of European modernity, has "bifurcated," or so Said tells
us with deadpan humor. Thus Traverso is simply trading in Said's
old wares. Traverso speaks of a "conservative turn," Said of a fork
in the road, Butler of "parting ways."[28] The road metaphor gets a
lot of traction, as it were. The figure of the Jew careening off the
proper path is no more than the postcolonialists' rehearsal of the
old trope of splitting the Jew: a split between the good and bad,
the ethical versus the ethnic Jew, the Jew according to the Spirit
and the Jew according to the flesh. Apparently, this notion holds
even though Said's Jew gone astray has betrayed his "Semitic"
ethnicity by becoming an anti-Semite. However, even if Europe
saw the Jew and the Arab (or Moor) as adversaries, it does not
necessarily follow that the two identities are interchangeable.
The hypothesis according to which the European precolonial or
colonial imaginary had constructed a hostile Jewish-Arab essence does not mean we should blindly accept this construct.
Postcolonial theory locks itself into an aporia by perpetuating the
imaginary categories of the discourse it claims to deconstruct.

THE PRISM METAPHOR

Let us return to Traverso for yet another variation on the theme of
good-Jew-bad-Jew, now borrowed from Isaiah Berlin's contrasting portraits of Benjamin Disraeli and Karl Marx. This example
invalidates the chronology of the "conservative turn," since the
so-called Jew of power exists simultaneously, synchronically,
with the Jew of revolution; there is thus no diachronic break in
the history of the Jewish world. Of Disraeli, the parvenu, and
Marx, the exiled revolutionary, Berlin writes: "the former [saw]
himself as a natural leader of an aristocratic élite, and the latter
the teacher and strategist of the world proletariat."[29] Traverso

glosses: "The first chose power, the second the radical critique of power." We can imagine which one Traverso prefers: the imaginary pariah and not the normalized bourgeois; the persecuted revolutionary as opposed to the British court Jew: "If the model of the critical intellectual embodied by Marx took precedence during the twentieth century, by its end the Disraelian model was in force, when the revolutionaries yielded their place to the kings' counselors and men of state."[30] "Jews of order" of this ilk work for think tanks linked to power. There can be no doubt that Traverso is alluding here to the neo-conservative ideologues of the Republican Party and former President George W. Bush. Regarding France, Traverso classifies as a Jew of order Alain Finkielkraut, with his supposedly Islamophobic and neoconservative remarks.

Only willful nearsightedness can explain Traverso's failure to appreciate the political and ideological diversity in the Jewish world today. How could that world be reduced to that of advisers to President George W. Bush, or contributors to the journal *Commentary,* or a notable French intellectual with a flair for polemics? What of Jewish radicals in the diaspora and Israel? Traverso ignores such personalities as the late Tony Judt, Rony Brauman, Odi Aphir, Zygmunt Bauman, and Gideon Levy, just to cite Jewish intellectuals from three geographical areas. For Traverso, it is as if universalist, internationalist, critical, anti-Zionist, and post-Zionist Jews had suddenly disappeared. Why does he focus on a handful of conservative, pro-American, pro-Israel Jews and neglect the others? Are great Israeli writers on the left, such as Amos Oz, A. B. Yehoshua, and David Grossman, to be considered Jews of order and lumped together with the likes of Ariel Sharon and Henry Kissinger? As for Europe, and particularly France with the largest Jewish population on the continent, Traverso seems to have forgotten the intellectuals from the 1950s to the 1980s, called by Eric Marty "the Moderns," who pursued the deconstruction of identity and of borders: think of Jacques Derrida or Hélène

Cixous. Regarding the United States, it seems hardly necessary to mention Noam Chomsky, one of the most influential intellectuals of the second half of the twentieth century. Is Chomsky to be reckoned as a conservative American Zionist?

Traverso refuses to see the diversity and heterogeneity of the Jewish world. The diaspora and Israel offer endless adherents to the entire gamut of ideological and political positions. Pronouncements such as *Jews are reactionaries, Jews are revolutionaries, Jews are Bolsheviks, Jews are plutocrats, Jews were revolutionaries, humanists, universalists; now they are reactionaries, imperialists, colonialists*—such judgments are at best superficial and at worst essentialist; they could be produced only by an ideologue of the most tendentious strain.

Moreover, Traverso adduces no evidence, no documents, no surveys, to prove that there is more conservatism among Jews now than before some presumed massive break from a revolutionary Jewish mindset. He draws wide-ranging conclusions from his mere impressions regarding the Jewish world today.

One should add that the idea of a Jewish "turn" or "break" in continuity is invalid. Traverso tacitly acknowledges as much in contrasting Disraeli and Marx, as mentioned above; in this portrayal, the Jewish world thus appears cleft synchronically and not diachronically, with the good Jews, the revolutionaries, on the side of good; those on the dark side are the Jews of order, of the state, of power. The dominated on the one hand, the dominators on the other.

The Jew who has gone rotten, turned bad, taken the road to perdition, would be a historical figure of Jewish "incongruity," part of the history of how diaspora Jewry, most of all in Europe, was perceived by non-Jewish society in the context of class conflict. This is clear from Anna Zuk's analysis of the socioeconomic alienation of Jews in her study of eighteenth-century Polish Jewry. Zygmunt Bauman, in his book on the Holocaust and modernity, summarizes Zuk's thesis as follows:

> What made the Jewish placement in the class war truly special
> was that *they had become objects of two mutually opposed and con-*
> *tradictory class antagonisms.* Each of the adversaries locked in the
> mutual class battle conceived of the Jewish mediators as sitting
> on the opposite side of the barricade. The metaphor of the prism,
> and hence the concept of *prismatic category,* seems to convey
> this situation better than that of the "mobile class." Depending
> on the side from which the Jews were looked at, they—like all
> prisms—unwittingly refracted altogether different sights; one of
> crude, unrefined and brutal lower classes, another of ruthless and
> haughty social superiors.[31] (original emphasis)

I hardly need to continue quoting, for we are well acquainted with
the history of alienation of European Jewry, of their ontological
incongruity resulting from prejudices against them in Christian
society. The same Jewish anomaly obtained in North Africa, on
linguistic and cultural as well as the socioeconomic planes, which
of course intersect. Albert Memmi's *Pillar of Salt* shows clearly
how Jews in Tunisia were perceived as colonizers by the Arabs,
even as they were colonized by Europeans.[32] In his preface to
Memmi's 1957 *The Colonizer and the Colonized,* Jean-Paul Sartre,
who always—almost always—got things right, paints a picture
of the "Arab Jew" in Tunisia during the colonial period:

> Exactly who is he? Colonizer or colonized? He would say "neither";
> you, perhaps, would say "both"—it amounts to the same thing.
> He belongs to one of those native but non-Muslim groups that are
> "more or less privileged in comparison with the colonized masses,
> but . . . rejected . . . by the colonizing group," which, however, "does
> not completely discourage" their efforts to integrate themselves
> into European society. Linked by actual liabilities to the subprole-
> tariat, but separated from it by meager privileges, the members of
> this group live in a constant state of uneasiness.[33]

This is existence in a prism, where perception depends on the
viewer's perspective. The prism metaphor is well suited as a portrayal of Jewish fate in the diaspora. For nineteenth- and twentieth-century antisemites, the Jew was a Bolshevik, a revolutionary,

a rootless cosmopolitan. But according to revolutionary dogma, for Marx and Proudhon, the Jew was a capitalist, and humanity had to free itself from Judaism and private property (seen as being the same thing), as encapsulated in Marx's well-known formula: "the *emancipation of the Jews*, in its ultimate meaning, is the emancipation of mankind from Judaism" (original emphasis).[34] The Jew as imagined by the revolutionary was the forerunner of today's conservative, Zionist-American Jew.

Thus, according to the viewpoint adopted, Jews are always on the wrong side of the barricade. If the wrong side is identified as American imperialism and capitalist globalization, Jews are on that side, through their ties to the United States and support of the state of Israel. Traverso, therefore, is just adding one more chapter to the tragic history of Jewish incongruity, a history ultimately inseparable from that of antisemitism. To take the case of France, while Traverso sees the Jewish world since the 1950s to be conservative, Jews have been seen by the French far right as supportive of an anti-French, nomadic, transnational, and antiracist ideology. To be convinced that the notion of prismatic category is still applicable to Jews today, it suffices to compare, side by side, Internet sites or publications of the Gallic far right and the far left.

Had Traverso studied "Jewish modernity" in interwar France, he would have come across the writings, in some cases posthumous, of such authors as Raymond-Raoul Lambert, Jean-Jacques Bernard, Hélène Berr, and Léon Werth.[35] All were assimilated Jews, "non-Jewish Jews," practically converted (this is especially true of Bernard), with an indubitably bourgeois, nationalist weltanschauung. Exemplary in this respect is Lambert's tragic *Carnet d'un témoin* (*Diary of a Witness*), which was composed in the months preceding his death at Auschwitz and includes quite unexpected homage to French nationalist writer Maurice Barrès.[36] We might recall as well the inglorious period when some assimilated Jews in western Europe (not all; once again, generalizations have to be avoided) desired normalization to such an extent that they regarded eastern European Jews as Oriental foreigners threatening their own wishfully seamless integration.[37]

These nuances in the positions of diaspora Jewry, this diversity of strategies sometimes clumsy or even (seen from today's standpoint) quite noxious, belie Traverso's philosemitic portrait of a homogenized, revolutionary, internationalist, and subversive Jewish modernity. The caricature, assigned a positive rather than a negative valence, enables Traverso most of all to paint today's Jews pejoratively. However, earlier times knew no shortage of well-established, bourgeois Jews who were obsessed with respectability and whose complacency was disturbed only by the war and anti-Jewish laws.

There is no doubt that European modernity had its "non-Jewish Jews," its revolutionary, subversive Jews, as well as Jews who strove to put an end to Judaism or, contrarily, to fulfill it by embracing all human kind (see Deutscher). There can also be no doubt regarding the presence of "Jews of order," "respectable" Jews who knew not the romantic notion of embodying "internal otherness" within the Western world. Such a portrayal—it bears repeating—is the brainchild of antisemitism and remains so even when put forward by philosemites from Charles Péguy to Enzo Traverso. It is no more than prejudice with a plus sign placed before it. Sartre may well have been wrong to assert that the antisemite's gaze is what creates the Jew, but we can be sure that the marginal, critical, subversive, revolutionary Jew is nothing other than the narcissistic projection of the philosemite.

Looking toward eastern Europe, Traverso could have focused on the Russian-speaking Polish philosopher Julius Margolin, a Zionist born in Pinsk, in West Belarus, a city that was part of the Russian Empire.[38] After emigration to Palestine in 1936, Margolin returned to visit his family in 1939. Lacking a passport that could satisfy Soviet authorities, he was sentenced to five years in a gulag. Traverso would have seen Margolin as a fierce defender of Western democracy and of Western values in general—called by our historian the "Party of Order." And since the East, for Margolin, was symbolized by the knout, the whip, and the Russian penchant for obedience and submission, Said would probably have characterized him as Orientalist and racist, thus reinforcing his identification of Zionism with racism and colonialism. To make matters worse, the selfsame Margolin published in 1947 his masterpiece, *The Inhuman Condition: Five Years in Soviet Concentration-Camps* (published in French as *La Condition inhumaine. Cinq ans dans les camps de concentration soviétiques* in 1949). In 1950, he testified on behalf of David Rousset, accused of having forged testimony on Stalinist camps on the basis of archival material from Nazi camps—so great was the unwillingness to criticize communism in immediate postwar France. As Sartre, who this time got things wrong, put it in a catchy phrase in the 1950s, "Il ne faut pas désespérer Billancourt." That is, intellectuals must not contradict utopian fantasies and thereby induce despair in workers (such as those employed by Renault in the Parisian suburb of Billancourt).

Thus, a totally different face of European "Jewish modernity" emerges following other evidence, other archives, but the view does not square with the romantic, subversive, and revolutionary image cherished by Traverso. For twentieth-century Jewish life was of kaleidoscopic breadth with assimilated, Christianized, bourgeois Jews; pro-Soviet Zionist Jews; anticommunist Zionists; anti-Zionist Ultra-Orthodox Jews; all manner of "un-Jewish Jews" and "Jewish Jews"; and so on. How ironic that in an age when cultural and ethnic diversity is celebrated, intellectual and political diversity is reduced to its bare minimum. In like measure, sheer human diversity—nuanced, and irreducible—finds itself subsumed, unspeakably reduced.

However, Traverso did not want to write a history of Jewish modernity, of the emancipation of German and European Jews, or of their tragic end. He preferred to exploit the tragic history of the failure of emancipation for purely polemical ends.

A NARRATIVE TRAP

The introduction to Traverso's book includes an account drawn from Isaac Deutscher's 1954 biography of Trotsky.[39] On December 24, 1917, the latter arrived as the Soviet minister of foreign affairs at Brest-Litovsk, "where negotiations were taking place with the Prussian Empire in view of achieving a separate peace."[40] I quote Traverso at length, for his narrative apparatus contains a trap, as literary scholar Louis Marin would have put it.[41] Even the slightest fall therein might cause the reader to accept the entirety of Traverso's argument. And if the narrative is a trap, so is the trap a narrative, a *captatio benevolentiae*, seeking to captivate, or capture, the reader.

In the account that appears at the threshold to Traverso's book, we read that Trotsky's "delegation included a certain Karl Radek, a Polish Jew and subject of the Habsburg Empire, who had been pursued in Germany for disseminating defeatist propaganda. As soon as they got off the train, they started distributing to enemy soldiers tracts calling for international revolution. The German diplomats observed them in amazement. Upon taking power, the Bolsheviks had begun publishing secret accords between the tsarists and Western powers; their objective was not to be admitted into international diplomacy, but to denounce it."[42] First, it is clear that, for Traverso, the Bolsheviks spread salutary disorder throughout the West. They denounced the Western powers' compromise of their own principles and broadcast the call for revolution. They are thus positive, exemplary, redemptive figures, good Jewish figures emblematized by Karl Radek. This internationalist, more or less stateless, Polish Jew who has taken up the cause of the revolution may well loom for the French reader as a forerunner to Pierre Goldman, a French 1970s radical of Polish Jewish origin, who joined Latin American rebels.[43]

Traverso continues: starting around 1919, the Bolsheviks were stigmatized in the West, and especially in Churchill's England, as enemies of civilization: "A warmongering conservative like Winston Churchill saw them [the Bolsheviks] as 'enemies of the human race,' as propagators of 'animal-like barbarism.' Civilization, wrote Churchill, 'is disappearing over immense territory, as Bolsheviks jump and bounce around like frightful baboons amidst cities in ruins and piles of dead bodies.' . . . Carried away by his rhetoric, Churchill did not hesitate to attribute Jewish traits to Lenin. This 'monster climbing on a pyramid of skulls' is nothing other than the leader of a 'vile group of cosmopolitan fanatics.'"[44] Traverso cites his source for the quotations from Churchill's speeches: the biography of the British statesman by French historian François Bédarida.[45]

However, the fact that Hitler used such rhetoric, with its analogies with animals, to designate Jews does not mean that Churchill's anti-Bolshevik rhetoric was antisemitic. Nowhere does Bédarida suggest that Churchill's anti-Bolshevik imprecations were anti-Jewish in the slightest; on the contrary, he speaks of Churchill's prescience, his anticipation of the threat posed by communism. But Traverso has so internalized Hitler's equating Jews and Bolsheviks that he reads anticommunist prose as antisemitic invective, for Bolsheviks and revolutionaries in general are, in his imagination, associated with Jews. And the great Jewish tradition is one of revolution.

Finally, Traverso offers an analogy. To the reader unversed in the history of the Russian Revolution and even more ignorant of early twentieth-century European diplomacy, he offers a kind of parable to illustrate what is at stake in the scene he recounts: "The state of mind of the German plenipotentiaries would be hard to understand now. One would have to imagine the arrival of an Al Qaeda delegation at a G8 summit. The Jews were then identified with Bolshevism, that is to say a worldwide conspiracy against civilization."[46] Let us try to unpack this complicated passage. What analogy is implicit in Traverso's narrative apparatus? The answer: the German plenipotentiaries of 1917 are the equivalent of the industrialized nations of the G8, who claim to represent civilization but actually embody plutocratic globalization. And the Bolsheviks—that is, the Jews, which is to say the revolutionaries—are today's equivalent of a delegation of Al Qaeda. The new Judeo-Bolsheviks are not just Muslims (as the thesis identifying Islamophobia as the new antisemitism would have it) but rather the most extremist movement within Islam: Al Qaeda, standing at the vanguard of a new worldwide, transnational, cosmopolitan revolution.

For Traverso, Islamist movements such as Hamas, Hezbollah, and even Al Qaeda pose only imaginary threats, fantasies of minds obsessed with the security concerns, xenophobia and Islamophobia propagated by the Americano-Zionist axis. We thus could ask about Traverso the following questions: Does he see the Bolsheviks as equivalent to Islamic terrorists, or bin Laden as a neorevolutionary, or even a new Radek? And as a corollary: do Jews embody for him the plutocratic, nationalist, and conservative resistance to a worldwide Islamist revolution? Those questions are neither futile nor facetious, especially if one considers Judith Butler's 2012 definition of Hamas and Hezbollah as "social movements that are progressive" and "part of a global left."[47]

The radical left, finding itself bereft of yesterday's proletariat, has now invested its hopes in former colonized peoples and the figure of the migrant. It views current political struggles through the messianic lenses of the past. While the international working class was endowed with millenarian expectations, some radical thinkers are now turning toward movements such as Hamas or Hezbollah to revive their confidence in the Hegelian work of the negative, another name for the meaning of history. Not only that; they yearn for redemption through violence and death, at the risk of playing into the hands of reactionary, even fascist movements.

Thus we have cause to ponder whether it is not "Jewish modernity" but actually the self-proclaimed "global left" that has veered to the right.

NOTES

1. On the Dieudonné affair, see Jean Birnbaum, "L'affaire Dieudonné, la gauche et l'antisémitisme," *Le Monde,* Jan. 13, 2014. Dieudonné M'bala M'bala is a French stand-up comedian, with a father from Cameroon and a mother from France. Together with self-proclaimed "national-socialist" ideologue Alain Soral, Dieudonné has become a leader of antisemitic and anti-Zionist campaigns in France since the beginning of the millennium. More recently, he has staged shows that ridicule Holocaust victims and that engage in Holocaust denial masqueraded as comedy. One such show was banned by the Conseil d'Etat for violation of human dignity.

2. "Manifestation antisémite à Paris 'Juif, la France n'est pas à toi!' . . . ," Jan. 26, 2014, http://www.youtube.com/watch?v=FdTkvAfOaMA. See also Geoffroy Clavel, "Jour de colère. Quenelles et saluts nazis dans les rues de Paris," Jan. 27, 2014, *Huffington Post,* http://www.huffingtonpost.fr/2014 /01/27/jour-colere-quenelles-saluts-nazis-rues-paris_n_4671985.html.

3. See Eric Hazan and Alain Badiou, *L'Antisémitisme partout, aujourd'hui en France* (Paris: La Fabrique, 2011); Guillaume Weill-Raynal, *Une Haine imaginaire. Contre-enquête sur le nouvel antisémitisme* (Paris: Colin, 2005); and Ivan Segré, *La Réaction philosémite* (Paris: Lignes, 2009).

4. Enzo Traverso, *La Fin de la modernité juive. Histoire d'un tournant conservateur* (Paris: La Découverte, 2013). All translations of this work are mine.

5. Traverso, *La Fin de la modernité juive,* 172.

6. Alain Badiou, *Portées du mot Juif* (Paris: Lignes, 2005.)

7. On "non-Jewish Jew," see Isaac Deutscher, *The Non-Jewish Jew and Other Essays* (London: Oxford University Press, 1968).

8. David Nirenberg, *Anti-Judaism: The Western Tradition* (New York: W. W. Norton, 2013).

9. Traverso, *La Fin de la modernité juive,* 8.

10. Ibid.

11. Ibid., 8.

12. Nathalie Azoulai, *Les Manifestations* (Paris: Éditions du Seuil, 2005), 136, my translation.

13. Léon Bloy, *Le Salut par les Juifs* (Paris: Mercure de France, Paris 1949), 29. See also Edouard Drumont, *La France juive devant l'opinion* (Paris: Marpon & Flammarion, 1886).

14. Raymond Aron, *Democracy and Totalitarianism,* trans. Valence Ionescu (New York: Praeger, 1969).

15. Traverso, *La Fin de la modernité juive,* 114–115.

16. Ibid., 114.

17. See "Le dernier voyage de Mohamed Merah" (Mohamed Merah's last trip), *Le Point,* March 26, 2012, http://www.lepoint.fr/societe/exclusif -le-dernier-voyage-de-mohamed-merah-26-03-2012-1445069_23.php.

18. See documentary by Mohamed Sifaoui, *Mohamed Merah, Itinéraire d'un terroriste français,* Groupe M6, November 2012.

19. Michel Wieviorka quoted by Traverso, *La Fin de la modernité juive,* 115.

20. Traverso, *La Fin de la modernité juive,* 117.

21. Ibid., 116.

22. Enzo Traverso, *La Pensée dispersée. Figures de l'exil judéo-allemand* (Paris: Lignes, 2004).

23. See Alain Finkielkraut, *L'Avenir d'une négation* (Paris: Éditions du Seuil, 1982), and Pierre Vidal-Naquet, *Les Assassins de la mémoire* (Paris: La Découverte, 1987).

24. See Gil Anidjar, *The Jew, the Arab: A History of the Enemy* (Stanford, Calif.: Stanford University Press, 2003). On page 193 Anidjar introduces the idea of Zionism as antisemitism.

25. Traverso, *La Fin de la modernité juive,* 122.

26. Edward Said, *Orientalism* (New York: Vintage Books, 1978).

27. Ibid., 286.

28. Judith Butler, *Parting Ways: Jewishness and the Critique of Zionism* (New York: Columbia University Press, 2013).

29. Isaiah Berlin, "Benjamin Disraeli, Karl Marx and the Search for Identity," *Midstream* 7 (1970): 29–49.

30. Traverso, *La Fin de la modernité juive,* 168.

31. Zygmunt Bauman, *Modernity and the Holocaust* (Ithaca, N.Y.: Cornell University Press, 1989), 43.

32. Albert Memmi, *La Statue de sel* (Paris: Corrêa, 1953).

33. Jean-Paul Sartre, introduction to Albert Memmi, *The Colonizer and the Colonized,* trans. Howard Greenfield (Boston: Beacon Press, 1965).

34. Karl Marx quoted by Nirenberg, Anti-Judaism, 436.

35. Raymond-Raoul Lambert, *Carnet d'un témoin* (Paris: Fayard, 1985); Jean-Jacques Bernard, *Le Camp de la mort lente* (Paris: Albin Michel, 1944); Hélène Berr, *Journal* (Paris: Tallandier, 2008); Léon Werth, *Déposition. Journal 1940–1944* (Paris: B. Grasset, 1946).

36. Raymond-Raoul Lambert, *Carnet d'un témoin: 1940–1943* ([Paris]: Fayard, 1985). Published in English as *Diary of a Witness: 1940–1943,* ed. Richard I. Cohen and trans. Isabel Best (Chicago: Ivan R. Dee, 2007).

37. See, for example, Bauman, *Modernity and the Holocaust,* 133–134.

38. See Julius Margolin's masterpiece, *Voyage au pays des Ze-Ka,* in its superb French translation by Luba Jurgenson (Paris: Le Bruit du temps, 2010). See also Julius Margolin, *Le Livre du retour* (Paris: Le Bruit du temps, 2012).

39. Isaac Deutscher, *Trotsky, le prophète armé* (1954; reprint Paris: Julliard), 1962), 5.

40. Traverso, *La Fin de la modernité juive,* 5.

41. Louis Marin, *Le Récit est un piège* (Paris: Éditions de Minuit, 1978). In that book, Marin was focusing on seventeenth-century rhetorical strategies meant to persuade the reader and on the articulation between rhetoric and power through a series of close readings of introits of fables, historiographies and memoirs. My analysis of Traverso's introduction is a humble tribute to Marin's heuristic method.

42. Traverso, *La Fin de la modernité juive,* 5.

43. See Pierre Goldman's memoir, *Souvenirs obscurs d'un Juif polonais né en France* (Paris: Éditions du Seuil, 1975).

44. Traverso, *La Fin de la modernité juive,* 5.

45. François Bédarida, *Churchill* (Paris: Fayard, 1999).

46. Traverso, *La Fin de la modernité juive.*

47. See Eva Illouz, "Judith Butler Gets a Taste of Her Own Politics," *Haaretz,* Sept. 20, 2012.

EIGHT

Anti-Zionism and the Anarchist Tradition

EIRIK EIGLAD

IT IS INITIALLY hard to see a connection between the anarchist tradition and the conflict between Israel and the Palestinians. On the surface, anarchism promises little explanation of this conflict over statehood and opposing national identities. Furthermore, in the world today, anarchism—or, in a broad sense, "antistate politics"—is nowhere on the public agenda. Even if it were, there would be no obvious reasons for anarchism to be concerned with Israel and Zionism. Anti-Zionism has been shaped primarily by ideological forces that are explicitly hostile to anarchism and its antistate aspirations.

Why then is it relevant to discuss the relationship between anti-Zionism and the anarchist tradition? First of all, because the anarchist perspective spurs a whole series of ideological motivations and analyses that cannot easily be countered by conventional criticisms of anti-Zionism. Scholars of antisemitism today are doing an excellent job in pointing out when and where anti-Zionism turns into antisemitism, or when it reveals itself as antisemitism. But there are forms of anti-Zionism that cannot easily be categorized as antisemitic. Anti-Zionism is often, but not always, a code name for antisemitism. This means that, unless we try to explore the underlying motivations, principles, and analyses that guide contemporary anti-Zionism, it will be difficult for us to understand it, much less challenge it. In particular, contemporary critics of antisemitism do not take into account what animates the anarchist critiques of Zionism and the state of Israel.

In recent years, anarchist or antistate arguments are increasingly used as a justification for anti-Zionist positions. Noam Chomsky has been a vocal and highly influential anti-Zionist since the early 1970s, but for a long time he was quite lonely in professing his anarchist sympathies.[1] Anti-Zionists framed their struggle against Israel not in traditional anarchist terms but in terms of Maoist, Trotskyist, or broader postcolonial analyses. After the turn of the millennium, however, antistate arguments seem to become increasingly popular. When Chomsky's friend Norman Finkelstein is charged with being dismissive of the Israeli state, he argues that he is dismissive of all states. The lessons of the Second World War and the Holocaust, Finkelstein claims, are that we should distrust all states and that we owe loyalty to none.[2] Judith Butler, a harsh critic of Zionism, in 2011 declared herself to be a "provisional anarchist."[3]

More important, however, is that we now see new forms of resistance to Israel and Zionism emerging. For more than a decade, activist networks like the International Solidarity Movement (ISM) and the Israeli-based Anarchists Against the Wall (AATW) have been highly influential in shaping radical opinion in the West, and we now see anarchists flock to the Palestinian cause. This is a relatively new phenomenon. Anarchists are neither the most vocal nor the most intransigent of the anti-Zionists today, but during the last decade there has been a distinct "anarchist turn" in anti-Zionist activism. The anarchist tradition provides a kind of reasoning and a new set of justifications that differ fundamentally from the crude maxims of anti-imperialism and national liberation that pestered the New Left in the 1960s and 1970s. While anti-imperialist and postcolonial theories provided

the New Left's ammunition against Israel, their support for national liberation struggles and for creating new states as a means
of fighting imperialism and the capitalist order were arguments
that anarchists always distrusted. There were exceptions, but this
was still the rule.

Today, anarchism in one form or another may contribute to
spreading anti-Zionist ideas to progressive circles that formerly
rejected anti-Zionism. If we are to decipher the new antisemitisms, it is crucial to understand how these changes came about
and why anti-Zionism gradually has become a staple of anarchism's antistate and anticapitalist creed. Anarchism may not
have a huge following today, but left-libertarian ideas have a
broad appeal to activists in social movements such as feminism,
ecology, and urban radicalism, particularly among activists who
adhere to no particular ideology. But in order to properly assess
how anarchism or antistate politics relate to anti-Zionism, we
first need to look briefly at how the anarchist tradition is related
to antisemitism. Any new idea must be judged against the backdrop of historical experience, particularly when dealing with a
cultural phenomenon as slippery and mutable—and deadly—as
antisemitism.

THE DARK SIDE OF ANARCHISM

Historically, antisemitism came predominantly from the political right. In its modern forms, it developed in reaction to the
ideas that nurtured the Enlightenment and the French Revolution.[4] Cosmopolitanism, egalitarianism, and republicanism
were modern ideas that reactionary theorists associated with
social turmoil and national decay—and with the Jacobin Terror. Still, the political left was never immune to antisemitic ideas
and sentiments, and it often shared a reservoir of images with
the right: images that played on deep-seated cultural prejudices
against Jewish exceptionalism transmitted from medieval Eu-

rope. This was also the case with anarchism: despite their fervent antinationalism, anarchism's founding fathers made deeply antisemitic remarks.

Anarchist ideology emerged in the aftermath of the French Revolution and came into its own during the 1840s. By anarchism, I refer to the radical, antiauthoritarian political tradition that seeks to build a new social order, not structured around states of any kind, but based on other types of human community, namely collectives, municipalities, cooperatives, and voluntary associations.[5] The first self-identifying anarchist was the Frenchman Pierre-Joseph Proudhon. His devotion to social equality and the rights of man led him to claim that he was "prepared to sacrifice his country to justice."[6] He was not a nationalist in a conventional sense but increasingly came to associate "the sacred land of Gaul" with the revolutionary idea, seeking to rid France of foreign influence.[7] Proudhon's vicious antisemitism, expressed in this statement from 1847, cannot be misinterpreted: "The Jew is the enemy of humankind. This race must be sent back to Asia or be exterminated. By steel or by fire or by expulsion the Jew must disappear."[8] In Proudhon's mind, Jews were inextricably linked to usury. Although Proudhon himself probably would have denied this, his antisemitism seems to have been rooted far more in French traditionalism and prejudice than in his anarchist ideology.[9] The same could be said about Leo Tolstoy's disdain for Jewish religion: his anti-Judaism is best understood in light of his Christianity and the widespread prejudices that existed in the Russia of his day, not primarily in his antistate creed.[10]

By contrast, the Russian émigré Mikhail Bakunin made antisemitic remarks that seem more directly derived from his anarchist analysis.[11] In his attacks on Marx, for instance, Bakunin wrote: "This whole Jewish world, comprising a single exploiting sect, a kind of bloodsucking people, a kind of organic destructive collective parasite, going beyond not only the frontiers of states, but of political opinion, this world is now, at least for the most part, at the disposal of Marx on the one hand, and of Rothschild on the other."[12] The crucial point for Bakunin was that both Marx and the capitalists called for the strong centralization of the state and a central state bank. Wherever "such a bank exists the parasitic Jewish nation, which speculates in the labor of the people will always find means to exist."[13] In the early days of anarchism, the adoption of a crude anticapitalism and anticlericalism made it difficult to distinguish between legitimate social critique and resistance to "foreign influence," notably by Jews. Given the ideological plasticity of the times—as well as "the broad back" of anarchist radicalism—it is difficult to estimate just how influential these ideas were, but the point is clear: early anarchist ideology was stained by anti-Jewish prejudices.

In Russia, Bakunin's legacy fed into populist antisemitism: "They make no distinction between Jews and gentry," one Jewish *narodnik* complained about his comrades; they were "preaching the extermination of both."[14] This problem was not in any way limited to anarchist circles; it was a broad populist problem that came to the fore during the wave of anti-Jewish riots and pogroms that swept southern Russia during the early 1880s.[15] Revolutionaries did not instigate these anti-Jewish riots, but few populists were prepared to condemn the riots due to their "revolutionary" and "mass" character; as Avrahm Yarmolinsky points out, they were not prepared to take "an indifferent, let alone negative, attitude towards a genuinely popular movement." Indeed, many populists condemned the repression of the riots more than the pogroms themselves; some even rejoiced "in the educational efforts of such occurrences."[16] Russian radicals also found it difficult to oppose antisemitism because their program required that they had the masses on their side, an approach that demanded a certain level of opportunism. "While the reactionaries would use Jewish blood to put out the fire of rebellion," it was noted, "their adversaries were not averse to using it to feed the flames."[17] The pogroms in the Pale of Settlement led many Jews to emigrate westward to countries like France, where Proudhon's followers had not yet resolved his tainted legacy. A shift was underway, forced on them by the public debacle that followed Alfred Dreyfus's trial in 1894, which neither anarchists nor socialists took seriously at first.[18] Prominent anarchists like Bernard Lazare and Sebastian Faure were among the first to speak out in Dreyfus's defense, and, shortly after the January 1998 publication of Émile Zola's seismic *J'Accuse,* anarchists organized the first public demonstrations for his acquittal. Although the pro-Dreyfusard anarchists initially met strong opposition from many of their comrades, the Dreyfus affair would eventually force French anarchists to take a definite stand on the issue of antisemitism.[19] Furthermore, the Jewish immigration from the East brought masses of poor artisans, proletarians, peasants, and déclassé elements among the Jews; these were strata anarchists and socialists readily identified with. Another important factor in this turn was that the political right during the period of the Dreyfus affair became more explicitly antisemitic.[20] By the turn of last century, antisemitism had arguably become one of the ideological issues that did in fact divide the left and the right.[21]

So what about anarchist practice? In contrast to Stalinism, Maoism, and Social Democracy, anarchism has never been victorious anywhere in the world, and has never controlled large territories over any period of time. Nowadays, however, it is difficult to appreciate just how influential anarchist ideology was in the formative years of the international labor movement.[22] In France, the failed rising in Lyon in September 1870, the defeat of the Paris Commune of 1871, and the demise of the First International in 1872, as well as the subsequent rise of anarchist individualism and terrorism, hampered the development of anarchism as a mass movement. By the outbreak of the First World War, anarchism's influence in most countries had waned. The only places anarchists had considerable impact were in the Ukraine during the Russian Civil War and in the Spanish Revolution of 1936.

Despite the significance of Bakunin, Tolstoy, and Kropotkin to the development of the international anarchist movement, Russian anarchists did not form any significant movement until after the February Revolution of 1917.[23] But although explicit anarchist groups and their influence were infinitesimal, genuinely libertarian and antistate ideas shaped early Russian socialism. Within Russian revolutionary populism, Isaiah Berlin remarks, "violent disputes took place about means and methods, about timing, but not about ultimate purposes. Anarchism, equality, a full life for all, these were universally accepted."[24] This broad left-libertarian legacy was carried forward by the massive Socialist Revolutionary Party, and eventually its offshoot, the Left Socialist-Revolutionaries.

In the buildup to the October Revolution of 1917, anarchist groups, collectives, and movements sprang up all over Russia, but none were more significant than the Ukrainian Makhnovshchina—a remarkable partisan army led by the anarchist Nestor Makhno—which was instrumental in defeating the White armies of Denikin and Wrangel in the Russian Civil War. The chaos and destruction of the Civil War brought tremendous violence directed against the Jews, both as spontaneous pogroms and systematic massacres, and this was certainly also the case in the Ukrainian theater of war. Civil war not only unleashed built-up popular resentment of Jews, but forces of the White Army systematically associated Jews with the revolution. Between 1918 and 1920 it is estimated that more than 60,000 Ukrainian Jews were murdered.[25] When the Whites were defeated, Trotsky's Red Army turned against the Makhnovists. Bolshevik media denounced Makhnovists as antisemites and instigators of pogroms, but the historical record instead seems to indicate that these were rumors started by the Bolsheviks to discredit anarchism in the eyes of radical Jews and diaspora communities.[26] Not only did Jews occupy leading positions in the Makhnovist cultural-educational section as well as its military command, but many Jews also fought alongside Ukrainians and Cossacks and in separate army detachments. Furthermore, although there were at times antisemitic elements among his partisans, Nestor Makhno himself consistently denounced antisemitism and anti-Jewish hatred.[27] His policy toward antisemitic transgressors was unmistakable: they were shot on the spot.[28] Saul Yanovsky, the editor of *Fraye Arbeter Schtime,* a major Yiddish journal in New York, accused Makhnovism of being an antisemitic movement, but he later acknowledged that he had been wrong on this point.[29]

Spain is the only country in the modern era where anarchism can credibly be said to have developed into a major social movement and to have seriously threatened the state.[30] In contrast to what most other countries on the continent experienced, classical antisemitism never gained the same foothold in the Spanish left, certainly not among the major anarchists and syndicalist tendencies. It is not hard to understand why. Not only had Spain essentially been a country without Jews since the Reconquista of 1492, but antisemitism was always fundamentally identified with the political right and the forces of clerical reaction.[31] To the Carlists and Franco's Falangists, the republican forces—and certainly the militantly anticlerical anarchists—embodied the fateful triad of Freemasons, Communists, and Jews.

Spanish anarchism was spearheaded by the large anarcho-syndicalist trade union Confederación Nacional del Trabajo (CNT, National Confederation of Labor), which claimed a membership of 1.4 million workers. Having defended the Spanish republic in July 1936 against the rebellion of the army generals, they then initiated a full-fledged revolution over large areas of republican-held Spain, championing proletarian internationalism against the nationalist forces of Franco. But even the CNT at times displayed a troublesome nationalism that prominent foreign anarchists in Spain at the time, among them Alexander M. Schapiro and Helmut Rüdiger, found problematic: they sharply condemned the "panegyric of revolutionary nationalism" and warned their comrades against a Spanish chauvinism they claimed had nothing to do with anarchism and proletarian universalism.[32] The CNT, explains Michael Seidman, was furthermore "not exempt from a xenophobia that occasionally degenerated into a rather familiar antisemitism."[33] In January 1937, at the height of the revolution, *Solidaridad Obrera,* a major CNT organ, accused Franco of looking like a Jew and condemned "Jewish plutocrats" and financiers of collaborating with Hitler.[34] More shamefully, in May 1938, a Sephardic Jew named Ben-Krimo asked the CNT to aid persecuted Jews who fled Central Europe, but he received only a cold response from Mariano Vázquez, the secretary of its national committee: Vázquez expressly refused to open Spain's doors "to all the Jews who wish to come here. It is impossible because it would undoubtedly be one of the most counterrevolutionary decisions that we could take." Vázquez's reasoning is telling; he was certain that admission of the Jews "would mean the immediate revival and strengthening of capitalism and the old exploitation."[35] Such occurrences to the contrary, the Spanish anarchists were perhaps the most class-conscious, idealistic, and internationalist proletariat the European left ever produced.

The black banners of anarchism not only symbolize fierce resistance to capitalism, but a fundamental rejection of all nations and all states. In its formative years, a crudely formulated hatred of capitalism fed on the popular images of Jews as "unproductive" and "parasitical" foreign elements. But when anarchism developed into a somewhat systematic set of ideas, antisemitism never became an integral part of its analysis or ideology.[36] For years on, however, an "anarchism of fools" persisted, and when ideologically grounded, it seems mainly influenced by Proudhon. In 1911, seeking to marry the revolutionary ideas of George Sorel with French *integralisme* and antisemitism, syndicalist theorists George Valois and Édouard Berth formed the Cercle Proudhon in France, where the group's influence provided continuous links between revolutionary syndicalism and fascism up to the days of the Vichy regime.[37] Historian Zeev Sternhell also traces how the ideology of the Cercle Proudhon would prefigure key ideological components of Italian fascism.[38] But as noted earlier, after the Dreyfus affair toward the end of the 1890s, these ideas were relegated to the margins of anarchism. Indeed, many of these individuals would soon find a more comfortable home on the political right, and ultimately in rising fascist movements. In general, then, from the turn of the last century, anarchism had developed a relatively consistent antinationalist and antistatist position that condemned antisemitism as a poison for working-class internationalism.

In order to make a proper assessment of anti-Zionism and the anarchist tradition, however, it is not sufficient to look at the dark side of anarchism. We must look also at its brighter side, not the least on the influence of anarchism on Jewish political movements and within Jewish communities. The truth is that there not only was a Spanish anarchism, Russian anarchism, and a French anarchism, but also a very important tradition of Jewish anarchism.

JEWISH ANARCHISM

Jews played a central role in all the revolutionary movements that emerged at the beginning of the twentieth century. In Russia, the Jewish Bund played an influential role, and in all diaspora communities Jews took major part in socialist and anarchist organizations. Furthermore, anarchism played an important role in fostering a Yiddish culture in both Europe and the United States. This did not contradict anarchist ideals of equality and human solidarity. As historian Paul Avrich says, anarchists, "cherishing diversity against standardization and conformity, have always prized the difference among peoples—cultural, linguistic, historical—quite as much as their common bonds."[39] Anarchist universalism and antinationalism was not simply calling for assimilation into the dominant culture, but about creating an alternative working-class culture that would encourage both cultural autonomy and universalism.

When the German anarchist Rudolf Rocker went into exile in 1892, he was introduced to Jewish anarchism in Paris, and although he initially thought the very idea of a specifically Jewish anarchism sounded like a travesty, he was completely taken by Jewish anarchists' egalitarianism, hospitality, and trust in debate.[40] Three years later, Rocker moved on to England, where he quickly began to learn Yiddish to be able to address and take part in the Jewish radical communities in London's East End. During the heyday of Britain's anarchist movement, the Jewish community was considered to be the largest anarchist group in the country.[41] Rocker soon became the editor of *Arbeter Fraynd*, the major Yiddish anarchist newspaper in Britain, and wrote a series of books and pamphlets in Yiddish. He was highly esteemed in the Jewish community and, to quote an East End Jew, he was "their rabbi."[42] The anarchist influence on early Jewish radicalism was considerable, but this exchange of ideas went both ways: Jewish influences on anarchism were not in any way less significant, because of the many Jewish luminaries of the international anarchist movement, such as Emma Goldman, Alexander Berkman, Bernard Lazare, Voline, and Gustav Landauer.[43]

Gustav Landauer, a towering figure in German anarchism, was to carry this legacy to Israel, most notably through Martin Buber, who was not only a personal friend of Landauer but the editor who brought his works to international attention.[44] Anarchism also shaped the theological politics of prominent Kabbalist Gershom Scholem.[45] Other pioneers, such as A. D. Gordon, also gave a distinct anarchist coloring to Hapoel Hatzair and the early kibbutzim.[46] It is commonly asserted that anarchism was a major political contender only in Spain and the Ukraine, and only for a short time, but an argument can be made that early Jewish settlements in Palestine were a vibrant example of antistate socialism.[47] James Horrox, for one, has brought new attention to the influence of anarchism in the Kibbutz movement, but even general accounts of the Kibbutzim convey the distinct libertarian character of their collectivism.[48] To illustrate how significant anarchist ideas were for early Zionism, Horrox refers to a fascinating correspondence between Nachum Goldman—then the leader of the German socialist Zionist organization and later president of the World Zionist Organization—and Landauer. Goldman asked Landauer for advice on how to implement exactly the kind of "decentralized community system" that Landauer had advocated, particularly in relation to the integration of industry and larger federalist structures.[49] The points Goldman raises in his correspondence reflect how closely their plans for the kibbutzim related to Landauer's future anarchist order. However, in May 1919, before Landauer could address these issues in full, he was seized by a mob of soldiers for his involvement in the Bavarian Socialist Republic and beaten to death. But his ideas, as well as those of Peter Kropotkin, were to shape early kibbutzim's social, economic, and ethical aspirations and practices in the 1920s and 1930s.[50]

According to Avrahm Yassour, during the first decades of its existence, Hashomer Hatzair, a network of *kvutsa* and kibbutzim, "dreamt of creating a state that was not a state, but rather a large confederation of communes."[51] To quote from the memoirs of Scholem: "The social and moral perception of anarchists like Tolstoy and Landauer was of inestimable importance in the building of new life in *Eretz Israel*."[52] As Meir Yaari, one of the early leaders the organization, stated in 1940, the "Hashomer Hatzair road to the Kibbutz was anarchistic."[53]

This was not lost on the anarchist movement. A 1962 article in the British anarchist journal *Freedom* stated that the Kibbutz "is one of the best examples of democracy and certainly the nearest thing to practicing anarchism that exists." James Horrox reminds us that anarchism strives to go beyond theory and begin "to build the elements of the new society in the present." He concludes his study with the observation that "the Kibbutz movement and the various forms of autonomous and quasi-autonomous communal organization that existed throughout pre–1948 Palestine represent probably the single most exemplary historical instance of such constructive activism in action."[54]

ANARCHISM, ZIONISM, AND ISRAEL

But what is anarchism's relationship to Zionism and the establishment of Israel? In general, anarchists were highly positive toward Zionist settlements in Palestine, though with some modifications. Landauer, and many other Jewish anarchists, were sympathetic to the settlements, and to the project of establishing a new Jewish culture in the land of Palestine, but skeptical about "political Zionism," the attempts to forge a new Jewish state.[55] They were more interested in the Zionist project as the creation of utopian social alternatives and a new society, untainted by traditions of state, nationalism, or capitalism. This was a notion that Martin Buber shared—despite his recognition of the need for a state, preferably as a "community of its communities"—and he pressed for a cultural Zionism, for the need to foster a visionary collectivism, and for a federalist relationship to the Jews' Arab neighbors.[56] This led many early Zionists to reject nationalism and aspirations to create a distinct Jewish state; they were probably more comfortable with Balfour's opaquely worded declaration of support for "the establishment in Palestine of a national home for the Jewish people." It is also true that anarchists like Emma Goldman were critical of nationalism and aspirations for state building, but not of Jewish settlements, working the land, and developing a distinct Jewish culture. She admitted opposing "Zionism as the dream of capitalist Jewry of the world for a Jewish state with all its trimmings, such as government, laws, police, militarism and the rest."[57] She did not want a Jewish state machinery. This was a commitment widely shared by Zionist settlers during the second and third aliyah, they certainly did not want to impose themselves as a new ruling class in Palestine; in fact that is precisely why the early *kvutsa* and kibbutzim took the radical egalitarian form they did. The land, they believed, should belong to those who tilled it, and only a radical egalitarianism could ensure the building of a new social order among the Jewish settlers.[58] In A. D. Gordon's view, "emigration to Palestine without radically revolutionizing Jewish social structures is nothing else than a transference of Exile to the land of Israel."[59]

Furthermore, criticisms of Zionism were not in any way limited to a principled anarchist antinationalism. Before the Second World War, the Bundists of Poland and Russia forcefully opposed political Zionism—they saw it as a form of "escapism" from the real challenge, namely to achieve certain degrees of territorial and cultural autonomy within other nation states. Zionism was also opposed by most European social democrats, who preferred assimilation into socialist parties and cultures.[60]

But the Jewish settlements could not mature in peace. "The doctrine of proletarian internationalism clashed with the cruel facts of life," Walter Laqueur points out, "as the young generation became aware of the vital importance of defense for which they ideologically had been quite unprepared."[61] Not only were their settlements attacked in 1929 and again in 1936–1939, but the onslaught of Hitler's armies and their annihilation of European Jewry meant that the settlements in Palestine had to consolidate themselves to be able to guarantee Jewish survival and security.[62]

After the experience of European Nazism and the Holocaust, many radicals accepted the establishment of Israel as a necessary historical fact, and erstwhile political differences cooled down, in comparison to the heated interwar debates. Jews were traumatized, as Colin Schindler asserts, both by the "inability of the civilized world to save them" as well as by the fact that "the international proletariat did not rise up against their masters."[63] This recognition created an existential gap that, in his view, essentially "divided the Jewish Left from the European Left."[64] This rift also haunted the anarchists, who faced yet another existential crisis. After the crushing of Spanish anarcho-syndicalism in the late 1930s, anarchists in Europe—who never believed in bourgeois republics, social democracy, Hitler, or Stalin—no longer had any viable social alternatives to point to. Mark Mratchny, the editor of *Fraye Arbeter Schtime* during the 1930s, expressed the defeat of Spain as a crushing disappointment. After that, he "felt like a rabbi in an empty synagogue."[65] Furthermore, it was clear that radical hopes for combating antisemitism without a new state formation had failed. Not only were anarchism itself and its constructive social solutions historically defeated, but assimilation policy in central Europe had obviously and disastrously failed, and so too had Bundist and socialist demands for cultural autonomy within Eastern European nations. As Colin Schindler points out, "The Allies may have won the war, but the Jews certainly lost it."[66] Confronted with the Shoah, Jewish survivors and exiles of all persuasions massively shifted toward supporting the establishment of a Jewish state.

There were anarchists who spoke up about the just cause of Israel's establishment and its just war of independence, but the discussions within the anarchist movement were heated and understandably painful.[67] For the most part, anarchists did not actively support Israel. But, as Mina Graur points out, despite the fact that journals like *Fraye Arbeter Schtime* continued to publish articles that on theoretical grounds challenged the existence of a Jewish state, "the State of Israel was accepted to be a historically necessary solution to the Jewish Question."[68] There were anarchists and veterans from the Spanish Civil War who left to fight for and live in Israel, but in general, the dwindling number of anarchists didn't have to come out publicly in support of a Jewish state. Neither did they have to play a tactical game in the emerging cold war configuration that shaped the political far left after the Second World War. And, unlike Maoists and Trotskyists, anarchists did not automatically justify or support national liberation struggles against "Western imperialism." Anarchists may not have seen any anarchist content in the establishment of the Israeli *state*—however sympathetic they were to the kibbutzim and the labor Zionism—but they responded to the establishment of Israel with what I interpret to be a respectful silence. Antistate socialism did not play a defining role in shaping the development of anti-Zionism in the West: We must remember that from 1948 and until very recently, all resistance to Israel and to Zionism was based on the claims that it was "an unnatural state," a colonizer of Arab land, and an imperialist bridgehead in the Middle East. Those who advanced anti-Zionism, it must be noted, *did not* object to either nationalism or state-formation; their problem was *Jewish* nationalism and the *Israeli* state.

Today, most anarchists have adopted an anti-Zionist stance. How was this at all possible? When did this happen? The perspectives of the anarchist movement did not change in 1948, when populations in Arab states cemented their antipathies toward "the Jewish entity" in their midst. Neither did they change in 1967, after the Six-Day War, when anti-Zionism came to predominate in the Maoist, Trotskyist, and Stalinist left. Neither did it change in 1982, after the Lebanon War, which, for the first time after the Second World War, saw major shifts in public opinion in western European countries, and was also the moment when many social democrats started questioning their support for Israel. Anarchists only started publicly shifting their opinions after 1987, when the First Intifada broke out in the West Bank and Gaza. Why? Because for the first time, it was not a war of Arab nations against the Israeli nation, but a popular revolt that pitted a civilian population against a military apparatus. This First Intifada was a popular insurrection "of the stones," to use the anarchist Alfredo M. Bonanno's description.[69] Since the student movements of the 1960s, the quintessential image of the anarchist rebel is the lone youth with a stone in his hand, ready to throw it at police forces. Now the twisted image of David and Goliath was available to new generations of activists: stone-throwing youths versus the Merkava.

To be sure, anarchism did play a role in the New Left, but I do not think that it played any role in *shaping* anti-imperialist theories that would nurture anti-Zionism.[70] Gradually, anarchists would—without much theorizing or historical analysis—adopt the view that Israel was a particularly illegitimate or unnatural state. By now, anarchists readily accept claims that Israel is fundamentally racist, colonialist, imperialist, capitalist, and militarist, and that it is an apartheid state. Unfortunately, these claims are all too common; not only are they held by anarchists but they constitute integral elements of the common myths and rituals shared by the left in our time.

But something new has happened. Previously, anarchists followed the anti-imperialist analyses of the Stalinist and Maoist left; recently, they developed their own peculiar brand of anti-Zionism, a process spearheaded by Israeli and Jewish activists. The International Solidarity Movement—this is the one Rachel Corrie and Tom Hurndall belonged to—is a Palestinian-led, nonviolent and consensus-based network that gained much attention in the early 2000s.[71] Even more interesting is the Israeli group called Anarchists Against the Wall. They aim to do their part in breaking down the fences and borders and ultimately all nation-states, and they do so by engaging in nonviolent protests on the West Bank and within Israel.[72]

The actions of these groups resonate with broad sectors among progressive movements in Europe and in the United States. Of course, they display a naïveté that would be unthinkable for the anarchists who fought the White and the Red Armies in Russia and the Ukraine, and who fought fascists in the streets of London and Vienna, in Asturias and Barcelona. But their actions today have a broad appeal to leftists who were not beguiled by the uncritical anti-imperialist support for national liberation struggles, for reactionary religious movements, and for open antisemitism. They speak to activists who are genuinely against nation-states, borders, and social privileges.

How important are groups like Anarchists Against the Wall? In numbers and activities, they are not at all significant. But as a *moral* factor, and as an example of "righteous Jews" who defy their national government to simply "do the right thing"—which is to protest the Israeli army and to socialize with Palestinians— they are in a position to delegitimize the state of Israel in a way that it seems to me that New Left anti-imperialism no longer can. Their position can be seen as comparable to that of Matzpen in the 1960s. In Israel, Matzpen was a minuscule group of Trotsky- ists who defined their views simply as "anticapitalist and anti- Zionist." They had no influence in Israeli society, but several of their leaders, such as Akiva Orr, emigrated to Europe, and their views became hugely popular among the New Left.[73] Here were Israelis who confirmed all the prejudices and "anti-imperialist" analyses espoused by the New Left. Daniel Cohn-Bendit, the famous German student leader, said, "Matzpen is the honor of Israel."[74]

It seems to me that the same is about to happen with new Israeli anarchist groups. I must emphasize the immensity of the ideo- logical shift that we are witnessing: a series of new coalitions like Ship to Gaza; the Israeli Apartheid Week; the Boycotts, Divest- ment and Sanctions campaigns; and the like understand the need for broad public appeal. These initiatives cannot, I believe, pres- ent their views in the "classical" anti-Zionist garb that appealed to the Stalinists, Maoists, and Trotskyists of the New Left in the 1960s and 1970s. To be sure, the same ideological framework still undergirds much of today's anti-Zionist activism, but when this is revealed it damages the public image and the potential for broad mobilizations. Ironically then, although anarchism does not have a broad appeal in Europe today, a new quasi-anarchistic rhetoric does: one that calls for joint actions and grassroots solidarity, and that is clearly skeptical or negative to all states, all borders, all kinds of nationalisms and racism, as well as every other form of oppression and violence. Groups like Anarchists Against the Wall are very useful to sustain the image of a humanitarian and progressive anti-Zionism. Their anarchist perspectives inform an anti-Zionism that is unlike any anti-Zionism we have encountered earlier. It is therefore difficult to counter anarchists' actions by using the same arguments that discredit other forms of anti-Zionist anti-imperialism or pro-Palestinian nationalism.

JEWS AGAINST GHETTOS

We should not, however, write off Anarchists Against the Wall as being just a stratagem for winning over public opinion. Uri Gordon, the most prominent representative of this organization, considers the experiences of Anarchists Against the Wall as a prime form of new anti-authoritarian politics.[75] So, what is their theory and practice?

The writings of AATW shed no light: "For better or worse, AATW is a pragmatic action initiative with no ideological platform, no manifesto, and no program for the future of the region."[76] Its criticisms are clear enough: it is against "ethnic cleansing" and "apartheid," and call for the removal of "national partitions" and, above all, resistance to "the military forces that cause mutual destruction and continuous slaughter." So far, there is nothing unique about this "analysis," it fits in well with the anti-Israeli perspectives that unite Maoists and anarchists with Christians and Islamists in anti-Israeli protests all over the world. AATW does, however, claim to be against all states, nations, and borders, as are other anarchists. But then again, this amounts to little, as Anarchists Against the Wall is not concerned with ideology: "Our primary moral duty is not to maintain ideological purity but rather to stand with Palestinians in their resistance to oppression," its activists emphasize.[77]

AATW maintains that they, the Israeli anarchists, "are not equal partners but rather occupiers who join the occupied in their struggle."[78] The Palestinian struggle, they insist, is entirely legitimate with or without their participation. But they do have two principles: "The first principle is that although the struggle is joint, Palestinians are affected more by the decisions taken within it, and therefore the ones who should make the important decisions. Second, Israelis have a special responsibility to respect Palestinian self-determination, including respecting social customs and keeping out of internal Palestinian politics."[79]

"When I encounter Palestinian nationalism or chauvinism," says AATW activist Roy Wagner, "it's easy for me to set it aside by telling myself that my solidarity is with their place as victims of occupation, and that I, an occupier, a participant in the violence that enables much of this nationalism and chauvinism, can't cast judgment."[80] Wagner's place is simply to express solidarity with the Palestinians who must "struggle on their terms." This, he believes, is how they can build the scaffolding for a better life "beyond the occupation." Queer activist Yossi Bartal agrees: "The struggle to change and challenge Palestinian culture with its patriarchal, militarist, and homophobic elements is not our task but instead that of our Palestinian comrades, to whom we must offer our solidarity." According to Bartal, this can be done "first and foremost by lifting the weight of the occupation from their shoulders, and by fighting the same elements in our own society. Liberation is always a process and it can evolve and intensify only by removing the biggest obstacle that stands in its way."[81] Kobi Snitz concludes that "the joint struggle faces only one main problem: The Israeli state."[82] By engaging—as far as I can understand, that means to be merely present—in joint meetings and demonstrations, anarchist activists claim to be "deconstructing the racist foundations of the conflict."[83] It is precisely this willingness to deploy "the body as an instrument of resistance" that makes Judith Butler so impressed "with Anarchists Against the Wall and other actions against the wall at Bi'lin which continue to divert the military and have solicited great support from global networks."[84] The anarchism that interests Butler "has to do with contesting the 'legal' dimensions of state power, and posing disturbing challenges about state legitimacy." The point, she explains, "is not to achieve anarchism as a state or as a final form for the political organization of society." Its value lies simply in its "disorganizing effect."[85] The anarchists "are there in solidarity, pure and simple. We are there supporting the antioccupation movement, we do not set the agenda."[86]

But what does Anarchists Against the Wall mean by "the occupation"? It certainly "doesn't stop at the checkpoint," says Bartal: "It is all around us, and thus there is no 'here' and 'there.' Israel is the occupation."[87]

Activists from Anarchists Against the Wall are present in meetings, demonstrations, and media, to build trust and to support Palestinian self-determination. As the activist Ilan Shalit puts it, "Success has been so great that even the leaders of Hamas in the West Bank supported our participating in the joint struggle with the local popular committees of the villages."[88] If they have "no ideological platform, no manifesto, and no program for the future of the region," and if they only commit themselves to "show solidarity with Palestinians," and pledge to respect all "social customs" and "keeping out of internal Palestinian politics," why should Hamas care if these anti-Zionists are "Jewish anarchist atheists"? Hamas, on the other hand, certainly do have a Charter and a plan for the future of the region.

When the group was initiated, they wanted a provocative name and ended up with Anarchists Against the Wall. We "don't all consider ourselves as anarchists, but all agree on an anarchist way of working," says Uri Ayalon.[89] Since ideology is not important to them, they also sometimes call themselves Jews Against Ghettos.[90] Provocative? Indeed. But then again, they agree with the anarchist Bonanno, who claimed the situation in the occupied territories is "like seeing an exact replica of the Warsaw ghetto."[91]

In 2013, Anarchists Against the Wall presented themselves to an English audience, and they honored Bonanno by asking him to write the foreword to the group's book. He immediately urged activists to take the next step: an "attack on the concrete targets that establish, nurture, guarantee, justify, and finance the management of such a monstrosity as the wall in question." Is he thinking of huge popular actions, bringing people into the streets, fraternizing between Jews and Palestinians? He answers: "Yes, *possibly* that too, but *also something else besides*" (emphasis added).[92] He insists "we have to attack. Everything else is just a form of support, essential but not of vital importance."[93]

So, who is Alfredo M. Bonanno? He is a veteran Italian iconoclast who has been the main ideologue of "insurrectionalism," a marginal but highly romanticized trend within contemporary anarchism. Coming from the violent class struggle in 1960s Italy, he calls for armed confrontation, propaganda of the deed, and immediate liberation. In his own book, *Armed Joy*, Bonanno encourages wanton murders of policemen, judges, bosses, and the wealthy. The Italian Supreme Court ordered his book retracted from libraries and destroyed, and he was incarcerated for eighteen months.[94] He has also been convicted several times for armed robberies in Italy and Greece. This is all justified according to his anarchist convictions, championing illegalism and armed insurrection.

In other writings, Bonanno offers his perspective on Arab-Israeli conflict. As far as Bonanno is concerned, the situation is simple: "There is a State (Israel) aggressive and militarist like many others but which wants to kill a whole people (the Palestinian one)."[95] The Israelis, through Zionism and through the international lobbies, "accepted their role as gendarme of the western project of world dominion," Bonanno says, echoing the crude anti-imperialist analyses of the Maoist left: this "lead[s] to an *extremism hitherto unequalled* in the *whole* of political-religious history" (emphasis added).⁹⁶ It is this extremism, he claims, that "rekindled anti-Semitism at world level." During the first Intifada, when a bookstore in Turin was attacked by Molotov cocktails by a renegade anarchist group, the anarchist groups of the city came out in defense of the bookstore and protested such vile acts of "anti-Semitism and intolerance of which anarchists have always fought." Bonanno ridiculed these statements in support of a pro-Israeli bookstore and defended the arsonists: "We know perfectly well that the struggle against the excessive power of Israel and its project to exterminate the Palestinian people" not only takes place "in that far off land." Fascists dominate the Israeli state, he claimed, and further: "Whoever defends the interests of the Israeli State at the present time should be attacked."⁹⁷

Sarah Assouline from AATW agrees that "Israeli fascism is a runaway train," and that Israeli citizens are the ones to blame. They "are the ones who do not revolt against racism, apartheid, and ethnic cleansing. In fact, all these are no more than a crystallization of Israeli public opinion." Israeli children are brainwashed from birth, Assouline explains, "to believe that Israel must be a Jewish State, Palestinians are the enemy, and military service is a sacred duty."⁹⁸

Since the Jews suffered the Nazi extermination project, then "by definition they deserve our sympathy," Bonanno claims, although "the mental rigidity of the Jews" has often "put our sympathies to the test." They are driven by an ideology of pessimism derived "from the millenarian isolation of the Jews and the persecution they have suffered," which "makes the politics of the Israeli State extremist and irresponsible, and makes the Israeli State itself even more dangerous than any other." But this claim is not antisemitism, he assures us, since it "is not a question of the Jews but of the Israeli State and, naturally, those of its subjects who are lending themselves to the extermination of the Palestinian people that is taking place."⁹⁹

Bonanno is adamantly clear when he states "that the enemy number one, the main obstacle to overcome, is today the State of Israel." When confronted by the brutal methods with which Palestinians were killing alleged collaborators, even by hacking them to pieces with axes, Bonanno admits that these were "drastic measures, to be sure, but which give an idea of what these people are suffering. When you get to certain levels, even feelings of pity and humanity begin to disappear."[100]

This, however, is not what Anarchists Against the Wall is about. "Now the Israeli and international anarchists take only non-violent action in Palestine," Uri Gordon emphasizes; at the same time, however, both the ISM and AATW "recognize the legitimacy of Palestinian armed resistance."[101] For Gordon, this "endorsement of a 'diversity of tactics' places anarchists in a more comfortable position in the landscape of struggle in Israel/Palestine than it would strict pacifists." But most important, perhaps, is that "Non-violence has the further goal of giving visibility to the non-violent aspects of Palestinian struggle, with which Western audiences can more easily identify."[102]

Still, the ideal solution for anarchists "would be the generalized insurrection." By that Bonanno means "an intifada starting from the Israeli people that is capable of destroying the institutions that govern them and of proposing peace based on collaboration and mutual respect to the Palestinian people directly, without intermediaries." But for the time being, he adds, "this perspective is only a dream. We must prepare for the worst."[103]

Bonanno later presents Israelis with an ultimatum: "Either the theocentric Israeli State disappears, giving life to another federalist kind of formation that is open to the possibility of a communitarian cohabitation with the Arab Palestinians and eventually with other peoples," he warns, or else "the Jews will be moving towards a catastrophe once again. But perhaps the shoah is precisely what they are waiting for, according to the forecasts of their profits [sic]. How can you disavow them?"[104]

THE STRUGGLE AGAINST ANTI-ZIONISM TODAY

The Jewish anarchists of old are gone. So too are the anarchist mass movements that confronted fascism in Spain, challenged the Bolsheviks in Russia, and helped create the first kibbutzim. The Old Left they belonged to was unable to stem the rise of Nazism, and they were overwhelmed by the horrors of the Second World War and the near-complete annihilation of the European Jews. When the Nazis were finally defeated in 1945, the international anarchist movement was spiritually broken.

Today, our world again faces a widespread upsurge of antisemitism. But an even more sinister trend is the diffusion and development of anti-Zionism, which I fear has far more explosive potential for cultivating a culture of indifference to the fate of Israel and the Jews today.[105] Unlike classical antisemitism, present anti-Zionism is predominantly a leftist phenomenon. Left-wing political tendencies have shaped the main tenets of today's anti-Zionist ideology—its imagery, prejudices, and hatred—although this ideology certainly cannot be seen as disconnected from the broader trajectories of antisemitism.[106] From the 1960s onward, Maoist anti-imperialism and Stalinist Cold War calculations did enormous damage in poisoning the aspirations of the New Left and of public discourse around Israel. I fear anarchism can play an even more destructive role delegitimizing Israel in the decades to come.

Therefore, to counter today's anti-Jewish politics, we need to decipher anti-Zionism—*as anti-Zionism,* not simply as a form of antisemitism—and understand its peculiarities and various mutations, of which various contemporary anarchist interpretations only form one part. Here it is crucial to acknowledge that anti-Zionism is not merely prejudice or hatred but a set of ideas and aspirations; it has, to use Saul Friedländer's term, a "redemptive dimension."[107] This, I believe, is crucial precisely because the greatest dangers of antisemitism and anti-Zionism lie in their promises of liberation, not in how they embody legacies of hatred and prejudice.

Such an inquiry would not interest Bonanno. He believes that, in the conflict between Israelis and Palestinians, "the only reality we can turn our attention to and support is that of hundreds of young people who are resisting the Israeli tanks that occupy their land by throwing stones." That this is a crude and simplistic image does not trouble Bonanno. He insists that there is "a time when Minerva's bird must go to sleep, and that is the time for action and the destruction of the enemy."[108]

Fortunately, however, the owl of Minerva is still awake, and can help orient us in the dusk. The last century showed how easily pandering to passions for unbridled activism and violence could be translated into destruction and total war: Sorel brought Bakunin uncomfortably close to Ernst Jünger. We also know that when political parties say that they are out to exterminate the Jews, or annihilate "the Zionist entity," they probably mean it. Today, we know that even Auschwitz is possible. As Imre Kertész succinctly pointed out, until Auschwitz occurred, it was not even a possibility. But it did happen, so now it is. "Since Auschwitz, nothing has happened that makes a new Auschwitz impossible," Kertész explains. "On the contrary. Because Auschwitz in fact occurred, it has now been established in our imaginations as a firm possibility. What we are able to imagine, especially because it once was, can be again."[109]

The anarchist tradition has a proud history of combatting antisemitism, but, ultimately, it failed to protect the Jews, as did socialist internationalism and republican assimilation. Those of us who are convinced that capitalism is a bad idea, who aspire for something better than the nation-state, and who still dream of the day the International will be the human race, we bear a special responsibility. We must revisit the historical struggles that socialists and anarchists waged against antisemitism and learn from their failures as well as from their successes. Today we see new forms of anti-Zionism develop in the guise of antistatism and antinationalism, much like earlier forms of antisemitism were developed in the guise of anticlericalism and anticapitalism. If we fail to decipher and confront anti-Zionism today—less than a century after Auschwitz—we will betray not only the victims of the Shoah, but the countless antifascists who gave their all to defend these ideals.

NOTES

1. See, for example, Noam Chomsky, *Chomsky on Anarchism,* ed. Barry Pateman (Oakland, Calif.: AK Press, 2005).

2. Finkelstein comes from a Maoist background but now claims that "No, I do not support a two-state solution. I don't support states. I remain an old-fashioned communist. I see no value whatsoever in states. If the borders were to disappear between every state in the world, I think it would be a much happier place." Finkelstein quoted in Jelle Bruinsma, "Norman Finkelstein in the Netherlands," *Counterpunch* (January 5–7, 2008).

3. Judith Butler quoted in Jamie Heckert, "On Anarchism: Interview with Judith Butler," in *Anarchism and Sexuality: Ethics, Relationships, and Power,* ed. Jamie Heckert and Richard Cleminson, 93–99 (New York: Routledge, 2011).

4. There are legitimate claims to denouncing antisemitism as "the longest hatred," as Robert S. Wistrich does: there certainly were widespread anti-Jewish and anti-Judaic sentiments long before antisemitism emerged as a distinctly modern doctrines in Germany, France, and Austria, particularly in its racist forms from the 1870s onward.

5. To be sure, there are a range of crucial distinctions within this broad anarchist tradition—notably between individualism and collectivism, between primitivism and syndicalism, and between pacifism and insurrectionalism, to just name a few. Several of these distinctions are important for how we should understand the relationship between anti-Zionism and antistate politics. This chapter, however, focuses not on the actual content of "anarchist politics" but on how anarchist arguments are used to delegitimize Israel and call for its dissolution or destruction.

6. Peter Marshall, *Demanding the Impossible: A History of Anarchism* (London: Fontana Press, 1992), 255, 257.

7. "Our race for too long has been subject to the influence of Greeks, Romans, Barbarians, Jews and Englishmen." Proudhon quoted in ibid, 255.

8. The full original quotation follows:

> Juifs. Faire un article contre cette race qui envenime tout, en se fourrant partout, sans jamais se fondre avec aucun peuple. Demander son expulsion de France, à l'exception des individus mariés avec des Françaises; abolir les synagogues, ne les admettre à aucun emploi, poursuivre enfin l'abolition de ce culte. Ce n'est pas pour rien que les chrétiens les ont appelés déicides. Le juif est l'ennemi du genre humain. Il faut renvoyer cette race en Asie, ou l'exterminer. H. Heine, A. Weil, et autres ne sont que des espions secrets; Rothschild, Crémieux, Marx, Fould, êtres méchants, bilieux, envieux, âcres, etc. etc. qui nous haïssent. . . . Par le fer, ou par la fusion, ou par l'expulsion, il faut que le juif disparaisse. . . . Toléres les viellards qui n'engendrent plus.

Pierre-Joseph Proudhon, Carnets de Proudhon, ed. Marcel Rivière (Paris: Pierre Haubtmann, 1961), 2:337–338.

9. "Ce que les peuples du Moyen Âge haïssaient d'instinct, je le hais avec réflexion, et irrévocablement." Proudhon, Carnets de Proudhon, 338.

10. Jürgen Mümken and Siegbert Wolf, eds., *"Antisemit, das geht nicht unter Menschen." Anarchistische Positionen zu Antisemitismus, Zionismus und Israel* (Hessen: Verlag Edition AV, 2013), 1:10. Tolstoy's "anarchism," furthermore, is more linked to medieval millenarianism than to anarchism as a modern political ideology.

11. The Bakunin passages containing these remarks are available in Michael Bakunin, "Persönliche Beziehungen zu Marx (Ende 1871)—Auszug," in Mümken and Wolf, *Anarchistische Positionen zu Antisemitismus, Zionismus und Israel,* 80–84.

12. Bakunin quoted in Francis Wheen, *Karl Marx* (London: Fourth Estate, 2000), 340.

13. Bakunin quoted in Steve Cohen, *That's Funny, You Don't Look Anti-Semitic: An Anti-Racist Analysis of Left Anti-Semitism* (Leeds: Beyond the Pale, 1984), 101.

14. Avrahm Yarmolinsky, *Road to Revolution: A Century of Russian Radicalism* (New York: Collier Books, 1962), 296.

15. Ibid., 294–298.

16. Ibid., 295, 297.

17. Ibid., 296. "You have already begun to rise against the Jews," said a proclamation of *Narodnaya Volya:* "That is fine. For soon a revolt will start all over Russia against the Czar, the landowners and the Jews." Ibid.

18. Robert S. Wistrich, *Between Redemption and Perdition: Modern Anti-semitism and Jewish Identity* (London: Routledge, 1990), 134.

19. Ibid., 135, 139–140; and Jean Maitron, *Le mouvement anarchiste en France* (Paris: Gallimard, 1975), 1:331–342.

20. Albert S. Lindemann, *The Jew Accused: Three Antisemitic Affairs (Dreyfus, Beilis, Frank), 1894–1915* (Cambridge: Cambridge University Press, 1991), 113–120.

21. Lindemann, however, does not consider the acquittal of Dreyfus to be a victory over antisemitism, only over the antisemites. Ibid., 124–128. Furthermore, the left never became immune to antisemitism, and the decades that followed would see antisemitism recurrently resurface, even within anarchist and syndicalist movements. See also Edmund Silberner, "Anti-Jewish Trends in French Revolutionary Syndicalism," *Jewish Social Studies* 15, no. 3/4 (July–October 1953): 195–202.

22. See, for example, G. D. H. Cole, *The History of Socialist Thought*, vol. 2 (London: Macmillan, 1954); and Milorad M. Drachkovitch, ed., *The Revolutionary Internationals, 1864–1943* (Stanford, Calif.: Stanford University Press, 1966), 3–92.

23. Paul Avrich, *The Russian Anarchists* (New York: W. W. Norton, 1978).

24. Isaiah Berlin, introduction to Franco Venturi, *Roots of Revolution: A History of the Populist and Socialist Movements in 19th Century Russia*, rev. ed. (London: Phoenix Press, 2001), xxviii.

25. Léon Poliakov, *The History of Anti-Semitism*, trans. George Klein (Philadelphia: University of Pennsylvania Press, 2003), 4:184.

26. Michael Malet, *Nestor Makhno in the Russian Civil War* (London: Macmillan, 1982), 168–174, 189; Alexandre Skirda, *Nestor Makhno, Anarchy's Cossack: The Struggle for Free Soviets in the Ukraine 1917–1921*, trans. Paul Sharkey (Oakland, Calif.: AK Press, 2004), 336–341. Note that during the heated July days of 1918, the Kerensky government announced that police searches found antisemitic material both among the Bolsheviks in their Kshessenky House and among the anarchists in their Durnovo Villa. Poliakov, *History of Antisemitism*, 178.

27. In English, see Nestor Makhno, *The Struggle against the State and Other Essays*, ed. Alexandre Skirda (Oakland, Calif.: AK Press, 1996), particularly 24–38; see also Piotr Arshinov, *History of the Makhnovist Movement, 1918–1921*, trans. Lorraine Perlman and Fredy Perlman (London: Freedom Press, 1987), 209–219.

28. Avrich, *Russian Anarchists*, 216; Paul Avrich, *Anarchist Portraits* (Princeton, N.J.: Princeton University Press, 1988), 123; Skirda, *Nestor Makhno, Anarchy's Cossack*, 338–339.

29. "My accusations of anti-semitism against Makhno were built entirely on the lies of the Bolsheviks and to the rest of their crimes must be added this great crime of killing his greatness and the purity of this fighter for freedom." Saul Yanovsky, "The Ever-Recurring Lie," Watchman, August 1934; reprinted as appendix in Nestor Makhno, My Visit to the Kremlin (London: Kate Sharpley Library, 1993), 36–37.

30. Marshall, Demanding the Impossible, 253.

31. Alejandro Baer, "Between Old and New Antisemitism: The Image of Jews in Present-Day Spain," in Resurgent Antisemitism: Global Perspectives, ed. Alvin H. Rosenfeld, 96–98 (Bloomington: Indiana University Press, 2013).

32. Federica Montseny, a CNT minister, claimed: "we are the true nationalists. We are a people . . . who lead all nations." Quoted in Michael Seidman, Workers against Work: Labor in Paris and Barcelona During the Popular Fronts (Berkeley: University of California Press, 1991), 98.

33. Seidman, Workers against Work, 336.

34. Ibid.

35. Mariano Vázquez quoted in ibid.

36. Indeed, despite the heinous quotations from Proudhon and Bakunin, which can be neither excused nor tolerated, antisemitism was arguably not an essential part of their body of ideas, and their followers, when aware of their anti-Jewish prejudices at all, could relatively easily excise them from their corpus. It is also worth noting, for example, that Proudhon's vilest antisemitic remarks were expressed in notebooks and personal correspondence, where they remained unpublished until well after his death. Robert Graham claims Proudhon's "truly horrific anti-semitic outburst" formed no part of Proudhon's revolutionary program. Robert Graham, introduction to Pierre-Joseph Proudhon, General Idea of the Revolution in the Nineteenth Century (London: Pluto Press, 1989), xxxvi. Bakunin's biographer Mark Leir claims: "Bakunin's anti-Semitism has been greatly misunderstood. At virtually every talk I've given on Bakunin, I'm asked about it. Where it exists, it is repellent, but it takes up about 5 pages of the thousands of pages he wrote, was written in the heat of his battles with Marx, where Bakunin was slandered viciously, and needs to be understood in the context of the 19th century." Mark Leir, "Bakunin for the 21st Century," interview by Iain McKay, Black Flag 229 (2009): 29. This attitude to situating Proudhon and Bakunin's politics, however, easily underestimates the force of anti-Jewish prejudice, and how they unconsciously shape less extrovert aspects of their ideology. But it remains a fact that some of Proudhon's greatest admirers were the anarchists Peter Kropotkin, Gustav

Landauer, and Rudolf Rocker, none of whom harbored antisemitic prejudices. And for many of the movements that followed them, Bakunin and
Proudhon's ideas were not valued because of their antisemitism.

37. George Sorel is a crucial link in this development, not only for his
ideas on syndicalism, bordering on corporativism, but for his glorification
of the purifying role of violence. Originally a Dreyfusard, Sorel took a radical turn to the right and came to openly embrace antisemitism. "Between
1908 and 1914," Wistrich explains, Sorel "was one of the driving forces of
Cercle Proudhon which attacked democracy as a 'Jewish' invention that
had substituted 'the laws of gold for the laws of blood.'" Robert S. Wistrich,
From Ambivalence to Betrayal: The Left, the Jews, and Israel (Lincoln: University of Nebraska Press, 2013), 200–201.

38. Zeev Sternhell, *Neither Right Nor Left: Fascist Ideology in France,*
trans. David Maisel (Princeton, N.J.: Princeton University Press, 1986).

39. Avrich, *Anarchist Portraits,* 176.

40. William J. Fishman, East End Jewish Radicals 1875–1914 (London:
Duckworth, 1975), 231–232.

41. Marshall, *Demanding the Impossible,* 490.

42. Fishman, East End Jewish Radicals, 229–275.

43. Mina Graur presents two excellent discussions of how anarchists
—and anarchist Jews—struggled with Zionism and Jewish identity politics at the turn of last century. See Mina Graur, "Anarchismus und Zionismus: Die Debatte über den jüdischen Nationalismus," in Mümken and
Wolf, *Anarchistische Positionen zu Antisemitismus, Zionismus und Israel,*
159–176; and Mina Graur, "Anarcho-Nationalism: Anarchist Attitudes
Towards Jewish Nationalism and Zionism," Modern Judaism 14, no. 1
(1994): 1–19.

44. Martin Buber, *Paths in Utopia* (Boston: Beacon Press, 1949), 39.
Marshall excludes Buber from the anarchist tradition proper, since Buber
"argued that the state can in certain instances have a legitimate role." Marshall, *Demanding the Impossible,* 574–575. Buber's book, it should be noted,
was completed in the spring of 1945.

45. Eric Jacobson, *Metaphysics of the Profane: The Political Theology of
Walter Benjamin and Gershom Scholem* (New York: Columbia University
Press, 2003), 52–81.

46. "He was the first significant Zionist thinker whose ideas emerged
through the confrontation with reality in Palestine itself," and "his thought
became the guiding ideology of Hapoel Hatzair" and the Labor Zionist
movement. Shlomo Avineri, *The Making of Modern Zionism: The Intellectual
Origins of the Jewish State* (New York: Basic Books, 1981), 151–152. Other sig-

nificant influences were Josef Trumpeldor and Franz Oppenheimer, and later figures like Chaim Arlosoroff. See James Horrox, *A Living Revolution: Anarchism in the Kibbutz Movement* (Oakland, Calif.: AK Press, 2009), 25–35, 50–53.

47. Horrox, *Living Revolution*, 9.

48. Ibid., and, for example, Daniel Gavron, *The Kibbutz: Awakening from Utopia* (Lanham, Md.: Rowman & Littlefield, 2000).

49. Horrox, *Living Revolution*, 42–43, 133–137.

50. The major sections of the Kibbutz movement were profoundly influenced by anarchist socialism, but not as an official ideology: their leading organs distanced themselves from anarchism in 1924, as its leaders turned toward "Marxism," and Zionism became the unifying ideology. Not until the mid-1960s were their anarchist roots recognized. Both anarchism and Marxism, however, found highly idiosyncratic expressions among the pioneers in the kibbutzim. See Yakoov Oved, "Anarchism in the Kibbutz Movement," *Kibbutz Trends* 38 (summer 2000). Anarchism as a distinct ideological current existed in Israel from the 1960s to the 1980s but has no major social impact: anarchists were largely grouped around the Yiddish anarchist circle that published the periodical *Problemen*. See, for example, Sam Dolgoff, *Fragments: A Memoir* (London: Refract, 1986), 152–159.

51. From Avrahm Yassour, "Introduction: Chapters in the History of the Kvutsa and Kibbutz," in *The History of the Kibbutz: A Selection of Sources, 1905–1929*, ed. Avrahm Yassour (Merhavia, 1995), 21. Quoted in Horrox, *Living Revolution*, 45.

52. Gershom Scholem quoted in Horrox, *Living Revolution*, 45.

53. Meir Yaari quoted in Oved, "Anarchism in the Kibbutz Movement."

54. Horrox, *Living Revolution*, 128, 9.

55. Graur, "Anarchismus und Zionismus," and "Anarcho-Nationalism"; and Sylvain Bouloque, "Les Paradoxes des anarchistes face au sionisme et à la naissance de l'État d'Israël," Archives juives 36, no. 1 (2003): 100–108.

56. Marshall, *Demanding the Impossible*, 574–575. For a treatment of Buber's position, see Siegbert Wolf, "Martin Bubers Konzeption der Binationalität," in Mümken and Wolf, *Anarchistische Positionen zu Antisemitismus, Zionismus und Israel*, 208–225.

57. Emma Goldman, "On Zionism," letter to the editor, 26 August 1938, *Spain and the World*, reprinted in *Dysophia* 3 (April 2012): 86.

58. Horrox, *Living Revolution*, particularly 11–58.

59. Gordon viewed "the gradual transformation of erstwhile pioneers into landowners and merchants dependent upon the labor of others" with "utter abhorrence." Avineri, *Making of Modern Zionism*, 153.

60. Walter Laqueur, *A History of Zionism: From the French Revolution to the State of Israel* (New York: Schocken Books, 2003), 270–337. For an excellent account of the troubled relationship the more mainstream European left had with Zionism, see Colin Schindler, *Israel and the European Left: Between Solidarity and Delegitimization* (London: Continuum, 2012), and Wistrich, *From Ambivalence to Betrayal*.

61. Laqueur, *History of Zionism*, 331.

62. Sternhell further problematizes how the various ideologies currents intermingled and were deployed in the years prior to 1948, providing an important corrective to my presentation here. Zeev Sternhell, The Founding Myths of Israel: Nationalism, Socialism, and the Making of the Jewish State, trans. David Maisel (Princeton, N.J.: Princeton University Press, 1998), particularly 74–133.

63. "Jews had fought in all the Allied armies as well as in the resistance in occupied Europe. Communist, Bundist and Zionist Jews had died together in the Warsaw Ghetto Uprising in 1943. In their desire to crush Nazism and end this terrible war, neither Capitalist nor Communist had seriously deflected the ultimate fate of the Jews." Schindler, *Israel and the European Left*, 123.

64. Schindler, *Israel and the European Left*, 120–137.

65. Mark Mratchny quoted in Avrich, *Anarchist Portraits*, 197.

66. Schindler, *Israel and the European Left*, 123.

67. Bouloque, "Les Paradoxes des anarchistes."

68. Graur, "Anarchismus und Zionismus," 176.

69. Alfredo M. Bonanno, *Palestine, Mon Amour* (London: Elephant Editions, 2003), 5.

70. Some, however, went to extreme lengths in their anti-Zionism. In Germany, an anarcho-communist group called Black Rats even justified the November 1969 bombing of a community center where the Jewish Congregation in West Berlin was gathered to commemorate Kristallnacht. See Robert S. Wistrich, *Hitler's Apocalypse: Jews and the Nazi Legacy* (New York: St. Martin's Press, 1985), 229–230. Although, overwhelmingly, the anti-Zionism of the New Left was developed and expounded primarily by Marxist-Leninists of groups like the Rote Arme Fraktion, there were also notorious antisemites among the student radicals, such as the anarchist Dieter Kunzelmann, who tried to "lead parts of the West German Left into a partisan struggle against the Jews in Germany." Interview with Tilman Fichter by Philip Gessler and Stefan Reinecke, "Wir haben das nicht ernst genommen," *Taz*, 25 October 2005. See also Hans Kundani, *Utopia or Auschwitz: Germany's 1968 Generation and the Holocaust* (London: Hurst, 2009).

71. U.S. activist Rachel Corrie was crushed to death by an Israeli bull-dozer during protests on 16 March 2003, and British activist Tom Hurndall was shot to death by an Israeli sniper 13 January 2004. Corrie and Hurndall remain important symbols for the nonviolent popular struggle that the ISM advocated.

72. See Uri Gordon and Ohal Grietzer, eds., *Anarchists Against the Wall: Direct Action and Solidarity with the Palestinian Popular Struggle* (Oakland, Calif.: AK Press and IAS, 2013).

73. In 1968, after he had left Israel, Orr turned to libertarian socialism and joined the London Solidarity group. Another member of Matzpen was Shlomo Sand, whose *The Invention of the Jewish People* (London: Verso, 2009) became an international bestseller.

74. Daniel Cohn-Bendit in Eran Torbiner's movie, *Matzpen: Anti-Zionist Israelis* (2003). It is worth noting that activists in Anarchists Against the Wall make this link to Matzpen explicit: See Uri Ayalon, "Means of Communication," in Gordon and Grietzer, *Anarchists Against the Wall,* 99–105.

75. Uri Gordon, *Anarchy Alive! Anti-Authoritarian Politics from Theory to Practice* (London: Pluto Press, 2008), particularly 139–164.

76. Uri Gordon and Ohal Grietzer, introduction, in Gordon and Grietzer, *Anarchists Against the Wall,* 11.

77. Anarchists Against the Wall, "The Carl von Ossietzky Medal Accep-tance Speech," in Gordon and Grietzer, *Anarchists Against the Wall,* 31.

78. Ibid.

79. Kobi Snitz, "Tear Gas and Tea," in Gordon and Grietzer, *Anarchists Against the Wall,* 56–57.

80. Roy Wagner, "Fear and Loathing at the Central Bus Station," in Gordon and Grietzer, *Anarchists Against the Wall,* 64.

81. Yossi Bartal, "Dykes and the Holy War," in Gordon and Grietzer, *Anarchists Against the Wall,* 113.

82. Snitz, "Tear Gas and Tea," 58.

83. Bartal, "Dykes and the Holy War," 113.

84. Judith Butler quoted in Heckert, "Interview with Judith Butler," 96.

85. Ibid., 94. Since "the legal regime is itself a violent regime, and legal violence consumes all recourse to due process or legal intervention, then anarchism becomes the way of contesting and opposing the violent opera-tion of the state."

86. Ruth Edmonds, "Hey Babe, Hope You're Not in Jail," in Gordon and Grietzer, *Anarchists Against the Wall,* 113.

87. Bartal, "Dykes and the Holy War," 109.

88. "Interview with Ilan Shalit," *Alasbarricadas*, August 26, 2010, available at http://news.infoshop.org.

89. Ayalon, "Means of Communication," 103.

90. Ibid., 99–105; Snitz, "Tear Gas and Tea," 50–59; Gordon, *Anarchy Alive!*, 145.

91. Bonanno, *Palestine, Mon Amour*, 31.

92. Alfredo M. Bonanno, foreword, in Gordon and Grietzer, *Anarchists Against the Wall*, 2–3, 3.

93. "After all, anarchists, even on their own, have historically been capable of carrying out actions of attack, which in their small dimensions and reproducibility have inspired those who have suffer exclusion, exploitation, and genocide." The fact is, Bonanno concludes, "that reality is right before our eyes. It does not need grand theories, or particular technical or strategic explanations. Just as that handful of women and men who became aware of its existence did not require any particular illumination." And "who would be able to stop our action, our action as anarchists?" Ibid., 3–4.

94. Alfredo M. Bonanno, *Armed Joy* (London: Elephant Editions, 1993), 3–4. Published first in Italian in 1977, it is still banned in Italy. Bonanno insists that his book remains pertinent because it "can point out the potent capabilities of the individual on his or her road, with joy, to the destruction of all that which oppresses and regulates them" (3).

95. Bonanno, *Palestine, Mon Amour*, 26. Commenting on the First Intifada, Bonanno said: "All the horrors of classical genocide have been used: mass deportation, concentration camps, indiscriminate massacre, destruction of individual houses or entire groups of houses, on the spot shootings, violence, rape, attacks on mosques, attacks on the Red Cross, prearranged massacres, the use of death squads made up of colons and plain clothes soldiers" (40). Furthermore, "No matter how clever the defenders of Israel are—and as we know they include a number of anarchists," there is nothing in the world that "would be able to eradicate the horrors of the last months" (34).

96. It was "the Zionist movement along with great Jewish-American and international, but mainly American, lobbies that pushed the Jewish people along this road in the land of Israel." Bonanno, *Palestine, Mon Amour*, 9.

97. Bonanno, *Palestine, Mon Amour*, 10, statement quoted 45–46, 43, 44.

98. Sarah Assouline, "Here Murderers are Heroes," in Gordon and Grietzer, *Anarchists Against the Wall*, 82.

99. Bonanno, *Palestine, Mon Amour*, 28, 8, 21, 28.

100. Ibid., 24, 28.

101. Gordon, *Anarchy Alive!*, 148. Curiously, the whole passage is worded as a defense for their lack of militancy to international anarchists. Gordon explains that it is precisely "because it takes place against the backdrop of a highly *violent* conflict, in which armed struggle is the norm rather than the exception," that anarchist activists in Palestine "can more comfortably accept nonviolence alongside armed struggle."

102. Gordon, *Anarchy Alive!*, 148.

103. Ibid.; Bonanno, *Palestine, Mon Amour*, 7.

104. Ibid., 78.

105. Jeffrey Herf, *The Jewish Enemy: Nazi Propaganda during World War II and the Holocaust* (Cambridge, Mass.: Belknap Press, 2006), vii–viii.

106. Antisemitism can be defined in a very broad sense, and anti-Zionism is certainly part of that tradition, but it still represents an entirely new ideological development that works in tandem with antisemitism. Eirik Eiglad, "Anti-Zionism and the Resurgence of Antisemitism in Norway," in Rosenfeld, *Resurgent Antisemitism*, 140–174.

107. Saul Friedländer, *The Years of Persecution: Nazi Germany and the Jews 1933–1939* (London: Phoenix, 1997).

108. Bonanno, *Palestine, Mon Amour*, 38, 40.

109. Imre Kertész quoted in Alvin H. Rosenfeld, *The End of the Holocaust* (Bloomington: Indiana University Press, 2011), 279.

Antisemitism and the Radical Catholic Traditionalist Movement

MARK WEITZMAN

THE TERM "the new antisemitism" has already led to much discussion of the different ways we can conceptualize antisemitism. For many experts, the "new antisemitism" is intrinsically connected to attempts to delegitimize Zionism, embracing what scholar Robert Wistrich has described as a focus that is "disproportionately centered on one tiny spot on the world's surface—the State of Israel."[1] In particular, a great deal of attention has been paid to the active and growing threat presented by the many radical violent Islamist movements that have spread to the West, where they have been joined by a coalition of elements of traditional right- and left-wing activists and thinkers in attacking Israel, Jews, and Judaism. This explosion of jihadist Islamic activity illustrated clearly the threat posed by the revival of a radical religion that is fueled by a core antisemitism. Yet our focus on the existential threat that is currently posed by those elements should not blind us to the presence of a Western version of a radical religious extremism that is also fueled by antisemitism. This movement is the loose constellation known as the radical Roman Catholic traditionalists.[2] And although the radical traditionalist Catholic movement is unlikely to manifest itself in mass violence, one of its primary goals is to restore antisemitism to dogma and thus to harness the power of religion to threaten the equality and safety of Jews and Israel. Since for these radical Catholic antisemites there is no valid separation of Church and State, their antisemitism has a clear political agenda and has also threatened to become part of mainstream political and religious discourse. Thus, in this chapter I use the concept of antisemitism as a form of political religion in order to closely examine the radical traditionalist Catholic movement. Antisemitism as a form of political religion is not a novel concept; while even Abraham Lincoln used the term *political religion,* which can be traced back to the French Revolution, the concept has long been applied to Nazi ideology, beginning perhaps with Eric Voegelin's work from the early 1930s.[3] The historian Uriel Tal wrote extensively on this theme, pointing out that "Hitler defined his political path in terms borrowed from religion" and described the Third Reich as a regime where "politics and state became sacred and served as an *ersatz* substitute religion."[4] Emilio Gentile has described political religion as

> a form of the sacralisation of politics of an exclusive and integralist character. It rejects coexistence with other political ideologies and movements, denies the autonomy of the individual with respect to the collective, prescribes the obligatory observance of its commandment and participation in its political cult, and sanctifies violence as a legitimate arm of the struggle against enemies, and as an instrument of regeneration. It adopts a hostile attitude toward traditional institutionalised religions . . . , in the sense that the political religion seeks to incorporate traditional religion within its own system of beliefs and myths, assigning it a subordinate and auxiliary role.[5]

Gentile's description, when linked to Tal's observation of the antisemitic possibilities inherent in some forms of political religion, aptly describes aspects of the radical traditional Catholic movement—especially those rejecting the reforms of Vatican II, and in particular those of *Nostra Aetate,* the document that revolutionized the relationship between the Church and the Jewish people. Following the sociologist Michael Cuneo, I define radical Catholic traditionalists as those who have rejected the reforms of Vatican II, and "entered into schism from the institutional church." This chapter, however, focuses on examining the attitudes of those extreme traditionalists toward Jews and Judaism.[6]

An unambiguous display of the extreme hostility of the radical Catholic traditionalists toward Jews occurred on November 12, 2013. That evening, a group of young Catholics began to disrupt a service of Jews and Catholics who had gathered in the Metropolitan Cathedral of Buenos Aires to commemorate the 1938 Kristallnacht pogrom in Nazi Germany in a ceremony inaugurated by Cardinal Jorge Mario Bergoglio, who in 2013 had become Pope Francis. The protesters were "shouting the rosary and the 'Our Father' prayer . . . (and) saying 'followers of false gods must be kept out of the sacred temple.'"[7] According to Buenos Aires Rabbi Abraham Skorka, who coauthored a book with the future pope on modern faith and family, the protestors "began to hand out little pieces of paper saying that Jews were blaspheming the place," and also made comments such as "the Jews killed Jesus."[8] The day after the event, the Reverend Christian Bouchacourt, the South American leader of the Society of Saint Pius X, identified the protesters as members of his organization, justifying their actions as "a reaction of faithful who are scandalized . . . the protesters have a right to feel outraged when rabbis preside over a ceremony in a Catholic cathedral."[9]

This incident was by no means the first time that the Society of Saint Pius X (SSPX) had been in the headlines, especially regarding its views on Jews, Judaism, and the Holocaust. Indeed, for most outside observers, the SSPX probably is best known for its controversial Bishop Richard Williamson, who in a 2009 interview on Swedish TV notoriously denied that the Holocaust took place. Ordained illicitly (in disobedience to papal authority) by SSPX founder Archbishop Marcel Lefebvre in 1988, Williamson was excommunicated from the Roman Catholic Church as a result of that act of defiance. As the storm over Williamson's Holocaust denial broke, the SSPX attempted to distance itself from the negative impression that his statements had made. In a press release issued immediately after the interview became toxic, Bernard Fellay, the Superior General of the SSPX, said that "Bishop Williamson's statements do not in any way reflect the position of our Society."[10]

For some Catholic defenders of the SSPX, Fellay's statement was sufficient to distance the SSPX from the charge of antisemitism. The blogger Jeffrey Mirus, writing in 2011, claimed that "The head of the SSPX, Bishop Bernard Fellay, has long since made it clear that Bishop Williamson's attitudes are not those of the Society as a whole ... it is really not fair for Jewish leaders to attempt to deny doctrinal reconciliation between the Church and the SSPX based on Richard Williamson's remarks."[11] Mirus was referring to the then-ongoing talks between the Vatican and the SSPX that attempted an official reconciliation between the two. However, in this chapter I demonstrate that, contrary to Bishop Fellay's disingenuous statement, antisemitism has been, and continues to be, an essential component in the theology of many radical Catholic traditionalists.

Among the many mainstream assessments of Pope Benedict XVI's papacy was the acknowledgment that, despite his obvious interest in steering the Church into a more traditional mode, he had failed to heal the rift between the Church and the radical Catholic traditionalist movement, particularly the Society of Saint Pius X. Indeed, one commentator refers to the SSPX as "Benedict's Unfinished Business" and suggests that the rift with the group "threatens the Vatican with what it fears the most: a small but permanent schism."[12] Ultimately, despite the Church having reached out to the traditionalists in an effort to restore them to its good graces, the radical beliefs of the schismatic SSPX proved to be too wide a gulf to bridge. A major breaking point appeared to be the group's insistent refusal to recognize the reforms of Vatican II, including the institutional shift in relations between the Church and the Jewish community.

These reforms have been so dramatic that the Israeli historian Israel J. Yuval writes that "the Christian-Jewish debate that started nineteen hundred years ago, in our day came to a conciliatory close. . . . In one fell swoop, the anti-Jewish position of Christianity became reprehensible and illegitimate. . . . Ours is thus the first generation of scholars that can and may discuss the Christian-Jewish debate from a certain remove . . . a post-polemical age."[13] Yuval bases his optimistic assessment on the strength of the reforms in Catholicism that stemmed from the adoption by the Second Vatican Council in 1965 of *Nostra Aetate,* which, in Michael Phayer's term, is "the revolutionary" document that signified "the Catholic Church's reversal of its 2,000 year tradition of anti-Semitism."[14]

Yet some Catholics within the Church still refuse to accept this seismic shift in theology. The SSPX, and others like them, so bitterly resented these changes that in some cases they even split with the Vatican and became vehement critics. Benedict made it a priority of his pontificate to try to heal the rift with the largest of these groups, the SSPX; indeed, it has been said "that he invested a large share of his personal charisma and political capital seeking reconciliation with the SSPX."[15] The announcement that the Vatican had broken off reconciliation talks with the SSPX signified the utter failure of this effort. Archbishop Gerhard Muller, the head of the Congregation for the Defense of the Faith, stated in October 2012 that "we cannot give away the Catholic faith . . . there will be no compromises here, I think there will be no new discussions," seemingly unambiguously signaling the end of negotiations.[16]

Even though the Catholic Church is officially committed to the teachings of *Nostra Aetate,* opponents of that document and of "modernity" in general have continued their fight and gained, if not a foothold, at least a hearing in the Vatican. As Michael

Davies, a leading radical Catholic apologist wrote, "international Judaism wants to radically defeat Christianity and to be its substitute," it is in their views on Jews and Judaism that we find the most profound expression of their radical rejection of *Nostra Aetate*, Vatican II, and the modern virtues of democracy and tolerance, as well as their continued affirmation of what French historian Jules Isaac labels "the teachings of contempt."[17]

The Society of Saint Pius X has become the locus of the extreme Catholic traditionalist world. It was created in 1970 by Archbishop Marcel Lefebvre, who first came to wide attention when he refused to sign on to the Vatican II statement, *Dignitatis Humanae* (Declaration on Religious Freedom).[18] After his refusal, he established a traditionalist seminary in Econe, Switzerland, and founded the Society of Saint Pius X. In 1973–1974 the SSPX expanded to the United States, establishing chapels in California, Texas, and New York. Lefebvre continued to publicly criticize Vatican II reforms, including the liturgical changes, which brought him increasingly into overt conflict with Rome. Pope Paul VI ordered him to close down his Swiss seminary in 1974, but Lefebvre refused, and as a result his priestly functions were suspended in 1976. Undeterred, in 1983 Lefebvre threatened to consecrate a successor.

A year later, Pope John Paul II reintroduced (under some conditions) the Tridentine (Latin) Mass, as a gesture of conciliation to the traditionalists. This failed to reconcile Lefebvre and his followers, and three years later he again threatened to consecrate a successor. This time the Vatican responded by entering into negotiations with the group, and indeed, on May 5, 1988, Lefebvre signed an agreement requiring him to acknowledge his loyalty to the Vatican and to accept the new Mass as legitimate. In return, the SSPX was to be recognized and allowed to continue to use the Tridentine Mass in its services. The very next day Lefebvre repudiated the agreement, and within two months, on June 30, 1988, he consecrated four bishops, defying Rome's authority. This time the Vatican responded forcefully, excommunicating Lefebvre and his priests and putting the SSPX into a state of schism.[19] Lefebvre died in 1991, but by then the group had become established and was able to withstand the loss of its founder. Swiss Bishop Bernard Fellay was elected as SSPX superior general in 1994 and was reelected in 2006.

Bishop Richard Williamson, one of the four SSPX bishops consecrated by Lefebvre in 1988, publicly questioned the reality of the Holocaust, bringing the SSPX into broader public scrutiny during the firestorm this statement caused. Nevertheless, in January 2009, Pope Benedict XVI lifted the excommunications; on that same day, the Swedish interview with Williamson aired in which he said "I believe that the historical evidence is strongly against, is hugely against six million Jews having been deliberately gassed in gas chambers as a deliberate policy of Adolf Hitler," and "I think that 200,000 to 300,000 Jews perished in Nazi concentration camps, but none of them in gas chambers."[20]

The reaction from outraged Jews and others was immediate. Indignation grew upon exposure of Williamson's history of antisemitic comments, which included a belief in the accuracy of the notoriously fraudulent work, *The Protocols of the Elders of Zion*.[21] The resulting storm of criticism caused the Vatican to insist on Williamson's renunciation of his Holocaust denial, which he has so far refused to do. However, in a February 2009 letter, Williamson wrote that "observing these consequences I can truthfully say that I regret having made such remarks."[22] This led one journalist, the BBC's religious affairs correspondent Robert Pigott, to note that "the apology stops short of fully recanting the bishop's earlier statements."[23] The negative import of Williamson's comments, coming amid the ongoing reconciliation discussions with the Vatican, was also not lost on the SSPX leadership. Fellay weighed in on the matter:

> It's clear that a Catholic bishop cannot speak with ecclesiastical authority except on questions that regard faith and morals. Our

Fraternity does not claim any authority on other matters. Its mission is the propagation and restoration of authentic Catholic doctrine, expressed in the dogmas of the faith. It's for this reason that we are known, accepted and respected in the entire world. The affirmations of Bishop Williamson do not reflect in any sense the position of our Fraternity. For this reason I have prohibited him, pending any new orders, from taking any public positions on political or historical questions.[24]

Yet Williamson's antisemitism was not new or even hidden. In a 1991 letter written when he was the rector of the SSPX seminary and posted on the seminary website, Williamson reflects on the first Gulf War. The war, he writes, was a creation of "the many friends of Israel in the U.S.A. . . . whooping for the United States to break the Arab strong man." Finally, Williamson puts these comments into a clear theological perspective: "Until (the Jews) recover their true messianic vocation (by accepting the Church) they may be expected to continue fanatically agitating, in accordance with their false messianic vocation of Jewish world domination. . . . So we may fear their continuing to play their major part in the agitation of the East and the corruption of the West."[25]

In another letter to his supporters written just a few months later, while discussing the media's debilitating influence on society (referring specifically to the confirmation hearings of Clarence Thomas for the Supreme Court), Williamson quotes the *Protocols of the Elders of Zion* approvingly: "it is indispensable to stir up the people's relations with their governments in all countries so as to utterly to exhaust humanity with dissension, hatred, struggle, envy . . . so that the goyim see no other course open to them than to take refuge in our complete sovereignty in money and all else."[26] In the same letter, Williamson also cites Protocol 14 ("in countries known as progressive and enlightened, we have created a senseless, filthy, abominable literature"), referring to the "alternative life-style" of homosexuality that, in Williamson's view, is "so horrible as to cry to heaven for vengeance." Williamson's belief in the *Protocols* has remained consistent. A decade later, in a letter of May 1, 2009, Williamson wrote that "God puts in men's hands the *'Protocols of the Sages of Sion'* . . . if men want to know the truth, but few do."[27]

Williamson's disseminated letters demonstrate not only his antisemitism but also his overt racism and sexism. In another letter, he explains the 2005 unrest in France: "So when white men give up on saving Jews, looking after other races and leading their womenfolk, it is altogether normal for them to be punished respectively by the domination of Jewish finance, by the refusal to follow of the non-white races and by rampant feminism."[28] In one letter Williamson even combines two of those themes, noting criticism of his September 1991 letter in which he condemned women for wearing pants and jocularly compared it to criticism of his Holocaust denial, beginning the letter, "Few of you will be surprised to learn that the September letter appealing to the women not to wear trousers caused a strong reaction, comparable only to the reaction of the Seminary letter which referred to scientific evidence that certain famous 'holocaust gas-chambers' in Poland cannot have served as gas-chambers at all."[29]

Thus, when Fellay issued his statement in 2009, it was clear that Williamson's antisemitism was evident and publicly disseminated to the membership of the SSPX for at least eighteen years prior to Fellay's public declaration. Further, barring any evidence of prior repudiation or discipline of Williamson for his antisemitism, it is evident that Fellay was being disingenuous at best when he claimed that "the affirmations of Bishop Williamson do not reflect in any sense the position of our Fraternity." Indeed, the SSPX and the extremist Catholic traditionalist movement in general are shot through with antisemitism to such an extent that it is possible to consider antisemitism as one of the foundational doctrines of the movement.

If we return to Lefebvre, we see that his record on Jews and Judaism is also highly questionable. He has been quoted as having spoken approvingly of "both the World War II–era Vichy

Regime in France and the far-right National Front" in an August 1985 letter to Pope John Paul II, and also characterizing the National Front as having identified the contemporary enemies of the faith as "Jews, Communists and Freemasons." In that letter, Lefebvre severely criticized "all the reforms carried out over 20 years within the church to please heretics, schismatics, false religions and declared enemies of the church, such as the Jews, the Communists and the Freemasons."[30]

After Pope John Paul II's dramatic 1986 visit to the synagogue in Rome, Lefebvre wrote, "And, most recently, the Pope has been into the synagogue of the Jews in Rome. How can the Pope pray with the *enemies* of Jesus Christ? These Jews know and say and believe that they are the successors of the Jews who killed Jesus Christ, and they continue to fight against Jesus Christ everywhere in the world."[31]

In an interview with the journal of the extreme right National Front in France, Lefebvre suggested that Catholic opposition to a residence of Carmelite nuns at the site of the Auschwitz concentration camp had been instigated by Jews.[32]

Lefebvre's followers often share this outlook. One of the four bishops ordained by him in 1988, Bernard Tissier de Mallerais, said in 1997, "The church for its part has at all times forbidden and condemned the killing of Jews, even when 'their grave defects rendered them odious to the nations among which they were established.' . . . All this makes us think that the Jews are the most active artisans for the coming of Antichrist."[33]

Nor has their record been confined simply to making statements. In 1989, Paul Touvier, a fugitive charged with ordering the execution of seven Jews in 1944 as a Nazi collaborator, was arrested in a priory of the Fraternity of St. Pius X in Nice, France. The fraternity stated at the time that Touvier had been granted asylum as "an act of charity to a homeless man." When Touvier died in 1996, a parish church operated by the fraternity offered a requiem Mass in his honor.[34] Similarly, in Italy in 2013, an SSPX priest offered the Mass at the funeral of convicted Nazi mass murderer Erich Priebke, an act that was defended by the SSPX even after public criticism.[35]

Prior to the Williamson controversy, the SSPX website had featured two postings that reflected and summed up the SSPX's position on Jews and Judaism. When Williamson's remarks came to public notice, these documents were expunged from the SSPX website.

In one SSPX post, the Vatican II teaching that "the Jews should not be spoken of as rejected or accursed as if this followed from Holy Scripture" is described as "outrageous."[36] Another online essay claims that "Judaism is inimical to all nations in general, and in a special manner to Christian nations" and that "the unrepentant Jewish people are disposed by God to be a theological enemy, the status of this opposition must be universal, inevitable, and terrible." There are claims that "the Talmud, which governs Jews, orders enmity with Christians" and that the "Jewish people persecute Christendom," "conspire against the Christian State," commit "usury," and even "are known to kill Christians!" Thus the essay defends the notion that Jews should not be "given equality of rights" but rather should be forced into ghettos ("isolated into its own neighborhoods").[37]

In a 1959 letter, Lefebvre's close ally, Bishop Gerald Sigaud, wrote, "Money, the media, and international politics are for a large part in the hands of Jews," and that "those who have revealed the atomic secrets of the U.S.A. were . . . all Jews. The founders of communism were Jew [sic]." Although written more than a decade before the society came into existence, this letter was also found fit to be posted on the SSPX website.[38]

These positions are not original to the SSPX, nor are they a theological innovation to current extremist Catholic traditionalists; indeed, they bear a striking similarity to the writings of an otherwise obscure Irish priest named Father Denis Fahey, whose work is one of the most, if not the most frequently cited by the members of the SSPX and similar believers. Mary Christine Athans, in her important book, *The Coughlin-Fahey Connection: Father Charles E. Coughlin, Father Denis Fahey, C. S. SP., and Religious Anti-Semitism in the United States, 1938–1954,* thoroughly explores Fahey's life and thought and how his theology of antisemitism made its way from Ireland to the United States.[39]

Fahey was born July 2, 1883, in Kilmore, Golden, County Tipperary, Ireland. In 1900 he was a novice of the Holy Ghost Congregation in France, which was still dealing with the impact of the Dreyfus Affair and the French government's anticlerical actions, particularly the Separation Law of 1905 that required religious congregations to be recognized by the government. At that time, France was an incubator for ecclesiastical antisemitism. As David Kertzer writes, "In the cauldron of Catholic resentment toward the republican state in the 1880s, the Jews, visible in national politics, in the civil service and in the economy, served as a lightning rod, a painful sign of all that was wrong with modern French society."[40] For all sorts of reactionaries, eventually including the Nazis, the French Revolution marked the moment the world was turned upside down. The historian Richard Wolin stresses the significance of this point: "As Goebbels pithily observed a few months after Hitler's rise to power, 'The year 1789 is hereby erased from history.'"[41]

Fahey traveled to Rome in 1908, obtaining two doctorates there (in philosophy and theology) and living at the Seminaire française. Ordained in 1911, Fahey returned the following year to Dublin, where he remained (except for 1916–1920, when he was in Switzerland for health reasons) as professor at the Holy Ghost Seminary until his death on January 24, 1954. Fahey maintained a high profile as a public intellectual in Ireland; upon his death, Irish prime minister Eamon de Valera attended his evening funeral Mass.[42]

During his four years in Rome, Fahey was heavily influenced by Father Henri Le Floch, the superior of the Seminaire Française (Pontifical French Seminary). Athans describes Le Floch "as an exponent of conservative right-wing French and Italian Catholic thought in those anti-Modernist years . . . Le Floch had substantial influence on Fahey. . . . He was later removed from his position as Rector because of his relationship to the controversial and anti-Semitic *Action Francaise* movement which was finally condemned by Pius XI in 1926."[43]

Le Floch was also a revered mentor to Lefebvre. Athans, who interviewed a number of Fahey's students and younger colleagues in Ireland, writes that "Some (priests) believe that Le Floch's influence can also be traced to Archbishop Marcel Lefebvre. . . . founder of the dissident traditionalist movement . . . known as the Fraternity of SPX."[44] Lefebvre himself acknowledged his debt to Le Floch; in his memoirs he describes Le Floch as one "to whom I owe much of my formation as a seminarian and as a priest" and remembers that he chose to speak "of Pere Le Floch at my consecration."[45]

In Fahey's Manichaean perspective, God is accessible only through the Catholic Church, which is "supra-national and su-pernatural"; however, God is locked in a cosmic struggle with Satan, who was, for Fahey, a very real antagonist. Although Judaism is the chief antagonist, Satan's agents in this world include "Bolshevism, as the most recent development in the age-long struggle waged by the Jewish nation against the Supernational Messias, our Lord Jesus Christ, and his Mystical Body, the Catholic Church." According to this theology, Judaism attempts, through the rejection of Jesus as Christ, to "recast (the world) in the mould of Jewish national life." Fahey concludes by asserting that this rejection "cannot but mean the complete undoing of the catholic organization of society," which is, in Fahey's view, the appropriate order of things.[46]

As already mentioned, Fahey saw Communism as just a tool used by the Jews: "The real forces behind Bolshevism in Russia are Jewish forces, and that Bolshevism is really an instrument in the hands of the Jews for the establishment of their future Messianic kingdom."[47]

This led Fahey in his 1940 tract, *The Rulers of Russia*,

> to contrast the Jewish idea of citizenship with the Catholic idea.
> . . . As members of their own "messianic" nation, they [the Jews] must strive for the domination of their nation over others, as thus alone, they hold, justice and peace can be achieved on earth. The Jew would fail in his duty to the Messias to come if he did not subordinate the interests of other nations to his own. But the Catholic Church, being supra-national and supernatural, does not aim at the obliteration of national characteristics and qualities by the imposition of a national form, but at their harmonious development by the elimination of the defects due to original sin.[48]

This reading of theological history views Judaism as a religion committed to ruling over the other nations, and its hunger for power and control make Jews unworthy of equal citizenship, while Catholicism by its nature is seen as less restrictive and thus deserves to be the dominant authority in society.

For Fahey, there is no concept of religious liberty; in fact, it is a tool of the devil that is used to take the state and society away from the true worship of the Church. An echo of this belief appears in Williamson's thought. In comments on Pope Benedict's December 2005 "Address to the Curia," Williamson writes that "what is wrong with freeing States from any obligation to Christ the King is that *implicitly you are denying that Jesus Christ is God*. . . . Religious liberty means in effect, a declaration of independence from God, which is directly opposed to the first Commandment. . . . However, where Catholics are in a sufficient majority, the State may physically prevent the *public* practice of false religion while tolerating their practice in private" (original emphasis).[49] This conviction was a fundamental tenet of Lefebvre's belief as well, as he held that the acceptance of the doctrine of religious liberty is "a scandal to Catholic souls (that) cannot be measured. The Church is shaken to its very foundation."[50]

In January 2008, Father Mathias Gaudron, an SSPX theologian, repeated this theme in his "Catechism of the Crisis of the Church." After posing the question, "Is there, then, no right to the free exercise of religion?," he offers this answer: "The true religion possesses the absolute right to develop and to be practiced freely, for no one can be impeded from serving God in the way He Himself has prescribed. It is an exigency of the natural law. The false religions, to the contrary, have no real right to be practiced precisely because they are false and erroneous. Error can never have any right; only the truth has rights." The same document succinctly sums up the SSPX's stance on tolerance; tolerance, it claims, is simply "the patient endurance of an evil."[51]

For Fahey and similar thinkers, political freedom, not only religious freedom, can only be found in and thus only given by the Church; therefore, the right order is one in which the Church reigns supreme and delegates those freedoms as she desires and for her benefit only; outside of the Church there are no rights and no freedom; and all in opposition or in nonbelief are regarded as agents of Satan.

This is one of the areas where today's radicals feel that Pope Benedict betrayed the Church. According to one of the more prolific traditionalist writers, John Vennari, "It is certainly difficult to reconcile Cardinal Ratzinger's words to the teaching of Pope Pius VII, who in his Encyclical Letter *Post tam diuturnas,* denounced indifferentism and the new concept of religious liberty: By the fact that the indiscriminate freedom of all forms of worship is proclaimed, truth is confused with error, and the Holy and Immaculate Spouse of Christ is placed on the same level as heretical sects and even as Jewish faithlessness." Vennari explicitly relies on Fahey for this insight.[52]

Fahey traces it all back to the original fall of humanity in the Garden of Eden, which was then followed by more recent tragic historical events, such as the Protestant Reformation and the

French Revolution, with equally disastrous results. Indeed, the Reformation, he writes, "broke the unity of European subjection to the supranational, supernatural Church of Christ." Since the Reformation failed to "install a naturalistic international organization," that task fell to the French Revolution, which initiated "the domination of the world by Masonic Naturalism." Fahey continues: "Behind Masonry, however (was) the other naturalistic force of the once chosen people.... The Jews everywhere made use of Freemasonry to secure the rights of becoming citizens of the once Christian states."[53]

Even the horrors of the Holocaust did not shatter Fahey's deep-rooted antisemitism. He did find it necessary after the Holocaust to attempt to draw a distinction between unacceptable antisemitism, which he defined as "hatred of the Jewish nation," and "opposition to the Jewish and Masonic naturalism," which he endorsed as a vital aspect of Catholicism.[54] For Fahey, naturalism was a source of evil precisely because it inevitably led to rejection of belief in God or any other form of supernaturalism. The revulsion felt by the world to the horrors of the Holocaust created the necessity for Fahey to try and distinguish his brand of antisemitism from that of the Third Reich. In the foreword to his last book, published in 1953, *The Kingship of Christ and the Conversion of the Jewish Nation*, he wrote of

> the confusion created in minds owing to the use of the term "Anti-Semitism." The Hitlerite naturalistic or anti-supernatural regime in Germany gave to the world the odious spectacle of a display of Anti-Semitism, that is hatred of the Jewish Nation. Yet all the propaganda about that display of Anti-Semitism should not have made Catholics forget the existence of age-long Jewish Naturalism and Anti-supernaturalism. Forgetfulness of the disorder of Jewish naturalistic opposition to Christ the King is keeping Catholics blind to the danger that is arising from the clever extension of the term "Anti-Semitism" with all its war connotation to the mind of the unthinking.[55]

In maintaining this position, Fahey remained true to the teachings of the church he grew up in. As Hubert Wolf has recently
stated in regard to the 1928 Vatican decree dissolving the group
Amici Israel, "In the opinion of these cardinals, this meant that
only racial antisemitism was condemned, whereas theological
antisemitism on the part of the Church would be considered legitimate and even necessary."[56] As some scholars have already
noticed, this was a distinction without a difference; in Birgit
Gregor's words, it "trivializes" the fact that the "racist antisemitism" grew out of the "religious anti-Judaism."[57]

In the body of that book, Fahey goes so far as to justify the Nazi
actions against the Jews on theological grounds, and to imply that
the Catholic Church was even more of a victim. In Fahey's words,
"One can readily conclude that the National-Socialist reaction
against the corroding influence of Jewish Naturalism on German
national life leads, not only to measures of repression against the
Jews but to a dire persecution of the Catholic Church. The deified
German race has attacked the rival natural deity, the Jewish race,
directly, and has proceeded systematically to get rid of it as cor-
rupting the very fount of deity, German blood." In other words,
the Nazis were only reacting to the Jewish threat, and their major
fault was not in the reaction, but rather the form it took. In the
same work, Fahey spells this out in even greater detail: "We have
seen that the Nazi movement in Germany is one of a number of
national reactions against the naturalistic Internationalism of the
Jewish Nation and of Freemasonry."[58] Thus, in Fahey's vision of
the Third Reich, the innate Jewish "naturalism" was recognized
by many as a danger that naturally would lead to defensive reactions, but it was the Church that was the ultimate opponent
and the ultimate victim of the Nazis.[59] In a very real sense, if
the results of the French Revolution, modernity and liberalism,
were both successfully erased, then there would be a need or
an opportunity for a weltanschauung that could dominate the
world. Recognizing this, Pius, del Val, and Fahey all hoped that

the Church would be the one to fill that vacuum, while the Nazis obviously saw themselves as the new vanguard. There were even some within the Church, or at least some high-ranking elements in the Church, who agreed that the results of 1789 had to be rolled back; and if the Nazis were also on the same wavelength, then there might be opportunity to try to find a modus vivendi, or a common ground between the two.[60] One of those who attempted to build such a bridge was Bishop Alois Hudal, who "staunchly defended the German states discrimination against Jews because of the dangers they posed for the 'German *Volk* spirit.'"[61] For those reactionaries, the division was over which ideology would be the victor that would successfully fill the vacated space and dominate the Western world.[62]

Fahey also published lists of Jews in the Russian Communist leadership, as well as a list of "Members of the Jewish Nations in the United Nations Organization. . . . As of last year (1951) this tiny but powerful group of Zionist nationalists hold the following key posts"; this list consisted of 86 names on five pages. A forerunner of many extremists today, Fahey wrote that "The real purpose of the UN is to pave the way for a 'World Government' to which all nations (but one?) surrender their sovereignty and independence."[63]

For Fahey, this alleged threat from Jews meant that the Church had to fight back by all available means, including depriving Jews of their civil rights, thus denying them the latitude and freedom they were using to undermine society as well as denying their own national aspirations. He believed that "A step to be taken to undo the naturalism of the French Revolution and, at the same time, prevent onslaughts on the Jews, is to withdraw citizenship of other States from all of them, and limit them to citizenship of some other State, their own. That State must not be Palestine, for the Jewish claim to Palestine is implicitly a denial that they have disobeyed God and missed their vocation by the rejection of the True Supernatural Messias."[64]

Finally, after the Holocaust, he worried that Catholic sympathy for Jews due to their terrible suffering would create a lessening of Catholic anti-Jewish vigilance. And, despite the growing awareness of the Nazi Holocaust, those crimes did not begin to compare to the ancient Jewish crime of deicide, the result of which should have ordained history and the structure of society ever since. "Some Catholics seem to forget that the Jews who, in their terrible opposition to God . . . were intent on the most awful crime ever committed, the crime of deicide."[65]

Fahey's theology was clearly formed in, and reflective of, the reactionary Church. However, as the Church began to change after World War II, his teachings might well have faded into obscurity but for the fact that he found a powerful ally in the United States in the person of Father Charles Coughlin, who brought Fahey to the attention of a receptive audience across the Atlantic. As Coughlin's aura dimmed, Fahey's teachings initially seemed to also wane, but in reality they had been well planted and were lying dormant, but still germinating and waiting the right circumstances to flower.

Athans, in her book *The Coughlin-Fahey Connection* and in other writings, has demonstrated how "the 'theologian' [that] Coughlin quoted most frequently was . . . Father Denis Fahey."[66] Coughlin did not just quote Fahey or even base his thought on the Irish priest's writings, but he took an even more active role, especially by reprinting and distributing Fahey's tract, *The Rulers of Russia,* through his Social Justice Publishing Company in 1940, when Coughlin was at the height of his powers. This distribution ensured Fahey's introduction to a mass U.S. audience.

Coughlin was easily the most prominent Catholic and antisemite in the United States at that time. As one of his biographers wrote, "Coughlin . . . dominated among antisemitic public figures in these years." His domination was reflected in his reach: "Not only did he reach millions with his weekly radio broadcasts, but he also disseminated his extremist messages through his widely read magazine *Social Justice,* which claimed 200,000 subscribers."[67] As a result, he popularized an antisemitism that had significant impact on U.S. popular discourse. Coughlin's fiery rhetoric spurred some of his followers into antisemitic acts that eventually even threatened public safety in Boston and New York.[68]

As Athans has clearly demonstrated, by bringing Fahey's writings to a U.S. audience, Coughlin allowed Fahey to become a bridge between the French and papal reactionary Catholic antisemitism of the early twentieth century and extreme right-wing groups and figures in the United States.[69]

One of Coughlin's chief supporters in the Catholic press was the *Brooklyn Tablet.* In a typical defense of Coughlin's antisemitism, editor Patrick Scanlon remarked, "Fr. Coughlin has fearlessly and courageously discussed the Jewish problem that others would pass by in cowardly silence . . . [no Catholic can honestly criticize] Fr. Coughlin's very temperate reference to the part that a Jewish *Weltanschauung* contributed to the untoward world conditions."[70]

What Scanlon called a "temperate reference" was translated by some of Coughlin's followers into the formation of a radical group called the Christian Front. In the late 1930s and early 1940s, members of the Christian Front were implicated in a series of disruptive and violent antisemitic acts that disturbed the peace and threatened the security of Jews throughout cities with large Irish Catholic populations, such as Boston and New York. In both cities, the wave of antisemitism was often ignored by sympathetic Catholic policemen and eventually had to be countered by official action by Massachusetts governor Leverett Saltonstall and New York mayor Fiorello LaGuardia.[71]

Even before the wave of antisemitism became overt, antisemitic discourse had become sufficiently heated and the issue became politically sensitive enough that it even reached the White House. In a 1941 memorandum to Myron Taylor, his personal representative to the Vatican, President Franklin D. Roosevelt wrote, "I forgot to mention that when you get the chance, you might express the thought that there is a great deal of anti-Jewish feeling in the dioceses of Brooklyn, Baltimore and Detroit and this feeling is said to be encouraged by the church. The point to make is that if anti-Jewish feeling is stirred up, it automatically stirs up anti-Catholic feeling and that makes a general mess."[72] Taylor did raise the issue but found the Vatican essentially non-responsive; the Vatican's resident American expert, Father Joseph Patrick Hurley, himself a virulent antisemite, had advised the Vatican to ignore Coughlin's antisemitism.[73]

While the Coughlin-Fahey correspondence continued in the same vein even after Coughlin's official silencing, the resulting lack of a public voice in the United States, as well as the beginning of the shift in Catholic thinking about Jews, certainly lowered Fahey's U.S. profile.[74] Richard Williamson also commented on the silencing of Coughlin's voice, writing in an 1987 letter, "Dear Friends and Benefactors . . . A great American priest, Fr. Charles E. Coughlin, as the famous 'Radio priest' of the late '30s and early '40s of this century, swung into action and took the Catholic battle right out into the public arena until the Church's own enemies had him silenced—through the Church's own hierarchy!"[75]

However, the damage had been done, and Fahey's influence had become entrenched in certain circles. While for the most part scholars have traced Fahey's influence in the extremist Catholic circles we have been examining, it is entirely possible that his connection with Coughlin allowed his influence to spread even wider. Among Coughlin's associates and allies were Gerald Winrod and Gerald L. K. Smith, both foundational figures in U.S. right-wing extremism. Smith, who was not a Catholic, first came to public notice as the chief lieutenant of Huey Long; he was also in direct contact with Fahey, with whom he exchanged letters in late 1940s and early '50s. Fahey wrote to an Irish follower that "the programme of Gerald L K Smith as taken from his paper *The Cross and the Flag* . . . declares unflinchingly and unequivocally for the Rights of Christ the King. Are his detractors and smearers for Christ the King or against Him? The Judaeo-Communists tried to brand every man who stood for American nationalism and against Communism during the war as pro-Nazis."[76]

The historian George Michael has also noted Coughlin's influence on Willis Carto, arguably the most important figure on the American far right in the last half century. Carto recalls Coughlin as a seminal figure from his childhood.

As a youth, Carto claims to have never heard of right-wing extremists "with the exception of Father Coughlin, to whose broadcasts he would listen with the whole family," and he "recalled listening to Coughlin's broadcasts with his family and described him as a spellbinding orator." Carto remembered "Coughlin as a genuine populist" and cited "opposition from Jewish organizations . . . as evidence of Coughlin's bona fides as a true American hero."[77]

Carto was also influenced by Francis Parker Yockey, a passionate antisemite, one of the early theorists of U.S. extremism, and a contributor of a 1938 article to Coughlin's *Social Justice*. Carto even visited Yockey in jail just before Yockey's suicide. As Michael writes, "Yockey left quite an impression on Carto; as he once remarked, 'I knew I was in the presence of a great force.'"[78]

This nexus between the extremist traditionalist Catholics and the far right has continued to the present, as Richard Williamson has also found himself championed by various current antisemitic figures. Among those who have adopted the bishop's cause are the notorious neo-Nazis and professional Holocaust denier, Mark Weber, the director of the Institute for Historical Review (IHR, the organizational center of Holocaust denial in the United States) who, in a 2009 article, "Bishop Williamson and 'Holocaust Denial': Why the Uproar?," concludes that "the Williamson affair underscores a well entrenched Jewish-Zionist bias in the cultural life of modern Western society, and reminds us, once again, of the power behind that bias."[79]

Robert Faurisson, the French academic Holocaust denier, in the midst of a 2009 squabble with Weber over the future of Holocaust negationism, also sprang to Williamson's defense. According to a posting on his blog, "The height of his enemies misfortune, and for the traditionalist Catholic he is . . . if he ever did fall to his knees before the new Inquisition he would immediately remind everyone of Galileo, the man whom science and history ended up acknowledging to be right despite his abjuration. Even if he wound up losing, Richard Williamson would thus have won."[80]

The links between the Holocaust deniers and Catholic extremists are not limited to Williamson. In one 1993 issue, the *Journal of Historical Review,* the organ of the IHR, published three short entries under the title "The Holocaust Issue: Three Christian Views." Two were by traditionalist Catholics (including the late Joseph Sobran, fired by William Buckley from his journal *National Review* for antisemitism) and the other by Bishop Louis Vezelis, described as the "editor of *The Seraph,* a traditionalist Catholic monthly." In his piece, Vezelis claims that "the preponderance of objective and factual evidence shows the promoters of the Holocaust story to be libelous frauds."[81] He had earlier contributed a piece to one of the first issues of the SSPX's official magazine in the United States, the *Angelus.*[82]

Sobran was being defended by the IHR as far back as 1987, and he spoke at the IHR 2002 conference.[83] His beliefs might be summed up by his statement that "History is replete with the lesson that a country in which the Jews get the upper hand is in danger. . . . Clearly, it is futile for the Church to try to mollify a hatred so ancient and so deep as the Jewish animus against Christianity."[84]

But while Sobran might have been a relatively minor figure, his friend Patrick Buchanan is a decidedly major figure in U.S. political discourse. Shifting between mass media and high political office, including his service in the Nixon, Ford, and Reagan administrations, where during the Reagan presidency he lobbied in defense of Nazi war criminals, Buchanan has made no secret of his often controversial views on many issues, such as stating "that it was impossible for 850,000 Jews to be killed by diesel exhaust fed into the gas chamber at Treblinka."[85]

Upon the ascension of Pope Benedict to the papacy, Buchanan wrote in 2007 that Benedict "acted to advance a reconciliation with traditionalists out of communion with the Holy See, including the 600,000 followers of the late Archbishop Marcel Lefebvre, excommunicated in 1988, who belong to his Society of Saint Pius X." Buchanan was describing a process where "the current head of SSPX, Bishop Bernard Fellay, has welcomed papal restoration of the Latin Mass. But he has called it a first step toward addressing all doctrinal disputes dating to Vatican II. Among these are the issues of ecumenism and religious liberty. If the true church is one, holy, catholic, and apostolic, then not all churches are equal."[86] It was comments like these that forced the late William F. Buckley, the patriarch of American political conservatism (and a nonradical traditionalist Catholic himself; as one friend observed, Buckley was "a devout Roman Catholic, [and] he loved the Latin mass"), to denounce both Sobran and Buchanan as antisemites.[87]

Thus, despite denunciations of Williamson's Holocaust denial, and even some pro forma condemnations of antisemitism from the SSPX, their own writings leave no question that the antisemitic teachings espoused by Fahey and repeated by Williamson and others still permeate the heart of the theology of the SSPX and many similar Catholic traditionalists. Indeed, in certain cases, these teachings even lead to connections with right-wing extremists.

Although the SSPX has tried to be more circumspect about these aspects of its theology in light of the negative publicity stemming from the Williamson affair, it has not succeeded in expunging its record. For example, still available in 2015 on the

Asia SSPX's website is a 2000 article by Bishop Salvador L. Lazo titled "My Return to the Traditional Latin Mass: Autobiography of a Traditional Catholic Bishop." In it Lazo lists books that inspired him on his spiritual journey, including Fahey's *The Kingship of Christ and the Conversion of the Jewish Nation,* as well as others about the dangers of Freemasonry. Lazo is candid about their impact on his thought:

> Reading these books gave me a better idea of the crisis and confusion in the Church today. It became clear to me who are the real enemies of the Catholic Church. Father Denis Fahey pinpointed them when he wrote: *"The enemies of the Catholic Church are three. One invisible, Satan, and two visible: a) Talmudic Judaism, and b) Freemasonry"*
>
> TALMUDIC JUDAISM
> [Lazo, following Fahey, defines Talmudic Judaism] *"That Judaism is the visible chief enemy of the Catholic Church, is evident from the Church history, from words and deeds of individuals, and groups and the teachings of the Talmud of which the Kabalah constitute the basis of Judaism."*[88] (original emphasis)

Williamson has also openly held up Fahey as an authority to be relied upon. Until recently the website of the SSPX's U.S. seminary had posted a letter written by Williamson from 1983, before he was even ordained as a bishop, in which, discussing a book written by a Protestant author, he advises his readers that "Catholics should be very wary of this kind of book. Let them keep to sound doctrine and proven authors, for instance the excellent Fr. Denis Fahey."[89]

Finally, it must be recognized that Fahey's baleful influence is alive today not only in the SSPX but also in similarly minded groups. E. Michael Jones, a significant figure in the radical Catholic movement over the past few decades, is one who relies on Fahey's distinctive definition of antisemitism. Jones, who holds a doctorate in literature, was described by Cuneo in his 1999 book as a "flamethrowing author . . . who employs a take-no-prisoners, slash-and-burn approach."[90] Over time, Jones has increasingly targeted Jews and Judaism, and in his journal, *Culture Wars,* he follows Fahey in drawing the distinction between "racial hatred" of Jews, which he claims to abhor, and hatred of the Jewish religion that is attempting, in his view, to overthrow Catholicism's natural position. In "The Conversion of the Revolutionary Jew," Jones quotes Fahey's definition and then sums up his own opinion that "Opposition to Jewish ambition 'to impose its rule on other nations' is not anti-Semitism, even if the Jews want to portray it that way. The Christian must oppose anti-Semitism, defined as hatred of the Jewish race, but he must also oppose the Jewish agenda of opposition to Logos. As many Catholics have done in the past, the Catholic must oppose the agenda of the revolutionary Jew, even now—nay, especially now—when Jews have adopted the tropes of conservatism to disguise their true aims."[91] In 2006, in an interview linked to his 1,200-page book, *The Jewish Revolutionary Spirit and Its Impact on World History,* Jones states that "Insofar as they rejected Christ, the Jews rejected Logos, and in rejecting Logos, they rejected the order of the universe, including its moral or political order," and that "Judaism is not the religion of the Old Testament. Catholicism is the religion of the Old Testament.... The Talmud is a systematic distortion of the Torah ... whose purpose is to keep the Jewish people away from Logos and in bondage to Jewish leaders."[92] Jones's antisemitism has led him into some strange company—such as the radical Palestinian American activist Hesham Tillawi, on whose cable television show Jones appeared in 2008. Tillawi's show has become an important forum for numerous antisemites, including such notorious figures as David Duke, Ted Pike, and Texe Marrs; Mark Weber and fellow Holocaust deniers Bradley Smith, Frederick Toben, and Willis Carto.[93] Jones has written about the cordial meeting he had with Carto at a 2007 conference that he, Carto, and Sobran all spoke at. Jones also published *L'affaire Williamson: The Catholic Church and Holocaust Denial,* in defense of Williamson, claiming that "Holocaust denial is another word for Jewish control of discourse."[94]

Another figure influenced by Fahey is Robert Sungenis, one of the most active internet proponents of radical traditionalist Catholic antisemitism. Sungenis, whose writings appear on Jones's website, is a polemicist whose early writings were contra Protestantism, but like Jones he has moved to targeting Jews. Reacting to accusations of antisemitism, Sungenis mounted a webpage titled "Ask Your Question about the Jews, Judaism, Zionism, etc.," where he gives his opinions to obviously set-up questions. However, his answers there are certainly revealing; for example, Sungenis denies being a Holocaust denier yet states that "I do not deny that Jews were killed by the Nazis. The Nazis killed many people. What I question is whether 6 million Jews were killed by the Nazis." Sungenis believes that Jewish-Catholic dialogue is part of a Jewish plot; he asserts that the reason for it "is philosemitism, a cultural malaise fostered by the semitically-dominated political and religious groups in America." Indeed, he defines philosemitism as a sin, stating "Hence, Jewish racism continues today, and it is a serious sin. I call it 'philosemitism,' the opposite of anti-semitism.") Sungenis believes that this plot is enforced because "the Jews control much of the politics, wealth, academia, media, sciences, arts, and culture today," and for their main weapon of control: "All they need do is brand someone who criticizes them as an 'antisemite,' publicize it at will in the media which they dominate, and the damage will be practically irreparable." Sungenis is open to blaming Jews for forcing Germany into World War II: "we should read accounts from people who see the events of World War I and II from a different angle. One of these issues concerns Germany's relationship with the Jews. According to various accounts, the Germans treated the Jews very nicely when the Jews were excised out of Russia and migrated to Germany. As the story goes, however, the Jews turned on the Germans because they got a better deal from someone else. This made the Germans very bitter against the Jews." He repeats the traditional supercessionist theology but also makes sure to use it against Zionism: "Conversely, any view of the Jews that sees them today as an exclusive and divinely blessed people whom God favors over other races and nations, or as a people who, based on selected historical events, still possess the deed, as it were, to the land of Palestine, is one the purest forms of racism. The Jews no longer are the Chosen People; the Church is. The Jews no longer own Palestine; the world does."[95] In another posting, Sungenis acknowledges his debt to Fahey: "Fr. Fahey has a lot of good things to say. He was a faithful priest who would not compromise with the latest fads in politics or culture."[96] Sungenis also has a positive view of Williamson; in an introduction to a 2004 interview with Williamson posted on his website, Sungenis states, "Although we do not subscribe nor endorse the present schismatic state of the SSPX, nevertheless, Bishop Williamson's comments about the state of the Church and what he calls the 'New Religion' are quite correct. Every Catholic, whether you are liberal, conservative or tradition, needs to read what he says." (Sungenis did part with Williamson over what he describes as "Williamson's insistence that Vatican II taught that man had the moral right to choose his own religion.")[97] The interview appeared originally in the *Remnant,* one of the earliest and most important traditionalist publications in the United States. However, in a column posted on the online *Remnant* on 1/26/09 that was devoted to the Williamson affair, one of their major writers and another follower of Fahey, Christopher Ferrara, pronounced himself "mortified" by Williamson's reliance on the discredited "Leuchter Report." Ferrara concludes that "In this defining moment we are being asked to define ourselves by declaring what we stand for, and what we will *not* stand for. To answer that question by rejecting what the Bishop has said is not to show weakness before the Church's foes."[98]

Like Fahey and Williamson, Sungenis also seems to have no problem relying on hard-core antisemitic sources. An entire blog is devoted to critiquing Sungenis's writings on Jews and Judaism, with one page showing Sungenis's reliance on antisemitic sources, and further, how he often plagiarized large sections of those sources. The sources include German Nazi authors like Robert Ley, modern antisemites like Jack Mohr or Holocaust deniers like Mark Weber (of Weber and his *Journal of Historical Review,* Sungenis writes, "*Journal of Historical Review* is a very credible source! . . . (it is) a highly prestigious and credible magazine. . . . You can't get much more credible than that, as far as history goes."[99] Finally, another blog on that website accuses Sungenis of plagiarizing from Fahey directly.[100] In January 2014 Sungenis stated that he is not an anti-Semite and would no longer discuss "Jewish political issues" and was removing all his posts related to Jews and Judaism. However, Sungenis still maintains that "the Jews, as a race, do not have a covenant with God any longer; the Jewish race of people are no longer the Chosen People, etc."[101]

Fittingly enough, the SSPX and other antisemitic traditionalists found themselves defended by what is probably the nation's most pseudo-academic far-right website, the *Occidental Observer.* The *Occidental Observer* is an offshoot of the *Occidental Quarterly,* which is edited by and reflects the views of the controversial professor Kevin MacDonald, who appeared as a defense witness for David Irving during Irving's lawsuit against Deborah Lipstadt. MacDonald has written extensively on Jews and Judaism from what he describes as an "evolutionary perspective," most notably in a trio of books.[102] The scholar of American right-wing extremism George Michael has described MacDonald's work as having "been well received by those in the racialist right, as it amounts to a theoretically sophisticated justification for anti-Semitism," with the result that MacDonald "has attained a near reverential status and is generally considered beyond reproach" by extremists.[103] In his 2009 article, "The Church and Anti-Semitism—Again," MacDonald defends the SSPX and other extremist Catholics traditionalists by describing how "The Catholic Church has played the role of ethnic and cultural defense in the past. It is certainly not surprising that Jewish organizations are alarmed by any sug-

gestion that it might be returning to its historic self-conception."
And he concludes by hoping that "the traditionalists don't give
in to what will be a furious onslaught to prevent any glimmer of
the resurgence of traditional Catholicism."[104]

Still another current follower of Fahey is John Sharpe, a rabid
traditionalist Catholic and former military officer. Sharpe sued
for libel a local newspaper that had publicized his antisemitic
beliefs. In the decision against him, the judge wrote in 2009, "No
reasonable person can read Sharpe's individual writings and conclude that he espouses anything other than a deep, abiding and
pervasive suspicion of and hostility toward Jews, whether considered as a collective people, religion, nation or ethnic group."[105]

In 2001, Sharpe founded IHS Press, with the proposed aim
"to bring back into print the classics of last century on the Social Doctrine of the Catholic Church and to spearhead a renewal
of interest in the true Catholic approach to politics, economics, and social affairs."[106] Sharpe's collaborator in this effort was
the Englishman Derek Holland. Holland, also known as Deric
O'Huallachain, is a longstanding member of the British far-right
movement. Holland authored a 1985 book, *Political Soldier,* which
has been described by the British scholar Roger Griffin as a prime
example of "fascist discourse" containing a "nebulous utopianism"
that continues to "foment racial hatred and orchestrate political
violence in contemporary society." Griffin concludes that Holland's thinking is "a blood relation of Nazism" and that Holland
himself is a "British fascist."[107]

Sharpe's website catalog promises a roster of authors that in-
cludes the leading lights of the traditionalist movement, and "will
include additional titles by Belloc, Chesterton, McNabb, and
Robbins, and new offerings by Frs. Denis Fahey, Edward Cahill,
Drs. George O'Brien and Charles Devas, and many of the other
Distributists and Social Catholics."[108]

Another speaker whose talks were being promoted in traditionalist circles was Jim Condit Jr., a radical traditionalist and for-

mer Ron Paul campaign worker. His activities included a series of three talks that were entirely based on the works of Denis Fahey (*Fr. Denis Fahey: Apostle for the Kingship of Christ in Our Time, the Mystical Body of Christ in the Modern World: An Introduction; The Mystical Body of Christ in the Modern World: Why the SPLC Is Afraid of Fr. Fahey*; and *From the Gristmill to Agri-bus: A Review of Fr. Denis Fahey's "The Church and Farming"*).

Condit, who worked for the Ron Paul presidential campaign in 2008, wrote after the election, "The Ron Paul Campaign failed because Ron Paul and the sincere part of his campaign team failed to recognize, or at least did nothing to strategically counter, the 'safeguards' erected by the NeoCon/Communist Jewish Crime Syndicate now pretty much running the U.S.A."[109] Condit's sister, Jennifer Condit Giroux, also was the leader of a movement that pressured movie theaters to show Mel Gibson's controversial film, *The Passion of the Christ.*[110]

Finally, in a 2003 article criticizing the 2001 Vatican document, *The Jewish People and Their Sacred Scriptures in the Christian Bible*, Sharpe concluded with a quotation from Fahey's *Mystical Body of Christ and the Reorganization of Society* (277–278), expressing his wish that "may we all have the courage to respond with the words of Fr. Fahey: 'In that sense, every sane thinker must be an anti-Semite.'"[111]

Sharpe's appropriation of Fahey's "courage" is also evident in the words of others in the movement, who have not relinquished their aim to restore the Catholic Church to their views. Speaking about the efforts by Rome to bring the group back into the Church, Bishop Tissier de Mallerais said, "we do not change our positions, but we have the intention of converting Rome, that is to lead Rome towards our positions."[112]

German Catholic theologian Rainer Bucher sums up the dangers inherent in political religion in *Hitler's Theology: A Study in Political Religion*, especially when considered in light of the history of Catholic-Jewish relations and antisemitism, thusly:

"Hitler's project allowed the taking up of certain elements of modernity without having to accept social plurality. Thus key concerns of the anti-pluralist modernization of Catholicism seemed reachable through Hitler." Bucher concludes that

> at the core of these politics ("politics of salvation") lies a project of purification, of "cleansing," of liberation—however not always from my own sins or my own mortality, but from the others and the imposition they represent. This God promises an "eliminatory salvation," salvation at the cost of the existence and others. This is salvation from the ills of this world by eliminating everything and everybody allegedly responsible for my suffering. This salvation certainly has one great advantage: it can be politically produced, or so at least it promises. . . . Hitler's God promised salvation to the many through mercilessness to others. . . . In order to experience themselves as a community, this God's "chosen people" had to exclude others to the point of death.[113]

The attempt by the Vatican to bring the radical Catholic traditionalists out of schism and into the Church failed, for the moment at least, because the Church held true to the reforms of Vatican II. As Archbishop Gerhard Muller said on the breakdown of the talks with the SSPX, "We cannot give away the Catholic faith in negotiations. . . . There will be no compromises here."[114] For the radicals, even to the very end of Benedict's papacy, there was hope that the Church would ultimately cave in. Fellay is on record as saying, "For a moment I thought that with his resignation, Benedict XVI would perhaps make a final gesture in our favor as pope."[115]

The distinction between "good" and "bad" antisemitism did not vanish from Catholic teaching even after the Holocaust.[116] It took the document *Nostra Aetate*, to create what the Catholic scholar, Gregory Baum (who also contributed to the document) to describe as "the most radical transformation of the Church's *ordinary magisterium* to emerge from Vatican II" by confronting the heritage of antisemitism within the "teachings of contempt" and their horrific result.[117] *Nostra Aetate*'s impact on Catholic antisemitism and the Church's recognition of religious liberty have caused what John Pawlikowski called "the fundamental reorientation on the Christian-Jewish question."[118]

Under Pope Benedict, during a conservative retrenchment of the Church on doctrinal and liturgical issues, the Vatican came close to reconciling with those who would turn back the clock before finally standing firm. So far, all indications are that Pope Francis will stand strong and continue to reject the approaches of the radicals.[119]

Yet we are left with unanswered questions: How did a blatantly antisemitic group like the SSPX come so close to being restored to the Church's good graces? How could the Vatican have been blind to the overwhelming evidence of the SSPX's antisemitism? And, although Pope Francis appears to be healthy and vigorous, he is in his late seventies, and what will happen after his papacy? After all, as one astute observer of the Vatican has written: "A principal result of the reconciliation effort has been to shift the center of gravity in the church to the far right, so that right wingers who might have been on the fringe in years past are considered sensible centrists."[120]

The continued presence of a large and vigorous Catholic movement that embraces antisemitism and rejects the concept of religious liberty for others poses a clear threat to the political and religious rights of Jews and other non-Catholics. Rooted in the dark history of Christian culture, it is an attempt to restore antisemitism to theological legitimacy, and ultimately, if successful, to political power. Even as we strive to meet the threat posed by radical Islam and its allies, we should not neglect the threats that still lurk in our culture.

NOTES

1. Robert Wistrich, *A Lethal Obsession: Anti-Semitism from Antiquity to the Global Jihad* (New York: Random House, 2010), 62.

2. In this chapter I use the term Catholic to refer both to the Roman Catholic Church as an institution and to the body of religious teachings that are generally identified with the beliefs expressed by that institution.

3. Eric Voegelin, *Political Religions, The New Science of Politics,* and *Science, Politics, and Gnosticism,* vol. 5, *Collected Works of Eric Voegelin* (Columbia: University of Missouri Press, 1999). Dietmar Herz notes that Voegelin's "*Die Politische Religionen* primarily analyses National Socialism" but concludes by warning against an over simplified acceptance of the concept, which can lead to a "Procrustean bed of simplification: modern history is a history of decay." Herz, *The Concept of "Political Religions" in the Thought of Eric Voegelin,* in Hans Meier, ed. *Totalitarianism and Political Religions,* ed. Hans Meier, 149–165, vol. 1, *Concepts for the Comparison of Dictatorships* (London: Routledge, 2004).

4. Uriel Tal, "'Political Faith' of Nazism Prior to the Holocaust," in *Religion, Politics and Ideology in the Third Reich* (London: Routledge, 2004), 16; Tal, "On the Study of the Holocaust and Genocide," in *Religion, Politics and Ideology in the Third Reich,* 73.

5. Emilio Gentile, "Political Religion: A Concept and Its Critics—A Critical Survey," *Totalitarian Movements and Political Religions* 6, no. 1 (June 2005): 19–32.

6. Michael Cuneo, *Smoke of Satan* (Baltimore, Md.: Johns Hopkins University Press, 1999), 6.

7. Michael Warren, "Saint Pius X Catholic Group Protests Kristallnacht Interfaith Memorial in Argentina, Challenging Pope Francis," *Huffington Post,* 11/13/2013, http://www.huffingtonpost.com/2013/11/13/catholic -protests-kristallnacht-argentina_n_4267655.html?ref=topbar, accessed 3/24/14. A video of the disruption posted by a traditionalist sympathizer can be found at "SSPX Priest Disrupts Vatican II New Religion Interfaith Service," *YouTube,* 11/23/2013, http://www.youtube.com/watch?v=Hbf N8JQLzFk.

8. Michael Warren, "Catholic Fringe Disrupts Kristallnacht Ceremony," 11/13/2013, http://news.yahoo.com/catholic-fringe-disrupts-kristallnacht -ceremony-170954080.html. See also Jorge Mario Bergoglio and Abraham Skorka, *Sobre el cielo y la tierra* (Buenos Aires: Editorial Sudamericana, 2012, ebook), published in English as *On Heaven and Earth: Pope Francis on Faith, Family, and the Church in the Twenty-First Century,* trans. Alejandro Bermudez and Howard Goodman (New York: Image, 2013).

9. "Buenos Aires Rosary Protest: The Facts," Society of Saint Pius X, 11/13/2013, http://sspx.org/en/news-events/news/buenos-aires-rosary -protest-facts-2799.

10. Bernard Fellay, "Press Release from Bishop Fellay Concerning Bishop Williamson's Interview," Society of Saint Pius X, District of Canada, 1/27/2009, http://fsspx.com/Documents/Bishop-Fellay/bishop_fellay_statement_re_bishop_williamson_english.pdf.

11. Jeff Mirus, "The SSPX, Jews, and Authority," CatholicCulture.org, 10/21/2011, http://www.catholicculture.org/commentary/otc.cfm?id=880.

12. Alessandro Speciale, "SSPX, Benedicts XVI's Unfinished Business," *Huffington Post*, 3/6/2013, www.huffingtonpost.com/2013/03/06/sspx-benedict-xvis-unfinished-business_n2816304.html, accessed 3/7/2013.

13. Israel J. Yuval, *Two Nations in Your Womb: Perceptions of Jews and Christians in Late Antiquity and the Middle Ages* (Berkeley: University of California Press, 2008), 20–21.

14. Michael Phayer, *The Catholic Church and the Holocaust, 1930–1965*, (Bloomington: Indiana University Press, 2001), 203.

15. Speciale, "SSPX, Benedicts XVI's Unfinished Business."

16. Tom Heneghan, "Vatican Plans No More Talks with SSPX Catholic Rebels: CDF Head Muller," *Reuters*, 10/5/2012, blogs.reuters.com/faith world/2012/10/05/vatican-plans-no-more-talks-with-sspx-catholic-rebels-cdf-head-muller/, accessed 3/7/12.

17. Michael Davies, *Apologia Pro Marcel Lefebvre, Part One* (Dickinson, Tex.: Angelus Press, 1979), 26. See Jules Isaac's seminal work, *The Teachings of Contempt* (New York: Holt, Rinehart and Winston, 1964).

18. Cuneo, *Smoke of Satan,* 91. Lefebvre's full perspective is in his *Religious Liberty Questioned,* trans. Jaime Pazat de Lys (Kansas City, Mo.: Angelus Press, 2001). A radical Catholic traditionalist reviews Lefebvre's book at Angelus Online, August 2002, http://www.angelusonline.org/index.php?section=articles&subsection=show_article&article_id=2152.

19. Cuneo, *Smoke of Satan,* 91–92.

20. "Vatican Urges Holocaust Denier to Recant," *World Today,* 5/2/2009, http://www.abc.net.au/worldtoday/content/2008/s2483182.htm, or "Holocaust-Denying Bishop Loses Court Battle," CNN, 9/2/2009, http://www.cnn.com/2009/WORLD/europe/02/09/germany.bishop/; "Pope to Cancel Excommunication of Rebel Bishops," *Telegraph,* 1/22/2009, http://www.telegraph.co.uk/news/worldnews/europe/vaticancityandholysee/4317996/Pope-to-cancel-excommunication-of-rebel-bishops.html.

21. "SSPX Expels Bishop Williamson," *Catholic Herald,* 10/24/2012, http://www.catholicherald.co.uk/news/2012/10/24/sspx-expels-bishop-williamson/. Also see Steven L. Jacobs and Mark Weitzman, *Dismantling the Big Lie: "The Protocols of the Elders of Zion"* (Los Angeles: Simon Wiesenthal Center in association with KTAV Pub. House, Jersey City, N.J.,

2003), for recent use of the Protocols, as well as a detailed refutation of the text.

22. Richard Williamson, quoted in "Vatican Rejects Bishop's Apology," BBC News, 2/27/2009, http://news.bbc.co.uk/2/hi/europe/7915022.stm.

23. "Vatican Rejects Bishop's Apology," BBC News.

24. Grant Gallicho, "Lefebvrites and Judaism (Updated)," Commonweal, 1/26/2009, http://www.commonwealmagazine.org/blog/?p=2721.

25. Richard Williamson, "The Gulf War and the State of the Catholic Church Today," Bishop Williamson's Letters, 2/1/1991, http://williamson letters.blogspot.com/2009/02/gulf-war-and-state-of-catholic-church.html.

26. Richard Williamson, letter Nov. 3, 1991, on letterhead of the SSPX's St. Thomas Aquinas Seminary in Winona, Minnesota, copy in my possession.

27. Richard Williamson, May 1, 2000, cited in Thomas C. Fox, "Lefebvre Movement: Long, Troubled History with Judaism," NCR Online, 1/26/2009, http://ncronline.org/news/lefebvre-movement-long-troubled-history -judaism.

28. Richard Williamson, "Denial of Christ Creates Chaos," Living in Tradition, 11/14/2005, http://www.dailycatholic.org/issue/05Nov/nov 141it.htm.

29. Williamson, letter Nov. 3, 1991.

30. Thomas C. Fox, "Lefebvre Movement: Long, Troubled History with Judaism," NCR Online, 1/26/2009, http://ncronline.org/news/lefebvre -movement-long-troubled-history-judaism. The full text of the 1985 letter is in "Letter of Lefebvre and De Castro Mayer to Holy Father (Aug. 31, 1985)," point 3, box 192, folder box 8, box 11, American Catholic History Research Center and University Archives (hereafter ACUA), Catholic University, Washington, D.C.

31. "The Archbishop Speaks," typescript, March 30 and April 18, 1986, box 192, folder 8, box 7, ACUA.

32. Fox, "Lefebvre Movement."

33. Ibid.

34. On Paul Touvier and his connection to the SSPX, see his obituary by David Stout, New York Times, July 18, 1996, reproduced at http://www .writing.upenn.edu/~afilreis/Holocaust/touvier-obit.html.

35. http://sspx.org/en/news-events/news/priebke-funeral-clarifying -interview-2703.

36. "Can It Truly Be Said that the Jewish Race Is Guilty of the Sin of Deicide, and that It Is Consequently Cursed by God, as Depicted in Gibson's Movie on the Passion?" Featured in the Q and A section, March 2004, http://www.salvationisfromthejews.com/g1.html.

37. Michael Crowley and Kenneth Novak, "Of the Jewish People in History," *Angelus,* April 1997. Available at http://holywar.org/mystery.htm.

38. Gerald Sigaud to Cardinal Tardini, "What Vatican II Should Have Done," August 22, 1959. Published in *Angelus,* it was later posted online on the SSPX website before being taken down. A copy is in my possession, but it can still be found online at http://aventors.blogspot.com/2010/04/what -vatican-ii-should-have-done.html.

39. Mary Christine Athans, *The Coughlin-Fahey Connection: Father Denis Fahey, C. S. SP., and Religious Anti-Semitism in the United States, 1938–1954* (New York: Peter Lang, 1991).

40. David Kertzer, *The Popes against the Jews* (New York: Alfred A. Knopf, 2001), 170.

41. Richard Wolin, *Seduction of Unreason,* 3, cited in David Dennis, *Inhumanities: Nazi Interpretations of Western Culture* (Cambridge: Cambridge University Press, 2012), 491n1. Dennis also cites Fritz Stern's similar observation that "they (the Nazis) appropriated something from every intellectual tradition of modern Germany, except one. They consistently warred against the ideas of the Enlightenment and the French Revolution." (Stern, *The Politics of Cultural Despair,* 277, quoted in Dennis, *Inhumanities,* 491n1).

42. Athans, *Coughlin-Fahey Connection,* 59.

43. Ibid., 22–23.

44. Ibid., 62–63, n25. Yves Congar, *Challenge to the Church: The Case of Archbishop Marcel Lefèbvre,* trans. Paul Inwood (Huntington, Ind.: Our Sunday Visitor, 1976), 16, 88–90; see also George Rutler, "1942—Complicated Loyalties," CatholiCity, 3/22/2010, http://www.catholicity.com /commentary/rutler/07849.html.

45. Davies, *Apologia Pro Marcel Lefebvre.*

46. Denis Fahey, *The Rulers of Russia* ([Detroit: Condon Printing Co.], 1940), 44–45.

47. Ibid., 22.

48. Ibid., 72.

49. "An Interview with Bishop Williamson on Pope Benedict XVI's Christmas Address to the Curia," *FishEaters Traditional Catholic Forum,* http://www.fisheaters.com/forums/index.php?topic=893264.0.

50. Marcel Lefebvre quoted in *Rome-SSPX, Background to the Doctrinal Discussions,* a traditionalist website.

51. Matthias Gaudron, "Catechism of the Crisis in the Church: Part 8," *Angelus,* January 2008, http://www.angelusonline.org/index.php?section =articles&subsection=show_article&article_id=2671.

52. John Vennari, "Judaism and the Church: Before and After Vatican II," http://www.sspx.org. Vennari is the editor of *Catholic Family News,* a monthly that is one of the most prominent radical publications. Vennari gives his source as Pope Pius VII, letter, "Post tam diurturnas," quoted in Denis Fahey, *The Kingship of Christ and Organized Naturalism* (1943; reprint Palmdale, Calif.: Christian Book Club of America, 1987), 10.

53. Fahey, *Rulers of Russia,* 50–51.

54. Denis Fahey, *What Really Is Anti-Semitism,* posted on the sspx website at http://www.salvationisfromthejews.com. The description that he quoted approvingly was taken from a review of his *The Kingship of Christ and the Conversion of the Jewish Nation* published in *La Civilta Cattolica,* March 1947.

55. Fahey, *Kingship of Christ,* 5–6. The body of the book was written before the war.

56. Hubert Wolf, *Pope and Devil: The Vatican's Archives and the Third Reich* 2nd ed. (Cambridge, Mass.: Belknap Press of Harvard University Press, 2012), 111. Wolf also links the opposition to the *Amici Israel,* spearheaded by the influential Vatican secretary of state Cardinal Merry del Val, to the Vatican's "antimodernism," as reflected in del Val's use of "code words (that) had been just two decades earlier used by Pius X in his condemnation of modernism" (107). John Connelly, *From Enemy to Brother: The Revolution in Catholic Teaching on the Jews, 1933–1965* (Cambridge, Mass.: Harvard University Press, 2012), 170, quotes del Val's 1928 statement that "Hebraism with all its sects inspired by the Talmud continues perfidiously to oppose Christianity," a statement that was mirrored in Fahey's works. According to Wolf's account of the *Amici Israel* incident, Pope Pius XI had by this time recognized the dangers of racial antisemitism and wanted to refer to it by using "the term anti-semitism, which del Val apparently wished to delete" (Wolf, *Pope and Devil,* 113).

57. Birgit Gregor, "Zum protestantischen Antisemitismus Evangelische Kirchen in der Zeit des Nationalsozialismus," in *Beseitigung des judischen Einfluss . . . : Antisemitische Forschung, Eliten und Karrieren in Nationalsozialismus,* ed. Fritz Bauer Institute (Frankfurt: Campus Verlag, 199), 174–177, cited in Wayne Meeks, "A Nazi New Testament Professor Reads the Bible: The Strange Case of Gerhard Kittel," in *The Idea of Biblical Interpretation: Essays in Honor of James L. Kugel,* ed. Hindy Najman and Judith H. Newman (Leiden: Brill, 2004), 539n68. Meeks also refers there to Paul Lawrence Rose's insight that "racist thinking was predicated on the notion of 'a national character' that is central to the evolution of modern antisemitism"

(and thus there was no major demarcation between religious and racial antisemitism). Paul Lawrence Rose, *Revolutionary Antisemitism in Germany from Kant to Wagner* (Princeton, N.J.: Princeton University Press, 1990), 15.

58. Fahey, *Kingship of Christ and the Conversion of the Jewish Nation*, 44–45, 57.

59. For a convincing exploration of the Nazis overwhelming obsession with and reliance on antisemitism as a driving force for World War II and the Holocaust, see Jeffrey Herf, *The Jewish Enemy: Nazi Propaganda during World War II and the Holocaust* (Cambridge, Mass.: Belknap Press of Harvard University Press, 2006.

60. Wolf, *Pope and Devil*, gives an excellent summary of del Val and Pacelli's position on these issues:

> In a letter dated December 9. 1926, Merry del Val . . . praised Pacelli's September letter to the German bishops as *zelante,* which from his perspective was an expression of the highest possible praise. This is surprising, at first glance because the word *zelante* has rather negative connotations and is usually translated as zealot. But in the Curia, the term *zelante* is associated with something considerably greater. . . . The *zelanti* . . . were religious hardliners who opposed all political compromise. . . . Not only had the *zelanti* taken up the cause against the Protestant heresy; they had at least since the French Revolution been in complete opposition to anything that even remotely smacked of *liberte, egalite* and *fraternite.* . . . One of the most important avowed twentieth-century *zelanti* happened to be Merry del Val, who as Pius X's cardinal secretary of state had been made responsible for rooting out modernists in the Catholic Church. Democracy, the emancipation of the Jews, and ecumenism were deeply abhorrent to him. By 'honoring' Pacelli as a *zelante,* Merry del Val was acknowledging him as a member of his party of fighters, unflinching in their advocacy of Catholic truth. (236–237)

61. Connelly, *From Enemy to Brother*, 26. Connelly also described Hudal as a "Catholic bridge builder to Nazism." After World War II, Hudal was a major figure in the notorious "rat line," the escape route for Nazis on the run from Europe to South American or Arab countries. On this see Gerald Steinacher, *Nazis on the Run: How Hitler's Henchmen Fled Justice,* trans. Shaun Whiteside (Oxford: Oxford University Press, 2011).

62. Wolf, *Pope and Devil*, notes that in Papal Nuncio Orsenigo's memo to the Vatican of his meeting with Hitler in 1933, "he assured us that he viewed the Jews as vermin, and recalling the position of the Catholic

Church up to the end of the fifteenth century, regretted that liberalism had not seen this danger" (205).

63. Fahey, *Kingship of Christ and the Conversion of the Jewish Nation,* 169–173, 174.

64. Fahey, *Rulers of Russia,* 75.

65. Fahey, *Kingship of Christ and the Conversion of the Jewish Nation,* 53.

66. Athans, *Coughlin-Fahey Connection,* 224.

67. Donald Warren, *Radio Priest: Charles Coughlin, the Father of Hate Radio* (New York: Free Press, 1996), 188–189, 305, cited in Joseph W. Bendersky, "Dissension in the Face of the Holocaust: The 1941 American Debate over Antisemitism," *Holocaust and Genocide Studies* 24, no. 1 (spring 2010): 96.

68. See, for example, David Bennett, *The Party of Fear* (New York: Vintage, 1995), 263–266.

69. Athans, *Coughlin-Fahey Connection.*

70. *Brooklyn Tablet,* Feb. 4, 1939, cited in Esther Feldblum, *The American Catholic Press and the Jewish State, 1917–1959* (New York: KTAV Publishing House, 1977), 46.

71. Leonard Dinnerstein, *Antisemitism in America* (New York: Oxford University Press, 1995), 120–123, 132–133. Philip Jenkins, *Hoods and Shirts: The Extreme Right in Pennsylvania 1925–1950* (Chapel Hill: University of North Carolina Press, 1997), examines the Christian Front and similar groups in one state.

72. FDR Papers, President's Secretary's File, 1941, box 51, Franklin D. Roosevelt Library, Hyde Park, New York.

73. Charles R. Gallagher, *Vatican Secret Diplomacy: Joseph P. Hurley and Pope Pius XII* (New Haven, Conn.: Yale University Press, 2008), 68–70; see also Charles R. Gallagher, "A Peculiar Brand of Patriotism: The Holy See, FDR, and the Case of Reverend Charles E. Coughlin," in *FDR, the Vatican, and the Roman Catholic Church in America, 1933–1945,* ed. David B. Woolner and Richard G. Kurial (New York: Palgrave Macmillan, 2003), 272–275. Gallagher also points out that Hurley "became the only bishop of the entire Second Vatican Council to officially and publicly protest the signing of Nostra Aetate" (275).

74. For example, see Coughlin's letter to Fahey: "while anti-Semitism is to abhorred in so far as it is related to hatred for the Jews as individuals and racials, nevertheless, *anti-Judaism, which means opposition to the Judaic concept of life, is not to be so condemned* . . . I cannot understand how so many amongst our hierarchy and clergy are demonstrating tolerance towards Judaism," Charles Coughlin to Denis Fahey, March 5, 1941, quoted in Athans, *Coughlin-Fahey Connection,* 188–189.

75. Williamson, "Letter from St Thomas Aquinas Seminary, Ridgefield, Conn, Aug. 10, 1987," box 192, 8,11, ACUA.

76. Denis Fahey, "Letter of May 3, 1949," in Athans, *New Perspectives,* 213. For more on Smith, see Glen Jeansonne's informative biography, *Gerald L. K. Smith: Minister of Hate* (Baton Rouge: Louisiana University Press, 1997).

77. George Michael, *Willis Carto and the American Far Right* (Gainesville: University Press of Florida, 2008), 20, 10, 154.

78. Ibid., 74.

79. Mark Weber, "Bishop Williamson and 'Holocaust Denial': Why the Uproar?," Institute for Historical Review, 3/4/2009, http://www.ihr.org/williamson_march09.html.

80. http://robertfaurisson.blogspot.com/2009/04/mark-weber-must-resign-from-institute.html.

81. Louis Vezelis, "Examine All the Evidence," *Journal of Historical Review* 13, no. 5 (September/October 1993): 34–35. Buckley's opinion of Sobran's antisemitism can be found in his *In Search of Anti-Semitism* (New York: Continuum, 1992). His conclusion there was that Sobran had indeed "written anti-semitic articles" (118–119).

82. Reverend Louis Vezelis, "A Sermon for the 10th Sunday after Pentecost—Domus Dei," *Angelus* 1, no. 7 (July 1978): 8–10.

83. Mark Weber, "Joseph Sobran and Historical Revisionism," *Journal of Historical Review* 7, no. 3 (fall 1986): 373–374, accessed at http://www.ihr.org/jhr/v07/v07p373_Weber.html; Joseph Sobran, "For Fear of the Jews," accessed at http://www.ihr.org/conference/14thconf/sobranconf.html.

84. Joseph Sobran, "The Church and Jewish Ideology," reprinted from *Sobran's,* May 1999, 4, accessed at http://sobran.com/jewid.shtml

85. "Is Pat Buchanan Anti-Semitic?," *Newsweek,* 12/22/91, accessed at http://www.newsweek.com/pat-buchanan-anti-semitic-201176.

86. Pat Buchanan, "A Triumph for Traditionalists," 2007, http://www.creators.com/opinion/pat-buchanan/a-triumph-for-traditionalists.html.

87. Lowell Ponte, "Memories of William F. Buckley Jr.," Newsmax, 2/28/2008, http://www.newsmax.com/LowellPonte/William-Buckley/2008/02/28/id/323027/. For Buckley's judgment on Sobran, see Buckley, *In Search of Anti-Semitism,* 119, where he concludes, "as for me, it was enough he had written anti-Semitic articles." Buckley's judgment of Buchanan was "I find it impossible to defend Pat Buchanan against the charge that what he did and said during the period under examination amounted to anti-Semitism" (44). The book originated as an extended essay that occupied a whole issue of Buckley's journal, *National Review* (Dec. 30, 1991).

88. Salvador L. Lazo, "My Return to the Traditional Latin Mass: Autobiography of a Traditional Catholic Bishop," Society of St, Pius X, District
of Asia, March–April 2000, http://www.sspxasia.com/Newsletters/2000
/March-April/Autobiography.htm.

89. The letter can now be found at http://www.leofec.com/bishop
-williamson/64.html.

90. Cuneo, *Smoke of Satan,* 40.

91. E. Michael Jones, "The Conversion of the Revolutionary Jew," accessed at http://www.culturewars.com/2006/Conversion.htm.

92. Martin Vianney, "An Interview with Dr. E. Michael Jones on *The
Jewish Revolutionary Spirit,*" *Culture Wars,* 2008, accessed at http://www
.culturewars.com/2008/JRSInterview.htm.

93. See Mark Weitzman, *Magical Logic: Globalization, Conspiracy Theory and the Shoah,* Posen Papers in Contemporary Antisemitism 10 (Jerusalem: Vidal Sassoon International Center for the Study of Antisemitism,
2008), 18, where I cite Tillawi as an example of one who is trying to bridge
the gap between the far left, the extreme right, and radical Islam.

94. E. Michael Jones, *L'affaire Williamson: The Catholic Church and
Holocaust Denial* ebook (South Bend, Ind.: Fidelity Press, [2012]).

95. To this point in the text paragraph, all quotations are from Sungenis's answers at "Ask Your Question about the Jews, Judaism, Zionism,
etc.," accessed from his website at http://www.catholicintl.com.

96. *Q&A's* April 2005, accessed at http://www.catholicintl.com.

97. "An Exclusive Interview with Bishop Richard Williamson," accessed
at http://forums.catholic.com/showthread.php?t=367176.

98. Christopher A. Ferrara, "Triumph and Tribulation: Pope under
Fire for Lifting Excommunication of SSPX Bishops," 1/26/09, accessed at
http://www.remnantnewspaper.com/Archives/2009-0131-ferrara-triumph
_and_tribulation.htm#_edn8. For Ferrara's reliance on Fahey, see Cardinal Ratzinger Fan Club, http://www.ratzingerfanclub.com/covenant_and
_mission.html.

99. A Catholic site that charges Sungenis with plagiarizing from those
antisemitic sources is William Cork, Robert Sungenis and the Jews, http://
sungenisandthejews.blogspot.com/search/label/plagiarism. There, Cork
does a side-by-side demonstration of Sungenis's writings and the original
uncredited sources.

100. David Palm, "Sources, Schoeman, and Sungenis," *Robert Sungenis
and the Jews,* 2/17/2007, http://sungenisandthejews.blogspot.com/2007
/02/sungenis-and-jews-sources-schoeman-and.html. Palm identifies himself as a traditionalist Catholic.

101. https://www.facebook.com/photo.php?fbid=619356591445593&set
=a.104545786260012.2844.100001137739551&type=1&comment_id=1885852
&offset=0&total_comments=364.

102. Kevin MacDonald, *The Culture of Critique: An Evolutionary Analysis of Jewish Involvement in Twentieth-Century Intellectual and Political Movements* (Westport, Conn.: Praeger, 1998); Kevin MacDonald, *Separation and Its Discontents Toward an Evolutionary Theory of Anti-Semitism,* (Westport, Conn.: Praeger, 1998); Kevin MacDonald, *A People That Shall Dwell Alone: Judaism as a Group Evolutionary Strategy, with Diaspora Peoples* (Westport, Conn.: Praeger, 1994).

103. George Michael, "Professor Kevin MacDonald's Critique of Judaism: Legitimate Scholarship or the Intellectualization of Anti-Semitism?," *Journal of Church and State,* 2006, 779–806, available online at http://www.kevinmacdonald.net/JC&S48-2006.pdf.

104. Kevin MacDonald, "The Church and anti-Semitism—Again," *Occidental Observer,* 2/2/2009, http://www.theoccidentalobserver.net/articles/MacDonald-sspx.html. MacDonald refers approvingly to claims by another radical Catholic traditionalist, James C. Russell, who MacDonald paraphrases as having said that "the Church was influenced by German culture." In 2010, Russell's writings became a matter of public controversy; he won the Republican and Conservative parties nomination to run against a long-term Democratic Congressional incumbent in a suburban New York district, however when one of his articles that was published in the *Occidental Quarterly* in 2001 became a matter of public record, the Republicans tried to drop him as their candidate. See Leah Rae, "Westchester GOP Drops Candidate over Inflammatory Essay," *Journal News,* 9/22/2010 and related stories available at http://www.lohud.com/article/20100922/NEWS01/9220350/Westchester%20GOP%20drops%20candidate%20over%20inflammatory%20essay.

105. *Sharpe v. Landmark* Opinion, 4/9/2009, Norfolk Circuit Court Office, http://www.icourt.info/Opinions/judge/Thomas/Sharpe-v-Landmark-Opinion.pdf.

106. IHS Press, http://www.ihspress.com/index1.htm.

107. Roger Griffin, *The Nature of Fascism* (London: Routledge, 2013), xii–xiii.

108. An interview with Derek Holland is available at the *"In the Spirit of Chartes" Committee* website. Identified there as codirector of IHS Press, the Gates of Vienna, and Light in the Darkness Publications (www.ihspress.com), he also appeared at a gathering of radical traditionalists held in Washington DC in September 2013.

109. "Topic: Jim Condit Jr.: Why Ron Paul Campaign Failed; Why Obama Campaign Succeeded," *Freedom Portal*, October 2008, http://www.freedomportal.net/forum/index.php?topic=9657.0.

110. Thom Patterson, "No Oscar Battle for 'Passion' Partisans," CNN *Entertainment*, 1/27/2005, http://www.cnn.com/2005/SHOWBIZ/Movies/01/26/oscar.passion/index.html?iref=newssearch.

111. John Sharpe, "Judaism and the Vatican," *Angelus*, March 2003, http://www.angelusonline.org/index.php?section=articles&subsection=show_article&article_id=2211.

112. "Tissier de Mallerais Speaks," *Rorate Cæli*, 2/1/2009, http://rorate-caeli.blogspot.com/2009/02/tissier-de-mallerais-speaks.html.

113. Rainer Bucher, *Hitler's Theology: A Study in Political Religion* (London: Continuum, 2011), 97, 113–114.

114. Heneghan, "Vatican Plans No More Talks with SSPX Catholic Rebels."

115. Interview by Pierre de Bellerive of *Nouvelles de France*, 2/15/2013, sspx.org/superior_generals_news/pope_benedicts_last_major_act_bishop_fellay_interview_2-15-2013.htm.

116. Elena Mazzini, "The Presence of Antisemitism in the Catholic World: The Case of the 'Enciclopedia Catholica' (1948–1954)," *Quest: Issues in Contemporary Jewish History* 1 (April 2010),accessed at http://www.quest-cdecjournal.it/focus.php?id=196, points out that the entry on anti-semitism in the authoritative, twelve-volume *Enciclopedia*, after condemning the crimes of Nazism, concludes by describing how "Only on these bases . . . is anti-Semitism legitimate in the field of ideas, and aimed at the watchful protection of the religious-moral and social heritage of Christianity." Mazzini further notes that the author of that entry, the Catholic priest-scholar Antonino Romeo, also referred to a 1951 article of his where he claimed "That many Israelites today . . . see His Kingdom in modern 'progress,' or they identify it with the triumph of the principles of the French Revolution." My thanks to Dr. Natalia Indrimi for this reference.

117. Gregory Baum, "The Social Context of American Catholic Theology," in *Proceedings of the Catholic Theological Society of America* 41 (1986): 87, cited in John Pawlikowski, "Vatican II's Nostra Aetate: Its Impact on the Church's Theological Self-Understanding," *New Theology Review* 25, no. 2 (March 2013). My thanks to Father Pawlikowski for this article. The journalist Adam Gopnik, writing about the iconic English traditionalist Catholic writer G. K. Chesterton, points out "The insistence that Chesterston's antisemitism needs to be understood 'in the context of his time' defines the problem, because his time—from the end of the Great War to the

mid-thirties—was the time that led to the extermination of the European Jews." Gopnik, "The Back of the World," *New Yorker* 7, no. 14 (July 2008).

118. Pawlikowski, "Vatican II's Nostra Aetate."

119. According to Fellay, a reported meeting this spring between Pope Francis and the SSPX leader was nothing more than "a brief exchange . . . that lasted a few seconds." Fellay added that for now "we stay as we are," indicating no more movement toward reconciliation. "About a Meeting: Pope Francis and Bishop Fellay," 5/12/2014, SSPX *News & Events,* http://sspx.org/en/news-events/news/about-meeting-pope-francis-and-bishop-fellay-4067, accessed 7/27/14.

120. David Gibson, "The Jews and the Masons, Again . . . ," *Commonweal,* 1/4/2013, www.Commonwealmagazine.org/blog/?p=22593.

PART III

Holocaust Denial, Evasion, Minimization

The Uniqueness Debate Revisited

BERNARD HARRISON

There is [in Holocaust studies] a distinct danger of escaping from the reality of the Nazi regime and its consequences into a nebulous general humanism, where all persecutions become holocausts, and where a general and meaningless condemnation of evil helps to establish a curtain between oneself and the real world. This escapism must of course be fought.

—Yehuda Bauer, *The Holocaust in Historical Perspective*

PRELIMINARIES

THE LONG-RUNNING dispute over the question of whether the Holocaust was a unique event has divided opinion since roughly the start of the 1990s to the present. An excellent account that surveys its various stages and its main contributors can be found in an outstanding book by Gavriel Rosenfeld.[1] My concern here is simply to tease out some of the more fundamental assumptions of the debate, in the process raising what I think are some pressing questions concerning their intellectual and moral solidity.

Several features of the uniqueness debate mark it out from the general run of academic, scholarly, controversies. There is, for instance, the unusual degree of acrimony with which it has frequently been conducted. Another curious feature of the debate is its power to unite the academic at one extreme with the scurrilous at the other. The academic end of this spectrum of opinion has, since 1996, found rich expression in Alan S. Rosenbaum's voluminous anthology, *Is the Holocaust Unique? Perspectives in Comparative Genocide,* which has now run into three editions.[2] The other, scurrilous, extreme can be encountered in the spatter of openly antisemitic and Holocaust-denial websites to be located by typing the words "was the Holocaust Unique?" into a search engine.

As putatively academic debates go, this one has proved unusually free, even for the present age of culture wars, of the disinterested objectivity popularly associated with the academy. On the contrary, it has been remarkable from the outset for the incessant and resolute grinding of political axes that has accompanied its various phases. Finally, it has been widely characterized, by journalistic and academic observers alike, as a dialogue, or rather a collection of dialogues, of the deaf, in which participants characteristically argue, not so much against, as past one another.

QUESTIONS OF DEFINITION

At its most abstract level, the dispute turns on the question of whether the terms "Holocaust" and "Genocide" are general terms, like "horse," or proper names, like Aristotle or Bismarck: whether, in short, given the nature of the thing named, there can be, in principle, more than one such thing.

When such abstruse, quite literally philosophical, issues become the focus of high emotions and pitched battles among nonphilosophers, there is generally a reason. In this case, the reason is itself philosophical. One of my teachers at the University of Michigan in the late 1950s was the late C. L. Stevenson. Stevenson was, and remains, famous for his book *Ethics and Language,* a monument of American Pragmatism that is still read, though not as much as it should be. His chapter 9 concerns what he calls "Persuasive Definitions." For Stevenson, the meaning of a moral term, for example *freedom,* has two components. First, there is a factual description, a statement of what constitutes a free society. Then, secondly, there is the emotional aura, of approval or disapproval, that surrounds the word; in the case of *murder,* a negative, disapproving one; in the case of *freedom,* a positive, approving one.

Stevenson takes from Hume the thought that these two components of meaning can be made, on occasion, to shift independently of one another. A term like *freedom* or *murder* thus becomes an instrument of political or moral persuasion to the extent that one can get people to accept a shift in its descriptive meaning while leaving its emotional aura unchanged. If one can persuade people, for instance, that abortion counts descriptively as murder, then the bleakly negative emotional aura surrounding the term *murder* can be successfully displaced onto the term *abortion.* If one can persuade people to accept that part of being free, descriptively speaking, is to possess a legally enforceable right to medical care, then the warm emotional aura surrounding the term *freedom* can be displaced on to the idea of state provision of medical care. As Stevenson puts it: "Our language abounds with words which, like 'culture,' have both a vague descriptive meaning and a rich emotive meaning. The descriptive meaning of them all is subject to constant redefinition. The words are prizes which each man seeks to bestow on the qualities of his own choice."[3]

THE CONTESTED POSITIONS

An understanding of Stevenson's distinction, it seems to me, is essential to making sense of the uniqueness debate. The debate exists only because the intense emotive auras surrounding the words "Holocaust" and "Genocide" have become covetable enough for the words themselves to become "prizes" in exactly the sense that Stevenson here exposes. What turns a word into a "prize" for political debate, he suggests, are the evaluative and associative structures that constitute its "emotive meaning." In the case of "Holocaust" and "Genocide," these include horror and revulsion against the perpetrators, on the one hand, and on the other, sympathy and fellow feeling for the victims.

These, of course, are responses of a kind that all of us would wish acts of mass murder to evoke. And recent history offers many episodes of mass murder, including many felt, by the communities involved, to be inadequately recognized or condemned. This has led some to seek redress for that situation in what Charles Stevenson would have called a persuasive redefinition of the terms "Holocaust" and "Genocide." If, such people feel, the *descriptive* meaning of those terms could only be redefined in such a way as to make them capture, descriptively, just *any* episode of mass killing, then the *emotive* meaning of the words, the responses of pity and horror indelibly associated with them, would transfer over to a multitude of eminently deserving cases in exactly the manner described by Stevenson.

The trouble, from the point of view of those who think like this, is that both "Holocaust" and "Genocide" are uniquely linked, in their origins with one specific episode of mass murder. And that episode has generally been supposed to stand, for reasons, some of which I attempt later in this chapter to unearth and examine, in a unique relationship to one particular people, namely, the Jews.

For the emotive connotations of the terms to transfer to other episodes of mass murder, involving other, non-Jewish groups, therefore, that link must be broken. To a degree it has been broken, since the events of the Second World War brought the word into being, in the case of the term *genocide*. Significant ambiguities attend the word, as they do all the contested terms in the uniqueness debate. It remains contestable, for instance, whether for an act of genocide to have occurred the *gens* in question must have undergone total extermination or "merely" have endured persecution *aiming at* total extermination, or "merely" great loss of life; or whether, for that matter, there can be such a thing as cultural genocide, where the people of a nation, or some of them, remain extant, but where everything that gave their nation its character as a special human group has been systematically extirpated. But on any of these readings of the term, historical instances both Jewish and non-Jewish can be found; for actual more or less total extermination (by systematic hunting, among other things), the Tasmanian aboriginals, for cultural genocide the Inca, or the inhabitants of a few mountain villages in Portugal, about whom I once read, survivors of successive persecutions of Jews, "new Christians" and Marranos, who know only that they once were, or were descended from, Jews, but nothing of Jewish religion of culture.

Genocide, then, has become, for better or worse, a general term. There can be, have been, genocides other than the Holocaust. The term "Holocaust," on the other hand, remains obstinately possessed, in common usage, of the logical characteristics of a proper name. A proper name, such as Bismarck, or Gandhi, names a single individual; in the case of those names, an individual person; in the case of "Holocaust," an individual act of mass murder, namely the Nazi destruction of the bulk of European Jewry between 1933 and 1945.

The uniqueness controversy has concerned, for the most part, the issue of whether that link, too, can and should be broken. Some—David E. Stannard, Ward Churchill, Norman Finkelstein, the late Tony Judt in some of his writing, and many others—consider that there is nothing about the murderous events commonly denominated by the term "Holocaust" that links those events specifically to the *Jewishness* of their Jewish victims. On such a view, "Holocaust" becomes to all intents and purposes a synonym for *genocide* and shares all the ambiguities, and the resulting subordination to a multitude of political uses, that have come to characterize the latter term.

The thought is that what happened to the Jewish victims of the Nazis happened also to even larger numbers of their non-Jewish victims, whose sufferings, it is then alleged, are diminished and obscured by the concentration, in commemorative activities of all kinds, from museums to educational programs, on the sufferings of the Jews. Should we not then, such reasoners suggest, universalize, so to speak, our conception of the Holocaust by recognizing that what made it a *crime against humanity* was that its victims, irrespective of whether they were Jew or Gentile, Germans, Poles, or Soviet prisoners of war, were *human beings*. And does not that eminently humane and reasonable shift of perspective, they conclude, commit one, further, to seeing the Holocaust not as something confined to the Second World War, or even to Europe, but as a type of human aberration that has had, and continues to have, many exemplars, from the Cambodian massacres under Pol Pot in Cambodia to Srebrenica, or for that matter to the history of Palestine since 1948.

Against this way of reconceiving the Holocaust, a wide spectrum of scholars, whose Jewish representatives include Elie Wiesel, Yehuda Bauer, Emil Fackenhein, Lucy Dawidowicz, Steven Katz, Deborah Lipstadt, Daniel Goldhagen, and Alvin Rosenfeld, have in general retorted that one cannot universalize the Holocaust in that way without de-Judaizing it in ways utterly false to the historical record.[4] The basic thrust of their objections is that to treat the Holocaust as a crime against humanity rather than against a specific people, the Jews, is not merely to render its nature and origins impossible to understand, except in terms of some vague and explanatorily vacuous notion of evil or the darkness of the human heart. It is to erase Jews and Jewishness from the historical record in a manner entirely agreeable to, and indeed reminiscent of, the ideology of National Socialism.

THE JEWS AS PUTATIVELY JEALOUS "PROPRIETORS" OF THE HOLOCAUST

Given the seemingly progressive and humanitarian note characteristically struck by opponents of the uniqueness claim, such as the Native American historians David E. Stannard or Ward Churchill, however, the evident attraction their views exercise for the promoters of openly antisemitic, revisionist, and white supremacist websites might appear surprising.[5] Codoh.com, for example, the website of a Holocaust-denial group calling itself the Committee for Open Debate on the Holocaust, posts a 1996 essay by the former, "The Dangers of Calling the Holocaust Unique," despite the fact that, in it, Stannard expressly dissociates himself at the outset from both Holocaust denial and antisemitism.

What strikes one about these caveats is that the internal logic of the enterprise of "universalizing," and thus necessarily de-Judaizing, the Holocaust itself works to defeat any such attempt at dissociation. Arguments involving what Stevenson called "persuasive definition" are, by their nature, arguments about *ownership*— even though the "asset" whose ownership they contest is no more than a word; or to be more accurate, the emotional connotations of a word. From this perspective, the attempt, especially when conducted by Jewish writers, to defend the singularity of the Holocaust considered as the attempt to destroy a specific people, the Jews, can only be perceived as an attempt to assert a *proprietary* claim to the word and its emotional connotations, and thus as an attempt to exclude other abused groups from enjoyment of any benefit that might accrue to them in consequence of the horror and sympathy widely evoked by the very word "Holocaust."

Once that thought has been introduced into the debate—as it must be if the debate is to get off the ground at all—it can hardly fail to ignite, by association, a familiar range of antisemitic stereotypes. There is, for a start, that of the obstinately "particularist" Jew, with no interest in anybody's suffering but his own, attached passionately to his own community, but chillingly unresponsive to wider humanitarian causes. Then, more darkly, there is the stereotype of the Jew as owner of assets that by rights should not belong to him at all; the Jew who uses his legendary business abilities, in underhanded ways that baffle the simple blond

Gentile, to acquire suspiciously vast assets of just the kind to afford him the means of exercising secret and illegitimate kinds of control over non-Jews: the Jew who "controls Hollywood" or "controls Wall Street"—and who also, it now appears, "controls" the history of the Second World War. And finally—one could extend the list further, but an end must be made somewhere—there is the stereotype of the Jew who, whenever anyone attempts to reclaim his ill-gotten assets in order to put them at the service of a wider suffering humanity, uses the craven and dishonest cry of "antisemitism" to smear and obscure the sterling nobility of his opponents' motives.

These stereotypes, and others related to them, have no particular political constituency. Historically important as they are, they figure nowadays, though usually in ways less overtly expressed, as frequently in the public discourse of far-left political groupings as of movements on the far right.[6] And they can certainly be found in putatively academic writing.

THE POLITICS OF MISPLACED UNIVERSALISM

Here I examine in some detail a specific contribution of this type to the debate, namely, David E. Stannard's lengthy closing contribution to the Rosenbaum volume, "Uniqueness as Denial: The Politics of Genocide Scholarship."[7]

First, however, a further question of definition needs to be gotten out of the way. It is customary in academic controversy for all parties to agree at the outset on common definitions of the main terms that define the debate, if for no other reason than to ensure that they are at least arguing about the same things. One of the oddest things about the uniqueness debate is the casual indifference shown by most of its participants to this elementary requirement. The terms "Holocaust" and "Genocide" appear to take on whatever meaning happens to suit the changing dialectical needs of each participant, as the moving sands of debate shift under him or her.

Such ambiguities extend to the term *unique* itself, where they are even less helpful to the cause of rational debate. Ludwig Wittgenstein, irritated by the philosophical deployment of the term *simple* as a name for a supposed class of metaphysical entities, pointed out that the adjective *simple* means little until we specify what kind of simplicity we have in mind. The term *unique* behaves in the same way: in any given context, that is to say, the question "Is X unique?" remains answerable, even in principle, until we answer the further question, *in what respect*? *Moby-Dick*, for instance, may be unique in respect of being a novel about a sea captain called Ahab, but it is not unique in respect of being a novel by Melville.

It matters, therefore, whether the parties to the uniqueness debate specify *in the same way* the sense in which the term "uniqueness" is to be attributed to, or denied of, the Holocaust. The briefest acquaintance with the main documents in the debate is sufficient to reveal that they do not. The specifically Jewish defenders of the uniqueness claim singled out for attack by Stannard, for instance, with one accord take the Holocaust to have been unique *in respect of the criteria used to select its victims for destruction*. A typical statement of this kind occurs in Elie Wiesel's response to the presentation of the Congressional Gold Medal, April 19, 1985: "I have learned that the Holocaust was a uniquely Jewish event, albeit with universal implications. Not all victims were Jews, but all Jews were victims."

Elsewhere Wiesel expands on this judgment as follows: "I believe the Holocaust was a unique event. For the very first time in history . . . a Jew was condemned to die not because of what beliefs he held . . . but because of who he was. For the very first time, a birth certificate became a death certificate."[8]

For Yehuda Bauer, what made the Holocaust a "totally new reality" was "the unique quality *of Nazi Jew-hatred*." He explains: "The *unique quality of Nazi Jew-hatred* was something so surprising, so outside of the experience of the civilized world, that the Jewish leadership, as well as the Jewish people could not comprehend it . . . the post-Holocaust generation has difficulty understanding this basic psychological barrier to action on the part of Jews—and non-Jews—during the Nazi period. We already know what happened, they, who lived at that time, did not. For them it was *a totally new reality* that was unfolding before their shocked eyes and paralysed minds" (added emphasis).[9]

Stannard, on the other hand, takes what is fundamentally at issue in the uniqueness debate to be, as he puts it, "the uniqueness *of Jewish suffering*" (emphasis added).[10] For Stannard, the claim that the Holocaust was unique equates with the claim that the Holocaust was unique *in respect of the quantity of suffering experienced by its Jewish victims;* a quantity of suffering that, he alleges, is considered, not merely by his selected Jewish opponents but by a wide spectrum of non-Jewish opinion, to have been grossly in excess of the quantity of suffering experienced by *any* other people, in *any* other of the numerous episodes of mass murder that have occurred in world history.

He takes this proposition to be at present accepted, and accepted as undeniable, moreover, by the bulk of informed opinion. Commenting on the fact that more is heard about the Holocaust than about the far more prolonged and numerically destructive processes of near-extermination that overtook the native peoples of the Americas following the arrival of the Europeans, and having ironically discounted the obvious explanation that the victims of the latter destruction were nonwhite, he adds,

> For those who might find such overt racial distinctions distasteful and preferably avoided, however, a more "reasonable" explanation exists for the grossly differential responses that are so commonplace regarding the American and the Nazi Holocausts. This explanation simply denies that there is any comparability between the Nazi violence against the Jews and the Euro-American violence against the Western Hemisphere's native peoples. *In fact, in most quarters it is held as beyond dispute that the attempted destruction of the Jews in Nazi-controlled Europe was unique, unprecedented and categorically incommensurable—not only with the torment endured*

by the indigenous peoples of North and South America, but also with the sufferings of any people at any time in any place during the entire history of humanity.[11] (emphasis added)

This claim for the uniqueness of the Holocaust does not, on the face of it, appear to be the claim that Wiesel, Bauer, Lipstadt, and other Jewish defenders of the uniqueness of the Holocaust, wish to advance. Their claim is that the Holocaust has a Jewish dimension that is essential to understanding it, and which is lost sight of when one "universalizes," and hence "de-Judaizes" the word "Holocaust." There is no inconsistency between claiming that and granting that other, even vaster episodes of mass murder have killed more people. So Stannard's proposed counterclaim is, it would seem, not a *counter*claim at all but merely an adroit change of ground. Small wonder, then, that the uniqueness debate should have struck many observers as a dialogue of the deaf, between antagonists who argue not with, but past, each other.

But this is clearly not the only thing wrong with Stannard's argument at this point. The claim Stannard takes to be "in most quarters... beyond dispute"—that the sufferings of Jewish victims of the Holocaust were greater *in sum* than (those of) *any people at any time in any place during the entire history of humanity*—is too vaunting in its generality to be seriously held by anyone, Jewish or non-Jewish. How could one possibly come to know something as magisterially exhaustive as that? And, even more fundamentally, how are "sufferings" to be quantified in any way capable of giving a clear meaning to a comparative judgment of any kind, let alone that kind? No one would, or could, assent to a proposal as crazily over-general and ludicrously under-defined as that.

BLAMING THE JEWS

Nevertheless, this is the claim Stannard takes to be "in most quarters . . . beyond dispute." And he takes its supposedly wide acceptance to be the outcome of "hegemonic" activity on the part of the Jews, those practiced pullers of wool over the eyes of honest but simple Gentiles. "This rarely examined, taken-for-granted assumption on the part of so many did not appear out of thin air. On the contrary, it is the hegemonic product of many years of strenuous intellectual labour by a handful of Jewish scholars and writers who have dedicated much if not all of their professional lives to the advancement of this exclusivist idea."[12]

Folded together in this sentence are two of the characteristic motifs of traditional antisemitism, together with a new one that has taken hold since the turn of the present century. First, there is the motif of Jewish "exclusivism," or as it is more usually phrased, particularism: the idea that Jews are exclusively concerned with the welfare of their own community, to the exclusion of any wider humanitarian goal or concern.

Second, there is the motif of secret, behind-the-scenes Jewish control of the non-Jewish world implicit in the adjective *hegemonic*. A tiny group of Jewish scholars, through "strenuous intellectual labour" absorbing—obsessively, it is to be supposed— "much if not all" of professional lives that might, by implication, have been better spent, has succeeded, we are assured, in establishing the "hegemony" over a multitude of non-Jewish minds of the idea that Jewish suffering in the Holocaust was "incomparably" worse than, and so, by implication, should be held to *matter* more than, the sum-total of *all other* human suffering, Jewish and non-Jewish, since the beginning of time.

Finally, if Stannard's "handful of Jewish scholars and writers" actually believed what he says they believe, then, irrespective of their success in getting others to believe it, they would be not unreasonable targets for the third, recently popular trope of antisemitism that I mentioned in the paragraph before last: that "Jews" believe Jewish blood, Jewish suffering, to be "worth more" than the blood and suffering of non-Jews.

It would be surprising if this last claim were actually true, since, as Gershon Weiler has pointed out, "it is fundamental to the whole Jewish Weltanschauung that no life is more valuable than any other. In the words of the Talmud: 'What makes you think your blood is redder? Perhaps his blood is redder.'" (Pesahim 25b).[13] Nevertheless, the canard that Jewish blood per se is held by "the Jews" to be redder than non-Jewish blood has of late years become part of the stock-in-trade of revisionist and antisemitic propaganda around the world. The following, from the Resistance Report, a U.S. antisemitic website (now dead), is typical:

> The Holocaust was crafted for two purposes.
> 1. To justify wiping Palestine off the map so that Jews can have a homeland there.
> 2. As a propaganda weapon to fool Gentiles into believing that Jews suffered more than any other people in the world.

Setting aside the relatively urbane and ostensibly academic style of Stannard's paper, it is not easy to see any difference in *content* between the above piece of gutter antisemitism and the following remark of Stannard's, à propos his observation that though a given revolution may display characteristics peculiar to it, no one would deny that all revolutions are *revolutions,* or consider one so special in nature as to require a special, capitalized word to designate it: "This has not been done, because to do so would be to depart from the world of scholarship and enter the world of propaganda and group hagiography—which in fact quite clearly is what Holocaust uniqueness proponents are up to: elevating the Jewish experience to a singular and exclusive hierarchical category, thereby reducing all other genocides to a thoroughly lesser and wholly separate substratum of classification."[14]

And the impression can only be deepened when this is followed up, a page later, with a passage asserting the classic antisemitic interpretation of Jewish chosenness as an assertion of superiority over all other peoples: "we are concerned with a small industry of Holocaust hagiographers arguing for the uniqueness of the Jewish experience with all the energy and ingenuity of theological zealots. For that is what they are: zealots who believe literally that they and their religious fellows are, in the words of Deuteronomy 7:6, 'a special people . . . above all people that are on the face of the earth,' interpreting in the only way thus possible their own community's encounter with mass death."[15]

A major motif of antisemitic propaganda has always been the myth of the Jewish conspiracy. In all versions of the myth, a tiny Jewish elite motivated by a belief in the innate superiority of Jew over non-Jew exerts power over non-Jewish affairs out of all proportion to its size. Stannard's thesis follows that pattern. A "small industry of Holocaust hagiographers," composed of "zealots" who take "literally" Deuteronomy 7:6, have succeeded, remarkably enough, in persuading the non-Jewish world that the sufferings of Jews in the Holocaust vastly outweigh all non-Jewish sufferings since the beginning of time, in consequence of which non-Jewish opinion has been led to consider the sufferings of non-Jewish groups in genocide after genocide as of little or no consequence compared to those endured by European Jews between 1933 and 1945.

As many contributors to the uniqueness debate pointed out at the time, the last claim appears in particular to stand reality on its head.[16] Not only the term *genocide* but also the concept itself owes their origins to the attempt, after 1945, to come to terms with the destruction of European Jewry. Prior to that, in the late 1940s, the Armenian genocide of 1915–1917 had sunk from European consciousness, while no general consciousness whatsoever existed of the full extent of the destruction visited upon non-European peoples by European expansion and colonialism from the late Middle Ages onward. All of that was still for the most part seen, as it had been for the preceding two centuries, as part of the Onward March of Civilization. The publication, in 1966, of Alan Moorhead's *The Fatal Impact,* which cataloged the ill effects, including massive losses of native populations, consequent to European invasion of the South Pacific from the mid-eighteenth century onward, marks, to my recollection, the first point at which the complacencies of Whig history in that respect began to be seriously doubted by large numbers of educated people.

Nor, since the 1960s, at least, has there been, *pace* Stannard's blank assertion to the contrary, any lack of consciousness among Western intellectuals of the long history of genocide to be laid at the door of European colonialism. To finger a supposed group of Jewish "zealots" as responsible for this entirely nonexistent lack of concern is not only absurd, but equally evidently it is antisemitic.

Since the Holocaust, the malignant absurdities of antisemitic calumny have tended—though with some surprising exceptions—to encounter, for obvious reasons, a less receptive mass audience than they did, say, in the 1930s and earlier. For that reason, no doubt, antisemitic discourse tends nowadays to be marked by a tendency to conclude each Judeophobic harangue with a complaint to the effect that innocent folk who merely attempt to tell the truth about "the Jews" always get accused of antisemitism, with a view to shutting them up. Here is a move of that type from the *Resistance Report* website: "They want us to think that they are always innocent and powerless, and anyone who disagrees with or hates even one Jew must be anti-Semitic. Yet if I say I hate White racists, does that make me anti-White? If not, then how does it make me anti-Semitic to say I hate Jewish racists? It doesn't, but they don't want you to know that." And here is the equivalent move in Stannard's essay: "In short, if you disagree with Deborah Lipstadt that the Jewish suffering in the Holocaust was unique, you are, by definition—and like David Duke—a crypto-Nazi. Needless to say, such intellectual thuggery usually has its intended chilling effect on further discussion."[17]

IN SEARCH OF TEXTUAL EVIDENCE

But does Deborah Lipstadt, or anyone else in Stannard's chosen band of Jewish "zealots," actually *say*, either in so many words or via some plausibly paraphrasable circumlocution, that what was "unique" about the Holocaust was the suffering it involved, taken—in terms of some suitable modulus—quantitatively?

Manifestly, Stannard stands in need of textual evidence to back up a claim like that. It is nowhere to be found in his essay. In its place we find repeated and forceful, but entirely unargued, assertions of the pair of implausible assumptions we have already repeatedly encountered, namely, (1) that non-Jewish Holocaust scholars who regard the Holocaust as without parallel (and there are, after all, plenty of them) do so only because of "pressure" from Jewish "Holocaust hagiographers"; and (2) that the only sense in which the Holocaust could intelligibly be deemed "unique," or "unparalleled," is in respect of the quantity of suffering (assuming "suffering," as distinct from number of persons killed, to be quantifiable) endured by its Jewish victims. These deeply dubious suggestions having been introduced into the unwary reader's mind by blank assertion alone, the remaining bulk of the essay is taken up with an attempt, in itself unexceptionable enough, though frequently cursory, to show that, in a range of other genocides, from the Ottoman massacres of Armenians between 1915 and 1917 to the accelerating destruction of the native peoples of the Americas in the decades and centuries following 1492, the sum total of the suffering endured, estimated by a variety of criteria (all of them conceptually parasitic on the idea of counting the dead, and including absolute number of dead, proportion of world population suffering death, and so on) may be reasonably supposed to have been as great or greater than that endured by the sum total of Jewish victims of the Holocaust.

There is, though, one point, late in the essay at which something at least resembling textual evidence is offered:

> According to uniqueness advocate Edward Alexander, for instance, the experience of the Holocaust provided "a Jewish claim to a specific suffering that was of the 'highest,' the most distinguished grade available." Even to mention the genocidal agonies

suffered by others, either during the Holocaust or at other times
and places is, Alexander says, "to plunder the moral capital which
the Jewish people, through its unparalleled suffering in World
War II, had unwittingly accumulated." One of the most ghastly
amassments of genocidal suffering ever experienced is thereby
made the literal equivalent for its victims of a great bounty of jealously guarded "capital" or wealth. It is unlikely that there exists
any more forthright expression than this of what Irving Louis
Horowitz calls Holocaust "moral bookkeeping."[18]

Stannard here equips Alexander, who happens to be Jewish,
with the character and motives of Shylock: the fictional Jew who
not only considers the sufferings of Jews "higher" and more "distinguished" than those of the non-Jew, but who can think in no
other terms than those of ownership, possession, wealth, "capital"
to describe not merely human suffering, but even the sufferings
of his own tribe, and who "jealously guards" both the word "Holocaust" and the thing itself, as uniquely Jewish *possessions*.

It thus becomes rather an important question whether Alexander's text, considered in extenso, will actually bear this ac-
cusatory interpretation. Alas, when the context of Alexander's
remarks is restored, the heightened colors capable of being bestowed by selective citation fade, as so often happens in such
cases, into the light of common day. The distinction between
"high" and "low" as applied to Jewish concerns, it turns out,
is not Alexander's at all, but George Eliot's, and the attaching
of central significance to suffering, in Alexander's opinion, not
to be Jewish, but rather Christian in character. Here is the full
sentence, in context:

> The uniqueness of Jewish suffering and of the Jewish catastrophe
> during the Second World War had no sooner been defined than it
> was called into question, by Jews as well as by Christians. The fact
> and the idea of suffering are central in Christianity, whose ethical
> values are based on the idea of a community of suffering. Many
> Christians also believe that, as Mary Ann Evans, later known as
> George Eliot, wrote in 1848, "Everything specifically Jewish is of a

low grade." Yet here was a specific suffering that was of the "highest," the most distinguished grade imaginable.[19]

Alexander's response to Eliot is ironic, which is why the word "highest" is in quotes. His point is that whatever nineteenth-century Christians may have thought concerning the "low-grade" nature of any concern specifically involving the Jews, the Holocaust, whatever else it has done, has at least rendered impossible that kind of airily patronizing dismissal. The point has, in short, no bearing whatsoever on the *meaning* of "uniqueness." Nor can the phrase "the uniqueness of Jewish suffering" be taken, as Stannard seems to imagine, to align Alexander's understanding of the term "uniqueness" with his. What Alexander takes the "uniqueness" of the Holocaust to consist in, as he makes clear in the first paragraph of the essay concerned, is not, as Stannard persistently asserts, the supposedly "incomparable" *extent* of Jewish suffering, but rather *the nature of the criteria by which its victims were selected.*

> The Jews held a unique position in the Nazi world because they alone, of all the peoples subject to German rule, had been marked for total destruction, not for anything they had done or failed to do, but because they had been born of three Jewish grandparents. Their guilt lay exclusively in having been born. Although only Jews could be guilty of being Jewish, the centrality of the Jews in the mental and political universe of the Nazis established a universal principle that involved every single person in German-ruled Europe: in order to be granted the fundamental human right, the right to live, one had to prove that he was not a Jew.[20]

That leaves Stannard with nothing to brandish but the phrase "moral capital," which he takes, by implication, to convict Alexander—in a manner, at the very least, highly redolent of one of the central motifs of traditional gutter antisemitism—of a willingness to see everything, including the sufferings of his fellow Jews, in the light of a "possession," of "capital," of "wealth." I lack access to the original Midstream version of Alexander's article, and I cannot locate the phrase, beginning "plunder the moral capital," that Stannard cites, in either of the versions of the essay that Alexander later reprinted (in *The Holocaust and the War of Ideas* and *The Jewish Idea and Its Enemies*).[21] But that hardly matters, since the phrase *moral capital,* expressing much the same thought, recurs in a passage in the version of the article included in *The Jewish Idea and Its Enemies,* in which Alexander is discussing the tendency, in recounting and dramatizing the *Diary of Anne Frank* for popular consumption, to downplay, in the interests of giving the work a "universal significance," its author's references to her own and her family's Jewishness as the cause of their predicament: "Cut free from her Jewish moorings, improperly understood by her own people, Anne Frank has become available for appropriation by those who have a sounder appreciation of the worth of moral capital, and know how to lay claim to sovereignty over it when the question of sovereignty has been left open."[22]

I think it is clear from context that the term *moral capital* refers here, not, as Stannard insists, to *quantity of suffering,* Jewish or otherwise, but rather to the recognition of the *causal role played by their Jewishness in the selection for persecution* of the Jewish victims of the Holocaust. It is, in short, *general recognition of the fact that Jews, unlike other victims of Nazi atrocity were killed just for being Jews,* that for Alexander, as for Bauer, Lipstadt, Rosenfeld, and other Jewish (and many non-Jewish) defenders of the uniqueness of the Holocaust, constitutes the "national asset" of which would-be "universalizers" and "de-Judaizers" of the Holocaust wish to deprive the Jewish people.

WHO "OWNS" WHICH ASPECTS OF THE HOLOCAUST?

If Alexander and Stannard agree about nothing else, they agree that the uniqueness debate was, and is, a debate about *ownership.* I conclude, therefore, by confronting this question afresh, and head-on. Who does "own" the Holocaust: the Jews alone, or all the victims of Nazi atrocity, of whatever kind or nation, or maybe all of suffering humanity? Evidently, one cannot answer that question without also confronting the central question of the uniqueness debate: *was the Jewish experience of the Holocaust unique?*

I have argued, following Wittgenstein, that the question of whether something X is or is not "unique" becomes answerable only if one has specified the characteristic or characteristics *in respect of which* uniqueness, for purposes of present discussion, is to be predicated of X.

So let's make the question a little more complex, by way of making the discussion a little more interesting, and maybe somewhat increasing the proportion of light over heat. *In what respects* was the Holocaust unique, and in what respects did it fail of uniqueness? And to whom, to the Jewish people or to others, does *the Holocaust considered in each of these respects* "belong"?

Bringing into play the notion that a thing can be unique in one respect and not in another opens up two possibilities that, simple and obvious as they are, appear, so far as I am aware, to be new to the debate. The first is that the Holocaust might turn out to have been unique among genocides in some respects and not unique in others. The second is that the respects in which it *was* unique, while they might turn out to "belong to the Jews," might on the contrary turn out to "belong to" others; that is to say, to the non-Jewish part of humanity. I believe that this second possibility is in fact the case.

Much has been made in the uniqueness debate, not only by David E. Stannard, but by many other contributors, of the uniqueness claim as a pretended attempt by Jews to exalt themselves above all other persecuted peoples, since the beginning of time, in respect of their *suffering*. One of the reasons why the bulk of Jewish (and, for that matter, non-Jewish) scholars have in fact made no such claim is, no doubt, that it would be an impossible claim to defend. Equally, I take it, the reason why those, like Stannard, hostile to the idea that there was anything unique about the Jewish experience of the Nazi persecution, emphasize the aspect of the Holocaust as suffering to the exclusion of all other aspects is that, by so doing they think to position themselves on strong ground.

Both sides are right, at least about this! Sadly, there is seldom anything unique about suffering. However great, however abominable the present form it takes, however satanically ingenious the modes of its present infliction, as bad or worse can generally be found in the long panorama of human barbarity.

But the proper conclusion to be drawn from that is not Stannard's. Rather, it is that if the Holocaust "belongs" to the Jews only *under the aspect of suffering,* then it belongs to them under an aspect that, far from dividing them from the rest of suffering humanity, unites them to it. No distinction arises between Jews and members of other nations *in that respect.* As victims of *suffering,* per se, we may all weep together.

But what about other aspects of the Holocaust? What, in particular, about its aspect as a persecution conducted against the members of a certain people *for no other reason than that they were members of that people,* and therefore, in logic, even if not always in practice, directed *against every member of that nation without exception?*

Here the Holocaust does seem to me—as it has to many others, Jewish and non-Jewish, including all of Stannard's "small industry of Holocaust hagiographers"—to have been unique.

But under that aspect, the aspect of *persecution upon the sole ground of birth,* the Holocaust in no way "belongs to" the Jews. It "belongs to" the rest of us, to non-Jews, simply because the *project* of the extermination on the sole ground of membership by birth of a given people *has no Jewish component.* It both took its rise, and arrived in time, at its attempted implementation entirely within non-Jewish circles.

We seem forced to conclude, in short, that what "belongs to the Jews," where the Holocaust is concerned, that is to say suffering so vast as not in practice to be remotely imaginable, is *not* the thing that makes the Holocaust "unique" but rather part of the common inheritance of mankind; whereas what *does* make the Holocaust unique, namely the nature of the grounds on which it was conceived and set in train, is in no sense the property of the Jews.

HEINSOHN ON HITLER'S MOTIVES

Let me now try to push that last thought a little further. What were the so-called grounds, what were the motives, of the Holocaust? In a paper on this difficult question by the German sociologist and economist Gunnar Heinsohn (more specifically, on the motives underlying Adolf Hitler's desire to be rid of the Jews), appears the following communication from Hitler to Martin Bormann, dated February 3, 1945:

> I have never been of the opinion that the Chinese or Japanese, for example, are racially inferior. Both belong to old cultures and I admit that their culture is superior to ours. [...] I even believe that I will find it all the easier to come to an understanding with the Chinese and the Japanese, the more they persevere in their racial pride. [...] Our Nordic racial consciousness is only aggressive towards the Jewish race. *We use the term Jewish race merely for reasons of linguistic convenience, for in the real sense of the word, and from a genetic point of view there is no Jewish race.* Present circumstances force upon us this characterization of the group of common race and *intellect,* to which all the Jews of the world profess their loyalty, regardless of the nationality identified in the passport of each individual. This group of persons we designate as the Jewish race [...] The Jewish race is above all a *community of the spirit.* [...] *Spiritual race is of a more solid and more durable kind than natural race.* Wherever he goes the Jew remains a Jew [...] presenting sad *proof of the superiority of the "spirit" over the flesh.*[23]

Heinsohn argues, from this and other textual evidence, that Hitler's antisemitism was not, in the ordinary sense *racially* based (a judgment that, as I have argued elsewhere, I would be inclined to extend to antisemitism in general).[24] Rather, Hitler believed that the Jews must be eliminated as the only way of eliminating *the malign spiritual influence* of Jewish culture. In what was this malign influence supposed to consist? Heinsohn marshals persuasive textual evidence to suggest that, in Hitler's mind, it consisted in the insinuation into European culture of ethical principles, notably that of the sanctity of life, which had sapped the capacity of the Nordic race (as it did historically, Hitler seems to have believed, that of the nations of the ancient world) to achieve their goals through the merciless destruction both of enemy combatants and of entire enemy peoples. Three of the passages Heinsohn cites in support of this reading of Hitler's motives are particularly telling. The first comes from an account by the Nazi leader of Danzig, Hermann Rausching, of conversations with Hitler at the start of the 1930s.

> We terminate a wrong path of mankind. *The tables of Mount Sinai have lost their validity. Conscience is a Jewish invention* […] It is our duty to depopulate, just as it is our duty to provide appropriate care to the German population […] What do I mean by depopulation, you will ask. Do I intend to eliminate entire peoples? Yes, more or less. That is where it will lead to. […] Natural instinct commands every living being not only to defeat the enemy but to destroy him. In earlier ages there existed *the good right of the victor to exterminate whole tribes, whole nations.*[25]

The second, from Hitler's table talk, records his belief that the Germans lost the First World War only because "Jewish" ethical inhibitions rendered them unable to pursue their aims with the absolute ferocity that, he supposes (arguably falsely, given the actual outcome of such tactics in World War II), would have brought victory in its train: "We experienced it during the World war: the only country that was religious was Germany, and that was the country that lost."[26]

The third, dating from August 7, 1920, records Hitler's conviction that it is because "the Jew" is, spiritually speaking, a *disease* of Western civilization that he must be treated as such: "Do not think that you can fight a disease without killing the causative agent, without destroying the bacillus, and do not think that you can fight racial tuberculosis without seeing to it that the nation is freed from the causative agent of racial tuberculosis. The influence of Judaism will never fade as long as its agent, the Jew, has not been removed from our midst."[27]

Heinsohn has two aims in his essay: first to elucidate Hitler's motives as a means of challenging the common view that the Holocaust is simply "inexplicable," and, second, to defend the idea that the Holocaust was indeed, in some sense, an utterly new and historically unique event. His proposal is that what made the Holocaust unique—or "uniquely unique," as he puts it—was that "it was a genocide for the purpose of reinstalling the right to genocide."[28] Hitler wished to abrogate the doctrine of the sanctity of life introduced to Western civilization by the Jews and reestablish a supposedly ancient right to kill without limit in the service of national, or "racial" self-interest: a right extending from the killing of the handicapped and the infanticide of surplus or unwanted children to the wholesale massacre of enemy populations.

THE FUNCTIONS OF THE MYTH OF JEWISH MALIGNANCY

The textual evidence that Heinsohn marshals, here and elsewhere, goes far to persuade me that he has much to teach us about the outlook and reasoning both of Hitler and of the party he founded. The main doubt I have concerning the paper under discussion is that it suggests the conclusion that the Holocaust was unique, if it was, mainly because it was the sole creation of one man, Hitler, whose reason for hating the Jews—that they had introduced into Western culture the principle of the sanctity of life—was indeed so singular as to be essentially sui generis: unique.

That this is a direction in which Heinsohn wishes to move is evidenced by the fact that he quotes with approval the following sentence from a *New Yorker* article strongly criticizing Daniel Goldhagen's *Hitler's Willing Executioners: Ordinary Germans and the Holocaust* (1996): "Hitler was the culprit who gave all the other culprits their chance."[29]

The doubts I feel concerning this are fueled by the fact that, aside from the issue of the sanctity of life, Hitler's thoughts on the Jews, as Heinsohn develops and documents them, seem not to have been in the least singular, but rather were entirely consonant with the broad current of European antisemitism that had developed during the previous century. Take, for example, the thought that the Jews are the source of a spiritual disease that cannot be cured without getting rid of the causative agents through which the body—the body politic in this case—is continually reinfected. We find the philosopher Ludwig Wittgenstein, in 1931, committing to his notebook a very similar thought, but this time as something that is so familiar an aspect of the history of the Jews in Europe as to go almost without saying.

> Within the history of the peoples of Europe the history of the Jews is not treated so circumstantially as their intervention in European affairs would actually merit, because within this history they are experienced as a sort of disease, anomaly, & nobody wants to put a disease on the same level as normal life. [and nobody wants to speak of a disease as though it had the same rights as healthy bodily processes (even painful ones)].
>
> We may say: this bump can be regarded as a limb of one's body only if our whole feeling for the body changes (if the whole national feeling for the body changes). Otherwise the best we can do is *put up with it.*
>
> You may expect an individual to display this sort of tolerance or even to disregard such things; but you cannot expect this of a nation since it is only a nation by virtue of not disregarding such things. I.e. there is a contradiction in expecting someone to retain the aesthetic feeling of his body and also to make the swelling welcome.[30]

Why, now, should the Jews in particular be regarded as the agents of a "spiritual disease" fatal to the integrity of a nation, or perhaps as constituting the "disease" itself, when, after all, no European nation possesses, historically, the cultural and spiritual integrity presumed by these remarks of Wittgenstein's? Why do the French not regard the Basques or the Bretons, or the English the Welsh, or the Scots the Orcadians or the Hebrideans, as carriers of a spiritual disease?

Part of the answer, I think, can be found in an excellent book by Brian Cheyette, *Constructions of the Jew in English Literature and Society: Racial Representations 1875–1945.* Cheyette surveys literary representations of "the Jew" by writers as various in their political and religious predilections as Matthew Arnold, John Buchan, Rudyard Kipling, George Bernard Shaw, H. G. Wells, Hillaire Belloc, G. K. Chesterton, James Joyce, and T. S. Eliot. Cheyette's interest in these writers is in part that they demonstrate the protean indeterminacy of non-Jewish characterizations of "the Jew." In his literary appearances, "the Jew" can signify, can symbolize, anything at all, from plutocracy to anarchic liberalism, depending on the political stance and narrative requirements of the particular writer.

One thing that these various and contradictory representations have in common, however, is the extent to which they embody responses of alarm and perceived danger *on the part of people who feel some favored conception of national unity, whatever that may be, to lie under some urgent threat that the image of "the Jew" serves to personify.*

Thus, for Shaw and Wells, with their disparate visions of a future of socialist order and world government, "Jews were constructed as an irrational and disorderly force . . . deemed to be standing in the way of world progress."[31] For Belloc, though French descended, a staunch Catholic Englishman, the Jew stands at the center of the world of international finance that threatens and is capable of bringing down the British Empire. For T. S. Eliot, notoriously, in *After Strange Gods*, it is Jewish free thought, rather than Jewish *plutocracy* or anarchic Jewish *indi-*

vidualism, that poses the problem: *"The population should be homogeneous;* where two or more cultures exist in the same place they are likely either to be fiercely self-conscious or both to become adulterate. What is still more important is unity of religious backgrounds; and reasons of race and religion combine to make any large number of free-thinking Jews undesirable. There must be a proper balance between urban and rural, industrial and agricultural development. And a spirit of excessive tolerance is to be deprecated" (emphasis added).[32]

If one sets these further, startlingly diverse, visions of Jewish threat beside Hitler's conviction, as documented by Heinsohn, that Germany lost the First World War because Germans were hamstrung as fighters by a superstitious and Jew-inculcated reverence for the supposed sanctity of human life, then I think, a certain pattern begins to emerge. All of them, and not merely T. S. Eliot, hanker after a *spiritually homogeneous* society: a society effectively united in the pursuit of certain desired goals. The goals envisaged by the different social thinkers in this short list are, of course very different. For Hitler they comprise the pursuit of Lebensraum and dominance over inferior races; for Wells, the transformation of social life in the direction of Reason, order and social justice; for Belloc and Chesterton, the exaltation of the values of empire and national honor over mere moneygrubbing. All of them, however, presume that it is possible not only to imagine in the abstract, but to envisage as a real possibility, a nation homogeneously united in the pursuit of national goals as specific as those of politically motivated theorists, activists, and writers tend to be. At the present moment, the same kind of presumption underlies the project, among Salafists and other Islamist groups, of reviving the society of the early Caliphate.

Reality, however, is not hospitable to the ideal of a nation homogeneously united in the pursuit of ideals common to all its citizens. Actual nations either possess political systems, like those of the United States or Britain, whose function is very largely to create a stable political space for the working out of large-scale differences of political opinion among its citizens, or else, like many Middle Eastern countries, political systems largely devoted to preventing, by repressive means, such differences from breaking out into civil war.

These humdrum, prosaic facts of political and social disagreement are, however, bad news to the messianic social theorist. To admit them means to admit the merely personal or sectional relevance of his most cherished beliefs. Therefore, some means must be found, especially in a moment of national crisis, when the possibility exists of representing this or that political nostrum as the path of national salvation, of plausibly representing the lack of national harmony and homogeneity *as an unnatural state of affairs.* But that means, in turn, representing it as a state of affairs produced by some agency *inherently foreign to the nation,* since if it were produced by some agency internal to, proper to, the nation *it would not be unnatural,* but rather part of the natural workings of national life!

The myth of national homogeneity, of national unity, needs, in short, to protect itself from unwanted and dangerous kinds of rational scrutiny—and needs more particularly at moments of national crisis—a correlative myth of alien malignancy. It is the misfortune of the Jewish people, I want to suggest, to have been selected, at an early point in the development of European civilization and culture, for a large and miscellaneous collection of historic religious and political reasons, to serve, for the future, as the putative objective correlate of this second, supporting myth.

What we confront in antisemitism, in short, is something in the nature of what the French philosopher and social theorist Michel Foucault called an "episteme," or more generally a "cultural formation." An "episteme," for Foucault, is some collection of supposedly—and often to a degree genuinely—cognitive or explanatory doctrines and practices, that, though it might be widely accepted as serving politically neutral goals of general enlightenment—and often to a degree does so—in fact (or in addition) serves hidden functions of power, social control, and manipulation. The entire body of generally accepted "knowledge" of Jews constantly exchanged and burnished by antisemites constitutes exactly this kind of "cognitive" structure. In its case, its contents add nothing to our *knowledge* of anything or anybody. Their role is, rather, to disseminate the idea that the Jews constitute just the kind of intrinsically alien, but immensely powerful, force needed to explain, to the messianic social theorist and his followers, why the society he and his friends wish to direct and dominate does not appear to be entirely and homogeneously animated by their chosen goals.

When both Wittgenstein and Hitler proclaim, in an eerily harmonious chorus, that "the Jews" cannot but be regarded by a nation as a "disease," then, it seems to me, neither is making an empirical claim. Both are, rather, exploring the internal logic of a Foucaultian episteme or, to put it in older terms, exploring the internal logical structure of a complex myth having less to do with knowledge than with the exercise of power. At one point in the passage cited earlier, Wittgenstein says that one cannot expect a nation to tolerate the diseased state constituted by the presence of Jews, because "it is only a nation by virtue of not disregarding such things." This is clearly not an empirical observation, but merely a further arbitrary definition, this time of the term "nation." Neither the "experience" of the Jew "as a sort of disease" nor the "nation" that "must," according to Wittgenstein, "experience" Jews in this way are, in short, *empirical realities.* Rather, they are merely *correlative poles within the structure of meanings that constitutes the myth of Jewish malignancy, given sense only by the mutual relationship to one another bestowed on them by the structure itself.*

An advantage of looking at antisemitism in this light is that it disengages the notion from questions of the moral disposition of individual minds. I have been criticized in the past for an inexplicable lack of readiness to finger this or that person as "an antisemite." Rael Jean Isaacs, for example, convicts me, in an otherwise positive review, of a "kid-glove treatment of . . . purveyors of anti-Semitism . . . [in whom] there is much that is contemptible, much to despise."[33] And she suggests, along with another reviewer, that my reason for eschewing direct accusation, in favor of textual analyses and investigations of pattern of argument from which the reader may be allowed to form his own opinion, must be that I imagine antisemites, implausibly, to be open to rational persuasion.

In fact, the reason is merely that it is indifferent to me whether or not this or that man or woman *is* an antisemite. It is indifferent to me not because the matter is not, in the bulk of cases, easily decidable one way or the other, but rather because that question itself fails to get to the heart of the matter. It fails to get to the heart of the matter because—as I see it—antisemitism is not, at least intrinsically, an aberration of the individual mind, but an aberration of Western civilization. Killing every antisemite, were such a thing possible, would not, in other words, rid the world of antisemitism, because vast and influential tracts of Western literature and public debate, sometimes openly, more often in thoroughly opaque and whitewashed ways, stink of it.

Antisemitism, in other words, understood as I understand it, is not, or not primarily, a pathological disposition or function of the individual mind, but rather a type of *social* or *cultural* pathology: a self-replicating structure of temptations and apparently explanatory delusions embodied, independently of the individual mind, in a multitude of enduring written and quasi-proverbial forms, that stands permanently ready to introduce itself, like the scrap of self-replicating genetic material that constitutes a virus, into the minds of people struggling to define their relationship to society, and of society to them, in moments of political crisis.

It is so deeply embedded in the culture that the only way to damage it, and perhaps in time get rid of it, is to attack it at the cultural, rather than the individual, level. For that, one must do the hard work of demonstrating, afresh each time, the intrinsically antisemitic underlying character of widely popular and persuasive patterns of thought: patterns of thought more than capable of making unconscious antisemites of large numbers of well-meaning people who simply fail to realize the delusive and dangerous character of what they are happily signing on to.

Looking at things in this way has, it seems to me, the further advantage of explaining why antisemitism, politically speaking, knows no frontiers; it crops up as regularly on the messianic left of the political spectrum as on the messianic right. Both wings of politics deal in the promise of a radical transformation of collective life; both base that promise on one or another persuasive theoretical representation of its workings. On the right, the entity envisaged as ripe for saving transformation has traditionally been the nation. Hence right-wing antisemitism equally envisages "the Jew" and Judaism as disruptive of an ideal national unity and homogeneity, however the latter may be conceived.

The messianic promises of the left, on the other hand, tend to be internationalist and to envisage humanity at large, or the world order, to be the objects ripe to undergo kinds of transformation that can only be plausibly introduced to possible converts, just as on the right, in terms of some complex explanatory theory. Because of the internationalism of the left, however, the theoretical structures required to render intelligible political action tend to be far wider in scope than their counterparts on the right, and thus to offer far more hostages to an unhelpful reality. For the left, therefore, Jews and Judaism tend to appear, in moments of political stress, less as disruptors of national unity than as disruptors of what would, in their absence, be a complete and satisfying conformity of reality to the demands of left-wing political conviction.

Thus, for example, Elhanan Yakira, in a remarkable book, offers the record of a fascinating discussion with Paul Guillaume, whose left wing bookshop and publishing house La Vielle Taupe (The Old Mole, a reference to a phase in Marx) published, among other things, the writings of the French Holocaust denier Robert

Faurisson.[34] Guillaume and his friends, Yakira makes clear, did not deny the Holocaust *despite* belonging to the radical left, ... but precisely *because* of it. Their motive lay, as Yakira ably documents, in their radical pacifism, which seemed to make it important to resist the demonization of Germany—which in turn made it necessary to find grounds for dismissing the Holocaust as a Jewish fabrication.

In much the same way, for those whose ideological stance commits them to the doctrine that the sources of armed conflict lie uniquely in capitalism and colonialism, Israel *must* be, as she is frequently accused of being, "the main threat to peace" in the Middle East. Over against Israel *must* stand, other things being equal, the absolutely unified and homogeneous Arab society frequently invoked by the late Edward Said and other spokesmen for Palestinian groups. And when, as at present, it becomes impossible to ignore the actual, and catastrophically violent, internal disharmony of the Islamic world (utterly unintelligible as that is, given its largely religious basis, in terms of the entire tradition of Western left-wing theory as that has developed since the mid-eighteenth century), then the machinations of "the Jews," as the supposed hidden hand behind, on the one hand the oil industry, and on the other United States foreign policy, must once again be invoked to explain it.

David E. Stannard's essay falls squarely into this tradition. Stannard's ideal America would presumably be a country deeply aware of the genocide against native peoples that formed the background to its early history, and anxious, as far as possible to remedy it. Sadly, the America we see around us is not like that. Why not? What can have caused this America to fall, if only in appearance, so far short of its own true reality, as the country Stannard would like to believe himself to belong to? The explanation lies—of course—in the machinations of a tiny coterie of Jews, who have succeeded in elevating their own sufferings in the public consciousness to a degree that permits them to downgrade the sufferings of others. Is Stannard an antisemite? Who am I to pry into his private motivations? And anyway, what does it matter? What matters is not pointing the finger of accusation at what he supposedly *is,* but pursuing the hard grind of argument and textual analysis necessary to reveal the meanness and the absurdity of what he *says.* In any case, he is certainly not an antisemite in the mold, say, of Hitler, or Reinhard Heydrich, or David Duke. He is a professor of American Studies who has, as I have tried to show, incautiously, and perhaps, for all I can say to the contrary, unconsciously, allowed his thinking to drift into the pattern prepared for it by a certain deeply socially and culturally embedded structure of self-propagating myth, and who has thereby chosen to subordinate both his powers and his academic standing to the cause of its further propagation.

CONCLUSION: HOLOCAUST MEMORY AS BOTH DUTY AND PRUDENCE

That is why, I think, Stannard and others like him are wrong to suppose that we can do without the term "Holocaust," understood as a singular term, a proper name referring uniquely to the destruction of European Jewry between 1933 and 1945. We need it, because it is an essential part of the work of Holocaust memory that includes museums, like the United States Holocaust Memorial Museum in Washington, D.C., along with Holocaust Days, research groups, university and school courses, books, and articles.

But why, it might still be asked, should all this effort be put into remembering the sufferings of the Jews, when others have suffered as much or more without being accorded this kind of attention?

The answer I have offered here is that what such things serve to keep alive is not the (alleged) uniqueness of the *suffering* inflicted in the Holocaust, but rather the (actual) uniqueness of the Holocaust *as a political crime.* The Holocaust was a unique, and (for the moment at least) uniquely European crime because it was the first moment in history at which an entire people was willed to destruction merely to save the credit of a political fantasy.[35]

No doubt we have a duty to the Jews, we who are non-Jews and members of nations the bulk of whose citizens are non-Jews, to remember these things as a duty to the Jews. But, non-Jews like me also stand under a duty of prudence, *a duty to ourselves, as non-Jews,* to remember these things. The Jewish world suffered the consequences of the Holocaust; the non-Jewish world, its mythic structures, its resources of secular political messianism, originated and contrived it. But those non-Jews who were not party to Hitler's war against the Jews, except through lack of vigilance, also paid a price for that lack of vigilance. Antisemitism is certainly part of what drew converts to the Nazi party, and so part of what served to bring Hitler to power. Hence, antisemitism lay causally at the root of many millions of non-Jewish, as well as Jewish deaths. Antisemitism, as long as it remains alive, retains the power it then showed, to blind many to the demonic character of messianic politics until it is too late.

That is why "the Holocaust Industry," as Norman Finkelstein derisively called it, is not, as he, Stannard, and others have wished to persuade us, a specifically *Jewish* enterprise. It is an enterprise for all of us, which we should pursue with all the industry we can muster, because it is in everyone's interest, the interest of all citizens of the world, Jewish and non-Jewish, to remember the specific nature and origins of the Holocaust *as a crime against the Jews.* To lose that memory, at the behest of a sophistical universalism, is to lose a precious bulwark against the perennial power of spurious moralizing to betray society into the bloody hands of political messianism.

NOTES

1. Gavriel D. Rosenfeld, *Hi Hitler! How the Nazi Past Is Being Normalized in Contemporary Culture* (Cambridge: Cambridge University Press, 2014), chapter 2.

2. Alan S. Rosenbaum, ed., *Is the Holocaust Unique?: Perspectives on Comparative Genocide,* 3rd ed. (Boulder, Colo.: Westview Press, 2009). Several of the essays in the Rosenbaum volume, including one by Ben Kiernan, director of the Genocide Studies Program at Yale, explore the question of possible analogies between the Holocaust and other genocides. Am I committed to regarding this as an illegitimate activity? Clearly not. The only claim I am committed to is that the Holocaust is rendered unique, whatever analogies may exist between it and other episodes of mass killing, interesting as those may be, by the strange but clearly causally determining relationship subsisting between it and the uniquely European system of politically active myth and delusion concerning the Jews.

3. C. L. Stevenson, *Ethics and Language* (New Haven, Conn.: Yale University Press, 1944), 212–213.

4. Alvin H. Rosenfeld, *The End of the Holocaust* (Bloomington and Indianapolis: Indiana University Press, 2011). See also Bernard Harrison, "Appropriating the Holocaust," *Israel Affairs* 17, no. 4 (October 2011): 644–650.

5. Among such websites are those of the Committee for Open Debate on the Holocaust (CODOH), Davidduke.com., Focal Point Publications (a site devoted to the writings of David Irving) and jewwatch.com.

6. On far-left political groupings, see Bernard Harrison, *The Resurgence of Anti-Semitism: Jews, Israel, and Liberal Opinion* (Lanham, Md.: Rowman and Littlefield, 2006), chapter 2 and beyond.

7. David E. Stannard, "Uniqueness as Denial: The Politics of Genocide Scholarship," in Rosenbaum, *Is the Holocaust Unique?,* 295–340.

8. Elie Wiesel quoted at "Wiesel Resources," PBS, www.pbs.org/eliewiesel /resources/.

9. Yehuda Bauer, *The Holocaust in Historical Perspective* (Seattle: University of Washington Press, 1978), 7.

10. Stannard, "Uniqueness as Denial," 301.

11. Ibid., 299.

12. Ibid.

13. Gershon Weiler, "The Jewish Establishment," letters section, *New York Review of Books,* March 17, 1966.

14. Stannard, "Uniqueness as Denial," 324.

15. Ibid., 325.

16. For contributors to the uniqueness debate, see, for example, Samantha Power, "To *Suffer* by Comparison," *Daedalus* 2 (spring 1999): 31–66; Alan Steinweis, "The Auschwitz Analogy: Holocaust Memory and American Debates over Intervention in Bosnia and Kosovo in the 1990s," *Holocaust and*

Genocide Studies, fall 2005, 276–289; John Torpey, "Making Whole What Has Been Smashed: Reflections on Reparations," *Journal of Modern History,* June 2001, 333–358. Further instances to be found in Rosenfeld, *Hi Hitler!*

17. Stannard, "Uniqueness as Denial," 300.

18. Ibid., 325.

19. Edward Alexander, "Stealing the Holocaust" (originally published in *Midstream: A Monthly Jewish Review,* November 1980), in *The Jewish Idea and Its Enemies: Personalities, Issues, Events* (New Brunswick, N.J.: Transaction, 1988), 101.

20. Alexander, "Stealing the Holocaust," 99.

21. Edward Alexander, *The Holocaust and the War of Ideas* (New Brunswick, N.J.: Transaction, 1994.

22. Alexander, "Stealing the Holocaust," 102.

23. Gunnar Heinsohn, "What Makes the Holocaust a Uniquely Unique Genocide?," *Journal of Genocide Research* 2, no. 3 (2000): 411–430, quote on 412. He is citing H. Trevor-Roper and A. François-Poncet, eds., *Hitlers Politisches testament. Die Bormann Diktate vom Februar und April 1945* (Hamburg: Albrecht Knaus, 1981), 66, 68, 69. The italics are Heinsohn's.

24. See Bernard Harrison, "Anti-Zionism, Antisemitism and the Rhetorical Manipulation of Reality," in *Resurgent Antisemitism: Global Perspectives,* ed. Alvin H. Rosenfeld, 8–41 (Bloomington and Indianapolis: Indiana University Press, 2013).

25. Heinsohn, "What Makes the Holocaust a Uniquely Unique Genocide?," 418. The italics are again Heinsohn's. He is citing H. Rauschning, *Gespräche mit Hitler* (1938; reprint Vienna: Europaverlag, 1988), 189, 210, 129ff.

26. Heinsohn, "What Makes the Holocaust a Uniquely Unique Genocide?," 419. He is citing H. Picker, *Hitlers Tischgespräche in Führerhauptquartier* (1951; reprint Stuttgart: Seewald, 1976), 77.

27. Heinsohn, "What Makes the Holocaust a Uniquely Unique Genocide?," 424. He is citing E. Jäckel and A. Kuhn, eds., *Hitler, Sämtliche Aufzeichnungen: 1905–1924* (Stuttgart: Deutsche Verlags-Anstalt, 1980).

28. Heinsohn, "What Makes the Holocaust a Uniquely Unique Genocide?," 425.

29. Ibid., 414. Heinsohn is citing C. James, "The Much Lauded Revisionist Study of the Holocaust [by Goldhagen] Goes Too Far," *New Yorker,* April 22, 1996, 7.

30. Ludwig Wittgenstein, *Culture and Value,* edited by G. H. von Wright, revised edition of the text by Alois Pichler (Oxford, U.K.: Blackwell, 2006), 18e.

31. Bryan Cheyette, *Constructions of "the Jew" in English Literature and Society* (Cambridge: Cambridge University Press, 1993), 148.

32. T. S. Eliot, *After Strange Gods: A Primer of Modern Heresy* (London, 1934), cited in ibid., 263.

33. Rael Jean Isaac, review of B. Harrison, *The Resurgence of Anti-Semitism: Jews, Israel and Liberal Opinion, Society,* January 2009.

34. Elhanan Yakira, *Post-Zionism, Post-Holocaust: Three Essays on Denial, Forgetting, and the Delegitimation of Israel* (Cambridge: Cambridge University Press, 2010), 1–36.

35. Several essays in the Rosenbaum volume, including one by Professor Ben Kiernan, director of a university genocide studies program, explore the question of possible analogies between the Holocaust and other genocides. Am I committed to regarding this as an illegitimate activity? Clearly not. The only claim I am committed to is that Holocaust is rendered unique, whatever analogies may exist between it and other episodes of mass killing, interesting as those may be, by the strange, but clearly causally determining relationship subsisting between it and the uniquely European system of politically active myth and delusion concerning the Jews.

ELEVEN

—ɷ—

Denial, Evasion, and Antihistorical Antisemitism

The Continuing Assault on Memory

DAVID PATTERSON

BOTH ELIE WIESEL AND PRIMO LEVI—two survivors from very different backgrounds—have described the Holocaust as a war against memory.[1] One dramatization of the Nazis' war against memory can be seen in Steven Spielberg's *Schindler's List* (1993), in a scene where SS-Hauptsturmführer Amon Göth addresses his troops on the liquidation of the Kraków Ghetto. "Jews have lived in Kraków for six hundred years," he proclaims. "By the end of the afternoon those six hundred years will be a rumor. They never happened."[2] If they never happened, then the Holocaust itself may be dismissed as a mere rumor in the continuing war against memory. Inasmuch as the war against the Jews is a war against memory, Holocaust deniers are among those who systematically and fervently heed the call of Hitler's dying words to "resist mercilessly the poisoner of all nations, international Jewry."[3] They deny the Holocaust not because they believe it never happened but precisely because they know it happened: they do not initiate but rather *continue* the war against the Jews in the mode of a war against memory.

That is why Holocaust denial is not about the evidence of history, as Michael Shermer and Alex Grobman suggest when they answer the deniers by presenting more evidence.[4] Nor is it precisely "a threat to all who believe in the ultimate power of reason," as historian Deborah Lipstadt maintains.[5] It has nothing to do with intelligence, rationality, education, political affiliation, social standing, religious inclination, or any other ontological contingencies. Holocaust denial is rooted in antisemitism, which is a hatred of the Jew as a *category* that *precedes* all contingencies; the Jew is always *already there* as a signifier of the immemorial testimony of Judaism that is beyond thematization. The denier's hatred or evasion of the Jew is also *already there*. What is needed is not a better explanation of the *cause* of the denier's antisemitism but a mode of thought that understands antisemitism to lie outside the coordinates of cause and effect, a mode of thinking that situates it in what Emmanuel Levinas refers to as the "immemorial," that is, as what is prior to all historical narratives, "the trace of a past which declines the present and representation, the trace of an immemorial past."[6] The Holocaust denier does not hate the Jews because they allegedly lie about the Holocaust; rather, he lies about the Holocaust because he hates the Jews. Antisemitism, then, is not caused by context or contingency, but rather the context or contingency occasions its manifestation.

Thus, the term *Jew* designates a metaphysical category and not an ethnic or racial group. As Emil Fackenheim has argued, the Nazis were not antisemites because they were racists—it is just the reverse: they were racists because they were antisemites.[7] In other words, the opposition to the teaching of Judaism has to be established in order to arrive at a racist position. "Never was a more exalted view of man conceived," writes Fackenheim, "than that of the divine image, and never one more radically antiracist. ... It was therefore grimly logical—if to be sure uniquely horrifying—that the most radical racists of all time decreed a unique fate for the Jewish people."[8] Kenneth Stern, therefore, is a bit mistaken in his view that, as a basis for Holocaust denial, "anti-Semitism is a form of human bigotry" and a "subset of human hatred."[9] Holocaust denial is indeed driven by antisemitism, rather than an argument over evidence, but it is not a form of bigotry—it is the *basis* for bigotry. Let us begin, then, with the bigots.

THE DEVELOPMENT OF RADICAL HOLOCAUST DENIAL

Harvard graduate David Hoggan and Professor Austin J. App, both born in the first quarter of the twentieth century, were two deniers whom Lipstadt regards as "the most significant figures in the evolution of Holocaust denial" in the United States.[10] Many of the earlier figures, all born before the end of the First World War—including French journalist Paul Rassinier, French fascist Maurice Bardèche, and U.S. political theorist Francis Parker Yockey—either blamed the Jews for perpetrating the Holocaust or accused the Zionists of perpetrating the hoax.[11] Hoggan and App are noteworthy as being among the first Americans to present their assault on memory under the guise of "scientific evidence." In *The Myth of the Six Million* (1969), Hoggan maintains that "there has never been even the slightest conclusive proof for such a campaign of promiscuous slaughter on the part of Germany, and, in the meantime, all reliable evidence continues to suggest with increasing volume and impact that this genocide legend is a deliberate and brazen falsification" perpetrated by the Jews.[12] In *The Six Million Swindle* (1973), App insists that "the charge that Hitler and the Third Reich wanted to exterminate all Jews is a totally fabricated, brazen lie," and that "the Talmudists have from the beginning used the six million swindle to blackmail West Germany into 'atoning' with the twenty billion dollars of indemnities to Israel."[13] His reference to the Jews as "the Talmudists" is indicative of his contempt for the Jews not only as a "race" but as witnesses to Judaism. On the U.S. scene, Hoggan and App were followed by engineering professor Arthur R. Butz, author of *The Hoax of the Twentieth Century: The Case against the Presumed Extermination of European Jewry* (1976); in a text littered with footnotes, Butz presents his "case" to demonstrate both that the Holocaust never happened and that the Jews perpetrated the hoax in order to further their Zionist aims.[14]

With the work of Butz, Auschwitz soon became the focus of the deniers' activity, a point that became all too clear with the testimony of British historian, author, and publisher David Irving at the trial held in 1996, when he filed a libel suit against Lipstadt for exposing him as a Holocaust denier; his activity as a denier dates from 1982, when he delivered a series of speeches in Germany denying the Holocaust. At the trial in England he reiterated a statement he had made in 1991, saying, "I don't see any reason to be tasteful about Auschwitz. It's baloney. It's a legend." In the development of strategy from Butz to Irving, one sees a shift from the pseudo-technical to the grossly tasteless. "Butz called for an attack on Auschwitz," Robert Jan van Pelt explains, "because the evidence provided enough technical data to refute the accepted historical record (he said). Irving aimed at Auschwitz because he recognized the great symbolic value of the camp for our knowledge and understanding of the Holocaust."[15] The Holocaust deniers began to realize that, for the vast majority of people, who are not researchers or analysts, undoing the symbol can be more effective than debunking the evidence.

Since the gas chambers of Auschwitz were emblematic of the six annihilation camps specifically designed to exterminate the Jews, the next phase in Holocaust denial was to deny the existence of the gas chambers.[16] Only the Jews were sent directly from the trains to the gas chambers in those camps as a matter of policy; hence, the Holocaust deniers generally do not deny that the Nazis murdered members of other groups, such as Gypsies, Communists, and homosexuals. For the Holocaust deniers, the matter of the gas chambers—indeed, their whole project—concerns only the Jews. In 1980, Robert Faurisson, a literature professor, published *The Problem of the Gas Chambers* (1980), with an introduction by Noam Chomsky. In 1985 and 1988, Canadian

Ernst Zündel was tried for hate speech crimes for his publication of Richard Verrall's (aka Richard Harwood) pamphlet *Did Six Million Really Die? The Truth at Last* and Fred A. Leuchter's *The Leuchter Report: An Engineering Report on the Alleged Execution Gas Chambers at Auschwitz, Birkenau, and Majdanek, Poland,* which was also published in a second edition by David Irving's publishing house Focal Point Publications.[17] Also worth noting in this connection is Gerd Honsik, the Austrian neo-Nazi author of *Freispruch für Hitler? 36 Ungehörte Zeugen wider die Gaskammer* (1988; Acquittal for Hitler? 36 unheard witnesses against the gas chambers).[18] Many of these and other works of Holocaust denial have been published by the Institute for Historical Review (IHR), founded in 1978 by William David McCalden and Willis A. Carto; the Anti-Defamation League labeled Carto as "the most important and powerful antisemite in the United States." Devoted to promoting Holocaust denial and inciting Jew hatred, among the stated aims of the IHR is to expose a worldwide Jewish conspiracy.[19]

A systematic response to the deniers came in 1992 with the publication of *The Assassins of Memory* by French historian Pierre Vidal-Naquet (1930–2006). For Vidal-Naquet, says Van Pelt, "the gas chambers represented more than the industrialization of death with its attendant anonymity. They also offered an epistemological shift by introducing the negation of the crime within the crime itself."[20] Elucidating this epistemological shift, Vidal-Naquet identifies eight axioms of the Holocaust deniers:

1. All testimony presented by a Jew is either a lie or a fantasy.
2. Any testimony or document from the war years is a forgery.
3. Documents based on firsthand information concerning Nazi methods are either forgeries or have been altered to suit a Jewish agenda.
4. Nazi documents written in coded language are taken at face value, but those that are written plainly are unacknowledged.

5. Anything that might render the Holocaust believable has been falsified.
6. Postwar testimony from the Nazis was obtained under torture or by intimidation.
7. Pseudo-technical evidence demonstrates the impossibility of mass gassings.
8. The gas chambers did not exist because nonexistence was one of their attributes.[21]

These axioms rest on a single premise, namely that the Jews are inherently evil, so that from Vidal-Naquet's eight axioms we may derive the corollary axioms of radical Holocaust denial:

1. Like Satan, world Jewry is ubiquitous, invisible, and behind every horror, including the horrors of the camps.
2. All Jews who were murdered deserved it, as they embody the essence of evil.
3. Jews control the media and are the arch disseminators of deception and corruption.
4. Because the Jews are evil by definition, the Nazis and any-one else who would eliminate the Jews are by definition good.

The Nazi outlook here is self-evident. Given the premises that shape the outlook, the Holocaust deniers could not help but adopt anti-Zionism as a central tenet of Holocaust denial. It is no coincidence, therefore, that anti-Zionism permeates the texts of the deniers.

Stern has observed that Holocaust denial "not only attacks Jewish history, its inherent anti-Zionism also targets the Jew-ish present and the Jewish future."[22] The logic is easy enough to follow: if Israel was established as a haven for an endangered Jewish people, and if they were not in fact so endangered, then there is no need for a Jewish haven; therefore, something else is at work in the establishment of a Jewish state—something like what Nazi ideologue Alfred Rosenberg described in his diatribe *Der staatsfeindliche Zionismus* (Zionism: enemy of the state, 1921), where he argues that Zionism is a Jewish strategy for world domination.[23] Similarly, Hitler claimed that during his years in Vienna (1907–1913) he discovered the true "national character of the Jews"—that is, the true evil of Jewish world domination—"in the Zionists." As though writing the script for the radical Holocaust deniers, he asserted, "It doesn't even enter their heads to build up a Jewish state in Palestine for the purpose of living there; all they want is a central organization for their international world swindle." Therefore, "the Jewish state," according to the Führer, "is completely unlimited as to territory."[24] And the measures taken to destroy the Jewish state must be equally unlimited, as the Islamic Holocaust deniers in particular insist. Thus, the Ayatollah Khomeini interpreted the Quran's injunction to "prepare against them whatever you can muster" (8:60) to mean that the Islamic state has a *religious duty* to gather "as much armed defensive force as possible," including nuclear weapons.[25] In many quarters of the Muslim world, Holocaust denial has a similar status of religious duty.

HOLOCAUST DENIAL IN THE MUSLIM WORLD

A transitional figure in the cult of Holocaust denial from the West to the Muslim world was Roger Garaudy, the French Communist who converted to Islam in 1982 and authored *The Founding Myths of Modern Israel* (1985).[26] When the French government charged him on 27 February 1998 with "complicity in contesting crimes against humanity," notes Robert Wistrich, "Palestinian professors, religious leaders, and journalists publicly protested," and "Lebanon's Arab Journalists Union called on fellow Arab intellectuals to rally to the man 'who had the courage to divulge Zionist lies.' All of Jordan's political parties issued a statement claiming that 'Zionists have fabricated the falsehoods about the extermination of the Jews in Germany to mislead the world and blackmail Western governments.'"[27] Here we discover at least one basic reason for distinguishing between radical Holocaust denial in the West and a similar phenomenon in the Muslim world: in the West, radical Holocaust denial is relatively marginal, while in the Muslim world it is relatively mainstream. There are numerous universities in the West where one can research and even earn a degree or a certificate in Holocaust studies. Nowhere in the Muslim world can a student do the same.

The antihistorical nature of Muslim animosity toward the Jews also provides a clue to the particular nature of the antisemitism that drives radical Holocaust denial. Indeed, the Muslim denial of Jewish history is as old as the Quran, where it is affirmed that Abraham was not a Jew but a Muslim (3:67) and that the Jews falsified the Scriptures (2:59; 3:78), which consist largely of the history of the Jewish people. Thus, from the time of Islam's inception to our own time, the Jews have been cast in the mold of falsifiers of history, so that article 20 of the PLO Charter states, "Claims of historical ties or religious ties of the Jews with Palestine are incompatible with the facts of history."[28] The Jews have no place in Palestine because the Jews have no place in history. There lies a significant part of the Palestinian objection to Jewish settlements in the West Bank; it has to do as much with antihistorical antisemitism as with Israeli occupation. Not surprisingly, therefore, Holocaust denial is an official position of the Palestinian Authority (PA). In 1983, the current Palestinian president Mahmoud Abbas published a book based on his doctoral dissertation from the Soviet Union's Patrice Lumumba University titled *The Other Side: The Secret Relationship between Nazism and the Zionist Movement*.[29] Focusing on the Haavara Agreement of August 1933, whereby the Nazis struck an arrangement with the Jewish Agency to facilitate Jewish emigration to Palestine, Abbas maintains that the Zionists worked in conjunction with the Nazis in the implementation of the Final Solution. Also typical is the sermon delivered by Palestinian Sheikh Ibrahim Madhi on 21 September 2001, in which the cleric proclaimed, "One of the cursed actions of the Jews is called the Holocaust, that is to say, the massacre of the Jews by Nazism. But revisionist historians have proved that this crime rumored against some was manipulated by Jewish leaders and became a political tactic" to justify the existence of the "Zionist entity."[30] Yes, "rumored": it never happened.

That the Holocaust was either perpetrated by the Jews or is a hoax promulgated by the Jews (with their compartmentalized thinking, Jihadist deniers hold both views simultaneously) is the official stance of the Muslim Brotherhood's offshoot Hamas, the terrorist group with whom the PA officially formed an alliance in June 2014. In 2003, Hamas leader Dr. Abdel Aziz al-Rantisi declared that the Holocaust was "the greatest of lies" spread by the Jews, and, if there was a Holocaust, the Jews were the true perpetrators.[31] Said Rantisi, "It is no longer a secret that the Zionists were behind the Nazis' murder of many Jews, and agreed to it, with the aim of intimidating them [other Jews] and forcing them to immigrate to Palestine. Every time they failed to persuade a group of Jews to immigrate, they unhesitatingly sentenced [them] to death."[32] The Holocaust did not happen, and yet the Jews did it. The antihistorical antisemitism underlying this thinking is illustrated by article 22 of the Hamas Charter, or "the Charter of Allah," with the implication that Hamas *is* Allah. The Jews, it states, "were behind the French Revolution, the Communist revolution and most of the revolutions we heard and hear about, here and there. With their money they formed secret societies, such as Freemasons, Rotary Clubs, the Lions and others in different parts of the world for the purpose of sabotaging societies and achieving Zionist interests. With their money they were able to control imperialistic countries and instigate them to colonize many countries in order to enable them to exploit their resources and spread corruption there."[33] The proof text cited as authoritative for these allegations is The Protocols of the Elders of Zion.

As the embodiment and origin of the evil that threatens all of humanity, the Jews lie about the Holocaust, which allegedly never happened; or if it happened, they did it; or, if Hitler did it, he was the instrument of Allah, who meted out to the Jews a just punishment. If the term *Nazi* has come to be a synonym for radical evil, then the Jews are the true Nazis. Thus, article 20 of the Charter of Allah describes the Jews as Nazis, a ploy used among other Holocaust deniers to veil the Nazi-like nature of their own ideology and to further incite hatred of the Jews. As Matthias Küntzel points out, the projection of "Nazi" onto the Jew is "a specific form of Holocaust denial, one which legitimates the pursuit of an anti-Jewish extermination policy, while projecting these murderous intentions onto the chosen victim."[34] Once they have been identified not only as an instance of evil but also as the source of evil, the extermination of the Jews becomes more a moral imperative—it is a religious obligation, as is the obligation to deny the Holocaust.

Meeting this obligation, several Muslim countries have hosted conferences on the theme of Holocaust denial. In April 2001, Lebanon provided a venue in Beirut for such a conference in partnership with the IHR and its Swiss counterpart, the L'Association Vérité et Justice. Featured speakers included Garaudy and Faurisson, with sessions in Arabic, French, and English.[35] A month later, the Jordanian Writers' Association held a meeting in Amman on the same theme; among its speakers was Jordanian university professor Dr. Ibrahim Alloush, who brought to his denial of the Holocaust all the authority of his academic standing. Then there was the International Conference to Review the Global Vision of the Holocaust held in Tehran in December 2006 and sponsored by the Iranian government. Among its attendees were Ku Klux Klansman David Duke, Robert Faurisson, and Ahmed Rami, a writer and radio broadcaster who Stephen Atkins describes as "the leading denier in the Muslim world."[36]

Iran is not the only government to adopt a policy of Holocaust denial. Atkins points out that the "Saudi regime has long been a

financial supporter for the Holocaust denial movement," and Lipstadt notes that "Saudi Arabia financed the publication of a number of books accusing the Jews of creating the Holocaust hoax."[37]
Gamal Baroodi, the Saudi representative to the United Nations,
has also openly denied that the Holocaust occurred.[38] Egypt is
another case in point, going back to Holocaust denier and head of
state Gamal Abdel Nasser.[39] A 29 April 2002 article in *Al-Akhbar*
by Egyptian journalist Fatma Abdullah Mahmoud proclaimed
that "French studies have shown that [the Holocaust] is nothing
more than a fabrication," complaining to Hitler, "If only you had
done it, brother, if only it had really happened, so that the world
could sigh in relief without their evil and sin."[40] It is no accident
that such statements arise in the country that produced the Muslim Brotherhood, the progenitor of Jihadist uprisings such as the
Islamic Revolution of Iran. Wistrich points out that "Iran is the
first example of a modern state since Hitler's Germany that has
officially adopted an active policy of anti-Semitism as a means to
promote its national interests. . . . This is the context in which one
must consider the relentless denial of the Nazi Holocaust that is
so rampant in Iran and much of the Arab world. Such a denial is
inextricably linked to the planned annihilation of Israel."[41] The
Iranian-spawned terrorist organization Hezbollah has embraced
the same position. True to the pattern, Hezbollah leader Hassan
Nasrallah first demonizes the Jews by labeling them Nazis and
then denies that the Nazis ever launched a program of extermination against them. In a 9 April 2000 speech, he cried out that
"the Jews invented the legend of the Nazi atrocities," a position
necessary to Hezbollah's stated aim of the destruction of the Zionist entity.[42]

The anti-Zionism of Holocaust denial, both in the West and
in the Muslim world, provides a link between the antisemitic
anti-Zionism that drives radical Holocaust denial and the antisemitic nature of the anti-Zionism that drives much of the liberal
left. In both instances, explains David Matas, "anti-Zionists move

from opposition to Israel to charges against Israel rather than from wrongdoing by Israel to anti-Zionism. . . . The reality of what happens in Israel is ignored. What matters is the condemnation itself. For anti-Zionists, the more repugnant the accusation made against Israel the better."[43] Among the most repugnant accusations made against Israel is that the Zionists are behind the Holocaust, if, indeed, there was a Holocaust. Just so, "hostility toward Israel and insensitivity to antisemitism make a neat package, especially for Europeans," notes Neil Kressel. The accusation shows that during the Holocaust the Jews "couldn't have been all that blameless; rescues its religious tradition; and proves that it is now more moral than ever by helping the Palestinian victims who suffer the onslaught of U.S.-Israeli power. . . . If facts about antisemitism get in the way, the facts be damned."[44] And so we have some intimation of what the assassins of memory set out to assassinate, and we catch a glimpse of the connection between the assassination of memory and the hatred of the Jews.

Israeli philosopher Elhanan Yakira offers this penetrating insight: "Both in Rassinier and his faithful followers on the radical French left one can find this syndrome: one must not allow the crime that was committed at Auschwitz, as it were, to blind us to the main thing, which is the suffering of those who are truly exploited—the workers, people of the Third World, the Palestinians. What happened at Auschwitz was, in the last analysis, just another instance, among many, of the true source of all crimes: colonialism, imperialism, capitalism, and Zionism. Thus, one cannot avoid the conclusion that nothing unique happened at Auschwitz."[45] Although they would never engage in overt Holocaust denial, some of the more fanatic left-wing preachers of tolerance—such as Michael Sinnot, Tony Judt, Mark Ellis, and others—find Holocaust denial tolerable because it serves the higher aim of removing the Jews from the stage of history.[46] Both the radical deniers of the Holocaust and the "virtuous" antisemites, as Yakira refers to them, would relegate the Jews to what David

Duke deems the "ashbin of history."[47] Indeed, the subtle denial of the Holocaust—the evasion of the Holocaust—is in some ways more insidious than its outright manifestations.

EVASION OF THE HOLOCAUST: PSYCHOLOGICAL DENIAL

A good working definition of psychological denial can be found in *The Freud Encyclopedia:* "Freud originally conceptualized denial as acting to ward off perceptions of external reality that would be upsetting. . . . At first, Freud explained [denial] in terms of the individual withdrawing attention from the stimulus. . . . Or the anxiety-arousing experience may be minimized, or ridiculed, or otherwise distorted so that the arousal of negative affect is diminished. . . . [Denial also arises in] situations in which external reality is overwhelmingly painful and immutable."[48] From this passage one can see that the psychological denial of the Holocaust is tied to the phenomenon that Alvin Rosenfeld describes as "the end of the Holocaust."[49] The Holocaust is coming to an end because many of us want it to come to an end. Although my evidence is admittedly anecdotal, I have personally encountered this phenomenon many times. Students in my Holocaust classes are often asked, "Why would you want to take a course on *that*? It is so depressing!" Colleagues say to me, "You're teaching a course on the Holocaust *again*? Can't we get over it?" Yet I have never heard anyone ask, "You're teaching a course on the Civil War *again*? Can't we get over it?" Historians hostile toward religious sensibilities, moreover, have declared to me that when discussing the Holocaust we must avoid the word evil because of its "religious baggage." Ethical implications, however, always come with religious baggage; if we fear the religious baggage, it may be because we fear the ethical implications. Indeed, the ethical implications above all must be avoided. And the ethical implications stem from the history that the Holocaust denier would deny.

There are other examples of the psychological evasion of the Holocaust, examples that can be found both in the popular culture that would trivialize the event and in the exhibits of the museums that would relativize it. For to relativize is to trivialize. Says Rosenfeld: "As the mass murder of millions of innocent people is trivialized and vulgarized, a catastrophic history, bloody to its core, is lightened of its historical burden and gives up the sense of scandal that necessarily should attend it. . . . The more successfully it enters the public mainstream, the more commonplace it becomes. A less taxing version of a tragic history begins to emerge—still full of suffering, to be sure, but a suffering relieved of its weightiest moral and intellectual demands."[50] The *weightiest* of the Holocaust's moral demands extend back to the absolute, divine prohibition against murder, to the ancient demands of Judaism (later taken up by other traditions), which are the demands of *history,* Jewishly understood—that is what makes the antisemitism of Holocaust denial antihistorical. As for the intellectual demands, although obvious, they are often ignored: for they include the demands of the study of history, religion, philosophy, languages, cultures, and many other areas. Relieved of its weightiest moral and intellectual demands, the Holocaust is relieved of its Jewish demands. Conference attendees and members of Holocaust museum boards tend more and more to speak less and less about the Jews. Instead, they speak of victims and trauma, dialogue and healing, representation and remembrance—everything except the singular assault on Jews and Judaism.

Thus de-Judaizing the Holocaust, one may ward off perceptions of external reality that would be upsetting and withdraw attention from the stimulus, so that the arousal of negative affect is diminished. Indeed, emptied of the demands of ethical absolutes, many among the left-wing, postmodern intellectuals can do no better than to echo the proclamation of Stanislas de Clermont-Tonnerre before the French Revolution's National Assembly in 1789: "It will be argued, the Jews have their own judges and particular laws. But, I answer, this is your fault and you should not permit it. Jews, as individuals, deserve everything; Jews as a nation nothing, . . . because it is inconceivable that there should be in the state a society of non-citizens, a nation within the nation."[51] Above all, there can be no Jewish state, the Holocaust notwithstanding. As individuals, Jews *as Jews* must be removed from history and swallowed up by the collective, so that they will no longer be a people apart. In short, the Jews must no longer be Jews, no longer represent the moral and intellectual demands that Rosenfeld so deftly points out.

One postmodernist scholar, Robert Eaglestone, understands that "Holocaust denial can most simply and clearly be understood as a form of anti-Semitism." At the same time, however, he questions the "empiricist view of history," that is, the view that objective observation is possible, adding that "historical knowledge is produced, and history books are written, as a genre." History, in other words, is nothing more than a narrative, void of any inherent or absolute ethical demand—a position that can play into the hands of Holocaust deniers. According to Eaglestone, the problem with Holocaust denial is that it "doesn't obey the rules of the genre."[52] And yet, to what end can the postmodernist privilege one set of rules over another? There is no escaping the postmodernist position that the survivor's "narrative" is no more than one narrative among many; indeed, one's status as a survivor is determined by the narrative. Once we are left with only the narrative, we are left without the historically grounded presence of the Jew. Left without the Jew, we are free to slip into a form of denial that the Jews were the targets of a program of complete annihilation.

One understands Lipstadt's complaint that, among postmodernists, "it became more difficult to talk about the objective truth of a text, legal concept, or even an event. In academic circles some scholars spoke of relative truths, rejecting the notion that there was one version of the world that was necessarily right while another was wrong." She adds that "because deconstructionism argued that experience was relative and nothing was fixed, it created an atmosphere of permissiveness toward questioning the meaning of historical events and made it hard for its proponents to assert that there was anything 'off limits' for this skeptical approach."[53] What she is describing here is precisely what makes the antisemitism of Holocaust denial antihistorical, in both its radical and psychological forms. What, then, is the counterpoint to this form of antihistorical antisemitism? It is the Judaism that from the whirlwind of the Holocaust shakes us from the comfort of our complacency. Therefore in our effort to relativize and trivialize the Holocaust, we invariably de-Judaize it. And de-Judaizing is a defining element of antisemitism, from Saint John Chrysostom (347–407), who described Judaizing as a "disease," to Martin Heidegger (1889–1976), arguably the father of postmodernism, who complained of the "Jewification" of the German mind.[54] And so the philosopher joined the party that would see to a Final Solution to the Jewification problem.

Heidegger's most famous respondent, the Jewish thinker Emmanuel Levinas, offers an insight that has serious implications for how we understand the evasion of the Holocaust on the part of so many of the left-wing heirs to Heideggerian philosophy: "Heideggerian philosophy precisely marks the apogee of a thought in which the finite does not refer to the infinite. . . . Heideggerian ontology subordinates the relation with the other to the relation with the neuter, Being, and it thus continues to exalt the will to power, whose legitimacy the other alone can unsettle, troubling good conscience."[55] In the cases at hand, the will to power—a power over history itself—finds its expression in various forms of Holocaust denial. In the post-Holocaust era, the "other" who unsettles and troubles the good consciences of both Holocaust deniers and Holocaust evaders is the Jew: xenophobia has come to pervade what I call "Holocaust studies without the Holocaust."

Those who seek to marginalize the Holocaust do not deal with the Jews because they do not want to have to respond to the first question put to the first human, the question that comes from on high and into the world through the testimony of the Jewish people: "Where are you?"

THE MEANING OF HOLOCAUST DENIAL
AS ANTIHISTORICAL ANTISEMITISM

Simply stated, antihistorical antisemitism lies in a principled opposition to a Jewish understanding of history, which is fundamentally an ethical understanding of history. This does not mean that someone who rejects a Jewish understanding of history rejects history's ethical dimension or hates Jews, nor does it mean that a refusal of a Jewish understanding of history leads to Holocaust denial. Historians from Raul Hilberg to Martin Gilbert engage their tasks in many different ways and are guided by different assumptions in their views of history itself; some, like Lucy Dawidowicz, see the Holocaust precisely as a war against the Jews, while others, such as Timothy Snyder, see it as part of a larger history of violence that unfolded in the blood lands of Eastern Europe. For all their differences, most historians of the Holocaust have a sense of ethical urgency about their task, and as soon as history takes on an ethical aspect, it takes on a philosophical aspect. Inasmuch as Jewish tradition is steeped in ethical concern, it has something in common with historians of the Holocaust who are driven by a sense of ethical urgency.

From the standpoint of the Jewish tradition that the denier would deny or the evader would evade, there is a historical narrative of transcendent meaning that the historian aspires to transmit, what might be called demand of the Good. The admitted assumption here is that the history of the Holocaust is a history of evil. If the historian should answer, "All I am trying to do is to get the facts straight," then, at least in the case of the Holocaust, getting the facts straight entails answering to an ethical demand. For one of the facts of the Holocaust, according to historian Yehuda Bauer, is that the Nazis accused the Jews of infecting the world with "unnatural concepts" such as moral conscience.[56] If history is to have an ethical aspect, if there is an ethical stake in what goes into the historical account of the Holocaust, and if the ethical imperative is grounded in something more than sheer power, then a transcendent meaning comes to bear. At the center of the historical narrative is an ethical narrative, which also becomes the object of denial. Without the absolute ethical imperative that emerges from the Holocaust, Holocaust denial has no ethical implications; at best, there is only the question of getting the story right, with nothing more at stake than political self-interest, descriptive accuracy, or the postmodernist compliance with the rules of the genre.

Here we realize that what Elie Wiesel and Primo Levi identify as a war against memory is in fact a war against accountability, in all its forms, from outright denial to turning away. It is, in short, a war against the absolute ethical injunction that, in this instance, enters the world through the Jews, which makes it a war against the memory of the Jews, both subjective and objective. Jewish history is, among other things, the history of a certain teaching on the absolute of human accountability, and the remembrance of that history lies in the remembrance of the tradition that the Nazis set out to destroy, the deniers deny, and others ignore. It is a history grounded, most basically, in an absolute prohibition against murder. If one aim of studying history is to curtail murder, then the historian must come to terms with that absolute— an absolute that Holocaust deniers tacitly deny.

Thus touching upon the transcendent within this historical, we encounter the absolute, which is a commandment that comes from outside of history, from an immemorial past that imparts meaning to history. This is where the historian might turn to the philosopher and the philosopher to the historian—a move necessitated wherever ethics enters the picture. Inasmuch as those who deny the Holocaust continue the Nazi assault on the memory of the ethical absolute, the war on memory is a war on the immemorial, which is encountered not through the study of history but the handing down of tradition. From a Jewish standpoint, it is very difficult to separate tradition from history. This is particularly true when it come to the history of the Holocaust. Why? Because, from a Jewish standpoint, to separate tradition from history is to separate the ethical from history, which is just what the Nazis and their allies among the Holocaust deniers would do. Whereas Holocaust deniers deny that there is anything to hand down, Jewish history entails handing down a meta-historical meser or "message," at the heart of masoret or "tradition," a message concerning the ethical responsibility as an expression of a higher relation. This view of history transforms the one to whom the testimony is handed down into a witness and a messenger, and those who maintain an engagement with the Holocaust have undergone that transformation. It means that the living remain in a relationship with the dead, and only if we are in such a relationship with the dead can the transmission of their memory be ethically charged, and not just a matter of academic curiosity. To deny or evade the Holocaust is to deny or evade the relationship with the dead in an abrogation of the ethical responsibility to the dead, to the living, and to the unborn.

The historian who would confront the Holocaust denier cannot ignore this ethical dimension of history. If the study of history is to take on an ethical aspect, then it must become what Levinas calls "a way of being against death," that is, against the death of the other human being.[57] Indeed, this ethical aspect of history imparts to it an orientation toward the future. As a struggle to answer to the ethical demand with which the Holocaust confronts us, the struggle for memory is a struggle for the future. The denial of Jewish history that characterizes Holocaust denial and Holocaust evasion, then, is a denial not only of the Jewish past but also of a Jewish future. As Wiesel has said, "the opposite of the past is not the future but the absence of future; the opposite of the future is not the past but the absence of past."[58] The war against memory, then, is a war against the child, who is the vessel of the future. Holocaust denial's refusal of a Jewish past is a denial not only of the Jewish child who was a first target of the Nazis' extermination project, but also of the ethical message transmitted to children yet unborn. That ethical message is what the antihistorical antisemite is anti. History is not reducible to generating this narrative or that, gathering data, or collecting archives; no, it is about bringing into the world children to whom we transmit history's meaning and the message concerning the ethical obligation to and for one another. For if we do not transmit it, we forget it.

CONCLUDING THOUGHTS

Antisemitism is a powerful word. That it applies to radical Holocaust deniers is self-evident. That it applies to those who evade all confrontation with the Holocaust—those who trivialize it, relativize, and otherwise render it irrelevant—may not be quite so self-evident. From the foregoing, however, two things about the evasion of the Holocaust perhaps come to light. First, it is rooted in a certain trauma that we experience when we collide with the Holocaust, not only in its graphic horror but, more importantly, in its inescapable ethical implications. Second, its ethical implications have a profound connection not just to Jewish history but to a Jewish understanding of history. And so deniers of every ilk deny not only what happened but, above all, the memory of the immemorial—of the infinite ethical responsibility—that makes it matter.

The real Jewish Question to be denied or avoided among the accomplices to the Nazis' Final Solution is couched in the two questions put to the first murderer: Where is your brother? And what have you done? The Jewish Question implicates each of us in what we stand for, why we live, and why we die. Holocaust denial is an attempt to silence the question that comes both from within and from beyond the Jewish people by turning them over to the silence of the grave. Or rather not even the silence of the grave: those turned over to the silence of the grave at least have a grave. The Holocaust deniers are literally grave robbers. They would remove the Jewish people from history altogether and turn them over to the silence of nonbeing: the Holocaust is nothing but a rumor—it never happened. The Jews never happened. The absolute prohibition against murder never happened. That is what the assassins of memory target for assassination.

NOTES

1. See Elie Wiesel, *Evil and Exile,* trans. Jon Rothschild (Notre Dame, Ind.: University of Notre Dame Press, 1990), 155; and Primo Levi, *The Drowned and the Saved,* trans. Raymond Rosenthal (New York: Vintage Books, 1989), 31.

2. It is worth noting that Jews had actually been in Kraków for eight hundred years.

3. Adolf Hitler quoted in David Welch, *Hitler* (London: UCL Press, 1998), 97.

4. Michael Shermer and Alex Grobman, *Denying History: Who Says the Holocaust Never Happened and Why Do They Say It?* (Berkeley: University of California Press, 2000), 2.

5. Deborah E. Lipstadt, *Denying the Holocaust: The Growing Assault on Truth and Memory* (New York: Free Press, 1993), 19–20.

6. Emmanuel Levinas, *Collected Philosophical Papers,* trans. Alfonso Lingis (The Hague: Martinus Nijhoff, 1987), 136.

7. Emil L. Fackenheim, "The Holocaust and the State of Israel," in *A Holocaust Reader: Responses to the Nazi Extermination,* ed. Michael L. Morgan (New York: Oxford University Press, 2001), 132.

8. Emil L. Fackenheim, *What Is Judaism?* (New York: Macmillan, 1987), 109.

9. Kenneth S. Stern, *Holocaust Denial* (New York: American Jewish Committee, 1993), 91–92.

10. Lipstadt, *Denying the Holocaust,* 102.

11. Bardèche maintains that the Jews were guilty of the atrocities of which the Nazis had been accused, saying that they "orchestrated the program"; see Maurice Bardèche, *Nuremberg ou la terre promise* (Paris: Le Sept Couleurs, 1948), 8. Yockey blames the "Culture-distorters," a code name for the Jews, for the Second World War and for the Holocaust propaganda that followed it; see Francis Parker Yockey, *Imperium—The Philosophy of History and Politics,* 4th ed. (Los Angeles: Noontide Press, 2008), 233. On accusations that the Holocaust was a hoax perpetrated by Zionists, see, for example, Paul Rassinier, *Le drame des Juifs européens* (Paris: Le Sept Couleurs, 1964), 59.

12. David Hoggan, *The Myth of the Six Million* (Los Angeles: Noontide Press, 1969), 104.

13. Austin J. App, *The Six Million Swindle: Blackmailing the German People for Hard Marks with Fabricated Corpses* (Takoma Park, Md.: Boniface Press, 1973), 3.

14. See Arthur R. Butz, *The Hoax of the Twentieth Century: The Case against the Presumed Extermination of European Jewry* (Torrance, Calif.: Historical Review Press, 1976), 87.

15. David Irving quoted in Robert Jan van Pelt, *The Case for Auschwitz: Evidence from the Irving Trial* (Bloomington: Indiana University Press, 2002), 1, 5.

16. The six camps are Treblinka, Chełmno, Bełżec, Sobibór, Majdanek, and Auschwitz-Birkenau.

17. Richard Harwood, *Did Six Million Really Die? The Truth at Last* (Torrance, Calif.: Historical Review Press, 1975); Fred A. Leuchter, Robert Faurisson, and Germar Rudolf, *The Leuchter Reports: Critical Edition* (Chicago: Theses and Dissertations Press, 2005).

18. See Gerd Honsik, *Freispruch für Hitler?: 36 Ungehörte Zeugen wider die Gaskammer* (Vienna: Burgenländischer Kulturverband, 1988).

19. Lipstadt, *Denying the Holocaust,* 144–145, 143.

20. Van Pelt, *Case for Auschwitz,* 8.

21. Pierre Vidal-Naquet, *Assassins of Memory: Essays on the Denial of the Holocaust,* trans. Jeffrey Mehlman (New York: Columbia University Press, 1992), 21–23.

22. Stern, *Holocaust Denial,* 52.

23. Alfred Rosenberg, *Der staatsfeindliche Zionismus* (München: Zentralverlag der NSDAP, 1938), 3.

24. Adolf Hitler, *Mein Kampf,* trans. Ralph Manheim (Boston: Houghton Mifflin, 1971), 56, 325, 301.

25. Ruhullah Khomeini, *Islamic Government* (New York: Manor Books, 1979), 46.

26. See Roger Garaudy, *The Founding Myths of Modern Israel* (Newport Beach, Calif.: Institute for Historical Review, 2000).

27. Robert S. Wistrich, *A Lethal Obsession: Anti-Semitism from Antiquity to the Global Jihad* (New York: Random House, 2010), 648.

28. See Leila S. Kadi, ed., *Basic Political Documents of the Armed Palestinian Resistance Movement* (Beirut: Palestine Research Centre, Beirut, 1969), 137–141.

29. See Anti-Defamation League, *Holocaust Denial in the Middle East: The Latest Anti-Israel Propaganda Theme* (New York: Anti-Defamation League, 2001), 5–6.

30. Sheikh Ibrahim Madhi quoted in David Matas, *Aftershock: Anti-Zionism and Anti-Semitism* (Toronto: Dundurn, 2005), 32.

31. "Hamas Leader Rantisi: The False Holocaust," MEMRI, 27 August 2003, http://www.memri.org/bin/articles.cgi?Page=subjects&Area=antisemitism&ID=SP55803.

32. Abdel Aziz al-Rantisi quoted in David Aaron, *In Their Own Words: Voices of Jihad* (Santa Monica, Calif.: Rand Corporation, 2008), 137.

33. "The Covenant of the Islamic Resistance Movement (HAMAS)," 18 August 1988, http://www.jewishvirtuallibrary.org/jsource/Terrorism/Hamas_covenant_complete.html.

34. Matthias Küntzel, *Jihad and Jew-Hatred: Islamism, Nazism and the Roots of 9/11,* trans. Colin Meade (New York: Telos Press, 2007), 118.

35. See Stephen E. Atkins, *Holocaust Denial as an International Movement* (Westport, Conn.: Praeger, 2009), 133.

36. Ibid., 129.

37. Ibid., 214; Lipstadt, *Denying the Holocaust,* 14.

38. Stern, *Holocaust Denial,* 49.

39. Atkins, *Holocaust Denial as an International Movement,* 213.

40. Küntzel, *Jihad and Jew-Hatred,* 61.

41. Wistrich, *Lethal Obsession,* 909.

42. Hassan Nasrallah, "Excerpts from Speech by Hizbullah Secretary-General Nasrallah," Israel Ministry of Foreign Affairs, 9 April 2000, http://www.mfa.gov.il/MFA/MFAArchive/2000_2009/2000/4/Excerpts%20from%20Speech%20by%20Hizbullah%20Secretary-Genera.

43. Matas, *Aftershock,* 53.

44. Neil J. Kressel, *"The Sons of Pigs and Apes": Muslim Antisemitism and the Conspiracy of Silence* (Dulles, Va.: Potomac Books, 2012), 151.

45. Elhanan Yakira, *Post-Zionism, Post-Holocaust: Three Essays on Denial, Forgetting, and the Delegitimation of Israel,* trans. Michael Swirsky (Cambridge: Cambridge University Press, 2010), 41.

46. For a lengthy discussion of the position of the fanatical left wing, see Manfred Gerstenfeld, "Academics against Israel and the Jews," in *Academics against Israel and the Jews,* ed. Manfred Gerstenfeld (Jerusalem: Jerusalem Center for Public Affairs, 2007), 17–82.

47. David Duke quoted in Lipstadt, *Denying the Holocaust,* 5.

48. Edward Erwin, ed., *The Freud Encyclopedia: Theory, Therapy, and Culture* (New York: Routledge, 2002), 142–143.

49. Alvin Rosenfeld, *The End of the Holocaust* (Bloomington: Indiana University Press, 2011).

50. Ibid., 11.

51. Stanislas de Clermont-Tonnerre quoted in Jacob Katz, *From Prejudice to Destruction: Anti-Semitism, 1700–1933* (Cambridge, Mass.: Harvard University Press, 1980), 109.

52. Robert Eaglestone, *Postmodernism and Holocaust Denial* (Duxford, U.K.: Icon Books, 2001), 9, 21, 39, 50.

53. Lipstadt, *Denying the Holocaust,* 18.

54. John Chrysostom, *Discourses against Judaizing Christians,* trans. Paul W. Harkins (Washington, D.C.: Catholic University Press of America, 1979), 15. Heidegger as reported in *Die Zeit,* 29 December 1989; see Theodore Kisiel, "Heidegger's Apology: Biography and Philosophy and Ideology," in *The Heidegger Case: On Philosophy and Politics,* ed. Tom Rockmore and Joseph Margolis (Philadelphia: Temple University Press, 1992), 12.

55. Levinas, *Collected Philosophical Papers,* 52.

56. Yehuda Bauer, *History of the Holocaust,* rev. ed. (New York: Franklin Watts, 2001), 98.

57. Emmanuel Levinas, *Totality and Infinity,* trans. Alphonso Lingis (Pittsburgh, Pa.: Duquesne University Press, 1969), 224.

58. Elie Wiesel, *From the Kingdom of Memory: Reminiscences* (New York: Summit Books, 1990), 239.

TWELVE

Generational Changes in the Holocaust Denial Movement in the United States

ARYEH TUCHMAN

AT ITS CORE, Holocaust denial argues that six million Jews were not killed—many with poison gas—by the Nazis during World War II. However, the style and methodologies of those arguments, and the rhetorical context in which they are expressed by the deniers, have evolved in the decades since Holocaust denial first emerged. From the 1940s through the 1960s, Holocaust denial was the province of pro-Nazi groups employing crude arguments and overtly antisemitic rhetoric. In the 1970s, Holocaust denial took up more sophisticated pseudoscientific methods and began to portray itself as a movement of historical revisionists in the tradition of the historian Harry Elmer Barnes, who argued that conventional historians had allowed their analyses of World War II to be influenced by Allied propaganda, and that a more accurate history needed to be written. Although the Holocaust denial movement in the United States continued to be dominated by right-wing extremists in the 1980s and 1990s, by the year 2000 and continuing to the present we have seen the movement expand to include other populations, including conspiracy theorists and anti-Zionists not affiliated with the extreme right. The methodological argumentation by a small group of hard-core deniers is as sophisticated as ever, but in a broader context the rhetoric of

Holocaust denial has shifted away from attempts to valorize the Nazis and rewrite the history of World War II. Instead, Holocaust denial now tends to be couched in arguments over free speech and the power of the "Jewish/Zionist lobby" to stifle debate and create "thought criminals" in the service of Israeli interests. How and why these generational shifts occurred can shed light on the development of both the extreme right in the United States and on the dramatic increase of what has been termed the "new antisemitism."

THE EARLY YEARS

Holocaust denial in the United States emerged in the years immediately after World War II. Throughout the 1950s and 1960s, neo-Nazi and white nationalist leaders, including Francis Parker Yockey, Gerald L. K. Smith, and George Lincoln Rockwell, all proclaimed their belief that the deaths of six million Jews at the hands of the Nazi regime was a hoax perpetrated by those same Jews to defame Hitler and advance their own interests.[1]

Despite the sometimes substantial ideological differences between them, Yockey, Smith, Rockwell, and their followers were united in their overt hatred of Jews and their avowed belief in the ideals of Hitler and National Socialism. Their denials of the Holocaust read either as transparent attempts at Jew baiting, as propaganda on the side of a war that Hitler had already lost, or as elements of neo-fascist, white supremacist manifestos. Their technical arguments against the Holocaust were usually no more sophisticated than comparing published population statistics in Europe before and after the war, on the basis of which they cast doubt on the six million figure.[2]

1970S–1990S

In the 1970s, Holocaust denial in the United States assimilated the more sophisticated, pseudoacademic claims pioneered by Paul

Rassinier in France during the 1950s and early 1960s. Rassinier's arguments included detailed analyses of survivor testimony and documentary evidence. Rassinier, an avowed leftist who was persecuted by the Nazis, may have been an unlikely champion of Holocaust denial. Whatever his motivation for his initial critique of the history of the destruction of European Jewry, over time it became clear that he was driven by conspiratorial beliefs about Jewish power. He differed from the likes of Yockey, Smith, and Rockwell, however, in that he was not a white nationalist with an overt agenda of rehabilitating Nazism as a practical and active political ideology. Rassinier was an antisemite, but not a neo-Nazi.[3]

Rassinier came to the attention of the English-speaking world due to the praise heaped on him by the controversial historian Harry Elmer Barnes, who inspired the publishing of a small run of an English translation of Rassinier's *Drame des Juifs Européens* in 1975.[4] Rassinier became even more accessible to the U.S. public due to the efforts of Willis Carto.[5] Carto had been an activist in the U.S. far-right scene since 1955 and had created an entity called Liberty Lobby in 1957. Though Carto himself was a devotee of the racist, antisemitic teachings of Francis Parker Yockey, Liberty Lobby eschewed the crude antisemitism of overt neo-Nazis in favor of anticommunist, racial segregationist, right-wing lobbying efforts in Washington, D.C. In his personal letters, Carto continued spewing overt antisemitism, and over the next two decades he devoted much of his activity to disseminating Holocaust denial.

The first vehicle Carto used for this purpose was Noontide Press. Among the earliest books Noontide printed was Yockey's magnum opus, *Imperium,* which denied the Holocaust, in 1963.[6] Over the next few years, the house published numerous racialist works, many of them by British anthropologist and right-wing extremist Roger Pearson. In 1969 it added what is probably the first book devoted to Holocaust denial in the United States: *The Myth of the Six Million* by David Hoggan. A student of Harry Elmer Barnes, Hoggan spent his professional career writing books in

German arguing that Germany was in fact the victim of Allied aggression during World War II and that the Holocaust was a hoax.

Through Carto's efforts, Holocaust denial began to develop into a cottage industry, which to some small degree had begun separating itself from its neo-Nazi roots in the 1950s and 1960s. In the following decade, Noontide Press published Arthur Butz's *The Hoax of the Twentieth Century* (1976), William Grimstad's *The Six Million Reconsidered* (1977), and Paul Rassinier's *Debunking the Genocide Myth* (1978). Carto advertised these texts in the pages of his newspaper, *Spotlight*.

A seminal moment in the development of Holocaust denial in the United States came in 1979, when *Spotlight* announced the formation of the Institute for Historical Review (IHR) and the convening of its first international Holocaust denial conference.[7] Some of the papers presented at that conference were printed in 1980 in the first issue of IHR's *Journal of Historical Review,* a journal that aped the look and feel of conventional academic publications. It was under the aegis of the IHR that Holocaust denial began to cohere into an international movement that could, albeit with some difficulty, be separated from the ideology and aims of the deniers from the 1950s and 1960s, many of whom had still held out hope of reviving overtly anti-Jewish, or even pro-Nazi, popular movements in the United States.

To be sure, IHR attracted its share of neo-Nazis and neo-fascists. The first editor of the *Journal of Historical Review* was David Mc-Calden, who had been a member of the British neo-fascist group called the National Front, before he came the United States and changed his name to Lewis Brandon.[8] Mark Weber, another early employee of IHR, had been a member of the neo-Nazi National Alliance and was the editor of its *National Vanguard.*[9] Revilo P. Oliver, also a member of the National Alliance, served on the editorial advisory board of the *Journal of Historical Review* throughout the 1980s.[10] Wolf Rudiger Hess, whose father was Rudolf Hess, attended IHR conferences and contributed articles to the journal, as did Otto Ernst Remer, who was a general in the Wehrmacht during World War II.[11] H. Keith Thompson, who had been a special agent for the Nazi Overseas Intelligence Unit during World War II, was also involved with the IHR.[12] According to a report from the Anti-Defamation League, during his speech at the 1983 IHR conference, Thompson "urged supporters to 'stand by the third Reich' because, 'if, in the end, the Holocaust did take place, then so much the better!'"[13]

However, not all the deniers attracted to the IHR and Holocaust denial at this time were neo-Nazis or neo-fascists. Many of these others, including many readers of Carto's *Spotlight,* had their ideological roots in less extreme right-wing populist movements. Examples of such deniers include Keith Stimely, who wrote Holocaust denial works and eventually became editor of the *Journal of Historical Review;* Michael A. Hoffman II, a freelance journalist and conspiracy theorist; Black Nationalist Robert L. Brock; and *Spotlight* writer Michael Collins Piper.[14]

Others came to Holocaust denial with no apparent connections to right-wing extremism other than participating in IHR conferences and writing for its journal. In this category, one might include ordained minister Robert Countess;[15] engineering professor Arthur Butz;[16] James J. Martin, a libertarian scholar;[17] Fred Leuchter, author of the famed *Leuchter Report;*[18] and the foremost French Holocaust denier, Robert Faurisson, whose influence on the IHR and Holocaust denial in the United States cannot be overstated.[19]

The Holocaust denial promoted by the IHR and its supporters featured Barnes-style World War II revisionism, as well as technical arguments for the impossibility of homicidal gas chambers. In many cases, the revisionist history was extreme. These deniers did not merely claim that Jews had not been gassed at Auschwitz or that Anne Frank's diary was a fabrication; they also argued that Dr. Mengele had noble intentions, that the SS was an honorable and heroic military unit, and that Nazism was a progressive, forward-looking movement that cared about its people and the environment.[20] Many of them believed that the Nazis were justified in interning the Jews in camps or executing them as potential communist sympathizers; moreover, they argued that Hitler alone among the world leaders saw the danger of communism and selflessly set his German armies to defend the West against the communist menace. The *Journal of Historical Review* serialized former SS Lieutenant Leon Degrelle's rhapsodies about Hitler and published the writings of other former Nazis, as well. Their revisionism extended to the Allies, whom they cast as the aggressors in World War II. They alleged that President Roosevelt knew in advance that the Japanese intended to attack Pearl Harbor but allowed the attack to occur in order to bring the United States into the war, and claimed that the Nazi admissions of guilt at Nuremberg were the result of torture.[21]

Of course, the core argument that deniers turned to time and again was the technical impossibility of the Nazis having killed six million Jews, many with poison gas. Articles in the *Journal of Historical Review* claimed to assess "Holocaust demographics," the distinction between cremation and incineration of bodies, the nature and construction of delousing chambers in the Nazi concentration camps, and the prevalence of typhus. Holocaust deniers craved any analysis that had the trappings of objective science. To take but one example: Fred Leuchter, a purported engineer and "gas chamber expert" who designed execution devices for several U.S. states, was hired by Canadian Holocaust denier Ernst Zundel to conduct a forensic analysis of Auschwitz. Leuchter concluded that the gas chambers there could not have been used for homicidal gassing, and his *Leuchter Report* became one of the foundational texts for the Holocaust denial movement.[22] Other deniers who specialized in producing technical studies on Nazi concentration camps without generally addressing larger issues pertaining to World War II revisionism were Carlo Mattogno, Friedrich Paul Berg, John Ball, and later, Germar Rudolf.

The IHR, and the constellation of deniers who surrounded it, was a hybrid mixture of neo-Nazis, white nationalists, conspiracy theorists, and antisemites. It produced pro-Hitler revisionist history, as well as sophisticated arguments against the existence of gas chambers, mass shootings, and other aspects of Holocaust history.

The 1980s and 1990s were the golden age of Holocaust denial in the United States. By this time, the IHR had refined its arguments to the point that its leadership felt it could take its message to the broader public. As the IHR launched its outreach campaigns, the mainstream U.S. media and the U.S. public learned of the existence of Holocaust denial.

Beginning in the 1980s, the IHR and its allies launched several stunts and outreach campaigns designed to increase the public's exposure to Holocaust denial. In 1980, the IHR sponsored a $50,000 challenge to anyone who could prove that Jews had been gassed at Auschwitz. A Holocaust survivor named Mel Mermelstein took up the challenge, which resulted in a lawsuit covered by newspapers in Los Angeles (where the suit took place), as well as by wire services, the *New York Times,* and the *Washington Post.*[23] IHR pamphlets and other Holocaust-denying literature were distributed at public libraries, and Holocaust deniers attempted to book meeting rooms on college campuses and in public libraries, sometimes attracting significant controversy.[24]

One of the most important promoters of Holocaust denial in the United States was Bradley Smith. In 1984, Smith, who had earlier aspired to become a journalist but had become enamored of Holocaust denial after reading the work of Robert Faurisson, convinced IHR leaders to underwrite a newsletter to journalists, arguing that the Holocaust never happened and urging them to write stories about it. He received virtually no responses from that enterprise, so in 1986 he became the first director of the IHR's Radio Project—quickly rebranded as the Media Project—in which he attempted to bring the message of Holocaust denial to radio and television broadcasts. Smith claims to have done over four hundred interviews during that period, although that number cannot be verified.[25]

In 1991, Smith hit on a strategy that would catapult Holocaust denial to a much larger audience. He created the Committee on Open Debate on the Holocaust (CODOH), whose mission was to place advertisements denying the Nazi genocide of European Jewry in college student newspapers. Smith hoped that the naïveté of college students would make them more likely to accept his propaganda, but his efforts paid off in another way: the local controversies that erupted when college newspaper editors wrestled with the decision of whether to publish Smith's ads themselves attracted intense coverage in regional and national media.[26] Smith even appeared on the television newsmagazine *48 Hours* on February 26, 1992, where he tried to convince a national audience that "there was no plan to exterminate the Jews of Europe, no order, no budget, no weapon—that is, no extermination gas chamber and no victim. . . . This false story is maintained by a cabal largely of Jewish organizations."[27] Two years later, Smith and an associate debated Michael Shermer, the editor of *Skeptic* magazine, on Phil Donahue's television show.[28]

The legal battles of Ernst Zundel in Canada, whose Holocaust denial was being prosecuted for violating the country's False News laws, also resulted in significant media coverage of "revisionist" theories in the United States. In a segment covering the Holocaust denial phenomenon on the March 20, 1994, edition of the television newsmagazine *60 Minutes,* Zundel allowed that Hitler had his "foibles," including that he "didn't particularly like Jews," but that no more than 300,000 Jews died during World War II. Clips of Bradley Smith also appeared in that segment.[29]

In the late 1990s, Holocaust denial again became a media phenomenon with U.S. coverage of the 1996 lawsuit filed by British historian David Irving against American academic Deborah Lipstadt after she described him as a Holocaust denier. Although the lawsuit was litigated in the United Kingdom, major U.S. newspapers and wire services covered the trial.

The concept that there was room to doubt the standard history of the Holocaust continued to appear in the media in other forms, as well. Conservative columnist Pat Buchanan questioned the notion that gas chambers at Treblinka could have been used to kill Jews, again provoking media controversy.[30]

The repeated references to Holocaust denial in U.S. media in the 1980s and 1990s exposed average Americans of the first, second, and third generations born after World War II that there were those who disputed the reality of the Holocaust about which they had learned in school or seen portrayed in many movies such as Claude Lanzmann's *Shoah* (1985) and Steven Spielberg's *Schindler's List* (1993).[31] I recall watching an evening newscast on the subject of Holocaust denial in the 1980s. I have a vivid memory of the news anchor earnestly warning his viewers that although there are those who deny the Holocaust, there are mountains of evidence that the Holocaust indeed happened. It was a remarkable departure from regular journalism, and in retrospect I think it spoke to a growing awareness of the existence of Holocaust deniers among mainstream Americans.

Although awareness of Holocaust denial swept through parts of the U.S. during these two decades, the connection that many of the deniers had to right-wing extremism made it easier for their opponents to discredit them. Jewish organizations and academics generally did not engage them on the substance of their spurious "historical" claims, preferring instead to focus on their general sympathy for Hitler, their racism, and their antisemitism. Time and again it was pointed out that if the deniers were not Nazis, like Leon Degrelle, they were neo-Nazis like David McCalden, Willis Carto, and Mark Weber. If they were not neo-Nazis, they were right-wing extremists, racists, and antisemites, predisposed to vindicating Hitler and obviously having a motive for discounting the destruction of European Jewry. The Anti-

Defamation League famously described Holocaust deniers as "Hitler's apologists" and included profiles of the most important deniers in its publications on right-wing extremism. The American Jewish Committee made this approach even more explicit in a publication on Holocaust denial published in 1993: "Holocaust deniers crave legitimacy above all else. As long as they are seen as neo-Nazi hacks, and not scholars, their task is harder. . . . The deniers' claims can and must be debunked—not with debate but with exposé. . . . It is important that people know that deniers want to rehabilitate Nazism and create a new world order based on the Third Reich."[32] This unequivocal formulation, while certainly true of the pro-Nazi Holocaust deniers of the 1950s and 1960s, and of some of the neo-Nazi Holocaust deniers of the 1980s and 1990s, was not necessarily true of many other Holocaust deniers. The armchair pseudo-historians and conspiracy theorists who became part of the Holocaust denial movement were almost certainly antisemites and anti-Zionists, but although they were interested in recasting the history of World War II and perhaps rehabilitating the image of Hitler, they had no desire to revive the Nazi movement. Moreover, several of the foremost Holocaust deniers, including Arthur Butz, Fred Leuchter, and Bradley Smith, did not have any discernible right-wing views or affiliations before they took up with the Holocaust denial movement. But because the Holocaust denial movement as a whole was predominantly composed of right-wing antisemites, calling them out for belonging to that ideology was a convenient way of conveying to the American people the disingenuousness and mendaciousness of their attempt to deny the existence of gas chambers.

2000–2014

Since 2000, the Holocaust denial movement in the United States has been disrupted and changed due to a number of factors. A conflict between the professional members of the IHR and their founder, Willis Carto, led to extended legal proceedings from 1993 to 2000, during which time the IHR's programming was sporadic and inconsistent. Although it held a large international conference in California in 2000, its plans to hold a 2001 conference in Beirut, Lebanon, collapsed.[33] In 2003, the IHR ceased publishing its *Journal of Historical Review*. The IHR is now essentially an organ for the promotion of its only professional staff member, Mark Weber. Its activities include an email newsletter with a collection of links to contemporary news sources and to old articles from the *Journal of Historical Review*. The IHR's only other activities are the convening of occasional lectures by Weber and one or another visiting Holocaust denier at small gatherings in California. Thus the umbrella that had united international Holocaust deniers beneath a canopy of right-wing extremism led by Willis Carto was closed.

There have also been generational changes of another, more basic kind: the old group of Holocaust deniers from the 1970s, 1980s, and 1990s has been aging and dying off. All of the former Nazis who had moved in Holocaust denial circles have died. Since 2000, at least ten major Holocaust deniers have died, including Doug Christie, Doug Collins, Robert Countess, Roger Garaudy, Russ Granata, James Martin, Eustace Mullins, Hans Schmidt, and Wilhelm Staglich. Although not all of these were based in the United States, they had all played a significant role in fomenting Holocaust denial in the United States in the 1980s and 1990s. Many of the other deniers from the 1980s and 1990s, in particular Butz, Carto, Faurisson, and Smith, are also aging.

Individual Holocaust deniers have also come upon hard times, which have disrupted their activities. After David Irving lost his lawsuit against Deborah Lipstadt in 2000, many publishers and bookstores stopped selling his books. He went bankrupt and states on his website that he now makes a living from donations and by driving throughout the United States and Europe selling books from the back of his car and, occasionally, by selling "authenticated" pieces of Nazi memorabilia, including what he claimed were Hitler's walking stick and locks of his hair.[34] Irving was also imprisoned in Austria for about a year for denying the Holocaust in that country.[35] Among other deniers encountering difficulties are Ernst Zundel, whose two Canadian trials allowed him to present a media circus, eventually prevailed in Canadian court but fell afoul of U.S. immigration rules. He was deported to Canada and from there back to his native Germany, where he served jail time for several years. He now lives in Germany, where the legal environment prevents him from returning to his old ways of disseminating Holocaust denial and serving as an apologist for Hitler. Ingrid Rimland, whose Zundelsite was ground zero for Holocaust denial on the internet in the 1990s, now uses the website for "archival purposes," while she quietly builds a pro-German library center in Tennessee.[36] Jürgen Graf, after facing jail time for his Holocaust denial activities in his native Switzerland, fled first to Iran and then to Belarus. Germar Rudolf, a young up-and-coming revisionist back in the 1990s and early 2000s, was also imprisoned in Germany for several years, though he has now settled in the United States.

Even in the United States, where the First Amendment protects free-speech rights, Holocaust deniers have nevertheless found it more difficult to use their old approaches to disseminating their ideology to the mainstream public. Where once Holocaust deniers like Bradley Smith could provoke national media controversies by running ads and placing inserts in college student newspapers, today's deniers find themselves largely locked out of these media. Editors are on the lookout for Smith and people like him.[37] Smith struggles now to have even simple, five-word text ads placed in college newspapers. He considers it a good month when he can have two comments posted on a story in an online newspaper without having them deleted within forty-eight hours.[38] Indeed, Smith has openly admitted that to get his message out, he compiles large email lists of students and

faculty at specific universities and then sends unsolicited messages to them. He admits that many, perhaps most, of his email
messages are relegated to the spam folders of their intended re-
cipients, unread.[39]

Probably the most important shift, which grows out of the
implosion of the IHR and the passing of the old guard, is that
Holocaust denial has moved away, in fits and starts to be sure,
and with many exceptions, from its earlier obsession with arguing in favor of a pro-Axis, Barnes-style revisionist history, which
was often linked to a nationalist, right-wing extremist orientation on the part of the deniers. The long, impassioned articles
and speeches from the first generations of Holocaust deniers in
the United States, which justified the conduct of the Axis nations during World War II, have subsided. Sixty years after World
War II ended, Holocaust denial as a movement is finally recognizing that the general historical narrative of the war has been
largely set.

Instead, the rhetorical focus of Holocaust deniers has shifted
primarily to what they perceive as infringements on their freedom of speech and on the power of "international Zionism" to
prevent them from receiving a fair hearing by governments and
in world media. Holocaust deniers today often cluster around
Bradley Smith, whose modus operandi is not generally the ven-
eration of Hitler but rather railing about the "professorial class"
that refuses to debate the historicity of the Holocaust, and about
Jewish organizations, from the ADL to the Holocaust Museum to
campus Hillels, which, he alleges, shut down debate.

The Holocaust denial movement's currently most active English-language journal, *Inconvenient History,* which was founded
by associates of Bradley Smith, explicitly states that although it
rejects the existence of the gas chambers and other aspects of the
extermination of European Jewry, its goal is not to rehabilitate
Hitler. In its mission statement, it avers twice that it is not the
intention of the journal to "whitewash totalitarian regimes."[40]

Indeed, a review of the journal from 2009 to the present shows that, with a few exceptions, the authors it publishes hew very closely to the driest, pseudoscientific style of Holocaust denial writing. The journal publishes articles densely packed with tables and figures purporting to prove that there could not have been homicidal gas chambers at Auschwitz, that the Aktion Reinhard camps could not have served as extermination centers, and that the Einsatzgruppen could not have been engaged in mass murder of Jews in the conquered Soviet territories. Throughout, it generally eschews broader, Barnes-style revisionist history of the war, Nazism, and Hitler.

When the antisemitic website Veterans Today published a piece that both denied the Holocaust and applauded Hitler for his treatment of European Jews, the site saw fit to include the following disclaimer: "This article is controversial and contains strong racial tones. It can upset some readers. This article reflects the view of the author exclusively and does NOT reflect the views of VT or any other VT authors, affiliates, sponsors, advertisers or partners. After extensive Editorial Board review, the board has deemed this piece something readers should read, investigate, study, and discuss. Be advised that VT stands for justice, equality, truth, and the U.S.A."[41] When Ingrid Rimland posted an article described by the site as "A Defense of Hitler the Veteran?" in 2013, a similar (albeit weaker) disclaimer by the editorial board was also posted.[42]

Virtually alone among contemporary U.S. Holocaust denial outlets, the *Barnes Review* magazine, published by the elderly Nazi apologist Willis Carto, continues to describe itself proudly as a "Journal of Nationalist Thought and History," and views among its core missions the denial of the Holocaust and the recasting of the history of World War II to castigate the Allies and applaud the Axis powers. In its most recent issues, it promoted books such as *The Myth of German Villainy* by Benton L. Bradberry; *Victims of Yalta: The Secret Betrayal of the Allies, 1944–1947* by Nikolai Tolstoy; and the *Illustrated Guide to Adolf Hitler and the Third Reich* by Stephen Goodson. In classical Barnes-style tradition, articles routinely blame the Allies for the barbarism of World War II; they depict Winston Churchill, Franklin D. Roosevelt, and Joseph Stalin as warmongers, and present Hitler as a defender of civilization against the Jewish-Bolshevik threat. The magazine takes for granted that the Holocaust is a myth, and periodically devotes special issues to the more technical arguments supporting that contention.

There are signs, however, that even the readers of the *Barnes Review* are losing their patience with Hitler apologetics. Its circulation numbers have been declining almost every year for the past fifteen years, from a high of about 11,000 to its current circulation of about 5,000. This may partly be due to the deaths of older readers, but recent issues have suggested that the incessant whitewashing of Hitler and the condemnation of the Allies have been losing their appeal to the audience. There are signs that the remaining readers, far from automatically defending Hitler from any and all charges, as deniers would have done twenty years ago, are themselves willing to include Hitler in other unsavory conspiracies even as they deny the existence of gas chambers. They accept as a matter of faith and fact that the Holocaust was faked, but they do not end up becoming Hitler apologists. In 2013, editor Michael Collins Piper, no doubt following Carto's directives, observed that

> TBR has taken a lot of heat for suggesting Hitler wasn't the devil incarnate and that it wasn't Hitler who started World War II, that the real demons in human form were the likes of Winston Churchill, Josef Stalin, and Franklin D. Roosevelt. . . . We've discovered time and again that there is a large number of TBR readers who also have a negative view of Mr. Hitler. . . . These folks believe some or all of the following (to one degree or another): That Hitler was a Jew or a "crypto-Jew." That Hitler was a spawn of the Rothschilds or some other Jewish dynasty. That Hitler was a tool—witting or unwitting—of Zionism, working to establish a Jewish state in

Palestine. That if Hitler wasn't a Rothschild by blood, he was certainly an agent of their interests. That Hitler was a tool of the New World Order. None of this is true. It is baseless rumor, cobbled together without regard for known facts.[43]

Despite this, Piper announced that the *Barnes Review* would redouble its efforts to present a nationalist, apologetic perspective on Hitler and World War II. The review called on its readers to distribute a sixteen-page pamphlet, written by Carto, titled *A Straight Look at the Second World War*. The very next issue was devoted to a "Defense of Adolf Hitler," and included a variety of articles on "Allied war crimes" and on justifying Hitler's response to "Judea's declaration of war against Germany." In an editorial, the review stated that it would begin serializing a book-length biography of Hitler in subsequent issues.[44] It remains to be seen how readers will react to these renewed efforts to supplement denial of the Holocaust with nationalist, pro-Nazi rhetoric of the kind that was more common in the old *Journal of Historical Review*.

An interesting case demonstrating the evolution of Holocaust denial in the United States is in *American Free Press,* a weekly tabloid also controlled by Willis Carto but designed to appeal to a less learned and overtly nationalist audience. In its pages, one often finds the assumption that the Holocaust did not happen, but here, as opposed to the *Barnes Review,* there is little or no effort to connect that assumption with Hitler himself. Most often, discussion of the falsehood of the Holocaust occurs in the context of complaints about the global power of Zionism, its persecution of revisionists, and the silencing of alternative views on history. To the readers of *American Free Press,* it is well established that the Holocaust is a hoax. The editors of that publication who promote this view do not appear to be seeking to change the textbooks on the history of World War II, but rather they use Holocaust denial as a weapon to wield against Zionism and to prove the power of the Jewish establishment to stifle debate.

Within the past decade, even the now-diminished Institute for Historical Review has altered its editorial line, shifting away from using Holocaust denial as a way to set the record straight on World War II, and toward using it as an aspect of an anti-Zionist and anti-Jewish agenda. In an article in 2009 that drew much debate within Holocaust denier circles, IHR director Mark Weber wrote that it had become clear to him that the Holocaust myth was only one facet of the larger societal problem of "Jewish-Zionist power." Therefore, he wrote, "debunking the Holocaust will not shatter that power." He also admitted that revisionists have been ineffective at altering the perception of the Holocaust and World War II among the general public. He concluded: "Setting straight the historical record about the wartime fate of Europe's Jews is a worthy endeavor. But there should be no illusions about its social-political relevance. In the real world struggle against Jewish-Zionist power, Holocaust revisionism has proved to be as much a hindrance as a help."[45]

In this decade, then, Holocaust denial has become just another conspiracy theory for many antisemites or anti-Zionists. It has become less and less connected with pro-Nazi ideology or even efforts to reargue the history of World War II. This is reflected in coverage of Holocaust denial in the U.S. media. The Holocaust denier who has made the most news in the past decade has been former Iranian president Mahmoud Ahmadinejad, who has little stake in the history of the Second World War per se but has a clear interest in casting the pervasiveness of the acceptance of the Holocaust "myth" as an indication of Jewish-Zionist power and the strength of the "Israel lobby." Outside Iran, Ahmadinejad did not attempt to convince the world of the alleged technical impossibility of the use of homicidal gas chambers, but focused instead on the power of Jews to stifle the dissenting opinions of "revisionist scholars," whom he usually left unnamed.

Indeed, Ahmadinejad was one of the prime figures in shifting the locus of Holocaust denial toward the Middle East. Although there had been Holocaust denial in the Middle East for quite some time before he came to power, Ahmadinejad courted and cultivated a number of Western Holocaust deniers.[46] He convened several international conferences devoted to denying the Holocaust, which were well attended by a cadre of international revisionists, including some of the old guard, such as Fredrick Toben, Bradley Smith, Mark Weber, and others.[47] Less well-known is that he brought individual deniers at various times to lecture to students at Tehran University.[48] Also under his leadership, a group of Western antisemites, many of whom deny the Holocaust, have become regular guests on the English-language Iranian television station, Press TV.[49] There is little overt Holocaust denial on Press TV, but a great deal of minimization, and some inveighing about Zionist power that holds down "Holocaust scholars," meaning revisionists.[50]

Other public discussions of Holocaust denial, such as the controversies over Facebook's policy about Holocaust-denial groups, tend to focus on censorship and freedom of speech, rather than discussing Holocaust denial on its "merits" or as part of the way it affects the narrative of World War II.[51]

Today, when Holocaust deniers express their ideas in public, they almost always do so in the context of condemning Zionist and Jewish power, opposing Israel as a colonialist apartheid state, and complaining that their free speech is being curtailed. In fact, by using the term "Israel lobby," or Zionists, deniers are able to dispense with the tedious job of arguing about Zyklon B pellets, or whether the water table at Auschwitz was low enough to allow for open-air incinerations, or about the number of bodies that will fit in a four-muffle crematorium. They can cut right to their main point, which today is not really about Hitler, but about Jewish power and perfidy.

To be sure, anti-Zionism has always been an important part of Holocaust denial, and deniers have always been quick to claim that they are being persecuted. But the balance has tipped. Holocaust denial today is invoked by people who in many cases do not really care how many Jews died during WWII. They are often not interested in rehabilitating Hitler's image. In fact, they prefer to keep Hitler as an expression of evil because it serves their propaganda technique of labeling Israelis—and Zionists around the world—as Nazis. Holocaust denial has become less an agenda and more of a tactic, a weapon in the service of anti-Zionism. As a result, organizations and individuals dedicated to opposing Holocaust denial may need to reconsider the tactics they used in the 1980s and 1990s, and to address the problem of Holocaust denial as an element of the "new antisemitism."

NOTES

1. Stephen Atkins, *Holocaust Denial as an International Movement* (Westport, Conn.: Praeger, 2009), 145–162; and Deborah E. Lipstadt, Denying the Holocaust: The Growing Assault on Truth and Memory (New York: Free Press, 1993), 65–67.

2. Lipstadt, Denying the Holocaust, 65–67.

3. On Rassinier, see Atkins, *Holocaust Denial as an International Movement,* 84–87; and Lipstadt, Denying the Holocaust, 49–54.

4. See for example Harry Elmer Barnes, "Zionist Fraud," *American Mercury,* fall 1968; Paul Rassinier, *The Drama of European Jews* (Silver Spring, Md.: Steppingstones Publications, 1975).

5. On Carto, see Leonard Zeskind, *Blood and Politics: The History of the White Nationalist Movement from the Margins to the Mainstream* (New York: Farrar, Straus and Giroux, 2009), 3–16; Lipstadt, Denying the Holocaust, 144–153.

6. Although the California secretary of state reports that Noontide Press was incorporated in 1965, the company published Yockey's *Imperium* in 1962. There is some evidence that Carto may have used the name Noontide Press as early as 1955.

7. Gail Gans, "Spotlight on Hate," ADL *Bulletin* 37, no. 6 (June 1980): 6–8.

8. *Hitler's Apologists: The Anti-Semitic Propaganda of Holocaust "Revisionism"* (New York: Anti-Defamation League, 1993), 6.

9. Atkins, *Holocaust Denial as an International Movement,* 170.

10. Ibid., 156.

11. Alan M. Schwartz, *Danger: Extremism: The Major Vehicles and Voices on America's Far-Right Fringe* (New York: Anti-Defamation League, 1996), 225.

12. Martin Lee, *The Beast Reawakens* (Boston: Little, Brown, 1997), 86.

13. Schwartz, *Danger,* 225.

14. Atkins, *Holocaust Denial as an International Movement,* 173–174, 177–179, 185–186, 172–173.

15. *Hitler's Apologists,* 71.

16. Lipstadt, Denying the Holocaust, 123–136.

17. Jeff Riggenbach, "James J. Martin, 1916–2004," *Antiwar.com,* May 18, 2004, http://www.antiwar.com/orig/riggenbach.php?articleid=2593. The obituary glosses over Martin's involvement with Holocaust denial.

18. Fred Leuchter, *The Leuchter Report: The End of a Myth, an Engineering Report on the Alleged Execution Gas Chambers at Auschwitz, Birkenau, and Majdanek, Poland* (Decatur, Ala.: David Clark, 1988).

19. Faurisson, a former literature professor, has been an energetic proponent of Holocaust denial in France since the early 1960s. He has also left a lasting impact on Holocaust deniers in the United States, attaining marquee status at numerous IHR conferences and writing influential articles in the *Journal of Historical Review.* His trademark phrase, "No holes, no Holocaust" (referring to the purported lack of delivery mechanisms for the Zyklon B gas into the gas chambers at Birkenau) has become a mantra in Holocaust denial circles. For more on Faurisson, see Atkins, *Holocaust Denial as an International Movement,* 92–95, and Lipstadt, Denying the Holocaust, 58–62.

20. On Anne Frank, see for example Robert Faurisson, "Analysis of the Anne Frank Diary," *Journal of Historical Review* 3, no. 2 (summer 1982): 147–209. On the Mengele affair, see Mark Weber, "Lessons of the Mengele Affair," *Journal of Historical Review* 6, no. 3 (fall 1985): 377–383.

21. On Pearl Harbor, see for example Charles Lutton, "Pearl Harbor: Fifty Years of Controversy," *Journal of Historical Review* 11, no. 4 (winter 1991–1992): 431–467.

22. Later it was revealed that Leuchter had fabricated his engineering credentials and had made serious methodological errors in his analysis of Auschwitz gas chambers. For an extensive description of Leuchter and his involvement in the Holocaust denial movement, see Lipstadt, Denying the Holocaust, 162–182. Leuchter's involvement with Holocaust denial was also the subject of a documentary film: Errol Morris, Michael Williams, David Collins, Dorothy Aufiero, and Caleb Sampson, Mr. Death: The Rise and Fall of Fred A. Leuchter, Jr., Lion's Gate Home Entertainment, 2003.

23. More on the Mermelstein lawsuit can be found in Lipstadt, Denying the Holocaust, 138–141; Hitler's Apologists, 33–34.

24. Kenneth Stern, Holocaust Denial (New York: American Jewish Committee, 1993), 15–16.

25. Bradley Smith, "Fragments: Another Ordinary Life," Smith's Report 197 (July 2013): 12.

26. In August 1991, shortly after the first of his ads ran in several college newspapers, Smith explained, "I don't want to spend time with adults anymore. I want to go to students. They are superficial. They are empty vessels to be filled." See Schwartz, Danger, 144.

27. "On Hate Street: College Paper Caught in Holocaust Flap," narr. Rita Braver, 48 Hours, CBS-WCBS, New York, February 26, 1992.

28. Michael Shermer and Alex Grobman, Denying History: Who Says the Holocaust Never Happened and Why Do They Say It? (Berkeley: University of California Press, 2000), 109–114.

29. "Who Says It Never Happened? Ernst Zundel and Other 'Holocaust Deniers' Promote Their Message that the Extermination of Millions of Jews during World War II Never Happened," narr. Mike Wallace, 60 Minutes, CBS-WCBS, New York, March 20, 1994.

30. From Columnist to Candidate: Pat Buchanan's Religious War, ADL Special Research Report (New York: Anti-Defamation League, 1992), 5–7.

31. Steven Spielberg, for his part, has stated that one of the reasons he created Schindler's List was to oppose the claims of Holocaust deniers. See Steven Spielberg, foreword to Schindler's List: Images of the Steven Spielberg Film by David James (New York: Newmarket Press, 2004), 9.

32. Stern, Holocaust Denial, 58–59.

33. Mark Weber, "Institute for Historical Review," Anti-Defamation League, April 24, 2004, http://archive.adl.org/learn/ext_us/historical _review.html

34. In early 2014, a British television show procured from Irving locks of what he assured them was Hitler's hair. The program subjected the hair to DNA testing and claimed that it could not have been Hitler's. See Susanna Lazarus, "Adolf Hitler Hair Sold to Channel 4 for £3,000 by Controversial Historian David Irving Was Fake," Radio Times, March 25, 2014, http://www.radiotimes.com/news/2014-03-25/adolf-hitler-hair-sold -to-channel-4-for-3000-by-controversial-historian-david-irving-was-fake. Pages on Irving's website continue to catalog the items he has sold. See http://www.fpp.co.uk/shop/Wuest/Taufbecher_Eddas/index.html and http://www.fpp.co.uk/shop/Ealing/photos_misc/index_1.html.

35. "Holocaust Denier Released from Prison: David Irving Free After 13 Months in Jail," *Spiegel Online,* December 20, 2006, http://www.spiegel .de/international/holocaust-denier-released-from-prison-david-irving -free-after-13-months-in-jail-a-455726.html.

36. Ingrid Rimland Zundel, "A Message to the Spartans of the Spirit," *Smith's Report* 199 (October 2013): 8–10.

37. To some extent, vigilance by editors may be due to efforts by Jewish organizations to sensitize students and their academic advisors to the existence of Smith and his efforts. See for example *Responding to Bigotry and Intergroup Strife on Campus: Guide for College and University Presidents and Senior Administrators* (New York: Anti-Defamation League, 2001), and *Fighting Holocaust Denial on Campuses: A Manual for Action* (New York: Anti-Defamation League and Hillel: The Foundation for Jewish Campus Life, 2010).

38. *Smith's Report* 196 (June 2013): 5.

39. See *Smith's Report* 189 (February 2012): 4, where he describes the continuous rejection of his online ad submissions by student newspapers and his effort to build email lists of students and faculty that can elude anti-spam software. In *Smith's Report* 196 (June 2013): 8, Smith admitted that the anti-spam software was getting the better of him.

40. Editorial, "Who We Are," http://inconvenienthistory.com/who_we _are/index.php.

41. J. P. Campbell, "What Was Hitler's Unforgiveable Sin?," *Veteranstoday .com,* May 11, 2011, http://www.veteranstoday.com/2011/05/11/jb-campbell -behind-the-holocaust/.

42. Ingrid Rimland, "War Veterans in Crisis: Then as Now," *Veteranstoday .com,* June 22, 2013, http://www.veteranstoday.com/2013/06/22/a-defense -of-hitler-the-veteran/.

43. Michael Collins Piper, "Hitler and the Big Lie(s)," *Barnes Review* 19, no. 6 (November/December 2013): 3.

44. Paul T. Angel, "Setting the Record Straight," *Barnes Review* 20, no. 1 (January/February 2014): 2.

45. Mark Weber, "How Relevant Is Holocaust Revisionism?," IHR.*org,* January 27, 2009, http://www.ihr.org/weber_revisionism_jan09.html.

46. *Holocaust Denial in the Middle East: The Latest Anti-Israel Propaganda Theme* (New York: Anti-Defamation League, 2001).

47. On the 2006 Tehran conference, see "Iran Hosts Anti-Semitic Hatefest in Tehran," ADL.*org,* December 14, 2006, http://archive.adl.org/main _international_affairs/iran_holocaust_conference.html#.U_NsTf11ySo.

Another Holocaust denial conference in Tehran took place in February 2013. See Mark Weber, "Another Productive Visit to Iran: Tehran Conference Critically Examines 'Hollywoodism,'" *IHR.org*, February-March 2013, http://www.ihr.org/news/iranvisit_feb2013.html.

48. Mark Weber of the IHR spoke at Tehran University in September 2012. See Mark Weber, "A Successful Visit to Iran," *IHR.org*, http://ihr.org /news/sept12ihrupdate. Australian Holocaust denier Fredrick Toben has visited Iran on several occasions since the 2006 conference, and spoke at an Iranian conference on bioethics in February 2011. See Fredrick Toben, *Adelaide Institute Newsletter* 554 (March 2011), http://www.adelaideinstitute .org/newsletters/Newsletter%20554.pdf.

49. *Iran's Press TV: Broadcasting Antisemitism to English Speaking World* (New York: Anti-Defamation League, 2013).

50. One notable exception to the lack of overt denialism is Brandon Martinez, "Zionist Perversion of History Threatens World Peace," *Press TV*, January 13, 2014, http://www.presstv.ir/detail/2014/01/13/345401/zionist -perversion-threatens-peace/.

51. For example, see "Facebook Urged to Remove Holocaust-Denial Groups," CNN.com, May 8, 2009, http://www.cnn.com/2009/TECH/05 /08/facebook.holocaust.denial/index.html?eref=time_us.

PART IV

Regional Manifestations

THIRTEEN

From Occupation to Occupy

Antisemitism and the Contemporary Left
in the United States

SINA ARNOLD

THE CONTEMPORARY political Left has often been described as one of the central actors of the "New Antisemitism" in the United States. So far, however, little empirical research has been conducted to analyze this specific political milieu. Writing on the topic often focuses on the German context (e.g., Imhoff 2011, Knothe 2009, Stein 2011, Ullrich 2013), but works looking at the history of the U.S. Left's uneasy relationship to antisemitism are few and far between (Liebman 1979, Norwood 2013). This lack of attention is surprising, since the current economic crisis has been met by various popular responses in the United States, including the emergence of the left-wing Occupy Wall Street (OWS) movement. Crises, however, are often times when antisemitic ideologies resurface, so the question of the relationship between antisemitism and the Left becomes even more relevant. Moreover, the success of the Boycott, Divestment, and Sanctions (BDS) movement and the proliferation of pro-Palestinian groups opposing the Israeli occupation—particularly on college campuses—have in recent years renewed questions as to the fine line between critiques of Israel and antisemitism.

This chapter addresses this issue by analyzing contemporary left social movements in the United States.[1] Based on qualitative interviews with political activists, it points to central characteristics of left antisemitism discourse, examines the main frames in these debates, and offers explanations for these positions. Finally, it draws methodological and theoretical conclusions regarding the nature of the New Antisemitism. Its empirical sources are thirty qualitative interviews with Jewish and non-Jewish activists, expert interviews conducted mostly with members of New York Jewish organizations, analysis of current movement literature, as well as participant observation at OWS protest sites and other political events.[2] Employing an anthropological approach, the chapter is also an attempt at a "thick description" (Geertz 1973) of the negotiation of antisemitism in everyday settings. The focus of the interviews is twofold: First, interviews explore what antisemitic topoi can be found among present-day left actors, which ones are most common, and how they are contextualized. Second, the interviews show activists' perspectives *on* antisemitism: How is antisemitism conceptualized? Is it considered a relevant problem? These issues are subsumed under the label "antisemitism discourses," meaning both antisemitic speech and speech about antisemitism.[3]

While this chapter takes contemporary left social movements in the United States as a case study, on a theoretical level it attempts to go beyond a descriptive approach by proposing a framework for analyzing antisemitic attitudes as well as attitudes toward antisemitism on the political Left. It sees left debates and their strategic outcomes as informed by international theoretical debates but also framed within a national setting. Rather than merely analyzing individual stereotypes, it explores which ideological and social factors *support* or *hinder* the emergence of antisemitic attitudes on the Left, that is, it uncovers the "enabling conditions" of antisemitism.

THE INVISIBLE PREJUDICE: CENTRAL FEATURES
OF LEFT ANTISEMITISM DISCOURSE

The dominant features of left antisemitism discourse can be summed up as follows: First, there *are* reoccurring instances of open antisemitism. These include, for example, a person at the New York Occupy Wall Street camp repeatedly holding signs like "Google: Jewish Bankers," or someone verbally assaulting a visibly Jewish man at the same place, or antisemitic conspiracy theories in the Occupy online forum (Arnold 2012). The protests against the wars in Iraq and Afghanistan regularly featured banners and posters with antisemitic imagery (Anti-Defamation League 2010). Likewise, several anti-Israel protests in the following years featured antisemitic tropes (Wistrich 2012, 472). However, such instances of open Jew hatred are in fact fairly marginal. In the interviews, only one person expressed a consistently antisemitic world view, while others occasionally reproduced single stereotypes mostly related to the image of disproportionate Jewish power in the economy and politics. Most forms of classical antisemitism, including ideas of dual loyalty, anti-Judaism, or stereotypical racial imagery—the process of "turning Jews into 'Jews,'" as Brian Klug (2003) put it—were absent.

A second feature of left antisemitism discourse is that an anti-Zionist position, or at least a critical orientation toward Israel, is the norm within the spectrum of the Left analyzed here, leading to a one-sided critique of Israel. While activists are often careful to distinguish between the categories Israel/Israelis/Jews, nonetheless a monoperspective and Manichaean view of the Middle East conflict is dominant. Thus, five common double standards can be identified:

- The double standard of *salience* leads to a situation where the Middle East conflict receives vastly more attention than other international conflicts in left debates.

- The double standard of *state foundation* marks Israel's establishment as artificial and violent, in contrast to other states, which are presumed to be peacefully and "organically" grown.
- The double standard of *state formation* sees Israel as anachronistic: it is depicted as a colonial and imperial regime that pursues an archaic form of expansionism.
- The double standard of *self-understanding* translates into Israel being criticized as a specifically ethnic-religious state while also ignoring that this holds true for several other states that exist today.
- And, finally, the double standard of *self-determination* results in acknowledging free choice of political means only for Palestinians: their feelings of rage and despair are seen as legitimate, sometimes leading to rationalization and understanding for suicide bombings; there is also support for groups like Hamas even when they may contradict personal political convictions, for example, nonviolence. In contrast, feelings of fear and insecurity among Jewish Israelis are not taken into account: Israel's militarization or political moves to the right are never interpreted in a similar way.

Third, antisemitism is not perceived as a relevant issue in its own right. Interview partners did often mention instances of antisemitism that they themselves—as Jews—experienced or—as non-Jews—witnessed. However, on a list of "isms" to target—capitalism, racism, sexism, and so on—antisemitism usually was not worth mentioning at all. One interview partner was critical of this fact and remembers his own political socialization into the Left:

> As a person raised this way I feel like the problem is no one talks about it. When I was coming into activism, you had to talk about race, you had to talk about these different things. You had to talk about gender, you had to criticize these things or people were

gonna call you out on it. So you have to really sit there and de-
compress and really read and understand where your power is and
how that affects other people. And you never really do that, you
never really understand how you are antisemitic or how you view
Jewish people.

As a consequence, antisemitism is considered, in the words of another interview partner, as "mostly a lighthearted thing." When
directly asked, "Do you think that antisemitism is a problem in
the United States today?," the activists hardly spent time talking
about antisemitism—examples, instances, observations—but
instead actively redirected the conversation so as to talk about
the problems they associate with this phenomenon: its supposedly strategic use or "misuse," typically understood as providing
justification for Israel. This avoidance or marginalization also
holds true for dealing with historical antisemitism, namely the
Holocaust. This phenomenon amounts to "antisemitism trivialization," and its dynamics have already been pointed out both
within intra-left debates and by outside critics: Ernest Volkman
speaks of an "anti-Semitism of indifference" within the New Left
(1982, 12); Jewish feminist Irena Klepfisz noted an "antisemitism
by omission" in the 1980s (1989, 52); and Arthur Liebman artic-
ulates the "insensitivity thesis of left antisemitism" (1986, 353).
Robert Fine has called this mechanism "antisemitism denial"
(2010), meaning an active tendency toward downplaying or denying the importance of antisemitism, a refusal to take seriously
the charge of antisemitism, the reflexive dissociation of the Left
and antisemitism, and a shift from talking about antisemitism to
talking about accusations of antisemitism unjustly experienced
as a left activist. To quote one interview partner's answer to the
aforementioned question: "Well, the biggest problem with antisemitism is that it's used as a rallying cry for supporting the state
of Israel and its horrors." In consequence, this attitude means that
the banners at demonstrations mentioned earlier and other expressions of antisemitism in left settings are often tolerated. This

stance is in stark contrast to how the Left deals with other "-isms": Occupy Wall Street, to take a recent example, triggered lively debates about white privilege and racism within the movement, and also debated how to address the sexual assaults and male dominance that occurred in some encampments. Understanding themselves as members of a structurally racist and patriarchal society, activists often show a high degree of sensitivity and self-criticism in these areas. Attempts at addressing antisemitism in a similar fashion, however, generally fail and are answered with rejection and hostility.

In some cases, this denial is so strong that it leads to mockery, for example, as expressed by philosophy professor Michael Neumann (2002, 1) in *The Politics of Anti-Semitism* (edited by Cockburn and St. Clair), which is often the only publication on the subject to be found in left-wing bookstores in the United States: "I think we should almost never take antisemitism seriously, and maybe we should have some fun with it."[4] Such mockery is accompanied by trivialization, as when Neumann writes "Undoubtedly there is genuine antisemitism in the Arab world: the distribution of the Protocols of the Elders of Zion, the myths about stealing the blood of gentile babies. This is utterly inexcusable. So was your failure to answer Aunt Bee's last letter" (ibid., 7). His article is but one of many such examples, both in the activist and the intellectual Left.[5] The sociology of social problems (Schetsche 2013) has long noted that any given circumstance is not perceived as a "problem" because of objective factors, but rather because a process of social definition allows it to be perceived as a "problem" by movements and individuals. The trivialization of antisemitism, its nonperception as a "problem," thus calls for an explanation.

A fourth feature of left antisemitism discourse, and closely related to this matter, is a mechanism David Hirsh (2010) has called the Livingstone Formulation, referring to former London mayor Ken Livingstone.[6] It describes a common reaction to accusations of antisemitism, namely the reflexive defense against any such accusations and the knee-jerk "counter-accusation that the person raising the issue of antisemitism is doing so in bad faith and dishonestly . . . in order to de-legitimize criticism of Israel" (ibid., 47). This formulation revealed an interesting recurring dynamic in the interviews: when asked about antisemitism, instead of talking about the issue, interview partners redirected the conversation to talk about accusations of antisemitism and its alleged abuse. Granted, these accusations are not always imagined: activists *do* sometimes experience denunciation as "self-hating Jews" or "Nazis" during demonstrations and events; they sometimes face critics who use overgeneralizing allegations. To take one example: In 2014, Tom Perkins, founder of venture capital firm Kleiner Perkins Caufield & Byers, suggested in a letter to the editor of the *Wall Street Journal* that the Occupy movement and the wider Left's campaign against the rich "one percent" was comparable to National Socialist politics against the Jewish "one percent." He asked furthermore: "Kristallnacht was unthinkable in 1930; is its descendent 'progressive' radicalism unthinkable now?" (Perkins 2014). To take another: On November 3, 2011, during the emergence of the Occupy movement, three cars were torched in a Jewish neighborhood in Brooklyn, with graffiti on surrounding benches—including swastikas and "KKK"—pointing to an antisemitic motivation. A local newspaper affirmatively quoted a resident who assumed the arson might have been committed by participants of Occupy Wall Street, given the supposedly frequent examples of antisemitism there (Burke, Rotondo, Siemasko 2011). However, such claims of rampant and overt Jew hatred within the Left are far-fetched. More prevalent is that accusations of antisemitism are almost always perceived as strategically motivated. As described above, this judgment stands in contrast to the perception of accusations of sexism or racism, which are far more likely to be taken at face value and critically evaluated.

BEYOND THE CHECKLIST: A THREE-LEVEL
ANALYSIS OF ANTISEMITISM

Debates around antisemitism and the Left in academia and the media often focus solely on the first of the aspects mentioned earlier: instances of open antisemitism. These debates are mostly characterized by simplified accusations. U.S. and Israeli commentators have accused the Occupy movement of "naked antisemitism," to quote Phyllis Chesler, or imagined a situation comparable to pre–World War II Germany, as in an article in *Israel Today*.[7] As these debates mostly revolve around the question of distinguishing between antisemitism and legitimate critiques of Israel, not surprisingly accusations often take the form of a "checklist approach." This approach analyzes a given statement by applying the "3D Test of Anti-Semitism" developed by Nathan Sharansky (2004), asking whether there are demonization, delegitimation, and double standards to be found to determine if a statement, and in extension a movement, is antisemitic. Indeed, when following the "3D Test of Antisemitism," all three Ds can be found, as is shown above.

Another tool for distinguishing between antisemitism and a critique of Israel is the internationally widely used "Working Definition of Antisemitism," adopted in 2005 by what was then the European Union Monitoring Centre on Racism and Xenophobia. While the definition does list several "examples of the ways in which antisemitism manifests itself with regard to the State of Israel," it adds that these have to be understood "taking into account the overall context."[8] This, however, is where the problem and thus the need for analysis arise.

While both the three Ds and the EUMC Working Definitions are useful tools for practical purposes, I suggest moving away from the "checklist" approach of analyzing left antisemitism to instead situate and contextualize an analysis against the backdrop of political-cultural opportunity structures, national history, and collective identity. Therefore, an analysis of antisemitism in social movements must focus not only on potential antisemitic topoi, but in order to gain a deeper understanding, also on its *enabling conditions.*

More concretely, a three-level approach for an analysis of these enabling conditions of left antisemitism discourses is suggested:

On the *macro level,* the unit of analysis would be the national context, meaning political-cultural opportunity structures—the conditions for mobilizing success, historical factors, current political development, social crisis, and so on.

On the *meso level,* the social movement is the focus, particularly its specific theoretical traditions and current interpretations of political events.

The *micro level* looks at the individual and analyzes forms of collective identity within a movement as well as individual psychological factors. Given that antisemitism is what Sartre (1994) termed "*Weltanschauung* and passion," this includes the analysis of authoritarian character structures and emotional involvement.[9] Each of these levels poses different central questions, as illustrated in table 13.1.

Of course, these levels are necessarily interlaced: Collective identities are shaped not only by subculture but also by national culture. Internal movement culture brings with it a distinct history that will influence any given position. Individual identity is shaped not only by the wider society, but—especially in social movements—by the dynamics of belonging to a very specific social milieu. This approach will therefore necessarily remain schematic. For the case study at hand, however, it can aid in explaining the four characteristics of the left antisemitism discourse, as mentioned in "The Invisible Prejudice" section above: the occasional appearance of antisemitic stereotypes; the one-sided critique and double standard in regard to Israel; antisemitism trivialization; and active forms of antisemitism denial.

TABLE 13.1. THREE-LEVEL APPROACH FOR ANALYSIS OF ENABLING CONDITIONS OF LEFT ANTISEMITISM

Level	Unit of Analysis	Analytical Content	Central Questions
Macro	National context	Political-cultural opportunity structures	What prevalence does antisemitism have in the general society?
			Which societal actors are addressing antisemitism?
			What is their motivation?
			What politics and attitudes toward Israel are politically dominant?
			Vis-à-vis the Holocaust, what commemorative culture is in place?
Meso	Social movement	Theoretical foundations	What theoretical traditions form the specific analysis of antisemitism, including its origins and explanations?
			What analytical categories frame current political action?
Micro	Individual	Identity	Against the backdrop of differing ethnic-religious identities, what identitarian needs are fulfilled by (not) addressing antisemitism?
			What meaning does anti-Zionism have as a "subcultural code"?

ANTISEMITISM IN CONTEXT: OFFERING EXPLANATIONS

I now turn to the characteristics of the given units of analysis and their content:

Macro Level Analysis. In the national context, a *relative absence of open antisemitism* in the United States since World War II can be noted, leading to the fact that this is not a subject where the political Left sees a particular need for intervention. Since leftists perceive antisemitism as simply one among many forms of racism, it becomes invisible compared to racism against Blacks and Muslims. By extension, Jews are not perceived as "victims," a central category for contemporary claims making.

Second, in the United States one finds generally *positive attitudes toward Israel in the general population.* According to a survey by the Anti-Defamation League (ADL), almost half of Americans were sympathetic to the Israeli side, whereas 18 percent sympathized with the Palestinians. Sixty-three percent of all respondents considered Israel an important ally of the United States (Anti-Defamation League 2011). Compared to many European countries, the image of Israel in the U.S. media fares better. Whereas, for example, in Germany popular anti-Israel attitudes provide an opportunity structure for open antisemitism (Bergmann 2008, 478), this is less possible in the United States. For leftists, the overall pro-Israel attitude in the general population leads to a counterreaction that focuses on the underrepresentation of the Palestinian side and to an ignorance of antisemitism as one of the many factors driving the Middle East conflict.

Third, the American national context provides a *visible commemorative culture with regard to the Holocaust.* Eighty percent of Americans support teaching and commemorating the Holocaust (Darnell 2010, 13). Commemoration ceremonies occur on the federal level; the Holocaust is a fixed part of school curricula; and the United States Holocaust Memorial Museum has had a prominent place on the Washington Mall for over twenty years, receiving two million visitors annually. In the Left's perception, there exists what one interview partner calls a "hierarchy of catastrophe": Holocaust commemoration is seen as happening at the expense of remembering slavery and the genocide of Native Americans. Moreover, Holocaust commemoration is typically understood as solely instrumental in support of U.S. or Israeli nationalism. The specific role the Holocaust plays in the United States leads not only to the invisibility of historical antisemitism for the Left, but also contributes to instances of its trivialization, and by extension, demonization in critiques of Israel—especially the equation of Israeli policies with Nazism, a trope that can often be found. However, these false equations are not always motivated by antisemitism, but more often by intent to scandalize. The fact that Holocaust comparisons are being put into use in U.S. political discourse by actors from different political camps supports this assumption. Former Vice President Al Gore, for example, spoke in environmental campaigns of an "ecological crystal night" and an "environmental Holocaust" (Novick 2001, 29); the Tea Party has repeatedly made comparisons between the politics of the Nazis and the Democratic Party;[10] influential right-wing talk show host Glenn Beck often uses similar imagery;[11] and in 2014 Republican Tennessee state senator Stacey Campfield on his blog compared the "Patient Protection and Affordable Care Act" with the deportation of Jews during National Socialism.[12] As Gulie Ne'eman Arad has pointed out (2002, 231), in the United States the Holocaust has become a highly popular moral-political metaphor, a multipurpose doctrine easily applicable for different purposes. When applied to Israel, it can further the antisemitic imagery of reversing victims and perpetrators, but is not necessarily motivated by an antisemitic stance.

Another influential factor is the specific *context of fighting antisemitism in the United States*. The topic is usually addressed by organizations such as the Anti-Defamation League and the American Jewish Committee, and often by Jewish individuals who lean more toward the conservative political spectrum. For leftists, this fact often leads to an erroneous automatic association between discussing antisemitism and political conservatism. Moreover, since these actors are often the only ones addressing antisemitism on the Left, but also in Muslim communities or Arab countries, the Livingstone Formulation, explained above, also applies here.

Meso Level Analysis. At the level of movement culture and its theoretical foundations, *correspondence-theoretical explanations of antisemitism* can be found, such as in the Leninist tradition, which see it either as a tool of the ruling class to drive a wedge between workers, or as a direct result of the actions of Israel and Zionist groups in the United States. Because the Israeli state and U.S.-Zionist groups carry out their politics in the name of global Jewry, for activists it is supposedly understandable that criticism of Israel or Zionism blends into anti-Jewish sentiments. In left analysis, a critique of Israel therefore becomes the best strategy against global antisemitism.[13]

Most importantly, *antiracism as a dominant frame and subject* in the Left also encourages the invisibility of antisemitism.[14] Since the time of the abolitionists, antiracism has been a central paradigm of the U.S. Left, continuing through the civil rights movement and becoming foundational for the emergence of the New Left (Zaretsky 2012). The black/white binary, the "color line" that W. E. B. Du Bois already theorized in 1903, has remained a central if not preeminent category for inequality in the United States. American Jews, however, have undergone a process of whitening in the general perception since the 1950s, as Karen Brodkin (1998) has pointed out. They are therefore—in the language of critical whiteness studies, the dominant theory of antiracism since the 1990s both in academia and activism—endowed with "white privilege." In the perception of the Left, white privilege for U.S. Jews entails social recognition and representation, personal security against attacks due to the possibility of "passing," economic security, and an exclusive victim status because of the experience of the Holocaust. Therefore, antisemitism ranks low compared to other forms of racism. As seen by people on the Left, Muslims, on the other hand, have come under increasing threat of racism since 9/11 (Kaplan 2006, Panagopoulos 2006). In the Left's perception, there is a competitive dynamic between antisemitism and anti-Muslim racism. This priority is made clear in interviews in sentences like "Today really what dominates politics is not antisemitism at all but Islamophobia" or "I haven't felt [antisemitism] is an urgent social justice problem in this country the way that Islamophobia and anti-Muslim oppression is." Speaking of antisemitism supposedly masks the real problem of Islamophobia. Yet at the same time, the frame of antiracism not only is an enabling condition for antisemitic stereotypes but also hinders it: open antisemitism in the form of Jew hatred rarely happens on the Left and, when it does, is usually countered. To return to an earlier example: The person with anti-Jewish banners at OWS was quickly met with protest. People stood next to him with signs stating that "This guy doesn't speak for me or Occupy Wall Street," another asking "Who's paying this guy?," or one that simply had an arrow next to the word "asshole."

The second dominant frame in left discourse is *anti-imperialism*. Jews, unlike Muslims, are not perceived as victims of imperialist states, but rather are supposedly its beneficiaries, through their inherent link to Israel. One interview partner critically summarized this perspective on the Left, stating: "Jews are the epitome of white imperialism." In the post–Cold War era, left anti-imperialism targets not only the United States, but also and especially Israel. While not necessarily leading to open antisemitism, this attitude has the imminent danger of singling out Jews via the Jewish state. With it comes a binary worldview that cannot see Palestinians as aggressors or actors but merely as victims or respondents, and will thus not see antisemitic ideology as one of many factors influencing the current situation in the Middle

East. The anti-imperialist frame also leads to an ignorance of the political content of the conflict parties: the logic of "my enemy's enemy is my friend" at times causes leftists to endorse reactionary groups like Hamas and to justify suicide attacks. This frame has become more prominent since the attacks of 9/11; Moishe Postone speaks of a "neo-antiimperialism" and "reawakened Manichaeism" (2006, 96f.). The traditional Marxist-Leninist anti-imperialist worldview is most prominent among socialist groups. Here, it goes hand in hand with pitting "bad," that is, Western, nationalism against "good" liberation nationalism.

Along with this often comes a "foreshortened" (Postone 1980), or rather an *analytically false critique of capitalism:* critiques characterized by a personified analysis and conspiratorial thinking. This view has been visible within the Occupy Wall Street movement, whose political analysis often targets capitalism not as a systemic organizing principle, but instead narrowly focuses on finance capital as the sole origin of the current crisis and the only aspect of capitalism that needs to be criticized, whereas the sphere of production—which includes Main Street, so to speak—is often seen as devoid of exploitation. This sort of analysis is often a critique of capitalists, not capitalism, and it can be an entry point for antisemitism, as Jews have traditionally been associated with this social arena. The praise given to OWS by former leading Ku Klux Klan member and Holocaust denier David Duke illustrates this danger dramatically: in a video titled *Occupy Zionist Wall Street,* Duke congratulates all those who attack the international banks supposedly holding America hostage.[15] In a similar fashion, the American Nazi Party offered its support to OWS, openly praising its potential for making "the Natives" aware of the influence of Jewish "Wall Street bankers" and stating that "this issue is TAYLOR [sic] MADE for National Socialists."[16] Several Nazi groups attempted to infiltrate Occupy encampments but were mostly turned away (Lyons 2011). However, their praise shows the antisemitic potential that can accompany foreshortened and personalistic critiques of capitalism. And less explicitly right-wing actors like the conspiracy theorist David Icke were welcomed with open arms in some Occupy camps (Sunshine 2011).

The frame of "American interests" is also prominent in left discourse. This perspective analyzes a given domestic or foreign policy issue to determine what the United States' interest in it is. This left logic of taking responsibility for the actions of one's government is certainly not specific to the United States. However, here it can have the unintended effect of rendering antisemitism invisible. To give an example: A critique of the dominant historical narratives often results in a critical take on Holocaust commemoration and a demand for more visible remembrance of the victims of the Vietnam War or the genocide of Native Americans. The intention is a heightened attention and visibility for U.S. imperialism and its victims. The unintended result, however, can be an ignorance and even relativization of the Holocaust. The frame of "American interests" also partly explains the disproportional engagement with the Middle East conflict, the "double standard of salience" mentioned in "The Invisible Prejudice" section. Israel is perceived as America's closest ally and the central recipient of U.S. foreign aid. As U.S. citizens and taxpayers, activists feel a special responsibility for criticizing American interests and politics in the region—and, by extension, Israel.

Micro Level Analysis. The third level is that of collective identity. Here, specifically *intra-Jewish debates* are relevant. For Jewish leftists in the United States, who are often highly represented within progressive movements, debates about Israel and antisemitism are also debates about ethnic identity and representation within the Jewish community. Jewish leftists often criticize mainstream Jewish advocacy organizations, their pro-Israel line, and their claims to represent all U.S. Jews. Using a form of strategic essentialism (Spivak 1988), these secular "non-Jewish Jews" (Deutscher 1977) speak *as* Jews to state their case. For many, their positions are related to reclaiming a specific Jewish identity within the American Jewish community, which they feel has been overdetermined via identification with Israel and through large Jewish advocacy organizations. Unlike the mainstream Jewish community, whose identity since World War II has rested on the two pillars of the Holocaust and Israel, theirs is also a struggle for an alternative definition of the very meaning of being Jewish in the United States, often resting on the prophetic tradition, on the principle of "tikkun olam," and on Jewish involvement in the socialist, communist, and civil rights movements. Reclaiming a progressive Jewish identity, therefore, means perceiving it as part of the left tradition. This is done in word but also in deed, through what Alvin Rosenfeld has called "new rituals of dissent" (2006, 18). These could most recently be observed in the Occupy movement, which had a clear and visible Jewish presence via a sub-movement called Occupy Judaism.[17] In several cities, Jewish activists initiated public prayers, erected sukkahs, or celebrated the Shabbat dinner, all the while linking Jewish traditions to the political demands of the ows movement. All these activities and debates revolve around "antisemitism" as a kind of proxy, whereby Jewish leftists accuse mainstream organizations of muting dissent and perpetuating the image of Jews as eternal victims, fueled by false accusations of antisemitism. Whereas antisemitism is not intentional in these debates, such debates can be misperceived in the wider society, where they reinforce images of disproportionate Jewish power or of the "Israel lobby" controlling U.S. politics. However, the fact that many Jews are active and visible in the Left also contributes to pluralistic and multifaceted images of Jews who are not overburdened by projection and stereotypes.

Finally, on the level of movement identity, we can observe the function of *anti-Zionism as a "subcultural code."* Almost twenty-five years ago, Shulamit Volkov applied the concept of antisemitism as a "cultural code," originally used to analyze the role of antisemitism in late-nineteenth-century Germany as a political marker, to the contemporary political Left. Rejection of Israel has become a distinctive mark of belonging to a specific subcultural milieu, it is part of a comprehensive ideological left "package deal," as Volkov put it (2000, 84). Anti-Zionism is more than a specific position taken toward the Middle East conflict; rather, it expresses that one is on the right side of history, thereby rejecting imperialism, colonialism, racism, nationalism. The counter principle is necessarily "Zionism," which allegedly stands for all of these forces. By extension, this attitude impacts the very meaning of "antisemitism." Jonathan Judaken (2013) notes that "'antisemitism' thus now serves as a proxy for differing positions on the Arab-Israeli conflict." Focusing analysis on collective identity provides a more accurate explanation for the strong anti-Zionism existing even among Jewish activists than psychologizing and necessarily speculative concepts such as "Jewish self-hatred."

Last, the political relevance of these questions should be pointed out: In some instances, it becomes impossible for Jews to talk about antisemitism without being accused by the Left of trying to push a Zionist agenda. Sometimes, Jews are allowed into activist circles only if they accept anti-Zionism, and are therefore singled out. In that vein an article in *Revolution,* the magazine of the Revolutionary Communist Party, has a suggestion for U.S. Jews (Goodman 2010): "Jewish people who resent being resented for Israel's crimes (like white people who resent being blamed for white racism and the history of the oppression of Black people in this country) need to loudly and unequivocally speak out against Israel's crimes." The author thereby draws a direct connection between Jewish individuals in the United States and the politics of the Israeli state. Moreover, he puts the blame for antisemitism on Jews themselves and thus participates in a form of "blaming the victim." Ziva, an interview partner from Berkeley who is the daughter of Holocaust survivors, comments on this mechanism:

I've been very silent. I think most Jews are silent. Because the Left
is very strongly pro-Palestine, and people who speak out against
that are being accused of being right-wing. And there is no room
for, it's so emotionally charged, there is no room for dialogue. [...]
So I have a different experience among the Left, I get really scared
because I hear antisemitism, and I hear this on demonstrations
I won't go to, because I hear so much hatred of Israel, so much
hatred of Jews, and I feel like leaving the country. In a way I feel
like I can't be here.

The account of this long-term feminist, antiwar activist, and
dedicated radical—who in her sixties considers leaving both her
political movement and country—is a chilling reminder that the
aforementioned positions are not just intellectual problems but
can have concrete, deeply negative effects on Jewish individuals.

CONCLUSIONS: TOWARD MUTUAL
LEARNING PROCESSES

To understand antisemitism discourse within the contemporary
political Left, this chapter suggests moving away from a "checklist approach" toward antisemitism, specifically in relation to critiques of Israel. Instead, it offers a multilevel approach focusing
on the enabling conditions of antisemitic discourse. In terms of
this case study, this means that in the perception of the Left, the
specific opportunity structures of the United States provide little
ground for the spread of antisemitism: the relative absence of
open antisemitism, a general pro-Israel orientation, widespread
Holocaust commemoration, and, finally, the perception that antisemitism is only a political issue for the Right. Taken together,
these factors make antisemitism a nonissue in left circles. Antisemitism is an "invisible prejudice" in the contemporary Left in
a twofold way: First, its occasional articulation is not generally
open and coherent but takes coded and fragmented forms. Second, it is a prejudice that cannot be seriously addressed.

On a subcultural level there are theoretical traditions—such as Marxist-Leninist analyses of imperialism and capitalism—that can feed into an antisemitic worldview. Others, such as the dominance of antiracist and anti-imperialist political frames, render Jewish positions in the Middle East conflict invisible. These analyses contribute to the various double standards outlined above. On the level of collective identity, one can observe how anti-Zionism functions as a cultural code for most of the Left. Moreover, one sees how Jewish identity struggles are an important underlying factor within left debates, which pose the ironic danger of actually reinforcing antisemitic stereotypes when transported into the different context of the general public.

The findings from this case study have both political and theoretical consequences regarding the role of the Left in the New Antisemitism: Wilhelm Kempf noted in an article in the *Journal for the Study of Antisemitism* that "one serious deficiency of antisemitism research [however] is that it seldom asks what alternative meanings statements that may express antisemitism could also have" (2012, 1505). Trying to understand the specific content, the intention behind it, and the possible reception of a given statement gives a better sense of the problem at hand and provides possible starting points for developing strategies for addressing problematic imagery and discourse on the Left. While it is necessary to analyze the semantic structures of an antisemitic worldview independent of context, in order for us to understand its global and historical continuities and functions, these insights need to be flexibly applied to different contexts, actors, their intentions, and varied levels of reception. Critiques of Israel or antiracist positions are only rarely coded forms of expressing antisemitism, as some authors have suggested (e.g., Taguieff 2004). Rather, they are positions in their own right that provide a possible "entry point" for genuine antisemitic positions.

These insights are even more important given the relevance of the topic at hand. Just as the Left often responds over hastily to criticism via the Livingstone Formulation, sometimes the criticism itself is also overly hasty. Some examples express oversimplified accusations, where the motivation appears less to fight antisemitism than to slander a whole movement. Such ad hominem attacks in bad faith happen on both sides. Critics should, therefore, be thorough in their arguments, as well: Why is a certain action or attitude considered antisemitic? What are the criteria for making such a determination? Where and why are the lines drawn between antisemitism and anti-Zionism? David Hirsh's (2013, 1410) suggestion holds true both for academia and political debates: "Sociology should not be content to 'prove' that anti-Zionism is antisemitic; instead, it can help us study distinct forms of anti-Zionism, their particular traditions and assumptions, to look at ways in which they actualize themselves in concrete political exclusions, and to explore the contradictions between the meanings social actors wish to communicate and the meanings with which their communications are heard, read, and interpreted in distinct contexts." The context is key, and it can be analyzed with the help of the three-level approach suggested above. While it seems unlikely that we are currently witnessing the reemergence of a specifically left antisemitism in response to the financial crisis, many factors point to existing enabling conditions for antisemitic discourse. They are theoretical and practical sites of fracture where antisemitism might grow and can be starting points for acceptance of antisemitic positions and actors within the Left. Rather than either alarmist or appeasing assessments, an analytical approach can give an estimate of the degree of antisemitic threat, the historical and contemporary reasons for specific positions, and thus the possibilities for changing the discourse. That this change in discourse is possible is proven by international examples, such as the German Left, a site of intense internal discussions since the mid-1990s, which has developed a more multifaceted perspective on the Middle East conflict and a stronger sensitization to antisemitism, as Peter

Ullrich (2013) has shown. Shift in discourse is also visible in historical and contemporary attempts at criticizing antisemitism
within the Left. These include the specific attempts of the short-
lived Jewish New Left of the 1970s, a loose network of groups,
magazines, and individual activists (Porter and Dreier 1973). This
offspring of the New Left consisted of Jewish radicals, who appropriated the language of the Black liberation movements prominent at the time in order to promote Zionism as a national liberation movement. Moreover, they battled antisemitism within the
Black Power movement and other currents of the New Left—all
while staying true to their radical left politics. Likewise, debates
initiated by Jewish feminists in the Second Wave of feminism a
decade later used the emerging language of identity politics to
speak about antisemitism (Bulkin, Pratt, and Smith 1984, Kaye-
Kantrowitz and Klepfisz 1989, Pogrebin 1982). Just as feminists of
color had claimed that the victims of racism should be the ones to
define what oppression meant to them, so Jewish feminists argued
that they needed more visibility *as Jews* and sought to define the
complex nature of antisemitism, including the fact that it sometimes expressed itself as anti-Zionism. And finally, some contemporary activists and political groups point to the possibility of
changing intra-left discourse. Since 9/11, a handful of publications
have come out of the radical Left with titles such as "The Past
Didn't Go Anywhere: Making Resistance to Antisemitism Part
of All of Our Movements" (Rosenblum 2007), and a left-wing blog
was established to collect texts on antisemitism and the Left.[18]
Meanwhile, selected authors and groups have criticized antisemitism in the alter-globalization movement (Anti-Fascist Forum
2001), within Occupy Wall Street (Marxist-Humanist Initiative
2011), or in the Left in general (Willis 2003), or translated articles
by German left-wing authors critical of antisemitism or anti-
Zionism.[19] Activists have occasionally organized workshops and
conferences on such topics, including "Finding Our Voice: The
Conference for Progressives Constructively Addressing Anti-

Semitism,"[20] "World Capitalist Crisis, Israel, and the Roots of Jew Hatred,"[21] or "Left Antisemitism: Building Bridges to the Right?"[22] Judy Andreas, a non-Jewish feminist activist, even organized two three-day conferences in 2004 and 2006 on both the East and West Coasts titled "Facing a Challenge Within: A Progressive Scholars' and Activists' Conference on Anti-Semitism and the Left" with the goal "to strengthen the Left by creating a new alternative to the existing polarization that isolates Jews and those who care about Jewish oppression."[23] Not surprisingly, each of these attempts was met with denial, skepticism, and rejection. These negative responses included emails to the conference organizers, internet comments, protests, angry counter articles, and a general questioning of the integrity and motivation behind such efforts. Nevertheless, these activities point to a potential that can draw both from history and international experience: Historically, one finds both the danger of antisemitism on the Left as well as potential for self-criticism and counter-activities, be it through the Old Left (Norwood 2013), the Jewish New Left, or lively debates within the feminist movement. Internationally, the German Left may provide a useful recent example of a successful learning process. The strengthening of that potential gives grounds for hope.

NOTES

1. When I speak of the "Left," I include actors labeling themselves as "progressive," "radical," "left" as well as those using more specific terms such as "anarchist" or "Marxist." This chapter mainly analyzes the extra-parliamentary Far Left, particularly its socialist and neo-anarchist wings. It is this part of the fragmented American Left that has in past debates mostly been accused of antisemitism, or that works on topics that in one way or the other touch on the issue, such as Palestine solidarity groups.

2. The interview partners come from five interrelated currents of the extraparliamentary far left: the antiwar movement, Palestine solidarity groups, Occupy Wall Street, and Jewish-identified groups. Moreover, three individuals active in the queer and anarchist scenes were part of the

sample. Many of these groups are also part of the BDS movement. This choice of groups was informed by my desire to analyze groups that have been accused of furthering antisemitic positions or that are in touch with the issue in their activism. The more prominent of these groups are World Can't Wait, the International Socialist Organization, the ANSWER Coalition, Code Pink, United for Peace and Justice, Women in Black, various Students for Justice in Palestine groups and Jewish Voice for Peace. The individuals interviewed were between nineteen and seventy-three years old and residents of either New York City or the San Francisco Bay Area. Sixteen interview partners identified as Jewish, most others as atheists with a Christian background, two as Muslim, and one as Mormon—although almost all declared themselves to be nonreligious. Most interview partners were white, three were Arab Americans, one was African American, and one Latina. Although a qualitative sample obviously can never be representative, in terms of age and race it mirrors the realities of the contemporary United States Left quite adequately.

3. In order to develop a thorough understanding of antisemitism discourses, the research explores related topics, including the Middle East conflict, the Holocaust and Holocaust remembrance, U.S. politics, and antiracism.

4. The work of prominent authors such as Uri Avnery, Edward Said, and Norman Finkelstein appear in *The Politics of Anti-Semitism*. Ten of the eighteen articles address the supposed "misuse" of antisemitism, grounded in false accusations towards pro-Palestinian activists. Not one single contribution deals with the historical background of antisemitism in general or the Left in particular. Instead, the basic assumption of many articles is that antisemitism, unlike Islamophobia, is an irrelevant issue worldwide. Some articles support the idea of a disproportionally influential "Israel Lobby." No article attempts to analyze the difference between antisemitism and a critique of Israel.

5. Other examples include verbal attacks against activists attempting to speak out against antisemitism, internet debates on left websites (such as www.indymedia.org suggesting that these attempts are mere Zionist public relations campaigns), and interrogating or even banning speakers critical of antisemitism from conferences or demonstrations.

6. Livingstone, after having been accused of antisemitism by a journalist after an argument, wrote in reply: "For far too long the accusation of anti-semitism has been used against anyone who is critical of the policies of the Israeli government, as I have been" (Livingstone 2006).

7. Phyllis Chesler, "Occupy Wall Street's Anti-Semitism Should Scare You," *Arutz Shiva,* 20.11.2011, http://www.israelnationalnews.com/Articles /Article.aspx/10737#.ToOeoHItgdZ, accessed 16.3.2015. Ryan Jones, "Israelis Worried by Anti-Semitic Flavor of 'Occupy Wall St.' Protests," *Israel Today,* 16.10.2011, http://www.israeltoday.co.il/News/tabid/178/nid/22978 /language/en-US/Default.aspx, accessed 16.3.2015.

8. European Forum on Antisemitism, "Working Definition of Antisemitism," http://www.european-forum-on-antisemitism.org/working -definition-of-antisemitism/english/, accessed 16.3.2015. The EUMC has since changed its name to the European Union Agency for Fundamental Rights (FRA).

9. This chapter does not engage in a micro-level analysis, which requires specific tools of analysis.

10. A call to "Stop America's Hitler" from February 2013 with a photo blends President Obama and Hitler, John Aravosis, "Tea Party: Obama Is Hitler," http://americablog.com/2013/02/tea-party-obama-is-hitler.html, accessed 16.3.2015. For other examples see Rosenfeld 2011: 35.

11. For an overview, see Lewis Black, "Glenn Beck Has Nazi Touettes [*sic*]," http://www.liveleak.com/view?i=d2a_1273833689, accessed 11.7.2013.

12. Stacey Campfield, "Thought of the Day," http://lastcar.blogspot.de /2014/05/thought-of-day_5.html, accessed 16.5.2014.

13. Interestingly enough, a similar position in regard to Muslims would clearly be called out for its inherent racism: the Left usually strongly and rightly condemns positions justifying resentments against Muslims because of terrorism carried out in the name of Islam. It rightly points to the fact that a distinction must be made between states (e.g., Iran, Saudi Arabia), political groups (e.g., Al-Qaida) and individuals (e.g., U.S. Muslims) so as to prevent essentializing and overgeneralizing viewpoints. The same standard, however, is seldom applied to Israel, Zionist groups, and Jews.

14. By labeling antiracism as a "frame," an approach from social movement studies is being applied. In the sense of Erving Goffman (1974), social movements have specific theoretical perspectives with which they look upon reality. These schemes of interpretation function like a picture frame: they lead the focus onto what is important and away from what is unimportant. Antiracism is such a mental filter.

15. "Occupy Zionist Wall Street by David Duke," http://youtube.com /watch?feature=player_profilepage&v=xKy22KsxX9k, accessed 14.3.2012.

16. "ANP Report for October 16, 2011," http://anp14.com/news/archives .php?report_date=2011-10-16, accessed 15.3.2012.

17. The self-proclaimed aim of this movement was "Bringing the Jews to Occupy Wall Street, Bringing Occupy Wall Street to the Jews," *Occupy Judaism,* www.facebook.com/occupyjudaism, accessed 21.2.2012.

18. See http://leftantisemitism.wordpress.com/, accessed 13.7.2014.

19. Cp. the texts featured in the *Platypus Review,* the newspaper of the Platypus Affiliated Society, a Marxist student group, http://platypus1917.org/, No. 28, 33, 49, 52, accessed 13.7.2014.

20. A daylong conference organized by left-wing Jewish activists in the San Francisco Bay Area in 2007.

21. A workshop criticizing BDS organized by the Socialist Workers Party at its 2010 annual conference.

22. A presentation by Spencer Sunshine at the Anti-Racist Action Conference in Portland, Oregon, in 2010.

23. Conference program, copy in author's possession.

BIBLIOGRAPHY

Anti-Defamation League. 2010. "2009 Audit of Anti-Semitic Incidents: Anti-Semitism at Anti-Israel Rallies." http://archive.adl.org/main_anti_semi tism_domestic/2009_audit76of.html#.UqHGNhl_sXw [6.12.2013].
————.2011. "American Attitudes Toward Israel, the Palestinians and Prospects for Peace in the Middle East." http://www.adl.org/israel /ADL-2011-Middle-East-11.9.11.pdf [16.6.2012].
Anti-Fascist Forum, ed. 2001. *My Enemy's Enemy: Essays on Globalization, Fascism and the Struggle against Capitalism.* Montreal: Kersplebedeb.
Arad, Gulie Ne'eman. 2002. "Nationalsozialismus und Zweiter Weltkrieg. Berichte zur Geschichte der Erinnerung: U.S.A." In *Verbrechen erin-nern. Die Auseinandersetzung mit Holocaust und Völkemord,* edited by Volkhard Knigge and Norbert Frei, 219–239. München: Verlag C. H. Beck.
Arnold, Sina. 2012. "'Bad for the Jews?' Antisemitismus und die 'Occupy'-Bewegung in den U.S.A." In *Jahrbuch für Antisemitismusforschung 21,* edited by Stefanie Schüler-Springorum, 370–391. Berlin: Metropol Verlag.
Bergmann, Werner. 2008. "Vergleichende Meinungsforschung zum Anti-semitismus in Europa und die Frage nach einem 'neuen europäischen Antisemitismus.'" In *Feindbild Judentum. Antisemitismus in Europa,* ed-ited by Lars Rensmann and Julius Schoeps, 472–507. Berlin: Verlag für Berlin-Brandenburg.

Brodkin, Karen. 1998. *How Jews Became White Folks and What That Says About Race in America*. New Brunswick, N.J.: Rutgers University Press.

Bulkin, Elly, Minnie Bruce Pratt, Barbara Smith. 1984. *Yours in Struggle: Three Feminist Perspectives on Anti-Semitism and Racism*. Ithaca, N.Y.: Firebrand Books.

Burke, Kerry, Christie Rotondo, and Corky Siemasko. 2011. "Anti-semitic vandals run wild in Brooklyn." *New York Daily News*, 11.11. http://www .nydailynews.com/news/crime/vandals-torch-vehicles-midwood -brooklyn-scrawl-anti-semitic-graffiti-article-1.976207 [12.11.2011].

Cockburn, Alexander, and Jeffrey St. Clair, eds. 2003. *The Politics of Anti-Semitism*. Petrolia/Oakland: Counterpunch/AK Press.

Darnell, Scott. 2010. *Measuring Holocaust Denial in the United States*. Policy Analysis Exercise, Harvard Kennedy School of Government, spring 2010. http://www.hks.harvard.edu/ ... /HolocaustDenialPAE.pdf [4.4.2011].

Deutscher, Isaac. 1977. *Der nichtjüdische Jude*. Berlin: Rotbuchverlag.

Du Bois, W. E. B. 1994 [1903]. *The Souls of Black Folk*. Mineola, N.Y.: Dover Publications.

Fine, Robert. 2010. "Antisemitism and discourses of denial." Presentation at the "Colloquium III: Patterns of Excuses for Antisemitism and Forms of Denial," International Institute for Education and Research on Anti-semitism, London, 28.10.

Geertz, Clifford. 1973. "Thick description: Toward an interpretative theory of culture." In *The Interpretation of Cultures*, 3–30. New York: Basic Books.

Goffman, Erving. 1974. *Frame Analysis: An Essay on the Organization of Experience*. New York: Harper & Row.

Goodman, Alan. 2010. "Behind the silencing of Helen Thomas: Covering up and carrying out great crimes." In *Revolution*, no. 203, http://revcom .us/a/203/Helen_Thomas-en.html [13.6.2010].

Hirsh, David. 2010. "Accusations of malicious intent in debates about the Palestine-Israel conflict and about antisemitism: The Livingstone For-mulation, 'playing the antisemitism card' and contesting the boundaries of antiracist discourse." In *Transversal*, no. 1: 47–77.

———. 2013. "Hostility to Israel and antisemitism: Toward a sociological approach." *Journal for the Study of Antisemitism* 5, no. 1: 1401–1422.

Imhoff, Max. 2011. *Antisemitismus in der Linken. Ergebnisse einer quantitativen Befragung*. Frankfurt am Main: Peter Lang.

Judaken, Jonathan. 2013. "Anti-antisemitic hitmen and the New Judeo-phobia." *Huffington Post Blog*, 2.4. http://www.huffingtonpost.com /jonathan-judaken/anti-antisemitic-hitmen_b_2617494.html [14.11.2013].

Kaplan, Jeffrey. 2006. "Islamophobia in America? September 11 and Islam-ophobic hate crime." *Terrorism & Political Violence* 18, no. 1: 1–33.

Kaye-Kantrowitz, Melanie, and Irena Klepfisz, eds. 1989. *The Tribe of Dina: A Jewish Women's Anthology*. Boston: Beacon Press.

Kempf, Wilhelm. 2012. "Antisemitism and criticism of Israel: A method-ological challenge for peace research." *Journal for the Study of Antisemi-tism* 4, no. 2: 1501–1518.

Klepfisz, Irena. 1989. "Anti-Semitism in the lesbian/feminist movement." In *Nice Jewish Girls. A Lesbian Anthology*, edited by Evelyn Torton Beck, 51–57. Boston: Beacon Press.

Klug, Brian. 2003. "The collective Jew: Israel and the new antisemitism." *Patterns of Prejudice* 37, no. 2: 117–138.

Knothe, Holger. 2009. *Eine andere Welt ist möglich—ohne Antisemitismus? Antisemitismus und Globalisierungskritik bei Attac*. Bielefeld: Transcript Verlag.

Liebman, Arthur. 1979. *Jews and the Left*. New York: John Wiley & Sons.

———. 1986. "Anti-semitism in the left?" In *Anti-Semitism in American History*, edited by Gerber, David, 329–359. Urbana: University of Illinois Press.

Livingstone, Ken. 2006. "An attack on voters' rights." *Guardian*, 1.3. http://www.theguardian.com/politics/2006/mar/01/society.london [25.1.2014].

Lyons, Matthew N. 2011. "Rightists woo the Occupy Wall Street move-ment," 8.11. http://threewayfight.blogspot.com/2011/11/rightists-woo-occupy-wall-street.htmlhttp://threewayfight.blogspot.com/2011/11/rightists-woo-occupy-wall-street.html [16.3.2012].

Marxist-Humanist Initiative. 2011. "Beware of left anti-semitism: Jew-hatred appears in conspiracy theories, anti-Americanism, lesser-evilism, and single-issue thinking." http://www.marxisthumanistinitiative.org/mhieditorial/condemn-left-anti-semitism-conspiracy-theories-and-other-limits-on-thought.html [23.11.2011].

Neumann, Michael. 2002. "What is anti-semitism?" In *The Politics of Anti-Semitism*, edited by Alexander Cockburn and Jeffrey St. Clair, 1–12. Petrolia, Calif.: Counterpunch.

Norwood, Stephen. 2013. *Antisemitism and the American Far Left*. New York: Cambridge University Press.

Novick, Peter. 2001. *Nach dem Holocaust. Der Umgang mit dem Massen-mord*. Stuttgart: Deutsche Verlagsanstalt.

Panagopoulos, Costas. 2006. "Arab and Muslim Americans and Islam in the aftermath of 9/11." *Public Opinion Quarterly* 70, no. 4: 608–624.

Perkins, Tom. 2014. "Progressive Kristallnacht coming?" *Wall Street Journal*, 24.1. http://online.wsj.com/news/articles/SB10001424052702304549 504579316913982034286 [26.1.2014].

Pogrebin, Letty Cottin. 1982. "Anti-semitism in the women's movement." *Ms. Magazine*, June 1982, 45–71.

Porter, Jack Nusan, and Peter Dreier, eds. 1973. *Jewish Radicalism: A Selected Anthology*. New York: Grove Press.

Postone, Moishe. 1980. "Anti-semitism and National Socialism: Notes on the German reaction to 'Holocaust.'" *New German Critique*, no. 19, special issue 1: 97–115.

———. 2006. "History and helplessness: Mass mobilization and contemporary forms of anticapitalism." *Public Culture* 18, no. 1: 93–110.

Rosenblum, April. 2007. "The past didn't go anywhere: Making resistance to antisemitism part of all of our movements." http://zinelibrary.info /past-didnt-go-anywhere-making-resistance-antisemitism-part-all-our -movements [5.12.2013].

Rosenfeld, Alvin H. 2006. "'Progressive' Jewish Thought and the New Anti-Semitism." American Jewish Committee.

———. 2011. *The End of the Holocaust*. Bloomington: Indiana University Press.

Sartre, Jean Paul. 1994. "Überlegungen zur Judenfrage." In *Gesammelte Werke in Einzelausgaben*. Politische Schriften, vol. 2. Reinbek b. Hamburg: Rowohlt, 9–91.

Schetsche, Michael. 2013. *Empirische Analyse sozialer Probleme. Das wissenssoziologische Programm*. 2nd ed. Wiesbaden: VS Verlag.

Sharansky, Natan. 2004. "3D test of anti-semitism: Demonization, double standards, delegitimization." *Jewish Political Studies Review* 16, no. 3–4.

Spivak, Gayatri. 1988. "Can the subaltern speak?" In *Marxism and the Interpretation of Culture*, edited by Cary Nelson and Lawrence Grossberg, 271–313. Chicago: University of Illinois Press.

Stein, Timo. 2011. *Zwischen Antisemitismus und Israelkritik. Antizionismus in der deutschen Linken*. Wiesbaden: VS Verlag.

Sunshine, Spencer. 2011. "Occupied with conspiracies? The Occupy Movement, populist anti-elitism, and the conspiracy theorists." *Shift Magazine*. http://libcom.org/library/occupied-conspiracies-occupy-movement -populist-anti-elitism-conspiracy-theorists [18.11.2013].

Taguieff, Pierre-André. 2004. *Rising from the Muck: The New Anti-Semitism in Europe*. Chicago: Ivan R. Dee.

Ullrich, Peter. 2013. *Deutsche, Linke und der Nahostkonflikt. Politik im Antisemitismus- und Erinnerungsdiskurs*. Göttingen: Wallstein Verlag.

Volkman, Ernest. 1982. *A Legacy of Hate: Anti-Semitism in America.* New York: Franklin Watts.

Volkov, Shulamit. 2000. *Antisemitismus als kultureller Code: zehn Essays.* 2nd ed. München: Verlag C. H. Beck.

Willis, Ellen. 2003. "Is there still a Jewish Question? Why I'm an anti-anti-Zionist." In *Wrestling with Zion: Progressive Jewish-American Responses to the Israeli-Palestinian Conflict,* edited by Tony Kushner and Alisa Solomon, 226–232. New York: Grove Press.

Wistrich, Robert. 2012. *From Ambivalence to Betrayal: The Left, the Jews, and Israel.* Lincoln: University of Nebraska Press.

Zaretsky, Eli. 2012. *Why America Needs a Left: A Historical Argument.* Cambridge: Polity Press.

—∿—

FOURTEEN

The EU's Responses to
Contemporary Antisemitism

A Shell Game?

R. AMY ELMAN

WHEN THE EUROPEAN UNION Agency for Fundamental Rights (FRA) released its survey report on antisemitism in 2013, a decade had passed since its predecessor (the European Union Monitoring Centre or EUMC) attempted to shelve its findings on the same subject.[1] If it appears that the European Union (EU) has come far since then to acknowledge the pervasiveness of a problem it earlier endeavored to downplay, consider this: the agency that released the 2013 report is the same one that withdrew its predecessor's "working definition of antisemitism" from its website and then insisted that the definition never really existed.

Deciphering the "new" antisemitism within the EU's transnational polity is like watching a shell game insofar as, like a glimpsed ball rapidly rotated beneath three shells, antisemitism is a swiftly moving object. Its composition and location seem obvious until you realize (if ever you do) that the others with whom you have been watching it move—those who seemingly had been paying as much (if not more) attention—may be the shills whose job it has been to distract you from finding it.

This chapter exposes a few of the grand gestures beneath which the "new" realities of antisemitism have been obscured. This requires that we understand that the most important element to any sleight of hand is misdirection. Misdirection involves diverting the public's attention away from that which one wishes to conceal. The intent behind magic and political maneuvers may differ, but the guiding principle is the same.[2] Grandiose, well-timed movements conceal smaller covert ones. The challenge, in watching (antisemitism), is discerning the difference between those moves.

Our focus is on a decade's worth of EU efforts said to identify and counter the escalation of prejudice against Jews in the aftermath of 9/11. It explores the informal adoption and later rejection of the EU's working definition of antisemitism and then examines the formal passage of a framework decision that criminalizes Holocaust denial. We consider whether these (official and informal) efforts offer Jews potential redress or mimic the mechanics of a shell game in which the "new" antisemitism is often glimpsed but rarely grasped.

Deciphering the "new" antisemitism within the EU first requires that we reveal the deceptions surrounding it—key among these is that this polity has long been, and continues to remain, active in the fight against antisemitism.[3] Not so. Like racism in general, antisemitism was seen as a uniquely national problem that the European Community had little interest in and no substantive authority to address because the unification of Europe was foremost, and has largely remained, an economically inspired plan.[4]

Stemming the economic disparities and tensions between states was the chief concern of the architects of "Europe's" integration; curtailing discrimination within them was far less important. Yet, well-meaning officials dedicated to a "redemptive" narrative of European unity often obscure this history. Consider, for instance, the EU's Ombudsman, Emily O'Reilly.[5] Speaking at a conference on "the branding of Europe," she explained that the best way to "spin a tale around the meaning of Europe that binds hearts and minds" is to "tell the tale of peace forged from the ashes of Auschwitz," because it is "harder to romanticise fiscal stability mechanisms."[6] Thus, the dangers of sentimentalizing Auschwitz notwithstanding, antisemitism offers retrospective utility. That is, antisemitism provided Europeans with a "learning experience" but it has been "tucked away safely in Europe's past, overcome by the defeat of fascism and the development of the European Union."[7] This tempting narrative brands European integration as an antidote against antisemitism.

It was not, however, until the turn of this century that any EU institution focused exclusively (or even primarily) on the very discrimination that had, decades ago, brought the continent to its knees. Even today, antisemitism may be regarded as antithetical to a "Europe" whose reputation is diminished by its association with it, although it remains one of the few forms of discrimination to have escaped the notice of the European Court of Justice, the EU's final arbiter of European law. Infrequently considered a significant problem in its own right, antisemitism was first addressed by the EUMC following 9/11, shortly after the institution was founded.

THE EUROPEAN UNION MONITORING CENTRE (EUMC)

When the EU's executive body, the European Commission, considered the EUMC's establishment, its 1996 memorandum explained: "The point is *not* to take specific measures to combat racism or xenophobia" (emphasis added). Indeed, the Commission insisted it would not "modify the system for protecting human rights in the Community or . . . [in] any of its Member States."[8] It may have wanted to avoid the perception that Brussels would unduly interfere in controversial matters where sovereignty dictates "core domestic preferences on ethical issues."[9] Thus the Centre was not to intrude on the internal affairs of the member states and, whatever appearances to the contrary may have been, it stayed true to the (memo's) original mission.

The following year, in 1997, the Centre's charge was clarified in the regulation that established it. Far from compelling member states to provide data or information to the EUMC, the Centre would "provide the Community and the Member States ... with objective, reliable and comparative data at the European level on the phenomenon of racism, xenophobia *and anti-Semitism* in order to help them *when* they take measures or formulate courses of action within their respective areas of competence" (emphasis added).[10]

In the case of antisemitism, the Centre remained a largely untapped source until after 9/11, when a noticeable increase in antisemitic acts in some member states prompted the Centre's director, Beate Winkler, to call for an investigation. In a coauthored foreword to that inquiry, she and the chair of the Centre's board (Bob Purkiss) explain: "It is important to listen sensitively to the fears of the Jewish communities, but also to identify the social context which gives rise to the hatred of the perpetrators."[11]

Having first proclaimed anti-Muslim discrimination their top concern following 9/11, the Centre lacked the political clout, if not the will, to address the antisemitic dimensions of 9/11.[12] Thus, it proved reluctant to recognize that some of the far right's traditional victims (viz., Muslims of African and Arab descent) had become antisemitism's leading proponents. Instead of confronting this complexity (one increasingly recognized as the "new" antisemitism), the Centre tried, in vain, to suppress the data relating to it. That effort at suppression was complicated by the relative autonomy enjoyed by the externally contracted researchers on whom the Centre relied, a problem resolved by the Centre's subsequent (from 2004) reliance on its own "in house" researchers for studies of a "politically very sensitive nature."[13]

In preparing for its first survey on antisemitism, however, the Centre tasked all fifteen of its national affiliates (known as National Focal Points) within its Racism and Xenophobia Network (RAXEN) to record for one month the number of violent attacks against Jews (from May 15 to June 15, 2002). It also requested information on subtler forms of antisemitism through additional surveys and the public's reactions.

With a minimal staff and no research division of its own at the time, the EUMC contracted expert researchers from the Centre for Research on Antisemitism (CRA) at the Technical University Berlin to synthesize these data for a single, comprehensive report. The subsequent CRA draft report established that the most violent attacks against Jews were tied to virulent anti-Zionism and to perpetrators who were "above all either right-wing extremists or radical Islamists or young muslims of Arab descent, who are often themselves victims of exclusion and racism."[14]

The EUMC refused to release the CRA's findings to the public, insisting that the one-month period covered in the CRA draft report was too short and that publishing the initial survey was never its intention. This explanation lacked heft. First, the Centre established the time frame and had already conducted a survey using the "rapid response" methodology to monitor conditions for Muslims (albeit over a four-month period) immediately following the terrorist attacks of 9/11. The Centre widely disseminated the results of that survey through its published report on Islamophobia. Moreover, the Centre's own annual report suggests that this earlier work was to serve as a template for the upcoming overview on antisemitism.[15]

The Centre's more serious claim was that the CRA research was methodologically unsound. This particular accusation led CRA researchers to respond that their focus on Muslim perpetrators of antisemitism and anti-Zionist attacks disturbed the EUMC, which endeavored to shield Muslims from such accusations.[16] Furthermore, the researchers revealed that the EUMC had repeatedly asked them to alter their "divisive" findings.[17] After the researchers refused to make these changes, the EUMC quashed the synthesis report.

The EUMC's response backfired in late November 2003 when news of the "shelved" report surfaced in the Financial Times. The chair of the EUMC's board responded to the critical coverage with a letter to that newspaper's editor. He insisted the report had not been shelved and that, instead, the CRA's work did not meet "the usual quality standards that all EUMC publications must adhere to."[18] That claim was questionable given that, months before, the Commission issued an excoriating review of the Centre's own research. According to its evaluation, "the Centre has clearly made significant improvements in the objectivity and reliability of its data over recent years," but "it is clear that the objective of comparability has not yet been achieved to any substantial degree."[19]

Its credibility further diminished by the *Financial Times* coverage, the Centre was embarrassed and on the defensive, its director and chairman conceded that the scandal over the report "present[ed] the strongest challenge for the EUMC since its foundation."[20] Several members of the European Parliament responded with a call for the report's immediate release. By December, the CRA experts released its draft online and exposed the Centre's countless efforts to alter its results. In turn, the EUMC resumed its research efforts and issued a final, lengthier study in April 2004. That report offered an extended time frame and substantiated some of the earlier results through in-depth interviews with representatives of Jewish communities within most of the member states.

Ironically, the most notable aspect of the Centre's final 2004 report on antisemitism was the controversy associated with the earlier version of it. And, given the countless similarities between the draft and final reports, the revisions can seem unremarkable, although many are not. For instance, the Centre deleted a reference from the draft report to Swedish Nazis who enthusiastically embraced Islamic antisemites. It similarly expunged evidence of the extreme left's role in violent attacks against Jews in Sweden and Denmark.[21]

The report's remaining references to the "extreme left" were speculative and relegated to a subsection entitled "the debate on the 'new antisemitism.'"[22] That section opens with a reference to

Robert Wistrich's 1984 lecture, which provided one of the earliest and most prescient warnings about the increasing inextricability of antisemitism and anti-Zionism. While ostensibly respectful, the gesture cast doubt on the novelty of the "new" antisemitism; at the same time, the report cited, but then ignored, Wistrich's synopsis of the two decades since. The final report thus omitted his more recent analysis of antisemitism as "more widespread, intense, radicalized, and 'Islamic.'"[23] With this omission, the report misleadingly pronounced the prolific scholar's views as dated, "differing somewhat from the ones drawn in recent debates."[24]

Of the nearly dozen other voices covered in the section on "the new antisemitism," the report refuted just two scholars (Elie Barnavi and Pierre-André Taguieff) by relying on the assessments of a third (Nonna Mayer).[25] Elie Barnavi, like Wistrich years prior, insists the "old antisemitism" has been replaced in France by a virulent anti-Zionism of the extreme left. Pierre André Taguieff's principal concern, by contrast, is with the massive manipulation of antiracist discourse for anti-Jewish purposes. He demonstrates that once antisemitism is excluded from the rubric of racism, Jews are referred to as racists.[26] Combined, their works underscore central elements of the "new" antisemitism—the denial of rights to Jews to live as a nation and the inversion of racism to conceal Jews as its victims.

Nonna Mayer received the last word in this "debate"; the report stated that her research contradicts the work of both Barnavi and Taguieff. Mayer finds that those who denied French Jews the status of being French were also the ones who are most apt to deny that status to Arabs, Muslims, and immigrants. With little to distinguish antisemitism from either racism or xenophobia, she depicts the majority of racists, xenophobes, and antisemites as followers of the extreme right.[27] Most fundamentally, one finds such conclusions were congenial to the EU's center left elite. In addition to assigning such prejudice entirely to the nationalistic far right, it absolved the left of any responsibility for antisemitism and maintained that Europe's integration is a prophylactic against antisemitism.[28]

In presenting the European Parliament the abbreviated version of the final report, the Centre's director issued a widely circulated statement that actually belied the report's key findings. It stated that the largest group of perpetrators were "young, disaffected white European[s], often stimulated by extreme right wing groups."[29] While none of the Centre's fifteen national experts discounted the involvement of far-right perpetrators in the countries they surveyed, the CRA researchers found their mobilization did *not* play a decisive role in the wave of antisemitism that engulfed Europe months prior to the report.[30] Indeed, some national experts observed a reduction in this segment's involvement with antisemitism. Consider France, home to Europe's largest Jewish and Muslim communities. Researchers there found that "the largest percentage of anti-Semitic violence attributable to the extreme-right was only 9% in 2002 (against 14% in 2001 and 68% in 1994)."[31]

Angered by the EUMC's manipulation of data and its persistent reticence to acknowledge the changing cast of antisemitism's leading characters, one of the researchers for the final report, Victor Weitzel, stepped forward. Like the CRA researchers before him, he acknowledged publicly that the EUMC had consistently manipulated his findings. For example, he explained, "When I told them that we need to monitor the inflammatory language being used by the Arab press in Europe, this was changed to the 'minority press.'"[32] The European Jewish Congress was one of many to publicly denounce the Centre for its deceptions.

Exposed as inadequate to monitor and analyze a prejudice it did not understand and had never defined, the Centre then attributed its shortcomings to its not having had an explicit definition of antisemitism for itself and its research network.[33] By emphasizing this methodological inadequacy in its final report on antisemitism, the Centre skirted the potentially more devastating charge of political bias. Nonetheless, this admission had some merit.

With only nine of the fifteen national reports employing an explicit definition of antisemitism and each using a different one, the Centre was unable to facilitate the cross-national comparisons essential to the development of the robust research that the Commission demanded and that a more sanguine public might have expected. However, as Mark Bell observes, "in retrospect the EUMC was placed in the invidious position of being charged with producing comparable data, but lacking the institutional resources to bring this about."[34] The question for us, however, is whether under such circumstances an explicit definition of antisemitism would enhance the data and hence credibility of the EUMC so that it could be effectively enjoined in advancing efforts against it.

THE MISSING DEFINITION: THE "WORKING DEFINITION OF ANTISEMITISM"

In the absence of any marked success for its initial efforts to address antisemitism, it is ironic that the Centre was enlisted to define it. But, that is what happened.

Following a 2004 international Organization for Security and Cooperation in Europe (OSCE) meeting in Berlin that forcefully condemned all manifestations of antisemitism, the Centre invited Jewish organizations to assist it in formulating a "Working Definition of Antisemitism."[35] Soon after, it presented the subsequent "working definition" to participants at a follow-up conference in Cordoba, where it was immediately received though *never formally* adopted. The definition reads: "Antisemitism is a certain perception of Jews, which may be expressed as hatred toward Jews. Rhetorical and physical manifestations of antisemitism are directed toward Jewish or non-Jewish individuals and/or their property, toward Jewish community institutions and religious facilities."[36]

In addition to informally adopting this working definition, the Centre incorporated it into a single-page document that also provided "a practical guide for identifying incidents, collecting data, and supporting the implementation and enforcement of legislation dealing with antisemitism." The Centre also made clear that manifestations of antisemitism "could also target the state of Israel, conceived as a Jewish collectivity." It continues: "Antisemitism frequently charges Jews with conspiring to harm humanity, and it is often used to blame Jews for 'why things go wrong.'"[37]

The Centre provided examples for clarification, focusing first on the expression of this prejudice in public life more generally and then on the antisemitic idiom specifically targeting Israel. It found that "holding Jews collectively responsible for actions in the state of Israel" and presenting caricatures of contemporary Israeli policy that draw comparisons to Nazi policy are antisemitic.[38] The Centre explained that when criticism of Israel is similar to that leveled against any other country, such criticism cannot be regarded as antisemitic.[39] However, it also acknowledged that the application of "double standards" for Israel (standards not expected of any other democratic state) and/or "denying the Jewish people their right to self-determination (e.g., by claiming that the existence of a state of Israel is a racist endeavour)" is antisemitic. Per Ahlmark, Sweden's former deputy prime minister, bluntly explains: "If anti-Semites once aspired to live in a world rid of Jews, today anti-Semitism's goal is apparently a world cleansed of the Jewish state."[40] That aspiration offers one the key elements of "new" antisemitism, which moved from *Judenrein* to *Judenstaatrein*.

Expecting that the definition might oblige member states to combat antisemitism, Jewish organizations and various state actors (perhaps especially those based outside of Europe) hailed its 2005 adoption.[41] For instance, when the U.S. Congress passed the Global Anti-Semitism Review Act of 2004, in response to rising antisemitism worldwide, it mandated a one-time investiga-

tion into antisemitic acts. The authors of that report adopted the
EUMC's working definition for their research.[42] When members
of the Canadian Parliament adopted a resolution to combat antisemitism in 2007, they too cited the EU's seemingly authoritative
definition, as did the Australian Online Hate Prevention Institute (OHPI) when it was established in 2012 to combat cyber hate.

Nonetheless, in 2008, the American Jewish Committee's European Forum on Anti-Semitism in Berlin found that "many Jewish
community and NGO leaders involved in monitoring antisemitism remain(ed) unaware of the working definition" or they were
hampered by its existence only in English.[43] This might help to
explain why Britain's All-Party Parliamentary Inquiry into Anti-
Semitism appears to have been the only European group to have
taken the definition to heart and recommended that the government adopt it.[44] To enhance the European public's knowledge of
this definition, the American Jewish Committee (AJC) translated
the definition into over two dozen languages and made it readily
available through its forum website, something that the Centre
did not do.

Rather than translate the working definition for adoption
throughout the member states, the Centre disseminated its Eng-
lish-only text to its national research network (RAXEN) and did
little else to promote it. The definition's *informal* adoption made it
possible for the Centre (and later others) to ignore it. Indeed, the
definition appeared in none of the Centre's annual reports that
detail important developments and responses to discrimination.

When asked about the definition's conspicuous absence from
the EU's myriad documents, an official from the Agency for Fundamental Rights (previously the EUMC) insisted that the definition was merely a "work in progress." This same official had
previously worked at the Centre as the "independent scholar"
largely responsible for the above-noted revisions to the draft report before becoming an "in-house" scholar. No novice on the
intricacies of EU antidiscrimination politics, he explained that,

as a "work in progress," the working definition of antisemitism required testing and further comment from throughout the EU before its practical use and effectiveness could be established and supported fully.[45] Yet, because the FRA repeatedly ignored the working definition, did not translate it, and omitted it from any of its reports, the definition's effectiveness could never be determined and, in turn, supported fully.

Far from being discredited for its dispiriting response to antisemitism, the Centre's powers were expanded in the midst of the controversies that surrounded it. In fact, shortly following the storm over the Centre's suppression of its first report on antisemitism, the European Council met for its routine December summit in 2003 to discuss the Centre's enlargement. Once assembled, the various heads of state and governments together stressed "the importance of human rights data collection and analysis" and thus agreed to extend the Centre's mandate to make it a human rights agency.[46] The Centre became the EU Agency for Fundamental Rights, a title that better reflected the Centre's expanded responsibilities for fundamental rights.

By 2009, the FRA had come no closer to acknowledging, much less revising or supporting the working definition of antisemitism than its predecessor. Instead, as the Centre before it, the agency's fortunes appear to be tethered to its abilities to deflect attention from the definition and any other instrument that might expose the shortcomings of the transnational polity and its member states. Thus, it touted Europe's meager accomplishments through dozens of glossy brochures, vivid websites, and vapid policy pronouncements concerning antidiscrimination and fundamental rights.

As the definition languished on its website, the FRA issued two brief overviews concerning antisemitism (in 2010 and 2011). Both lamented that, because so few member state authorities had bothered to define antisemitism, there was a dearth of statistical data related to it.[47] This was a puzzling admission given that the Centre's earlier adoption of a working definition might have resolved this conundrum. Nonetheless, the agency revisited—without the least irony—the methodological quandaries that stemmed from reporting a problem its researchers had yet to define.

Then, just months prior to the high-profile release of its latest and most comprehensive report on antisemitism in 2013, the FRA quietly withdrew the definition from its website. That act was first reported by the pro-Palestinian website Electronic Intifada.

By the time Europe's Jewish community and its allies discovered the working definition's disappearance and appealed to the agency to reinstate it, an FRA spokesperson insisted she was "not aware of any *official* definition." Moreover, she submitted, "The agency does not need to develop its own definition of antisemitism to research these issues."[48] Despite the outcry these answers provoked, she was technically correct. The EU had never adopted an official (and thus legal) definition of antisemitism, and its 2013 report testified to the comparable data that could be generated without one. Advocates against antisemitism had been misdirected and had wrongly assumed that a working definition posted to an official EU website constituted its official recognition. Although many knew that the definition was not "directed at governments for incorporation into national legislation," they held out hope and "nevertheless expected that it [would] seep into universal usage via adoption by the relevant parties."[49]

Despite evidence to the contrary, outspoken opponents of antisemitism (e.g., the Simon Wiesenthal Center) insisted that the definition offered an effective weapon in the arsenal against antisemitism. Thus, when the measure's proponents mobilized for the definition's reinstatement, members of the European Parliament joined in although they were in a privileged position to understand the limitations of this demand. That is, the *formal* adoption of the working definition was never on the table.

The question at this stage is whether an official act, such as the 2008 Framework Decision, proves any more effective in offering Jews redress from antisemitism. A brief inquiry into the EU's adoption and consequences of that legislation might shed light on this question.

FRAMEWORK DECISION

The Framework Decision arose from the commission's increasing alarm in late 2001 over the persistence of racist crimes and the rapid dissemination of Holocaust denial through the internet, including within those member states that had restrictions against it. The Commission expressed concern that Holocaust deniers and others had gained the upper hand by exploiting the legislative differences between the member states. Though it offered no concrete data on either "forum shopping" or the transnational dimensions of these crimes, the commission stressed the need to both reinforce punitive measures and enhance judicial cooperation throughout the EU.

To accomplish a more integrated approach while balancing the union's commitments to free expression, the commission proposed a Framework Decision.[50] Decisions generally function as advice given governments and are significantly less coercive than other EU laws (like Directives or Regulations).[51] Interestingly, it is exactly this weakness that can encourage flexible, effective implementation. Decisions may also go largely ignored, but is impossible to insist they do not exist.

After a turbulent and lengthy legislative history in which several states expressed their reservations about that decision's compatibility with their domestic protections for free speech, the legislation passed in 2008.[52] The decision stipulates that the same criminal racist and antisemitic behavior constitutes a common offense in all member states.[53] The FRA embraced it as "an important tool for the EU-wide condemnation of racist and xenophobic crime."[54] Its only criticism was that it did not extend to cover other vulnerable social groups (e.g., the disabled and

LGBT community). Those found in violation of the decision were to receive no less than one year and no more than three years of imprisonment for their wrongdoings, a penalty intended to be effective, proportionate, and dissuasive.

To accommodate the persistent concerns of several member states about overreach and potential challenges to free expression, the 2008 Framework Decision allowed for several significant exceptions. First, the decision "is *limited to* combating *particularly serious forms of racism and xenophobia* by means of criminal law" (emphasis added).[55] Hence, member states may criminalize only conduct that "is either carried out in a manner *likely* to disturb public order or which is threatening, abusive or insulting" (emphasis added).[56] In the absence of clear EU guidelines on what constitutes "public order," "insulting," "abusive," or "threatening," the EU legal scholar Laurent Pech suggests that national authorities are "free to decide when, for instance, a statement denying the Holocaust becomes likely to disturb the public order." This, he warns, might lead to "the distressing possibility of a person being extradited for having engaged in lawful conduct in his/her country of residence but constitutive of a racist offense in another EU member State."[57]

As states step in where EU institutions fear to tread, the Union's 2008 Framework Decision could exacerbate the legislative disparities it sought to remedy. Additionally, Laurent and others worry that the decision's restrictions on free expression today could lead to greater ones tomorrow, a concern better known as the "slippery slope effect."[58]

Perhaps the most contentious and significant exception turns on article 7(2): "This Framework Decision *shall not have the effect of requiring Member States to take measures in contradiction to fundamental principles relating to freedom of association and freedom of expression,* in particular freedom of the press and the freedom of expression in other media as they result from constitutional traditions or rules governing the rights and responsibilities of, and the procedural guarantees for, the press or other media where these rules relate to the determination or limitation of liability" (emphasis added).

Since all member states have legislation outlawing hate speech and a majority of them "have long considered that the fundamental right to freedom of expression *inter alia* precludes the criminalization of Holocaust denial per se," it is unlikely their governments will incorporate, much less implement, those provisions of the decision that might afford Jews further protection.[59] Indeed, three years after the decision was adopted, an impatient Moshe Kantor, the president of the European Jewish Congress (EJC), insisted that not one member state adopted reforms in keeping with this ambition.[60] In 2014, the Commission could not demonstrate that conditions had improved. By its own account, "national provisions against denial, condoning or grossly trivializing certain crimes—such as crimes against humanity—remained inadequate in 20 [of 28] Member States."[61] Considering that the heaviest tolls for Europe's toleration of hate speech and genocide have been borne by its Jewish communities, Kantor's frustration is warranted. The FRA's 2013 online survey on antisemitism found that antisemitism on the Internet was "a significant concern for a majority of respondents."[62] Not only did 75 percent of respondents consider it a problem, but 73 percent believed that online antisemitism had worsened in the last five years since the definition was first placed on the web and the Framework Decision was issued.[63]

While space constraints preclude a more comprehensive review of the 2008 Framework Decision, it is sufficient to stress that the extensive proliferation of online antisemitism, the "escape clause" noted above, and enduring conflicts over freedom's requirements, suggest that member states will continue to enjoy considerable latitude in implementing the decision's symbolic aspirations.[64] That is, rather than a valuable instrument against antisemitism and other prejudices, the legal scholar Jenia Iontcheva

Turner insists the Framework Decision may best be understood as a "tool to express the Union's commitment to human rights and equal treatment." Are these separate? If "the EU is using the Framework Decision primarily to make a statement about the values for which it stands," the question is how we measure its commitment to these values.[65]

The gulf between the EU's rhetoric of human rights and the often-disappointing reality of its lax enforcement at the state level may be wide, but let us turn again to the EU institution charged with advancing the promotion and protection of human rights, the Agency for Fundamental Rights. It may be imprudent to expect more from member states in mitigating antisemitism when the FRA has failed to provide leadership on the matter. Indeed, the agency's aversion to identifying antisemitism as a human-rights violation was evidenced, somewhat incongruously, through a brochure it distributed in Jerusalem at the 4th International Conference of the Global Forum for Combatting Antisemitism in 2013.

That brochure, *Human Rights Education at Holocaust Memorial Sites across the European Union,* was ostensibly about the Holocaust but contained little information on antisemitism and no analysis of Holocaust denial or its inversion and those EU instruments (such as the working definition and Framework Decision) that were supposed to alleviate it. Instead, the FRA's chief concern, as expressed by its brochure, was that "*most of the memorial sites . . . do not systematically include education on human rights in their work*" (emphasis added).[66] For those who doubted whether Jewish rights are "human rights," the FRA synopsis on "Holocaust education" is revealing. That its distribution in Jerusalem resulted in no public outcry signals the pervasive success of antisemitism in numbing us to a reality we have begun to glimpse but not fully grasp—the (discursive) exclusion of Jews from the EU panoply of fundamental rights.

This chapter began with the assertion that deciphering the "new" antisemitism necessitates that we reveal the deceptive gestures that inhibit that ability. Its focus has been on the "branding" of an integrated Europe as foundationally antithetical to antisemitism. To this end it considered the establishment of two EU agencies (the EUMC and the FRA) and their subsequent efforts to stem antisemitism. The first of these involved the EUMC's scandalous manipulation of data from initial reports on the subject. The chapter then followed the Centre's reason for and subsequent effort to define antisemitism. This second effort gave rise to a working definition that proved so illusive that the Centre's successor agency (the FRA) later denied its existence.

The chapter's last case centered on the EU's criminalization of Holocaust denial (through the Framework Decision), a seemingly promising development that is likely to fall short. After all, without the benefit of the working definition of antisemitism, which explicitly condemned holding Jews responsible for actions in the state of Israel and caricaturing that state as a Nazi regime, this last effort is anachronistic. That is because today's most virulent antisemitism is expressed less through denying the Holocaust than in accusing Jews of perpetrating crimes similar to it. Thus, Jews are ridiculed as opponents of fundamental rights, a position that went unchallenged by the FRA when it claimed that Holocaust memorials offered no systematic insights into fundamental rights.

Whether through the EU's misleading branding, altered research, or the renunciation of its explicit definition, antisemitism is a swiftly moving object on the European agenda. It is addressed and rarely grasped, concealed by the bluster of seemingly sensitive but nonetheless contradictory discourse.

NOTES

I am indebted to Alvin H. Rosenfeld for organizing and contributing to the intellectual exchanges that made this work possible. I must also acknowledge the many helpful comments I received from Günther Jikeli, Lesley Klaff, Jonathan L. Laurans, and Susan Weinger.

1. Throughout this work, I use "EUMC" and "Centre" interchangeably. When referring to the EU's Agency for Fundamental Rights (FRA), I often employ the term "agency."

2. Magic entertains audiences, whereas political maneuvers deceits and cheats them.

3. This position was perhaps most clearly expressed by Romano Prodi, former president of the European Commission, in a speech he gave on February 19, 2004 (see http://europa.eu/rapid/press-release_SPEECH -04-85_en.htm).

4. Only after 1993 and the adoption of the Treaty on European Union (aka the Maastricht Treaty) did the European Community (EC) begin to be referred to as the European Union (EU).

5. The European Ombudsman is charged with mitigating the maladministration of myriad EU bodies when they contravene the law and/or violate human rights.

6. "Civil Society Media Seminar 2013—European Economic and Social Committee—Address by the European Ombudsman, Emily O'Reilly," Brussels, November 25, 2013, http://www.ombudsman.europa.eu/activities /speech.faces/en/52642/html.bookmark (viewed July 14, 2014).

7. Robert Fine, "Fighting with Phantoms: A Contribution to the Debate on Antisemitism in Europe," *Patterns of Prejudice* 43, no. 5 (2009): 460, 463.

8. European Commission, *Proposal for a Council Regulation (EC) establishing a European Monitoring Centre for Racism and Xenophobia*, COM (96), 615, 27.11.96, 3.

9. Cécile Leconte, "The EU Fundamental Rights Policy as a Source of Euroscepticism." *Human Rights Review* 15 (2014): 83. Leconte attributes the recent rise in "value based Euroscepticism" to the "perception that the EU via its fundamental rights policy, unduly interferes with matters where value systems and core domestic preferences on ethical issues are at stake." She continues: "This happens in a context where the EU is resented, by some segments of political elites, for allegedly empowering diverse groups (such as ethnic minorities, immigrants' rights associations, judges, and so on) at the expense of popular sovereignty." Overlooked are the ways that Europe's disappointing interventions might bolster skepticism among those who are presumed to be its benefactors.

10. Council Regulation (EC) No. 1035/97, 2 June 1997, establishing a European Monitoring Centre on Racism and Xenophobia OJ L 151, 10/06/1997, article 2(1).

11. European Monitoring Centre on Racism and Xenophobia, *Manifestations of Anti-Semitism in the EU 2002–2003: Based on Information by the*

National Focal Points of the EUMC-RAXEN *Information Network* (Vienna: EUMC, 2004).

12. See Matthias Küntzel, *Jihad and Jew-Hatred: Islamism, Nazism and the Roots of 9/11* (New York: Telos Press, 2007).

13. Andreas Accardo, "Fundamental Rights Agency Can Learn from EUMC experiences: Interview with Anastasia Crickley, New Chair of the EUMC Management," *Equal Voices* 15 (2004): 5–6. *Equal Voices* was the Centre's in-house magazine.

14. Werner Bergmann and Juliane Wetzel, *Manifestations of Anti-Semitism in the European Union: First Synthesis Report* (Vienna: EUMC, 2003), 7.

15. See European Monitoring Centre on Racism and Xenophobia, *Activities of the European Monitoring Centre on Racism and Xenophobia—Annual Report 2002* (Luxembourg: OOPEC, 2003), 11–12.

16. Juliane Wetzel quoted in Bertrand Benoit and Silke Mertins, "Brussels Urged to Publish Report on Anti-Semitism," *Financial Times,* November 22, 2003, 4.

17. Hannah Cleaver, "Race Report Team 'Told to Change Findings on Muslims,'" *Telegraph,* November 27, 2003, http://www.telegraph.co.uk/news/worldnews/europe/1447915/Race-report-team-told-to-change-findings-on-Muslims.html (viewed July 14, 2014).

18. Bob Purkiss, "Letter from Bob Purkiss to Mr. Andre Gowers, Editor of the *Financial Times* on the FT Reports Dated 22/23 and 24 November on 'EU Racism Body Shelves Report on Anti-Semitism' and 'Brussels Urged to Publish Anti-Semitism Report,'" EUMC, November 25, 2003.

19. European Commission, "Communication from the Commission to the Council, the European Parliament, the European Economic and Social Committee and the Committee of the Regions on the Activities of the European Monitoring Centre on Racism and Xenophobia, Together with Proposals to Recast Council Regulation (EC) 1035/97," 2003, 4. See also note 21.

20. Bob Purkiss and Beate Winkler, "EUMC Media Release, Issue 194-03-03-12-01-EN," EUMC, December 2, 2003. The blow to the EUMC's image proved so severe that, years later, others affiliated with it echoed this assessment. See Martin Groenleer, *The Anatomy of European Union Agencies: A Comparative Study of Institutional Development* (Delt: Euburon), 259.

21. After interviewing nearly a dozen board members of and experts within the EUMC and FRA, Martijn Groenleer discovered that individual members of the EUMC's board had "interfered with the contents of reports, particularly the data for their respective countries" in Groenleer, *Anatomy of European Union Agencies,* 258. One wonders if that occurred in this subsection of the final report. After all, the board member representing

Denmark had earlier defended the Centre to the *Financial Times* reporter by characterizing the draft report as "unsatisfactory." In the same article, he insisted that "anti-Semitism is non-existent in my country. Jews are very highly thought of here." He continued: "but, we have a lot of problems with hostility towards Muslims." Ole Espersen, quoted in Bertrand Benoit, "EU Racism Group Shelves Anti-Semitism Study," *Financial Times,* November 25, 2003, 9.

22. European Monitoring Centre on Racism and Xenophobia, *Manifestations of Anti-Semitism in the EU 2002–2003,* 232–236.

23. Robert S. Wistrich, *Muslim Anti-Semitism: A Clear and Present Danger* (New York: American Jewish Committee, 2002), 46.

24. European Monitoring Centre on Racism and Xenophobia, *Manifestations of Anti-Semitism in the EU 2002–2003,* 232–233.

25. Ibid., 234–235.

26. Pierre-André Taguieff, *Rising from the Muck: The New Anti-Semitism in Europe* (Chicago: Ivan R. Dee, 2004), 67.

27. European Monitoring Centre on Racism and Xenophobia, *Manifestations of Anti-Semitism in the EU 2002–2003,* 235–236.

28. The conclusion absolving the left has once again been contradicted by Wistrich's later insights into the EU's western member states. He writes: "In Western Europe (unlike in the Muslim World, Russia or Eastern Europe) contemporary Judeophobia is more postnational than narrowly nationalist, most anti-American than anticommunist, more 'liberal' and leftist than illiberal and antidemocratic." Robert S. Wistrich, *European Anti-Semitism Reinvents Itself* (New York: American Jewish Committee, 2005), 9. My book on the politics of EU integration similarly counters the common notion that Europe's integration is an inherently progressive force that helps inoculate society against antisemitism. It reveals that this received wisdom persists despite the limited evidence to sustain it. R. Amy Elman, *The European Union, Antisemitism and the Politics of Denial* (Lincoln: University of Nebraska Press, 2014).

29. Beate Winkler, "Presentation on 31 March 2004 in the European Parliament," paper presented at the Parliamentary Session, Strasbourg, March 31, 2004.

30. Bergmann and Wetzel, *Manifestations of Anti-Semitism in the European Union,* 5.

31. European Monitoring Centre on Racism and Xenophobia, *Manifestations of Anti-Semitism in the EU 2002–2003,* 21.

32. Victor Weitzel quoted in Ambrose Evans-Pritchard, "EU 'Covered Up' Attacks on Jews by Young Muslims," *Daily Telegraph,* April 1, 2004,

http://www.telegraph.co.uk/news/worldnews/europe/1458300/EU
-covered-up-attacks-on-Jews-by-young-Muslims.html (viewed July 14,
2014).

33. European Monitoring Centre on Racism and Xenophobia, *Manifestations of Anti-Semitism in the EU 2002–2003*, 320.

34. Mark Bell, "EU Anti-Racism Policy: The Leader of the Pack?," in
*Equality Law in an Enlarged European Union: Understanding the Article 13
Directives*, ed. Helen Meenan (Cambridge: Cambridge University Press,
2007), 195.

35. The OSCE was the first international organization to treat antisemitism as a "distinct human rights issue."

36. European Union Monitoring Centre, "Working Definition of Antisemitism," European Commission, Vienna, 2005.

37. Ibid.

38. Ibid.

39. Still, Israel receives more than its fair share of criticism, a point
evidenced by comparing casualties since World War II. Since then, 25 mil-
lion people were killed in internal conflicts, of them, 8,000 in the Israel-
Palestinian conflict—ranking it 46th in a list of victims. Nonetheless, the
UN and other international groups have condemned Israel more than all
the other nations combined. See Walter Laqueur, *The Changing Face of
Antisemitism: From Ancient Times to the Present Day* (New York: Oxford
University Press, 2006), 8.

40. Per Ahlmark quoted in Yair Sheleg, "A World Cleansed of the Jewish State," *Haaretz*, April 18, 2002, http://www.haaretz.com/print-edition
/features/a-world-cleansed-of-the-jewish-state-1.47537 (viewed July 15, 2014).

41. On the feared compulsion of states to fight antisemitism, note, for
example, Dina Porat, *The Road that Led to an Internationally Accepted Definition of Antisemitism* (Tel Aviv: Rosenberg School of Jewish Studies and
the Stephen Roth Institute, 2006), 16.

42. United States Department of State, *Contemporary Global Anti-Semitism: A Report Provided to the United States Congress*, 2008, 81, http://www
.state.gov/j/drl/rls/102406.htm.

43. European Forum on Antisemitism, "Working Definition of Antisemitism," 2008, http://www.european-forum-on-antisemitism.org
/working-definition-of-antisemitism/ (viewed July 14, 2014).

44. The government's refusal to heed that advice was apparent when, in
2013, Alistair Carmichael, a senior member of the coalition and a member
of the Liberal Democrat Friends of Israel, admitted he had never heard of
the definition. As Lesley Klaff notes, the admission proved particularly

discouraging because Carmichael was responsible for disciplining David Ward, an MP from his own party. Lesley Klaff, "Holocaust Inversion in Great Britain: Defining the Limits of Acceptable Political Discourse in Parliament," paper delivered at the conference, "Anti-Judiasm, Antisemitism and Delegitimizing Israel," Vidal Sassoon International Center for the Study of Antisemitism, Hebrew University, Jerusalem, May 2014. After signing a book of remembrance in Parliament on Holocaust Memorial Day, Ward insisted that Israel inflicts atrocities on Palestinians in a manner reminiscent of Auschwitz. In her earlier article on this matter, Klaff explains how such inversions "involve the abuse of Holocaust memory to issue a *moral stricture* aimed at Israel and 'the Jews,' imposing upon them a *uniquely* onerous moral responsibility and accountability in their treatment of others." Lesley Klaff, "Holocaust Inversion," *Fathom* 3 (February 2014), http://www.fathomjournal.org/policy-politics/holocaust-inversion/ (viewed July 14, 2014). According to the working definition, Holocaust inversion meets the definition of antisemitism and the definition might have offered the clarity Carmichael needed to denounce Ward's statements as unequivocally antisemitic, see Klaff, "Holocaust Inversion in Great Britain" (2014).

45. Alexander Pollak, interview with Fundamental Rights Agency civil servant, Fundamental Rights Agency, Vienna, May 28, 2009.

46. European Council, "Presidency Conclusions," 12–13 December, 5381/03, Brussels, 2003, 27. The council earlier considered the establishment of a human rights–oriented agency at its summit in 1999 but appeared to lack the momentum. See European Council, "Presidency Conclusions," 3–4 June, 150/99 REV 1, Cologne, 1999, paragraph 46.

47. European Union Agency for Fundamental Rights (FRA), *Anti-Semitism: Summary Overview of the Situation in the European Union 2001–2009* (Vienna: European Union Agency for Fundamental Rights, 2010); European Union Agency for Fundamental Rights (FRA), *Anti-Semitism: Summary Overview of the Situation in the European Union 2001–2010* (Vienna: European Union Agency for Fundamental Rights, 2011).

48. In Shimon Samuels, "EU Disowns the 'EU working Definition of Anti-Semitism,'" *Times of Israel Blog*, December 3, 2013, http://blogs.times ofisrael.com/e-u-denies-validity-of-eu-working-definition-of-antisemitism (viewed July 14, 2014).

49. Michael Whine, "Progress in the Struggle against Anti-Semitism in Europe: The Berlin Declaration and the European Union Monitoring Centre on Racism and Xenophobia's Working Definition of Anti-Semitism," Jerusalem Center for Public Affairs, February 1, 2006, http://jcpa.org/article

/progress-in-the-struggle-against-anti-semitism-in-europe-the-berlin
-declaration-and-the-european-union-monitoring-centre-on-racism-and
-xenophobias-working-definition-of-anti-semitism/ (viewed July 14, 2014).

50. European Commission, *Proposal for a Council Framework Decision on combating racism and xenophobia,* COM (2001) 664 final, Brussels, 28.11.01.

51. Directives introduce broad binding objectives that call on Member States to implement them, each in its own way. By contrast, regulations (which are also binding) are automatically incorporated within the national legal systems of the member states.

52. Mark Bell, *Racism and Equality in the European Union* (Oxford: Oxford University Press, 2008), chapter 8; Erik Bleich, *The Freedom to Be Racist? How the United States and Europe Struggle to Preserve Freedom and Combat Racism* (New York: Oxford University Press, 2011); Jenia Iontcheva Turner, "The Expressive Dimension of EU Criminal Law," *American Journal of Comparative Law* 60, no. 2 (2012): 555–584.

53. Council Framework Decision 2008/913/JHA of 28 November 2008 on combating certain forms and expressions of racism and xenophobia by means of criminal law, OJL 328, 6.12.08, 55–58.

54. FRA Media Team, "FRA Welcomes New EU Framework Decision on Combating Racism and Xenophobia," December 2, 2008, https://groups .google.com/forum (viewed July 14, 2014).

55. Ibid., paragraph 6, emphasis added.

56. Ibid., article 1(2), emphasis added.

57. Laurent Pech, "The Law of Holocaust Denial in Europe: Towards a (Qualified) EU-Wide Criminal Prohibition," in *Genocide Denials and the Law,* ed. Ludovic Hennebel and Thomas Hochmann (Oxford: Oxford University Press, 2011), 230, 231.

58. On restrictions of free expression, see Bleich, *Freedom to Be Racist?,* 135.

59. Pech, "Law of Holocaust Denial in Europe," 185.

60. Moshe Kantor, "Dealing with Europe's Soul, Not Just Economies," *Jerusalem Post,* December 6, 2011.

61. European Commission, "International Holocaust Remembrance Day: Commission Calls on Member States to Criminalise Denial of Crimes against Humanity," IP/14/75, Brussels, January 27, 2014.

62. That survey is the EU's most comprehensive to date although, like previous EU surveys on antisemitism, it shares a reluctance to identify the perpetrators of antisemitism. See European Union Agency for Fundamental Rights (FRA), *Discrimination and Hate Crimes against Jews in EU Member*

States: Experiences and Perceptions of Antisemitism (Vienna: European Union Agency for Fundamental Rights, 2013). The survey specifically focused on the experiences and perceptions of antisemitism among nearly 6,000 self-identified Jews from eight member states *without differentiating perpetrators by country* as it did for other data such as those on victims, their concerns, and experiences. I am indebted to Günther Jikeli for pointing this out. Thus, one notices, as well, that within the agency's fact sheet summary of the methodology and key findings of the 2013 report, data pertaining to the perceived perpetrators is conspicuously absent. In withholding these data, the FRA obstructs information on antisemitism's perpetrator categories that might help mitigate antisemitism. See European Union Agency for Fundamental Rights (FRA), "Jewish people's experience of discrimination and hate crime in European Union Member States" (Vienna: European Union Agency for Fundamental Rights, November 2013), http://fra.europa .eu/en/publication/2013/jewish-peoples-experience-discrimination-and -hate-crime-european-union-member (viewed July 15, 2014). For further analysis of the survey, see the epilogue of my forthcoming book on the EU and antisemitism, *The European Union, Antisemitism and the Politics of Denial.*

63. European Union Agency for Fundamental Rights (FRA), *Discrimination and Hate Crimes against Jews in EU Member States*, 12.

64. Turner, "Expressive Dimension of EU Criminal Law," 555–584.

65. Ibid., 557, 572.

66. European Union Agency for Fundamental Rights (FRA), *Human Rights Education at Holocaust Memorial Sites across the European Union* (Vienna: European Union Agency for Fundamental Rights, 2011), 31.

FIFTEEN

Anti-Israeli Boycotts

European and International
Human Rights Law Perspectives

ALEKSANDRA GLISZCZYNSKA-GRABIAS

CALLS FOR BOYCOTTS against Israeli goods, individual scholars, or academic institutions carry a significant legal irony: while appealing to the desire to compel Israel to cease violating human rights, boycott campaigners themselves may breach various principles of international human rights law. At the same time, legal actions undertaken by Israel in order to reduce the effects of boycotts, namely, the antiboycott law of 2011, are highly questionable from the point of view of international law. The problem of anti-Israeli boycotts arises also in certain bodies of the UN system of human rights protection, and such boycotts can be in violation of the UN Charter.[1]

Several international and regional human rights bodies, including the European Court of Human Rights, have tackled similar dilemmas. In such cases it was established under what circumstances a boycott may amount to discrimination. However, what is also central for this issue is the question of what legally qualifies as antisemitism. This question is not easily answered as it requires an adequate legal determination of the point at which, to quote André Glucksmann, the "anti-Israeli anger" turns into "anti-Jewish anger."[2] In this chapter I try to pinpoint the all-too-frequent cases in which the thin red line between criticism and discrimination, or even hatred, of Israel and Israelis has been crossed.

As boycott campaigns are announced around the world (a significant initiative was launched by the American Studies Association in December 2013), they seem to negatively affect Jewish communities, including those not directly harmed by the boycotts.[3] As indicated in the report of the European Union Agency for Fundamental Rights, released in November 2013, as many as 73 percent of French Jews pointed out that the Arab-Israeli conflict and its repercussions (such as the boycott, divestment, and sanctions movement, known as BDS) significantly affected their feeling of safety in France. In turn, nearly 60 percent of Belgian and Italian Jews said that the guilt associated with certain political and military decisions of Israeli authorities was "nearly always" or "often" ascribed to them.[4] Answers recorded in the survey help clarify how antisemitism destructively affects the life of the people who experience it nearly every day. At the same time, the results show the depth and complexity of the social problem. The words of one respondent, a woman from the United Kingdom, are a fitting example here: "I feel worried about antisemitism now in a way that I did not thirty years ago. Something that should have disappeared from social acceptability is instead becoming stronger."[5]

This chapter begins with an overview of the main legal resources available in the key instruments of international law that condemn boycotts as illegal. I next analyze at some length a landmark case on the issue before the European Court of Human Rights, which announced a strong condemnation of calls for boycotts and refused to protect them under the right to freedom of expression. I then briefly discuss both boycotts of Israel in the UN Forum and academic boycotts. Finally, I reflect on the Israeli legislative response to boycotts and offer some concluding remarks.

BOYCOTTS UNDER INTERNATIONAL
HUMAN RIGHTS LAW STANDARDS

Free, democratic, and pluralist states and societies, such as those in Europe and the United States, allow everyone to follow his or her conscience, common sense, and free will in making choices. No one can prevent a person from abstaining from buying Israeli products, for instance Israeli food produce or medications, or from using Israeli technology. This general idea, stated in terms of international law then in force, had been articulated by Hersch Lauterpacht in his classic article of over eighty years ago: "As a matter of international duty, a government cannot be expected to dictate to private individuals from whom they shall buy the goods they need."[6] But already at the time the article was published, the principle expounded by Lauterpacht was unduly formalistic, ignoring as it did various ways in which governments could directly or indirectly support "private" boycotts.[7] More importantly, however, the transformations of international law and, in particular, the emergence of the international law of human rights, in which individuals and not only states are protected subjects and also bearers of responsibility, dealt a fatal blow to Lauterpacht's principle. An individual person can still, of course, buy or refuse to buy whatever he or she wants, no matter on what grounds, but when a boycott is extrapolated into the public sphere, it ceases to be just a question of a free individual choice and can become an act of discrimination based on nationality, or even (as the case may be) incitement to hatred or violence against Israelis. For instance, boycotting Israeli products in supermarkets in some countries has been carried out in a "robbery"-like manner, by masked "commando units," who mark Israeli products with anti-Israeli labels.[8] Any international human-rights court, when considering a complaint regarding such actions, would have to take into account their impact on Israeli nationals, even if they did not directly witness such illegal actions. Protecting individuals and vulnerable groups from a hostile, intimidating, and humiliating atmosphere and social attitude has been recognized as an element of human rights protection in the jurisprudence of human rights tribunals for more than half a century.[9]

The main argument of the present chapter is thus to claim that the boycotts of Israeli goods, institutions, and persons and of Israel itself can amount to a violation of a number of legal rules belonging to the body of international human rights law. What are those rules? At the level of the UN-based universal human rights protection, these are mainly the provisions of the UN Charter and the International Covenant on Civil and Political Rights as well as the International Convention on the Elimination of Racial Discrimination (ICERD).[10] As far as the UN Charter is concerned, sanctions in the form of boycotts against a particular state can be undertaken in some cases, after a determination issued by the UN Security Council. Such measures can be undertaken only by governmental authorities acting within the framework of article 41 of chapter 8 of the charter, which envisages, among other things, "complete or partial interruption of economic relations" in cases of "the existence of any threat to the peace, breach of the peace, or act of aggression," that is, the conditions mentioned in article 39. Moving now to the International Covenant, article 20 is of particular relevance: it imposes on state parties to the covenant an obligation to prohibit by law any advocacy of national, racial, or religious hatred that constitutes incitement to discrimination, hostility, or violence. In turn, the ICERD contains a number of obligations for the signatory states:

- Engage in no act or practice of racial discrimination against persons, groups of persons or institutions and to ensure that all public authorities and public institutions, national and local, shall act in conformity with this obligation.
- Take effective measures to review governmental, national, and local policies, and to amend, rescind, or nullify any

laws and regulations which have the effect of creating or perpetuating racial discrimination wherever it exists.

- Prohibit and bring to an end, by all appropriate means, including legislation as required by circumstances, racial discrimination by any persons, group, or organization.
- Refrain from sponsoring, defending, or supporting racial discrimination by any persons or organizations.[11]

Further, it must be emphasized that in the ICERD the term "racial discrimination" shall mean "any distinction, exclusion, restriction or preference based on race, colour, descent, or *national or ethnic origin* which has the purpose or effect of nullifying or impairing the recognition, enjoyment or exercise, on an equal footing, of human rights and fundamental freedoms in the political, economic, social, cultural or any other field of public life" (emphasis added). Thus, the definition is clearly applicable to cases of discrimination directed against Israeli citizens, if they are singled out and discriminated against on the basis of their national or ethnic (Israeli) origin.

A similar, strict antidiscrimination principle is contained in the European Convention on Human Rights and Fundamental Freedoms (ECHR) and its additional protocols.[12] Article 14 of the convention stipulates that "The enjoyment of the rights and freedoms set forth in the Convention shall be secured without discrimination on any ground such as, among others, sex, race, colour, language, religion, national or social origin, association with a national minority."[13] In addition, the ECHR prohibits any actions that may destroy its axiological foundations; hence, it prohibits incitement to hatred or violence against any person or group as identified by their national origins. EU law is also pertinent in this regard: a number of antidiscrimination directives have proclaimed prohibitions of ethnic-based or nationality-based discrimination.[14]

WILLEM V. FRANCE: BOYCOTT = DISCRIMINATION

The most important confirmation of the proposition that various calls for boycott of Israeli products or citizens may constitute violations of international human rights law can be found in the judgment of the European Court of Human Rights (ECTHR) in the case of *Willem v. France*.[15] For several reasons I consider this case at some length. First, it is so far the most elaborate, powerful, and authoritative statement of a supranational judicial authority on the issue discussed in this chapter. Second, the ECTHR is a court of great prestige and reputation, and the persuasive impact of its judgments goes far beyond its area of jurisdiction; in fact, it is generally considered to be the most impressive and respectable international judicial body in the world.[16] Third, the judgment has been handed down by an overwhelming majority (six to one), which suggests that the doctrine announced by the court is unlikely to be overruled in the foreseeable future. Fourth, the presence of a dissent—lonely but eloquent—provides an opportunity to analyze the argument also from the point of view of an opponent, which is always helpful when judicial decisions (and those of the ECTHR are no exception) are marred by formalism and legal technicalities.

In 2002, Jean-Claude Willem—at the time, the mayor of the municipality of Seclin, in France, during a session of the town council and in the presence of journalists, announced that he intended to boycott Israeli products in his municipality. He stated that he had taken this decision to protest against what he considered anti-Palestinian policies of the Israeli government. Representatives of the Jewish community in the Département du Nord filed a complaint with the public prosecutor, who charged the applicant with inciting discrimination on national, racial, and religious grounds, under the Press Act of 29 July 1881. Willem was acquitted by the Lille Criminal Court but was sentenced on appeal on 11 September 2003 and fined 1,000 euros. His appeal against conviction was unsuccessful.

In his complaint lodged to the ECTHR, Willem claimed that his call to boycott Israeli products was part of a political debate concerning the Israeli-Palestinian conflict and was a matter of general and public interest. He complained that his conviction had thus constituted a violation of his right to freedom of expression within the meaning of article 10 of the European Convention.

However, the ECTHR found no violation by France of Willem's right to freedom of expression. The court acknowledged that the applicant's conviction amounted to an "interference" with his freedom of expression, but under the European Convention's standards it was not a conclusive violation of the convention.[17] The conviction had been based on the Press Act of 1881, which referred to the provisions of the Criminal Code. The aim of the court's interference had been to protect the rights of others, in this case, Israeli producers. The court restated its established doctrine that any interference with the freedom of expression, especially in the domain of political speech on public issues, required the court to show particular vigilance.[18] However, the ECTHR found that in this case the applicant had not been convicted for his political opinions but for inciting the commission of a discriminatory act.[19] He had not stopped at denouncing the policy of Ariel Sharon's government at the time, but had gone further and called for a boycott of food products from Israel. Furthermore, as the European court approvingly noted, the French Court of Cassation had taken into account not only the call for a boycott made orally at the council meeting but also the message posted on the municipal internet site, which had aggravated the discriminatory nature of the applicant's position. In his capacity as mayor, the applicant had certain duties and responsibilities. He should have shown a degree of neutrality, and he had special duties when acting on behalf of the community he represented.[20] In particular, the mayor was in charge of the spending of public funds, and in this capacity he should not "advocate spending them along the lines of a discriminatory logic."[21] The court conceded that the applicant's intention may have been to protest against the policy of Israel's prime minister, but the reasons given for the boycott, both at the meeting and on the internet site, were discriminatory and therefore reprehensible. In so doing, by means of a statement at a municipal council meeting, with no debate or vote on the matter, and on the municipal Internet site, Willem could not claim to have been encouraging the free discussion of a subject of general interest.[22]

As a secondary argument, the European court considered the issue of the competences of the mayor, in the French system of vertical division of powers. The court noted the French public prosecutor's submissions to the domestic courts, stating that the mayor was not entitled to take the place of the governmental authorities by declaring an embargo on products from a foreign country.[23] In such circumstances, the reasons given by the French courts to justify interference with the applicant's freedom of expression had been "relevant and sufficient" for the purposes of article 10 §2 of the convention. In addition, the fine imposed had been relatively moderate and proportionate to the aim pursued. That being so, and showing a proper deference (in ECHR terminology: "the margin of appreciation") to the national authorities in such matters, the European court concluded that the impugned interference had been proportionate to the legitimate aims pursued.[24]

As already mentioned, there was only one dissenting opinion attached to the judgment, but it was a strong and eloquent one, and it is worth considering in some detail. Judge Karel Jungwiert (of the Czech Republic) started from the premise, which was also the basis of the court's decision, that freedom of speech in the context of public debate is of the highest importance and can only be restricted for "compelling reasons" (des raisons impérieuses). But what are "compelling reasons," asked Judge Jungwiert, and immediately responded, referring to the incident under scrutiny: "all that happened in Seclin and what may happen elsewhere in the future must be considered to be public debate of general interest within the framework of which it is permitted to resort to a certain degree of exaggeration or provocation." He then proposed a hypothetical scenario: What about a mayor (who usually is a member of a political party) who advocates a boycott of U.S. products in order to protest the war in Iraq, or products from Russia because of the conflict in Chechnya, or against Chinese merchandise in order to support Tibet? "I am strongly convinced that a democratic society must tolerate and sometimes even support such a debate or an advocacy of action," said Judge Jungwiert. Contrary both to the French law and also to the majority of the Court, he believed that the statements of the complainant in this case constituted, taking into account the circumstances of the event and the tone of his remarks, "the expression by an elected representative of an opinion or a political position on a current international issue."[25]

Having set the stage for a legal analysis in this way, Judge Jungwiert then turned to the French Press Act of 1881 and the way it was applied to this case by the French Court of Cassation. The press law's proviso about "provocation to discrimination" (which constituted a ground for exceptions to the protection of freedom of speech in the media) was said by the French court to refer to the penal code, but according to Judge Jungwiert no specific explanation of that "reference" was made, and, as he declared, there is no legal proviso referring to discrimination for "economic motives." But even if, as Judge Jungwiert admitted, the case law of the Court of Cassation provided the grounds for subsuming an "economic boycott" within the "provocation to discrimination" concept, in this particular case, according to him, such an exception to freedom of speech should not apply because (1) the statements by the mayor were relatively vague, (2) the impact of such measures would be limited (basically provisions of foodstuff to a small commune), and (3) the concrete effects of such a decision (of boycott) were never demonstrated. For all these reasons, the impugned statements by the mayor could not be interpreted as "measures of economic boycott" in the sense of the French penal code, and should be properly understood as "an expression of a political position relying on freedom of opinion, which is an essence of the right guaranteed by Article 10 [of the European Convention]."[26]

Weaknesses in this part of the argument by Judge Jungwiert may explain why he was so isolated in his dissent (despite an institutional tradition of the Strasbourg Court of multiauthored dissents). The fact that the calls for discrimination in French law embrace also "economic discrimination" (something questioned in the dissenting opinion) has been well-established by the French case law.[27] As to the "vagueness" of the mayor's calls for boycott (argument 1)—there was nothing "vague" about his statements, as evidenced by the summary in the judgment of the ECTHR:[28] the statements were meant to be, and were understood to be, calls for boycotts of importation of Israeli products to his municipality. Nothing more specific or detailed was needed to make his advocacy perfectly determinate. To use a deliberately exaggerated analogy: an advocacy of violence does not have to be particularly specific (e.g., accompanied by detailed instructions about the tools and methods of violence) in order to be punishable. As to the limited character of the impact of the boycott (argument 2), in case it was to be undertaken—that was entirely begging the question: a call by one municipality might have strong persuasive effects on other authorities and territorial units. In any event, it is not the actual extent of the economic effect that counts but rather the symbolic impact of such a statement. The harm of discrimination consists not only, and not necessarily, in the material effects but in the mental and psychological harm to its victims. Finally, regarding the absence of any evidence of possible economic effects of such a boycott (argument 3), the defects of this argument follow from the weakness of argument 2. The fact that a single illegal action may have minor effects (other than symbolic) does not count against its illegality when, replicated in large numbers, collective actions of this sort would precipitate disastrous effects on their target.

At the end of his dissenting opinion, Judge Jungwiert added a political dimension to his otherwise legal argument by emphasizing that the mayor's statements had to be understood in a broader context of the "escalation of violence in the Israeli-Palestinian conflict" and, puzzlingly enough, against the background of "a unanimous position of international organizations in 2002." No clarification of this background is given: What particular "international organizations" are included in this alleged "unanimity"? The only way to interpret this statement by the dissenting judge is as a rhetorical flourish meant to create an impression that Mayor Willem's remarks aligned themselves with some sort of international consensus, and hence were politically acceptable. If so understood, the rhetoric is disingenuous. Further, Judge Jungwiert emphasizes the circumstances of the office of the speaker and the place where the speech was made: the speech was given "by the mayor during a session of the municipal council, a privileged site of public debate."[29] But the fact that the call for boycott was made by the highest local official in a highly ceremonial setting *adds to* rather than *detracts from* the symbolic harm of his speech. If French law had an institution analogous to a "parliamentary privilege" extended to local authorities, according to which a speech made during a municipal council session would be fully immune to any legal prosecution, the mayor's advocacy of boycott would be exempt from any liability, but that clearly was not the case.

The final salvo in the dissent by Judge Jungwiert concerns the standard of "necessity in a democratic society," which is a test, based on a heightened proportionality requirement, used by the ECTHR in assessing the legitimacy of interference with article 10 rights. Judge Jungwiert observes, not inaccurately, that the judgment of the majority merely asserts, without demonstrating, that the sanctioning of the mayor's speech was "necessary in a democratic society." But neither does he attempt to demonstrate that such legal restriction was not necessary in a democratic society. The last sentence of his dissenting opinion reads: "In conclusion, in the light of the totality of elements of the case, it seems to me evident that the condemnation of the complainant can be seen as an interference which was not necessary and disproportionate with the right to freedom of expression."[30] But this is a mere assertion, not an argument. And that is the whole point of the standard of "necessity" used by the ECTHR: it usually serves as a *conclusion* of a prior argument to the effect that an interference with a right matches one or more of the legal grounds of restricting the right. The fact that this conclusion is usually presented by the court in a formulaic and ritual way, as it was done by the majority in *Willem v. France,* is, ironically, confirmed by the way Judge Jungwiert challenged this conclusion in his dissent, without any attempt at an argument that such interference was *not* necessary.

With just the single dissenting opinion of Judge Jungwiert (and a rather weak and unconvincing one at that), this ruling offers a strong voice in the boycott debate stating clearly that this type of incitement to discrimination will not be protected by the European Convention on Human Rights. No doubt, if a call for a boycott was addressed to a particular person, the court's judgment would have been even harsher: the court would have doubtlessly referred to its earlier case law in which it was established that contributing to an atmosphere of intimidation and exclusion of a particular national or ethnic group constitutes a blatant violation of the rights and freedom of members of these groups, and that each member state of the Council of Europe has an obligation to counteract such actions, including by legal means.[31]

However, before leaving the issue of the ECTHR position as revealed in *Willem v. France,* a word of caution is in order. By the very end of its reasoning, the court appealed, as one of the grounds for its conclusion, to the "margin of appreciation." In the doctrine of the ECTHR, this is equivalent to the principle of deference to national authorities, especially when no pan-European consensus has been formed on particular standards for interpretations of rights. The fact that the court chose to mention the "margin of appreciation" may be seen as an ominous signal: it may be read as saying that some other state, where local sensibilities about standards of freedom of expression are different, may receive a different treatment, and that persecution for advocacy of boycotts may be seen as violating article 10 if the overall legal traditions in another state are more libertarian.

In the case of France, the European Court was aware of a domestic case law that was strongly intolerant of advocacy of boycotts—including of boycotts against Israel. In 1994, the French Court of Cassation determined that the requirement of a certificate stating that the delivery of goods exported from France would not use any Israeli transport company or would not pass through Israel constituted a discriminatory action.[32] More recently, in a judgment of 18 December 2007, the Penal Chamber of the Court of Cassation determined that in trade transactions, any distinction between persons, in particular in terms of their nationality, constituted a punishable discrimination under penal code articles 225-1 and 225-2.[33] The facts of the case were as follows: a French company that wanted to deal with a company based in the United Arab Emirates submitted certificates to that UAR company that the products were manufactured without any Israeli material or Israeli labor, and were delivered without the use of any Israeli transport companies. The court determined that this practice constituted economic discrimination which resembles a "prohibited boycott" of the sort that articles 225-1 and 225-2 of the French Penal Code aim to eliminate.

The point of mentioning this line of cases in France is that, combined with the reference to the "margin of appreciation" in *Willem,* they may suggest that the European court had a relatively easy task in sustaining the punishment for the advocacy of boycotts because of local legal sensibility in France, and that the same "margin of appreciation" may cause the court to take a different approach in the future, in cases originating in other member states of the Council of Europe.

Interestingly, an (anonymous) legal commentator in a UK-based journal issued the following caustic opinion about *Willem v. France:* "To British eyes this judgment is surprising. . . . It is interesting to consider whether mayors or council leaders in [the UK] would expose themselves to any sanction if they were to call for a boycott of goods from a particular country. Clearly, calling for a boycott could not of itself give rise to a criminal prosecution."[34] But then, the author of that comment hypothesized that a British local official, in a position equivalent to that of Jean-Claude Willem, might be liable for a breach of section 30 of the Race Relations Act of 1976, which provides for liability when someone who has authority over another instructs that person to commit a discriminatory act.[35]

It remains to be seen how the ECTHR would react to a complaint for such a sanction from a country that, in contrast to France, provides for no *criminal* liability for discrimination on the basis of nationality where the discrimination takes the form of interfering with the normal exercise of any economic activity. It may well be that, ex post facto, if and when similar cases reach Strasbourg from other European countries, we see that the ECTHR *did* announce a strong principle in *Willem,* and that it really did not rely on "margin of appreciation" but rather on its own strong conviction that the French law expresses well the European Convention's balance between freedom of speech and competing values. The use of the "margin of appreciation" in *Willem* is rather timid and ritualistic: it is mentioned in the entire judgment only once, in the very last paragraph of the reasoning, which is in clear contrast to those judgments of the ECTHR where this notion of deference is effectively relied upon, and where the reasons for the use of the "margin of appreciation" (pointing at a lack of the European consensus on a given standard) are usually explicated at length in the body of the reasoning.[36]

It is also useful to refer to several judgments by other international tribunals. In one of its landmark judgments (*Feryn*), the Court of Justice of the European Union ruled that publicly expressed statements by an employer, claiming that he would not employ individuals of Moroccan origin, constitutes an act of direct discrimination and is forbidden by EU law.[37] Furthermore, the UN Committee on the Elimination of Racial Discrimination (CERD), reviewing the case of *Ziad Ben Ahmed Habassi v. Denmark,* in which the applicant—a national of Tunisia residing in Denmark—was refused a loan by a Danish bank on the sole ground of his non-Danish nationality, clearly found a violation of the applicant's rights and freedoms under the ICERD.[38] Additionally, it decided that the state was responsible for ensuring that such discrimination did not take place.

BOYCOTTS OF ISRAEL IN THE UN FORUM

Both the boycott and the calls for a boycott of the state of Israel by other states in the forum of the UN may constitute a violation of the international law in its very core, namely, they may be seen as a breach of the UN Charter, which guarantees equal treatment to all nations.[39] That Israel has been boycotted and that attempts at isolating Israel in various UN circles as allegedly the worst violator of human rights in the world, is evident to anyone who has had an opportunity to listen to the sessions of the UN Human Rights Council (HRC) or of its predecessor, the Commission of Human Rights.[40] This fact was pointed out by, among others, the former UN secretary general Kofi Annan when he expressed the hope that the Human Rights Council, set up to replace the commission in 2006, would not repeat the commission's former practices and would cease to condemn one state only, namely Israel.[41]

Unfortunately, the hope expressed by Kofi Annan has not been fulfilled. As a drastic example of the fact that nothing has really changed, one must consider the speech by the representative of Syria during the session of the HRC on 8 June 2010, in which she accused Israel in the following way: "Let me quote a song that a group of children on a school bus in Israel sing merrily as they go to school: 'With my teeth I will rip your flesh, with my mouth I will suck your blood.'"[42]

From the perspective of respect for international law, as expressed in the UN Charter, it would seem that the reaction (or rather, the lack of one) by the chair of the session, Alex Van Meeuwen, was even worse than the very statement just quoted—the content of which refers to one of the most ancient antisemitic myths about ritual drinking of blood of non-Jews by Jews. But all the chairman did was to thank the delegate of Syria for her speech. A few minutes earlier, the chairman had reacted harshly to a statement by the Canadian representative who used the word "regime" when referring to the military junta of Burma, which had been persistently violating the human rights of its population for decades; the chairman pointed out that such terms should be avoided when describing other governments. The contrasting, discriminatory treatment of Israel in this case is striking.

ACADEMIC BOYCOTTS

In 2003, Andrew Wilkie, a professor in England, refused an Israeli student's employment in his laboratory. In his email to the student, Wilkie wrote:

> Thank you for contacting me, but I don't think this would work. I have a huge problem with the way that the Israelis take the moral high ground from their appalling treatment in the Holocaust, and then inflict gross human rights abuses on the Palestinians because the Palestinians wish to live in their own country. I am sure that you are perfectly nice at a personal level, but no way would I take

on somebody who had served in the Israeli army. As you may be aware, I am not the only U.K. scientist with these views but I'm sure you will find another suitable lab if you look around.[43]

Is Wilkie, who committed an obvious act of discrimination based on nationality, an antisemite? Whether this is true could be determined by a court inquiring into this case. However, the very language of the letter quoted, the group-based responsibility mentioned, and the reference to an oft-repeated antisemitic theme about Jews abusing the Holocaust, prove that Wilkie participated in the kind of social exclusion that antisemites have always practiced against Jews.[44] In 1939, a famous Polish writer, Kazimierz Brandys, wrote a moving letter to the dean of the Faculty of Law at the University of Warsaw protesting his implementation of the university senate's decision concerning the removal of Jewish students from the student list and against exclusion, discrimination, and violence, verbal and physical, against Jewish students, which prevailed at Polish universities at that time:

> You have not hesitated, Sir, to endanger the loss of one year of studies by 20-year old Jewish boys who, regardless of violence and intimidation have persisted in their protest . . . and have not accepted to be confined to a university ghetto. To the representatives sent to you to plea on that matter you have explained that you were unable to infringe legal principles. . . . Legal principles? So why have your legal principles not moved you, Sir, to condemn unlawfulness and violence which are not rare in our university life and which . . . undermine the order and the law of social coexistence to a higher degree than a silent, peaceful protest by the defenceless Jewish students?[45]

It was a dramatic expression of defiance against the social exclusion of Jews caused by the boycott.

Any attempt at isolation and exclusion beyond the circle of mutual contacts and interpersonal relations promotes an atmosphere of suspicion, fear, contempt, and, in consequence, verbal or physical aggression against the group concerned. Such actions are not only discriminatory but also violate one of the most fundamental human right: a right to dignity.

ISRAEL'S LEGISLATIVE RESPONSE

The Israeli Anti-Boycott Bill, passed into law in July 2011, allows citizens to bring civil suits against persons and organizations that call for economic, cultural, or academic boycotts against Israel, Israeli institutions, or regions under Israeli control.[46] The second part of the law says that a person or a company that declares a boycott of Israel or the Israeli settlements will not be able to bid in government tenders. The most controversial aspect of this law concerns the lack of definition of actions and expressions that constitute a boycott. Although it does not impose any criminal law sanctions, this provision is vague and overly broad and thus seems contrary to international human rights law standards. As a result, two fundamental freedoms, freedom of speech and freedom of association, are likely to be infringed.[47] An Amnesty International official observes, for instance, that "the broad definition of boycott could apply to anyone seeking to use this nonviolent means of dissent to criticize any individual or institution involved in human rights violations or violations of international law in Israel or the Occupied Palestinian Territories."[48] Undoubtedly, if an individual whose rights have been violated by the antiboycott law filed a complaint to the international human rights protection bodies, such as the UN Human Rights Council, Israel would have been found guilty of such a violation.[49]

At the same time, one must notice that the fierce accusations against Israel that emerged after the adoption of this law were lacking in both proportion and merit.[50] Some comments were clearly false and misleading, for instance the claim that the law "criminalizes freedom of speech" (the New Israel Fund); and some were wildly exaggerated, for instance, the alarming insistence that the law is "a death sentence for the right to freedom of expression" (Gush Shalom).[51] Intense and turbulent public debate and discussion about the new law in Israel and the court motions challenging the law which were initiated by many of its opponents prove more than anything else that Israel is a democratic state.

It seems useful to refer here to an example of a controversial Polish provision of criminal law. While the provision was not directly about boycotts, it nevertheless illustrates different types of responses by an international and domestic public opinion to a problematic law. In 2006, the Polish Parliament, with the votes of the right-nationalist coalition then in power, incorporated into the criminal code a new provision which instituted the crime of the so-called "defamation of Polish nation" which could be committed by blaming Poland for involvement in Nazi and communist crimes. To a large extent this regulation was a legal response to the truth, described by Jan Tomasz Gross in his books published around that time, about the crimes of "blackmail, extortion, denunciation, betrayal, and plunder of the living and the dead," committed by Poles against the Jews in many places in Poland during and just after the Second World War.[52] This provision, fortunately no longer in force, was a clear violation of all possible standards of free speech and academic freedom, enforcing historical lies with the authority of the law. Does it mean that by adopting this law Poland turned from being a democracy into a kind of totalitarian regime that violates human rights? No reasonable person would ever advance such an opinion. In the case of Israeli antiboycott laws, however, such accusations appeared on a regular basis. The analogy is, of course, imperfect: the intensity of interest seen in public opinion—both internationally and nationally—in the Israeli-Palestinian conflict is incomparably higher than any concern about Polish legislation just mentioned. Nevertheless, the fact that legislative errors of a similar character and potential effects are treated so differently by public opinion only confirms that Israel is measured by much tougher standards whenever its authorities and policies are being assessed.

CONCLUSION

The individual choices we make in our personal relations or in deciding not to purchase products from a particular country are outside the scope of legal rules, and rightly so. When, however, they are made beyond the purely private realm of individuals, the state must interfere in order to prevent acts of discrimination. After all, as the Court of Justice of the European Union ruled, not even a private employer is allowed to announce that candidates of Moroccan background need not apply for a job; neither may a university professor refuse supervision to a student on the basis that the student holds an Israeli passport.

Both the universal and the European systems of human rights protection are founded on a few fundamental principles that cannot be suspended and that allow no exceptions. Those principles have become part and parcel of national legal systems in all democratic states. One principle is a prohibition of discrimination based on nationality, race, or ethnic origin, and a ban on incitement to hatred and the advocacy of violence against individuals or groups based on their racial, ethnic, or national characteristics. Clearly, the exclusion of an Israeli scholar from a research team based purely on his or her nationality is an act of discrimination prohibited by international human rights law. In this case, it really does not matter whether the exclusionary conduct was at the same time antisemitic. But if it was the case, international human rights law provides extra protection to the victim; its provisions and case law clearly prohibit the spreading of hatred based on race, ethnic, or national membership. A time may have arrived when those harmed by the boycott, divestment, and sanctions movement should claim their rights using the instruments of international law. And the same should be undertaken by the state of Israel, which should demand equal treatment in the forum of international organizations while rigorously complying with the international standards of human rights protection.

NOTES

1. For detailed analysis of the antisemitic and anti-Israeli attitudes at the UN forum, see *The United Nations and Anti-Semitism 2004–2007 Report Card*, UN Watch Report, 1 November 2007, http://www.unwatch.org/site/apps/nl/content2.asp?c=bdKKISNqEmG&b=1330819&ct=.

2. André Glucksmann, *Le Discours de la haine* (Paris: Plon 2004).

3. "ASA National Council Votes Unanimously to Endorse Academic Boycott of Israel," 4 December 2013, http://www.theasa.net/from_the_editors/item/council_statement_on_the_academic_boycott_of_israel_resolution/.

4. The FRA report presents the problem of antisemitism as seen by its victims, who precisely describe how antisemitic attitudes and actions affect their everyday life. For the first time ever, this detailed, direct, and large-scale survey covered responses from nearly six thousand Jewish people in the eight countries with the largest Jewish communities (Belgium, Denmark, France, Hungary, Italy, Latvia, Sweden, and the United Kingdom). For the full report, see "Discrimination and Hate Crime against Jews in EU Member States: Experiences and Perceptions of Anti-Semitism," 8 November 2013, http://fra.europa.eu/en/press-release/2013/combating-antisemitism-more-targeted-measures-needed.

5. FRA Report, *Discrimination and Hate Crimes against Jews in EU Member States: Experiences and Perceptions of Anti-Semitism,* 8 November 2013, 16.

6. H. Lauterpacht, "Boycott in International Relations," *British Year Book of International Law* 14 (1933): 125–140, 128.

7. For a contemporary critique of Lauterpacht's principle along these lines, see Wolfgang Friedmann, "The Growth of State Control Over the Individual and Its Effect upon the Rules of International State Responsibility," *British Year Book of International Law* 19 (1938): 118–150.

8. Peter Martino, *France Penalizes Boycott of Israeli Products,* Gatestone Institute, 12 July 2012, http://www.gatestoneinstitute.org/3164/france-penalizes-boycott-israeli-products.

9. See Jeremy Waldron, *The Harm in Hate Speech* (Cambridge, Mass.: Harvard University Press, 2012).

10. "International Covenant on Civil and Political Rights, New York, 16 December 1966," United Nations, Treaty Series 999, 171. International Convention on the Elimination of All Forms of Racial Discrimination, New York, 7 March 1966, United Nations, Treaty Series 660, 195.

11. Ibid., article 2, para. 1.

12. Convention for the Protection of Human Rights and Fundamental Freedoms, CETS No. 005, Council of Europe, 4 November 1950.

13. For the detailed information on the ECTHR's landmark jurisprudence concerning racial, ethnic and national discrimination, see "Factsheet—Racial Discrimination," April 2013, http://www.echr.coe.int/Documents /FS_Racial_discrimination_ENG.pdf.

14. See in particular the Council Directive 2000/43/EC of 29 June 2000 implementing the principle of equal treatment between persons irrespective of racial or ethnic origin, Official Journal L 180, 19/07/2000, 0022–0026.

15. *Willem v. France,* application no. 10883/05, ECTHR judgment of 10 December 2009. There is no official English translation of the French-language judgment, and all the translations of the excerpts from the judgment in this chapter are my own. Strangely enough, the only official translation of the judgment available at the ECTHR website is in Armenian.

16. The ECHR system, with the European Court at its epicenter, has been described as "the most effective human rights regime in the world." Alec Stone Sweet and Helen Keller, "The Reception of the ECHR in National Legal Orders," in *A Europe of Rights: The Impact of the ECHR on National Legal Systems,* ed. Helen Keller and Alec Stone Sweet, 3–28 (Oxford: Oxford University Press 2008), 3.

17. *Willem v. France,* para. 28.

18. Ibid., para. 33.

19. Ibid., para. 35.

20. Ibid., para. 37.

21. Ibid., para. 37.

22. Ibid., para. 38.

23. Ibid., para. 39.

24. Ibid., para. 42.

25. *Willem v. France,* dissenting opinion of Judge Jungwiert.

26. Ibid.

27. In fact, it was also covered by the explicit text of the Penal Code which, in article 225-2 (as in force at the time of the events) extended unlawful discrimination upon actions contrary to an "ordinary exercise of any economic activities" (*l'exercice normal d'une activité économique quelconque*), see *Willem v. France,* para. 20.

452   ALEKSANDRA GLISZCZYNSKA-GRABIAS

28. *Willem v. France,* para. 7. The statement by Willem had even mentioned "fruit juices" as the merchandised to be specially targeted—so it is hard to be more detailed than that.

29. *Willem v. France,* dissenting opinion of Judge Jungwiert.

30. Ibid.

31. See, in particular, the judgment concerning the Holocaust denial case: *Garaudy v. France,* application 65831/01, ECTHR decision on inadmissibility of 23 June 2003.

32. Decision of the Court of Cassation summarized in *Willem v. France,* para. 20.

33. Decision summarized in *Willem v. France,* para. 20.

34. Comment, *Willem v. France, European Human Rights Law Review,* 2009, 825–827, 827.

35. Ibid.

36. *Willem v. France,* para. 42. To be sure, the concept of the "margin of appreciation" appears also in para. 26, but only in a summary of the French government's position, which, naturally enough, wanted to exploit to its advantage the concept of deference by the court to national authorities.

37. *Centrum voor gelijkheid van kansen en voor racismebestrijding v. Feryn NV,* case c-54/07, CJEU judgment of 10 July 2008.

38. *Ziad Ben Ahmed Habassi v. Denmark,* application no. 10/1997, CERD judgment of 17 March 1999.

39. UN Charter, articles 1(2) and 2(1).

40. See *United Nations and Anti-Semitism 2004–2007 Report Card.*

41. See "Transcript of Press Conference by Secretary-General Kofi Annan at United Nations Headquarters, 15 June 2006," http://www.un.org/News/Press/docs/2006/sgsm10516.doc.htm.

42. See the recordings of the Human Rights Council Fourteenth session and Organizational Session of the Human Rights Council for its 5th Cycle, 8 June 2010, http://www.un.org/webcast/unhrc/archive.asp?go=100608.

43. See Geoffrey Short, "Antisemitism on Campus: A View from Britain," in *Antisemitism: The Generic Hatred. Essays in Memory of Simon Wiesenthal,* ed. M. Fineberg, S. Samuels, and M. Weitzman (London: Vallentine Mitchell, 2007).

44. On this aspect of antisemitic hatred, see in particular Alvin H. Rosenfeld, "The End of the Holocaust and the Beginnings of a New Antisemitism," in *Resurgent Antisemitism: Global Perspectives,* ed. Alvin H. Rosenfeld (Bloomington: Indiana University Press, 2013).

45. Reprinted in Adam Michnik, ed., *Przeciw antysemityzmowi 1936–2009* (Kraków: Universitas, 2010), my translation.

46. The Law for Prevention of Damage to State of Israel through Boycott was approved in the Knesset on 11 July 2011. The unofficial English translation of the Law is available at http://www.acri.org.il/en/wp-content /uploads/2011/07/Boycott-Law-Final-Version-ENG-120711.pdf.

47. See, among others, the critique of the law by Amnesty International, "Israel Anti-Boycott Law an Attack on Freedom of Expression," 12 July 2011, http://tbinternet.ohchr.org/Treaties/CCPR/Shared%20Documents /ISR/INT_CCPR_NGO_ISR_105_9108_E.doc (inactive). A statement on an official Amnesty website declares that "Amnesty International has taken no position on boycotts anywhere in the world, but fears that this law will lead to violations of the right to freedom of expression of those calling for boycotts," ibid.

48. Philip Luther, Amnesty International's deputy director for the Middle East and North Africa, quoted in Amnesty International, "Israel Anti-Boycott Law an Attack on Freedom of Expression."

49. On the UN Committee standards concerning freedom of speech, see its General Comment no. 34, 12 September 2011, http://www2.ohchr .org/english/bodies/hrc/docs/GC34.pdf.

50. The selection of comments is available in "Background and Analysis Regarding Knesset 'Anti-Boycott Law,'" NGO Monitor, 13 July 2011, http:// www.ngo-monitor.org/article/background_and_analysis_regarding _knesset_anti_boycott_law_#media.

51. "Background and Analysis Regarding Knesset 'Anti-Boycott Law.'"

52. See, in particular, Jan T. Gross, *Neighbors: The Destruction of the Jewish Community in Jedwabne, Poland* (New York: Penguin Books, 2002).

SIXTEEN

Delegitimizing Israel in Germany and Austria

*Past Politics, the Iranian Threat,
and Post-national Anti-Zionism*

STEPHAN GRIGAT

OVER THE LAST DECADE or two, calls for an end to Israel as a Jewish state have become increasingly acceptable, even in the political discourse of the Western mainstream. Although loss of life through terrorist and rocket attacks—particularly the possibility of a future attack by the Iranian regime—is the most imminent threat Israel faces today, its delegitimization as a Jewish state not only presents a serious problem for Israel, but also encourages antisemitism globally. The emergence and growth of the delegitimization campaign against Israel is a vital indicator of contemporary antisemitism in Europe in general and in the successor states of National Socialist Germany in particular. An analysis of this phenomenon can contribute significantly to a better understanding of contemporary antisemitism.

In this essay I cover three points. First, I discuss the delegitimization of Israel and Zionism in Germany and Austria and outline the relationship between the politics of the past and present criticism of Israel. Second, I discuss the delegitimization of Israel in Austria and Germany in light of the Iranian threat. Third, I offer some thoughts on the theoretical and philosophical justifications of Israel's delegitimization, examining post-nationalism, post-structuralism, and cultural relativism.

Prime elements of efforts to delegitimize Israel are specific to the successor states of National Socialist Germany. German and Austrian politicians and scholars tend to avoid *direct* condemnations of Israeli actions. Because of Germany's and Austria's Nazi past, relatively soft accusations—such as the charge of "using disproportionate force" instead of calling for boycott, divestment, and sanctions, or criticism of Israel's consistent self-defense instead of denial of the country's right to exist—are more common there than in other European countries.

Nonetheless, there are people on the lunatic fringe, especially among the anti-imperialist left wing, who openly call for the "destruction" of Israel. In a November 2012 announcement in Vienna, for example, an activist belonging to the Trotskyist group Revolutionary Communist Organization for Liberation (Revolutionär-Kommunistische Organisation zur Befreiung), demanded that Israel be "annihilated."[1] However, a more central problem is mainstream magazines and newspapers as well as people such as columnist Jakob Augstein and Nobel Prize–winning author Günter Grass, the latter who received broad support when he declared Israel to be a "danger for world peace."[2]

Of course, one can find many branches of the boycott, divestment, and sanctions (BDS) movement in Germany, and there can be absolutely no doubt that the BDS movement seeks to destroy Israel.[3] Supporters of BDS publicly admit that when they demand solely that Israel end the occupation of the West Bank, it is merely strategic—a strategy aimed at putting an end to Israel once and for all.[4] In Austria, however, the BDS movement is almost non-existent (the first official BDS chapter in Austria was founded in May 2014), and in Germany BDS is criticized even within the left-wing party Die Linke, which is known to have members of the Bundestag who openly oppose Israel.[5] However, antisemitic criticism of Israel in Germany is not limited to extreme left- or right-wing groups. Consider the caricature that portrays Benjamin Netanyahu as saying "I need bird poison and poisonous pellets to kill snails." Meant to evoke the Israeli prime minister's attitude toward the nuclear production talks with the Iranian regime in Geneva, the cartoon employs the classical blood libel image of the Jewish poisoner. The caricature did not appear in the extreme left-wing daily paper, *Junge Welt,* which expresses anti-Israeli views openly, nor did it appear in the Nazi paper, *Deutsche Stimme.* Rather, it was published in the well-known *Badische Zeitung,* whose editorial staff defended the cartoonist against accusations of antisemitism.[6]

Columnist and editor Jakob Augstein exemplifies this point of view. The political analyst Samuel Salzborn cautiously, but rightly, attested that some of Augstein's almost obsessive statements on Israel in his column "Im Zweifel links" (When in doubt, turn left), published over a period of months in 2011 and 2012, contained "a series of antisemitic terms."[7] But, in Germany, Augstein hardly stands alone. His anti-Israel statements correspond to the views of many of his colleagues and of much of the German public. Augstein's view of Israel as a danger for "world peace," his false depictions and belittling of the antisemitic Iranian regime's expressed intention to annihilate Israel, the parallels he draws between orthodox Israeli Jews and jihad murderers, his labeling the Gaza strip as a "camp," and his mumblings of conspiracy theories, with Israel being behind just about everything, earned him ninth place on the Simon Wiesenthal Center's list of "2012 Top Ten Anti-Israel/Anti-Semitic Slurs."[8] Yet, across the German political spectrum he was widely defended in the press against accusations of antisemitism. Representatives of Die Linke defended him just as strongly as executive committee members of the conservative Christliche Demokratische Union (CDU). In the *Frankfurter Rundschau* and the *Berliner Zeitung,* writers speculated about throwing Augstein's critics, such as the journalist Henryk M. Broder, into jail.[9] From *Die Tageszeitung* to *Die Zeit,* from the left-wing liberal *Süddeutsche Zeitung* to the conservative *Frankfurter Allgemeine Zeitung,* almost no one in the print media seriously discussed the accusations leveled against Augstein by the Simon Wiesenthal Center. (One of the few exceptions was Josef Joffe, who rightly contended that it is more condemned today "to call someone antisemitic than actually to be antisemitic yourself.")[10]

The wide-ranging defense of Augstein probably resulted from a feeling on the part of many authors that they had been personally exposed. The statements of the co-owner of one of Germany's most important publishing houses made the antisemitic nature of "Israel criticism" in Germany and Austria even more evident than it already was.

When Israel is discussed in postwar Germany and Austria, National Socialist history is always lurking in the background. When discussion points to "Israeli crimes," the German-Austrian conscience is put to rest: in the end, everyone has some sort of a skeleton in the closet. And Germans are pleased to underscore that they have already dealt with *their* crimes in an exemplary manner.

One utterance by a German historian aptly illustrates what post-Nazi normality means in Germany today. At the anniversary celebrations for the architect Peter Eisenman's Holocaust memorial in Berlin, which Chancellor Gerhard Schröder (Sozialdemokratische Partei Deutschlands, SPD) wished to be a monument "people will enjoy visiting," the historian Eberhard Jäckel said in May 2010: "Some people in other countries envy the Germans for this monument."[11] In light of the Citizen's Festival at the Field of Stelae, the Berlin daily *Tagesspiegel* was genuinely pleased with the "history of success of the Holocaust memorial."[12]

What was still being criticized in the 1980s and 1990s by authors such as Wolfgang Pohrt or Eike Geisel, in hopes that criticism at an early stage would not pervade society as a whole, is what shapes the self-image of the entire German nation today.[13]

Varying Paul Celan's verse from "Fugue of Death," "Death is a master from Germany," the fitting motto for Germany's self-image today could be "Germany is a master at coping with the past."[14] To talk about everything but to understand absolutely nothing, that is *Vergangenheitsbewältigung* in today's Germany. Indeed, the majority of Germans know what they reaped from mass murdering European Jews and how to create politically added value by dealing with Germany's past extermination policies: The more the National Socialist past is dealt with publicly, the easier it is to preach moral behavior to the surviving victims of Hitler's Germany. The more commemorations for murdered Jews, the more tightly you can embrace today's antisemites, for example the Iranian regime.

At the beginning of the 1980s, the Israeli prime minister Menachem Begin (Likud) let the German chancellor Helmut Schmidt (SPD) know that whoever served as an officer in the war of annihilation at the Eastern Front should hold his tongue once and for all concerning problems in the Middle East. For the former first lieutenant of the German Wehrmacht, that seems to have fallen on deaf ears. Schmidt is among twenty-six European ex-politicians who, at the end of 2010, wanted to dictate policy to Israel on construction in the West Bank and on how to prevent further armament in the Gaza Strip. Another former officer of the German Wehrmacht stood by his side: former president Richard von Weizsäcker (CDU), who to this day defends his father, Ernst von Weizsäcker, who had been state secretary in the Federal Foreign Office during the Nazi era and was sentenced for crimes against humanity because of his involvement in the deportation of French Jews to Auschwitz. Both Schmidt and Weizsäcker were complicit in starving to death over a million people in Leningrad. They fought in the hinterland of the Eastern Front, where the systematic murder of European Jews was perpetrated. Today, as angry "elder statesmen," they demand sanctions against the very country founded as a reaction to the German crimes. Claiming to have already dealt with their own history, they feel justified in dictating behavior to the state of the Shoah survivors and their offspring. Schmidt, who according to Die Zeit is "the most popular German politician in recent history," openly stated the consequence of this approach for German foreign policy: "Germany is not responsible for Israel."[15] Hence, Schmidt and Weizsäcker, together with an entire squad of former, primarily Social Democratic top-ranking politicians, have pleaded for "sanctions" and "concrete measures"[16]—not against the Iranian regime or its allies Hamas, Islamic Jihad, and Hezbollah that aim to annihilate Israel—but against the Jewish state.

In any case, that stance is more honest than the policy of Schmidt's successor, Angela Merkel, who rhetorically stands at Israel's side but has changed nothing about the fact that, despite sanctions, the Federal Republic of Germany remains the most important Western supporter of the Iranian regime to this day.[17] No one in post-Nazi Germany wants to say with any certainty how great the secret admiration is for the anti-West rage of the Iranian regime. On the contrary, what the majority of Germans think of Israel, the state upon which the rulers in Teheran wish death, has been well-known for many years: in 2003, 65 percent of Germans considered Israel to be the greatest threat to world peace—at the same level of threat, that is, of North Korea, and distinctly ahead of Iran.[18] According to a 2008 BBC poll, 77 percent of the population exhibited a negative attitude toward Israel, a more negative outcome than in the case of either North Korea or Iran.[19] In 2004, over half of Germans declared that "what the state of Israel is doing with the Palestinians today is principally no different than what the Nazis did with the Jews in the Third Reich." Almost 70 percent believed that Israel was carrying out a "war of annihilation against the Palestinians."[20]

In this context, it should not be surprising that Israel by its very existence reminds Germans and Austrians of Dachau, Mauthausen, Auschwitz, and Treblinka. This expression of guilt-defensiveness that critical theory terms secondary antisemitism is one of the main features of German attacks on Israel.

In Austria the situation is in some respects even worse. While 59 percent of EU citizens considered Israel the greatest danger for world peace at the time of the Second Intifada, in Austria that statistic was 69 percent.[21] In 2011, 42 percent of Austrians thought that Israelis acted "just as inhumanely to the Palestinians as the Nazis once did to the Jews."[22]

This Israel-related antisemitism correlates with classical hostility toward Jews: 43 percent of Austrians hold the Jews accountable for the current financial crisis. Their delusional projections are topped currently only by Hungary, which ranks in first place with 46 percent.[23] In 2011, 44 percent of Austrians thought that "the Jews ruled the business world," a finding that can be considered great progress in that country: in 1986, when Kurt Waldheim (Österreichische Volkspartei, ÖVP) campaigned for the Austrian presidency, it was 64 percent.[24]

Based on a discourse analysis of news coverage of Israeli military operations in the Gaza Strip in 2008–2009, the communications research specialist Maximilian Gottschlich concluded that not only had tabloids such as *Kronenzeitung* succumbed to the "communication strategy calculations of Hamas," but the left-wing liberal newspaper, *Der Standard,* had too—in such a way that anti-Zionist and "exuberant Israel criticism," which spilled over into antisemitism, had become a normal part of "public discourse in Austria" today.[25]

What Gottschlich concluded using the Gaza War of 2008–2009 as a paradigm has since been confirmed by the Media Monitoring Center for the Middle East (Medienbeobachtungsstelle Naher Osten, or MENA), which was founded in Vienna in 2011. Its daily comments on and analysis of Austrian news coverage of Israel can be considered as current validation of Gottschlich's findings. According to him, numerous examples for that "noxious mixture of various antisemitic and anti-Israeli stereotypes" can be clearly placed into the category of antisemitic propaganda against Israel.[26] He does not in any way limit himself to the usual suspects, but also criticizes liberal opinion makers such as columnist Hans Rauscher, who assailed Israel using terms such as "aggressor," "Banana Republic," and "ruthless occupying power" under the title "Black Times for Israel's Friends."[27] With such "friends," Israel no longer has the need for enemies.

The obviously anti-Israel attitudes held by a majority in Germany hardly affect the Middle Eastern policies of the German government. However, this is primarily the result of the special relationship with Israel that had been imposed upon Germany in the postwar period.[28] The differences between German and Austrian post-Nazisms can be clearly seen in both countries' relations to the Jewish state: Germany saw itself forced to generally support Israel when relevant issues arose in international bodies, and in fact it still widely does, as long as such issues do not run counter to German economic interests. On the other hand, as a result of the pervasive fiction that Austria was the first victim of the Nazis,[29] it has not only abstained in such votes, but even voted to the disadvantage of Israel, as when "Palestine" was admitted to UNESCO at the end of 2011.[30]

While the Germans acted as if they suddenly loved Jews and wanted to provide for the well-being of the Jewish state because of genuine shame over Germany's history, Israelis act as if they believe Germans have turned into staunch campaigners against antisemitism. For Israel, it is naturally important to have a more or less dependable ally in Europe, in order to at least moderate anti-Israeli decisions in international forums. In turn, by lending its partial support, Germany hopes to be able to act on the world stage without being hindered by the burdens of its history.

This pragmatism on both sides, however, has never prevented the heir to the Nazi legacy from issuing one brazen statement after another. The first postwar chancellor, Konrad Adenauer (CDU), indicated that one of the reasons for the so-called *Wiedergutma-*

chung (reparations) was his claim of 1965 that one should not underestimate "the power of the Jews even today and in America in particular."[31] During Willy Brandt's (SPD) term his foreign minister Walter Scheel (Freie Demokratische Partei, FDP) tried to prevent U.S. arms deliveries via Germany to Israel in the Yom Kippur War. Helmut Schmidt called Menachem Begin "a danger for world peace."[32] Helmut Kohl (CDU) broke the international isolation of the Austrian federal president Kurt Waldheim, who had a past as a Wehrmacht officer and visited the Iranian regime as the first Western head of state in 1991, placing a wreath on the sarcophagus of Ayatollah Ruhollah Khomeini.[33] Chancellor Gerhard Schröder "honored" the German Wehrmacht by placing a photo of his uniformed father on his desk.[34]

Nevertheless, the notion of the special relationship continues to be cited. Remarkably, then, the German Bundestag was the sole European parliament to unanimously adopt a resolution against the actions of the Israel Defense Forces (IDF) after the Israeli army disrupted the so-called Gaza Freedom Flotilla in the summer of 2010. A resolution approved unanimously by all parties of Vienna's city council in the summer of 2010, on a like subject, represents a kind of provincial-political complement to the German parliamentary decision. The latter can be seen as a step toward a break in post–National Socialist normality, in which the ever-asserted "obligation" to Israel is one of the last visible remains of German memory of guilt.

Today, in Germany—and also in Austria from a different perspective—the remnants of National Socialism manifest themselves no longer in the threat of fascistic mass marches or in a classical historical revisionism, but in the appeasement of Islamic Jihadists and in the delegitimization of Zionism. This is a delegitimization that is articulated in the political mainstream as a criticism of Israel's resolute self-defense. At the same time, the frontal attack on the Jewish state is generally left to Islamists, Nazis, and alleged radical left-wingers.

In the decades after 1945, it was the left wing that transformed the dictum "Never again Auschwitz, never again War"—where "war" meant German aggression and war of annihilation—into that of "Never again War against Antisemitism." However, after Israel has been repeatedly forced to wage war, this dogma has become one of the key justifications for delegitimizing Zionism. This leads to the absurd conclusion that, as a lesson learned from National Socialism, criticism of Israel's military posture is called for. The state of Shoah survivors and their offspring, as this tenet would have it, is obliged to seek security through peaceful means only.

THE IRANIAN THREAT AND THE DELEGITIMIZATION OF ISRAEL

The German-language discussion of the Islamic Republic of Iran repeatedly asserts that the Iranian regime is being "demonized." In Austria, Georg Hoffmann-Ostenhof, former international policy editor at Austria's most important weekly newspaper, labeled the criticism of Mahmoud Ahmadinejad "hysteria."[35] Gudrun Harrer, international policy editor at a left-liberal Austrian daily, employs the term "Iranophobia," used by the Iranian regime to delegitimize any criticism directed against the Islamic revolution and law in Iran.[36]

On days of remembrance, such as November 9 or January 27, representatives of nearly all political factions in Austria and Germany fully condemn their countries' National Socialist past. But criticism of contemporary antisemitism in its Islamic and Iranian form is scarcely heard during such commemorative events. In today's Austria and Germany, only dead Jews are commemorated, while there is no expression of solidarity with the Jewish state as it faces a lethal threat from Iran. Leading political analysts in Germany have been calling for dialogue or even "strategic partnership" with the Iranian regime and allied jihadist groups such as Hamas or Hezbollah. Again, it is simple to find culprits among the lunatic fringe. For example, the Austrian Trotskyist League of the Socialist Revolution (Liga der Sozialistischen Revolution), which is known as the Worker's Power Group (Gruppe Arbeitermacht) in Germany and was the predecessor of the Revolutionary Communist Organization for Liberation, declaims: "For the right of Iran to establish and utilize nuclear facilities—for peaceful as well as military means!" and "For the military defense of Iran against imperialist aggression!"[37]

In the political mainstream, Muriel Asseburg, a Middle East expert at a think-tank that advises the German government and parliament on foreign policy, regards "the present policy of isolation [...] towards Iran" as "counterproductive."[38] Volker Perthes, head of the most influential think tank in Germany, pursues the same approach and demands consideration of the "interests of all relevant actors" in the conflict with Iran.[39] In Austria, Georg Hoffmann-Ostenhof speaks of the "legitimate security interests" of the Islamic Republic, as does Michael Lüders, a leading German expert on the Middle East.[40] This language, originating in the realist school of international relations, turns the character of the Iranian regime into a complete abstraction. It pretends that Iran is just another state, akin to Iceland or Ireland, say, and not an Islamo-Fascist dictatorship, whose founder openly stated that his interpretation of Islam—which is driven by antisemitism—called for global domination.[41] And still, influential voices in Austria and Germany systematically repudiate the menace that emanates from this dictatorship and its nuclear program.

Christoph Bertram, who used to head the most important German think tank for international and security affairs, declared: "The danger of a nuclear armed Iran would be [...] manageable." And: "The contemporary development amounts neither to a clear nor to an immediate danger."[42] The Austrian political expert Gerhard Mangott also argues that a nuclear-armed Iran would present no existential threat to Israel.[43]

These authors exemplify an entire bloc of scholars. Their pronouncements routinely appear in the most important Austrian and German media, and they strongly influence the discussion on the Iranian regime there. Their main argument for an all-clear signal regarding Iranian nuclear weapons implies that the military deterrence capability of Israel and its assumed arsenal of nuclear weaponry would even contain an Iranian regime in possession of such weapons. According to their views, Iran is a rational actor who would never employ a nuclear bomb.

Many participants in the German-language discussion underestimate the concurrence of pragmatism and irrationality that characterizes the Iranian regime. Further, the apocalyptic and messianic elements of the Iranian ideology go unheeded. The same holds true in regard to the ideology of martyrdom. In German and Austrian discussions, the Tehran rulers frequently figure on the same level as authoritarian regimes such as Russia or Algeria.[44] Very few authors in either country discuss the *specific* danger inherent in the Iranian regime, one that results from its combination of apocalyptic martyrdom, antisemitism, and aspirations to perfect the technology of mass destruction.[45]

In addition, these authors ignore the fact that Iran would not have to use nuclear weapons to endanger Israel's existence and to change the rules of the game of international relations in favor of Islamic Jihadism. The Iranian bomb, in contrast to the assumed Israeli nuclear weapons, would lead to a nuclear arms race in the Middle East. The Austrian and German discussions rarely mention the consequences of an Iranian bomb that Yossi Klein Halevi and Michael Oren outlined in the *New Republic*: "No Arab partner will be able to make concessions to Israel with a nuclear Iran standing over them. Israel will find its military options severely limited. Foreign investors will flee the country, and many Israelis will, too. In one poll, 27 percent of Israelis said they would consider leaving if Iran went nuclear." Oren and Halevi summarize: "The promise of Zionism to create a Jewish refuge will have failed, and, instead, Jews will see the diaspora as a more trustworthy option for both personal and collective survival."[46] Instead of taking such prognoses seriously, leading German and Austrian political analysts and commentators advise Israel to resign itself to a nuclear-armed Iran.

Iranian threats of annihilation against Israel, they contend, are mere rhetoric, intended to serve "internal purposes" only, a means employed by the regime to distract from economic and social problems.[47] It escapes these opinion leaders' attention that antisemitism does not just represent one tactic among others; it lies at the ideological core of Islamic Jihadism. In respect to the threats of annihilation against Israel, such authors suggest that a "solution" to the Middle East conflict or an improvement of the situation of the Palestinians would end Iran's lethal threats.[48]

On the one hand, these explanations ignore that the entire Iranian regime calls for the extermination of Israel. Few articles in Germany and Austria mention precisely such utterances by the strong man of Iran, the Supreme Leader Ali Khamenei. They also fail to take into account that, in regard to the Middle East conflict, the Iranian regime has no interest whatsoever in improving the situation of the Palestinians. It also displays no disposition toward a compromise settlement, or even a two-state solution, but rather promotes and pursues the "liberation of the whole of Palestine," a euphemism for the annihilation of the Jewish state. These activities started not with Mahmoud Ahmadinejad's presidency, but with the Islamic Revolution in 1979. As David Meshari put it, "Iran's attitude to Israel was one of the rare examples of adherence to dogma."[49] The concurrence of pragmatism and irrationality led to a kind of flip-flopping in many areas of politics over the last three decades, but never when it comes to the slogan "Marg bar Israel" (Death to Israel).

In sum, the German and Austrian perceptions of the Islamic Republic of Iran show both the trivialization of the antisemitic character of the regime by downplaying the threats of the Iranian nuclear program to Israel and the West and—this an aspect worthy of further, detailed investigation—ignoring those voices of the secular opposition in Iran and in exile who oppose such trivializations.

Why is this kind of perception of the Iranian regime flourishing throughout Austria and Germany? First, Austria and Germany are pursuing economic and political goals through their policy toward Iran.[50] Second, present within various sectors of public opinion, in the media, and even within the political arena, a certain level of naïveté regarding Islamist ideology predominates. Obviously, displeasure associated with confronting a serious threat and thereby bringing about unwanted consequences exists. This is discernible in the comparatively reluctant courses of action against Islamist organizations within Austria and Germany. Third, because the utterly skewed perception of the Middle Eastern conflict always perceives Israel as the troublemaker, it colors the perception of the Iranian regime: public opinion in Austria and Germany is more than willing to take the statements of Iranian politicians and clerics, who aim to see Israel exterminated, as essentially justifiable criticism of Israeli behavior toward the Palestinians, and explain away the more candid statements as "translation issues."[51]

Beyond superficial amendments to their Iran policies, indications of a substantial change have yet to emerge. Austria and Germany, the successor states of National Socialism, still oblige the Iranian regime through economic cooperation and policies of appeasement. Despite the threats emanating from the Iranian regime, Germany remains Iran's most important trading partner in the West. Since the election of Hassan Rouhani and the disastrous nuclear agreement made in Geneva in November 2013, the situation has become even worse: Rouhani, who can be best described as the friendly face of terror, was first characterized as a "moderate." Now, even papers like Der Standard refer to him as a "liberal reformist." The German Tageszeitung called him a "bearded bearer of hope with heart."[52]

Through nuclear negotiations with the Iranian regime and the Geneva agreement, with a shrug of its shoulders Germany has also made clear that it is ignoring the massive concern of Israel with regard to a nuclear-armed Iran. And again: Germany and Austria are at the forefront when it comes to making billions through trade with the sworn enemy of Israel. Their relentless will to accept a dangerous compromise with the Iranian regime expresses a desire that is as naive as it is enterprising. This ominous development quite pleases European lobbyists for trade with Iran. The Austrian energy giant OMV sought to conclude a 22-billion euro trade agreement with the Iranian regime even during Mahmoud Ahmadinejad's presidency but had to put it on hold after massive criticism from the Israeli and the U.S. governments, as well as from the European coalition Stop the Bomb, which campaigns for effective economic and political sanctions against the Iranian regime. Now, however, OMV is back in the starting gates, as is German industry. The Austrian Chamber of Commerce, which also tried its best to explain to Austrian companies during Ahmadinejad's presidency how they could do huge business with the antisemitic regime in Teheran despite all of the sanctions, sent a large delegation to Iran in November 2013. In late February 2014, the same institution began a new campaign with a daylong seminar in Vienna to encourage companies to take up business that the rulers in Iran urgently need in order to continue their projects and stay in power. The German-Iranian Chamber of Commerce in Hamburg held a similar seminar only a day later.

Hassan Rouhani and his foreign minister Mohammad Javad Zarif are exactly the right men at the right time for the Iranian regime to achieve its endeavors with regard to the nuclear option. For Germany and Austria, which have both maintained very close economic and political ties to the dictatorship of the Ayatollahs, the election of the allegedly "moderate" Rouhani conveniently excuse them from undertaking any serious steps against the Iranian regime. Thus, Israel finds itself threatened by a dangerous compromise with respect to the Iranian nuclear program, negotiated with the significant involvement of German and Austrian diplomats, namely Helga Schmidt and Stephan Klement. This confirms to the Jewish state that it must prepare for the possibility of being on its own should it need to act against Iranian nuclear armament.

DELEGITIMIZATION AND POST-NATIONALISM

Those on the political Left who contribute to delegitimizing the Jewish state operate within a distinct theoretical framework. The concepts upon which they draw for their anti-Israel project merit scrutiny, particularly since in the last twenty years anti-Zionist thinking has been subject to change. During the last decades of the Cold War, from the late 1960s until the collapse of the Soviet bloc at the beginning of the 1990s, an anti-imperialist "nationalism of liberation," as Marxist-Leninist thought puts it, was its main point of reference. In the past two decades an abstract antinationalism has emerged that is strongly influenced by certain anarchist theoretical traditions with roots in post-structuralism. It has become the primary legitimization of anti-Zionism and strongly influences the political mainstream through the social sciences, which are currently occupied with post-national constellations.

The Nazis declared that the Jews were incapable of establishing a "true" state. The core National Socialist writing on Zionism stems from Adolf Hitler's senior philosopher, Alfred Rosenberg. He claimed that the project of founding a Jewish state was in itself "adverse to statehood."[53] The Führer, too, maintained that the Jews were incapable of "building a state in a spatially perceived manner" (*Staatsbau räumlich empfundener Art*) due to their "lack of productive capability."[54] During the 1970s and 1980s, this doctrine resonated among the Left, with the Arab Nationalist and later Islamist condemnation of Israel as an "artificial creation."

But today, Zionist Jews are accused of stubbornly clinging to their allegedly obsolete concept of nationhood.

In recent years, Europe's post-nationalism has been elevated to an intellectual virtue. Israel embodies national self-determination as an answer to antisemitism from its founding until today. The Jewish state constantly reminds Europe in general and the successor states of National Socialist Germany in particular *why* Jewish national self-determination is necessary. In recent years, debates about post-nationalism and blindness to resurgent antisemitism have led to calls on Israel to overcome its "outdated nationalistic ideology." Among others, the late influential scholar Tony Judt, who is also widely read in Austria and Germany, described Israel as an "anachronism" and declared that there is "no place" for a Jewish state.[55] Although the persistence of antisemitism remains one of the strongest arguments for the necessity of Zionism and a strong Jewish state, it comes as no surprise that the trivialization and even denial of contemporary European and Islamic antisemitism has become central to both demonizing and delegitimizing Israel.

In both Germany and Austria, Jewish and Israeli leftists play key roles in the delegitimization campaigns. In Austria, the political scientist John Bunzl is a major inspirer of anti-Israeli sentiment. Most recently in Germany, drawing on Martin Buber's objections to early statehood, Micha Brumlik played a key role in making the "one-state solution," that is, the dissolution of Israel into a binational state, acceptable again.[56] In the 1960s, both Brumlik and Bunzl had been members of the Israeli Matzpen group, which was calling for the "de-Zionization" of Israel.[57] However, significant differences also separate the two. While Bunzl eagerly gave interviews to Iranian regime media even during the presidency of Ahmadinejad and campaigned for European political leaders' contact with Hamas, despite Brumlik's harsh criticism of Israel, he has taken a clear position against the rulers in Teheran and their allies on Israel's border, such as Hamas and Hezbollah.

Further important sources of inspiration for the left-wing dele-gitimization of Israel in Germany and Austria include anti-Zion-ist activist and author (and former Matzpen member) Michael Warschawski,[58] as well as Moshe Zuckermann, who has opposed Israeli policies numerous times in both countries and nearly all of whose books have been released in German.[59] Zuckermann op-poses a doctrine of universalism to the particularism of Zionism, inappropriately drawing on Adorno for scholarly, philosophical, and theoretical support. Compared to Warschawski and his like, he represents a sort of "moderate anti-Zionism" that fits much better into the German debate than do open calls for the destruc-tion of the Jewish state. As a consequence, he plays an especially decisive role in discrediting Israel.

Currently, the reception of Judith Butler commands lively in-terest in the German and Austrian debates, not only on the Left or among left-wing radicals, especially after she received the re-nowned Theodor W. Adorno Prize from the City of Frankfurt am Main in 2012. The enthusiasm for Butler raises a series of ques-tions, not only with regard to her anti-Zionism: Why should an author who favors U.S. gender scholar Lila Abu-Lughod's praise of the burka be recognized as a paragon of feminism? According to Judith Butler, Abu-Lughod sees "important cultural meanings of the burka." In *Precarious Life,* (published in German in 2005 as Gefährdetes Leben), Butler draws on Abu-Lughod's protest against the "decimation of Islamic culture" and the "extension of U.S. cultural assumptions about how sexuality and agency ought to be organized and represented" in an attempt to denounce pictures of non-veiled Afghan girls and women. Veiling should be understood, Abu-Lughod declares, as "an exercise of mod-esty and pride" and serves as "a veil behind which, and through which, feminine agency can and does work." Butler declares any critical view of the Islamist terroristic imposition of "virtues" to be a "culturally imperialist exploitation of feminism."[60] The fitting answer to this kind of cultural relativism was given in

1979 by those exceptionally brave women who demonstrated for weeks against forced veiling in Khomeini's Iran under the slogan "Emancipation is not Western, emancipation is not Eastern, it is universal!"[61]

Those of Butler's followers who still take feminism seriously found it hard to turn a blind eye to statements that clearly nullify the universal idea of freedom. Something similar took place when the city of Frankfurt am Main awarded Butler the Adorno Prize. During the debates stirred by her anti-Israeli statements, the Frankfurt jury and many of Butler's German admirers tried to defend her by claiming that she had only attacked the continuous settlement building and other specific actions of the Israeli government. If this defense strategy was hardly stable then, after the publication of Butler's *Parting Ways* in 2012 it completely collapsed.

Translated into German in 2013, the book starts with the grand delusion that the allegedly omnipotent community of Israel defenders will stigmatize as antisemitic all anti-Zionists, who portray themselves as victims of merciless persecution. For Butler, the fact that there have always been Jewish opponents of Zionism confirms her own opposition to Israel, which, she asserts, takes courage to express. She cites Jewish criticism of Zionism by Hermann Cohen, Franz Rosenzweig, or Hannah Arendt in order to justify her opposition to Israel.

Quoting the Shoah survivor Primo Levi's protest against the Lebanon war of 1982, Butler tries to justify her extreme disapproval of the Zionist project. Against this background, like her ideological ally Edward Said, she aims at nothing less than the abolition of Israel. Unsurprisingly, her Jewish witnesses to the evils of Zionism are not radical enough for Butler: The binational proposals of Hannah Arendt, Martin Buber, and Judah Magnes "did not go far enough," she remonstrates.[62] She demands a "dismantling of political Zionism" and the "dismantling of the structure of Jewish sovereignty."[63]

Thus, Butler argues for the abolition of the Law of Return, which guarantees all Jews the right to immigrate to Israel, and the implementation of the "right of return" for Palestinians, which would spell doom for Israel as a Jewish state. In *Parting Ways,* Butler advances her passionate defamation of Israel's legitimacy by supporting the BDS movement, as she has for many years, a fact always downplayed by her German and Austrian supporters. Meanwhile, even the radical defamers of Israel Noam Chomsky and Norman Finkelstein have backed off from the BDS movement.

Butler clarifies that her aim is not only to boycott products from West Bank settlements but to boycott the state of Israel totally. Anything less would mean giving up the Palestinian "claims of 1948" and their "right of return."[64] Butler's objectives are unmistakable: like Ali Khamenei's, the Sunnite Islamists, and the PFLP's, albeit with a different vision of future cohabitation in that region, Butler's concern is the "liberation" of "Palestine" in its entirety. Thus, she even strongly disagrees with left-wing versions of Zionism.

Butler's objections to Zionism provide any type of person in Austria and Germany who hates Israel, mostly pseudo-critical liberals, with ample ammunition. They delight in the set of notions and the pretentious language of the post-structural mastermind. Her book is another milestone along the course of delegitimizing and ultimately destroying Israel. Unless I am mistaken, Butler's fans in Austria and Germany, who claimed during the Adorno Prize debate that her polemics were confined to Israel's presence in the West Bank, should find themselves with little ground left. The professor of rhetoric and comparative literature points out: "It is important to note that for Said and for my own argument here, binationalism leads not to a two-state solution, but to a single state."[65]

Butler ignores not only the current resurgence of antisemitism in Europe, but the entire history that led to the founding of the state of Israel. For her, the displacement of Palestinians in 1948 did not result from a decades-long conflict essentially fueled by Arab antisemitism and was not the outcome of a war triggered by the Arab-Palestinian axis, but rather it was due to the nature of Zionism. Butler says nothing about the displacement of some 800,000 Jews originating from Arab countries. The history of Arab antisemitism and Israel's constant threat from the Iranian regime are never mentioned within the 250 pages of *Parting Ways*, not to speak of the anti-Jewish rage of Hamas or Hezbollah, which Butler takes for "progressive" and "part of a global left."[66] Undisturbed by facts, she erases a hundred years of Middle Eastern conflict with her self-defined ethics of conviction, while gangs of Jihadist killers find place as allies in her fight against Israel.

Not only in her defense of the burka but in her radical verdict on Zionism, as well, Butler refers to Lila Abu-Lughod and her struggle against something she calls "Jewish exceptionalism."[67] In the main, Butler mobilizes an abstract and ahistorical universalism against what she sees as Zionist particularism. Her universalistic pseudo-morality easily gives way to crude cultural relativism, as can be seen, for example, in her earlier noted apology for veiling. She not only fails to recognize the tension between particularism and universalism which has always been present in various manifestations of Judaism, but she also ignores the decades-long debate among various strains of Zionist thought regarding separatism, cosmopolitism, universalistic aspirations, and necessarily particularist practice.

Butler and her entourage refuse to see that Zionist particularism—despite diverging tendencies within the Zionist movement—has been imposed by hostility from without and was not voluntarily chosen. Whoever opposes it must address the root of the problem: the antisemitism that Butler fuels with her own variety of "Jewish exceptionalism." Whatever she refuses Israel, whether it be sovereignty, nationalism, or safeguarding of territories, despite her post-nationalistic notions, Butler freely grants the Palestinians. The substance of their political intentions and their nationalism go unmentioned, as if these were uncharted waters and beyond reproach. Her uncritical alignment with the cause of "Palestine" reveals the intimacy of her antinationalist political theory with barbarism.

Not only Butler, but still other key actors in the delegitimation campaign come from the Left. However, in Austria and Germany especially, a clear split among the Left has emerged. There, some of the most outspoken defenders of Israel and strongest critics of delegitimation come from the left wing, especially from the radical left wing.[68] This split is also reflected in their theoretical positions. To put it simply: those who base their views on critical theory lean toward defending Zionism as a necessary response to antisemitism, while the proponents of post-structuralism and postcolonial theory lean toward defending the so-called legitimate rights of the Palestinians and toward attacking the legitimacy of Israel and Zionism.

Adorno wrote that "a new categorical imperative has been imposed by Hitler upon unfree mankind: to arrange their thoughts and actions so that Auschwitz will not repeat itself, so that nothing similar will happen."[69] If the Left were to take the categorical imperative of Adorno seriously it would have to be on the frontline fighting against the delegitimization of Israel, against the threats emanating from the Iranian regime, and against the support of the Ayatollahs by Austrian and German companies, politicians, and scholars. Unfortunately, we are miles away from that fight in both countries, as well as globally.

NOTES

1. "Free Palestine. Rede von Johannes Wiener auf der Demonstration am 16. November 2012," November 16, 2012, http://www.rkob.net/multimedia /video-gaza-16-nov-2012. The date of last access for all websites is July 13, 2014, unless stated otherwise.

2. Günter Grass, *Was gesagt werden muss,* April 10, 2012, http://www
.sueddeutsche.de/kultur/gedicht-zum-konflikt-zwischen-israel-und-iran
-was-gesagt-werden-muss-1.1325809.

3. See, for instance, Rima Najjar Kapitan, a civil rights attorney and BDS
activist in Chicago, January 7, 2014, https://www.youtube.com/watch?v
=1nGARsFnwbI.

4. See, for instance, a discussion among Norman Finkelstein, Jonathan
Rosenhead (British Committee for Universities in Palestine), and several
BDS activists at University College London, November 11, 2011, https://
www.youtube.com/watch?v=nMoD9ME5VtY.

5. See, for instance, Kathrin Vogler, "Boykott? Israel ist nicht Südafrika,"
in *Königsweg der Befreiung oder Sackgasse der Geschichte? BDS: Boykott,
Desinvestition und Sanktionen. Annäherung an eine aktuelle Debatte,* ed.
Kathrin Vogler, Martin Forberg, and Peter Ullrich (Berlin: AphorismA,
2011), 7–14.

6. Thomas Fricker, "Umstrittene Karikatur. Nicht jede Kritik ist antisemitisch," November 15, 2013, http://www.badische-zeitung.de/karika
turen/umstrittene-karikatur-nicht-jede-kritik-ist-antisemitismus—6089
8246.html.

7. "Dämonisierung mit dem Ziel der Delegitimierung. Interview mit
Samuel Salzborn," January 16, 2013, http://www.welt.de/politik/deutschland
/article112787522/Daemonisierung-mit-dem-Ziel-der-Delegitimierung
.html.

8. On his views, see Jakob Augstein, "Es musste gesagt werden," April 6,
2012, http://www.spiegel.de/politik/deutschland/jakob-augstein-ueber
-guenter-grass-israel-gedicht-a-826163.html, and "Gesetz der Rache," November 11, 2012, http://www.spiegel.de/politik/ausland/jakob-augstein
-ueber-israels-gaza-offensive-gesetz-der-rache-a-868015.html.

9. Christian Bommarius, "Broder diffamiert Augstein," January 2,
2013, http://www.berliner-zeitung.de/medien/antisemitismus-broder
-diffamiert-augstein,10809188,21374630.html and http://www.fr-online
.de/medien/antisemitismus-broder-diffamiert-augstein,1473342,21374630
.html.

10. Josef Joffe, "Antisemitismus-Knüppel. Israel-Kritik oder Dämonisierung?," *Die Zeit* 3 (2013).

11. Gerhard Schröder quoted in Jan Feddersen, "Die Erinnerung-
slücken bleiben," *Die Tageszeitung,* May 10, 2006, http://www.taz.de/index
.php?id=archivseite&dig=2006/05/10/a0136; "From Allah to Osama (Part
2-1)," *Entweder Broder* 2, Entweder Broder Video, 14:30. ARD, November 14,
2010, https://www.youtube.com/watch?v=Z3yGxV09DDk.

12. Claudia Keller, "Bürgerfest am Stehlenfeld," *Der Tagesspiegel,* May 5, 2010.

13. Wolfgang Pohrt, *Harte Zeiten. Neues vom Dauerzustand* (Berlin: Edition Tiamat, 1993); Eike Geisel, *Triumph des guten Willens. Gute Nazis und selbsternannte Opfer. Die Nationalisierung der Erinnerung* (Berlin: Edition Tiamat, 1998).

14. Paul Celan, "Todesfuge," 1948, http://www.celan-projekt.de/todes fuge-deutsch.html.

15. Helmut Schmidt quoted in Peter Dausend, "Kanzler und Krise," *Die Zeit* 44 (2011); Helmut Schmidt and Fritz Stern, "Verantwortung für Israel? Ein Gespräch," April 16, 2010, http://www.cicero.de/schmidt-stern -verantwortung-für-israel/40774.

16. Chris Patten et al., "EU Must Sanction Israel over Its Refusal to Obey International Law and Must Recognize the State of Palestine. Letter to the President of the European Council," December 13, 2010, http:// www.romanoprodi.it/documenti/eu-must-sanction-israel-over-its-refusal -to-obey-international-law-and-must-recognize-the-state-of-palestine _2401.html.

17. See Stephan Grigat, *Die Einsamkeit Israels. Zionismus, die israelische Linke und die iranische Bedrohung* (Hamburg: Konkret, 2014), 137–140 and 168–175.

18. See Alex Feuerherdt, "Die Agenda der 'Israelkritiker,'" June 8, 2011, http://kamo.blogsport.de/images/IsraelkritikerMoers.pdr.

19. Ibid.

20. Martin Kloke, "40 Jahre deutsch-israelische Beziehungen," May 5, 2005, http://www.bpb.de/popup/popup_druckversion.html?guid=EV50 UI&page=0.

21. See Matthias Küntzel, "'Affen und Schweine.' Der islamische Antisemitismus und die deutsche Politik," *Jungle World* 3 (2008), http://jungle -world.com/artikel/2008/01/20952.html.

22. Maximilian Gottschlich, *Die große Abneigung. Wie antisemitisch ist Österreich? Kritische Befunde zu einer sozialen Krankheit* (Wien: Czernin, 2012), 180.

23. Ibid., 242.

24. Ibid., 65.

25. Ibid., 211, 231.

26. Ibid., 275.

27. Hans Rauscher, "Schwere Zeiten für Freunde Israels," *Der Standard,* June 1, 2010, http://derstandard.at/1271377993127/ Schwere-Zeiten-fuer-Freunde-Israels.

28. See Yves Pallade, *Germany and Israel in the 1990s and Beyond: Still a "Special Relationship"?* (Frankfurt am Main: Peter Lang, 2005).

29. See Stephan Grigat and Florian Markl, "Österreichische Normalität. Postfaschismus, Postnazismus und der Aufstieg der Freiheitlichen Partei Österreichs unter Jörg Haider," in *Postnazismus revisited. Das Nachleben des Nationalsozialismus im 21. Jahrhundert*, ed. Stephan Grigat, 229–250 (Freiburg: Ça Ira, 2012).

30. For an overview of Austrian-Israeli relations, see Helga Embacher and Margit Reiter, *Gratwanderungen. Die Beziehungen zwischen Österreich und Israel im Schatten der Vergangenheit* (Wien: Picus, 1998).

31. See Rolf Schleyer, "'Wir haben da Zusagen gemacht.' Anmerkungen zu den deutsch-israelischen Beziehungen," in *Insel der Aufklärung. Israel im Kontext*, ed. Alexandra Kurth (Giessen: NBKK, 2005), 113.

32. Quoted by Michael Wolffsohn, "Ohne Hitler kein Israel. Der Staat der Juden und die Deutschen," *Der Spiegel*, February 2, 1992, http://www.spiegel.de/spiegel/spiegelspecial/d-52498300.html.

33. See Gerhard Schweizer, *Iran. Drehscheibe zwischen Ost und West* (Stuttgart: Klett-Cotta, 1991), 405.

34. See Götz Aly, "Ehre für Fritz Schröder," *Süddeutsche Zeitung*, May 17, 2010, http://www.sueddeutsche.de/politik/der-kanzler-am-grab-seines -vaters-ehre-fuer-fritz-schroeder-1.417128.

35. Georg Hoffmann-Ostenhof, "Dr. Seltsam. Wer hat Angst vor Mahmoud Ahmadinejad?," *Profil* 40 (2007).

36. See Gudrun Harrer, "Im Dschungel der iranischen Politik," *Der Standard*, March 14, 2008, http://derstandard.at/3263844/Analyse-Im-Dschun gel-der-iranischen-Politik, "Tehran Defeated Enemies Iranophobia Campaign," December 18, 2013, http://www.presstv.ir/detail/2013/12/18/340598 /tehran-defeated-iranophobia-campaign/. The term Iranophobia was first used by a left-wing Israeli scholar, Haggai Ram, *Iranophobia: The Logic of an Israeli Obsession* (Stanford, Calif.: Stanford University Press, 2009).

37. Michael Pröbsting, "Zu den Waffen! U.S.A. und Israel drohen mit neuen Krieg gegen den Iran," August 27, 2007, http://www.arbeiterin nenstandpunkt.net/, last accessed October 10, 2007.

38. Muriel Asseburg, "Wie weiter nach der Waffenruhe?," *Internationale Politik*, September 2006, 104f.

39. Volker Perthes, *Iran. Eine politische Herausforderung* (Frankfurt am Main: Suhrkamp, 2008), 121.

40. Georg Hoffmann-Ostenhof, "Aufwind für die Tauben. Entwarnung an der Iran-Front," *Profil* 50 (2007); Michael Lüders, *Iran: Der falsche Krieg. Wie der Westen seine Zukunft verspielt* (München: C. H. Beck, 2012), 85.

41. Recently, historian Jeffrey Herf again pointed out the antisemitic character of the Iranian regime: "Taking Iran's Anti-Semitism Seriously," June 2, 2014, http://www.the-american-interest.com/articles/2014/06/02 /taking-irans-anti-semitism-seriously/. In Germany, a young scholar recently did the same in her dissertation: Ulrike Marz, *Kritik des islamischen Antisemitismus, Zur gesellschaftlichen Genese und Semantik des Antisemitismus in der Islamischen Republik Iran* (Berlin: Lit, 2014).

42. Christoph Bertram, *Partner, nicht Gegner. Für eine andere Iran-Politik* (Hamburg: Edition Körber, 2008), 86, 10.

43. See Gerhard Mangott, "Über die Rationalität iranischen Erdgases," *Die Presse,* December 22, 2007.

44. Ibid.

45. Two of these rare examples are Matthias Küntzel, *Deutschland, Iran und die Bombe. Eine Entgegnung—auch auf Günter Grass* (Münster: Lit, 2012), and Wahied Wahdat-Hagh, *Der islamistische Totalitarismus. Über Antisemitismus, Anti-Bahaismus, Christenverfolgung und geschlechtsspezifische Apartheid in der "Islamischen Republik Iran"* (Frankfurt am Main: Peter Lang, 2012).

46. Michael Oren and Yossi Klein Halevi, "Israel's Worst Nightmare," March 22, 2009, http://www.aish.com/jewishissues/middleeast/Israels _Worst_Nightmare.asp. In German, see Michael Oren and Yossi Klein Halevi, "Israels Alptraum. Zur Rezeption der iranischen Gefahr im Staat der Shoahüberlebenden," in *Der Iran—Analyse einer islamischen Diktatur und ihrer europäischen Förderer,* ed. Stephan Grigat and Simone Dinah Hartmann, 90–101 (Innsbruck: Studienverlag, 2008).

47. For examples, see Gerhard Mangott, "Das Interesse Israels," *Die Presse,* September 14, 2007; and Katajun Amirpur, "Religiöse Minderheit unter Druck," *Die Tageszeitung,* February 10, 2009.

48. For example, see Sarah Shokouhbeen, "Die Islamische Republik Iran. Regimestabilität und Atomkonflikt," in *Von Marokko bis Afghanistan. Krieg und Frieden im Nahen und Mittleren Osten,* ed. Jochen Hippler (Hamburg: Konkret Literatur Verlag, 2008), 121.

49. David Menashri, *Post-Revolutionary Politics in Iran. Religion, Society and Power* (New York: Routledge, 2001), 281.

50. Stephan Grigat, "In die Bresche springen. Aktuelle Entwicklungen im österreichischen und schweizerischen Verhältnis zum iranischen Regime," in *Iran im Weltsystem. Bündnisse des Regimes und Perspektiven der Freiheitsbewegung,* ed. Stephan Grigat and Simone Dinah Hartmann, 136–153 (Innsbruck: Studienverlag, 2010). Stephan Grigat and Simone Dinah Hartmann, "Freundschaft statt Freiheit. Warum die Mullahs Deutschland lieben und die Bundesrepublik Israel im Stich lässt," in *Verratene Freiheit.*

Der Aufstand im Iran und die Antwort des Westens, ed. Thomas von der Osten-Sacken et al., 47–73 (Berlin: Verbrecher, 2010).

51. For example, Katajun Amirpur, "Der iranische Schlüsselsatz," May 11, 2010, http://www.sueddeutsche.de/kultur/umstrittenes-zitat-von-ahmadinedschad-der-iranische-schluesselsatz-1.287333.

52. Eric Frey, "Reform und Charakter," June 20, 2013, http://derstandard.at/1371170164099/Reform-und-Charakter. Bahman Nirumand, "Irans neuer Präsident," June 16, 2013, http://www.taz.de/!118223/.

53. Alfred Rosenberg, *Der staatsfeindliche Zionismus* (München: Eher, 1938).

54. Gerhard L. Weinberg, ed., *Hitlers Zweites Buch. Ein Dokument aus dem Jahr 1928* (Stuttgart: DVA, 1961), 220.

55. Tony Judt, "Israel: The Alternative," *New York Review of Books,* October 2003. His essay has been published in German in *Blätter für deutsche und internationale Politik* 12 (2003) and the German edition of *Le Monde diplomatique* 7208 (2003).

56. Micha Brumlik, "Plan B," *Konkret* 7 (2013): 16–20.

57. See Ari Bober, ed., *The Other Israel: The Radical Case against Zionism* (New York: Anchor Books, 1972). In 2013, for the first time the collected writings of a leading *Matzpen* member was published in German: Moshe Machover, *Israelis und Palästinenser—Konflikt und Lösung* (Hamburg: Laika, 2013).

58. Michael Warschawski, *An der Grenze* (Hamburg: Edition Nautilus, 2003). Michael Warschawski, *Mit Höllentempo. Die Krise der israelischen Gesellschaft* (Hamburg: Edition Nautilus, 2004).

59. Moshe Zuckermann: *Zweierlei Israel? Auskünfte eines marxistischen Juden an Thomas Ebermann, Hermann L. Gremliza und Volker Weiß* (Hamburg: Konkret, 2003); "Einleitung. Kritische Theorie in Israel—Analyse einer Nichtrezeption," in *Theodor W. Adorno. Philosoph des beschädigten Lebens,* ed. Moshe Zuckermann (Göttingen: Wallstein, 2004); *Israel—Deutschland—Israel. Reflexionen eines Heimatlosen* (Wien: Passagen, 2006); *Sechzig Jahre Israel. Die Genese einer politischen Krise des Zionismus* (Köln: Pahl Rugenstein, 2009); *"Antisemit!" Ein Vorwurf als Herrschaftsinstrument* (Wien: Promedia, 2010); *Israels Schicksal. Wie der Zionismus seinen Untergang betreibt* (Wien: Promedia, 2014).

60. Judith Butler, *Precarious Life: The Powers of Mourning and Violence* (New York: Verso, 2006), 142, 41.

61. See Andreas Benl, "Delegierte Regression. Der europäische Kulturrelativismus: Eine Form der Kollaboration mit dem Islamismus," in Grigat and Hartmann, *Der Iran,* 246.

62. Judith Butler, *Parting Ways: Jewishness and the Critique of Zionism* (New York: Columbia University Press, 2012), 242. The German edition was published as *Am Scheideweg. Judentum und die Kritik am Zionismus* (Frankfurt am Main: Campus, 2013).

63. Butler, *Parting Ways*, 7, 214.

64. Ibid., 216.

65. Ibid., 208.

66. "'In diesem Kampf gibt es keinen Platz für Rassismus.' Interview mit Judith Butler," July 29, 2010, http://jungle-world.com/artikel/2010 /30/41420.html.

67. Butler, *Parting Ways*, 113.

68. See Simon Erlanger, "'The Anti-Germans'—The Pro-Israel German Left," *Jewish Political Studies Review* 21, no. 1–2 (spring 2009). Stephan Grigat, "'Projektion'—'Überidentifikation'—'Philozionismus.' Der Vorwurf des Philosemitismus an die antideutsche Linke," in *Geliebter Feind— Gehasster Freund. Philosemitismus in Geschichte und Gegenwart*, ed. Irene A. Diekmann and Elke-Vera Kotowski, 467–485 (Berlin: VBB, 2009).

69. Theodor W. Adorno, *Negative Dialectics* (New York: Seabury Press, 1973), 365. The German original is *Negative Dialektik*, vol. 6 of *Gesammelte Schriften* (Frankfurt am Main: Suhrkamp, 1997 [1966]), 358.

Antisemitism and Antiurbanism, Past and Present

Empirical and Theoretical Approaches

BODO KAHMANN

STUDIES ON ANTISEMITISM have highlighted, on several occasions, that modern Jew hatred opposes urbanization and urban
life. Although the importance of antiurban sentiments for antisemitism is highly accepted in the field of antisemitism studies,
there have been very few attempts at developing theoretical and
empirical approaches concerning the relationship of these two
phenomena. The question of the character and origin of antiurbanism, in particular, has been left unanswered. This chapter
seeks to provide some initial theoretical and empirical insights
regarding the relationship between antisemitism and city hatred.
I focus mainly on German history because city and Jew hatred
had its most radical proponents in Germany. The field of German
history is the place where an understanding of antisemitic antiurbanism can most clearly be understood. This applies especially for
the Völkisch and National Socialist movement. The Nazi government's attitude toward modern big cities was the most negative
and radical among all European fascist governments in the 1920s
and 1930s.

The first part of the chapter presents an overview of the development of antiurban and antisemitic thought in Germany from

the 1850s until 1945. The following section explores manifestations of antisemitic city hatred in Germany and Hungary as well as in Islamist ideology after the Holocaust. Finally, the chapter develops a theoretical approach to the connection between antisemitism and antiurbanism. Both theoretical texts and empirical studies that deal with antiurbanism as a social phenomenon and with its causal relationship to modern antisemitism are discussed.

GERMAN ANTISEMITISM AND ANTIURBANISM BEFORE 1945

The tradition of antiurbanism goes back to the 1850s, a time when Germany had only three cities with more than a hundred thousand inhabitants. Antiurbanism first emerged as a coherent ideology in the writings of the folklorist Wilhelm Heinrich Riehl (1823–1897).[1] He became one of the most influential proponents of city hatred in Germany, reaching hundreds of thousands with his texts and speeches. Later antiurbanists regularly referred back to his writings. In his four-volume *Die Naturgeschichte des Volkes als Grundlage einer deutschen Social-Politik,* he formulated the basic arguments against modern city life.[2] At its core, his antiurbanism was an expression of agrarian romanticism that perceived the peasant as a natural conservative element guaranteeing the survival of the German people through high birth rates. Riehl considered large cities, in contrast, as the dark ghost of the social future of Germany.[3] Without actually knowing how the process of urbanization would alter people's lives, he predicted that the rise of cities would cause the decline of society and of the German nation. Riehl's antiurbanism reveals that negative sentiments toward cities are not essentially based on an evaluation of actual living conditions.

A great wave of antiurbanism began to form, as stressed by historian Andrew Lees, in the last decade of the nineteenth century.

Several works, based on demographic arguments concerning the impact of urbanization on the size and health of the German population, were published at that time. They claimed that big cities were unable to effectively reproduce their populations on their own; rather, their survival depended on immigration from the countryside. The most influential social biology books were written by Georg Hansen, a Bavarian statistician, and Otto Ammon (1842–1916), a Social Darwinist with ties to the Völkisch movement, who also influenced later theorists of race.[4] Hansen's *Die drei Bevölkerungsstufen* was published in 1889, and Ammon's main work, *Die Gesellschaftsordnung und ihrer natürlichen Grundlagen,* was released six years later in 1895.[5] Both authors claimed that families who had moved from the countryside to the city would die out within two generations. Robert A. Nye highlights the importance of antiurbanism for social biologists. According to Nye, social biologists shared the belief that city life and disease were linked on a European scale: "Social biologists often disagreed vigorously on the 'positive' and 'negative' effects of war, religion, occupation and race-mixing, but they universally agreed on the generally pathological influence of one social artifact: the city."[6] The assumption that cities exploit the countryside and are unable to survive without it, was an assertion that "became one of the most pervasive and compelling arguments against the city among German antiurbanists of all sorts."[7]

Sociobiologist discourse on cities not only affected Völkisch circles but also figured prominently in the ideas of the alternative Lebensreform movement. The Lebensreformbewegung was established as a counterculture to industrialization and urbanization in Germany. According to historian Wolfgang R. Krabbe, all factions of this movement agreed that the urban population was essentially rootless and had to be reconnected with the soil and nature.[8] The Lebensreformbewegung attempted to develop a temporary escape from cities by creating rural settlements. Historian Ulrich Linse calls this attempt a form of "practical antiurbanism."[9] These settlements were intended to counterbalance the alleged negative impact imposed by urban life rather than to replace the cities. There existed in addition to Völkisch and religiously oriented settlements socialist and anarchist ones. Elements of the radical left showed great interest in establishing rural settlements in order to shape a new society on the basis of a small community. Although antisemitic theories about the alleged urban character of the Jews were also formulated by leftist settlers like eco-socialist Raul Robien,[10] Linse asserts that racism and antisemitism were far more dominant in right-wing antiurbanism.[11] After World War I, the idea of rural settlements became an obsession for youth movements in Germany, including those of Völkisch, religious, socialist, and anarchistic orientations.[12] At the end of the 1920s, Völkisch-oriented settlements made up the majority of such attempts in the German youth movement.

Starting with the Wilhelminian Empire, cities were referred to as "mass graves" or "graves for the race" in sociobiological and demographic discourse in Völkisch thought.[13] The farming community was held up as a counter-ideal to city life and was declared to be the foundation for the survival of the race. The Völkisch ideal of an independent Germany and of the purity and strength of the German race were therefore projected onto the countryside and farming life. It was argued that Germans, both by nature and according to history, were not city dwellers and would eventually perish if they were to become urbanized. The most influential group opposing urbanization and rural depopulation was the so-called Artamanen. Founded by Bruno Tanzmann in the 1920s, the Artamanen was a part of the Weimar Republic's youth movement. Its main goal was to create rural settlements in the eastern part of Germany in order to replace and expel Polish migrant workers. The peasant settlements were to be run by city dwellers doing voluntary fatigue duty. The Artamanen sought expansion beyond Germany's eastern borders. The anti-Slavic, antiurban, and imperialist ideology of the Artamanen was later adapted for the SS by Heinrich Himmler, who was a member of the Artamanen (alongside other Nazi leaders).[14]

The supposed bond Germans had with the soil and with agricultural life was in direct contrast to the alleged urban character of the Jews. Voelkisch and Nazi authors were not the only ones who claimed that Jews had always been urban people; antisemites maintained that Jews lacked the ability to connect to the mother soil, characterizing them as rootless and cosmopolitan. In contrast to Germans, Jews were seen as capable of living and reproducing in the concrete environment of large cities. Unlike the "northern race," they were able to successfully exist in an urban setting because city life did not impact their health negatively. Nazi writer Hans F. K. Günther, a leading theorist of race, claimed that Jews were the only group able to survive in cities.[15] His *Urbanization* was one of the most important antiurban works published in the Third Reich. Jews were also accused of being hostile toward farmers. According to Völkisch and Nazi writings, Jews aimed to destroy the farming community in order to weaken the "Aryan race." Thus, by destroying or denying the rural origin of Germans, Jews were supposedly attempting to uproot and urbanize the whole of the German population. The conclusion that followed placed Jews at the center of urbanization in that they were both responsible for and benefitted from the growth of cities. Richard Walther Darré (1895–1953), Reichsminister of Food and Agriculture, for instance, referred regularly to this kind of argument.[16]

All aspects of modern urban life were identified as "Jewish." In antisemitic texts, the German word "Asphalt" became a synonym for both big cities and Jews. It was juxtaposed with the notion of soil and supposedly expressed the rootlessness of the urban population, especially the rootlessness of the Jew as a city dweller par excellence. Antisemites created neologisms by linking the term to phenomena they associated with Jews and with city life. Common expressions were "asphalt democracy," "asphalt novelist," or "asphalt press." In the context of right-wing agitation, the term "Asphalt" received an antisemitic, antiurban, and anti-intellectual connotation.[17] Antiurbanism therefore became part of a specific antiliberal and antidemocratic culture symbolized by antisemitism. In this regard, antiurbanism can be seen as part of a culture for which antisemitism served as a cultural code—as described by Shulamit Volkov.[18]

Negative remarks about Jews and modern city life can be found in the texts of prominent National Socialists, including Alfred Rosenberg, Joseph Goebbels, Richard Walther Darré, and Heinrich Himmler. Although there are many examples of antiurbanism in the writings of prominent Nazi thinkers, the National Socialist movement's attitude toward big cities is often described as ambivalent or even contradictory. On the one hand, the antiurban blood-and-soil-ideology affected urban planning in the Third Reich: Urban development, particularly in the first three years after 1933, was guided by the ideal of rural and suburban settlements for the working class. These settlements were to provide every German family with a house and garden, strengthening the rural origin of the "Aryan race" by reconnecting the urban population with the soil. The establishment of such settlements must be seen in the context of serious attempts at spatial ruralization of German cities as well as a decentralization of industry.[19] These efforts were accompanied by propaganda that idealized small-town life, depicting the small town as a perfect Nazi community. The state-controlled leisure organization Kraft durch Freude (KdF, Strength through Joy) arranged trips to Rothenburg ob der Tauber, a Bavarian town that served as a symbol for Germany's medieval history. Joshua Hagen emphasizes that since the foundation of the German Reich in 1871 the town appeared "as a living relic of medieval Germany and quickly evolved into a romanticized symbol of rootedness, community, and continuity with this perceived golden age of national greatness."[20]

In 1936 there was a shift in the politics of settlement. Although Nazi propaganda continued the ideal of a deep-rooted life in settlements outside the city, urban planning was focused on the creation of cheap apartments, which fit the demands of the war industry. In October 1937, the Nazi government enacted a law for the re-creation of German cities (Gesetz zur Neugestaltung deutscher Städte). The Nazis intended to construct massive buildings as a symbol of the NSDAP's universal power. The most well-known examples were plans to reshape Berlin as the world capital "Germania." At first glance, the Third Reich's intention to build a huge metropolis may seem to contradict efforts at ruralization; Dieter Münk, however, emphasizes that in this context the quantitatively oriented concept of National Socialist big cities lacked a specific urban quality.[21] Klaus Bergmann makes the same point when he argues that the Nazis tried to destroy the form and character of the modern metropolis, which was considered responsible for negative developments such as liberalism and Marxism.[22] According to Robert A. Taylor, Berlin should be turned into an oversized garden city.[23] The Nazi government's ideology concerning the creation of a monumental city must therefore also be seen as an expression of antiurbanism. The idea of redesigning cities following a reactionary agenda can be understood in reference to the term "reactionary modernism" coined by Jeffrey Herf.[24] Here, idealization of small-town life is not inconsistent with plans for the creation of a mega city. Taylor stated that "not only major cities, but small villages as well, were to express the achievement and the nature of the German people."[25] This is how both concepts were able to coexist without being contradictory. Antisemitism was the common basis for the Nazi attitude toward modern big cities: all National Socialists shared the belief that the modern metropolis represented ideas marked as "Jewish" such as liberalism, Marxism, cosmopolitism, or parliamentarianism.

In this regard, one can criticize some theoretical approaches in the literature about antiurbanism and National Socialism;

the thesis that the Nazis did not adapt an antiurban agenda after coming into power should be rejected.[26] The agitation against big cities before 1933 was far more than just an ideological veneer. George L. Mosse argued that the antiurbanism of the Nazis ended when German cities were destroyed during World War II. The experience altered Völkisch thought, and cities were perceived as being equal in importance to rural life.[27] This view is problematic, however, because it implies that Völkisch and Nazi thought rejected cities in general. Hillel J. Kieval is correct in his criticism when he states that Mosse adapted the self-manifestation of the Völkisch movement as a rural movement that attacked cities from the outside.[28] Bernhard Marchand also argues that the Nazis abandoned their antiurbanism during the war. According to him, the Nazis had no reason to hate cities following the deportation of German Jews.[29] This approach presents two problems, however. First, it overlooks Nazi attempts to re-create German cities because of their perceived hatred towards modern metropolises. In Marchand's view, the Nazis did not hate cities for their representation of modernity and liberalism; they loathed the Jewish population living in these cities. This leads to the second point: modern anti-Semitism is not a function of the actual living conditions of Jews. The connection between antisemitism and antiurbanism cannot be explained exclusively by an actual Jewish presence in urban areas. This approach misses the complexity of modern antisemitism.

POST-HOLOCAUST ANTISEMITIC ANTIURBANISM

Following the Holocaust, neither antisemitism nor antiurbanism disappeared from Germany's political culture. Fear and loathing toward cities coupled with an idealization of country and peasant life persisted in the cultural memory of many Germans. The most radical proponents of racist, antisemitic city hatred developed in the Federal Republic, once again within far-right extremism.

Negative statements about city life as well as positive sentiments toward peasant life can be found among different factions of the German far-right scene.

Antiurbanism became especially dominant and characteristic of a part of the movement known as eco-fascism or brown ecology.[30] City hatred plays a crucial role in radical ecological thinking in general, with cities serving as both a symbol for and the most visible symptom of life detached from nature.[31] Ecological antiurbanists thus seek a decentralization of cities into small living units intended to restore a symbiotic relationship between nature and humanity. The most influential of the "brown ecology" groups was the Independent Ecologist of Germany (Unabhängige Ökologen Deutschlands). Founded in 1991, the group supports a racist and antiurban program. One of its founders, Baldur Springmann (1912–2003), was a member of the Sturmabteilung (SA) and self-proclaimed eco-peasant. Springmann was highly influential in the German ecological movement of the 1970s and 1980s. He participated in the foundation of the Green Party in 1980 but left it shortly thereafter because the party lacked a nationalistic orientation. He wrote a book detailing his beliefs and experience as a peasant, which was briefly sold by the publishing house of the neo-Nazi party, National Democrats of Germany (NPD). In his book, Spingmann combines his radical antiurbanism with nationalism, racism, and spirituality.[32]

Antiurbanism is an integral part of the beliefs of German new-age and neo-pagan Völkisch groups. In 2009 the Völkisch and esoteric religious group Die Artgemeinschaft—GGG republished Günther's *Urbanization,* an antisemitic and antiurban book. Jürgen Rieger, an influential neo-Nazi and head of the Artgemeinschaft until his death in 2009, stated, in response to why the book was being sold, that cities embodied an environment threatening children and the life of the "Nordic race."[33] Rieger was also well-known for his attempts to create rural facilities for racist purposes. He sought to revitalize the idea of the SS-Lebensborn association of the Third Reich in order to increase the birth rate of the "Aryan race."

The belief that life in rural settlements or small villages—far away from urban areas—can strengthen resilience against the negative influences of modern society is still upheld in neo-Nazi writings and practices. In fact, recent years saw renewed efforts in neo-Völkisch circles to adapt the Artamanen idea of founding rural settlements. In the 1960s a so-called Circle of Friends of the Artamanen was launched to maintain contacts and provide a positive image of Artamanen activity in the Weimar Republic. Upon the circle's dissolution in 2001, right-wing families began making arrangements to buy farm land in the eastern parts of Germany, especially in the state of Mecklenburg-Vorpommern.[34] In 2010, Stephan Jurisch, a neo-Nazi, published an article titled "The Return" in a magazine with ties to the NPD in which he cites the Artamanen as an example of an alternative way of life. He calls for the creation of a peasant settlement in eastern Germany.[35] The importance that the idealization of the farming community has for the ideology of the NPD is indicated by its party platform. The latest program of 2013 calls for state protection for the farming community because of its economic and cultural importance.[36] It is therefore not surprising that leading party thinkers refer to antisemitic and antiurban arguments of the Völkisch and Nazi movements. In 2007, Jürgen Gansel, a member of the NPD, published a text that unified central antisemitic theses concerning urbanization and the character of rural and small town life.[37] Gansel describes globalization as a threat because it causes urbanization. The decline of nonurban areas supposedly weakens the German populace since, compared to city dwellers, people who live in villages or small towns are more resistant to the negative influences imposed by globalization. Rural people, Gansel writes, are more aware of the threats facing the German population as they are the last group to remain rooted in the soil and to still live within the strong boundaries

of a local community (Gemeinschaft). Conversely, inhabitants
of urban areas are rootless, suffering from a lack of identity and
an inability to integrate into a community, leaving them open to
the "anti-national" forces of globalization. Gansel also claims that
"a certain group" benefits from this process of urbanization; he
calls this group the "globalists from the East Coast of the United
States." The "East Coast" is a common antisemitic code for Jews.
Gansel combines basic arguments of antisemitic antiurbanism
by asserting that Germans were weakened by urbanization and
that Jews took advantage of this process in order to destroy and
control the German population.

The connection between antisemitism and antiurbanism does
not exist exclusively in Germany. A tradition of anti-Jewish city
hatred can be found in other countries, as well. A comparable
history of hatred toward Jews and urban life exists in Hungary.
According to Magdalena Marsovszky, a political scientist, antiurbanism remains an integral part of nationalism in Hungary.
Budapest, the country's capital, is the focus of hate; it is considered "not Hungarian" in contrast to the rest of the country.[38] The
stereotype concerning the sinful character of cities in general and
of Budapest in particular can be traced back to the literature of the
late nineteenth century. In the time between the world wars, antiurbanism found its expression in a dispute between two groups
of literary figures.[39] The so-called Völkischen idealized the rural
population and hated the city on account of its allegedly sinful
character. The so-called Urban identified themselves as cosmopolitan and pro-Western. The result of the dispute, a semantic
equation between "urban" and "Jewish," did not disappear during
socialist times, and the antisemitic stereotype of the decadence
of the urban way of life, especially with regard to Budapest, was
revitalized in 1998 by the first Orbán administration. The existence of radical antiurbanism in Hungarian Völkisch thought
recently surfaced in the antisemitic propaganda of the right-wing

extremist Jobbik Party. Adapting an antisemitic slur, first used by Karl Luegner (1844–1910), the antisemitic mayor of Vienna, the Jobbik Party uses the German neologism "Judapest" to refer to Budapest. The term is meant to express the antisemitic idea that the modern metropolis has a "Jewish character" and is based on a perceived "Jewish principle."

The stereotype of the sinful city as well as the association of Jews with money, commerce, and large urban areas played a crucial part in the ideology behind the terror attacks in the United States on 9/11. Ian Buruma and Avishai Margalit believe that negative sentiments about the city are a basic element of anti-Western ideology, which they call Occidentalism. Identification of modern city life with the West in general and with the United States and the Jews in particular originated in Western thought and was adapted by political and religious movements in the non-Western world. The spectrum of movements that adapted antiurban ideas spans from the Khmer Rouge to jihadist circles. They all see the modern city as a symbol of the renunciation of a divine or native-traditional order. Write Buruma and Margalit: "Hubris, empire building, secularism and the power and attraction of money—all these are connected to the idea of the sinful City of Man."[40] The fact that the 9/11 attacks had an antisemitic background is not surprising: Abdul Rahman Yasin, who participated in the first terror attack on the World Trade Center in 1993, admitted in an interview that the Twin Towers were chosen because he and his partner were convinced that a majority of the employees were Jews.[41] Another horrific example of Islamic antiurbanism can be seen in the terrorist attacks on the Indian city of Mumbai, which caused the loss of 174 lives. Mumbai, as the center of both commerce and the movie industry, is regularly referred to as the most Western city in India. During the attacks, a group of terrorists assaulted a Jewish community center and murdered a rabbi and his wife.

THEORETICAL AND EMPIRICAL APPROACHES
TO ANTISEMITISM AND ANTIURBANISM

When seeking a theoretical approach to the connection between antisemitism and antiurbanism, one soon realizes that theories about antisemitism do not include many references to this subject. One exception is an essay written in 1948 by sociologist Arnold Rose, entitled *Antisemitism's Root in City-Hatred*, in which Rose asserts that antisemitism is based on hatred toward life in the metropolis. He claims that "Jews are hated today [. . .], primarily because they serve as a symbol of city life." They are not associated with sexual desirability like African Americans, but with traits referring to city life: "Rather the Jews are associated with economic success, political radicalism, and quick adaptiveness to a rapidly changing world. Historically such traits are connected with life in cities, and so are the Jews. The Jews are the urban people *par excellence.*"[42] Rose highlights that the association of Jews with city life is based not merely on hatred but also on envy. For Rose, emotions that form the basis of prejudices generally arise from hatred and fear, as well as envy and desire; prejudice is predicated on the projection of unattainable desires onto groups, which results in relief from a mental conflict. Furthermore, he states that this is why attitudes about a group that is a symbol of something that is both hated and loved can change without questioning symbolic identification. The antisemitic identification of Jews with life in cites can therefore change into philosemitic attitudes. Rose's theory has certain similarities to the social psychological approaches to antisemitism proposed by the critical theory or Frankfurt School. In his study *Prophets of Deceit,* published in 1949, sociologist Leo Löwenthal referred to the same psychological processes, while also declaring that antisemitism includes both hatred and envy.[43]

In the case of antisemitism, Rose states that people admire cities while simultaneously hating and fearing them. They hate cities because they cannot adjust to them, or—if they are successful—they feel that adjusting to them is immoral. For these people, the Jews became a symbol of undeserved and perfect acclimatization to city life. According to Rose, Jews are associated with urban life and therefore envied by antisemites because of the historical connection between Jews and urbanity: anti-Jewish laws imposed in Europe in the Middle Ages forced Jews to live within city boundaries and to choose professions that bound them to urban life. As a result, Jews had a head start within the rise of capitalist society. Such generalizations are problematic, however. Rose's historical remarks, for instance, do not apply to the urbanization history of German Jewry. From the late Middle Ages until the nineteenth century, the majority of German Jews, especially in the south, lived in small villages (*Landjudentum*). A rapid urbanization of German Jewry occurred around 1871, when legal restrictions were retracted.[44] In this context, Hillel Kieval opposes the view that the presence and stake of Jews "in urban culture has been so high as to render them the symbolic equivalent of the city itself."[45]

Rose's theoretical approach does not focus on the Jewish contribution to urban life as an explanation of antisemitic city hatred. He points out that antisemitism emerges from a mental conflict; antisemites project their mixed feelings about the city onto Jews, leaving the city itself untouched. Those who fear and hate the city can thus still be urban residents: "The symbolic projection of hatred of the city onto Jews allows the prejudiced person to destroy the city and to escape the city, and at the same time to keep it and live in it."[46] Hence antiurbanism, for Rose, is a phenomenon that occurs primarily among city dwellers.

In a book on the culture and politics of antiurbanism, sociologist Michael J. Thompson develops a totally different approach to antiurbanism's theoretical understanding. He argues that hatred toward cities depends on a nonurban socialization, and highlights the impact of spatial factors on the mental constitution of subjects: "The link between the material/spatial organization of society and the experiential and mental organization of the subjects that inhabit it is therefore the place where an understanding of antiurbanism can be most clearly understood. [...] I think that the spatial organization of nonurban life is a central explanatory variable leading to distinct attitudes and sensibilities that shape certain cognitive (specifically social) views toward urban areas."[47] The assertion of a direct causality between spatial structure and cognitive constitution is highly controversial in social science, especially in the field of urban studies. Many authors have stressed that differences in political attitudes and lifestyle segmentation that separate city life from rural life cannot simply be traced back to different spatial organization. Further empirical research is required in order to ascertain whether these effects are not simply a result of people with liberal attitudes being attracted to urban areas. Thompson's argument also lacks empirical proof in other respects: an overwhelming majority of antiurban movements had their origin within the metropolis; members of rural settlements came from cities; antiurban literature was successful especially in large cities. Antiurbanism then cannot be understood with reference to an actual rural-urban divide. Existing differences between urban and rural areas have a low impact on the constitution of antiurban thought. The disparity between urban and rural life has doubtlessly shrunk since industrialization. The question, however, is to what extent. In his famous 1938 article "Urbanism as a Way of Life," sociologist Louis Wirth stated that urbanity was no longer bound to life in the big cities.[48] Thus, for some social scientists, antiurbanism disappeared as the urban way of life spread into rural areas. *The Oxford Dictionary of Sociology* gives the following definition under the term *antiurbanism*: "Contemporary sociology largely rejects anti-urbanism. It is now generally recognized that the growth of cities, and the varied forms of social association occurring within them, are both consequences of the emergence of modern industrial societies."[49]

This definition is unconvincing when applied to the development of antiurban thought in Germany. Antiurbanism reached its peak at the end of the 1920s and in the 1930s when the Nazis came to power. The initial process of urbanization and industrialization was accomplished at that time. Large cities remained a target of hate beyond the process of transformation from an agricultural to a modern industrial society.

The claim that city life is merely a mirror for modern social life emphasizes that the traits Rose mentions can hardly be considered specific for city life; rather, they can be recognized as characterizing modern society itself. Economic success, political radicalism, and quick adaptation to a rapidly changing world are not applicable exclusively to life in the metropolis. The crucial point, however, is that this reality does not affect the perception of city life as an antithesis of rural life. Although the distinction between urban and nonurban areas has decreased in importance, the big cities have been a target of hatred and fear throughout the twentieth century until the present day.

In an ethnographic study, anthropologist Susanne Spülbeck provided empirical proof for Rose's assumption that Jews are associated with traits that are considered urban. Shortly after Germany's reunification, a group of Jewish refugees from the Soviet Union was housed in a refugee home located in a village in eastern Germany. At the same time, another group of refugees arrived in the village. This group belonged to a so-called ethnic German minority in eastern Europe. Spülbeck spent several weeks in the village in order to study how the locals reacted to the temporary housing of Jewish refugees. One of her basic insights was that the Jews were considered city dwellers, whereas the other group of refugees was regarded as rural folk. The two groups were seen in a distinct light and were ascribed contrary traits: The Jews, as city dwellers, were described as egoistic and rootless. The eastern European ethnic Germans, in contrast, were described as honest, rooted in the soil, and hardworking. Spülbeck explains this association of Jews with urbanity by means of an ideological connection between the identification of Jews with money and trade and their perception as city dwellers. With respect to this connection, she writes: "In Winterfeld [the name of the village] the discourse about the urbanity of Jews from the former Soviet Union was bound to the old stereotype of the 'rich Jew' and the 'Jew as merchant' as an explanation for their urban lifestyle. The reference to the rural-urban-divide and its anti-Semitic content was evident because another group of strangers appeared at the same time. This group [ethnic Germans], whose traits were defined by their non-Jewish and rural origin, were put in contrast to the Jews."[50] In this case, the antisemitic ascription of an urban character is detached from the question of whether the members of the group actually lived in cities. It is characteristic of antiurban sentiments that the attribute of being urban is seen ontologically. There is a lot of empirical evidence indicating that Jews are accused of leading an urban lifestyle regardless of whether they live in cities or rural areas. The second basic insight of Spülbeck's empirical study concerns the link between the personification of the sphere of economic circulation as Jewish, as described by Moishe Postone's theory, and the perception of Jews as representatives of urbanity.[51]

Völkisch and Nazi authors allege that Jews are urban because they have no bond to the soil. Rather, antisemites see Jews as rootless, mobile, universal, and intangible. Postone shows that these are characteristics of the value dimension of the social forms analyzed by Marx. In antisemitic and antiurban thought, the characteristics of value are contrasted with the ideal of rural and peasant life. Money, economy, and commerce are identified with large urban areas; the financial sector does not appear to be organically rooted and concrete and is therefore considered urban. In contrast to the financial sector, Postone argues, technology and industrial capitalism are seen by antisemites as an integral part of the blood-and-soil-ideology. Jeffrey Herf called attention to the fact that influential conservative thinkers in 1920s Germany, such as Ernst Jünger, Werner Sombart, and Oswald Spengler, admired technology and industrial capitalism while simultaneously detesting the modern metropolis, especially Berlin, as a symbol of cosmopolitism and liberalism.[52] For this reason, most far-right and antisemitic antiurbanism is not primarily focused on hatred toward technology or industrial capitalism. The Third Reich's early attempts at a spatial ruralization of German cities along with its plans to decentralize industry show that the Nazis' blood-and-soil-ideology aimed to integrate the idea of industrial capitalism. Günther's book, *Urbanization,* stresses that his statements against big cities should not be understood as an expression of hostility toward German industry and the German worker in general, as long as they are part of blood-and-soil-ideology.[53] Antiurbanism in its most common manifestation should therefore not be confused with simple antimodernism. One of the main reasons for antiurban antisemitism must be seen in the association of urban life with financial capital.

The connection between urban life and the modern money economy was popularized by Oswald Spengler (1880–1936) in his famous *The Decline of the West,* published at the end of World War I.[54] Spengler drew a distinction between rural life, rooted in the soil with an economy characterized by commodities, and a rootless life in the large city, based on the modern money economy.[55] Although Spengler rejected the racist antisemitism of the Nazis, his writings influenced Völkisch and Nazi ideology, especially with regard to the terms in which antiurbanism is expressed. For Spengler, a finance-based economy is a social phenomenon that appears exclusively in the city. Spengler views money as abstract and artificial, in contrast to the soil, which is tangible and concrete. As a result, the peasant, living symbiotically with the soil, has no relationship with money. Furthermore, Spengler claims that people in the countryside think in terms of commodities, while people in cities think in terms of money. He even goes so far as to declare that the difference between peasants and members of the urban middle class is based not only on the distinction between countryside and city but also on commodity and money.

Spengler's claims had a major impact on the antisemitic antiurbanism of the Nazi movement. The peasant was, and still is, upheld as the counterimage of the Jew. The association of rootlessness, money, and urbanity is projected onto Jews. This opposition is found not only in antisemitic texts but also in antisemitic caricatures. In her study of cartoons found in the Nazi newspaper *Der Stürmer*, Dorota Gornik showed that the skyline of New York City was frequently used as a symbol for the city.[56] By means of this image, Nazi cartoonists tried to illustrate the connection they had created between urbanity and Jews. The cartoons of *Der Stürmer* depicting the city of New York all have the same structure: they show a stockbroker, usually referred to as a "Wallstreet-Jud," who appears to be floating above New York's skyline—a figure definitely not rooted in soil. Moreover, the cartoons are full of references to the world of finance and commerce.

ANTISEMITIC HATRED OF NEW YORK CITY

It is not surprising that neo-Nazis and antisemites all over the world welcomed the terror attacks of 9/11, even before the first antisemitic conspiracy theories were formulated.[57] Hatred of New York City has a long tradition among members of the far right in Germany. It can be traced back to Oswald Spengler's book, *The Decline of the West*, in which he sought to establish a connection between the decline of Western societies and the growth of cities. He alleged that this development would be irreversible once cities became cosmopolitan metropolises (*Weltstadt*)—in the end, all cities would be virtually indistinguishable.

According to Spengler, there was always one city that served as an example for all others—in modern times this is the city of New York. The rise of New York City to the status of a global metropolis in the aftermath of the U.S. Civil War is described by Spengler as the most important event of the nineteenth century. Following Spengler's work, New York City has regularly served as a negative example of urban development in the writings of antiurbanists. Spengler had a particularly strong influence on Alfred Rosenberg, despite Rosenberg's criticism of Spengler. In his main work, *Der Mythus des 20 Jahrhunderts,* Rosenberg regards the uncontrolled growth of German cities, following the model of New York City, as a major threat. Consequently, he suggests limiting the size of urban populations, with only a few cities permitted a half million inhabitants at most.[58]

Hatred of New York City also reveals that antiurbanism is a connecting element between antisemitism and anti-Americanism. Both Jews and Americans are considered to be rootless and thus urban, a connection that originates in the association of money and finance capital with the United States.[59] The stereotype concerning the "Jewish character" of New York City belongs to one of the most pervasive beliefs of antisemites the world over.[60]

The economic crisis in 2009 caused a newly negative perception of Wall Street when left-wing and antiglobalization groups like Occupy Wall Street made financial capital responsible for the crisis. It was not surprising that antisemitic incidents occurred during the occupation of Zuccotti Park in Manhattan. Further research is needed to answer the question of whether the movement was also partially dominated by antiurban attitudes. This would be the case if not only Wall Street is described as immoral but also the City of New York and urban life in itself. It is possible that negative images of financial capital are linked by some groups of the antiglobalization movement to negative images of urbanity in general.

Big cities have been an object of hatred since the nineteenth century. In regard to German history, one can conclude that antiurbanism became more radical the more urbanized society became. City hatred therefore cannot be understood as a phenomenon that occurs only during the time of transformation from an agrarian to an industrial state. The image of the farming community as a naturally conservative and nationalistic group, rooted in native soil, was never real. It served in antisemitic discourse as a counterimage of the Jew, who was identified with urban life. With reference to the social psychological approach of Arnold Rose, Jews not only represent what is hated about urbanity but also features that are admired about city life. Jews serve in this context as a symbol for the promises and the allure of urban life because they represent an ability to adapt perfectly to the city. Antisemites project their suppressed fascination with urban life onto Jews. They have the feeling that they cannot successfully adjust to urban settings despite being part of them. This is the reason they experience both hatred and admiration for city life and therefore antipathy and envy for Jews. Antisemitic literature about modern cities reveals the obsessive way antisemites deal with urbanization and urban life.

The examples and empirical studies discussed reveal a link between the personification of the financial sphere as Jews and the perception of Jews as an urban population. This connection can be expressed through the claim that Jews are characterized by urban traits. Jews are therefore seen as urban people par excellence, regardless of whether or not they actually live in cities.[61] In the case of the *Stürmer* cartoons, Jews emerge as an abstract power behind the skylines of the metropolis, creating the appearance of cities as "Jewish" entities. Postone wrote in this respect that "International Jewry" is "perceived to be centered in the 'asphalt jungles' of the newly emergent urban megalipoli, to be behind 'vulgar, materialist, modern culture' and, in general, all forces contributing to the decline of traditional social groupings, values and institutions."[62] Thus the distinction made by antisemites between urban and rural life is based on the perception that rural life is something concrete and that life in the metropolis is characterized by abstract forms of social relationships. This is why big cities are associated with the modern financial economy and intellectualism.

This point is especially important for an understanding of contemporary attacks on New York City, which are still evident in antisemitic propaganda in the Western and non-Western world. The widespread use of the "East Coast" as a code for "international Jewry" refers to the antisemitic belief in the unlimited and global power of money as personified by the Jews. This abstract power is symbolized by the city of New York and by the skyline of Manhattan. Antisemitic images of New York City and Wall Street are based on the identification of Jews with money, commerce, and urbanity. To understand the origins of hatred toward the city of New York, it is necessary to reflect on the history of the connection between antisemitism and antiurbanism.

NOTES

1. Klaus Bergmann, *Agrarromantik und Großstadtfeindschaft* (Meisenheim am Glan: Anton Hain, 1970); Andrew Lees, "Critics of Urban Society in Germany, 1854–1914," *Journal of the History of Ideas* 40, no. 1 (1979): 62; Andrew Lees, *Cities Perceived: Urban Society in American and European Thought, 1820–1940* (Manchester, U.K.: Manchester University Press, 1985).

2. Wilhelm Heinrich Riehl, *Die Naturgeschichte des deutschen Volkes als Grundlage einer deutschen Social-Politik* 4 vols. (Stuttgart: J. G. Cotta, 1851–1869).

3. Wilhelm Heinrich Riehl, *Die Naturgeschichte des deutschen Volkes als Grundlage einer deutschen Social-Politik*, vol. 1, *Land und Leute* (Stuttgart: J.G. Cotta, 1861), 67.

4. Richard Weikart, "Progress through Racial Extermination: Social Darwinism, Eugenics, and Pacifism in Germany, 1860–1918," *German Studies Review* 26, no. 2 (2003): 279–280.

5. Georg Hansen, *Die drei Bevölkerungsstufen. Ein Versuch, die Ursachen für das Blühen und Altern der Völker nachzuweisen* (München: J. Lindauersche Buchhandlung, 1889); Otto Ammon, *Die Gesellschaftsordnung und ihre natürlichen Grundlagen. Entwurf einer Sozial-Anthropologie zum Gebrauch*

für alle Gebildeten, die sich mit sozialen Fragen befassen (Jena: Gustav Fischer Verlag, 1895).

6.   Robert A. Nye, "The Bio-Medical Origins of Urban Sociology," *Journal of Contemporary History* 20, no. 4 (1985): 666.

7.   Lees, *Cities Perceived,* 143.

8.   Wolfgang R. Krabbe, *Gesellschaftsveränderung durch Lebensreform. Strukturmerkmale einer sozialreformerischen Bewegung im Deutschland der Industrialisierungsperiode* (Göttingen: Vandenhoeck & Ruprecht, 1974), 28.

9.   Ulrich Linse, "Antiurbane Bestrebungen in der Weimarer Republik," in *Im Banne der Metropolen. Berlin und London in den zwanziger Jahren,* ed. Peter Alter (Göttingen: Vandenhoeck & Ruprecht, 1993), 314–347.

10.   Ulrich Linse, "Die Anfänge der deutschen Ökologiebewegung," *Arch plus. Zeitschrift für Architektur und Städtebau* 78 (1984): 63–64.

11.   Linse, "Antiurbane Bestrebungen in der Weimarer Republik," 319.

12.   Ulrich Linse, *Zurück, o Mensch, zur Mutter Erde. Landkommunen in Deutschland 1890–1933* (München: DTV, 1983).

13.   Uwe Puschner, *Die völkische Bewegung im wilhelminischen Kaiserreich. Sprache-Rasse-Religion* (Darmstadt: Wissenschaftliche Buchgesellschaft, 2001), 115–119.

14.   Michael H. Kater, "Die Artamanen—Völkische Jugend in der Weimarer Republik," *Historische Zeitschrift* 213 (1971): 577–638.

15.   Hans F. K. Günther, *Die Verstädterung. Ihre Gefahren für Volk und Staat vom Standpunkte der Lebensforschung und der Gesellschaftswissenschaft* (Leipzig: Teubner, 1942), 34.

16.   Richard Walther Darré, *Um Blut und Boden. Reden und Aufsätze* (München: Zentral Verlag der NSDAP, 1940).

17.   Dietz Bering, *Die Intellektuellen. Geschichte eines Schimpfwortes* (Stuttgart: Klett-Cotta, 1978).

18.   Shulamit Volkov, "Antisemitism as a Cultural Code: Reflections on the History and Historiography of Antisemitism in Imperial Germany," *Leo Baeck Institute Year Book* 23, no. 1 (1978): 25–46.

19.   Dieter Münk, *Die Organisation des Raumes im Nationalsozialismus. Eine soziologische Untersuchung ideologisch fundierter Leitbilder in Architektur, Städtebau und Raumplanung des Dritten Reiches* (Bonn: Pahl-Rugenstein, 1993); Tilman Harlander, *Zwischen Heimstätte und Wohnungsmaschine. Wohnungsbau und Wohnungspolitik in der Zeit des Nationalsozialismus* (Basel: Birkäuser, 1995), 39–86; Manfred Walz, "Gegenbilder zur Großstadt. Von den nationalsozialistischen Versuchen zur Auflösung der Stadt bis zu den Wiederaufbauphasen nach 1945," *Stadtbauwelt. Vierteljahresheft der Bauwelt* 71, no. 65 (1980): 473–482.

20. Joshua Hagen, "The Most German of Towns: Creating an Ideal Nazi Community in Rothenburg ob der Tauber," *Annals of the Association of American Geographers* 94, no. 1 (2004): 208.

21. Münk, *Die Organisation des Raumes im Nationalsozialismus,* 334.

22. Bergmann, *Agrarromantik und Großstadtfeindschaft,* 354–360.

23. Robert R. Taylor, *The Word in Stone: The Role of Architecture in the National Socialist Ideology* (Berkley: University of California Press, 1974), 260.

24. Jeffrey Herf, *Reactionary Modernism. Technology, Culture and Politics in Weimar and the Third Reich* (Cambridge: Cambridge University Press, 1987).

25. Taylor, *Word in Stone,* 11.

26. Bernhard Dietz, "Countryside-versus-City in European Thought: German and British Anti-Urbanism between the Wars," *European Legacy: Toward New Paradigms* 13, no. 7 (2008)" 810–811.

27. George L. Mosse, *The Crisis of German Ideology. Intellectual Origins of the Third Reich* (New York: Grosset & Dunlap, 1964), 23.

28. Hillel J. Kieval, "Antisemitism and the City: A Beginner's Guide," in *People of the City: Jews and the Urban Challenge,* ed. Ezra Mendelsohn (New York: Oxford University Press, 1999), 5.

29. Bernhard Marchand, "Nationalsozialismus und Großstadtfeindschaft," *Die alte Stadt. Zeitschrift für Stadtgeschichte, Stadtsoziologie und Denkmalpflege* 26, no. 1 (1999): 49.

30. Jutta Ditfurth, *Entspannt in die Barbarei. Esoterik, (Öko-)Faschismus und Biozentrismus* (Hamburg: Konkret Verlag, 1996), 144.

31. Christoph Laimer, "Antiurbanismus und der Mythos vom natürlichen Leben," *Derivé. Zeitschrift für Stadtforschung,* no. 4 (2001).

32. Baldur Springmann, *Bauer mit Leib und Seele,* vol. 2 (Koblenz: Bublies, 1995).

33. Jürgen Rieger, 2009, http://asatru.de/versand/main_bigware_34.php?bigPfad=22&items_id=86.

34. Stefan Brauckmann, "Nach dem Vorbild der Artamanen: völkische Siedlungsbewegung," *Politische Ökologie* 131 (2012): 52–58; Andreas Speit, "Projekte und Positionen völkischer Ideologie," in *Braune Ökologen. Hintergründe und Strukturen am Beispiel Mecklenburg-Vorpommerns,* ed. Heinrich Böll Stiftung Mecklenburg Vorpommern, 62–75 (Berlin: Heinrich-Böll-Stiftung, 2012).

35. Stephan Jurisch, "Rückkehr—Die Artamanenbewegung als Beispiel alternativer Lebensgestaltung," *Hier & Jetzt. Radikal Rechte Zeitung,* 2010.

36. NPD Parteiprogramm, 2010, http://npd.de/inhalte/daten/dateiablage/br_parteiprogramm_a4.pdf.

37. Jürgen Gansel, "Der Globalisierungs-Angriff auf den ländlichen Raum," 2007, http://www.ab-rhein-neckar.de/frankfurt/dateien/unter seiten/hintergrund/artikel/globalisierungsangriff.html.

38. Magdalena Marsovzky, "Antisemitismus in Ungarn nach 1989. De-mokratiedefizit und kulturpolitische Herausforderung für Europa," 2005, http://www.zeithistorische-forschungen.de/zol/_rainbow/documents /pdf/asm_oeu/marsovszky_asm.pdf, 10.

39. Magdalena Marsovzky, "Neue völkische Bewegung und Antisemitis-mus in Ungarn," in *Minderheitenkonflikte in Europa. Fallbeispiele und Lösung-sansätze*, ed. Samuel Salzborn (Innsbruck: Studien Verlag, 2006), 201–222.

40. Ian Buruma and Avishai Margalit, *Occidentalism: The West in the Eyes of Its Enemies* (New York: Penguin Books, 2004), 16.

41. Matthias Küntzel, *Djihad und Judenhaß. Über den neuen antijüdischen Krieg* (Freiburg: Ça Ira Verlag, 2003), 128–129.

42. Arnold M. Rose, "Antisemitism's Root in City-Hatred. A Clue to the Jew's Position as Scapegoat," *Commentary* 3, no. 6 (1948): 376, 375.

43. Leo Löwenthal and Norbert Gutermann, *Prophets of Deceit: A Study of the Techniques of the American Agitator* (New York: Harper, 1949).

44. Steven M. Lovenstein, "The Rural Community and the Urbaniza-tion of German Jewry," *Central European History* 8, no. 1 (1980): 218–235; Monika Richarz, "Landjuden—ein bürgerliches Element im Dorf?," in *Idylle oder Aufbruch? Das Dorf im bürgerlichen 19. Jahrhundert. Ein euro-päischer Vergleich*, ed. Wolfgang Jacobeit, Josef Mooser, and Bo Strath, 181–190 (Berlin: Akademie Verlag, 1990); Monika Richarz, "Vom Land in die Stadt. Aspekte der Urbanisierung deutscher Juden im 19. Jahrhundert," in *Juden in der Stadt*, ed. Fritz Mayrhofer, 327–339 (Linz: Österreich. Arbe-itskreis für Stadtgeschichtsforschung, 1999).

45. Kieval, "Antisemitism and the City," 4.

46. Rose, "Antisemitism's Root in City-Hatred," 377.

47. Michael J. Thompson, "What Is Antiurbanism? A Theoretical Per-spective," in *Fleeing the City: Studies in the Culture and Politics of Antiurban-ism*, ed. Michael J. Thompson, 9–34 (New York: Palgrave Macmillan, 2009).

48. Louis Wirth, "Urbanism as a Way of Life," *American Journal of Soci-ology* 44, no. 1 (1938): 14.

49. John Scott and Gordon Marshall, "Anti-Urbanism," *A Dictionary of Sociology* (Oxford: Oxford University Press, 2009), http://www.oxford reference.com/view/10.1093/oi/authority.20110803095417637.

50. Susanne Spülbeck, *Ordnung und Angst. Russische Juden aus der Sicht eines ostdeutschen Dorfes nach der Wende: Eine ethnologische Studie* (Frank-furt, New York: Campus, 1997), 134–135. My translation.

51. Moishe Postone, "Anti-Semitism and National Socialism: Notes on the German Reaction to 'Holocaust,'" *New German Critique* 19, special issue 1, *Germans and Jews 1980*, 97–115.

52. Jeffrey Herf, "Reaktionäre Modernisten und Berlin. Die Ablehnung der kosmopolitischen Metropole," in *Im Banne der Metropolen. Berlin und London in den zwanziger Jahren*, ed. Peter Alter, 237–285 (Göttingen: Vandenhoeck & Ruprecht, 1993).

53. Günther, *Die Verstädterung*, 47.

54. Oswald Spengler, *The Decline of the West* (New York: Oxford University Press, 1991).

55. The sociologist Georg Simmel also asserted in his famous essay "The Metropolis and Mental Life" that urban economy is characterized by modern money economy. Unlike Spengler and other antiurbanists, he did not see an insuperable contrast between urban life and rural life. He saw the metropolis as a place to study and analyze social developments. Georg Simmel, "The Metropolis and Mental Life," in *The Sociology of Georg Simmel*, ed. K. H. Wolff, 409–424 (New York: Free Press, 1957).

56. Dorota Gornik, *Anstiftung zum Hass. Antiamerikanismus in den Karikaturen des Stürmers während des 2. Weltkrieges* (Saarbrücken: VDM Müller, 2007).

57. Mark Weitzmann, "Antisemitismus und Holocaust-Leugnung: Permanente Elemente des globalen Rechtsextremismus," in *Globalisierter Rechtsextremismus? Die extremistische Rechte in der Ära der Globalisierung*, ed. Thomas Greven and Thomas Grumke (Wiesbaden: VS Verlag, 2006); Anton Maegerle, *Globalisierung aus Sicht der extremen Rechten* (Braunschweig: Bildungsvereinigung Arbeit Und Leben Niedersachsen, 2005), 32–68.

58. Alfred Rosenberg, *Der Mythus des 20. Jahrhunderts. Eine Wertung der seelisch-geistigen Gestaltungskämpfe unserer Zeit* (München: Hoheneichen-Verlag, 1934), 550–558.

59. Bodo Kahmann, "Antiurbanismus und Antisemitismus. Zur Geschichte und Aktualität eines innigen Verhältnisses," *Tribüne. Zeitschrift zum Verständnis des Judentums* 50, no. 197 (2011): 108–115.

60. Andrei S. Markovits, *Amerika, dich haßt sichs besser. Antiamerikanismus und Antisemitismus in Europa* (Hamburg: Konkret Verlag, 2008), 90–91.

61. Joachim Schlör, "Der Urbantyp. Stadtbewohner par excellence," in *Antisemitismus. Vorurteile und Mythen*, ed. Julius H. Schoeps and Joachim Schlör, 229–240 (München: Piper, 1995).

62. Postone, "Anti-Semitism and National Socialism," 106.

EIGHTEEN

Tehran's Efforts to Mobilize Antisemitism

The Global Impact

MATTHIAS KÜNTZEL

MORE JEWS live in Iran than in any other Muslim country in the world. Its leadership insists that it is not antisemitic but a friend of the Jews. "My colleagues and I are telling the world that Iran is opposed to antisemitism and genocide," emphasized Foreign Minister Mohammad Zarif in May 2014.[1] Well-known critics of the Islamic regime tend to defend Iran in this respect. Thus, Baham Nirumand, an influential Iranian exile in Germany, has claimed that even Ahmadinejad's call to eliminate Israel had "little to do" with antisemitism. "Up to now, Ahmadinejad has never criticized Jews as such, but above all the 'Zionist occupation power,' Israel."[2] Why then is it nonetheless right to talk of Iranian antisemitism?

A second major question concerns Iran's foreign policy. The negative image of the Ahmadinejad years (2005–2013) has been changing with the advent of Hassan Rouhani, Ahmadinejad's successor to the Iranian presidency. Rouhani's "vision aims to move Iran away from confrontation and toward dialogue, constructive interaction, and understanding," claims his foreign minister.[3] Does this new image of Iran correspond to a real shift in its hitherto ideology-driven foreign policy?

These are important questions that deserve answers. This chapter, therefore, deals first with the specific form of Iranian antisemitism and second with the particular nature of Iran's foreign policy. It then goes on to try to identify the links between the two—Iranian foreign policy and antisemitism.

KHOMEINI'S ANTISEMITISM

In the 1960s, Ruhollah Khomeini was the first Iranian to speak about Jewish world domination and to discover the mobilizing power of Jew hatred. His antisemitism was characterized by three features.

First, it was directed not only against Zionists, but also against Jews. "I know that you do not want Iran to be under the boot of the Jews," he cried out to his supporters in April 1963.[4] In the same year, he called the Shah a Jew in disguise and accused him of taking orders from Israel.[5] The response was positive, tremendously so. From then on, hatred of Jews has remained a central component of Iranian Islamist ideology. "The Jews . . . wish to establish Jewish domination throughout the world," Khomeini wrote in 1970 in his main work *Islamic Government*. "Since they are a cunning and resourceful group of people, I fear that . . . they may one day achieve their goal."[6] In September 1977, he declared: "The Jews have grasped the world with both hands and are devouring it with an insatiable appetite, they are devouring America and have now turned their attention to Iran and still they are not satisfied."[7]

The second feature of his antisemitism was that Khomeini propagated the extinction of Israel for religious reasons—as a precondition for Muslim unity and Islamic revival and as a core duty in the struggle against the "moral corruption" embodied by a decadent Western culture. He drew a direct link between Zionism and secularization, describing Israel as the "germ of corruption . . . the destructive impulses of which threaten the entire Islamic world every day."[8] Thus, a political conflict was changed into a struggle between righteousness and falsehood, between premodern Islamic culture and cultural Westernization, in which no compromise was possible. Khomeini thus "islamized" the Arab-Israeli conflict and transformed the political-national conflict into a religious crusade.[9]

Third, Khomeini viewed Israel through the prism of the *Protocols of the Elders of Zion*. In a speech in June 1963, he claimed that "Israel does not wish the Qur'an to exist in this country. Israel does not wish the 'ulama to exist in this country. Israel does not wish a single learned man to exist in this country. . . . It wishes to seize your economy, to destroy your trade and agriculture, to appropriate your wealth."[10]

Khomeini was not the first to combine crude antisemitism with anti-Zionism. In 1925, Hitler likewise attacked Zionism in *Mein Kampf,* warning that "a Jewish state in Palestine" would only serve as an "organization centre for their international world-swindling, . . . place of refuge for convicted scoundrels and a university for up-and-coming swindlers."[11] Fifty years later, Khomeini designated Israel as a "festering sore and a cancerous tumour on the body of the Islamic countries," as a "man-eating giant and a pagan usurper," as a "monster aspiring to world domination," as a "germ of corruption in the heart of the Arab world" and an "enemy of all mankind." These quotes are taken from a 1996 brochure that was disseminated by the Iranian state in an edition of five thousand copies in the German language.[12] It is difficult, according to Robert Wistrich, the leading historian of antisemitism research, "to imagine a more dehumanizing and repulsive terminology, yet the significance of its usage is widely ignored by the Western world."[13]

After the victory of the revolution in 1979, three major changes took place with regard to Iranian antisemitism.

IRANIAN ANTISEMITISM

First, the rhetoric against Jews was toned down. Khomeini could ignore neither the signs of submission given by the Iranian Jewish community nor the precept of tolerance laid down in the Koran.

In May 1979, he declared: "We distinguish between Jews and Zionists. Zionism has nothing to do with religion."[14] From now on, Jews (like the Armenian Christians and Zoroastrians) were treated as wards of a traditional Islamic state—Dhimmis—according to the "principles of Islamic justice." The fundamental antisemitism, however, did not vanish. Iranian copies of the *Protocols of the Elders of Zion*—Hitler's textbook for the Holocaust—spread all over the world. Some examples:

- In 1984, the journal *Imam*, published by the Iranian Embassy in London, reproduced parts of the *Protocols* in a series of articles.[15]

- In 2005, at the Iranian stand at the Frankfurt Book Fair, this author purchased a complete English edition of the *Protocols of the Elders of Zion*, published by the Islamic Propagation Organization of the Islamic Republic of Iran. Its foreword explains the purpose of this publication: "to expose the real visage of this satanic enemy" in order to "awaken the Moslems to this great danger." Zionism, the editors continue, is a "deadly, cancerous tumor" that must be eliminated. There then follows a collection of citations, among them this one: "The United Nations is Zionism. It is the Super Government mentioned many times in the Protocols of the Learned Elders of Zion." After a call to "Jihad against this menace," the English text of the antisemitic tract follows.[16]

- At the same Iranian stand at the Frankfurt Book Fair, this author also bought an English copy of Henry Ford's *The International Jew*, published by the Tehran-based Islamic Culture and Relations Organization in 1997. In the preface, the editor wrote that "the grip of the Jewish parasitic influence has been growing stronger and stronger ever since [Henry Ford's time]. The Jewish danger—now called Zionism—is . . . directed against the entire humanity." The numerous footnotes added to the text by the Iranian publisher are particularly interesting. Here we find talk of an "expansion of power" of the Jews during the Second World War and of German "resistance" against this "Jewish control" while Salman Rushdie is presented as an example of the insidiousness of Jewish calumny.[17]

- In 2000, the Iranian government published a special edition of the *Protocols* whose introduction was designed to show "the Zionist . . . inveterate rancor against Islam and Muslims," as well as their "boundless passion for usurpation and hegemony."[18]

- "In 2004, the Iranian TV station al-Alam aired a documentary . . . which purported to explain how the Jews control Hollywood by the directives set out in the *Protocols*."[19]

- In 2012, the Iranian daily *Resalat* claimed that the *Protocols* were "the most dangerous collection of laws and regulations in history" while the regime's English-language website *Press TV* published articles attributing the economic crisis in Europe to a scheme by the "Jewish Banking Cartel."[20]

- In August 2014, Hassan Rouhani, the new and allegedly moderate Iranian president, blamed Zionism for pulling the strings against the interests of the American people: "Unfortunately, a pressure group in the U.S., which is a warmongering group and is against constructive talks, is [pursuing] the interests of a foreign country and mostly receives its orders from that foreign country. . . . The interests of one foreign country and one group have been imposed on the members of the U.S. Congress."[21]

It is true that the Iranian regime distinguishes between Zionism as a menace and Judaism as a legitimate religion and at holiday time, wishes "all Jews, especially Iranian Jews, a blessed Rosh Hashana."[22] However, a "Jew" is here characterized as someone who is willing to support Tehran's antisemitic program and Israel's elimination. Only this kind of Jew—the fanatical followers of the

Neturei Karta sect, the intimidated leaders of the Iranian Jewish community, or the useful idiots of the Jewish radical left—are acceptable to Tehran.

The second major change since the Islamic revolution is that Iranian antisemitism has been radicalized in several ways: Some of Iran's leading clergymen, such as Grand Ayatollah Nuri-Hamadani, infused a messianic element into their struggle against the Jews. He insisted that it was necessary to "fight the Jews and vanquish them so that the conditions for the advent of the Hidden Imam [i.e., the Shiite messiah] be met." Thus he hinged the redemption of the Muslims or even of the whole world on the destruction of Israel.[23]

Mahmoud Ahmadinejad, a supporter of the messianic approach, radicalized the idea of a Jewish conspiracy. In a presidential speech for Al Quds Day in August 2012, he maintained that "the Zionists planned World Wars I and II . . . with the aim of controlling others." He continued: "All the main centers of power, the strong governments, the banks, and the major media in the world are in the hands of the Zionists, and they exploit them all, with the aim of destroying cultures, values, nations, and the existence of states. The Zionists are behind every [instance of] extensive moral destruction, war, conflict, or massacre."[24]

Another escalation, never conceived by Khomeini, related to the denial of the Holocaust. Whoever calls the Holocaust a "myth" implicitly portrays the Jews as a group of people who for filthy lucre have been duping the rest of humanity for the past seventy years. It started in April 1998, when the Supreme Leader Ali Khamenei met Roger Garaudy, a French Holocaust denier, for the first time. Later, he claimed, that the "exaggerated numbers" of Jews killed in the Holocaust, were "fabricated." While Rouhani's current government avoids this issue, Holocaust denial has remained an essential component of Iran's official doctrine. "It's not clear what the reality is about it [the Holocaust], whether it even has a reality, or how it happened," declared Ali Khamenei in March 2014.[25]

The third major change is that after the revolution, Khomeini's paranoid attitude toward Israel became the policy of a powerful state. Before 1979, Israel and Iran had cooperated successfully for several decades, not only on security issues but also in the fields of agriculture, hydraulic engineering, health, and industry. The two nations had no territorial disputes or any kind of refugee problem. Indeed, throughout history, Iranians have viewed the Arabs as their adversaries, whereas Iranian Jews and non-Jews have lived together for more than 2,500 years. In 1979, however, "in one of the most rapid and dramatic shifts of alliance in modern Middle Eastern history, Iran went from being an important strategic partner of Israel . . . to becoming its most dangerous and implacable enemy," writes Robert Wistrich. "With no other country were Iran's relations overturned so speedily and drastically."[26]

Already during Yassir Arafat's visit to Iran shortly after the revolution, Khomeini proclaimed "imruz iran, farad felestin" ("today Iran, tomorrow Palestine"), implying that the "liberation of Palestine" would come next.[27] Khomeini and his followers had (and have) no doubt that this "liberation" requires the elimination of Israel and an Islamic revolution in Palestine.

NO PEACE, BUT MARTYRDOM

Since 1979, Tehran has been committed to destroying any peace process. Whenever a compromise between Arabs and Israel "threatens" to mitigate the Middle East conflict, Tehran does everything to thwart the peaceful solution. Nadia von Maltzahn gives an example: "In September 1993, after Israel and the PLO signed the Declaration of Principles in Washington, President Rafsanjani at once condemned the agreement and called it 'the biggest treason committed by the PLO against the Palestinian people.' Rafsanjani sent his Deputy Foreign Minister, Sheikholeslam, to Damascus to deliver a message to Assad and discuss the implications of the Israeli-PLO accords."[28] Iran's activism was successful. Syria and Lebanon joined the rejection front, and the peace initiative did indeed fail. Other efforts to destroy a peaceful solution have focused on shipping weapons and ammunition to militant Jew haters such as Hezbollah and Hamas.[29]

The antisemitic hatred behind this behavior has a long tradition. "All Arabs who collaborate with the Jews should be destroyed before they help the Jews destroy us," announced Nazi Germany's Arabic-language radio program back in April 1943.[30] A generation later, Khomeini declared it "the duty of all Islamic countries to completely eradicate Israel. . . . Any relation with Israel and its agents . . . is religiously prohibited and constitutes a hostility to Islam."[31] A generation later, Ahmadinejad exclaimed: "If someone . . . recognize[s] the Zionist regime—he should know that he will burn in the fire of the Islamic *Ummah* [nation]."[32]

This abhorrence of peace with Israel and the concomitant disregard for the vital interests of the Palestinian population is facilitated by a radicalized version of martyrdom ideology. Mahdi Mohammad Nia vividly describes the contrast between the Western and the Iranian worldview in Tehran's official journal, *Iranian Review of Foreign Affairs.*

On the one hand, "according to the Holy Quran, a martyr has a guaranteed place in Paradise. Martyrdom-seekers and Jihadists are not afraid of death at all in a battle front." On the other hand, the "fear factor is a serious dilemma in mundane and materialistic societies in which the life is defined solely within the boundaries of the physical existence. They regard the happiness and well-being within the short span of life on earth. This culture is completely opposite to the cult of martyrdom." Thus there is a different understanding of war: "The martyrdom shows Shia attitudes toward war which is *less goal-oriented* than the western concepts. . . . In this context, *defeat is not necessarily equated with failure.* This emphasis on continuing the struggle against oppression and injustice (as an Islamic duty) rather than on achieving 'victory' is seen as producing a *high tolerance of pain* in Iran. The cult of martyrdom inherent in Shi'ism, specifically, the honor accorded those who give their life to defend the faith, may give Iran certain practical military advantages" (emphasis added).[33]

In other words: Iran's foreign policy with regards to Israel is not motivated by the desire to provide the Palestinians with "happiness and well-being" but by the desire to conduct a religious war and to fulfill an Islamic duty even if defeat is inevitable and a reward only obtainable "in Paradise." This program of inhumanity represents the counter-concept to Judaism par excellence.

"Shia culture . . . drives Iranian behavior in ways that are not readily understood by the West" continues Mahdi Mohammad Nia, "some objectives of Iranian foreign policy are most difficult for some to understand, unless we interpret them within the ideological context."[34] This is true. Let us now take a closer look at this peculiarity of Iranian foreign policy.

REVOLUTIONARY FOREIGN POLICY

Antisemitism is rampant in many countries. One of the worst examples today is certainly Egypt. Nevertheless, if we ask whether Egypt also practices an antisemitic foreign policy, our answer would have to be no. Why? Because in Egypt, there is no totalitarianism, no triumphalism, no expansionism at work.

Iran's antisemitism, in contrast, is a revolutionary antisemitism, and Iran's foreign policy is a revolutionary policy. Its scope is global, its program chiliastic, and its goal revolutionary.

Its scope is global: The Islamic revolution was publicly characterized as being neither Iranian nor Shiite, but rather Islamic and universal. "We will export our revolution to the whole world because it is an Islamic revolution," declared Khomeini in February 1980. "The struggle will continue until the calls 'there is no god but God' and 'Muhammad is the messenger of God' are heard all over the world."[35]

This missionary zeal is not only embodied in the emblem of the Islamic Republic—the word "Allah" written in Arabic script so as to form a stylized globe[36]—but is also dictated by Iran's constitution, which outlines "the country's foreign policy on the basis of the Islamic criteria: fraternal alignment towards all Moslems and unsparing support" for "any rightful struggle of the weak against the strong on the face of the globe."[37] Thus, Ali Khamenei's homepage is currently translated into twelve languages: English, French, Spanish, Indonesian, Azeri, Russian, Kiswahili, Turkish, Hindi, Arabic, Urdu, and German.

Its program is chiliastic: Ali Khamenei describes the Islamic revolution as "the turning point in modern world history" that carries a precise message: "the message of salvation of humanity." And he adds, "Our historical movement is creating a new civilization."[38] The creation of this new civilization depends—as always—on the annihilation of its enemies—in this case Israel and the United States. "Preservation of the safety and revival of world peace," writes Monouchehr Mohammadi, a former deputy minister of defense in 2012, "is only possible through the destruction and defeat of the hegemonic powers." Ahmadinejad expressed the same idea in this way: "The Zionist regime will be wiped out, and humanity will be liberated."[39]

Regardless of any day-to-day pragmatism, Iran's foreign policy is still inspired by this kind of expectancy, based on an alleged spiritual superiority.

Its goal is revolutionary rather than accommodating and *idealistic* rather than status quo–oriented.[40]

Iran displayed its rejection of the pillars of international relations when it violated diplomatic immunity and took hostage more than fifty U.S. embassy personnel in Tehran. It negated the very basis of the international state system when Khomeini issued a fatwa against Salman Rushdie, a British citizen. In both cases, Iran was isolated within the international community because it placed so-called divine law above secular international law.

"Revolutionary states often do not engage in cost-benefit analysis that other states do," explained the Tehran-based *Iranian Review of Foreign Affairs* in 2012. "The main goal of such states is to pursue their revolutionary mission and to construct a particular identity based on a certain set of norms and values. . . . Hence, this country [Iran] can be considered as a mission-oriented state rather than interest-oriented."[41]

Are we today, under Rouhani's presidency, entering a more pragmatic phase, in which considerations of national interest are prioritized over mission-oriented considerations? Mohammad Javad Zarif, the new Iranian Foreign Minister and figurehead for an alleged moderation, says no: "We are claimants of a mission, which has a global dimension," he writes in Farsi in his memoirs, published in early 2014. "We have defined a global vocation, both in the Constitution and in the ultimate objectives of the Islamic revolution . . . I believe that we do not exist without our revolutionary goals."[42]

Advancing this global mission, however, does not exclude the semblance of conventional diplomacy. Instead, Iranian foreign policy zigzags between moderation and militancy—a pattern determined "by the total interdependence of state-making and revolutionism." Kaveh L. Afrasiabi, therefore, calls the Islamic Republic of Iran a quasi-state: "Quasi-state refers to a state-movement characterized by a dual logic of action in which the disparate interests of revolutionism and national state-making are fused; moreover, the quasi-regime is uniquely resistant to diplomacy as usual."[43]

This analysis captures accurately the particularity of the current nuclear negotiations with Iran. This is not diplomacy as usual: at the same time that Foreign Minister Zarif is claiming that his "vision aims to move Iran away from confrontation," Supreme Leader Khamenei is calling the United States an "eternal enemy" and identifying these negotiations as a form of warfare: "Every step, forward and reverse, is similar to a battlefield and must be decided upon in advance in order to achieve the goal."[44] Khamenei's cost-benefit analysis, however, is based on ideological values rather than material interests.

But what about the anti-Jewish impact of this foreign policy approach? In what follows, we consider a number of facets of Iranian foreign policy—international media, mobilization, terrorism, and diplomacy from the point of view of their relationship to antisemitism.

INCITEMENT

Iran's international mouthpiece is Press TV, a TV channel founded in summer 2007 with four hundred staff members and twenty-six reporters worldwide.[45] Headquartered in Tehran, it broadcasts in North America, Europe, the Middle East, Asia, and parts of Africa and Latin America via a number of television satellite providers.

Some years ago the following advertisement decorated the red buses of London: "*Press TV*. Giving a voice to the voiceless. 24/7. News. Truth. The World is changing. People are changing. Opinions are changing. The News is changing. Why do you still watch the same tired news channel? GET THE FULL STORY AT PRESS TV."[46]

What does this slogan mean? What is the "full story?" A collection of Press TV headlines reveals the slant:

"Dirty Zionist game in Syria"
"Jewish Mafia tied to death in America"
"Zionist fingerprints all over 9/11 attacks"
"Israeli lobbies dominate U.S. system"
"Netanyahu still has his hands on the strings that control puppets around the world, the press, entertainment industry, key world leaders"
"Only war satisfies Israel lobby in U.S."
"I wouldn't say Israel is running the U.S., I would say Jews in America are running the U.S. Israel is a euphemism for that."

In October 2013, the Anti-Defamation League published an updated version of its documentation "Iran's *Press TV:* Broadcasting Anti-Semitism to the English Speaking World." "The antisemitic themes frequently broadcast on Press TV . . . fall into five major categories of classic anti-Jewish conspiracy theories," states this study. "1. Allegations of Zionist Control over World Events. 2. Allegations of 'Israeli Lobby' Control of America. 3. Allegations of Excessive Jewish/Zionist Influences as a Result of Disproportionate Wealth. 4. Allegations of 'False Flag' Conspiracy Theories. 5. Allegations that Israel is Committing a 'Holocaust' in Gaza."[47]

Press TV gives the impression of being highly professional. It pretends to be a credible and independent channel. Its programs include information about criticisms of Iran's nuclear program. However, it is not dedicated to spreading reliable information but is used as a revolutionary tool. Its reporters, for example, are not allowed to use the term "state of Israel." They are instructed to stick with "Israel" or "the Zionist entity."[48]

At the beginning of 2012, the Islamic Republic of Iran Broadcasting Company (IRIB) established a similar channel for the Spanish-speaking world: Hispan TV.[49] Broadcast from the Venezuelan satellite Simón Bolívar, this channel now has a growing audience in South America.[50]

The Iranian propaganda machine has been successful but has also suffered setbacks. In 2009, the mullahs tried to launch their own Arabic-language movie channel, al-Alam. However, by order of Saudi Arabia, two Arab-controlled satellite companies—Nilesat and Arabsat—took this channel off the air.[51] In October 2012, the European satellite Hotbird also stopped broadcasting Iranian channels. Russian satellites have stepped in to fill the gap.[52]

MOBILIZATION

In 1979, Khomeini declared the last Friday of the month of Ramadan as Jerusalem (Quds) Day, and called on the Muslims of the world to participate. Since then this day has marked an international high point of antisemitic mobilization, when demonstrators all over the world call for the annihilation of Israel.

In South Africa, demonstrations on Al Quds Day are regularly held in Cape Town. In November 2002, the march was led by children disguised as suicide bombers or armed Hezbollah fighters. In Nigeria, Al Quds demonstrations, led by Muslim Brotherhood activists, take place each year in the Northern federal states where the population is predominantly Muslim.[53]

The biggest Al Quds demonstrations take place in countries with a high proportion of Shiite Muslims, such as Iran, Lebanon, Pakistan, Bahrain, and Iraq. In 2005, during Al Quds Day in Beirut, thousands of uniformed militia, which included children, formed battalions marching in lockstep. Broadcast worldwide live via satellite over the Hizbullah channel Al-Manar; the festive proceedings were attended by representatives of the Lebanese president, the prime minister, and the president of the parliament.[54]

In Turkey, only a few hundred people took part in demonstrations on the 2005 Al Quds Day in Istanbul and the Kurdish town of Batman. In Western countries, Al Quds Day demonstrations are mostly organized by Shiite activists. In Berlin, in December 2000, more than two thousand demonstrators—separated according to gender—called for "the liberation of Palestine." In London, the 2005 Al Quds Day rally was supported by the Jewish sect Neturei Karta, while in the United States supporters of radical Sunni organizations joined the rallies. In recent years, however, Al Quds Day demonstrations in Western countries have become smaller.

The annual Al Quds Day is also used by Iran's Islamic Culture and Relations Organization (ICRO). Set up in 1995, ICRO has the sole responsibility for coordinating Iran's cultural foreign policy. It is affiliated with the Ministry of Culture and Islamic Guidance under the ultimate guidance of the Supreme Leader. ICRO has set up cultural centers across the world, in particular in countries with a Muslim majority. "These centers, of which there exist over 60 worldwide, are formally attached to the Iranian embassy or consulate in each country," writes Nadia von Maltzahn. "ICRO published over 20 journals in different languages inside Iran, to be distributed in the representations outside Iran; and over 30 of its cultural centers abroad have their own publications."[55]

Von Maltzahn's study concentrates on Iran's cultural policies vis-à-vis Syria. Here, the Iranians launched a quarterly journal—*Islamic Culture*—which between 1985 and 2006 published thirty-five articles on "Palestine and the crimes of Zionism and imperialism." In 2010, Iranian officials also organized an Iranian cinema festival in Damascus. At the opening night, a Syrian-Iranian coproduction called *Al-Ghuraba* (Strangers) was screened that defended suicide bombing and "clearly fed into the discourse on resistance, Anti-Zionism and anti-imperialism."[56]

Antisemitic words, spread by Press TV and by films such as *Al-Ghuraba,* are intended to trigger antisemitic deeds, which brings us to the next topic: Anti-Jewish terrorist operations.

TERRORISM

The killing of five Israeli tourists in Bulgaria in 2012 and the attacks or planned attacks in Thailand, Georgia, and India perpetrated by Hezbollah terrorists and Iranian agents made headlines.[57] Iran has also made other attempts to kill Jews that are less well known.

In 2012, two members of the Iranian Revolutionary Guards were arrested in the coastal city of Mombasa, Kenya, in possession of extremely powerful explosives. They were obviously planning to attack Jewish targets in Kenya, several hotels on that coast being Israeli-owned.

In 2013, security forces in Nigeria exposed another terror cell. Their leader had been paid and trained in Iran. The planned attacks were aimed at the Chabad Cultural Center and an Israeli company in Lagos.[58]

In 2014, Hezbollah terrorists were planning to carry out attacks at six locations in Bangkok during Passover. One of two suspected Hezbollah members "confessed that he and at least two others entered Thailand to carry out a bombing against Israeli tourists in Bangkok as well as other Israeli groups."[59]

The 1994 suicide bombing of the Asociación Mutual Israelita Argentina (AMIA), the Jewish center in Buenos Aires, caused the death of eighty-five persons, injured more than 150 and destroyed or damaged the surrounding buildings in a radius of 200 meters. This was the most deadly terror attack against Jews since World War II, and it was the Iranian leadership including Khamenei and Rafsanjani that made this decision and instructed Hezbollah to commit the crime. The sole reason was Argentina's unwillingness to continue its nuclear cooperation with Iran. Who, however, should be blamed and punished for Argentina's independent decision? Jews were the scapegoat, of course.

Once the suicide operation had been approved, the revolutionary and spiritual leader issued a fatwa authorizing the action from the standpoint of Islamic Law. Argentina's attorney general, Alberto Nisman, wrote a 650-page report about this case. Although mostly ignored by the media, it is shocking. Nisman's examination shows "beyond a shadow of doubt that the realization of acts of terrorism abroad was not the outgrowth of an unusual foreign policy instrument, but was instead based on the principles of the Iranian revolution of February 1979."[60] That is to say: based on antisemitic principles. The AMIA example clearly shows that the anti-Jewish paranoid pattern contains a call to kill. If the Jews of Argentina are responsible for the government's decisions, you have to kill them in revenge. If Israel is responsible for the wars in the world, you have to wipe it out in order to secure peace. Iran's diplomacy is just another tool to this end.

DIPLOMACY

"It is necessary to be present in all world forums and to defend Islam and Iran effectively in all international tribunals and conventions," explained former Iranian president Mohammad Khatami. "But we cannot ultimately flourish and make our weight felt in the international scene . . . unless we maintain our unique idealism."[61] Here it is again: The particular mixture of terrorism, idealism, and pragmatism that characterizes Iran's foreign policy. Every forum of the United Nations is misused for this end. To present just one example of "unique idealism": In January 2007, the Iranian government filed a complaint with the UN Human Rights Council against those who do *not* deny the Holocaust. Let me quote from Iran's official letter of complaint: "History cannot be rewritten as it pleases [the] Israeli regime. It cannot be manipulated and hand-picked selectively and it cannot be reformatted based on [the] political agenda or historical ambitions of this regime."[62] Here, the UN, of all organizations, which was founded in the 1940s in response to the horrors of the World War II, is being urged to oppose all those who do not deny the greatest horror of that war.

Iran, however, is not only present in world forums but also organizes international events in Tehran. A case in point is the annual Conference of the International Revolutionary and Liberation Movements of the World, organized by Iran's Ministry of Foreign Affairs, which later developed into annual international conferences in support of Palestine. "A common feature of all these conferences was the rejection of Israeli-Palestinian peace negotiations and the praising of 'martyrdom operations' such as suicide bombings," states Udo Wolter, a German Iran expert.[63]

This applies to the 2006 conference "On Al-Quds and Support of the Rights of Palestinian People," as well. According to IRNA, Iran's official news agency, this conference was attended by six hundred foreign officials, including twenty parliamentary speakers from Islamic as well as non-Islamic countries like Zimbabwe, Cuba, Sri Lanka, and Venezuela.[64]

More effective, however, is the hidden part of Tehran's diplomacy. It serves the purpose of isolating Israel.

My first example relates to a Sunni Muslim country: Mauritania. In 1999, Mauritania established diplomatic relations with Israel and was one of the few Arab League countries to have done so. In 2000, the Ministry of Health decided to establish an advanced center for cancer research in the country's capital, Nouakchott. This project was partly funded by the Israeli government and partly by the America Jewish Committee and was considered as a symbol of Israeli-Mauritanian cooperation. A team of Israeli doctors was planning to travel to Mauritania to train local physicians in the treatment of cancer patients.

In 2009, some months before the opening of the cancer center, Mauritania decided to suspend diplomatic ties with Israel. The country recalled its ambassador to Israel and requested Israel to close its embassy in Nouakchott. Following these steps, the hospital project was stalled. The Iranian government praised these steps. There were reports that Iran paid the Mauritanian government about $10 million U.S. to expel the Israel ambassador. In March 2009, Iranian foreign minister Manouchehr Mottaki came to Mauritania and promised to boost trade with Mauritania and increase cooperation in health, oil, energy, business, agriculture, and mines. He visited the nearly completed hospital, known by locals as "the Israeli hospital." "We'll equip the hospital with whatever gear it needs," the Iranian minister was quoted by the Mauritanian news agency. The cancer research center was inaugurated in 2010.[65]

My second example deals with a deeply Roman Catholic country, Venezuela, which was among the founding members of OPEC but had always maintained a neutral position on Israel and had no history of antisemitism. This changed as soon as Presidents Hugo Chávez and Mahmoud Ahmadinejad struck up a friendship in 2006. The Chávez administration subsequently broke off relations with Israel. This step was accompanied by the outbreak in Venezuela of an antisemitic wave.

In 2009, vandals broke into a temple in Caracas and desecrated the sacred space with graffiti calling for the death of Jews.[66] A series of raids on Jewish schools and synagogues added to the insecurity of the Jewish community. During 2013, Venezuela's Jewish umbrella body witnessed and recorded 4,033 antisemitic expressions in various media and in social networks.[67] While in the 1990s some 25,000 Jews are thought to have lived in Venezuela, that number is today estimated to be as low as 9,000. In other words: Venezuela's Jewish community has shrunk by more than half over the last decade.[68]

My third and last example of antisemitic diplomacy deals with the new relationship between Tehran and Washington, D.C. It would be good if a real rapprochement between Iran and the United States were to take place. That, however, would require a new Iranian attitude toward the Jewish state. But Tehran does not intend to lessen its enmity toward Israel in exchange for the so-called bilateral thaw. On the contrary, "the Islamic Republic is offering to diminish its enmity toward the West in exchange for the latter's abandonment of Israel," writes Ze'en Maghen.[69]

Iran's calculus is to lure the United States away from its alliance with Israel. Mahmoud Ahmadinejad's letter to U.S. president George W. Bush was revealing in this respect: "The Zionists . . . would even sacrifice the Western regimes for their own sake," he claimed. "I say to the leaders of some Western countries: Stop supporting these corrupt people." Ahmadinejad's successor, Hassan Rouhani, has maintained Ahmadinejad's approach by making Israel and its supporters in the U.S. Congress responsible for difficulties during the nuclear talks: "The interests of one foreign country and one group have been imposed on the members of the U.S. Congress."[70] Tehran seems to hope that one day Washington might sacrifice the Jewish state on the altar of a temporary Muslim-Christian rapprochement.

The Iranian attempt to isolate the Jewish state by driving a wedge between Jerusalem and Washington has intensified against the background of the Geneva talks about Iran's nuclear program. In May 2014, Iran's foreign minister Zarif boasted of the damage his new diplomacy had inflicted on Israel. It "had stolen Israel's thunder" and "put an end to Israel's portrayal of Iran as a danger." In order to underline the success of his anti-Israel diplomacy, Zarif stated "that forces in the region, including Hamas and Hizbollah, had thanked him for this 'success.'"[71]

At the same time, there seems to be a new dimension of Western indifference toward Iranian attacks against Israel. In November 2014, Ali Khamenei ranted and raved at the Jewish state, calling it a "sinister, unclean rabid dog" and added that "Israelis should not be called humans."[72] Khamenei used this language just hours before the negotiations about the nuclear program between Iran and the six world powers were set to resume in Geneva.

Previously, such ranting had led Western diplomats to leave the conference room of the UN General Assembly. Now, the leader of an U.S. dialogue partner had used language that recalls Nazi incitement, but the Western powers did not even address it during the talks at Geneva. The fact that Khamenei's provocation went unheeded was a success for Iran's diplomacy.[73]

THE ABSENCE OF CLARITY

This chapter shows that Iran's attitude vis-à-vis Israel is based on an antisemitic world view, which is older than the Islamic revolution. Iran is no status quo power like Egypt. It tries to incite nations and peoples against Israel and seeks to spread antisemitism worldwide.

The effects of this policy are devastating, as was evident in July 2014: countless people, innocent and guilty, were dying because of Hamas's decision to attack Jerusalem, Tel Aviv, and Haifa with rockets. The real perpetrator, however, was Iran: Tehran delivers not only advanced missiles and money to Hamas but also a murderous ideology: the momentous call to destroy Israel with suicidal activities originates from Tehran.

The crucial question, however—*why* does Tehran wants to wipe Israel off the map?—is not raised within the West, and Iranian antisemitism is downplayed or ignored. The absence of clarity, however, is the beginning of complicity. The greatest success of Iranian foreign policy to this date is the fact that the international community seems to believe Tehran's bogus claim to be "opposed to antisemitism."

NOTES

1. Iran's Zarif says new diplomacy has isolated Israel, May 6, 2014, http://www.ynetnews.com/articles/0,7340,L-4516775,00.html.

2. Baham Nirumand, "Der Verrückte aus Teheran," *Tageszeitung,* June 23, 2006.

3. Mohammad Javad Zarif, "What Iran Really Wants: Iranian Foreign Policy in the Rouhani Era," *Foreign Affairs,* May/June 2014.

4. Cheryl Benard and Zalmay Khalilzad, *Gott in Teheran: Irans Islamische Republik* (Frankfurt am Main: Suhrkamp, 1988), 260n26.

5. Gabriele Thoß and Franz-Helmut Richter, *Ayatollah Khomeini. Zur Biographie und Hagiographie eines islamischen Revolutionsführers* (Münster: Wurf-Verlag, 1991), 95.

6. Ayatollah Rouhollah Mousavi Khomeini, *Islamic Government: Governance of the Jurist,* Institute for the Compilation and Publication of Imam Khomeini's Works (International Affairs Division), 79. See http://www.iranchamber.com/history/rkhomeini/books/velayat_faqeeh.pdf.

7. International Affair Division (ed.), *Kauthar,* vol. 1 of *An Anthology of the Speeches of Imam Khomeini Including an Account of the Events of the Revolution 1962–1978* (Tehran: Institute for the Compilation and Publication of the Works of Imam Khomeini, 1995), 370.

8. Institution zur Koordination und Publikation der Werke Imam Khomeinis, *Abteilung Internationale Beziehungen, Das Palästinaproblem aus der Sicht Imam Khomeinis,* Teheran: N.p., 1996, 97.

9. David Menashri, *Iran, Political Islam, and Israel: Challenge and Response,* Working Paper No. 64, American University of Paris, April 2008, 3.

10. Robert Wistrich, *A Lethal Obsession: Anti-Semitism from Antiquity to the Global Jihad* (New York: Random House, 2010), 856.

11. Adolf Hitler, *Mein Kampf,* vol. 1 (München: Verlag Franz Eher Nachfolger, 1934), 356.

12. Institution zur Koordination, *Abteilung Internationale Beziehungen,* 38, 182, 197, 241.

13. Wistrich, *Lethal Obsession,* 862.

14. David Menashri, "The Jews of Iran," in *Antisemitism in Times of Crisis,* ed. Sander L. Gilman and Steven T. Katz (New York: New York University Press, 1991), 363.

15. Robert Wistrich, *Hitler's Apocalypse: Jews and the Nazi Legacy* (London: Weidenfeld & Nicolson, 1985), 180.

16. Matthias Küntzel, "The Booksellers of Tehran," *Wall Street Journal,* October 28, 2005.

17. Ibid.

18. Meir Litvak, "The Islamic Republic of Iran and the Holocaust: Anti-Semitism and Anti-Zionism," *Journal of Israeli History* 25, no. 1 (March 2006): 272.

19. Ibid.

20. Middle East Media Research Institute (MEMRI), "The Image of the Jew in the Eyes of Iran's Islamic Regime—Part II: The Blood Libel and *The Protocols of the Elders of Zion,*" Inquiry and Analysis Series Report No. 944, March 6, 2013, 1.

21. "Rouhani: U.S. Officials Still Do Not Fully Grasp the [*sic*] Iran's Realities," *Iran Daily Brief,* August 9, 2013.

22. Yoel Goldman, "Iranian President Tweets Rosh Hashana Greeting," *Times of Israel,* September 4, 2013.

23. Meir Litvak, "Islamic Republic of Iran and the Holocaust," 272.

24. MEMRI, "Image of the Jew in the Eyes of Iran's Islamic Regime," 4.

25. Reuel Marc Gerecht, "Holocaust Denial and the Iranian Regime," *Wall Street Journal,* April 25, 2014.

26. Wistrich, *Lethal Obsession,* 853.

27. Nadia von Maltzahn, *The Syria-Iran Axis* (London: Tauris, 2013), 78.

28. Ibid., 41–42.

29. "Iran's Hand in Gaza," *Wall Street Journal,* July 8, 2014.

30. Jeffrey Herf, *Nazi-Propaganda for the Arab World* (New Haven, Conn.: Yale University Press, 2009), 171.

31. Institution zur Koordination, *Abteilung Internationale Beziehungen,* 97. This statement was made on June 8, 1967.

32. MEMRI, "Iranian President at Tehran Conference," MEMRI Special Dispatch Series No. 1013, October 28, 2005.

33. Mahdi Mohammad Nia, "Discourse and Identity in Iran's Foreign Policy," *Iranian Review of Foreign Affairs* 3, no. 3 (fall 2012): 53.

34. Ibid., 39.

35. Farhang Rajaee, *Islamic Values and World View* (Lanham, Md.: University Press of America, 1983), 83.

36. Karl Binswanger, "Das Selbstverständnis der Islamischen Republik Iran im Spiegel ihrer Verfassung," *Orient* 3 (1980): 330.

37. Article 3, paragraph 16, and article 154, see Henner Fürtig, *Islamische Weltauffassung und außenpolitische Konzeption,* Studie 8 (Berlin: Verlag Das Arabische Buch, 1998), 269.

38. Ibid., 148.

39. Yigal Carmon, "The Role of Holocaust Denial in the Ideology and Strategy of the Iranian Regime," MEMRI, Inquiry and Analysis Series, No. 307, December 15, 2006.

40. Arshin Adib-Moghaddam, "Islamic Utopian Romanticism and the Foreign Policy Culture of Iran," *Critical Middle Eastern Studies* 14, no. 3 (fall 2005): 265–292, 280.

41. Nia, "Discourse and Identity in Iran's Foreign Policy," 31, 38.

42. Ali Alfoneh and Reuel Marc Gerecht, "An Iranian Moderate Exposed: Everyone Thought Iran's Foreign Minister Was a Pragmatist. They Were Wrong," *New Republic,* January 23, 2014.

43. Kaveh L. Afrasiabi, *After Khomeini: New Directions in Iran's Foreign Policy* (Boulder, Colo.: Westview Press, 1994), 29–30, 16.

44. "Khamenei: I Told the Negotiating Team that the Nuclear Talks Have Red Lines that Must Not Be Crossed," *Iran Daily Brief,* November 20, 2013.

45. Nazila Fathi, "Iran Expands Role in Media, via Satellite and in English," *New York Times,* July 3, 2007.

46. John Plunkett, "Press TV Can Say It Tells the Full Story, Rules Ad Watchdog," Guardian, December 2, 2009.

47. Anti-Defamation League, "Iran's Press TV: Broadcasting Anti-Semitism To English-Speaking World," October 21, 2013, http://www.adl.org /anti-semitism/united-states/c/press-tv-iran.html.

48. Nathan Guttman, "All the News Iran Sees Fit to Broadcast Is Aired on Press TV," www.forward.com, May 5, 2010.

49. "Iran Officially Launches Hispan IV," *Press TV,* January 31, 2012.

50. Sammy Eppel communication with the author, March 24, 2014.

51. "Iran Arabic Channel Taken Off Air," BBC News, November 4, 2009.

52. "Russia Steps in to Broadcast Iranian Channels," *Radiozamaneh,* November 4, 2012.

53. Arne Behrensen, "International Dimensions of Al Quds Day," in American Jewish Committee, *Antisemitism "Made in Iran": The International Dimensions of Al Quds Day* (Berlin: American Jewish Committee Berlin Office Lawrence and Lee Ramer Center for German-Jewish Relations, 2006), 19–20.

54. Mira Dietz, "Lebanon," in American Jewish Committee, *Antisemitism "Made in Iran,"* 21.

55. Von Maltzahn, *Syria-Iran Axis,* 67–69.

56. Ibid., 102–115.

57. Nicholas Kulish and Eric Schmitt, "Hezbollah Is Blamed for Attack on Israeli Tourists in Bulgaria," *New York Times,* July 19, 2012; Kate Hodal, "Bangkok Bombers Planned to Attack Israeli Diplomats, Say Thai Police," *Guardian,* February 16, 2012; Ernest Petrosyan, "Car Bombs in Tblisi and New Delhi Linked to Iran-Israel Conflict," *Messenger Online,* February 15, 2012.

58. "Iranische Terrorzelle in Nigeria verhaftet," *Tachles,* February 21, 2013.

59. Times of Israel staff and Aron Donzis, "Lebanese Man Cops to Thai Terror Plot against Israelis," *Times of Israel,* April 18, 2014, and Wassayos Ngamkham and Anucha Charoenpo, "Israel Calls for Extra Security after Thwarted 'Terror Plot,'" *Bangkok Post,* April 20, 2014.

60. Alberto Nisman and Marcelo Martinez Burgos, Office of Criminal Investigations: AMIA CASE, October 25, 2006, 20. See: www.peaceand tolerance.org/docs/nismanindict.pdf.

61. Adib-Moghaddam, "Islamic Utopian Romanticism and the Foreign Policy Culture of Iran," 285.

62. Ambassador Alireza Moayera, Permanent Representative of Iran to the Council, Geneva, to Ambassador Luis Alfonso De Alba, President of the Human Rights Council, letter January 8, 2007, as documented by UNWatch.org, "Iran's UN Human Right Envoy Questions Holocaust, Ban Ki-moon Urged to Respond," Geneva, January 11, 2007.

63. Udo Wolter, "April 2006: A New Conference against Israel in Tehran," in American Jewish Committee, *Antisemitism "Made in Iran,"* 12.

64. Ibid.

65. "A Search for Allies in a Hostile World," *Economist,* February 4, 2010; Barak Ravid, "Iran to Complete Hospital that Israel Started Building in Mauritania," *Haaretz,* March 29, 2009; and Media Line News Agency, "Iran Steps into Israeli Void in Mauritania," *Jerusalem Post,* March 26, 2009.

66. Mary Anastasia O'Grady, "Revolutionary Anti-Semitism: Chávez Imports Ahmadinejad's Ideology to Latin America," *Wall Street Journal,*

October 4, 2009; Frank Jack Daniel, "Venezuela's Chavez Calls Israel 'Murderous' U.S. Arm," *Reuters*, November 25, 2009.

67. "Over 4,000 Anti-Semitic Expressions Recorded in Venezuela in 2013, Study Finds," World Jewish Congress, May 6, 2014.

68. "Jews Flee Venezuela Amid Security Fears," *Ynet*, January 31, 2014.

69. Ze'ev Maghen, "Eradicating the 'Little Satan,'" *Commentary*, January 1, 2009.

70. "Rouhani."

71. "Iran's Parliament 'Satisfied' with Minister's Holocaust Explanation," Radio Free Europe/Radio Liberty, May 6, 2014, http://www.rferl.org /content/iran-parliament-zarif-holocaust/25375405.html.

72. AP and Times of Israel, "Iran's 'Rabid Dog' Insults to Israel Complicate Nuke Talks," *Times of Israel*, November 20, 2013.

73. According to Marie Harf, deputy speaker of the state department, the negotiations had not addressed the topic of inflammatory language used by Iranian officials against Israel. See Rebecca Shimoni Stoil, "P5+1 Talks on Iran's Nukes to Resume on Monday," *Times of Israel*, December 7, 2013.

Contributors

SINA ARNOLD studied Social Anthropology, Political Science, and Pedagogy in Berlin and Manchester. She received her PhD from the Center for Research on Antisemitism at the Technical University of Berlin and is currently a postdoctoral researcher at the Berlin Institute for Migration and Integration Research (BIM) at Humboldt University. Her academic work has focused on antisemitism among Arab youth and in left-wing social movements, on anti-Muslim racism, as well as on new forms of migration and belonging in Germany.

DORON BEN-ATAR is Professor of History at Fordham University and a playwright. The author of five books, his most recent work is *Taming Lust: Crimes against Nature in the Early Republic*.

PASCAL BRUCKNER, author of more than twenty books of fiction and nonfiction, is one of France's most prominent writers and influential social critics. Among his books in English translation, *The Tears of the White Man, The Temptation of Innocence,* and *The Tyranny of Guilt* have won particular praise.

JEAN AXELRAD CAHAN is Senior Lecturer in Philosophy and Director of the Norman and Bernice Harris Center for Judaic Studies at the University of Nebraska-Lincoln. Her research focuses on various aspects of modern Jewish thought. She is currently working on a book-length study that proposes a metaphysical interpretation of antisemitism.

BRUNO CHAOUAT is Professor of French at the University of Minnesota. He has published two books and several edited volumes and numerous essays in French and in English. His forthcoming took is titled *Is Theory Good for the Jews? Responses to the New Antisemitism in France.*

EIRIK EIGLAD is an independent scholar located in Telemark, Norway. A writer, editor, translator, and longtime activist in the Scandinavian ecology movement, Eiglad's writings include *The Anti-Jewish Riots in Oslo* (2010).

R. AMY ELMAN is the Weber Professor in Social Science at Kalamazoo College. She is author of *The European Union, Antisemitism, and the Politics of Denial* (2014) and *Sexual Equality in an Integrated Europe: Virtual Equality* (2007).

ALEKSANDRA GLISZCZYNSKA-GRABIAS is Senior Researcher at the Institute of Legal Studies of the Polish Academy of Sciences, where in 2012 she defended her PhD on counteracting antisemitism with legal instruments of the international human rights law. She is a recipient of the 2012 Fellowship of the Foundation for Polish Science for outstanding achievements in science and research and a 2014 Bohdan Winiarski Fellowship at the Lauterpacht Centre of the University of Cambridge. Gliszczynska-Grabias is also a legal advisor for the Open Republic Association against Antisemitism and Xenophobia, a leading Polish NGO active in the field of counteracting intolerance, hatred, and prejudice.

STEPHAN GRIGAT received his PhD from the Free University of Berlin and currently lectures at the Institutes for Political Science, Philosophy, and Jewish Studies at the University of Vienna and the Center for Jewish Studies at the University of Graz. The author and editor of numerous books and articles on antisemitism and related subjects, his latest work is *Die Einsamkeit Israels. Zionismus, die israelische Linke und die iranische Bedrohung* (2014).

BERNARD HARRISON is author of *The Resurgence of Antisemitism: Jews, Israel and Liberal Opinion* (2006) and a number of shorter pieces on contemporary antisemitism and other aspects of the relationship between Jewish and non-Jewish culture. Other recent work includes *Word and World: Practice and the Foundations of Language* (2004) and *What Is Fiction For? Literary Humanism Restored* (2015). A number of critical studies of his work have recently appeared in Patricia Hanna's edited volume *Reality and Culture: Essays on the Philosophy of Bernard Harrison* (2014). Married, with three children, he lives in England.

GÜNTHER JIKELI is a research fellow at the Moses Mendelssohn Center for European-Jewish Studies, Potsdam University, and at the Groupe Sociétés, Religions, Laïcités at the Centre National de la Recherche Scientifique (GSRL/CNRS), Paris. In 2013, he was awarded the Raoul Wallenberg Prize in Human Rights and Holocaust Studies by the International Raoul Wallenberg Foundation and Tel Aviv University. His latest book, *European Muslim Antisemitism: Why Young Urban Males Say They Don't Like Jews*, was published by Indiana University Press (2015).

BODO KAHMANN holds a master's degree in Political Science and Sociology. He is currently a lecturer and PhD researcher at the University of Göttingen (Germany). His research focuses on antisemitism, social theory, and urban studies. In 2015 he published an essay about Norbert Elias's sociology of antisemitism.

MATTHIAS KÜNTZEL is a political scientist in Hamburg, Germany, and an external Research Associate of the Vidal Sassoon International Center for the Study of Antisemitism at the Hebrew University of Jerusalem. He is author of *Jihad and Jew-Hatred: Islamism, Nazism and the Roots of 9/11* (2007) and of *Germany and Iran: From the Aryan Axis to the Nuclear Threshold* (2014).

KENNETH L. MARCUS is President and General Counsel of the Louis D. Brandeis Center for Human Rights Under Law and a former Staff Director of the U.S. Commission on Civil Rights. He is author of *The Definition of Anti-Semitism* (forthcoming) and *Jewish Identity and Civil Rights in America* (2010).

DAVID PATTERSON holds the Feinberg Chair in Holocaust Studies at the University of Texas at Dallas. A winner of the National Jewish Book Award and the Koret Jewish Book Award, he has published thirty-five books and more than 150 articles and book chapters.

ALVIN H. ROSENFELD, Professor of English and Jewish Studies at Indiana University, holds the Irving M. Glazer Chair in Jewish Studies and is the Director of the Institute for the Study of Contemporary Antisemitism. He is the author of numerous books and articles on American poetry, Jewish literature, Holocaust literature, and contemporary antisemitism, including *A Double Dying, Imagining Hitler, The End of the Holocaust,* and *Resurgent Antisemitism: Global Perspectives.*

ARYEH TUCHMAN is Adjunct Lecturer in Jewish History at Hunter College. He served as Research Analyst at the Anti-Defamation League from 2000 to 2005 and then served as Director of ADL's Library and Research Center through 2010, where he created a digitization program for ADL's collection of U.S. antisemitic literature and designed and implemented a nationwide system for reporting antisemitic incidents. He holds bachelor's and master's degrees from Yeshiva University and received rabbinic ordination at the Rabbi Isaac Elchanan Theological Seminary in New York.

MARK WEITZMAN is Director of Government Affairs for the Simon Wiesenthal Center. He is a member of the official U.S. delegation to the International Holocaust Remembrance Authority (IHRA, formerly the Task Force for International Cooperation on Holocaust Education, Remembrance and Research), where he chairs the Committee on Antisemitism and Holocaust Denial and was lead author of the IHRA's Working Definition of Holocaust Denial and Distortion, which was officially adopted by the thirty-one member countries of the IHRA. His writings on antisemitism include *Antisemitism, the Generic Hatred: Essays in Memory of Simon Wiesenthal,* which won a 2007 National Jewish Book Award; *Jews and Judaism in the Political Theology of Radical Catholic Traditionalists;* and *Dismantling the Big Lie: the Protocols of the Elders of Zion.*

ELHANAN YAKIRA is Professor Emeritus at the Department of Philosophy at the Hebrew University of Jerusalem. His latest book is *Spinoza and the Case for Philosophy* (2014). He has been engaged in recent years in research, reflection, and critique of anti-Zionism and the delegitimation campaigns against Israel. His book *Post-Zionism, Post-Holocaust,* which deals with this subject, was published in the United States in 2010.

Index